INTERNATIONAL LAW STUDIES

Volume 78

Legal and Ethical Lessons of
NATO's Kosovo Campaign

Andru E. Wall
Editor

Naval War College
Newport, Rhode Island
2002

INTERNATIONAL LAW STUDIES

Volume 78

Library of Congress Cataloging-in-Publication Data

Legal and ethical lessons of NATO's Kosovo campaign / Andru E. Wall, editor.
    p. cm. -- (International law studies ; v. 78)
Includes index.
  ISBN 1-884733-25-5 (alk. paper)
  1. Kosovo (Serbia)—History—Civil War, 1998—Law and legislation. 2. North Atlantic Treaty Organization—Armed Forces—Yugoslavia—Kosovo (Serbia) I. Wall, Andru E., 1968- II. Series.
  JX1295 .U4 vol. 78
  [KZ6377.5]
  341 s—dc21
  [949.7

2002153487

Table of Contents

Foreword ix
Introduction xi
Preface xiii

PART I: KEYNOTE ADDRESSES

Opening Remarks
   Vice Admiral Arthur Cebrowski 3

Judging Kosovo: The Legal Process, the Law of Armed Conflict, and the Commander In Chief
   The Honorable James E. Baker 7

Operation Allied Force from the Perspective of the NATO Air Commander
   Lieutenant General Michael Short, USAF (Ret) 19

Discussion 27

PART II: THE APPLICABILITY OF THE LAW OF ARMED CONFLICT

Introduction
   Scott Silliman 33

The Applicability of International Humanitarian Law and the Law of Neutrality to the Kosovo Campaign
   Christopher Greenwood 35

Rules of Conduct During Humanitarian Intervention
   Ivan Shearer 71

Application of the Law of Armed Conflict During Operation Allied Force: Maritime Interdiction and Prisoner of War Issues
   George Walker 85

Commentary
   Judith A. Miller 107

Commentary
   Natalino Ronzitti 113

Commentary
   Richard Sorenson 121

Discussion
   The UN Security Council and the Creation of International Law . . . 125
   The Law of Neutrality Under the UN Charter 125
   Peacekeepers or an Occupying Force? 126
   The Legality of Blockade or Visit & Search 127
   Applying the LOAC: A Question of Intent or Act?. 130
   Enforcement of the Laws of Armed Conflict and 20/20 Hindsight . . . 131
   Are the Laws of War a Constraint? 133

PART III: TARGETING

Introduction
   Robert F. Turner 137
Legitimate Military Objectives Under the Current *Jus In Bello*
   Yoram Dinstein 139
Targeting
   Michael Bothe 173
Legal Pespective from the EUCOM Targeting Cell
   Tony Montgomery 189
Commentary
   Harvey Dalton 199
Commentary
   Wolff H. von Heinegg 203
Commentary
   Henry Shue 207
Discussion
   Reasonable Military Commanders and Reasonable Civilians 211
   Legal Advisors and Time-Sensitive Targets. 213
   Coalition Approval of Targets. 214
   When Civilian Objects Become Military Objectives 214
   Relating the Permissible Mission to the Military Advantage 216
   "Dual-Purpose" Targets. 218
   Targeting Regime Elites. 220

PART IV: COLLATERAL DAMAGE

Introduction
   John Norton Moore 225

Some Legal (And A Few Ethical) Dimensions of the Collateral Damage Resulting from Nato's Kosovo Campaign
   John F. Murphy 229
International Humanitarian Law after Kosovo: Is *Lex Lata* Sufficient?
   Ove Bring 257
Commentary
   Yves Sandoz 273
Commentary
   W. Hays Parks 281
Commentary
   Barry Strauss 293
Discussion
   Modern Technology: Is There An Obligation to Use It? 297
   Human Shields: Can Abuse of the Law of War Be a Force Multiplier? . 298
   Do We Need An Additional Protocol For Humanitarian Intervention? 300
   Reciprocity in War and the Law of War. 302
   Target Priority and Collateral Damage 304
   "No Body Bags" War and the Value of Human Lives 304
   Does Kosovo Provide Lessons for the Future?. 306
   Cluster Bombs and Long-Term Collateral Damage. 306
   The Principle of Proportionality. 308
   Flying At 15,000 Feet 309

PART V: COALITION OPERATIONS

Introduction
   Nicholas Rostow 313
Coalition Warfare and Differing Legal Obligations of Coalition Members Under International Humanitarian Law
   Torsten Stein 315
To What Extent Is Protocol I Customary International Law?
   The Honorable Fausto Pocar 337
Commentary
   Rudolph Dolzer 353
Commentary
   Leslie C. Green 361
Commentary
   David Graham 377

Discussion
- Can a Coalition Member Be Held Responsible for the Actions of Other Members? 387
- The United States and Protocol I 388
- The Status of Protocol I As Customary International Law 389
- Reprisals 390
- The Martens Clause and the Margin of Appreciation 391
- The Relationship Between Human Rights Law and the Law of Armed Conflict 392

PART VI: THE ROAD AHEAD

Introduction
Joel Rosenthal 399

The Laws of War After Kosovo
Adam Roberts 401

Propositions on the Law of War after the Kosovo Campaign
Ruth Wedgwood 433

Commentary
Rein Müllerson 443

Commentary
Horace B. Robertson, Jr. 457

Commentary
Harvey Dalton 463

Discussion
- Does the US Have a Unilateralist Approach to International Law? 467
- Is There a Right of Humanitarian Intervention? 469
- Humanitarian Intervention: Ethically Right, Although Legally Wrong? 469
- Is There a Link Between the *Jus ad Bellum* and the *Jus in Bello*? 474
- Critiquing the Report to the Prosecutor 477
- Applying the Law of Armed Conflict in the Future 477

Appendix A
Final Report to the Prosecutor by the Committee Established to Review the NATO Bombing Campaign Against the Federal Republic of Yugoslavia 483

Appendix B
Contributors 533

Index 547

Foreword

The International Studies "Blue Book" series was initiated by the Naval War College in 1901 to publish essays, treatises, and articles that contribute to the broader understanding of international law. This, the seventy-eighth volume of the historic series, contains the proceedings from a scholarly colloquium entitled *Legal and Ethical Lessons of NATO's Kosovo Campaign*, which was hosted here at the Naval War College on 8–10 August 2001.

The colloquium's mission was to examine the international legal and ethical lessons to be learned from NATO's Kosovo conflict from the standpoint of the *jus in bello*, that is, issues relating to the conduct of hostilities, rather than the *jus ad bellum* questions regarding the legal justification for NATO's initiation of the air operation in Kosovo. Renowned international scholars and practitioners, both military and civilian, representing government and academic institutions, participated. The colloquium and this Blue Book were co-sponsored by the Carnegie Council on Ethics and International Affairs; the Center on Law, Ethics and National Security, Duke University School of Law; the Center for National Security Law, University of Virginia School of Law; and the International Law Department (then the Oceans Law and Policy Department) of the Center for Naval Warfare Studies, United States Naval War College.

On behalf of the Secretary of the Navy, the Chief of Naval Operations, and the Commandant of the Marine Corps, I thank the co-sponsors and participants for their invaluable contributions to this project and to the future understanding of the laws of war.

RODNEY P. REMPT
Rear Admiral, U.S. Navy
President, Naval War College

Introduction

After every clash of arms, it is important to review the actual application of the laws of armed conflict, especially the *jus in bello*. The NATO campaign in Kosovo is no exception and, as allied forces were accused of having committed various violations of the law of armed conflict, examining what happened in Kosovo is particularly valuable. While the Prosecutor for the International Criminal Tribunal for the former Yugoslavia conducted a preliminary inquiry into NATO's actions and concluded that there was insufficient evidence to conduct a formal investigation, there remained significant concerns in the international community over the lawfulness of NATO's actions. Moreover, even if NATO did comply with the laws of armed conflict, are those laws properly suited for today's high-technology battlefield and do they encourage the maintenance of international peace and security? These issues warranted examination by scholars in the fields of both ethics and international law.

For over one hundred years, the United States Naval War College has committed itself to combining a scholarly understanding of the laws of war with an appreciation for and insight into the perspective of the warfighter—the one who must apply those laws to the battlefield. As such, the Naval War College was uniquely suited to convene an array of scholars and practitioners to examine the legal and ethical lessons of NATO's Kosovo campaign. We are indebted to Lieutenant Andru Wall of the International Law Department faculty for the energy and enthusiasm he displayed in organizing our conference and in editing this volume of the International Law Studies (Blue Book) series. Well done!

Special thanks also are due to Yoram Dinstein and the Israel Yearbook on Human Rights, Joel Rosenthal and the Carnegie Council on Ethics & International Affairs, John Norton Moore and Bob Turner and the Center for National Security Law at the University of Virginia, and Scott Silliman and the Center on Law, Ethics, and National Security at the Duke University School

Introduction

of Law. Without their co-sponsorship and invaluable assistance the colloquium and this Blue Book would not have been possible.

Funding for this book and the colloquium was also provided by Dean Alberto R. Coll, Center for Naval Warfare Studies of the Naval War College. His leadership and support are key to the Blue Book series. Invaluable contributions were also made by Captain Ralph Thomas, JAGC, USN (Ret.), who volunteered many hours of his personal time in reviewing manuscripts and offering advice. Further assistance was provided by the rest of the faculty and staff of the International Law Department and our associated reserve unit.

Volume 78 will serve as a standard reference work of case studies in this area, continuing the solid, scholarly tradition of the "Blue Books." The series is published by the Naval War College and distributed throughout the world to academic institutions, libraries, and both U.S. and foreign military commands.

DENNIS MANDSAGER
Professor of Law & Chairman
International Law Department

Preface

Andru E. Wall

When an international group of military officers, judges, political scientists, philosophers, historians and lawyers gathered at the United States Naval War College in early August 2001 to discuss the legal and ethical lessons to be learned from NATO's Kosovo campaign, no one could have imagined the horrific attacks that would take place in the United States just one month later. Much of the discussion centered on whether Operation Allied Force represented a new kind of war—what many term humanitarian intervention—or simply an aberration with limited lessons for the future. Some suggested that Kosovo was nothing like the battlefields of the future would be, and so the lessons to be gleaned would be of limited use.

There is no question that the global war on terrorism that the United States and its allies throughout the world are actively engaged in at the time of this writing is dramatically different from Operation Allied Force. Most significantly, the war on terrorism is a conflict fought primarily against non-State actors and the States that aid, harbor, or support them, while the war over Kosovo was more traditionally fought against a sovereign State. Some scholars mused over whether humanitarian intervention wasn't really war at all, yet it was, classically stated, a matter of politics by another means. A group of sovereign States (NATO) used military force in order to impose their political will (the cessation of the oppression of Kosovar Albanians) on another sovereign State (Serbia).

The goal of the colloquium was to examine how the law of armed conflict should be applied in modern warfare—focusing not just on the law, but also the crucial operational perspective of the warfighter. As Judge James E. Baker pointed out during his keynote luncheon address, the law of armed conflict is

Preface

not for the specialist, it is not for the lawyer; it must be capable of application at the tactical level by the most junior of military personnel.[1] As Professor Dolzer's wisely cautions: "We are living through a period of fundamental changes in the laws of armed conflict, and it is important that the implication of all these changes are thought through in a broad debate where the requirements of criminal law are discussed, where the realities of military conduct are taken into account and where not only the noble humanitarian aspirations in an isolated sense are highlighted."[2]

The theme of the colloquium and, thus, this volume, is simply that while the politics and the modalities of force employed in Kosovo may have been unique, the legal and ethical lessons to be learned are applicable to any international armed conflict. So what are the *jus in bello* lessons to be learned from Operation Allied Force? First, the law of armed conflict applies to any clash of arms between two or more States. Secondly, only military objectives may be lawfully targeted and they are defined within the temporal context of the given conflict. Thirdly, the principle of proportionality prohibits excessive collateral damage, yet the law does not impose absolute rules regarding implementation of weapons and tactics. Fourthly, despite the proliferation of treaties on the law of armed conflict, customary international law will continue to define major elements and interpretations of the law of armed conflict. Thus, it is essential that the development and determination of customary international law be properly understood and the continuing relevance of state practice be fully appreciated.

The Applicability of the Law of Armed Conflict

1. The existence of an international armed conflict

While there was some debate contemporaneous with the Kosovo campaign over whether "humanitarian intervention" triggered the applicability of the law of armed conflict, Professor Christopher Greenwood abruptly answers the question without qualification: while there is no definition of international armed conflict in any law of armed conflict treaty, it is agreed to be a factual determination based on the existence of actual hostilities between two or more States.[3] This is irrespective of a declaration of war and of the justification for the hostilities. An international armed conflict "exists from the first

---

1. Baker, *infra*, at 9.
2. Dolzer, *infra*, at 358.
3. Greenwood, *infra*, at 39.

moment after an exchange of fire" between two States.[4] *Opinio juris* supports this, as NATO certainly believed the law of armed conflict was fully applicable and defined and incorporated the legal limits on the use of force within the NATO rules of engagement.[5]

2. The internationalization of an internal armed conflict

The more challenging question is whether intervention by outside States (e.g., NATO) on behalf of an organized armed group within a State (e.g., the Kosovo Liberation Army) "internationalizes" the conflict between that group and the State it is in conflict with (e.g., Serbia). Professor Greenwood argues that it does "only if there is a clear relationship between the non-governmental party to the conflict and one of the States party to the international conflict."[6] In the present case, there was not a sufficient link between the KLA and NATO to internationalize the conflict between the KLA and Serbia.[7] As such, the members of the KLA were not entitled to combatant immunity nor were they entitled to prisoner of war status if captured.

3. The interdiction of maritime shipping

The issue of whether NATO could lawfully intercept and divert neutral vessels carrying strategic commodities was a political question more than a legal one. The "customary law of armed conflict still permits a State engaged in an international armed conflict to prevent strategic commodities such as oil from reaching its opponent by sea, even if carried by neutral flagged vessels."[8] The law of neutrality was not abolished by the UN Charter, but belligerent rights still permit warring States to interdict shipping—even that from neutral States.[9] While not disputing the continuing viability of customary belligerent rights, Professors Greenwood and Bring urge caution in applying them in the post-UN Charter era.[10] NATO chose not to interdict shipping bound for Serbia, not because doing so would have been illegal, but because certain political

---

4. Shearer, *infra*, at 76.
5. Miller, *infra*, at 109.
6. Greenwood, *infra*, at 45.
7. Greenwood, *infra*, at 44–6; Ronzitti, *infra*, at 114.
8. Greenwood, *infra*, at 56. *See also* Walker, *infra*, at 92 and discussion comments by Professor Wolff H. Von Heinegg at 127–8.
9. Ronzitti, *infra*, at 117–8.
10. *See* Discussion, *infra*, at 127–30.

leaders within the alliance were "trying to damp down expectations of the level of violence" that would be applied.[11]

4. Is it the law of armed conflict or international humanitarian law?

Professor Stein acknowledges the confusion created by "re-naming the 'laws of war' or 'law of armed conflict' as 'international humanitarian law' thus blurring the distinction between 'humanitarian' and 'human rights' law."[12] For Colonel Graham this "renaming" indicates that some people think that elements of human rights law are included in the law of armed conflict—a troubling proposition for those who have to advise military commanders on their legal obligations given that human rights law is much less well-defined than the law of armed conflict.[13] The US military prefers the term "law of armed conflict" as its obligations are better understood and because, as a matter of policy, the US military applies the law of armed conflict to all military operations regardless of their characterization.

Professors Bothe and Green, among others, engaged in a lively debate over whether humanitarian law, or the law of armed conflict, is *lex specialis* vis-à-vis human rights law.[14] A *lex specialis* implies the existence of a *lex generalis*. However, because many human rights treaties do not apply during armed conflicts, it is incorrect to label human rights law a *lex generalis* and the law of armed conflict a *lex specialis*. They are two separate bodies of international law with, at times and depending on the treaties a State is party to, overlapping jurisdiction.

The drafters of Protocol I and other more recent law of armed conflict treaties did draw from the realm of human rights law and incorporated certain human rights concepts into the law of armed conflict. What must remain clear is that these concepts are then implemented from the standpoint of the law of armed conflict. Where there is overlapping jurisdiction and the actions of a military commander are subject to review under both human rights law and the law of armed conflict, then the greater specificity of the latter must be determinative.

5. Is there a link between the *jus ad bellum* and the *jus in bello*?

It is a well-established maxim that the law of armed conflict applies equally to both sides of a conflict, although some have argued that there may be a relationship between the degree of force that may be used and the "purpose for

---

11. See the comments by Professor Greenwood, *infra*, at 127.
12. Stein, *infra*, at 319.
13. Graham, *infra*, at 381.
14. *See* Discussion, *infra*, at 392–6.

which force is permitted under the *jus ad bellum*."[15] Professor Bothe agrees that the "*jus ad bellum* and *jus in bello* have to be kept separate" because the equality of the parties is an essential precondition to the objective application of the law of armed conflict, however, he proffers the caveat that "[m]ilitary advantage . . . is a contextual notion."[16] This, to Professor Von Heinegg, amounts to simply paying "lip service" to the principle that the two bodies of law are separate.[17] He counters that "the overall aim that led one of the parties to an armed conflict to resort to the use of armed force is irrelevant when it comes to the question whether certain objects effectively contribute to military action of the adversary or whether their neutralization offers a definite military advantage."[18]

Professor Greenwood emphatically rejects the "heresy" that NATO's humanitarian motives entitled it to greater latitude in choosing targets and the "rival heresy" that "because the campaign was fought for a humanitarian objective, international humanitarian law has to be interpreted as imposing upon NATO more extensive restrictions than would otherwise have been the case."[19] Both these "heretical" views "involve an unjustified muddling of *jus ad bellum* and *jus in bello* issues in a way which is contrary to principle and unsupported by authority."[20]

"The law of armed conflict does not ask for motives, political aims, or the legality of the first use of force," Professor Von Heinegg states: "[i]t takes as a fact that the jus ad bellum has failed to function properly."[21] Any time consideration of the *jus ad bellum* plays a role in the *jus in bello*, the latter is weakened.[22] Even if violations of the *jus in bello* can justify intervention as some have argued, that remains a matter of the *jus ad bellum* and the *jus in bello* remains equally binding on both parties in any resulting hostilities.[23]

Nevertheless, Professor Bothe identifies this as the "fundamental issue: how far does the context of the military operation have an impact on the notion of military advantage?"[24] In this regard, Professor Müllerson points out

---

15. Greenwood, *infra*, at 52.
16. Bothe, *infra*, at 186.
17. Von Heinegg, *infra*, at 205.
18. Id.
19. Greenwood, *infra*, at 48–9.
20 Greenwood, *infra*, at 53.
21. Von Heinegg, *infra*, at 206.
22. See comments by Professor Von Heinegg, *infra*, at 221.
23. See Robertson, *infra*, at 457; *see also*, Roberts, *infra*, at 409–13. Professor Roberts states: "Quite simply, massive violations of *jus in bello* by a belligerent can help to legitimize certain threats and uses of force by outside powers intervening to stop the violations." *Id.* at 410.
24. See Discussion, *infra*, at 216.

that the International Court of Justice in its advisory opinion on Nuclear Weapons "created a novelty distinguishing between 'an extreme circumstance of self-defense, in which the very survival of a State would be at stake' and other circumstances."[25] This implies that "a wrong done in light of *jus ad bellum* has an impact on the *jus in bello*" applicable in the resulting conflict, because an aggressor would not be entitled to argue that it was acting under such "extreme circumstance of self-defense."[26]

Notwithstanding the ICJ's advisory opinion, "it remains certain that all parties have to equally abide by the requirements of *jus in bello*" and in "that sense these branches of the law are separate."[27] If there is a "bridge between the two branches of international law" it "is the requirement of adequacy" because "an act justified by the necessity of humanitarian intervention must be limited by that necessity and kept clearly within it."[28] In the final analysis, it is important to distinguish between political or moral reasons for applying a "maximum standard" of compliance with the law of armed conflict, and a legal obligation to do so.[29]

Targeting Military Objectives

1. Defining military objectives

Perhaps the most fundamental principle of the law of armed conflict is that of distinction. Professor Michael Bothe traces the development of the principle of distinction from Jean Jacques Rousseau's conception of the sovereign's war. War is between States and their rulers, not their peoples, thus conflict should be limited to combatants and military objectives.[30] Article 52(2) of Protocol I contains the "binding definition of military objective:"[31]

> In so far as objects are concerned, military objectives are limited to those objects which by their nature, location, purpose or use make an effective contribution to military action and whose total or partial destruction, capture or neutralization, in the circumstances ruling at the time, offers a definite military advantage.

---

25. Müllerson, *infra*, at 443.
26. Müllerson, *infra*, at 444.
27. Müllerson, *infra*, at 445.
28. Müllerson, *infra*, at 452–3.
29. Stein, *infra*, at 326–7.
30. Bothe, *infra*, at 173–4.
31. Dinstein, *infra*, at 140.

While there should "be no doubt" that this definition "corresponds to existing principles as reflected in customary law and simply clarifies them," some of the clarifications could be "open to different interpretations of the scope of the obligations imposed on the attacker" and, thus, "incompatible with a consideration of the provision as fully reflecting customary international law."[32] Judge Pocar offers as examples of imprecise clarifications the expressions "effective contribution to military action" and "definite military advantage."[33]

"The difficulty of the Article 52(2) definition" of military objective, Professor Bothe writes, "is its general character" particularly with respect to "dual-use objects."[34] Professor Dinstein is "not enamored" by the phrase "dual use" and argues that legally the fact that an object may have both a military use and a civilian use does "not alter its singular and unequivocal status as a military objective."[35]

Professor Bothe asks how "the general principle of distinction" can be rendered "more concrete in order to have secure standards for targeting" and then agrees that an illustrative list of military objectives could be a possible solution.[36] Professor Dinstein proffers that "only a composite definition—combining an abstract statement with a non-exhaustive catalogue of illustrations—can effectively avoid vagueness, on the one hand, and inability to anticipate future scenarios, on the other."[37] The likelihood of States ever reaching agreement on such a list, however useful, is doubtful. Given what Professor Dinstein himself identifies as the "temporal framework" within which military objectives are defined—what may be legitimately attacked at one time may not be at another time—a list could include objects which by their "nature" are military objectives, but would not likely include the myriad of objects that become military objectives by their location, purpose or use.[38]

2. Presuming civilian purpose

While the general definition of military objective contained in Article 52(2) of Protocol I can be considered customary international law, it is doubtful that the same can be said about the requirement to assume civilian purpose

---

32. Pocar, *infra*, at 348.
33. *Id.*
34. Bothe, *infra*, at 177.
35. See comments by Professor Dinstein in the Discussion, *infra*, at 218–9.
36. Bothe, *infra*, at 177.
37. Dinstein, *infra*, at 142 (footnote omitted).
38. Dinstein, *infra*, at 144; *see also* Von Heinegg, *infra*, at 204.

contained in Article 52(3).[39] This was an issue that was much debated during the drafting process and some argue that it "may reflect a '[r]efusal to recognize the realities of combat' in some situations."[40] Professor Dinstein points out, however, that the presumption only arises in cases of doubt regarding the civilian purpose. "The degree of doubt that has to exist prior to the emergence of the (rebuttable) presumption is by no means clear. But surely that doubt has to exist in the mind of the attacker, based upon 'the circumstances ruling at the time.'"[41]

3. Effects-based targeting

The target selection and review process in Operational Allied Force was premised on "effects based targeting," which articulates a desired objective, then seeks to identify "specific links, nodes, or objects" that, if attacked, will achieve the objective.[42] Judge Baker warned of "the impending collision among the law of armed conflict, the doctrine of effects-based targeting, and a shared desire to limit collateral casualties and consequences to the fullest extent possible."[43] The focus of the collaborative targeting sessions seems to validate Judge Bakers fears, as they "revolved around three issues: 1) the linkage to military effects—the key to obtaining legal approval, 2) the collateral damage estimate, and 3) the unintended civilian casualty estimate."[44] "[E]ffects-based targeting and the law of armed conflict may be on a collision course" with respect to critical infrastructure, particularly factories owned by supporters of regimes that could be quickly converted to military use.[45] A focus on desired effects could lead military commanders to target certain objects for effect, rather than because of their "effective contribution to military action."

4. Presidential review of targets

Contrary to popular belief, the president of the United States did not review and approve all targets, but rather a "smaller subset" of the 200–300

---

39. Bring, *infra*, at 261; Pocar, *infra*, at 348.
40. Dinsetin, *infra*, at 149 *quoting* W. Hays Parks, *Air War and the Laws of War*, 32 AIR FORCE LAW REVIEW 1, 137 (1990).
41. Dinsetin, *infra*, at 150.
42. Montgomery, *infra*, at 190.
43. Baker, *infra*, at 8.
44. Montgomery, *infra*, at 193.
45. Baker, *infra*, at 16.

targets that were reviewed by the National Security Council.[46] Traditional military objectives were approved in theater, while military industrial, electric power grid, critical infrastructure, and targets with a high likelihood of collateral damage were reviewed by the Pentagon. Of these, maybe ten targets were submitted for presidential review every four to five days.[47]

Nevertheless, General Short believes there was too much involvement by civilians in the targeting process. He argues that because targets were chosen by civilians rather than by military officers, NATO "bombed targets that were frankly inappropriate for bringing Milosevic to the table."[48] General Short asks "whose responsibility should targeting be?" Answering his own question, he asserts that the president should restrict himself to selecting target sets and leave it to "professional military officers" to select individual targets in accordance with the strategic guidance and the law of armed conflict.[49]

5. Targeting the will of the people

> The morale of the population and of the political decision-makers is not a contribution to 'military action.' Thus, the advantage of softening the adversary's will to resist is not a 'military' one and, thus, cannot be used as a legitimation for any targeting decision. If it were otherwise, it would be too easy to legitimize military action which uses bombing just as a psychological weapon—and there are other words for this.[50]

NATO did not target the will of the civilian population, but neither was it so naive as to fail to see that there are valid military objectives that can be targeted, a peripheral result of which will be to make the civilian population unhappy with their leadership for choosing a course of action that allowed this to happen.[51] NATO did seek to impose "discomfort" on the civilian population, but this was secondary to targeting lawful military objectives.[52]

---

46. Baker, *infra*, at 13.
47. Dalton, *infra*, at 201.
48. Short, *infra*, at 20.
49. Short, *infra*, at 20. For more on this "'normal' theory of civil-military relations" and the relationship between military leaders and political leaders during times of war, see ELIOT A. COHEN, SUPREME COMMAND: SOLDIERS, STATESMEN, AND LEADERSHIP IN WARTIME (Free Press 2002).
50. Bothe, *infra*, at 180.
51. *See* Short, *infra*, at 29–30.
52. Miller, *infra*, at 110.

Collateral Damage and the Principle of Proportionality

1. The principle of proportionality

The principle of proportionality, while codified for the first time in Article 51(5)(b) of Protocol I, is one of the core principles of the customary law of armed conflict. While the Protocol I formulation of proportionality may have included specifications that cannot be found in prior declarations of the principle, these "specifications are aimed at clarifying the scope . . . rather than at adding new elements that would lead to the modification of their contents or effects."[53] Simply put, the principle of proportionality prohibits attacks that cause injury to civilians or damage to civilian objects "which is excessive in relation to the concrete and direct military advantage anticipated."[54]

The principle of proportionality rests on the presumption that the attacker is complying with the principle of distinction, thus implicitly acknowledging that some collateral damage is unavoidable.[55] Yet many fail to recognize or acknowledge this simple fact. Professor Dinstein agues that they make the mistake of confusing extensive with excessive: "injury/damage to noncombatants can be exceedingly extensive without being excessive, simply because the military advantage anticipated is of paramount important."[56]

"[S]ome have used Kosovo to advance a legal view that the law of armed conflict virtually prohibits collateral casualties. This is an honorable and worthy aspiration, but not the law. Nor should it be the law, or the tyrants of the world will operate with impunity."[57] Professor Dinstein reminds us that "[o]ne has to constantly bear in mind that war is war; not a chess game. There is always a price-tag in human suffering."[58] Rather than focusing on the unrealistic goal of eliminating civilian casualties, the goal should be on their mitigation—understanding their inevitability and the reality of mistakes, "accidents and just sheer bad luck."[59]

The principle of proportionality was "the guiding principle of paramount importance" for US forces during Operation Allied Force.[60] "Concern for collateral damage drove us to an extraordinary degree," General Short states,

---

53. Pocar, *infra*, at 346.
54. Protocol I, Article 51(5)(b).
55. Bring, *infra*, at 262–3.
56. See Discussion, *infra*, at 215.
57. Baker, *infra*, at 17.
58. See Discussion, *infra*, at 219.
59. *Id.*
60. Miller, *infra*, at 308–9.

"and it will drive the next generation of warriors even more so, because whereas I see this as an extraordinary failure, the leadership within the NATO senior administrations would say this was indeed an extraordinary success."[61] General Short emphasizes that NATO did its "very, very best to limit collateral damage" but "[e]very time we failed in that effort, the reaction by political leaders was hysterical."[62] The political leadership of NATO could not stand collateral damage and "they did not understand war. They thought it was a video game, and that no one ever dies. . . . Did you ever see anyone die in the films from the Gulf War? I never did. I just saw crosshairs on a target in downtown Baghdad, and then it blew up."[63]

2. Responsibility for civilian casualties

There is a very real danger in misplacing responsibility for civilian casualties. It is wrong to place "the entire responsibility for civilian casualties on the party to the conflict that has the least control over them."[64] As an example, Mr Parks argues that civilians "killed within an obvious military objective" should not be counted as "collateral civilian casualties."[65] To count them as such "would only encourage increased civilian presence in a military objective in order to make its attack prohibitive in terms of collateral civilian casualties."[66] In the same sense, placing too many targets off-limits because of the presence of human shields would create the perverse effect of rewarding the use of human shields.

3. The use of precision-guided munitions

Contrary to the arguments made by some, there is no obligation, in customary international law or treaty law, to use precision-guided munitions in attacks on urban areas.[67] Such a rule would be "dysfunctional" and a far better standard would be "to rely on the judgment of the commander."[68] Nowhere in the law of armed conflict is there a requirement to use specific weapons, rather there is a legal standard of reasonableness that remains constant. A doctor in a developing country has the same legal standard of care as a doctor in a

---

61. Short, *infra*, at 24.
62. Short, *infra*, at 23.
63. *Id.*
64. Parks, *infra*, at 288.
65. Parks, *infra*, at 291.
66. *Id.*
67. Murphy, *infra*, 231–43.
68. Murphy, *infra*, 241.

Preface

developed country, but the doctor in the developed country may be expected to perform more tests or expend more resources in order to properly treat his patient. Mr Sandoz argues that this is an apt analogy to apply in analyzing the reasonableness of a military commander's choice of weapons.[69] Yet one wonders whether this isn't a false analogy. The doctor has no choice in whether to treat his patient, yet the military commander always has a choice in whether to target a particular military objective. If the commander does not have the technological capability to attack the target without causing disproportionate damage, then the law of armed conflict prohibits him from attacking it. Thus the law simultaneously protects civilians and provides an incentive for the acquisition of technology that increases the commanders freedom of action.

4. Flying above 15,000 feet

Collateral damage concerns must be balanced against "the risk that you are asking your pilots to take."[70] Professor Murphy noted that NATO's "decision to engage in high-altitude bombing did not by itself constitute a violation of the law of armed conflict."[71] Colonel Sorenson is more blunt: it "sells newspapers, airtime and interviews, but the facts just simply aren't there to suggest that by keeping our pilots at 15,000 feet to protect them that we were engaging in basically carpet bombing."[72]

5. The environment

For those States that are party to Protocol I without reservation to Articles 35 and 56, causing damage to the environment is a war crime only if it reaches "the triple cumulative threshold" of being "widespread, long-term and severe."[73] Professor Bothe suggests that a lower threshold could be reached if the "collateral environmental damage was excessive in relation to a military advantage anticipated."[74] However, Professor Von Heinegg counters that customary international law would still not consider wanton destruction of the environment a prosecutable war crime.[75] Judge Pocar agrees noting that the provisions have "no clear precedent in customary law."[76]

---

69. Sandoz, *infra*, at 278.
70. Short, *infra*, at 22.
71. Murphy, *infra*, at 249.
72. *See* Discussion, *infra*, at 310.
73. Bothe, *infra*, at 181–3.
74. Id.
75. Von Heinegg, *infra*, at 204.
76. Pocar, *infra*, at 348–9.

6. Collateral damage and future conflicts

Professor Bring asserts that NATO's "no-body bags policy . . . implies that the lives of your own pilots are worth more than the lives of the innocent civilians on the ground."[77] Yet Professor Adam Roberts cautions that this desire to protect one's own servicemen was "entirely understandable" and, looking at the speeches made by NATO leaders prior to the start of the air campaign, it was not presumed going in to be a "no body bags war."[78] Those who argue that NATO should have accepted an increase risk to their military service members lose sight of the goals of democracy to stop democide, genocide, and aggressive war. "The reality," Professor John Norton Moore points out, is that we want to achieve those goals "as rapidly as we possibly can at the lowest cost to all involved."[79] By arguing that democracies must be willing to accept greater risks to their personnel, proponents of humanitarian goals may in fact raise barriers in a manner that would lead to increased suffering.

Professor Murphy closes his paper on collateral damage with the prescient observation that future wars will increasingly see a "'happy congruence' between the needs of military efficiency and the avoidance of unnecessary injury to civilian persons or property"; however, "the protections the law of armed conflict affords to civilian persons and property are likely to be less and less effective in practice. This is because the technologically weaker States, as well as terrorists or other non-governmental actors, may increasingly conclude that they must attack the civilian population of the enemy State to offset the latter's great advantage in firepower."[80]

Customary International Law and the Law of Armed Conflict

1. The Martens Clause

The Martens Clause, which was codified in the 1899 and 1907 Hague conventions as well as the 1977 Additional Protocol I, recognizes the importance of customary international law to the law of armed conflict. It reads:

> Until a more complete code of the laws of war is issued, the high contracting parties think it right to declare that in cases not included in the Regulations adopted by them, populations and belligerents remain under the protection and empire of the principles of international law, as they result from the usages

---

77. Bring, *infra*, at 266.
78. Discussion, *infra*, at 304–5.
79. Discussion, *infra*, at 303.
80. Murphy, *infra*, at 254–5.

established between civilized nations, from the laws of humanity and the requirements of the public conscience.[81]

"The Martens Clause," Professor Shearer writes, "is a powerful reminder that in situations of armed conflict, of whatever kind, there is never a total gap in the law, never a situation in which there cannot be an appeal to law in order to mitigate the horror and the suffering."[82] The powerful rhetoric invoking the dictates of the public conscience should not be misunderstood as creating a new source of customary international law, but rather as a safeguard thereof. Anytime one discusses the application of the laws of armed conflict to new, or perceived new, types of conflicts, it must never be forgotten that there is at the very least customary law that regulates the application of military force.

Professor Dolzer notes that much of the "humanitarian law community" emphasizes the "principles of humanity and . . . dictates of public conscience" aspect of the Martens Clause, while the military tends to be primarily concerned with the customary practice provision.[83] This is understandable as customary practice tends to be more easily defined, which is of primary importance when potential criminal liability is at stake. The two approaches should converge, however, upon the realization that the Martens Clause encourages the view that customary international law is based not just on battlefield practice, but rather on *opinio juris*—battlefield practice combined with a concurrent belief that it is lawful. It is upon the State's subjective belief in the legality of its actions that "the principles of humanity and dictates of public conscience" weigh most heavily. In any event, no tribunal has ever trumped customary law by resting an opinion on the "dictates of the public conscience."

2. The formulation of customary international law

Following the North Sea Continental Shelf case and the Nicaragua case, "there is no doubt that for a rule to exist as a norm of customary international law both its recognition as a legal obligation by States and the latter's conduct which is consistent with the rule are required."[84] The "cannon of principles laid down in Article 38 of the Statute of the International Court of Justice" are as applicable to the law of armed conflict as they are to other areas of public

---

81. Preamble, Convention (II) with Respect to the Laws and Customs of War on Land, July 29, 1899, U.S.T.S. 403, 32 Stat. 1803, 1 Bevans 247.
82. Shearer, *infra*, at 72.
83. Dolzer, *infra*, at 356.
84. Pocar, *infra*, at 340 (footnote omitted).

international law.[85] Thus, "[w]idespread practice and corresponding *opinio juris* will be required for the formulation of customary law, with or without parallel treaty law."[86]

The importance of State practice cannot be overstated as this is the first of the three components of customary law listed in the Martens Clause.[87] However, equally important is the corresponding *opinio juris*. On this point it must be noted that many of the steps taken by the United States during Operation Allied Force to limit collateral damage were taken because they *could* be taken, not because there was any sense of a legal obligation to do so. Thus, these actions provide little in the way of clarifying customary international law.[88] The "positivist approach" taken by the Permanent Court of International Justice in the Lotus case, which argues that "restrictions on the practice of States cannot be presumed," may be "particularly well-suited to issues of the law of armed conflict, which, by their very nature, implicate the vital interests of States."[89]

Professor Stein observes that the International Court of Justice and the International Criminal Tribunal for the former Yugoslavia (ICTY) have looked beyond traditional sources for "evidence" of customary international law, which the ICTY said could include "the number of ratifications to international treaties and the dictates of military manuals."[90] However, a "long list of signatories" has very little to do with determining State practice in the area of the law of armed conflict because the "vast majority of signatories of Protocol I are at best interested observers—bystanders if you will—when it comes to the actual application of the law of armed conflict in combat situations."[91]

On the issue of the precedential value of international case law, Judge Pocar writes:

> [I]t has to be stressed that previous decisions of international courts cannot be relied on as having the authority of precedents in order to establish a principle of law. The current structure of the international community, which clearly lacks a hierarchical judicial system, does not allow consideration of judicial precedent as a distinct source of law. Therefore, prior case law may only constitute evidence of a customary rule in that it may reflect the existence of *opinio juris*

---

85. Dolzer, *infra*, at 353.
86. Dolzer, *infra*, at 354.
87. Graham, *infra*, at 384.
88. *See* Parks, *infra*, at 281–2.
89. Murphy, *infra*, at 235.
90. Stein, *infra*, at 318–9.
91. Graham, *infra*, at 383.

and international practice, but cannot be regarded per se as having precedential authority in international criminal jurisdiction.[92]

Finally, the traditional rules protecting the persistent objector still allow a State to protect itself from a developing norm it finds objectionable.[93]

3. The customary nature of provisions of Protocol I

It is "undisputed" that Protocol I in part reaffirms and clarifies customary international law and in part develops that law.[94] "For the first part [its] rules bind all States, for the second only the State parties to the Protocols are bound."[95] The "fundamental principles" of "distinction between civilians and combatants, the prohibition against directly attacking civilians, and the rule of proportionality, are customary international law," Professor Stein writes, but "it is very doubtful whether the same can be said about other provisions of Protocol I—in particular those dealing with collateral damage."[96]

Three points are important to this debate: 1) the status of a particular provision in Protocol I (whether it is new law or customary international law) may change with time, 2) if the provision is customary international law, it is customary international law that is binding "not the treaty provision as such" and 3) the codification process necessarily involves new or more precise elements which must themselves be distinguished from the customary principle.[97] In the final analysis, "there is a trend in the increasing number of ratifications and some case law in some international tribunals" towards recognition of Protocol I as customary law; however, there is also significant State practice involving the "major actors" that prevents consideration of many provisions of Protocol I as customary international law.[98]

Reasonableness and Implementation of the Law of Armed Conflict

It has become a popular mantra for commentators to decry the perceived increasing influence of lawyers over the planning and execution of military operations. Yet, "[w]hether actors like it or not, Kosovo may serve as a harbinger

---

92. Pocar, *infra*, at 342.
93. Dolzer, *infra*, at 354.
94. Pocar, *infra*, at 338–9.
95. Sandoz, *infra*, at 273.
96. Stein, *infra*, at 321–2.
97. Pocar, infra, at 338–9.
98. See comments by Judge Pocar, Discussion, *infra*, at 389–90.

of the manner in which specific US military actions—down to the tactical sortie—will receive legal scrutiny, from non-governmental organizations, ad hoc tribunals, and the International Criminal Court."[99] The concern, however, is not so much that military operations are subject to legal review, but what standard will be applied in evaluating the wartime actions of military commanders? Is it that of the reasonable man or the reasonable military commander? As Professor Green wryly observes, a "reasonable man is the man on a downtown bus; that is not the reasonable soldier."[100] Reasonableness during times of armed conflict must be judged through the eyes of the man involved in that armed conflict.

A particular challenge arises in the context of proportionality, the determination of which often gives rise to a "clash between the military and humanitarian 'value genres'."[101] Can a "reasonable civilian" ever properly determine military necessity and proportionality? Professor Bothe thinks they could with proper training, but Professor Green is less confident that civilian judges could ever appreciate "the circumstances that were prevailing at the time that led to the soldier's actions."[102] This, of course, raises the issue of whether civilian judges should try military cases. Professor Ronzitti offers a solution by distinguishing between wartime crimes that are battlefield crimes (war crimes) and those that are not (crimes against humanity and genocide). He suggests that special chambers be established to hear the former.[103]

Conclusion

There are many people to thank for their role in bringing this work to fruition, foremost are the co-sponsors and participants in the colloquium from which this book is derived. Many thanks to Professor Dennis Mandsager for entrusting me with the opportunity to coordinate the colloquium and edit this volume—for seeing through rank to the individual that holds it. I am also grateful for two wise and experienced hands who patiently shepherded a first-time editor from first-draft to completion: Ms Susan Meyer for her patient and precise desktop publishing assistance, and Captain A. Ralph Thomas, JAGC, USN (Ret.) for his indefatigable editorial input and assistance. Thanks are also due Ms Pat Goodrich, Ms Erin Poe, Ms Margaret Richard,

---

99. Baker, *infra*, at 15.
100. Discussion, *infra*, at 212.
101. Murphy, *infra*, at 247 (footnote omitted).
102. Discussion, *infra*, at 211–2.
103. *Id.* at 212.

Preface

and Mr Jeremiah Lenihan for their proofreading and publication support. While they all kept me from countless mistakes, those that remain are solely my own.

During my nearly three years here at the Naval War College, I have had the privilege of learning from many of the greatest minds in international law, including the contributors to this volume. The most recent holders of the Charles H. Stockton Chair of International Law, Ruth Wedgwood, Ivan Shearer, Nicholas Rostow and Yoram Dinstein, have selflessly illuminated me with their brilliance and guided me with their mentoring wisdom. For that I am forever grateful.

A note of personal thanks to my grandfather, Earl Wall, whose words of wisdom led me to pursue my dream of military service and, in turn, to discover a passion for international law, and to my beautiful wife, Yashmin, whose unconditional love is a source of continual strength and encouragement. This book is dedicated to their honor.

PART I

KEYNOTE ADDRESSES

Opening Remarks

Vice Admiral Arthur Cebrowski

The Naval War College is thrilled to have such a distinguished and diverse group of participants in this colloquium. You represent the preeminent international law and ethics scholars and the top military lawyers and warfighters from the United States and at least ten of our friends and allies—including Australia, Belgium, Canada, the Netherlands, Germany, Israel, Italy, Sweden, Switzerland, and the United Kingdom.

This colloquium, Legal and Ethical Lessons of NATO's Kosovo Campaign, is unique in that it is the first time that warfighters and international law scholars alike have gathered to specifically address the *jus in bello* issues that arose during Operation Allied Force. The opportunity to study, reflect, discuss and debate the issues involved is a rare one that must be seized with zeal and determination. The mission for this colloquium is simple: to examine the legal and ethical lessons of NATO's Kosovo Campaign—focusing exclusively on the *jus in bello* aspect of the campaign. Notice that we have not said lessons learned, for only the future will reveal if they have in fact been learned. Your work will lay the foundation that is necessary for policy makers and warfighters to comply with international law today, tomorrow and for years into the future.

The Information Age and Modern Warfare

How does law and ethics impact where we are headed with modern warfare? We here at the US Naval War College, whether looking at ancient battles or modern technology, always ask the question: what are the implications for the military and its activities in the future?

Opening Remarks

Admiral Jay Johnson, the former Chief of Naval Operations for the United States Navy, has described the future as being shaped by three increasing and irreversible trends: networking, greater globalization and economic interdependence, and technology assimilation. Each has enormous implications for militaries and societies throughout the world.

Obviously, these trends have enormous implications for the armed forces. We are now in the midst of a revolution in military affairs unlike any seen since the Napoleonic Age. In that period, the practice of maintaining small professional armies to fight wars was replaced by the mobilization of citizen armies composed of much of a nation's adult population. Henceforth, societies as a whole would, perhaps tragically, become intricately vested in warfare. The character of armed conflict had changed fundamentally.

Today we are witnessing an analogous change in the character of war and warfare—an information revolution that enables a shift from what we call platform-centric warfare to network-centric warfare. Understanding of these new operations remains nascent. No great body of collated wisdom has emerged to explain how this revolution will alter national and international security dynamics.

Allow me to briefly explain what network-centric warfare is, then raise some concerns with how it intersects with law and ethics. Perhaps most notably, network-centric warfare enables a shift from attrition-based warfare to a much faster effects-based warfighting style, one characterized not only by operating inside an opponent's decision loop by speed of command, but by an ability to change the warfare context or ecosystem. At least in theory, the result may well be decisional paralysis.

How might this be achieved? The approach is premised on achieving three objectives:

- First, the force achieves information superiority, having a dramatically better awareness or understanding of the battlespace.
- Second, forces acting with speed, precision, and the ability to reach out long distances with their weapons achieve the massing of effects versus the massing of the forces themselves.
- Finally, the results that follow are the rapid reduction of the enemy's options and the shock of rapid and closely coupled effects in his forces. This disrupts the enemy's strategy and, it is hoped, forecloses the options available to him.

Underlying this ability is an alteration in the dynamics of command and control. The key to this possibility is the ability to provide information access to those force levels that need it most. In a sense, the middle-man is cut out.

Traditionally, military commanders engaged in top-down direction to achieve the required level of forces and weapons at the point of contact with the enemy. However, top-down coordination inevitably results in delays and errors in force disposition. It is an unwieldy process that denies flexibility to subordinate commands. Combat power is needlessly reduced and opportunities present themselves to one's enemy. In contrast, bottom-up execution permits combat to move to a high-speed continuum in which the enemy is denied operational pause to regroup and redeploy.

Challenges

There are several challenges that arise from the information age and the resulting bottom-up organizational structure. The ones you will address during this colloquium concern the law of armed conflict as it relates to the conduct of hostilities, rather than the *jus ad bellum* or legality of the conflict. Two concerns related to targeting come immediately to mind. First is consistency: as you are delegating decision-making down to the lowest levels, how do you ensure that commanders are uniformly applying the same standards of military necessity and proportionality? The second concern related to targeting is accountability: the information age ensures that we as warfighters will have more and better information, but it also means that everyone else will as well. Thus, our decision making—our targeting decisions—will continue to be scrutinized in ever-increasing detail.

Allow me to remind you of an incident that occurred during Operation Allied Force. On April 12, 1999 a NATO fighter was given the mission to destroy the Leskovac railway bridge over the Grdelica Gorge and Juzna Morava River in eastern Serbia. The fighter was to drop two electro-optically guided bombs—one on each end of the bridge. The first bomb was launched and as it was being remotely guided in to the aimpoint, at the last instant before impact, a train came into view. It was too late to divert the bomb and the train and bridge were struck. The fighter then circled around to complete his mission by dropping the second bomb on the opposite end of the bridge as planned. The bomb was dropped and as it broke through the clouds and smoke, again at the last instant before impact, it became apparent that the train was covering the expanse of the bridge. The train was struck a second time. All told 15 civilians lost their lives.

The laws of armed conflict judge military commanders on the basis of the information they have available to them at the time decisions are made. Now the decision to target and destroy this particular railway bridge was reviewed and approved by the US National Command Authorities and, in general, by the North Atlantic Council. The bridge was a valid military objective because it was an integrated part of the communications and logistics networks in Serbia. It was determined that the military necessity of destroying the bridge was not outweighed by the potential incidental injury or collateral damage that would occur should civilians be on or near the bridge at the time of the attack.

That was a reasonable determination consistent with the laws of armed conflict. The challenge arose during the execution of the mission when the pilot acquired information that the planners did not have—i.e. that a train, possibly a civilian passenger train, was on or near the bridge. The pilot then made a split-second decision under the pressures of combat, while flying in enemy airspace that he would execute his mission as planned. He was properly assuming that the possibility of incidental injury or collateral damage had been accounted for during the target approval process. But while the pilot made that decision as he flew above the clouds, at an altitude above 15,000 feet, in enemy airspace, and while guiding the bomb on a five-inch screen in his cockpit, the public—including eventually the Prosecutor's Office for the International Criminal Tribunal for the former Yugoslavia—had the luxury of hindsight and of viewing the cockpit video in slow-motion on large-screen televisions in the comfort of their own homes or offices. Many critics were appalled by the sight of crosshairs seemingly locked-on to a civilian passenger train. The pilot was accused by many of having committed a war crime—of having intentionally targeted civilians or recklessly disregarded the fact that they would be struck.

So as our actions as warfighters will be increasingly analyzed in ever greater detail, it is important that we reflect back on Operation Allied Force and identify the legal and ethical lessons to be learned. There is no better venue for this colloquium than here at the Naval War College. Here we have a proud tradition of bringing the preeminent legal minds together with the leading warfighters and policy makers. Together we can ensure that the law of armed conflict is not only expertly articulated, but also applied to real world scenarios in a manner that incorporates the crucial operational perspective and realities. You will go even further by not just asking "what is lawful?" but also "what is ethical?" Not just what *can* we do, but what *should* we do.

Judging Kosovo: The Legal Process, the Law of Armed Conflict, and the Commander In Chief

The Honorable James E. Baker

My objective is to give you some personal insights into the application of the law of armed conflict to the Kosovo air campaign from the perspective of a lawyer serving the United States' commander in chief. I am not here out of any desire to tell my story. Almost all of my instincts as a lawyer, former national security official, and judge run against my participation in this forum. However, I have overcome my reticence because I am committed to constitutional government, and I believe that national level legal review is critical to military operations, not just in determining whether the commander in chief has domestic and international legal authority to resort to force, but also in shaping the manner in which the United States employs force, which is the focus of this colloquium.

In short, Kosovo was a campaign during which the law of armed conflict was assiduously followed. The campaign was conducted with uncommon, if not unprecedented, discrimination. I believe the process for reviewing targets within the US government worked well. Where there were mistakes, they were not mistakes of analytic framework or law. Where the process did not work smoothly or effectively, the idiosyncratic nature of a NATO campaign likely came into play. And, let us not lose sight of the fact that the combination of diplomacy and military operations that comprised the campaign was successful in achieving NATO's objectives.

I would like to focus on a particular aspect of Kosovo—the process of reviewing targets going to the president. At the outset I would like to correct a misperception. In preparing for the opportunity to comment here today, I asked military friends what they would be interested in hearing if they were in the audience. I was struck by the number of times thoughtful officers asked me why the president insisted upon approving all air targets; invoking images of President Johnson crouched over maps of Vietnam. As a matter of fact, the commander in chief did not approve all targets during Kosovo, but rather a smaller subset, which I will describe later. Carrying the analysis to the next step, in my opinion presidential review did not impede effective military operations in Kosovo. Rather, such review was efficient, contributed to the rule of law, and allowed the president to engage more effectively with NATO allies.

During my preparation for this speech, I was also (perhaps as a courtesy) asked about the role of lawyers, and particularly the role of a civilian lawyer at the National Security Council. Therefore, I will begin by describing and assessing my role in applying the law of armed conflict. I will close with a few concerns about the impending collision among the law of armed conflict, the doctrine of effects-based targeting, and a shared desire to limit collateral casualties and consequences to the fullest extent possible.

The Targeting Process

Before, during and after the air campaign, I performed three integrated roles with respect to the law of armed conflict.

1. Preparation

First, I educated and advised the president, the national security advisor, the principals and deputies committees,[1] and the attorney general on the law of armed conflict before (as well as during and after) the air campaign. As with any client, the time you spend educating them up front pays huge dividends when it comes time to apply the law in a live situation. (0400 on a secure

---

1. The Principals Committee, chaired by the Assistant to the President for National Security Affairs, included the following core members during the Kosovo conflict: the Secretary of State, Secretary of Defense, Assistant to the Vice President for National Security Affairs, Chairman of the Joint Chiefs of Staff, United States Representative to the United Nations, and the Director of Central Intelligence. The Deputies Committee, chaired by the Deputy Assistant to the President for National Security Affairs, included the Deputy Secretary of State or Under Secretary of State for Political Affairs, the Undersecretary of Defense for Policy, Assistant to the Vice President for National Security Affairs, Vice Chairman of the Joint Chiefs of Staff, United States Representative to the United Nations, and Deputy Director of Central Intelligence.

conference call is not the time to introduce any client, especially the national decision-maker, to the concepts of proportionality, necessity and discrimination.)

At the most practical level, I provided background and advice in the form of memoranda, e-mail, and oral input. My sources were customary international law (including those portions of Protocol I recognized by the United States as customary international law), the Geneva conventions, the commentaries on the Geneva conventions, US military manuals and academic treatises, and all who taught me along the way, including a number of the participants in this colloquium.

I have often thought that questions about the president's domestic authority to resort to force are driven by one's constitutional perspective and doctrinal convictions. In contrast, and I know this is risky to say in a room full of experts who have done so much to shape our understanding of the law of armed conflict, the principles underlying the law of armed conflict are generally agreed upon: necessity, proportionality, discrimination, and military objective. It is the different application of these principles to decisions to resort to force and to decisions regarding how force is used that generates most debate.

The law of armed conflict is not law exclusively for specialists. We expect junior personnel to apply these same principles on a tactical level. These are principles that policymakers must understand and apply to their most solemn responsibility: the exercise of force and the taking of human life. I would add, particularly to this audience, that in this respect government lawyers share a common duty with law professors and other experts to educate the policymaker of today and tomorrow in advance of the crisis—and not just to comment after the fact.

Advance guidance on the law of armed conflict also helps establish lines of communication and a common vocabulary of nuance between lawyer and client. In a larger, more layered bureaucracy than the president's national security staff, I imagine that the teaching process is even more important where the lawyer may be less proximate to the decision-maker. Not only does a good advance law of armed conflict brief educate the policymaker, any policymaker who hears such a brief will be sure his or her lawyer fully participates in the targeting process. In addition, the policymaker will understand in a live situation that the lawyer is applying hard law, and not kibitzing on operational matters.

I say that in part because some policymakers treat international law as soft law, and domestic, particularly criminal law, as hard law. The law of armed conflict is, of course, both. Indeed, reading some of the literature on Kosovo, limitations on collateral casualties and consequences seem always to be referred to as a political constraint and rarely as the legal constraint that it also is. Whether this reflects lack of knowledge about the law, or merely recognition that the policy hurdle was often the first encountered, is hard to say. But as you well know, pursuant to 18 U.S.C. §2441, war crimes committed by or against US persons violate US criminal law.

2. Target Categories

My second law of armed conflict related role was the review of target categories, such as air defense or lines of communication, under which rubric specific targets were almost always approved in theater. Among other things, I would ensure that such categories were consistent with the president's constitutional authority and with his prior direction.

How did I play this role in practice? To the extent specific targets or categories of targets were briefed, suggested or debated at deputies or principals committee meetings, I was immediately available in the room to identify issues and guide officials around legal rocks and shoals.

You may ask why principals were discussing military targets at all. First, as General Wesley Clark makes clear in his book *Waging Modern War*, NATO alliance operations involved the careful orchestration of nineteen national policies and, I will add, nineteen legal perspectives, many of which hinged on the nature of targets selected and the risk of collateral casualties. If the secretary of state was to address an appeal from one foreign minister or another to change the course of the campaign, she needed to understand the campaign.

Second, policymakers brought to bear extraordinary regional knowledge, including insight into Serbian pressure points. The principals had special knowledge into the effects of targeting that a military staff officer might not have.

Principals also bore a heavy responsibility for the outcome of a policy carried out through Operation Allied Force. I believe it was their duty to test the scope of operations to ensure we were doing all that we should do to achieve NATO's objectives, but in a way that would hold the alliance together. This was a duty fulfilled.

3. Targets

My third law of armed conflict related role was to review specific targets. If the president was going to approve or concur in a target, it was my duty to ensure the target was lawful. Time and again I returned to the same checklist: What is the military objective? Are there collateral consequences? Have we taken all appropriate measures to minimize those consequences and to discriminate between military objectives and civilian objects? Does the target brief quickly and clearly identify the issues for the president and principals?

You might ask why the NSC legal adviser and not military lawyers was doing this. There are at least three reasons. First, the European Command staff judge advocate (EUCOM SJA) and legal counsel to the Chairman of the Joint Chiefs of Staff (Chairman's legal counsel) were performing these reviews. The system of legal review, however, was sufficiently streamlined that I served as a fail-safe to ensure legal review had occurred on targets going to the president. Moreover, the authority to approve is also the authority to modify or to change, and it was essential that any such changes receive legal review prior to final approval and execution.

As you know, there is a propensity in government to adopt smaller and smaller decision-making circles in the interest of operational security. The circle can become too small. A decision-making process limited to cabinet principals may ask too much of too few if those principals are to address issues of policy and law on operational timelines. In my view, there should be a lawyer at the senior most policy level who is directly responsible at that level (in addition to the indispensable legal reviews conducted at other levels) for applying the law of armed conflict to each decision involving the use of force.

Second, it was in Washington at the Pentagon, the State Department and at the White House that issues of law, policy, and operations came together. A NATO alliance objection to a particular target, at the "political" level, might be couched in both policy and legal terms. Having a lawyer involved helped to avoid a "default judgment" when legal issues were raised.

Finally, and importantly, I implicitly assumed an additional role as a trustee to the process. I was not self-appointed; rather, this is what the national security advisor expected from his lawyer. In short, it was my job to make sure that in doing the right thing the US government was doing it the right way.

I had a standard mental checklist: Are all the relevant facts on the table—do the president and his principal officials know what they are reviewing? Are the longer-term repercussions of striking a target identified? Have the right process steps been taken? These are, of course, not inherently legal questions, but the lawyer in the room may be the staff person best positioned to test the process with policy detachment.

It is also important to think broadly about whom may be missing from a particular process. For example, I would ask, is this a matter that the attorney general should review? If not, will the attorney general nonetheless be asked by the press or the congress for her legal view on whether an action is consistent with the president's constitutional authority. Did this lead to the attorney general substituting her military judgment for those of the commanders? Of course not. Understanding the military objective for an action is not to question the military recommendation. It is, however, central to evaluating constitutional authority and the application of US law to particular facts, and that is a lawyer's task.

At the level of practice points and lessons learned, the critical process link was with the Chairman's legal counsel working closely with the Department of Defense (DoD) general counsel. As the national level lawyer closest to the operational line, Admiral Mike Lohr served as the primary communications channel with whom I could track and review briefs as they came to the White House. This ensured that I was ahead of, or at least even with, the operational timeline and that the president and not just the Pentagon had the benefit of military and DoD general counsel legal expertise. It also provided for one chain of legal communication, avoiding confusion. Because I had the familiarity of working with one person on hundreds of targets, we understood each other's vocabulary, tone and expression.

Where I could, I provided my input and advice in writing. First, I felt I should be no less accountable for my legal concurrence than the president for his decision. Second, I wanted to make sure my advice was received. Relying only on oral communication is to run the risk that the process will move forward without your input, given the competing pressures for principals' time. Finally, I found that my advice was cumulative and that policymakers were ready to apply the law of armed conflict principles in other contexts, including during conversations and meetings that I might not attend.

Assessment

Having given you a sense of the legal process in the White House involving target review, let me now give you my assessment as to how that process worked, focusing first on the role of the commander in chief and then on the role of lawyers.

1. Role of the Commander in Chief

As part of the president's brief on military operations, he was briefed on all categories of targets (that is, he concurred in the framework for addressing certain classes of target such as air defense or ground force targets in Kosovo), and he reviewed a sub-category of specific targets. These were for the most part targets raising heightened policy concerns, because of, among other factors, potential allied reactions, and especially because of potential risk to US personnel and collateral casualties. Not surprisingly, these were the targets that also raised more difficult law of armed conflict questions. Of the approximately 10,000 strike sorties involving some 2,000 targets, review of targets by the national security advisor and his legal adviser reached into the hundreds of targets (200-300), with the president reviewing a smaller subset of this number.

From my vantage-point, the president's review of targets was crisp; he would hear the description, review the briefing materials and at times raise a question he wanted answered. He expected issues to be addressed before they reached him, or alternatively, that the issue—perhaps with an ally—be quickly and clearly presented. This was not a ponderous process, but rather a decision-making process that one would expect of a commander in chief.

There is a school of thought that would have preferred that the commander in chief not review as many targets or the particular ones that he did, because such review amounts to micromanagement of the armed forces. Under this school, which has its genesis in the Vietnam era, the president should issue strategic guidance, a presidential mission statement of commander's intent, and give the authorization to pursue necessary targets.

While I think it is prudent to test whether the right balance was struck between military efficacy and civilian control, I disagree with the "minimal review" school as applied to Kosovo. In my view, the right balance was struck between national level and theater approved targets. I believe the success of the campaign is highly relevant in this debate—the alliance was sustained and NATO's objectives were achieved.

Why was presidential review important? As General Jumper, and others, have pointed out, this was a highly idiosyncratic campaign involving coalition warfare by nineteen democracies—fourteen with deployed forces. In this context, some individual target decisions assumed strategic policy implications. A government might fall. A runway might close. Or, NATO consensus might collapse. In my view, those are implications of presidential dimension. Not surprisingly, when there were allied concerns about targets, the president would get called.

Further, some of the targets the president reviewed required his approval. At the very least, his review removed any possible question of legal authority with respect to targets reaching beyond the scope of what he had already reviewed.

Finally, whether legally required or not, the president was accountable to the American people for US operations and casualties. Whether a target was approved at the tactical, operational or national level, its consequences would ultimately, and usually immediately, rest with NATO's political leadership—and no leader more than the US president. This last argument is not particular to Kosovo. Perhaps it is a truism, but it applies to an analysis of Kosovo just the same.

If I were to strengthen the process, I would make doubly sure that national level target suggestions, or nominations, were processed in the same manner as targets originating in the military chain of command; no shortcuts and no deference to grade or policy position. This would ensure that all targets receive the same measure of staff review and analytic scrutiny. Frankly, I am not in a position to state whether this was a novel or recurring problem during Kosovo. But there were times during the campaign when I would hear that so and so was pushing for a certain proposed target to be included in the next presidential brief. If I was aware of such "advice" I would channel it into the normal process of selection and review. In any event, the potential for error will diminish if target nominations all receive the same stepped process of review. Where operational necessity dictates speed, my answer is to make the process work faster, but do not adopt shortcuts.

2. Lawyers' Role

Although I think legal review at the NSC worked well with respect to Kosovo targets, there is no one answer to good process. Indeed, the policy and military context of one scenario is likely to be so different from the next that it would be dangerous to generalize—or to insist on one shoe size for all conflicts. Kosovo was not Desert Storm. And Desert Storm was not Desert Fox. One has to maintain situational awareness. If there is no one right way to lawyer, however, there is a wrong way and that is to absent yourself from the decision-making process or be prone simply to defer to others' conclusions.

Lawyers are not always readily accepted into the military targeting team. This reluctance has to do with concerns about secrecy, delay, lawyer creep (the legal version of mission creep, whereby one legal question becomes 17, which requires not one lawyer but 43 to answer). And, of course, fear that the lawyer may "just say no" to something the policymaker wants to do. I was fortunate that the national security advisor, secretary of defense and chairman and vice chairman of the joint chiefs of staff needed no persuading on the need for close-up lawyering. During the Kosovo campaign, legal advice may not have always received warm and generous thanks, but policymakers never hid from it or sought to shut it out.

In return, I think the lawyers fulfilled their responsibilities under the contract. We kept the number of participants to the absolute minimum; for example, if a matter of domestic legal authority needed to be limited within the Justice Department to the attorney general alone, then the attorney general alone it was. And, within the US government, NSC legal review met all but one operational deadline. One target was put on the president's brief before legal review was complete. Therefore, when the president reached the target during an Oval Office briefing, I asked that it be set aside until that review could be completed.

While I always felt pressure, I never let pressure dictate my analysis. One such pressure I did not fully anticipate was the extent to which US actions would receive international legal scrutiny. In any event, we applied the law, because it was the law, not because there was an audience.

Whether actors like it or not, Kosovo may serve as a harbinger of the manner in which specific US military actions—down to the tactical sortie—will receive legal scrutiny, from NGOs, ad hoc tribunals, and the International Criminal Court, the latter two of which may attempt to assert jurisdiction over US actors. As a result, policymakers should anticipate that the same public statement intended to influence an adversary might also influence the legal observer. Policymakers, and not lawyers, should surely decide what points to emphasize in public statements, but they should do so conscious of the legal implications of what is being said. As the International Criminal Tribunal for the former Yugoslavia (ICTY) review of NATO action illustrates, although that review concluded our actions were indeed lawful, merely doing the right thing and doing it well and carefully will not necessarily immunize actors from law of armed conflict scrutiny.

Areas of Future Tension

I will close with a few words of caution involving three areas where I would forecast tension in the future between doctrine, policy and the law of armed conflict.

1. Proportionality, Necessity, and "Going Downtown"

First, there is a potential tension between proportionality and necessity on the one hand, and on the other hand, the military importance of striking hard at the outset of a conflict to surprise, to shock, and thus to effect a rapid end to conflict. There has been commentary about the incremental nature of the air campaign, and the merits of "going downtown" earlier. On one level this aspect of the campaign was dictated by NATO's phased air campaign; that is what NATO approved and therefore that was the limit of alliance authority and consensus.

Legal considerations did not drive this result. Indeed, the political constraint agreed to by the alliance was reached well before any legal constraint based on necessity or proportionality, particularly so given NATO's objectives of preventing ethnic cleansing and avoiding a larger regional war. But looking forward, we should not lose sight that there is a legal facet to any decision to "go downtown." Legal judgments depend on factual predicate. If policymakers believe a symbolic show of force alone will accomplish the permitted goal, a lawyer would find it difficult to concur in the bombing of national level military targets in a nation's capital.

2. Dual-Use Targets

Similarly, so called "dual-use targets" present any number of inherent tensions. The law of armed conflict attempts to posit a clarity in the distinction between military objective and civilian object that may not exist on the ground. I found that dual-use targets largely appeared on a continuum. This seemed particularly true because we were dealing with a dictatorship with broad, but not always total, control over potential dual-use targets, like media relay towers or factories. In such an environment, facilities can be rapidly converted from civilian to military to civilian use at the direction of a government not bound by Youngstown Sheet and Tube.

In such a context, effects-based targeting and the law of armed conflict may be on a collision course. The tension is particularly apparent where a facility financially sustains an adversary's regime, and therefore the regime's military operations, but does not make a product that directly and effectively contributes to an adversary's military operations. The policy frustration is that in a dictatorial context, these may be exactly the targets that not only might persuade an adversary of one's determination, but more importantly striking such targets may shorten the conflict and therefore limit the number of collateral casualties that will otherwise occur.

I am not arguing here for a change in the law; I am very conscious that too malleable a doctrine of military objective will send the law hurdling down the slippery slope toward collateral calamity. Nor, I should be clear, am I suggesting that the United States applied anything other than a strict test of military objective as recognized in customary international law and by those states that have adopted Protocol I. My purpose is to identify to you a very real area of tension that warrants further review and that will confront lawyers in the future.

3. Protection of Noncombatants and Traditional Understanding of Military Objective

The law of armed conflict generates a number of ironic results in the interest of a higher principle or in the interest of clarity. For example, "treacherous" killing of military leaders (as that term is understood under the law of armed conflict) is prohibited, but the law of armed conflict permits the use of more dramatic force, even with significant collateral consequences, to attack a military headquarters with essentially the same objective of disrupting command and control. During the Kosovo campaign, lawyers were never squarely confronted with the target that would have the effect of ending the conflict with minimal collateral consequences, but which nonetheless failed a traditional test of military objective. But I sensed that such an issue could have arisen.

Without diminishing the paramount principle of protection for noncombatants, I wonder whether the definition of military objective deserves another look, in the interest of limiting collateral casualties. Are traditional definitions adequate, or do they drive military operations toward prolonged conflict and ground combat? Do they provide enough guidance to shield the commander from prosecution where the commander has made legal judgments in good faith?

These are more than academic questions of passing interest. The potentially poor fit between traditional categories of military objective and the reality of a conflict where targets fall on a continuum of judgment between military and civilian, becomes more perilous in an age of international scrutiny where good faith differences of view can take on criminal implications. Those who do evaluate such actions should do so aware of the factual and temporal context in which decisions are made. National security decision-making is not judicial decision-making. Time is more of the essence, and information is not necessarily of evidentiary quality.

Further, as much as I would hope that the United States is not engaged in armed conflict in the future, there are no doubt national interests that will require the exercise of force. As Air Vice-Marshal Mason has said, it is honorable for democracies to strive to the fullest extent possible to eliminate collateral casualties from armed conflict. Just as low and no casualty conflicts have resulted in a public expectation, and some suggest a de facto policy constraint, regarding US military action, some have used Kosovo to advance a legal view that the law of armed conflict virtually prohibits collateral casualties. This is an honorable and worthy aspiration, but not law. Nor should it be law, or the tyrants of the world will operate with impunity.

The law of armed conflict does not prohibit collateral casualties any more than international law prohibits armed conflict. It constrains, regulates, and limits. War is almost never casualty free and we will be extraordinarily lucky if the next conflict incurs as few collateral casualties as Kosovo.

Conclusion

In closing, I hope I have given you some insight into the process of legal review at the commander in chief level during the Kosovo air campaign. I also hope I have given you a sense of the issues, at least in a manner consistent with my duty to safeguard deliberations.

My message is clear. First, lawyers are integral to the conduct of military operations at the national command level. They must be in the physical and metaphorical decision-making room. And, they can perform their duties to the law in a timely and secure way that meets operational deadlines and needs. Those who uphold the law of armed conflict bring honor to the profession and to the armed forces.

Second, the law of armed conflict is hard law. It is US criminal law. Increasingly, it will also serve as an international measure by which the United States is judged. The law of armed conflict addresses the noblest objective of law—the protection of innocent life. And the United States should be second to none in compliance, as was the case with Kosovo.

Finally, application of the law of armed conflict is a moral imperative. If international law regulates, but does not prohibit war, the law of armed conflict helps to ensure that force is used in the most economical manner possible. Whether we agree on the precise definition of military objective, or on each and every Kosovo target, I am confident that we all agree on the moral imperative of minimizing civilian casualties and suffering to the fullest extent possible.

Operation Allied Force from the Perspective of the NATO Air Commander

Lieutenant General Michael Short, USAF (Ret)

The forces that I was privileged to command bombed Milosevic for seventy-eight days flying over thirty-eight thousand sorties without the loss of a single pilot, after which Milosevic accepted all of NATO's terms. Those terms were: number one, the killing would stop in Kosovo; number two, the professional military forces of the Serb Army and the paramilitary police would leave Kosovo; number three, a NATO commander would come in on the ground with a predominantly NATO force to occupy the province (this was General Mike Jackson and the NATO forces that came in shortly after the bombing campaign was over); number four, the Kosovar Albanians would return to their homes; and, number five, we would facilitate the ICTY (International Criminal Tribunal for the former Yugoslavia) process. We did all that despite some extraordinary restraints that were placed upon the warfighters in this effort.

I would like to talk quite frankly tonight about three of the issues coming out of Kosovo that are of most concern to me personally and for the future of the US armed forces. I am not a lawyer. I will hopefully share with you some things that will be of value to you who are military lawyers, or civilian lawyers who impact the Department of Defense, about how the next generation of my profession does its business. But I am not a lawyer. I am a professional soldier. I did that for thirty-five years. The three things that are of particular interest to me are targeting, collateral damage and coalition warfare.

Targeting

Let's talk first about targeting. A lot has been said in a lot of different publications and by a lot of different people about how we did our targeting. Let me first assure you that the professionals in the American and NATO militaries understand the concept of effects-based targeting. We know what we were trying to do. We were trying to compel Milosevic to accept NATO's terms as rapidly as possible with as little destruction of Serbian property as possible and with as little loss of life on both sides as was humanly possible. That is what we were trying to do. Unfortunately, because NATO was an alliance of nineteen nations, you get the lowest common denominator. All those folks have to agree on something.

Targeting became something that was not in my control. I spent thirty-four years in my profession thinking that when I was in charge of an air effort, I would indeed be in charge of targeting. I thought that the president of the United States and the leaders of whatever alliance we were associated with would give me broad guidance—political objectives that they wanted to achieve. I thought that my boss, the combatant commander, would translate those into military objectives for me. I thought I would perhaps brief the president of the United States on target categories that I intended to strike, but that individual targets would be mine to decide and mine to destroy. And, thereby, I would achieve the effect of bringing Milosevic to the table as rapidly as possible. As all of you understand, that was not the case.

Targeting was not mine to decide. Targeting decisions were made in the White House, at Number Ten Downing Street, and in Paris, Rome and Berlin. The senior political leaders of the alliance approved individual fixed targets—a fixed target being something that doesn't move. Mobile targets were mine to decide upon. I could decide to attack tanks and armored personnel carriers any time I thought it was appropriate. Quite frankly I never thought it to be appropriate, because the center of gravity was not the third army in Kosovo. The center of gravity was Milosevic, the circle of leadership around him, and the ruling elite. But that was not the way NATO wanted to wage war.

We did our level best to target those things that we thought would have the effect of bringing Milosevic to the table. Instead, because those targets were not picked by professional soldiers and professional sailors and professional airmen, we bombed targets that were quite frankly inappropriate for bringing Milosevic to the table. I would say to you that in terms of targeting, this was victory by happenstance more than victory by design.

We had a video teleconference (VTC) every day for seventy-eight days—clearly the highlight of my day—between myself and my staff and the combatant commander, General Wesley Clark, and his staff. One of my favorite video teleconferences occurred when General Clark was haranguing Admiral Jim Ellis, a great American. (No one in this audience, no one in this country will ever understand the extraordinary difficulties that Jim Ellis put up with and the incredible difficult position he was placed in.) General Clark was telling Jim and I what we needed to do that day and at the end of his guidance he said to us: "Mike, Jim, I hope this will work." Jim Ellis looked at the Supreme Allied Commander Europe (SACEUR) on the VTC and said: "SACEUR, hope is not a course of action." Course of action is kind of a military term—maybe some of you are unfamiliar with it—but it is what we are going to do today. Hope is not something we would like to be doing today. We like to know what we are doing.

We were accused by a lot of folks of inaccurate targeting and not understanding what we were targeting. The fact of the matter is that every target we intended to strike had passed an extraordinary series of tests, perhaps the most important one being whether it fit with our definition of military objective under the law of armed conflict. We had some targeting failures. We acknowledge that. The Chinese embassy was a failure of intelligence, not a targeting failure. The young men who worked for me hit exactly what I told them to hit. It wasn't until two or three or four in the morning that I found out we had hit the Chinese embassy as opposed to the Serbian logistics headquarters that we thought we had struck.

As for the convoy that we struck early in the operations against the third army in Kosovo, I reviewed that tape five times before it became clear to me that those were indeed tractors hauling wagons as opposed to eighteen-wheel military vehicles. The young man that dropped those bombs was flying at 450 miles an hour in bad weather and he was being shot at. He had one chance to make identification and he made a mistake. That was not a war crime. He had no intent to kill people he was not supposed to kill. He made a mistake.

The issue I would lay in front of you—particularly you youngsters who will be the next generation in the civilian hierarchy or in the uniformed military—is whose responsibility should targeting be. Should targeting be the responsibility of the president of the United States—someone not trained in my profession, who does not fully understanding what I am trying to do in terms of military objectives and the targets that he has given me? Should he approve target sets? I believe he should. I believe we should have gone to Mr Clinton and Mr Blair and Mr Chirac and Mr Schroeder and Mr D'Alema and said:

"Gentlemen, we intend to target these sets. We will target the military production capability. We will target command and control nodes. We will target power grids. We will target lines of communication. We will target field forces. And we will target the integrated air defense capability of the nation. Now if there are targets within those sets that you don't want me to strike, tell me, and I will place those individual targets on a no-strike list. But once you have done that, then give me that totality of target set, and let me achieve the effect you want achieved as rapidly and with as little loss of life and as little destruction of property as possible."

Collateral Damage

Now let me move to the issue of collateral damage. It is inconceivable to me that anyone who understands anything about modern warfare would think that as a responsible commander that I would not take every step within my command to limit collateral damage; that I would not provide to my air crews from all the participating nations and all the American forces the most precise guidance I could provide to them on limiting collateral damage; that I would not package the forces we send into battle every day with collateral damage foremost in my mind. But it becomes my job, your job as the next generation of commanders and the commanders' advisers, to balance concern for collateral damage and concern for loss of life on the one hand with the risk that you are asking your pilots to take.

On about the fiftieth day of the war, we bombed the bridge outside the city of Nis in broad daylight on a Saturday afternoon. It was a valid line of communication. We had seen Serbian troops moving across that bridge in reinforcement efforts to Kosovo. Two F-16's dropped laser guided bombs on that bridge. The first aircraft hit the right stanchion and the second aircraft hit the left stanchion. Predictably, the bridge dropped in the river. That is what I had told the pilots to do. Unfortunately, on or near the bridge were about twenty Serb civilians. It was market day. It was Saturday. The young pilots could do nothing about that. The next day Milosevic stretched the bodies out on the street, called the press down from Belgrade, and announced that the NATO war criminals had done their thing once again. As a result of that incident, this was the guidance I got from the very highest levels of the NATO military political leadership: you will no longer bomb bridges in daylight, you will no longer bomb bridges on market days, on holidays or on weekends. In fact, you will only bomb bridges between ten o'clock at night and three o'clock in the morning in order to ensure that we do not kill civilians crossing those bridges.

Lieutenant General Michael Short, USAF (Ret)

I will grant you that that may indeed lessen the possibility of killing civilians crossing the bridges, but what does it do to your aircrews? Number one, it creates sanctuary for the enemy. It will take Milosevic about forty-eight hours to figure out that no bridges are being bombed except between ten o'clock at night and three o'clock in the morning; that they are not being bombed on weekends or on market days. So he does not need to protect those bridges except for between ten o'clock at night and three o'clock in the morning. At ten o'clock at night the NATO aircrews become totally predictable because that is the five hour limit that the air commander is allowed to send those young men into harm's way to attack those bridges that must be struck. So the risk for NATO aircrews is raised by a magnitude of three or four or five times what it would have been if I were allowed to conduct the conflict the way I wish to. No responsible commander wishes to kill civilians. Let me say that to you again. No responsible commander wearing the NATO uniform wishes to kill civilians. Never in seventy-eight days did we target Serb civilians, but unfortunately in war civilians are sometimes where you would like them not to be. Unfortunately sometimes in a war civilians are a very key part of the establishment that you're targeting.

There are civilian workers on every one of our air fields in this country and every shipyard and every aircraft factory. There are civilian workers who would die if they were attacked by an adversary of the United States of America. Every day we did our very, very best to limit collateral damage and limit the loss of life on the adversary's side. Every time we failed in that effort, the reaction by political leaders was hysterical—along the lines I just outlined for you. The restrictions that were placed on the young men and women who were going in harm's way every day were extraordinary—losing all sight of what effect we were trying to achieve. In fact, we got to the point that during the last ten days of the war I was instructed to attack only those targets that had a potential for low collateral damage. I was given no instruction with regard to the impact this might have on Milosevic, whether this would injure the war machine, whether this would bring the conflict to a close. Our young people were to only to strike those targets that had the potential for a low collateral damage, because the leaders of the nineteen nation alliance could no longer stand collateral damage incidents and because they did not understand war. They thought it was a video game, and that no one ever dies.

Did you ever see anybody die in the films from the Gulf War? I never did. I just saw crosshairs on the target in downtown Baghdad, and then it blew up. I never saw a body in the street. But Milosevic was extraordinarily good at putting bodies in the street of people that we had in all probability killed. That is, maybe a hundred Serbs, not in all cases did we kill who he said we killed. We were on the defensive and our political leaders could not stand the heat. They could not grit their teeth and say simply "get this done—do it as well as you can, don't kill folks you don't have to kill, and don't blow up things you don't have to blow up, but go ahead and get it done—you know how to do this, we do not, but we have given you the basic guidance." That is not what happened. Concern for collateral damage drove us to extraordinary degree, and it will drive the next generation of warriors even more so, because whereas I see this as an extraordinary failure, the leadership within the NATO senior administrations would say this was indeed an extraordinary success. We bombed for seventy-eight days; nobody died on our side; and Milosevic accepted all our terms. What in the world is that burned-out old three star whining about? This was an extraordinary success, they would say, yet indeed it was not.

Coalition Warfare

Finally, let me turn to the issue of coalition warfare. We do not want to fight by ourselves. My country wants to fight as part of the coalition. We want to be with our allies. We want to share the risk. We do not want just young Americans to die on the first night and the second night and the third night. We want our friends to be there with us. We do not want to be the lone wolf going out striking wherever we think we need to strike. We need to represent the considered opinion of the NATO alliance, or the Western community of nations, or whoever it happens to be, if we choose to employ military action. We want to be part of a coalition. However, as a professional soldier, I would tell you I prefer to be a member of a coalition of the willing as we had in the Gulf War.

In 1991 if you chose to throw in your forces with us and the Saudis and the Kuwaitis and the Brits, you were welcome, but you came under our terms. We explained to you how we were going to make war and if you did not like that explanation, or if you could not sign up for those terms, then you did not need to be part of our coalition. However, in 1999 it was NATO, not a coalition of the willing. All nineteen nations had to agree, and so we ended up with the lowest common denominator. That is how it was that a nation that was providing less than 10% of the total effort could say to the most powerful nation on the face of the earth "you cannot bomb that target."

The United States of America lost its leverage on the first night. On the first night of the war we lost any leverage we had, and we ended up being leveraged. What was the US interest in Operation Allied Force? Was there a US national interest? I make the case that our only national interest was the continuance of the NATO alliance in some successful form. If NATO had been defeated by a third-rate war criminal and murderer, then I think NATO would cease to exist. Before the war started, the United States of America enjoyed ultimate leverage over its NATO allies. NATO wanted to go to war. The Europeans were saying, "we need to do something about this tragedy that is occurring in Europe's backyard." NATO wanted to go to war. There was no maritime option and NATO did not want to commit ground troops, so the only option was the air option. I do not wish to offend any of my NATO friends in the audience, but NATO cannot make war without the United States of America. It is just that simple. You do not have the technology. You do not have the numbers. You do not have the precision. You do not have the forces that allow you to do it. So if the United States of America was not going to participate in that air war in Kosovo, it was not going to be a successful air war in Kosovo. So we had the ultimate leverage. We were in the same position we were in 1991 to dictate how this should be done. We did not do that because it was going to be a three night war. We were going to demonstrate resolve. Who cared what we bombed, because it was going to be over in three nights. So we threw that leverage away and we ended up being leveraged.

Now what do the lawyers have to do with all of this? I expected that I would be the targeteer, and so the advice of my lawyer would be extraordinarily important to me because everything I struck had to be a valid military target for all the coalition members. Concern for the law of armed conflict was absolutely paramount in my mind. However, as I said to you earlier, those target decisions were taken out of our hands. Target decisions were made by the president of the United States, the prime minister of Great Britain, the president of France, and the president of Germany, and targets were just issued to me. So I really did not need to go to my lawyer and say "do you think this passes the test? Is this a valid military target?" What my lawyers say is a valid military target and consistent with the law of armed conflict, nation X's lawyers may disagree with. So every day I put together what was called the air tasking order which sent out to the thousand or more NATO airplanes what targets they were going to strike that next day. I had to wait for the individual nations to answer back, having gone to their capitals and asked whether they should accept that target. And, indeed, in many capitals the answer was no—we do not define that as a valid military target. Now if I could get that answer back in a timely fashion, I could assign that target to a nation that had a less restrictive view of the law of armed conflict, but if I got that information late, and the aircraft were already airborne, then I ended up canceling the strike.

Perspective of the NATO Air Commander

Great Britain exercised control over all US airplanes stationed on UK soil. All B-52's and all B-1's stationed at Fairford and all F-15E's stationed at Lakenheath had to have their targets approved by the British parliament before they could be struck. US aircraft had to have their targets approved by other nations because we were based on British soil. As many of you know, the French exercised total veto over targets. They would take the position that not only would their aircraft not strike the "Rock-and-roll Bridge," no one could strike the "Rock-and-roll Bridge." That makes it very, very difficult to fight within a coalition. It makes it very, very difficult for your lawyer to do his business.

Concluding Thoughts For Lawyers

A young man asked me earlier this evening what advice I would give an up-and-coming young operational lawyer wearing the uniform in defense of this country. Understand what your commander is up against. Understand and participate in the development of his rules of engagement. Understand what special instructions he is providing as supplemental to his rules of engagement, to his troops in the field, or his men and women at sea, or his men and women in the air. Then, do not be afraid to tell him what he really does not want to hear—that he has put together this exquisite plan, but his targets indeed are not valid ones or his targets may in fact violate the law of armed conflict.

Every target that we bombed for seventy-eight days had been reviewed at some level by professional military lawyers and that is the way it has to be. I want to bomb the targets. I want to get this thing done, but I must have advisers sitting at my right hand telling me whether I am doing this properly or not. Am I breaking laws? Am I doing things that are unacceptable? Will the eyes of a professional soldier believe that to be a valid target or a valid target set? It will take enormous courage to do that in particular circumstances because you're always going to be junior to your boss. My lawyer most of the time was a lieutenant colonel. It is very difficult for him to come in and say to a three star "you are out of bounds, sir, you are about to break the law." But you have got to be able to do that. You have got to know your business inside and out and you have got to think like an operator. Your job as a military lawyer is not to prevent me from doing my job, your job as a military lawyer is to make it possible for me to do my job without breaking the law, without blowing up things I should not blow up, without killing people I should not kill and without committing war crimes. I want to get this done. You have got to help me. Do not be a hindrance. Tell me the truth. Tell me when I have pushed it too far. Tell me when I am in the gray area, but help me get this thing done that our country wants to get done for the alliance. That's it.

Discussion

Brian O'Donnell:
General, did you ever feel constrained in the bombing campaign not to strike a target because you did not have a precision-guided munition?

Michael Short:
We started this fight out as a totally precision-munitions fight. A lot has been made in the press about the fifteen thousand foot floor that I placed on my people. You need to understand that when we started this fight, we were only going to attack fixed targets. We were not going to attack tanks. We were not going to attack troops in the field. We were going to attack buildings and airfields and aircraft shelters and bridges and those sorts of things, which are easily identifiable from fifteen thousand feet. Restrictions were placed on me that I could not lose any aircraft and any aircrews. So I had enormous concern for force protection. You cannot fly high enough to avoid the radar of a surface-to-air missile. But you can fly high enough to avoid small arms and light triple-A (anti-aircraft artillery) and the IR (infra-red) missile. Fifteen thousand feet was that floor, so that's where we started out.

Every bomb that was dropped for the first X number of days in Serbia and Kosovo was a guided munition. There were a number of NATO nations that did not carry precision-guided munitions, and they were not allowed to drop bombs. Then as we moved into the next phase, which was attacking the Third Army in Kosovo, we continued to use nothing but precision munitions. Then we found that if we controlled it properly and used the correct force that we could drop a certain number of unguided munitions—what you and I call dumb bombs. We did indeed drop a number of dumb bombs, particularly from B-1s and B-52s. I understand there was a discussion earlier today about so-called carpet bombing B-52s. No carpet bombing occurred. Outside of Kosovo, again with the exception of the B-52 and the B-1, we dropped nothing that wasn't precision guided. Everything that hit Serbia proper was precision-guided munitions in an attempt to control collateral damage and in attempt to control loss of civilian life.

Leslie Green:
Do you not think that it is time we took the line that we want the military representative with perhaps their legal advisers from the members of the coalition to get together and say, putting it brutally, to hell with our constitutional political advisers—we are going to decide, not somebody sitting three-and-a-half thousand miles away who has not the vaguest idea of what is going on anyway?

Michael Short:
No, sir, I can never imagine giving up civilian control of the military.

Leslie Green:
It is the constitutional control that worries me, not the civilian control.

Michael Short:
No, as strongly as I feel about men and women in my profession being allowed to do their jobs, and as strongly as I would advise against micromanagement by political appointed or elected leaders, if that is the role they choose to play, then I have to accept that role. I advise against it. I hope that what my own country and I saw during the last eight years was an aberration driven by a particular administration that I will not see again. But you need to understand, I hoped the same thing in 1967 when Lyndon Johnson was on his hands and knees in the Oval Office reviewing targets with Robert McNamara. Remember that my generation swore that would never happen again. In the Gulf War, in fact, it did not. George Bush the elder gave us mission-type orders. That was not the case in 1999. But I cannot imagine a military professional saying to hell with the constitution and to hell with our elected and appointed leaders, we'll do this as we see fit. That is not how we do business.

Leslie Green:
What if the constitution of one country interferes with the military operations of the coalition?

Discussion

Michael Short:
I believe, sir, you've got to set those rules beforehand with that particular country. In the case of the Canadians, there were targets I knew the Canadian F-18s were not allowed to attack. Their pilots were dying to do it, but Ottawa was not going to allow them. So it was my job to assign those targets to a nation with less restrictive guidance. I could still use the Canadians in many roles. It is my job to fold all those capabilities together and produce a coherent war-making effort. Now I agree with you that before the fact is when we have to agree on what the rules are. I would take the position that before the fact we say "nation X, if you don't wish to attack any of these targets, that's fine, but you cannot prohibit the rest of us from attacking those targets." But as far as I can tell, that conversation never took place, and once the fight started, we lost that leverage.

Ruth Wedgwood:
You said that the center of gravity to really win the campaign was the ruling elite in Belgrade.

Michael Short:
Milosevic and the men and women around him who depend upon him and who he, in turn, depends upon.

Ruth Wedgwood:
We had a big debate this afternoon about whether civilian morale as such is ever an allowable target. From an operational point of view, fill me in on what you make of that.

Michael Short:
Let me give you my perspective, and Colonel Sorenson who was my lawyer will leap to his feet if I get out of bounds here even though I am retired now. You cannot target civilians—pure and simple. Now, as a professional soldier, I will target the power grid, which I believe will significantly impact command and control of all Serb forces throughout the entire country. We will prohibit their ability to move on trains, and we will make it very, very difficult for them to do their military business. Now when I sit with my planners, I am not going to think that you are so naive that I do not say to myself and to my planners that this will also make the Serb population unhappy with their senior leadership because they allowed this to happen. But that is a spin-off—a peripheral result—of me targeting a valid military target.

Discussion

If I had gone to my bosses with Colonel Sorenson and said I want to target something because it will impact the Serb civilian population, from my perspective, that would be totally out of bounds. That would be unacceptable. But any thinking military professional knows that there are certain target sets that if targeted are going to have an effect on the population which in turn will pressure the senior leadership. There were factories that we were never able to get to for a number of different reasons that were dual-use factories. They produced Yugos from midnight until noon and tank turrets from noon to midnight. That is a valid military target. Now if I blow that up, two thousand Serbs probably just lost their jobs, and they will demonstrate outside Milosevic's palace because they would be unhappy. I know that, but that is not why I targeted that facility. I will stand in any court in the land and swear to that because that is how we hit our targets. But certainly we understand the peripheral in that.

Christopher Greenwood:
My question is this General: Britain would have been in the dock along with the United States, so can you see any circumstances in which it would have been responsible for a British government not to have insisted on reviewing targets? Can you think of any circumstances in which the United States would allow British aircraft to fly from a US air base to attack a target without the United States checking to see whether it would be attacking a lawful target?

Michael Short:
No, I understand your position. There were strange aircraft taking off from Germany every day and the Germans did not exercise their prerogative to approve the targets of those aircraft. The vast majority of US strike aircraft were stationed at Aviano, Italy and Mr D'Alema, who was struggling with extraordinary skills to hold together a coalition government, never approached us and asked to review the targets of our aircraft taking off from Aviano. So while I certainly understand the position taken by the British government, when the rest of my allies did not take that position, then the British position stands out to me as a problem. Okay? I was able to work around this as long as I got a notification time or as long as I was able to understand the sensitivity of what Britain thought was good, bad, or indifferent. But on more than one occasion when the system wasn't working, I had dozens of strike aircraft on the tanker within ten minutes of pushing into Serbian airspace when the word came through from Ten Downing Street that the target was not acceptable to the British.

PART II

THE APPLICABILITY OF THE LAW OF ARMED CONFLICT

Introduction

Scott Silliman

This first panel will address the overall applicability of the law of armed conflict, also called international humanitarian law, to the NATO operation in Kosovo. We are also going to be focusing on several specific issues that arose during that campaign, one being the legal status of the three Army soldiers who were captured while on a routine mission near the border. As you recall, immediately after they were captured, our State Department announced to the press that the three were "illegal detainees" and many of us—and several are here at this conference—responded vehemently that they were clearly prisoners of war under the Third Geneva Convention, and that to consider them otherwise was to denude them of the protections afforded them under international law.

I'd like to lay a foundation by reading from a portion of the very controversial Final Report to the Prosecutor by the Committee Established to Review the NATO Bombing Campaign Against the Federal Republic of Yugoslavia[1] on this linkage between the *jus ad bellum*, which is a very large debate as all of you know, and the more particular *jus in bello*, which is the focus of this colloquium. It reads:

> 32. The precise linkage between *jus ad bellum* and *jus in bello* is not completely resolved. . . . [I]n the 1950's there was a debate concerning whether UN authorized forces were required to comply with the *jus in bello* as they represented the good side in a battle between good and evil. This debate died out as the participants realized that a certain crude reciprocity was essential if the law was to have any positive impact. An argument that the 'bad' side had to

---

1. Final Report to the Prosecutor by the Committee Established to Review the NATO Bombing Campaign Against the Federal Republic of Yugoslavia, 39 INTERNATIONAL LEGAL MATERIALS 1257 (2000), *reprinted* herein as Appendix A [hereinafter Report to the Prosecutor].

comply with the law while the 'good' side could violate it at will would be most unlikely to reduce human suffering in conflict.

33. More recently, a refined approach to the linkage issue has been advocated by certain law of war scholars. Using their approach, assuming that the only lawful basis for recourse to force is self defence, each use of force during a conflict must be measured by whether or not it complies with the *jus in bello* and by whether or not it complies with the necessity and proportionality requirements of self defence. The difficulty with this approach is that it does not adequately address what should be done when it is unclear who is acting in self defence and it does not clarify the obligations of the 'bad' side.[2]

The Report to the Prosecutor went on to say that the Committee deliberately refrained from assessing *jus ad bellum* issues and focused exclusively on whether violations of the law of war occurred within the confines of the *jus in bello*. It concluded that there was no basis for further investigation and no basis whatsoever for the referral of war crimes charges against any of the NATO combatants.

With regard to the question of linkage between the *jus ad bellum* and the *jus in bello*, though, there seems to be no ambiguity in the United States position. If there is an armed conflict, whether deemed just or unjust, right or wrong under the *jus ad bellum*, the *jus in bello* applies equally to both sides. That's the position I personally take, but I know that many will disagree with that.

---

2. Id.

The Applicability of International Humanitarian Law and the Law of Neutrality to the Kosovo Campaign

Christopher Greenwood

The purpose of this paper[1] is to examine the applicability of international humanitarian law and the law of neutrality to Operation Allied Force, the NATO campaign over Kosovo in 1999. The paper is thus chiefly about *jus in bello* (which is treated here as synonymous with the law of armed conflict and international humanitarian law), not about *jus ad bellum*. It is not intended, therefore, to enter into the controversy regarding the legality of the decision to resort to force over Kosovo or the long-running debate over whether contemporary international law recognizes a right of humanitarian intervention in the face of large scale violations of human rights. The present writer has already made clear in other publications his view that a right of humanitarian intervention (albeit one of a strictly limited character) exists in

---

1. This paper has been revised since the colloquium in order to take account of points made by a number of commentators in the immensely valuable discussion periods, although the responsibility for the views here expressed remain mine alone. I have also taken the opportunity to take account of the decision of the European Court of Human Rights in *Bankovic v. Belgium and Others* delivered on December 19, 2001 since that decision is directly concerned with the Kosovo conflict. Conflicts occurring since Kosovo are not discussed here.

international law and that the conditions for the exercise of that right were present in Kosovo in 1999,[2] although that view is by no means universal.[3] That, however, is a debate for another occasion. For present purposes, it is sufficient—but also necessary—to note three points regarding the legal justification advanced by the NATO States for their resort to force, since these points have a bearing on the application of international humanitarian law and the law of neutrality during the campaign.

First, the Kosovo campaign was one in which some actions against the Federal Republic of Yugoslavia (FRY) were undertaken pursuant to a mandate from the United Nations Security Council, while others were taken by the

---

2. See Christopher Greenwood, *Evidence to the House of Commons Foreign Affairs Committee*, Foreign Affairs Committee Fourth Report, 1999-2000, HC Paper 28-II, p. 137, reprinted in 49 INTERNATIONAL AND COMPARATIVE LAW QUARTERLY 926 (2000), and *Humanitarian Intervention: the Case of Kosovo*, 10 FINNISH YEAR BOOK OF INTERNATIONAL LAW (forthcoming).

3. Amongst the literature on the subject, which reflects the very different positions taken by a wide range of international lawyers, see the evidence given by Ian Brownlie, Christine Chinkin and Vaughan Lowe to the Foreign Affairs Committee of the United Kingdom House of Commons, *supra* note 2, reprinted in 49 INTERNATIONAL AND COMPARATIVE LAW QUARTERLY 876–943 (2000); Louis Henkin, Ruth Wedgwood, Jonathan Charney, Christine Chinkin, Richard Falk, Thomas Franck and W. Michael Reisman, *Editorial Comments: NATO's Kosovo Intervention*, 93 AMERICAN JOURNAL OF INTERNATIONAL LAW 824–878 (1999); Bruno Simma, *NATO, the UN and the Use of Force: Legal Aspects*, 10 EUROPEAN JOURNAL OF INTERNATIONAL LAW 1 (1999); Antonio Cassese, *Ex iniuria ius oritur: Are We Moving towards International Legitimation of Forcible Humanitarian Countermeasures in the World Community?*, 10 EUROPEAN JOURNAL OF INTERNATIONAL LAW 23 (1999) and *A Follow-Up: Forcible Humanitarian Countermeasures and Opinio Necessitatis*, *id.*, at 791; Nico Krisch, *Unilateral Enforcement of the Collective Will: Kosovo, Iraq, and the Security Council*, 3 YEARBOOK OF UNITED NATIONS LAW 59 (1999); Dino Kritsiotis, *The Kosovo Crisis and NATO's Application of Armed Force Against the Federal Republic of Yugoslavia*, 49 INTERNATIONAL AND COMPARATIVE LAW QUARTERLY 330 (2000); Steven Blockmans, *Moving into UNchartered Waters: An Emerging Right of Unilateral Intervention?*, 12 LEIDEN JOURNAL OF INTERNATIONAL LAW 759 (1999); and Francesco Francioni, *Of War, Humanity and Justice: International Law After Kosovo*, 4 YEARBOOK OF UNITED NATIONS LAW 107 (2000). The Kosovo crisis has also attracted an unusual number of studies by official and semi-official bodies. These include the report of the Foreign Affairs Committee of the United Kingdom House of Commons, HOUSE OF COMMONS PAPER (1999–2000) NO. 28-I together with the response by the United Kingdom Government at COMMAND PAPERS 4825 (August 2000); the report of the Advisory Council on International Affairs and the Advisory Committee on Issues of Public International Law of the Netherlands Government, Report No. 13 (April 2000), available at http://www.aiv-advice.nl (reviewed by Ige Dekker in 6 JOURNAL OF CONFLICT AND SECURITY LAW 115 (2001)); the report of the Danish Institute of International Affairs, Humanitarian Intervention: Legal and Political Aspects (1999); and the Kosovo Report published by the Independent International Commission on Kosovo (2000).

NATO States on their own initiative. The Security Council had imposed an arms embargo on the FRY when it adopted Resolution 1160 in 1998, a year before the NATO military action commenced. After the cessation of the bombing campaign on June 10, 1999, the Council adopted Resolution 1244, which provided the legal basis for ground forces led by NATO and known as KFOR, to enter Kosovo and assume responsibility for the security situation there, to the exclusion of the armed forces and paramilitary police of the FRY. The bombing campaign itself, however, was not authorized by the Council. Although that campaign was undertaken by NATO in support of goals identified by the Security Council in Resolutions 1160, 1199 and 1203 (all of which contained provisions which were legally binding upon all States, including the FRY), none of those resolutions authorized military action. Unlike the situation in the 1990–91 Gulf conflict, therefore, Operation Allied Force was not a case of enforcement action taken with the authority of the Security Council. A distinction must accordingly be drawn between the bombing campaign which occurred between March 24, 1999 and June 10, 1999, on the one hand, and the military presence in Kosovo thereafter. As will be seen, this distinction is of some importance in considering the law applicable to military operations after June 10, 1999.

Secondly, while some members of NATO were more forthright on this matter than were others, the only substantial justification advanced for the decision to resort to military action was that such action was justified as a response to the humanitarian situation which had been created in Kosovo in the immediate run-up to the commencement of Operation Allied Force on March 24, 1999. For example, the United Kingdom's Permanent Representative to the United Nations told the Security Council, on the day that the military operation commenced, that:

> The action being taken is legal. It is justified as an exceptional measure to prevent an overwhelming humanitarian catastrophe. Under present circumstances in Kosovo, there is convincing evidence that such a catastrophe is imminent. Renewed acts of repression by the authorities of the Federal Republic of Yugoslavia would cause further loss of civilian life and would lead to displacement of the civilian population on a large scale and in hostile conditions.
>
> Every means short of force has been tried to avert this situation. In these circumstances, and as an exceptional measure on grounds of overwhelming humanitarian necessity, military intervention is legally justifiable. The force

now proposed is directed exclusively to averting a humanitarian catastrophe, and is the minimum judged necessary for that purpose.[4]

The emphasis on the limited purpose for which force was being employed and the reference, inherent in that statement, to the requirement that the force used should be proportionate to that goal has led some commentators to argue that the application of international humanitarian law in the NATO operation should have been different from that required of States engaged in a "normal" armed conflict. That argument is considered later in this paper.

Finally, it needs to be remembered that, while the *jus ad bellum* and the *jus in bello* are separate bodies of law (a fact which has important legal consequences), for military action by a State to be lawful, it must comply with both bodies of law. The Gulf conflict of 1990–91 may be used as an illustration. Iraq's invasion of Kuwait was the clearest possible violation of the *jus ad bellum*. It followed that the subsequent occupation of Kuwait and the Iraqi resistance to the coalition campaign to liberate Kuwait were also a violation of the *jus ad bellum*, even though some aspects of Iraq's behavior (e.g., some of the property requisitions which occurred or the missile attacks on the Dahran airbase) complied with the *jus in bello*.[5] Thus, Iraq's liability to make reparation in accordance with the provisions of Security Council Resolution 687 for the consequences of its unlawful invasion is not confined to damages caused by acts unlawful under the *jus in bello*.

In this context, it has to be recognized that there was considerable controversy about the legal justification advanced by the NATO States for their resort to force against the FRY. That controversy about the application of the *jus ad bellum* may have affected the way in which certain issues regarding the *jus in bello* and, in particular, the law of neutrality were perceived. Specifically, it may have affected the approach of various governments to the question whether the NATO States would have been entitled to impose an embargo on

---

4. U.N. Doc. S/PV.3988, at 12. See also the views expressed in the same debate by the Permanent Representatives of the United States of America (4-5), Canada (6) and the Netherlands (8). In the cases concerning *Legality of Use of Force* brought by the FRY against ten of the NATO States in the International Court of Justice, Belgium advanced the same justification for military action; see Oral Pleadings of Belgium (Yugo. v. Belg.), 1999 I.C.J. CR/99/15, *available at* http://www.icj-cij.org/icjwww/idocket/iybe/iybeframe.htm. The other respondent States did not address this issue during that phase of the case.

5. For a discussion of these issues, see Christopher Greenwood, *New World Order or Old? The Invasion of Kuwait and the Rule of Law*, 55 MODERN LAW REVIEW 153–178 (1992) and the articles cited at note 38, *infra*.

shipments of oil and other supplies to the FRY, even where those supplies were carried in ships flying the flags of States not involved in the conflict.

This paper will first consider the applicability of international humanitarian law to Operation Allied Force before examining certain general issues regarding the manner in which that law had to be applied in the Kosovo campaign. The question whether persons captured during the operation were prisoners of war within the Third Geneva Convention will be addressed next, followed by discussion of the issue of a naval embargo and the law of neutrality. The legal regime applicable to KFOR operations in Kosovo since June 10, 1999 will be briefly considered before closing with a discussion of the various judicial proceedings relating to the conduct of the Kosovo conflict. Questions of targeting and proportionality are considered only in passing, as these are the subject of other papers in the present volume.[6]

The Applicability of International Humanitarian Law

1. The Existence of an Armed Conflict between the NATO States and the FRY

The first question to consider is whether international humanitarian law was applicable to Operation Allied Force. Though much discussed at the time, there is less to this question than meets the eye. The answer—which can be given without qualification—is that international humanitarian law was fully applicable from the moment that Operation Allied Force began on March 24, 1999 until the cessation of hostilities on June 10, 1999. Throughout that period an international armed conflict existed between the FRY on the one hand and the NATO States on the other.

There is no definition of an international armed conflict in any of the treaties on international humanitarian law. It is agreed, however, that the concept is a factual one based on the existence of actual hostilities between two or more States, even if those hostilities are at a low level and of short duration. The Appeals Chamber of the International Criminal Tribunal for the former Yugoslavia (ICTY) has stated that an "armed conflict exists whenever there is a resort to armed force between States."[7] That test was undoubtedly satisfied in the case of Operation Allied Force. The fact that no declaration of war was made was, of course, irrelevant to the applicability of international humanitarian law

---

6. See the papers by Professors Bothe and Dinstein and Lieutenant Colonel Montgomery on targeting and by Professors Bring and Murphy on collateral damage.
7. Prosecutor v. Tadic, Jurisdiction, 105 INTERNATIONAL LAW REPORTS 453, ¶ 70 (1997). See also COMMENTARY ON GENEVA CONVENTION III 23 (Jean Pictet ed., 1960).

to that conflict. It is well established that it is the fact of armed conflict between two or more States, not the formality of a declaration of war (which has been almost unknown since 1945) which triggers the application of that law.[8]

Nor does it make any difference to the applicability of international humanitarian law that the decision to resort to force was taken by the North Atlantic Council, the governing body of NATO, or that the military conduct of the campaign was in the hands of the Supreme Allied Commander Europe (SACEUR) and the NATO military authorities, who acted in consultation with the NATO Secretary-General under the authority given them by the North Atlantic Council. While NATO is an international organization which possesses a legal personality separate from those of its members, that separate personality does not affect the applicability of international humanitarian law to the armed forces of any member State which implements a NATO decision.[9] That fact was expressly recognized both by NATO and the member States during Operation Allied Force. Thus, the North Atlantic Council's authorization to SACEUR and the military authorities expressly required that operations were to be conducted in accordance with international humanitarian law. Similarly, the United Kingdom Government stated that "action by our forces is in strict conformity with international humanitarian law, including the 1949 Geneva Conventions and their Additional Protocols."[10] Other NATO governments adopted a similar position.

The fact that NATO acted for humanitarian reasons, so that the legal justification offered for the decision to resort to force was different from the reliance on self-defense or Security Council authorization which has been characteristic of most armed conflicts since 1945, is also irrelevant to the applicability of international humanitarian law. The principle that international humanitarian law

---

8. *See* Christopher Greenwood, *The Concept of War in International Law*, 36 INTERNATIONAL AND COMPARATIVE LAW QUARTERLY 283 (1987). US forces are specifically required to comply with international humanitarian law in any armed conflict, irrespective of its formal characterization; *see* Department of Defense, DoD Law of War Program, DoD Directive 5100.77, Dec. 9, 1998 and ANNOTATED SUPPLEMENT TO THE COMMANDER'S HANDBOOK ON THE LAW OF NAVAL OPERATIONS 290–1 (A.R. Thomas and James Duncan eds., 1999) (Vol. 73, US Naval War College International Law Studies).

9. Whether it affects the issue of State responsibility for a violation of those rules is currently under consideration in the proceedings in the International Court of Justice and the European Court of Human Rights discussed later in this paper. No one, however, has suggested that armed forces operating under NATO command and control are not subject to customary international humanitarian law and the treaty provisions binding upon the State concerned.

10. Answer to a Parliamentary question on May 18, 1999 by Baroness Symons, Parliamentary Under-Secretary of State, Foreign and Commonwealth Office, 70 BRITISH YEAR BOOK OF INTERNATIONAL LAW 605 (1999).

applies equally to both sides of a conflict irrespective of the reasons for resort to force or its legality is one of the best established principles of the *jus in bello*.[11]

It follows that the humanitarian law of international armed conflicts was applicable throughout the period March 24, 1999 to June 10, 1999 to the hostilities between the NATO States and the FRY. Two questions, however, require further consideration.

2. The Status of the FRY as a Party to the Geneva Conventions and Protocol I

The first question concerns the applicability of the 1949 Geneva Conventions and Protocol I of 1977.[12] This question arises because of the peculiar status of the FRY at the relevant time. The FRY was one of the States which emerged from the former Socialist Federal Republic of Yugoslavia (SFRY) when that State collapsed in 1991–92. Of the six republics which had made up the SFRY, four—Bosnia-Herzegovina, Croatia, Macedonia and Slovenia—had declared their independence between June 1991 and May 1992 and had, in due course, been recognized and admitted as members of the United Nations. The two remaining republics, Serbia and Montenegro, formed the FRY. The Government of the FRY from its foundation until the overthrow of Slobodan Milosevic in 2000 considered the FRY to be the continuation of the old SFRY (just as the Russian Federation was the continuation of the USSR) and not a successor State. It therefore maintained that the FRY continued the SFRY's membership in all international organizations and

---

11. See, e.g., the decision of the United States Military Tribunal in United States v. List, 8 LAW REPORTS OF TRIALS OF WAR CRIMINALS 1234, 1247. See also Protocol I to the 1949 Geneva Conventions, the Preamble to which states that "the provisions of the Geneva Conventions ... and of this Protocol must be fully applied in all circumstances to all persons who are protected by those instruments, without any adverse distinction based on the nature or origin of the armed conflict or on the causes espoused by or attributed to the parties to the conflict." Protocol Additional (I) to the Geneva Conventions of 12 August 1949, and Relating to the Protection of Victims of International Conflicts, Jun. 8, 1977, 1125 U.N.T.S. 3, DOCUMENTS ON THE LAWS OF WAR 422 (Adam Roberts & Richard Guelff eds., 3d ed. 2000) [hereinafter Protocol I].

12. Geneva Convention for the Amelioration of the Condition of the Wounded and Sick in Armed Forces in the Field, Aug. 12, 1949, 6 U.S.T. 3114, 75 U.N.T.S. 31, DOCUMENTS ON THE LAWS OF WAR *supra* note 11, at 197 [hereinafter Geneva I]; Geneva Convention for the Amelioration of the Condition of the Wounded, Sick and Shipwrecked Members of the Armed Forces at Sea, Aug. 12, 1949, 6 U.S.T. 3217, 75 U.N.T.S. 85, *id.* at 222 [hereinafter Geneva II]; Geneva Convention Relative to the Treatment of Prisoners of War, Aug. 12, 1949, 6 U.S.T. 3316, 75 U.N.T.S. 135, *id.* at 244 [hereinafter Geneva III]; Geneva Convention Relative to the Protection of Civilian Persons in Time of War, Aug. 12, 1949, 6 U.S.T. 3516, 75 U.N.T.S. 287, *id.* at 301 [hereinafter Geneva IV]. Protocol I, *supra* note 11.

that all treaties concluded by the SFRY, including the Geneva Conventions and Protocol I, continued to apply to the FRY without any need for an act of succession. Accordingly, whereas the other States which emerged from the SFRY each made a declaration of succession to the Conventions and Protocols, the FRY did not.

The FRY's claim to be the continuation of the SFRY was not, however, accepted by the rest of the international community. Thus, the Arbitration Commission of the Peace Conference for the Former Yugoslavia (known as "the Badinter Commission" after the name of its Chairman, Judge Robert Badinter of the French Constitutional Court) rejected the FRY's claim and gave the opinion that the States which emerged from the SFRY were all successor States, none of which had any special claim to continue the personality of the old State.[13] The United Nations Security Council and General Assembly also rejected the FRY's claim and stated that it should apply for membership of the United Nations.[14] The then Government of the FRY, however, adhered to its position that it continued the personality of the SFRY and thus continued to be bound by, and to have the benefit of, all of the latter's treaty obligations. Thus, in the cases brought against it in the International Court of Justice by Bosnia-Herzegovina and Croatia for alleged violations of the Genocide Convention, it did not contest that it was bound by that Convention.[15] The FRY took the same position in the cases which it brought against ten NATO States in 1999.[16]

The change of government in the FRY in 2000 brought a complete reversal of this position. The post-Milosevic government accepted that the FRY was a new State, one of five successors to the SFRY. In October 2000 it applied for,

---

13. Opinions 9 and 10, 92 INTERNATIONAL LAW REPORTS 203, 206 (1998); 31 INTERNATIONAL LEGAL MATERIALS 1488 (1998). See Michael Wood, *Participation of Former Yugoslav States in the United Nations and in Multilateral Treaties*, 1 YEARBOOK OF UNITED NATIONS LAW 231 (1997).
14. S.C. Res. 757 (May 30, 1992), U.N. Doc. S/RES/757 (1992); S.C. Res. 777 (Sep. 19, 1992), U.N. Doc. S/RES/777 (1992); S.C. Res. 821 (Apr. 28, 1993), U.N. Doc. S/RES/821 (1993); and G.A. Res. 47/1 (Sep. 22, 1992), U.N. Doc. A/RES/47/1 (1992).
15. Application of the Convention on the Prevention and Punishment of the Crime of Genocide (Bosn. & Herz. v. Yugo.) 1996 I.C.J. 595 (Preliminary Objections) and 1997 I.C.J. 243 (Counter-claims); Application of the Convention on the Prevention and Punishment of the Crime of Genocide (Croat. v. Yugo.), *available* on the ICJ website *at* http://www.icj-cij.org. At the time this was written, the Court had not held hearings on the merits of the Bosnian case or taken any substantive decision in the Croatian case.
16. *See infra* note 56 and accompanying text.

and was admitted to, membership of the United Nations.[17] On March 8, 2001, the new government deposited an instrument of accession to the Genocide Convention, which became effective ninety days later in accordance with Article XIII of the Convention. By the same instrument, the FRY entered a reservation to Article IX (the provision which confers jurisdiction on the International Court of Justice). The FRY subsequently applied to the International Court under Article 61 of the Court's Statute to re-open the jurisdiction phase of the *Bosnia* case on the grounds that the FRY had not been bound by the Genocide Convention at the relevant times and had never been bound by Article IX.[18] At the time of writing, the Court had not taken any decision regarding this application.

The FRY had, however, been treated throughout the Kosovo conflict as a party to the Geneva Conventions and Protocols both by other States (including the NATO States) and by the ICRC, which sent a formal note to the FRY and the NATO member States on March 24, 1999 reminding them of their obligations under the Geneva Conventions.[19]

On October 16, 2001, the new government of the FRY deposited with the Swiss Federal Government a declaration regarding the Geneva Conventions and Protocols. In contrast to the position taken by the new government with regard to the Genocide Convention, however, this declaration was an instrument of succession, not accession. Moreover, it was expressly made retrospective, stating that it took effect as from April 27, 1992. Any element of doubt which might therefore have arisen regarding the status of the FRY as a party to the Geneva Conventions and Protocols is therefore removed. The new government had earlier deposited instruments of succession to a large number of multilateral conventions.

Accordingly, the Geneva Conventions were applicable to all the States involved in the conflict, while Protocol I applied as between the FRY and those NATO States which were parties to it (all of them except France, Turkey and

---

17. S.C. Res. 1326 (Oct. 31, 2000), U.N. Doc. S/RES/1326 (2000); G.S. Res. 55/12 (Nov. 1, 2000), U.N. Doc. A/RES/55/12 (2000).
18. Application of the Convention on the Prevention and Punishment of the Crime of Genocide (Bosn. & Herz. v. Yugo.), Application for Revision of Judgment of 11 July 1996 (23 April 2001), *available at* http://www.icj-cij.org.
19. ICRC Press Release 99/15, Mar. 24, 1999, *available at* http://www.icrc.org/eng/news_by_date.

the United States of America).[20] The customary law of armed conflict was also applicable.

3. The Relationship between NATO and the KLA/UCK

The second question concerns the extent to which the hostilities between the FRY and the Kosovo Liberation Army (KLA or UCK) were governed by international humanitarian law. There is little doubt that, even before the start of Operation Allied Force, an armed conflict existed in Kosovo between the FRY and the KLA/UCK. The possibility that such a conflict might exist was impliedly recognized by the Security Council as early as March 1998, when it urged the Prosecutor of the International Criminal Tribunal for the former Yugoslavia (ICTY) "to begin gathering information relating to the violence in Kosovo that may fall within its jurisdiction."[21] Since the Tribunal's jurisdiction is largely confined to crimes committed in armed conflict,[22] this invitation appears to have proceeded on the basis that, at least, an armed conflict might already exist. The events of early 1999 also strongly suggested that an armed conflict existed within Kosovo.[23]

At least until March 24, 1999, that conflict was of a non-international character, since it consisted of "protracted armed violence between governmental

---

20. France became a party to Protocol I in 2001. Peter Kovacs, *Intervention armée des forces del'OTAN au Kosovo*, 82 INTERNATIONAL REVIEW OF THE RED CROSS 103 (2000), argues that the United States had agreed to comply with Protocol I and was therefore bound by it. This argument is unconvincing. It confuses the willingness (and, indeed, the obligation) of the United States to apply the rules of customary international law codified in some of the provisions of Protocol I with a declaration of readiness to apply the entire Protocol as such. The United States has never agreed to apply all of the provisions of Protocol I.
21. S.C. Res. 1160 ¶ 17 (Mar. 31, 1998), U.N. Doc. S/RES/1160 (1998).
22. The existence of an armed conflict is an inherent feature of grave breaches (Article 2 of the Tribunal's Statute) and war crimes (Article 3); it is also expressly required as a condition for jurisdiction over crimes against humanity (Article 5). Only genocide (Article 4) can be prosecuted in the Tribunal without the need to demonstrate the existence of an armed conflict. The ICTY was created by the United Nations Security Council in Resolution 827 (May 25, 1993), U.N. Doc. S/RES/827 (1993). The ICTY Statute and the Secretary-General's Commentaries are contained in the Report of the Secretary-General Pursuant to Paragraph 2 of Security Council Resolution 808 (May 3, 1993), U.N. Doc. S/25704, *reprinted in* 32 INTERNATIONAL LEGAL MATERIALS 1163, 1192 (1993).
23. See the indictment against Slobodan Milosevic and others issued by the Prosecutor on May 22, 1999 and confirmed by Judge Hunt on May 24, 1999 (IT-99-37-I). Note also the ICRC statement of January 18, 1999 regarding the massacre at Racak, which called on "both sides to comply with international humanitarian law and to spare those not, or no longer, involved in the fighting." ICRC Press Release 99/04, Jan. 18, 1999, *available at* the ICRC website, *supra* note 19.

authorities and organized armed groups . . . within a State."[24] As such, it was governed by the provisions of common Article 3 and the customary law applicable to non-international conflicts.[25] Although the KLA/UCK has at times claimed to be a national liberation movement, so that its struggle for self-determination would constitute an international armed conflict under Article 1(4) of Protocol I, that claim has not been accepted by the international community.[26]

The question is whether the intervention of NATO on March 24, 1999 "internationalized" that conflict, so that all the hostilities became subject to the law applicable to international armed conflicts considered above. The ICTY has recognized, in its two decisions in the *Tadic* case,[27] that an international armed conflict can co-exist alongside a non-international one and that the latter will be internationalized only if there is a clear relationship between the non-governmental party to that conflict and one of the States party to the international conflict. While the reasoning of the Appeals Chamber on the nature of that relationship is open to criticism, the requirement that some kind of relationship exist is surely right—the mere fact that a conflict between States comes into being alongside a conflict within one of those States cannot, in and of itself, be sufficient to make the law of international armed conflicts applicable to the latter. At least until the end of May 1999, however, NATO kept its distance from the KLA/UCK and even after that time it is far from clear that the relations between them were sufficiently close for the conflict

---

24. The definition of a non-international armed conflict given by the Appeals Chamber of the International Criminal Tribunal for the former Yugoslavia in *Tadic, supra* note 7, ¶ 70.

25. It is more doubtful whether Protocol II applied. Until the closing stages of the fighting, it is unclear whether the KLA/UCK exercised sufficient control over a defined area of territory to meet the requirements of Article 1(1) of Protocol II. Protocol Additional to the Geneva Conventions of 12 August 1949, and Relating to the Protection of Victims of Non-International Armed Conflicts, Jun. 8, 1977, 1125 U.N.T.S. 609, DOCUMENTS ON THE LAWS OF WAR, *supra* note 11, at 483 [hereinafter Protocol II].

26. It is noticeable, for example, that none of the NATO States argued that the KLA/UCK was a national liberation movement or that the population of Kosovo had a right to self-determination, nor is such a view reflected in the various UN Security Council resolutions regarding Kosovo. The Prosecutor has not charged Slobodan Milosevic with grave breaches under Article 2 of the ICTY Statute—the only offense within the jurisdiction of the Tribunal which can only be committed in an international armed conflict (*Tadic, supra* note 7)—in respect of Kosovo, even though some of the incidents in Kosovo in early 1999 (such as the massacre of forty-five villagers at Racak on January 15, 1999 (U.N. Doc. S/PRST/1999/2)) would appear to have qualified as a grave breach had there been an international conflict.

27. Prosecutor v. Tadic (Jurisdiction) (2 October 1995), 105 INTERNATIONAL LAW REVIEW 419 (1997); Prosecutor v. Tadic (Merits), 38 INTERNATIONAL LEGAL MATERIALS 1518 (1999).

between the KLA/UCK and the FRY to be regarded as part of the international armed conflict, rather than a separate internal conflict governed by a different set of rules.[28]

Application of International Humanitarian Law in the Kosovo Conflict

The preceding discussion leads to the conclusion that the law of international armed conflicts (both the customary law and that contained in the relevant treaties) was applicable to the Kosovo conflict. Since it is a well established principle that international humanitarian law applies equally to both sides in a conflict, irrespective of the lawfulness of the resort to force or the purpose for which force is used, it should follow that there was nothing special about the application of international humanitarian law in the Kosovo campaign.[29]

That means, in particular, that the two main principles of targeting—distinction and proportionality—were applicable throughout. While these principles are discussed in greater detail in other papers in the present volume, it is useful to recall the way in which they are formulated in Protocol I, which is generally regarded as stating the customary law on the subject. The principle of distinction is evident throughout Articles 48 to 58 of the Protocol but three provisions are particularly important:

Article 48
In order to ensure respect for and protection of the civilian population and civilian objects, the Parties to the conflict shall at all times distinguish between the civilian population and combatants and between civilian objects and military objectives and accordingly shall direct their operations only against military objectives.

Article 51(2)
The civilian population as such, as well as individual civilians, shall not be the object of attack. Acts or threats of violence the primary purpose of which is to spread terror among the civilian population are prohibited.

---

28. On the subject of prisoners captured by the KLA and handed over to NATO forces, see *infra* this paper.
29. The principle of equal application is clearly stated in the *List* case, *supra* note 11, and was more recently reaffirmed in the Preamble to Protocol I, *supra* note 11.

Article 52(2)
Attacks shall be strictly limited to military objectives. In so far as objects are concerned, military objectives are limited to those objects which by their nature, location, purpose or use make an effective contribution to military action and whose total or partial destruction, capture or neutralization, in the circumstances ruling at the time, offers a definite military advantage.

The principle of proportionality is succinctly stated in Article 51(5)(b), which prohibits "an attack which may be expected to cause incidental loss of civilian life, injury to civilians, damage to civilian objects, or a combination thereof, which would be excessive in relation to the concrete and direct military advantage anticipated."

Two very different schools of thought have suggested that the purpose of the NATO intervention and the unusual character of the conflict meant that the rules of international humanitarian law—and, in particular, these rules of distinction and proportionality—were to be applied in a manner different from that in other recent conflicts such as the 1990–91 hostilities in the Gulf.

The purpose for which NATO employed force—to halt the attacks on the Kosovars and to reverse the effects of ethnic cleansing in Kosovo—has already been considered. The unusual character of the conflict may be said to have manifested itself in two ways. First, for most of the period of Operation Allied Force, the ability of the NATO States directly to influence events on the ground in Kosovo was very limited. With no ground forces available for immediate deployment, they were obliged to rely on air power and their ability to strike effectively at the FRY forces engaged in the process of ethnic cleansing in Kosovo was limited, at least until the closing stages of the conflict. Instead, their strategy was to attack targets throughout much of the FRY in order to bring about a change of policy on the part of the FRY government.

Secondly, while the FRY's anti-aircraft defenses continued to attack NATO aircraft throughout the conflict, the FRY did not attack the territory of any of the NATO States, nor, apart from the capture of a US patrol on the border between the FRY and Macedonia, did it conduct any operations against NATO forces anywhere outside the FRY. The result was that the conflict was exceptionally one-sided—in contrast, for example, to the Gulf conflict, where Iraq launched missile attacks against Saudi Arabia and other coalition States, as well as against Israel.

The purpose for which NATO resorted to force and these unusual characteristics of the conflict have led to two very different theories, each of which suggests a departure from the normal principles of the law of armed conflict and each of which, in this writer's view, is a heresy which demands emphatic rejection.

The first of these heresies is that NATO's motives and the manner in which it was obliged to fight the conflict permitted it a greater latitude in choosing the targets which it would attack than would otherwise be the case. In particular, since the purpose of the bombing campaign was not to defeat the FRY armed forces (in the normal sense of that term, i.e., by successfully engaging them in battle) but to produce a change of policy on the part of the FRY Government, objects whose destruction was particularly likely to increase the pressure on the FRY Government were legitimate targets in this conflict irrespective of whether they fell within the definition of military objectives codified in Article 52(2) of Protocol I. An important part of this thesis is that attacks carried out in order to undermine support amongst the enemy civilian population for the policy of its government would be lawful.

Tempting though such an approach may be, it is difficult to reconcile with contemporary international humanitarian law. As demonstrated above, the principle that the enemy civilian population and individual civilians are not themselves legitimate targets is now clearly established in that law.[30] Moreover, the definition of a military objective requires both that the object in question make an effective contribution to the enemy's *military* action and that the destruction or damage of the object offers a definite *military* advantage to the State whose forces attack it.[31] Nothing in any of the treaties on the law of armed conflict or the practice of States suggests that a State's motives or the fact that it seeks to procure a change in its adversary's policy rather than that adversary's total defeat can expand the range of targets which is lawfully open to it. It follows that an object does not become a target simply because of its political significance or the effect which its destruction is likely to have on civilian morale and support for a hostile government. Only something which meets the criteria of a military objective laid down by international humanitarian law may lawfully be attacked.

That does not mean that the political effect (including the effect on enemy morale) of attacking a particular target cannot legitimately be taken into consideration. Provided that the target constitutes a military objective and the

---

30. See, e.g., the provision to that effect in Protocol I, Articles 48, 50 and 51(2), *supra* note 11, and the statement in ¶ 8.1.2 of Naval Doctrine Command, THE COMMANDER'S HANDBOOK ON THE LAW OF NAVAL OPERATIONS (NWP 1-14M/MCWP 5-2.1/COMDTPUB P5800.1) (1995), *reprinted in* the ANNOTATED SUPPLEMENT, *supra* note 8, at 403.
31. Protocol I, Article 52(2), *supra* note 11, at 450; COMMANDER'S HANDBOOK, *supra* note 30, ¶ 8.1.1 (the wording of which is slightly different).

principle of proportionality contained in humanitarian law is respected,[32] it is entirely legitimate to seek to undermine the will of and support for the enemy's government. But the desire to achieve that goal cannot convert into a lawful target something which does not otherwise meet those criteria. It is noteworthy that none of the NATO governments suggested otherwise.[33]

The rival heresy is that, because the campaign was fought for a humanitarian objective, international humanitarian law has to be interpreted as imposing upon NATO more extensive restrictions than would otherwise have been the case. Such an approach is apparent in the report of the Independent International Commission on Kosovo (an unofficial body of non-governmental commentators established at the initiative of the Prime Minister of Sweden). As part of what it describes as a "Framework for Principled Humanitarian Intervention," the Report proposes that in cases of humanitarian intervention "there must be even stricter adherence to the laws of war and international humanitarian law than in standard military operations."[34]

This suggestion (which is admittedly made *de lege ferenda*) is open to criticism on at least three grounds. First, there is something distinctly woolly-minded about the whole idea. The Report does not appear to suggest that the rules of international humanitarian law applicable to a force engaging in humanitarian intervention should differ from those applicable to forces engaged in other military operations, but rather that those rules should be more strictly applied. Yet the idea that the law can prescribe the same rules for all types of military operations but require a higher standard of adherence in some cases than in others is untenable. International humanitarian law requires that, whenever it applies, it should be complied with. One violation may, of course, be less serious than another and, as a matter of fact, one force may have a better record of compliance than another. It is, however, illogical and contrary to principle to say that the law requires one party to comply with all of the rules which are binding upon it but requires another party—albeit bound by all of the same rules—to comply only with some, or to comply with all but to a lesser degree. In reality what the Commission is proposing is that different—and stricter—rules should apply to a State which resorts to force by way

---

32. See Protocol I, Article 51(5)(b), *supra* note 11, at 448–9; COMMANDER'S HANDBOOK, *supra* note 30, ¶ 8.1.2.1.
33. See also the article by James Burger, *International Humanitarian Law and the Kosovo Crisis: Lessons Learned or to be Learned*, 82 INTERNATIONAL REVIEW OF THE RED CROSS 129, 131–2 (2000).
34. INDEPENDENT INTERNATIONAL COMMISSION ON KOSOVO, THE KOSOVO REPORT 195 (2000); see also page 179.

of humanitarian intervention than to one which resorts to force for any other purpose. But the Commission's proposal begs many questions about which rules are involved and what degree of modification might be involved.

Secondly, whichever way the Commission's suggestion is put, it would have the effect of driving a coach and horses through the principle that international humanitarian law applies equally to both sides in any conflict, without regard to the cause which they espouse or the legality of their action under the *jus ad bellum*. A State whose forces were resisting humanitarian intervention by another State or group of States would, presumably, be required to comply with the normal rules of international humanitarian law (or to display the normally required degree of adherence). It would therefore be entitled to a greater degree of latitude than its opponent. The implications of the Commission's proposal in this respect are concealed by the unusual circumstances of the Kosovo conflict. As has already been noted, the FRY did not respond by force against the NATO States (other than by the use of anti-aircraft fire) and did not attack the NATO States themselves. It would be naive, however, to assume that the same conditions will necessarily apply in any future humanitarian intervention. Indeed, had NATO proceeded to a ground campaign, it would not have been the case in the Kosovo conflict, as the FRY could, and almost certainly would, have put up a strenuous resistance to NATO ground forces.

Thirdly, the effect of the Commission's suggestion would be that international humanitarian law would impose greater constraints on a State engaging in humanitarian intervention than on a State which acted in self-defense or even one which invaded a neighbor in clear violation of Article 2(4) of the United Nations Charter. It is not immediately obvious why an aggressor should be subject to less rigorous rules in respect, for example, of targeting than a State which intervenes to prevent genocide or other large-scale violations of human rights.

A more sophisticated suggestion is canvassed by Professor Bothe in a critique of the Report to the Prosecutor.[35] After examining the Report's findings regarding the NATO campaign, Professor Bothe states:

> Both in relation to the question of the definition of the military objective and in relation to the proportionality principle, the report fails to raise yet another fundamental question. Do traditional considerations of military necessity and

---

35. Final Report to the Prosecutor by the Committee Established to Review the NATO Bombing Campaign Against the Federal Republic of Yugoslavia, 39 INTERNATIONAL LEGAL MATERIALS 1257 (2000), *reprinted* herein as Appendix A [hereinafter Report to the Prosecutor]. The Report is discussed *infra* this paper.

military advantage have a legitimate place in a conflict the declared purpose of which is a humanitarian one, namely to promote the cause of human rights? The thought would deserve further consideration that in such a conflict, more severe restraints would be imposed on the choice of military targets and of the balancing test applied for the purposes of the proportionality principle than in a 'normal' armed conflict.[36]

The reasoning which seems to underlie this proposal can be summarized as follows: humanitarian intervention, in so far as it justifies military action at all, does so only for strictly limited purposes. It follows that only military action which serves those limited purposes is legitimate and the traditional considerations of military advantage and military necessity must be adapted (and circumscribed) accordingly. In effect, it requires reading the definition of a military objective codified in Article 52(2) of Protocol I and the statement of the proportionality principle in Article 51(5)(b) as though they referred to a *legitimate* military advantage.

Professor Bothe's approach[37] avoids the first objection raised in relation to the Kosovo Commission proposals but it still falls foul of the other two objections and must therefore be rejected. As soon as one qualifies the concept of military advantage (or military necessity) by reference to considerations of legitimacy drawn from the purpose for which a party resorts to force, the *jus ad bellum* and the *jus in bello* become inextricably mixed and the principle of equal application of international humanitarian law is fatally compromised. If a State, whose resort to force is in *jus ad bellum* terms lawful only for strictly limited purposes, violates the *jus in bello* whenever it attacks a target whose destruction will not contribute to the achievement of those purposes, it follows that a State whose resort to force is unlawful under the *jus ad bellum* will violate the *jus in bello* whenever it targets anything. Yet that is precisely the argument which was advanced and comprehensively rejected both in the trials at the end of World War Two and in the negotiation of Protocol I.

The difficulties, both practical and theoretical, of such an approach are obvious when one asks what standards would have been applicable to attacks by the FRY on targets in the NATO States had such attacks been carried out during the Kosovo conflict. The FRY was plainly not acting by way of humanitarian intervention. Would its actions therefore have been judged by

---

36. Michael Bothe, *The Protection of the Civilian Population and NATO Bombing on Yugoslavia: Comments on the Report to the Prosecutor of the ICTY*, 12 EUROPEAN JOURNAL OF INTERNATIONAL LAW 531, 535 (2001).
37. See the papers by Professors Bothe and Bring in the present volume.

reference to the modified *jus in bello* considered to apply to a humanitarian intervention or would they have been subject to the *jus in bello* applicable in a "normal" armed conflict? Neither answer would be at all satisfactory, for the first treats the FRY as engaged in an activity which was entirely alien to it while the second would mean that the FRY would enjoy greater latitude in targeting than the NATO States for no apparent reason. It is only because the circumstances of the Kosovo conflict were such that the FRY was not, in practice, able to attack the NATO States that these difficulties were obscured.

That is not to say that the legal basis for resort to force has no bearing on the manner in which that force may be used. As the statement by the United Kingdom Representative, quoted in Part I above, makes clear, the force used in humanitarian intervention has to be necessary in order to achieve the goal of ending (or preventing) the humanitarian emergency. In other words, the purpose for which force is permitted under the *jus ad bellum*—in the case of Kosovo, a humanitarian purpose—limits the degree of force which may be used. However, this recognition of the relationship between the degree of force used and the goal to be achieved is different from the suggestion advanced by Professor Bothe in two important respects.

First, considerations of necessity and proportionality here operate as part of the *jus ad bellum*, not the *jus in bello*. This is much more than a theoretical distinction and has important practical consequences. It leaves intact the *jus in bello* definition of what constitutes a military objective and such concepts as military necessity and proportionality for the purposes of Article 51(5)(b). The proportionality limitation in the *jus ad bellum* measures the use of force *as a whole* against the yardstick of what is proportionate to the *overall* goal to be achieved; it does not require analysis of each individual attack by reference to that overall goal. Moreover, the limits of the *jus ad bellum*, unlike those of the *jus in bello*, do not carry with them the possibility of criminal sanctions for individual servicemen. Secondly, a requirement that the force used must be proportionate to the goal to be achieved is not confined to humanitarian intervention. Proportionality in this sense is also a requirement of the law of self-defense.[38]

---

38. See, e.g., the decision of the International Court of Justice in Military and Paramilitary Activities in and against Nicaragua (Nicar. v. U.S.), 1986 I.C.J. 14, ¶ 194 (June 27); this principle was common ground between the United States of America and Nicaragua. For further discussion of the principle of proportionality in self-defense and its relationship to the *jus in bello*, see Christopher Greenwood, *The Relationship Between Ius ad Bellum and Ius in Bello*, 9 REVIEW OF INTERNATIONAL STUDIES 221–34 (1983) and *Self-Defence and the Conduct of International Armed Conflict*, in INTERNATIONAL LAW AT A TIME OF PERPLEXITY 273–88 (Yoram Dinstein ed., 1989).

Both of the "heretical" views considered here are the product of understandable (though largely contradictory) concerns but they involve an unjustified muddling of *jus ad bellum* and *jus in bello* issues in a way which is contrary to principle and unsupported by authority. In this writer's view, the true position can be stated very simply: the NATO States and the FRY were bound to comply with the relevant rules of international humanitarian law in this conflict, as they would have been in any other—nothing more or less.

Prisoners of War

Issues concerning prisoners of war arose in two contexts during the Kosovo conflict. First, three US soldiers serving with the multinational peacekeeping force in the Former Yugoslav Republic of Macedonia (FYROM) were captured by FRY forces on March 31, 1999. Secondly, two members of the FRY forces captured by the KLA/UCK were subsequently handed over to United States forces who held them for a short period. Both cases gave rise to a degree of confusion about the status of the prisoners, which is surprising in view of the clarity of the Third Geneva Convention. In both cases the status of those concerned as prisoners of war entitled to the full protection of the Convention should never have been in doubt.

At the time of their capture, the three US soldiers were serving in a multinational peacekeeping force in the FYROM. That force had originally been a United Nations one (UN Preventative Deployment Force (UNPREDEP)) but in February 1999 the People's Republic of China had vetoed the Security Council resolution required to renew the mandate of UNPREDEP, because of the FYROM's diplomatic links with Taiwan. The contingents which had composed UNPREDEP had remained in the FYROM at the request of its government and had reconstituted themselves as a multinational force outside United Nations control. At the time of their capture, the three US soldiers were not involved in the military operations against the FRY and were conducting a patrol as part of the multinational force's operations. There was some doubt as to whether at the time of their capture they had inadvertently strayed into the FRY or whether they were captured in the territory of the FYROM.

Neither their membership in the multinational force nor the place of their capture, however, affects their status. Under Article 4A(1) of the Third Convention, members of the armed forces of a party to the conflict who have "fallen into the power of the enemy" automatically have the status of prisoners of war. The three US servicemen were undoubtedly members of the US armed forces and the United States was clearly a party to an armed conflict with the FRY at the time of their capture. Moreover, it is difficult to think of words more apt to describe what happened to the three than that they had "fallen into the power of the enemy." Nothing in the Convention, or the subsequent practice in its interpretation leaves any room for excluding them on the ground that they were not involved in the conflict itself or that they were members of a non-United Nations peacekeeping force.

Nor would their status be affected by the fact that they were captured in the FYROM. Whether the FYROM was, strictly speaking, a neutral State is a controversial question but even if it was, the place of their capture does not affect the applicability of the Convention. If the FYROM was properly regarded as a neutral State, then the FRY incursion into its territory which resulted in the capture of the three would have been unlawful but the status of prisoner of war is made contingent on the fact of being in the hands of an enemy, not the legality of the means by which that was accomplished.

In these circumstances, it is surprising and disturbing that there was ever any doubt about the status of the three captured soldiers. James Burger has commented that "[s]ome persons thought initially that it would be better to assert that the captured soldiers were illegal detainees, allowing the United States to demand their immediate release, rather than waiting until the end of active hostilities"[39] but that the United States instead took the position that the men were prisoners of war, which he describes as "the right decision." It was certainly that but the point needs to be emphasized that the status of the three as prisoners of war was an automatic consequence of the fact that they met the requirements of the Convention, not the result of a policy choice. The status of a detainee as a prisoner of war is not something dependent upon the choice of either his or her own State or the detaining power. The initial uncertainty may have contributed to the refusal by the FRY to allow access by the ICRC to the three until more than three weeks after their capture, a clear breach of the Convention.[40]

In passing, it should be noted that, had the force in which the three men been serving remained a United Nations peacekeeping force, then the answer would probably have been different. In principle, when a national unit is assigned to the United Nations for a mission under United Nations command—i.e., a "blue beret" operation—the members of the unit are, for the

---

39. Burger, *supra* note 33, at 136.
40. ICRC Press Releases 99/21, Apr. 23, 1999 (protesting lack of access) and 99/25, Apr. 27, 1999 (recording a visit by the ICRC to the three men) *available at* ICRC website, *supra* note 19.

duration of their assignment and at least as long as they do not act outside the scope of the United Nations mandate (e.g., by engaging in surveillance activities unauthorized by the United Nations), to be considered as United Nations personnel, not members of the armed forces of their own State. In those circumstances, they would be protected by the provisions of the Convention on the Safety of United Nations and Associated Personnel of 1994, assuming that the States concerned were parties, or the Convention on Privileges and Immunities of 1946.

The position of the FRY soldiers captured by the KLA/UCK is also straightforward, at least once they came into the custody of the United States. Assuming that, at the time of their capture, the conflict between the KLA/UCK and the FRY was still an internal conflict (a matter considered above), the captured soldiers did not become prisoners of war when they fell into the hands of the KLA/UCK, as that status does not apply to prisoners in internal conflicts. Nevertheless, once they were transferred to the custody of a State which was engaged in an international armed conflict against their own State, they fulfilled the requirements of Article 4A(1) of the Third Convention and were thus entitled to treatment as prisoners of war. It appears that they were treated as such throughout the time they were held by the United States and access by the ICRC was allowed in accordance with the Convention.[41]

The Naval Embargo

By contrast, the naval operations against the FRY gave rise to more serious legal questions. The focus of discussion was the proposal—in fact never implemented—that the considerable naval forces available in the Adriatic should prevent shipments of oil to the FRY, even where the oil was being carried by ships flying the flag of States not involved in the conflict. There was obviously no obstacle in international law to the NATO States preventing ships flying their own flags from engaging in this trade.[42] Nor was there any such obstacle where the flag State, though not a member of NATO, consented to NATO warships intercepting its vessels, as a number of States did. The question which gave rise to difficulty was whether NATO could lawfully intercept and

---

41. *See* ICRC Press Releases 99/20, Apr. 18, 1999 and 99/29, May 18, 1999; *available at* ICRC website, *supra* note 19.
42. Whether the national laws of the States concerned permitted such action is another matter and one which falls outside the scope of this study.

divert ships flying the flag of a neutral State which did not consent to such action, such as Russian merchant ships.

The problem was, in part, of a political, rather than a legal, character. There was an understandable desire on the part of NATO not to risk an escalation of the conflict or further to embitter their relations with Russia. A further political complication was that the FRY's only port, Bar, was in Montenegro, not Serbia. Throughout the conflict, the Government of Montenegro sought to distance itself to the greatest extent possible from the actions of the FRY Federal Government and the Government of Serbia. While Montenegro, as part of the FRY, could not be regarded as a neutral in the legal sense of the term, it nevertheless sought something akin to a neutral status in political terms. NATO, although it bombed some targets in Montenegro, wished to bolster the position of the Montenegro Government and thus to minimize military action against Montenegro.

By contrast, international law appeared to present few problems. Although the matter is not entirely free of controversy, the general view is that the customary international law of armed conflict still permits a State engaged in an international armed conflict to prevent strategic commodities such as oil from reaching its opponent by sea, even if carried in neutral flagged vessels. The majority view is that that can be done either by the imposition of a blockade[43] or by less drastic measures of visit, search and capture designed to prevent the flow of contraband to an enemy.[44] Since the NATO States were engaged in an armed conflict with the FRY, the imposition of an oil embargo (with or without a general blockade) would, in principle, have been compatible with the *jus in bello*.

It would, however, be wrong to dismiss the doubts about the proposed embargo as having no legal basis. Two different legal issues need to be considered. First, in order to be lawful an oil embargo would have had to comply not only with the *jus in bello* but also with the *jus ad bellum*. A blockade of Saudi Arabia by the Iraqi navy (had that been possible) during the 1990–91 Gulf conflict might well have complied with the requirements of the *jus in bello* but it would nevertheless have been unlawful, because the entire Iraqi resort to force contravened the *jus ad bellum*. The need to comply with the *jus ad bellum* is particularly important when the measures in question are taken against

---

43. *See, e.g.,* COMMANDER'S HANDBOOK, *supra* note 30, ¶ 7.7; SAN REMO MANUAL ON INTERNATIONAL LAW APPLICABLE TO ARMED CONFLICTS AT SEA ¶¶ 93–104 (Louise Doswald-Beck ed., 1995).
44. COMMANDER'S HANDBOOK, *supra* note 30, ¶ 7.4.1; SAN REMO MANUAL, *supra* note 43, ¶¶ 146–152.

neutral States. An oil embargo of the FRY would have involved enforcing restrictions on the exercise by the shipping of neutral States of the normal rights of freedom of navigation under international law. Accordingly, while it is necessary to show that those restrictions were compatible with the *jus in bello*, it is not sufficient to do so; they must also be within the limits of the *jus ad bellum*.

The uncertainty about the possible imposition of an oil embargo was therefore, for many, the reflection of their uncertainty about whether NATO had a solid legal justification for resorting to force at all. In addition, even if international law does recognize a right to use force by way of humanitarian intervention, it is still necessary to ask whether that extends to the exercise of belligerent rights over the shipping of neutral States. As was made clear earlier in this paper, the present writer is firmly of the view that there is a right of humanitarian intervention in an extreme case. Moreover, if international law permits States to use force in such a case against the State responsible for the humanitarian crisis, then it is logical that it should also permit the taking of action which is both necessary and proportionate against neutral shipping to prevent that State from acquiring supplies needed to continue its human rights abuses or resist attempts to prevent them. But it is in considerations of this kind, and not just in references to the traditional rights of belligerents at sea, that the justification for an oil embargo needed to be found.

Secondly, both the *jus ad bellum* and the *jus in bello* require that action taken against neutral shipping be necessary and proportionate. In view of the limited port facilities at Bar, the difficulty of moving oil from the port to the rest of the FRY and the relative ease with which the NATO States could have disrupted links between Bar and the rest of the FRY, it is questionable whether interference with neutral shipping was really necessary on the facts of the case.

The Military Presence in Kosovo after June 10, 1999

On June 10, 1999 the NATO airstrikes were suspended and active hostilities came to an end. The FRY Government accepted the principles on a settlement presented to it by the European Union envoy, Mr Ahtisaari, and the Russian Federation envoy, Mr Chernomyrdin, on June 2, 1999, themselves based on an earlier set of principles laid down by the G-8 foreign ministers.[45] On June 9, 1999, a military technical agreement was concluded between NATO and FRY commanders. United Nations Security Council Resolution

---

45. Annexes 1 and 2 to S.C. Res. 1244 (June 10, 1999), U.N. Doc. S/RES/1244 (1999).

1244, adopted under Chapter VII of the Charter on June 10, 1999 approved these steps. The resolution went on, in paragraph 7, to authorize "member States and relevant international organizations to establish the international security presence in Kosovo . . . with all necessary means to fulfill its responsibilities." The responsibilities of KFOR, as the security presence became known, were set out in paragraph 9 of the resolution as follows:

(a) Deterring renewed hostilities, maintaining and where necessary enforcing a ceasefire, and ensuring the withdrawal and preventing the return into Kosovo of Federal and Republic military, police and paramilitary forces, except as provided in point 6 of annex 2;

(b) Demilitarising the Kosovo Liberation Army (KLA) and other armed Kosovo Albanian groups;

(c) Establishing a secure environment in which refugees and displaced persons can return home in safety, the international civil presence can operate, a transitional administration can be established, and humanitarian aid can be delivered;

(d) Ensuring public safety and order until the international civil presence can take responsibility for this task;

(e) Supervising demining until the international civil presence can, as appropriate, take over responsibility for this task;

(f) Supporting, as appropriate, and coordinating closely with the work of the international civil presence;

(g) Conducting border monitoring duties as required;

(h) Ensuring the protection and freedom of movement of itself, the international civil presence, and other international organisations.

Although NATO was not expressly mentioned, the reference in paragraph 7 to "relevant international organizations" was clearly intended to mean NATO and KFOR was, from the start, largely NATO-led. While KFOR derived its legal authority from the Security Council, it was not a United Nations force and was not subject to United Nations command and control.

By contrast, the international civil presence, UNMIK, was a United Nations body, created and controlled by the United Nations. It is worthwhile noting UNMIK's terms of reference. Paragraph 10 of Resolution 1244 authorized the United Nations Secretary-General, with the assistance of relevant international organizations (a reference not confined to NATO) to establish a civil presence:

[I]n order to provide an interim administration for Kosovo under which the people of Kosovo can enjoy substantial autonomy within the Federal Republic of Yugoslavia, and which will provide transitional administration while establishing and overseeing the development of provisional democratic self-governing institutions to ensure conditions for a peaceful and normal life for all inhabitants of Kosovo.

Under paragraph 11, the responsibilities given to the international civil presence were:

(a) Promoting the establishment, pending a final settlement, of substantial autonomy and self-government in Kosovo, taking full account of annex 2 and of the Rambouillet accords (S/1999/648);

(b) Performing basic civilian administrative functions where and as long as required;

(c) Organising and overseeing the development of provisional institutions for democratic and autonomous self-government pending a political settlement, including the holding of elections;

(d) Transferring, as these institutions are established, its administrative responsibilities while overseeing and supporting the consolidation of Kosovo's local provisional institutions and other peace-building activities;

(e) Facilitating a political process designed to determine Kosovo's future status, taking into account the Rambouillet accords (S/1999/648);

(f) In a final stage, overseeing the transfer of authority from Kosovo's provisional institutions to institutions established under a political settlement;

(g) Supporting the reconstruction of key infrastructure and other economic reconstruction;

(h) Supporting, in coordination with international humanitarian organisations, humanitarian and disaster relief aid;

(i) Maintaining civil law and order, including establishing local police forces and meanwhile through the deployment of international police personnel to serve in Kosovo;

(j) Protecting and promoting human rights;

(k) Assuring the safe and unimpeded return of all refugees and displaced persons to their homes in Kosovo.

Resolution 1244 (1999) is of the utmost importance. By using its powers under Chapter VII of the Charter to create a civilian administration for

Kosovo and to authorize an international military presence there, the Security Council ensured that Kosovo did not fall under a regime which was subject to the law of belligerent occupation. Whatever the doubts regarding the applicability of international humanitarian law to United Nations military operations generally,[46] the United Nations is not bound by the basic framework of the law of belligerent occupation (in particular, the duty codified in Article 43 of the Hague Regulations on Land Warfare to respect "unless absolutely prevented" the law in force in the occupied territory) where it establishes a new administration for a territory after a conflict. To hold otherwise would place a wholly unreasonable fetter on the power of the Council to provide for political change in territories such as Kosovo and East Timor. Resolution 1244 has to be seen as an exercise of that power and the legal regime governing both the security and civil presences is derived primarily from that Resolution, not from the law of belligerent occupation.[47] That said, individual principles of the law of belligerent occupation, such as those requiring humane treatment of detainees, would be applicable.

International Proceedings Relating to the Kosovo Conflict

One of the unusual features of the Kosovo conflict was the extent to which the military operations became the subject of scrutiny by international courts and tribunals. Three different tribunals have considered different aspects of the Kosovo conflict (and, at the time of writing, proceedings were continuing in two of them). While space does not permit a detailed analysis of these proceedings, it is nonetheless important briefly to consider each of them.

1. The International Criminal Tribunal for the former Yugoslavia

International humanitarian law has long expressly provided for its enforcement through criminal proceedings against individuals. Nevertheless, while the grave breaches machinery established by the Geneva Conventions and

---

46. On which, see the *Observance by United Nations forces of international humanitarian law, Secretary-General's Bulletin*, U.N. Doc. ST/SGB/1999/13 (Aug. 6, 1999), *reprinted in* 2 YEARBOOK OF INTERNATIONAL HUMANITARIAN LAW 563 (1999); Christopher Greenwood, *International Humanitarian Law and United Nations Military Operations*, 1 YEARBOOK OF INTERNATIONAL HUMANITARIAN LAW 3-34 (1998).

47. For a contrary view, see John Cerone, *Minding the Gap: Outlining KFOR Accountability in Post-Conflict Kosovo*, 12 EUROPEAN JOURNAL OF INTERNATIONAL LAW 469 (2001).

Protocol I[48] requires States to take action in cases of grave breaches and to bring offenders to justice irrespective of nationality, proceedings of this kind have in fact been almost unknown. In the case of Kosovo, however, there was already in existence an international tribunal able to exercise criminal jurisdiction. The ICTY, which was established by United Nations Security Council Resolution 827 (1993), had "the power to prosecute persons responsible for serious violations of international humanitarian law committed in the territory of the former Yugoslavia since 1991."[49] Although drawn up with the conflicts in Bosnia-Herzegovina and Croatia in the early 1990's in mind, the Statute was not limited to those conflicts and was clearly applicable to events in Kosovo (as the Security Council recognized in Resolutions 1160 and 1199 (1998)).

The attacks by the FRY armed forces and police on the majority community in Kosovo led to the indictment, on May 22, 1999, by the ICTY Prosecutor of the then FRY President, Slobodan Milosevic, and a number of other prominent political and military figures on charges of war crimes and crimes against humanity.[50] While this indictment was dismissed as a political gesture by Milosevic at the time, the new government of the FRY surrendered him to the custody of the Tribunal in 2001. At the time of writing, Milosevic was standing trial on these and other charges.

The Prosecutor also considered that the ICTY had jurisdiction over any serious violations of humanitarian law which might have occurred in the NATO air campaign. Although her stance in this regard attracted some criticism in political circles, it was plainly correct. The ICTY's jurisdiction under Article 1 of its Statute is confined to the territory of the former Yugoslavia but it is not limited to offenses committed there by Yugoslavs and clearly extends to offenses by NATO personnel. The Prosecutor established a committee to inquire into various allegations that NATO forces had violated international humanitarian law and to advise whether there was "a sufficient basis to proceed with an investigation into some or all of the allegations or into other incidents related to the NATO bombing."[51] The committee concluded

---

48. *See* Geneva I (Article 49), Geneva II (Article 50), Geneva III (Article 129), and Geneva IV (Article 146), *supra* note 12. *See also* Protocol I (Article 85), *supra* note 11.
49. Statute of the Tribunal, Article 1, *supra* note 22.
50. The indictment is *available on* the ICTY website at http://www.un.org/icty/indictment/english/mil-ii990524e.htm. On May 24, 1999, Judge Hunt confirmed the indictment, Case No. IT-99-37-I.
51. Report to the Prosecutor, Appendix A, ¶ 3.

that no investigation should be commenced.[52] The Prosecutor accepted that recommendation and told the Security Council that:

> [T]here is no basis for opening an investigation into any of those allegations or into other incidents related to the NATO bombing. Although some mistakes were made by NATO, I am very satisfied that there was no deliberate targeting of civilians or of unlawful military targets by NATO during the bombing campaign.[53]

The committee's report and the conclusions drawn by the Prosecutor have attracted much criticism. Most of that criticism has come from those who wanted to see charges brought against members of the NATO armed forces and who accused the committee of adopting too lenient a stance in its appraisal of the NATO actions.[54] More surprisingly, however, others have criticized the committee for subjecting decisions taken in the heat of the moment and sometimes in conditions of considerable danger to too close and detached a scrutiny.[55] In the opinion of this writer, both criticisms are misconceived. The report suggests neither undue leniency nor an excessive dose of hindsight. While scrutiny of military decisions with a view to prosecution is never a comfortable experience for those who might be the subject of charges, it is what the Geneva Conventions and Protocol I envisage and what has been applied to non-NATO defendants by the ICTY for several years. What the report shows is that armed forces today cannot expect to be immune from the kind of legal scrutiny—seeking to apply rules which have long been binding on all States—which has become commonplace in other walks of life. It also shows that a body like the committee established by the Prosecutor of the ICTY is capable of applying those rules in a fair and sensible manner.

2. The International Court of Justice

The NATO air campaign was also the subject of proceedings instituted by the FRY before the International Court of Justice against ten of the NATO

---

52. Id., ¶ 91.
53. United Nations Security Council 4150th Meeting; S/PV.4150, at 3, col. 1.
54. See, e.g., Paolo Benvenuti, *The ICTY Prosecutor and the Review of the NATO Bombing Campaign against the Federal Republic of Yugoslavia*, 12 EUROPEAN JOURNAL OF INTERNATIONAL LAW 503 (2001) and, for more moderate criticism, see the article by Professor Bothe, *supra* note 36.
55. See the Commentary by Judith Miller in the present volume.

States while the campaign was in progress.[56] The FRY maintained both that the NATO resort to force was a violation of the principles of *jus ad bellum* enshrined in the United Nations Charter and that the conduct of the campaign violated obligations contained in a wide variety of treaties ranging from the Geneva Conventions to the Convention on Navigation on the River Danube. In each case the FRY sought provisional measures in the form of an order that the respondent State should immediately cease military action against the FRY pending the hearing of the merits. In order to obtain provisional measures, however, an applicant must demonstrate the existence of a prima facie basis for jurisdiction on the merits. The Court held, by large majorities, that the FRY had failed to satisfy this threshold requirement.

The result is scarcely surprising. None of the treaties which were the basis for the FRY's substantive claim contain provisions conferring jurisdiction on the International Court and the two bases for jurisdiction advanced by the FRY[57]—Article IX of the Genocide Convention of 1948 (which was invoked against all the respondents) and Article 36(2) of the Statute of the Court, the so-called "Optional Clause" (which was invoked against six out of the ten)—were rightly rejected by the Court.

Even assuming that the FRY was a party to the Genocide Convention, a position which it has subsequently repudiated, Article IX manifestly offered no basis for jurisdiction against Spain and the United States of America, both of which had entered reservations rejecting the application of that provision when they became party to the Convention. Moreover, Article IX confers jurisdiction only with regard to a dispute "relating to the interpretation,

---

56. Belgium, Canada, France, Germany, Italy, the Netherlands, Portugal, Spain, the United Kingdom and the United States of America. The Orders of the Court refusing the FRY's request for provisional measures of protection and ordering the removal of the cases against Spain and the United States of America from the Court's list are each reported under the title *Case concerning Legality of Use of Force*, 1999 I.C.J. 124 (Belgium), 259 (Canada), 363 (France), 422 (Germany), 481 (Italy), 542 (the Netherlands), 656 (Portugal), 761 (Spain), 826 (United Kingdom) and 916 (United States of America). At the time of writing, the cases against the respondents, other than Spain and the United States of America, were still before the Court. The eight remaining respondents have all objected to the jurisdiction of the Court and the admissibility of the applications. The writer acted as counsel for the United Kingdom in these proceedings; the present paper represents his personal views.

57. In the cases against Belgium and the Netherlands, the FRY also attempted at a late stage to rely upon a bilateral treaty. The Court held that this treaty had been invoked too late in the proceedings; see, e.g., *Case concerning Legality of Use of Force* (FRY v. Belgium), 1999 I.C.J. 124 (Jun. 2) (Order—Request for the Indication of Provisional Measures), ¶ 44.

application or fulfillment" of the Genocide Convention. Not surprisingly, the Court held that:

> [T]he essential characteristic [of genocide] is the intended destruction of a 'national, ethnical, racial or religious group' (*Application of the Convention on the Prevention and Punishment of Genocide, Provisional Measures Order of 13 September 1993*, ICJ Reports 1993, p. 345, para. 42); ... the threat or use of force against a State cannot in itself constitute an act of genocide within the meaning of Article II of the Genocide Convention; and ... in the opinion of the Court, it does not appear at the present stage of the proceedings that the bombings which form the subject of the Yugoslav Application 'indeed entail the element of intent, towards a group as such, required by [Article II]' (*Legality of the Threat or Use of Nuclear Weapons, Advisory Opinion*, ICJ Reports, 1996 (I), p. 240, para. 26).[58]

In effect, the FRY was seeking to use Article IX of the Genocide Convention as a device to establish jurisdiction over complaints relating to quite different agreements. The FRY's interpretation of the Genocide Convention would have entailed watering down the crime of genocide to the point that it was deprived of its separate identity as the most serious of international crimes.

The other provision relied on by the FRY—Article 36(2) of the Statute of the Court—could afford jurisdiction only in the event that both the FRY and the respondent State in question had each made a valid declaration accepting the Court's jurisdiction under that provision and the dispute fell within the scope of both declarations. The FRY had purported to make a declaration under Article 36(2) on April 25, 1999 (a month after the commencement of the NATO campaign and three days before the FRY filed its applications against the respondent States). It then sought to rely upon that declaration as a basis for jurisdiction in the proceedings against those respondent States which had extant declarations under Article 36(2) (Belgium, Canada, the Netherlands, Portugal, Spain and the United Kingdom).

In view of the dispute regarding the status of the FRY, the question immediately arose whether the FRY declaration was valid. If, as the Security Council and the General Assembly had decided,[59] the respondent States claimed and the FRY has now accepted, the FRY was not at the relevant time a member of the United Nations, then it was not a party to the Statute of the Court and could not have made a valid declaration under Article 36(2) of that

---

58. *Id.*, ¶ 40.
59. See *supra* note 14.

Statute. The Court, however, understandably chose not to decide that question in provisional measures proceedings when there were other, more obvious, reasons for holding that there was no basis for jurisdiction. In the cases against Spain and the United Kingdom, Article 36(2) of the Statute could not have provided a basis for jurisdiction, because those two States had accepted the jurisdiction of the Court only as between themselves and another State which had made a similar declaration not less than one year earlier. The FRY's declaration, even if valid, plainly did not fulfill that requirement.

The Court's reason for holding that Article 36(2) did not afford a basis for jurisdiction in the cases against Belgium, Canada, the Netherlands and Portugal is of more general interest. The FRY declaration accepted the jurisdiction of the Court as between the FRY and other States with Article 36(2) declarations "in all disputes arising or which may arise after the signature of the present declaration [i.e., after April 25, 1999], with regard to the situations or facts subsequent to this signature."[60] The Court held that the dispute which the FRY wished to bring before the Court had arisen before April 25, 1999. That was clear from the terms of the FRY applications, which referred primarily to events before that date, and from the debates in the Security Council on March 24 and 26, 1999 in which the legality of the NATO action was the subject of extensive discussion. The Court rejected the suggestion that the air campaign could be sliced up like salami, so that each air raid gave rise to a fresh dispute. The decision is not a technical one. The temporal reservation in the FRY's declaration was carefully drafted to ensure that no proceedings could be brought against the FRY in respect of the abuses in Kosovo which had led to the NATO campaign. It was entirely in accordance with precedent and principle that the FRY was not allowed, in the words of the old saying, "to have its cake and eat it too."

The International Court proceedings are, nevertheless, an important reminder that military action can be the subject of scrutiny by the International Court not merely after the action has ended but while it is in progress. Provisional measures proceedings can be brought before the Court in a comparatively short time and the Court has now held that an order for provisional measures is legally binding.[61] Since it cannot be assumed that there will always be a jurisdictional ground for dismissing a request for provisional measures in

---

60. The full text of the FRY declaration is quoted in Order in the case against Belgium, *supra* note 57, ¶ 23.
61. LaGrand Case (Germany v. United States of America), 40 INTERNATIONAL LEGAL MATERIALS 1069 (2001) (Judgment of June 27, 2001).

such a case, the possibility clearly exists that States involved in ongoing military operations might be forced to defend them before the Court in such proceedings. The stakes, in such an event, could be very high indeed. Moreover, the Court's findings were, for the most part, provisional and, at the time of writing, the proceedings against all of the respondent States except for Spain and the United States of America remained on the Court's list.

3. The European Court of Human Rights

The third proceedings were in the European Court of Human Rights. The case of *Bankovic* v. *Belgium* concerned the attack on the building in Belgrade housing the studios of *Radio Televizije Srbije* (RTS).[62] That building was hit in an air raid on April 23, 1999. Sixteen people were killed and sixteen injured. The application was brought by one of those injured and relatives of some of those killed against the seventeen NATO States which were also parties to the European Convention on Human Rights (i.e., all of the NATO States except Canada and the United States). The applicants alleged that the attack had violated the right to life, under Article 2 of the Convention, and the right to freedom of expression, under Article 10, of those killed or injured. They maintained that the respondent States were responsible for those violations even though they had occurred outside the territory of any of them (and, indeed, in the territory of a State not party to the European Convention). In arguing that the Convention was not confined to events occurring on the territory of the States parties, the applicants relied on the decisions in *Loizidou* v. *Turkey*, in which the European Court had held Turkey responsible for violations of the Convention occurring in the north of Cyprus where large numbers of Turkish forces have been stationed since 1974 and in which the Court found that Turkey exercised effective control.[63] In addition they argued that the respondents were responsible for the alleged violations irrespective of which State's forces had actually carried out the attack, because they contended that NATO operated on the basis that any NATO State could have

---

62. The decision of the Grand Chamber of the Court on December 12, 2001 (Bankovic et al. v. Belgium et al.) 11 BUTTERWORTHS HUMAN RIGHTS CASES 435 (2002) is also *available at* the website of the Court, http://www.echr.coe.int. The present writer was counsel for the United Kingdom in those proceedings; this paper represents his personal views.

63. Loizidou v. Turkey (Preliminary Objections), 103 INTERNATIONAL LAW REPORTS 622 (1995); Loizidou v. Turkey (Merits), 108 INTERNATIONAL LAW REPORTS 443 (1996). These decisions were confirmed by the Court's decision in Cyprus v. Turkey (10 May 2001), *available on* the Court's website, *supra* note 62.

vetoed the decision to attack the RTS building.[64] In doing so, they highlighted the whole issue of the geographical extent of the European Convention and its applicability to operations involving the armed forces of States party to the Convention which occur outside the territory of those States.

The case also raised important questions about the relationship between the principles of international humanitarian law and international human rights law. The applicants contended that human rights law and international humanitarian law were not mutually exclusive and denied that military operations in an international armed conflict were governed solely by humanitarian law.[65] The first argument of the applicants was that the legality of the attack on the RTS building had to be assessed by reference to provisions of the European Convention, quite independently of whether that attack complied with international humanitarian law, although they also contended, in the alternative, that the Convention in effect incorporated the principles of humanitarian law, so that the Convention would have been violated if the attack on the RTS building had been in breach of international humanitarian law.

These are arguments of very considerable breadth which, had they been accepted, would radically have altered the legal framework within which military operations have to be conducted. A Grand Chamber of the Court,[66] however, rejected the applicants' arguments and unanimously declared the application inadmissible. The Grand Chamber accepted the respondents' argument that the case fell outside the scope of the Convention. Article 1 of the Convention defines that scope by providing that "the High Contracting Parties shall secure to everyone within their jurisdiction the rights and freedoms defined in Section I of this Convention." The Court held that this provision reflected a largely (though not exclusively) territorial concept of jurisdiction and that it was only in exceptional cases that persons outside the territory of one of the High Contracting Parties would be considered as falling within the jurisdiction of that Party. The Court contrasted Article 1 of the European Convention with common Article 1 of the Geneva Conventions,

---

64. Benvenuti, *supra* note 54, at 526–9, broadly supports these propositions.
65. They relied in part on the report of the Inter-American Commission of Human Rights in Coard et al. v. United States of America, Case 10, 951 (Sept. 29, 1999) 9 BUTTERWORTHS HUMAN RIGHTS CASES 150 (2001), which considered that the detention by United States forces of persons captured in the Grenada operation was subject to the American Convention on Human Rights. *Available at* http://www.cidh.oas.org/annualrep/99eng/merits/unitedstates10.95.htm.
66. While most cases in the Court are heard by a Chamber of seven judges, the Chamber originally constituted to hear *Bankovic* relinquished jurisdiction to the Grand Chamber of seventeen judges because of the importance of the issues raised by the case.

under which "the High Contracting Parties undertake to respect and ensure respect for the present Convention in all circumstances." The parties to the Geneva Conventions were expressly required to respect the Conventions in all their military operations and could be held responsible for any failure on the part of their forces anywhere in the world to observe those Conventions. By contrast, Article 1 of the European Convention was clearly narrower and imposed responsibility only in respect of treatment of a person who was within the jurisdiction of the State concerned at the relevant time. The Court held that a person was not to be treated as falling within the jurisdiction of a State merely because he or she was affected by the military operations of that State's forces.

The *Bankovic* judgment removed the possibility that military operations by the European members of NATO would henceforth be measured not only against the yardstick of international humanitarian law but also by reference to the very different standards of the European Convention on Human Rights. Indeed, had the applicants' arguments been accepted it would not only have been NATO that would have been affected. Coalition military operations in the Gulf and United Nations operations in, for example, East Timor would also presumably have come within the purview of the European Court and the provisions of a regional human rights treaty would have been superimposed on the requirements of international humanitarian law. The Court did not reverse its earlier decisions in the Cyprus cases, but it noted that the circumstances in Cyprus were unusual in that both Cyprus and Turkey were parties to the European Convention so that the inhabitants of northern Cyprus should not be deprived of the benefits of the Convention by reason of the changes brought about by the Turkish intervention of 1974. It remains to be seen what attitude the Court would take in a case where armed forces of a party to the European Convention occupied territory of a non-Convention country.

Conclusions

The Kosovo conflict raised important questions about the *jus in bello* in addition to the difficult issues of the *jus ad bellum* which have already attracted so much attention. Indeed, in one sense the former group of questions are more important, because they may have a wider impact. Although, for the reasons given above, the Kosovo conflict was unusual in certain respects (notably its asymmetric character), many of the lessons learned should be relevant to future conflicts.

The following conclusions seem warranted:

1. International humanitarian law applies to a conflict between two or more States irrespective of what that conflict is called or the cause for which force is used; the use of force by way of humanitarian intervention is no different in this respect from the use of force for other purposes.

2. While the *jus ad bellum* requires that the use of force be proportionate to the goals which the State or States using force are permitted to pursue, that does not mean that the *jus in bello* principles on such issues as targeting are to be interpreted or applied differently and it should never be used as an excuse to undermine the principle of the equal application of the *jus in bello*.

3. Members of the armed forces of a party to an international conflict who find themselves in the power of the enemy are prisoners of war, irrespective of the purpose for which the conflict is waged, whether prisoner of war status is claimed on their behalf or how or where they were captured.

4. It might have been lawful for the NATO States to have imposed an oil embargo on the FRY but the legal issues involved went beyond a simple application of the law of neutrality.

5. The KFOR and UNMIK presence in Kosovo pursuant to Security Council Resolution 1244 (1999) was not governed by the law of belligerent occupation.

6. Scrutiny by international courts and tribunals of military operations was a fact of life even before the establishment of the International Criminal Court. The approach of the three tribunals which considered the conduct of the Kosovo conflict suggests that much of the concern which has been expressed on this subject is misplaced.

Rules of Conduct During Humanitarian Intervention

Ivan Shearer

The Russian Orthodox Church recently canonized the last Czar of Russia, Nicholas II. A fantasy of mine is that the Church will at some point also consider for sainthood (assuming his private life met appropriate standards) the czar's legal adviser, Baron Feodor de Martens, who was responsible for the wording of what has come down to us as the "Martens Clause."

As it first appeared in the Preamble to the Second Hague Convention of 1899, the Martens Clause reads:

> Until a more complete code of the laws of war is issued, the high contracting parties think it right to declare that in cases not included in the Regulations adopted by them, populations and belligerents remain under the protection and empire of the principles of international law, as they result from the usages established between civilized nations, from the laws of humanity and the requirements of the public conscience.[1]

In common articles of the 1949 Geneva Conventions, the Martens Clause is substantially repeated, with the substitution of the word "dictates"

---

1. Preamble, Convention (II) with Respect to the Laws and Customs of War on Land, July 29, 1899, U.S.T.S. 403, 32 Stat. 1803, 1 Bevans 247.

for "requirements" in relation to the public conscience.[2] The Clause also appears in the 1977 Additional Protocols to the Geneva Conventions.[3]

The Martens Clause is a powerful reminder that in situations of armed conflict, of whatever kind, there is never a total gap in the law, never a situation in which there cannot be an appeal to law in order to mitigate the horror and the suffering. Baron de Martens correctly foresaw in 1899, and again in 1907, that unscrupulous commanders and their cunning legal advisers might seek to exploit loopholes or ambiguities in the written law. An egregious example is the "general participation clause" of the Hague Conventions of 1907, according to which the provisions of the Conventions did not apply to any of the belligerents unless all of them were parties to the Conventions. Thus, the detailed Hague Regulations might not apply but, according to the Martens Clause, standards of civilized behavior deriving from custom, humanity and the public conscience do.

---

2. Geneva Convention for the Amelioration of the Condition of the Wounded and Sick in Armed Forces in the Field, Aug. 12, 1949, Article 63, 6 U.S.T. 3114, 75 U.N.T.S. 31, DOCUMENTS ON THE LAWS OF WAR 197 (Adam Roberts & Richard Guelff eds., 3d ed., 2000) [hereinafter Geneva I]; Geneva Convention for the Amelioration of the Condition of the Wounded, Sick and Shipwrecked Members of the Armed Forces at Sea, Aug. 12, 1949, Article 142, 6 U.S.T. 3217, 75 U.N.T.S. 85, *id.* at 222 [hereinafter Geneva II]; Geneva Convention Relative to the Treatment of Prisoners of War, Aug. 12, 1949, Article 142, 6 U.S.T. 3316, 75 U.N.T.S. 135, *id.* at 244 [hereinafter Geneva III]; Geneva Convention Relative to the Protection of Civilian Persons in Time of War, Aug. 12, 1949, Article 158, 6 U.S.T. 3516, 75 U.N.T.S. 287, *id.* at 301 [hereinafter Geneva IV].
3. Protocol Additional to the Geneva Conventions of 12 August 1949, and Relating to the Protection of Victims of International Conflicts, Jun. 8, 1977, Article 1(2), 1125 U.N.T.S. 3, *id.* at 422 [hereinafter Protocol I]. Protocol Additional to the Geneva Conventions of 12 August 1949, and Relating to the Protection of Victims of Non-International Armed Conflicts, Dec. 12, 1977, Preamble, 1125 U.N.T.S. 609, *id.* at 483 [hereinafter Protocol II].

I take this as my starting point in the discussion of the *jus in bello* in relation to humanitarian intervention operations.[4] Whatever may be the uncertainties in the identification and application of this law to a relatively new form of armed conflict, at least we can be confident that we start from a firm, albeit general, basis in humanitarian law. That basis is indeed becoming more detailed in content as consensus emerges that certain principles and rules of the *jus in bello* have achieved recognized status in customary law. Note should be taken in this regard of ongoing discussions in Geneva to identify those parts of Protocol I that may be regarded as customary, notwithstanding the inability of certain States to ratify the Protocol by reason of particular objections.[5]

The other firm foundation for my approach is that the application of the *jus in bello* is not dependent upon the demonstration of a legal basis for the resort to armed force in the *jus ad bellum*. The law of armed conflict (which term I regard as including international humanitarian law) applies its protection equally to the just and the unjust sides to a conflict. This is an established and undoubted proposition.

What is "Intervention"?

We may consider first a number of actions that constitute (for the most part) non-forcible and thus uncontroversial forms of intervention. These are sometimes listed under the heading "Military Operations Other than War" (MOOTW) and include disaster relief, humanitarian assistance, peace

---

4. Some recent literature on the topic includes: Hilaire McCoubrey and Nigel White, THE BLUE HELMETS: LEGAL REGULATION OF UNITED NATIONS MILITARY OPERATIONS (1996); Daphna Shraga and Ralph Zacklin, *The applicability of international humanitarian law to UN peacekeeping operations: conceptual, legal and practical issues*, in SYMPOSIUM ON HUMANITARIAN ACTION AND PEACE-KEEPING OPERATIONS (Umesh Palwankar, ed., 1994); Willy Lubin, *Towards the international responsibility of the UN in human rights violations during peace-keeping operations: the case of Somalia*, 52 BULLETIN OF THE INTERNATIONAL COMMISSION OF JURISTS 47 (1994); Julianne Peck, Note: *The UN and the Laws of War: How Can the World's Peacekeepers Be Held Accountable?*, 21 SYRACUSE JOURNAL OF INTERNATIONAL AND COMPARATIVE LAW 283 (1995); Brian Tittemore, *Belligerents in Blue Helmets: Applying International Humanitarian Law to UN Peace Operations*, 33 STANFORD JOURNAL OF INTERNATIONAL LAW (1997); Garth Cartledge, *Legal constraints on military personnel deployed on peace-keeping operations*, in THE CHANGING FACE OF CONFLICT AND THE EFFICACY OF INTERNATIONAL HUMANITARIAN LAW (Helen Durham and Timothy L.H. McCormack eds., 1999).
5. Yoram Dinstein, *The Thirteenth Waldemar A. Solf Lecture in International Law*, 166 MILITARY LAW REVIEW 93 (2000).

operations, arms control, military support to the civil authorities, enforcement of sanctions, foreign internal defense, counter-drug operations, evacuation of noncombatants, hostage rescue, and others.[6] The law applicable to such operations consists principally of the norms of human rights, as recognized in the major international covenants and conventions, and established as general international law. The domestic law of the country where the intervention takes place will also call for respect, except in so far as it may conflict with established international human rights law or the provisions of a higher law, such as a resolution of the United Nations Security Council.

Some of these examples may, of course, in the circumstances, involve the use of armed force or grow through "mission creep" to require the use of armed force. A hostage rescue almost certainly requires the use of armed force, but the swiftness of the insertion and withdrawal of force hardly allows for the application of the law of armed conflict as such: only the general principles of proportionality and humanity guide us here. Lengthier presences, such as the operation in Somalia, may come to pose questions of the applicability of the laws of armed conflict as the situation escalates from a peaceable and unopposed intervention to armed conflict. A peacekeeping operation authorized by the United Nations may envisage the necessity of the use of force beyond the elementary right of UN forces to defend themselves against armed attack.[7] These are sometimes referred to as "robust" peacekeeping operations. This type of operation also raises the question of application of the laws of armed conflict.

Finally, intervention may be avowedly a forcible action—a peace enforcement action usually authorized by the UN Security Council (as in the case of Iraq's invasion of Kuwait), but in certain cases not authorized by it (as in the case of the bombing by NATO forces of Yugoslavia by reason of the situation in Kosovo). This is the type of intervention most clearly requiring the applicability of the laws of armed conflict. But what laws?

---

6. Chairman of the Joint Chiefs of Staff, U.S. Department of Defense, Joint Publication 3-07, JOINT DOCTRINE FOR MILITARY OPERATIONS OTHER THAN WAR (1995).
7. In September 1992 the Secretary-General of the United Nations announced that peacekeeping troops in Bosnia-Herzegovina "would follow normal peace-keeping rules of engagement [and] would thus be authorized to use force in self-defense.... It is to be noted that in this context self-defense is deemed to include situations in which armed persons attempt by force to prevent UN troops from carrying out their mandate." Cited by LESLIE GREEN, THE CONTEMPORARY LAW OF ARMED CONFLICT 344 (2d ed. 2000).

The Applicability of the Conventional Laws of Armed Conflict to Forcible Intervention

We speak more narrowly of the law of armed conflict (LOAC) as "Hague Law," since it finds its principal elaboration in the now rather dated Hague Conventions of 1907. We speak of international humanitarian law (IHL) as "Geneva Law", since it derives principally from the Geneva (Red Cross) Conventions of 1949. These two sets of laws, of separate origin in the nineteenth century and flowing in separate if parallel streams through most of the twentieth century, were brought together in one stream and updated in Additional Protocols I and II to the Geneva Conventions, adopted in 1977.[8] Those Protocols have since been widely (although not universally) ratified. It is now usual to speak of "the law of armed conflict" and "international humanitarian law" interchangeably. Either expression generally includes the other.

What is the threshold of application of these laws? The Hague Conventions are silent on the point, assuming that their application to "war" was objectively ascertainable by reason of a declaration to that effect by one or more parties. The Charter of the United Nations no longer envisages declarations of war as a right of States and restricts the use of force by States against other States to situations of self-defense and actions authorized by the Security Council under Chapter VII of the Charter. (Some also believe that there is a limited range of uses of armed force which are not prohibited by Article 2(4) of the Charter, such as "humanitarian intervention.") Hence, the UN Charter does not establish a definition of a state of war or armed conflict. The Geneva Conventions of 1949, however, adopted soon after the creation of the United Nations, do establish a threshold in general terms, a threshold that is also adopted in Protocol I. Common Article 2 of the Geneva Conventions provides:

> In addition to the provisions which shall be implemented in peacetime, the present Convention[s] shall apply to all cases of declared war or of any other armed conflict which may arise between two or more of the High Contracting Parties, even if the state of war is not recognized by one of them.
>
> . . .
>
> The Convention[s] shall also apply to all cases of partial or total occupation of the territory of a High Contracting Party, even if the said occupation meets with no armed resistance.[9]

---

8. Protocol I and Protocol II, *supra* note 3.
9. See Article 2 in each of the four Geneva Conventions, *supra* note 2.

The threshold of application of the Geneva Conventions and of Protocol I is thus not set high: it merely requires the objective existence of an "armed conflict," which presumably exists from the first moment after an exchange of fire.

The Conventions and Protocol I apply between "the Contracting Parties." Can the United Nations, as such, be a Contracting Party? Following the Advisory Opinion of the International Court of Justice in the *Reparations for Injuries Suffered in the Service of the United Nations* case,[10] the United Nations could, if it chose, become a party to such conventions. But it has not done so for reasons to be discussed further below. The national contingents of UN forces participating in an armed conflict would, however, be bound by the conventions to which their States are parties.

It is also necessary to note that under the Geneva Conventions and Protocol I they may apply between Contracting Parties and other parties to the conflict which are not represented by a government or an authority recognized by the adverse party. These latter forces must, however, "be subject to an internal disciplinary system which, *inter alia*, shall enforce compliance with the rules of international law applicable in armed conflict."[11] Essentially this means voluntary de facto compliance by a entity not competent to become a Contracting Party to the Conventions, which—if offered—must be reciprocated. More formal status, however, is accorded by Protocol I, Article 96(3) to the particular case of an "authority representing a people engaged against a High Contracting Party in an armed conflict of the type referred to in Article 1, paragraph 4 [self-determination struggles against colonial, alien, or racist regimes]" provided that the authority undertakes to apply the Conventions and the Protocol by means of a declaration addressed to the depositary (the Swiss Federal Council).

So far as non-international armed conflicts (civil wars) are concerned, Common Article 3 of the Geneva Conventions similarly refers merely to the objective existence of an armed conflict, and applies as between "the parties to the conflict," an expression distinct from, and wider than, "Contracting Parties." Protocol II supplements this by defining such a conflict in terms of the parties being the armed forces of the Contracting Party in whose territory the conflict takes place and "dissident armed forces or other organized armed groups which, under responsible command, exercise such control over

---

10. 1949 I.C.J. 174 (Apr. 11).
11. Protocol I, *supra* note 3, art. 43.

a part of its territory as to enable them to carry out sustained and concerted military operation and to implement this Protocol." Thus, police-type actions against armed individuals or bands that do not fulfill these conditions do not engage the application of Common Article 3 of the Geneva Conventions or Protocol II.

As can be seen, there are a number of issues of interpretation and application of the above instruments to particular situations. Notwithstanding these, one must always remember the Martens Clause and the growing body of customary law of armed conflict and human rights law as relevant sources of law to apply to any situation.

The United Nations and International Conventions Relating to Armed Conflict

The United Nations is not, as an international personality in its own right, a party to any of the conventions relating to armed conflict. It is sometimes suggested that it should become a party. This, however, could impede its peacekeeping missions. The problem is the threshold of application of the conventions. There are situations in peacekeeping, especially those that require—or come to require—"robust" measures, that may cross the threshold, but it may be undesirable for the operation to "change gears" notionally from a peacekeeping mission into an armed conflict. This could well be escalatory in effect. Moreover, there would be something odd about a situation in which the United Nations, in the name of the international community, is conducting an essentially peaceful operation in accordance with the United Nations Charter, which could be characterized nonetheless as an "armed conflict" in which United Nations forces and opposed forces are equally "combatants." It has rightly been suggested that the threshold of armed conflict must be set higher than that set by the Geneva Conventions and Protocols where United Nations peacekeeping operations are concerned.[12]

Notwithstanding that understandable view, the United Nations has consistently taken the view that "the principles and spirit of general international

---

12. JOSEPH BIALKE, UNITED NATIONS PEACE OPERATIONS: THE APPLICABLE NORMS AND THE APPLICATION OF THE LAW OF ARMED CONFLICT, LL.M thesis, University of Iowa College of Law, published by Defense Information Systems Agency, Defense Technical Information Center, Ft. Belvoir, Virginia, AD No. ADA380930 (2000); Joseph Bialke, *United Nations Peace Operations: Applicable Norms and the Application of the Law of Armed Conflict*, 50 AIR FORCE LAW REVIEW 1 (2001).

conventions applicable to the conduct of military personnel" shall be observed by forces participating in United Nations peacekeeping operations.[13] This, of course, is to underline the fundamental consideration that the absence of formal applicability of the laws of armed conflict/international humanitarian law does not open up a vacuum in which no laws apply.

It might stick in the throats of right-thinking people that there should be an equality of arms (and the equal moral stature that might be implied by the formal applicability of international conventions relevant to armed conflict) in the case of enforcement actions carried out under the authority of the United Nations Security Council acting under Chapter VII of the Charter. After all, in such a case there is a party clearly identified by the Security Council as being in the wrong, and United Nations forces are being deployed to right that wrong. That, however, would be a wrong approach, if it led to the proposition that the conventions could not apply. Both the law of armed conflict and international humanitarian law have throughout their development been consistently agnostic so far as the rightness or wrongness of a belligerent party's position is concerned. The *jus in bello* applies equally among the parties however strong or weak their claims may be to have the right to resort to force under the *jus ad bellum*. And of course that must be so, otherwise the conflict could be fought without restraint.

Peace enforcement personnel acting on behalf of the United Nations are essentially engaged in hostilities as belligerents and "are treated in exactly the same way as the armed forces of a state."[14] Looked at from the practical point of view, as Professor Greenwood has remarked, if those laws did not apply

---

13. In 1991 the United Nations formulated a Model Participation Agreement, to be concluded between itself and Member States contributing forces, to be used in peacekeeping operations. Paragraph 28 of the Model Agreement provides:

> [The United Nations peacekeeping forces] shall observe and respect the principles and the spirit of the general international conventions applicable to the conduct of military personnel. The international conventions referred to above include the four Geneva Conventions of 12 August 1949 and their Additional Protocols of 8 June 1977 and the UNESCO Convention of 14 May 1954 on the Protection of Cultural Property in the Event of Armed Conflict. [The participating State] shall therefore ensure that the members of its national contingent serving with [the UN peacekeeping force] be fully acquainted with the principles and spirit of the Conventions.

U.N. DOC. A/46/185 (1991).
14. Christopher Greenwood, *Protection of peacekeepers: the legal regime*, 7 DUKE JOURNAL OF COMPARATIVE AND INTERNATIONAL LAW 185, 189 (1996).

then a commander of the force opposed to the UN force could well conclude that he "might as well be hanged for a sheep as for a lamb."[15]

The Convention on the Safety of United Nations and Associated Personnel

The difference between peacekeeping and peace enforcement operations is clearly marked by the Convention on the Safety of United Nations and Associated Personnel, adopted by the General Assembly and opened for signature on December 9, 1994.[16] The convention applies to protect military, police or civilian personnel engaged or deployed in a "United Nations operation." It is made a crime for any person to murder, kidnap, or otherwise attack personnel so engaged or deployed. The convention provides for quasi-universal jurisdiction over offenders.[17] The term "United Nations operation" is defined to mean:

> [A]n operation established by the competent organ of the United Nations in accordance with the Charter of the United Nations and conducted under United Nations authority and control:
>
> where the operation is for the purpose of maintaining or restoring international peace and security; or
>
> where the Security Council or the General Assembly has declared, for the purposes of this Convention, that there exists an exceptional risk to the safety of the personnel participating in the operation.

Thus there is no "equality of arms" between UN personnel and others in peacekeeping operations authorized under what Secretary-General Dag Hammarskjold, referring to the situation in the Congo, once dubbed "Chapter VI and a half"—even "robust" ones under what some others have dubbed "Chapter VI and three quarters." However, as mentioned above, the policy of the United

---

15. Id.
16. 34 INTERNATIONAL LEGAL MATERIALS 482 (1995). Note also the protection of peacekeepers contained in Protocol I (1977), art. 37(1)(d), *supra* note 3.
17. By "quasi-universal jurisdiction" is meant jurisdiction of a pattern common in modern conventions creating international crimes (aircraft hijacking, torture, etc.) which provide that any State may exercise jurisdiction over offenders in accordance with its national law. If a suspected offender is in the territory of any contracting State, that State must either prosecute the offender itself or extradite to a State competent and willing to prosecute: *aut dedere aut judicare*. It is not truly universal jurisdiction as in the case of piracy.

Nations is that "the principles and the spirit of the general conventions applicable to the conduct of military personnel" apply to those operations.

In relation to peace enforcement operations the situation is different. Article 2(2) of the Convention provides:

> This Convention shall not apply to a United Nations operation authorized by the Security Council as an enforcement action under Chapter VII of the Charter of the United Nations in which any of the personnel are engaged as combatants against organized armed forces and to which the law of international armed conflict applies.

This provision thus indirectly recognizes that while the principles and spirit of LOAC/IHL apply to peacekeeping, the letter of that law applies to peace enforcement.

The UN Secretary-General's Bulletin of 1999

On August 6, 1999 the Secretary-General of the United Nations issued a Bulletin entitled "Observance by United Nations forces of international humanitarian law."[18] In this document one can discern that United Nations parlance has come out of the shadows of "the principles and spirit" formula and has embraced "international humanitarian law" as such, which the document then proceeds to summarize in substance (sections 5 to 9). These sections are "promulgated" by the Secretary-General "for the purpose of setting out fundamental principles and rules of international humanitarian law applicable to UN forces conducting operations under United Nations command and control."

It will be noted that these principles and rules apply only to UN forces "conducting operations under United Nations command and control." While this covers most UN peace operations, it would not have applied in the case of Iraq, where the Security Council approved the operations of a "coalition of the able and willing," led by the United States, acting in support of the right to self-defense of Kuwait. Nor does it apply to current operations in the Balkans, which have been approved by the UN Security Council but the command of which has been entrusted to NATO.

---

18. *Observance by United Nations forces of international humanitarian law*, Secretary-General's Bulletin, U.N. Doc. ST/SGB/1999/13 (Aug. 6, 1999), *reprinted in* 2 YEARBOOK OF INTERNATIONAL HUMANITARIAN LAW 563 (1999).

The statement in Section 1 of the Bulletin—"Field of application"—is of importance. It provides:

> 1.1 The fundamental principles and rules of international humanitarian law set out in the present bulletin are applicable to United Nations forces when in situations of armed conflict they are actively engaged as combatants, to the extent and for the duration of their engagement. They are accordingly applicable in enforcement actions, or in peacekeeping operations when the use of force is permitted in self-defence.
>
> 1.2 The promulgation of this bulletin does not affect the protected status of members of peacekeeping operations under the 1994 Convention on the Safety of United Nations and Associated Personnel or their status as non-combatants, as long as they are entitled to the protection given to civilians under the law of armed conflict.

There are some possible problems of interpretation of the first paragraph of this provision. In the first place, one wonders whether, in the course of a single operation, UN forces can move in and out of "situations of armed conflict" and "engagement" as the paragraph implies. Thresholds of application are not so neatly marked in situations of the kind likely to be encountered. In the second place, rather than to search for some more polite and more exact definition of "robust peacekeeping," such situations are described as "peacekeeping operations when the use of force is permitted in self-defence." Just as self-defense is described in the UN Charter, Article 51, as an "inherent" right of States, it is also in all major legal systems of the world an inherent right of individuals to use necessary, proportionate and reasonable force in personal self-defense. The right of members of UN forces to use force in immediate personal and unit self-defense in all operations should be assumed; it should not be used in order to characterize a particular type of operation.

Conclusions

While the difference between interventions authorized by the United Nations and those not so authorized may have everything to do with the debate regarding the *jus ad bellum*—the right to use force—it is, for all the reasons given above, not relevant to the *jus in bello*—the law applicable in armed conflict. Whether an intervention is carried out under the authority of the United Nations, or by a single State, or by a coalition of States (e.g., NATO) without the authority of the United Nations, the participants are equally bound by the law of armed conflict.

The effect of the various statements and documents discussed above regarding the applicability of the law of armed conflict and international humanitarian law to forces acting under the authority of the United Nations is to make the entire corpus of that law, as presently understood to represent customary international law, applicable. National contingents may, in addition, apply various rules and interpretations of that law contained in conventions binding on them (notably Protocol I) that may not have reached customary law status. In the interests of consistency in adopting combined rules of engagement among the participating forces and for the avoidance of disagreement, US forces acting against Iraq in 1991 applied certain of the provisions of Protocol I de facto, even though that instrument has not been ratified by the United States.

The application of the law relating to armed conflict is not a difficult matter, at least for most of the armed forces of the world likely to contribute forces to UN operations. They are trained constantly in their use, secured through rules of engagement. It would be difficult indeed for them to act in any other way.

Michael Ignatieff has recently observed that "legal constraints are necessary if wars are to preserve public support. The real problem with the entry of lawyers into the prosecution of warfare is that it encourages the illusion that war is clean if the lawyers say so. A further illusion is that if we play by the rules, the enemy will too." Then, after describing the way in which Serbian forces behaved in Kosovo, he concludes: "The lesson is clear: it is a form of hubris to suppose that the way we choose to wage a war will determine how the other side fights. Our choice to wage 'clean' war may result in wars of exceptional dirtiness."[19] That may be so, but neither public opinion nor the training and instincts of modern armed forces in civilized countries would have it any other way.

The real problem may lie elsewhere. It lies not so much in the observance of the laws of armed conflict as in the manner of conducting operations. The problems of discrimination in targeting, illustrated by certain tragic errors in the bombing campaign against Yugoslavia, do not result in any sense from a desire to ignore or avoid the law, but may have more to do with the tendency of forces, especially Western forces, to be averse to taking casualties. As another writer has observed: "In recent years the key results of these concerns

---

19. MICHAEL IGNATIEFF, VIRTUAL WAR: KOSOVO AND BEYOND 200 (2000).

for the military have been rules of engagement and force-protection directives—designed largely to protect political and military leaders from recriminations that often follow casualties."[20] "*Dulce et decorum est pro patria mori.*" But human sentiment, and public opinion, may be less understanding when a life is lost in the course of nasty wars between other peoples. To die, or suffer injury, for the human rights of other people is indeed a noble, even heroic, act.

---

20. John Gentry, *Complex Civil-Military Operations: A U.S. Military-centric Perspective*, 53 NAVAL WAR COLLEGE REVIEW 57, 61 (2000).

Application of the Law of Armed Conflict During Operation Allied Force: Maritime Interdiction and Prisoner of War Issues

George Walker

Introduction

NATO's 1999 Operation Allied Force, to succor Albanian Kosovars and others (e.g., Roma) indigenous to the former Yugoslavia's[1] Kosovo province subjected to brutal actions, including murder, rape and displacement from their homes by Serbian forces under SFRY President Slobodan Milosevic's direction, was a legitimate collective action for humanitarian intervention pursuant to principles of state of necessity under circumstances known at the time.[2] NATO's Kosovo intervention was but one of those crises where States, individually or collectively, succored indigenous nationals, as part of a rescue operation for their own or other non-State nationals, or with the sole

---

1. Hereinafter referred to as SFRY. There may be no "Yugoslavia" in the future. A March 14, 2002 agreement, which must be approved by Serbia and Montenegro, declares the area of the former Yugoslavia will be known as Serbia and Montenegro. *See* Ian Fisher, *Serbia and Montenegro Sign a Plan for Yugoslavia's Demise*, N.Y. TIMES, Mar. 15, 2002, at A3.
2. For analysis of principles of the state of necessity doctrine for collective humanitarian intervention and its application to Operation Allied Force in Kosovo, *see* George Walker, *Principles for Collective Humanitarian Intervention to Succor Other Countries' Imperiled Indigenous Nationals*, published in the American University International Law Review (2002). Milosevic raised the issue of the NATO campaign's lawfulness in his opening statement in his genocide and war crimes trial in The Hague. *See* Ian Fisher & Marlise Simons, *Defiant, Milosevic Begins His Defense by Assailing NATO*, N.Y. TIMES, Feb. 15, 2002, at A1.

goal of protecting indigenous nationals. Some occurred during the nineteenth and twentieth centuries before the United Nations Charter era, in some cases pursuant to the Concert of Europe, which lasted in one form or another from 1815 through most of the nineteenth century. Scholars have traced these principles to ancient times.[3] Others have arisen since 1945, i.e., after the Charter became effective for interState relations.[4] Among the more important of the latter was NATO's bombing and sea interdiction campaigns, conducted pursuant to UN Security Council decisions authorizing them, that led to the 1995 Dayton Accords for Bosnia-Herzegovina, which included protection for indigenous peoples. NATO's 1999 Operation Allied Force action was among the latest of this kind of campaign. What made Allied Force unique was that it was the first time a collective self-defense organization constituted under Article 51 of the Charter intervened while the Security Council was seized of a crisis the Council had said threatened international peace and security.

A. Relevance of the General Law of Armed Conflict and Neutrality Law

Other papers in this volume discuss the lawfulness of particular NATO attacks. A more fundamental question is whether the law of armed conflict and the law of neutrality, which apply during war in the traditional sense, govern during operations like Operation Allied Force.

There is a developing view that military operations operating under UN Security Council decisions pursuant to Articles 25 and 48 of the Charter do not necessarily follow the law of armed conflict. When a Council decision is contrary to law of armed conflict principles, particularly those in a treaty, the decision must be followed. This rule, rooted in Article 103 of the Charter and the obligatory nature of Council decisions, does not account for contrary

---

3. See Walker, *supra* note 2.
4. See id.

customary or general principles norms, nor does it consider the possibility of a *jus cogens* norm in the law of armed conflict.[5] If a Council decision does not specify rules of conduct for conducting military operations that would appear to contradict the law of armed conflict, and this is the usual case, the law of armed conflict should be followed. If non-mandatory UN resolutions[6] are contrary to law of armed conflict rules, the only established body of law for standards is the law of armed conflict, and it should be followed. The same is true for Council decisions authorizing force with unspecified standards; the law of armed conflict should be followed. Thus although the law of armed conflict, strictly speaking, does not govern because a UN resolution-authorized

---

5. UN CHARTER arts. 25, 48, 103. *Jus cogens*, i.e., a peremptory norm that trumps inconsistent treaty, customary and general principles rules, is a vague doctrine whose contours are less than certain; it is not cited in traditional international law sources, e.g., Statute of the International Court of Justice, Articles 38, 59; RESTATEMENT (THIRD) OF FOREIGN RELATIONS LAW OF THE UNITED STATES §§ 102–03 (1987). *See generally* Vienna Convention on the Law of Treaties, May 23, 1969, arts. 53, 64, 1155 U.N.T.S. 331, 345, 347; IAN BROWNLIE, PRINCIPLES OF PUBLIC INTERNATIONAL LAW 4, 19, 514–17 (5th ed. 1998); T. ELIAS, THE MODERN LAW OF TREATIES 177–87 (1974); 1 OPPENHEIM'S INTERNATIONAL LAW §§ 2, 642, 653 (Robert Jennings & Arthur Watts eds., 8th ed. 1992); RESTATEMENT (THIRD), *supra*, §§ 102 r.n.6, 323 cmt. b, 331(2), 338(2); THE CHARTER OF THE UNITED NATIONS 1118–19 (Bruno Simma ed., 1994); IAN SINCLAIR, THE VIENNA CONVENTION ON THE LAW OF TREATIES 17–18, 85–87, 94–95, 160, 184–85, 218–26, 246 (2d ed. 1984) (Vienna Convention, *supra* is progressive development); GRIGORII I. TUNKIN, THEORY OF INTERNATIONAL LAW 98 (William E. Butler trans., 1974); Levan Alexidze, *Legal Nature of Jus Cogens in Contemporary International Law*, 172 RECUEIL DES COURS 219, 262–63 (1981); John Hazard, *Soviet Tactics in International Lawmaking*, 7 DENVER JOURNAL OF INTERNATIONAL LAW AND POLICY 9, 25–29 (1977); Eduardo Jimenez de Arechaga, *International Law in the Past Third of a Century*, 159 RECUEIL DES COURS 1, 64–69 (1978); George Walker, *Integration and Disintegration in Europe: Reordering the Treaty Map of the Continent*, 6 THE TRANSNATIONAL LAWYER 1, 60, 63 (1993); Mark Weisburd, *The Emptiness of the Concept of Jus Cogens, As Illustrated by the War in Bosnia-Herzegovina*, 17 MICHIGAN JOURNAL OF INTERNATIONAL LAW 1 (1995). For UN Charter Article 103 analysis, see generally LELAND GOODRICH ET AL., CHARTER OF THE UNITED NATIONS 614–17 (3d ed. 1969); THE CHARTER OF THE UNITED NATIONS, *supra* at 1116–25; W. Reisman, *The Constitutional Crisis in the United Nations*, 87 AMERICAN JOURNAL OF INTERNATIONAL LAW 83 (1993).

6. Non-mandatory UN resolutions include General Assembly resolutions and Council resolutions recommending action. Assembly or Council recommendations passed pursuant to UN Charter Articles 10–11, 13–14 and Chapters VI–VII are non-mandatory, although they may strengthen preexisting customary and treaty norms recited in them. SYDNEY BAILEY & SAM DAWS, THE PROCEDURE OF THE UN SECURITY COUNCIL ch. 1.5 (3d ed. 1998); BROWNLIE, *supra* note 5, at 14–15, 694; JORGE CASTENEDA, LEGAL EFFECTS OF UNITED NATIONS RESOLUTIONS ch. 3 (Alba Amoia trans., 1969); GOODRICH ET AL., *supra* note 5, at 126, 144, 290-314; 1 OPPENHEIM, *supra* note 5, § 16, at 47–49; RESTATEMENT (THIRD), *supra* note 5, § 103(2)(d), cmt. c, r.n.2; THE CHARTER OF THE UNITED NATIONS, *supra* note 5, at 284, 407–18, 605–36, 652.

operation is not a conflict between States in the traditional sense of war, the law of armed conflict should govern in these situations. If UN resolution-governed operations grow in number and complexity and intensity of conflict, an ultimate result may be a parallel body of law that should be, and hopefully will be, the same as the law of armed conflict for war.

Humanitarian intervention under Operation Allied Force stood on footing similar to the latter situations. The campaign was not war in the classical sense, although there are reports the United Kingdom's Prime Minister and maybe others characterized later phases of the NATO campaign as war. Participants, whether the collectively intervening States or the affected State, should have applied the law of armed conflict as in the case of UN resolution-authorized actions. No Council decision governed the Allied Force situation with respect to humanitarian intervention. Humanitarian law issues covered by, e.g., the 1949 Geneva Conventions, stand in a special place.[7] The same principles of applying the law of armed conflict and neutrality law should govern during collective humanitarian interventions operating under state of necessity principles.

Standards of necessity and proportionality in self-defense situations may be different from law of armed conflict standards of necessity and proportionality for attacks during traditional armed conflict. What is necessary or proportional for a self-defense response may not be necessary or proportional in an armed conflict situation. The reverse is also true; what is necessary or proportional under the law of armed conflict for attacks may not be necessary or proportional in a self-defense context. The same is true for humanitarian intervention pursuant to state of necessity. What is necessary or proportional for humanitarian intervention may not be necessary or proportional in a self-defense or law of armed conflict situation, and what is necessary or proportional in a self-defense or law of armed conflict situation may not be necessary or proportional in attacks incident to a particular humanitarian intervention. Depending on the scope of the intervention and the timing of attacks (immediately after a decision to intervene is made as distinguished from attacks made well into a campaign), the law of self-defense or the law of armed conflict may be examined as guides.

---

7. See *infra* this paper.

There are some per se forbidden targets, e.g., cultural property unless used for military purposes.[8] Under the law of armed conflict, there are some methods of warfare, e.g., no first use of poison gas,[9] that are per se indiscriminate under the law of armed conflict. These targets or methods and means of warfare, forbidden under the law of armed conflict, should also be followed in humanitarian intervention operations under state of necessity.

Decision makers should only be held accountable for what is known, or reasonably should have been known, at the time a decision to attack is made. Hindsight can be 20/20; decisions at the time may be clouded with the fog of war.[10] Declarations of understanding by countries party to Protocol I[11] to the

---

8. *See generally, e.g.*, Convention for Protection of Cultural Property in Event of Armed Conflict, May 14, 1954, 249 U.N.T.S. 240 [hereinafter Cultural Property Convention]; Protocol for Protection of Cultural Property in Event of Armed Conflict, May 14, 1954, 249 U.N.T.S. 358; Second Protocol to Hague Convention of 1954 for Protection of Cultural Property in Event of Armed Conflict, Mar. 26, 1999, art. 1(f), 38 INTERNATIONAL LEGAL MATERIALS 769 (1999) [hereinafter Second Protocol]; Treaty on Protection of Artistic & Scientific Institutions & Historic Monuments, Apr. 15, 1935, 49 Stat. 3267, 167 L.N.T.S. 290; JIRI TOMAN, THE PROTECTION OF CULTURAL PROPERTY IN THE EVENT OF ARMED CONFLICT (1996); GEORGE WALKER, THE TANKER WAR, 1980–88: LAW AND POLICY 507–11 (2000) (Vol. 74, US Naval War College International Law Studies).
9. Protocol for Prohibition of Use in War of Asphyxiating, Poisonous or Other Gases, & of Bacteriological Methods of Warfare, June 17, 1965, & US Reservation, 26 U.S.T. 571, 94 L.N.T.S. 65. *See also* ANNOTATED SUPPLEMENT TO THE COMMANDER'S HANDBOOK ON THE LAW OF NAVAL OPERATIONS ¶¶ 10.3–10.4.2 (A. Thomas & J. Duncan eds., 1999) (Vol. 73., US Naval War College International Law Studies).
10. CARL VON CLAUSEWITZ, ON WAR 117–21 (Michael Howard & Peter Paret ed. & trans., 1976).
11. Protocol Additional (I) to the Geneva Conventions of 12 August 1949, & Relating to the Protection of Victims of International Armed Conflicts, June 8, 1977, 1125 U.N.T.S. 3 [hereinafter Protocol I].

1949 Geneva Conventions state that for civilians' protection in Article 51,[12] protection of civilian objects in Article 52,[13] and precautions to be taken in attacks, stated in Article 57,[14] a commander should be liable based on that commander's assessment of information available at the relevant time, i.e., when a

---

12. Protocol I, *id.*, art. 51, 1125 U.N.T.S. 26. Articles 51(2) and 51(5) prohibitions on attacks on civilians, absent other considerations, e.g., civilians who take up arms, restate customary law. MICHAEL BOTHE ET AL., NEW RULES FOR VICTIMS OF ARMED CONFLICT 299 & n.3 (1982); SAN REMO MANUAL ON INTERNATIONAL LAW APPLICABLE TO ARMED CONFLICTS AT SEA ¶ 39 (Louise Doswald-Beck ed., 1995); ANNOTATED SUPPLEMENT, *supra* note 9, ¶ 6.2.3.2; 1 JEAN PICTET, THE GENEVA CONVENTIONS OF 12 AUGUST 1949, at 224–29 (1952); CLAUDE PILLOUD ET AL., COMMENTARY ON THE ADDITIONAL PROTOCOLS OF 8 JUNE 1977 TO THE GENEVA CONVENTIONS OF 12 AUGUST 1949, at 618, 623–26 (1987); JULIUS STONE, LEGAL CONTROLS OF INTERNATIONAL CONFLICT 684–732 (1959); Michael Matheson, *Remarks*, in Session One: The United States' Position on the Relation of Customary International Law to the 1977 Protocols Additional to the Geneva Conventions, in Symposium, *The Sixth Annual American Red Cross - Washington College of Law Conference on International Humanitarian Law: A Workshop on Customary International Law and the 1977 Protocols Additional to the 1949 Geneva Conventions*, 2 AMERICAN UNIVERSITY JOURNAL OF INTERNATIONAL LAW AND POLICY 423, 426 (1987); William Schmidt, *The Protection of Victims of International Armed Conflicts: Protocol I Additional to the Geneva Conventions*, 24 AIR FORCE LAW REVIEW 225–32 (1984); Waldemar Solf, *Protection of Civilians Against the Effects of Hostilities Under Customary International Law and Under Protocol I*, 1 AMERICAN UNIVERSITY JOURNAL OF INTERNATIONAL LAW AND POLICY 130–31 (1986).
13. Article 52 states a general customary norm, except its Article 52(1) prohibition on reprisals against civilians, upon which commentators divide. *See generally* BOTHE ET AL., *supra* note 12, at 320–27; C. COLOMBOS, THE INTERNATIONAL LAW OF THE SEA §§ 510–11, 524–25, 528–29 (6th rev. ed. 1967); ANNOTATED SUPPLEMENT, *supra* note 9, ¶¶ 6.2.3 & n.36, 6.2.3.2, 8.1.1 & n.9, 8.1.2 & n.12 (noting U.S. position that Protocol I Article 52(1) "creates new law"); 2 D. O'CONNELL, THE INTERNATIONAL LAW OF THE SEA 1105–06 (I. Shearer ed., 1984); 4 PICTET, *supra* note 12, at 131 (1958); PILLOUD ET AL., *supra* note 12, at 630–38; Matheson, *supra* note 12, at 426; Horace B. Robertson, Jr., *The Principle of the Military Objective in the Law of Armed Conflict*, in THE LAW OF MILITARY OPERATIONS: LIBER AMICORUM PROFESSOR JACK GRUNAWALT 197 (Michael Schmitt ed., 1998) (Vol. 72, US Naval War College International Law Studies); Solf, *supra* note 12, at 131. Frank Russo, Jr., *Targeting Theory in the Law of Naval Warfare*, 30 NAVAL LAW REVIEW 1, 17 n.36 (1992) rejects applying Protocol I Article 52(2) to naval warfare.
14. *See also* ANNOTATED SUPPLEMENT, *supra* note 9, ¶¶ 8.1-8.1.2.1; BOTHE ET AL., *supra* note 12, at 359–69; PILLOUD ET AL., *supra* note 12, at 678–89. Rules of distinction, necessity and proportionality, with the concomitant risk of collateral damage inherent in any attack, recited in Article 57, generally restate customary norms. *See supra* note 12.

decision is made.[15] Two 1980 Conventional Weapons Convention[16] protocols have similar terms, i.e., a commander is only bound by information available when a decision to attack is made.[17] The Second Protocol to the 1954 Hague Cultural Property Convention also recites this principle.[18]

Protocol I, with its understandings, and the Conventional Weapons Convention protocols are on their way to acceptance among States.[19] These treaties' common statement, in text or declarations, that commanders are held

---

15. Declaration of Belgium, May 20, 1986, *reprinted in* THE LAWS OF ARMED CONFLICTS: A COLLECTION OF CONVENTIONS, RESOLUTIONS AND OTHER DOCUMENTS 706, 707 (Dietrich Schindler & Jiri Toman eds., 3d ed. 1988); Declaration of Italy, Feb. 27, 1986, *reprinted in id* at 712; Declaration of the Netherlands, June 26, 1977, *reprinted in id.* at 713, 714; Declaration of the United Kingdom, Dec. 12, 1977, *reprinted in id.* at 717.
16. Convention on Prohibitions or Restrictions on Use of Certain Conventional Weapons Which May Be Deemed Excessively Injurious or to Have Indiscriminate Effects, Oct. 10, 1980, T.I.A.S. No. ———, 1342 U.N.T.S. 137 [hereinafter Conventional Weapons Convention].
17. Protocol on Prohibitions or Restrictions on Use of Mines, Booby Traps & Other Devices, Oct. 10, 1980, art. 2(4), 1342 U.N.T.S. 168 (Protocol II (Mines)); as amended, May 3, 1996, art. 2(6), 35 INTERNATIONAL LEGAL MATERIALS 1206, 1209 (1996) (Amended Protocol II); Protocol on Prohibitions or Restrictions on Use of Incendiary Weapons (Protocol III), Oct. 10, 1980, art. 1(3), 1342 U.N.T.S. 171, 172. The United States has ratified the Convention and Protocols I and II (Mines) *supra*; Protocol III is not in force for the United States. United States Department of State, Treaties in Force 478–79 (2000) [hereinafter TIF]. Amended Protocol II, Protocol III and Protocol IV on Blinding Laser Weapons, May 3, 1995, 35 INTERNATIONAL LEGAL MATERIALS 1218 (1996) are now before the US Senate. Marian Leich, *Contemporary Practice of the United States Relating to International Law*, 91 AMERICAN JOURNAL OF INTERNATIONAL LAW 325 (1997). Protocol IV and Protocol on Non-Detectable Fragments (Protocol I), Oct. 10, 1980, 1342 U.N.T.S. 168, do not have these provisions. Protocol II (Mines) and III commentators say little about these provisions; they state the obvious. *See* Burrus Carnahan, *The Law of Land Warfare: Protocol II to the United Nations Convention on Certain Conventional Weapons*, 105 MILITARY LAW REVIEW 73 (1984); W. Fenrick, Comment, *New Developments in the Law Concerning the Use of Conventional Weapons in Armed Conflict*, 19 CANADIAN YEAR BOOK OF INTERNATIONAL LAW 229 (1981); Howard Levie, *Prohibitions and Restrictions on the Use of Conventional Weapons*, 68 ST. JOHN'S LAW REVIEW 643 (1994); J. Roach, *Certain Conventional Weapons Convention: Arms Control or Humanitarian Law?*, 105 MILITARY LAW REVIEW 1 (1984); William Schmidt, *The Conventional Weapons Convention: Implications for the American Soldier*, 24 AIR FORCE LAW REVIEW 279 (1984).
18. Second Protocol, *supra* note 8, art. 1(f). Second Protocol is not in force; 10 States are party, and 101 have ratified the Hague Cultural Property Convention, *supra* note 8. International Committee of the Red Cross website as of March 24, 2002, *available at* http://www.icrc.org/eng/party_gc.
19. 159 States are party to Protocol I, but not the United States. *See* International Committee of the Red Cross website, *supra* note 18. International Committee of the Red Cross website, *id.*, listed 88 States as parties to the Conventional Weapons Convention, *supra* note 16; 79 for Protocol II (Mines), 63 for Amended Protocol II, 81 for Protocol III, *supra* note 17, as of March 24, 2002.

accountable based on information they have at the time for determining whether attacks are necessary and proportional has become a nearly universal norm. The San Remo Manual recognizes it as the naval warfare standard.[20] It can be said with fair confidence that this is the *jus in bello* customary standard. It is also the standard for self-defense situations. It was the standard for Allied Force.

Collective action after a decision to intervene raises problems of consensus on action within a campaign. Even as collective self-defense situations may raise scope and definitional problems (i.e., whether anticipatory self-defense is admissible in the Charter era, what are proportional and necessary responses), and the same kinds of issues can surface in the law of armed conflict under collective action situations, analogous problems will arise during collective humanitarian intervention under state of necessity. What are proper targets? Is the proposed attack necessary and proportional? These issues arose with respect to targeting during Allied Force and were resolved, like the decision to mount the campaign, by consensus among the 19 NATO member States.

One issue, perhaps for Operation Allied Force and certainly for the future, is how far consensus decision making should penetrate into operational matters. To take an extreme example from a hypothetical ground campaign, must a NATO squad leader seek a necessity and proportionality determination all the way up the chain of command to take a particular building, with almost assured damage to it? US commentators and military commanders have decried the "rudder orders" approach to military command and control; is there a collective consensus decision version of it? Should there be one? How does a rudder orders policy, or the opposite of letting field and at sea commanders and perhaps lower echelon commanders decide, affect accountability under international law if things go wrong?

B. NATO's Right to Conduct Maritime Interdiction as Part of Allied Force

NATO considered but did not implement visit and search of ships that may have carried goods to the SFRY through Adriatic Sea ports. Nothing in the law of state of necessity or the law of armed conflict forbade these kinds of operations if they had been ordered.

---

20. SAN REMO MANUAL, *supra* note 12, ¶ 46(b) & Commentary 46.3. *See also* BEN CHENG, GENERAL PRINCIPLES OF LAW AS APPLIED BY INTERNATIONAL COURTS AND TRIBUNALS 90 (1983); MYRES MCDOUGAL & FLORENTINO FELICIANO, LAW AND MINIMUM WORLD PUBLIC ORDER 220 (1961).

1. NATO Naval Assets Available; Naval Operations during Allied Force

There were no naval engagements at or under the sea connected with Allied Force; some apparently had been projected.[21] But, as the following indicates, naval forces had a role:

> NATO forces provided defense and logistics support [undoubtedly including sealift after the campaign,] for the alliance forces deployed in Italy, Albania, and ... Yugoslavia; ... and carried out naval operations in the Adriatic Sea. The latter included, at one time, aircraft carriers, submarines, and surface ships from four nations, all operating within the same confined space.[22]

These vessels included the US Navy's USS *Kitty Hawk* and USS *Theodore Roosevelt* battle groups and UK Royal Navy units, including a missile-launching submarine.[23] When Allied Force began the USS *Enterprise* battle group was in the Persian Gulf; there was no other battle group within bombing range of Serbia.[24] In late March 1999, incident to sponsoring a Security Council resolution condemning Operation Allied Force and conversations with Yugoslavia, Russia sent several naval vessels to the Mediterranean where they could enter the Adriatic. This caused tension between NATO and Russia, leading to worries that the SFRY might get information on NATO flight operations from these ships.[25] The *Roosevelt* battle group arrived April 5, the first in the area since mid-March.[26] There is no record of NATO-Russian maritime confrontations. There is also no report of blue-water NATO-SFRY naval confrontations.[27]

---

21. General Wesley Clark, while Supreme Allied Commander Europe (SACEUR), spoke to the Yugoslav Chief of Staff [by telephone] at least once during the campaign, warning him that if he sent any of his navy out into the Adriatic it would be sunk. WESLEY CLARK, WAGING MODERN WAR 184 (2001); MICHAEL IGNATIEFF, VIRTUAL WAR: KOSOVO AND BEYOND 137 (2000).
22. United States Department of Defense, Report to Congress: Kosovo/Operation Allied Force After-Action Report xiv (Jan. 31, 2000) [hereinafter After-Action Report]; *but see id.* at 41 (little reliance on sealift).
23. *Id.* at 92; North Atlantic Council, Statement on Kosovo, Apr. 23, 1999, *reprinted in* IVO DAALDER & MICHAEL O'HANLON, WINNING UGLY: NATO'S WAR TO SAVE KOSOVO 104 (2000). The *Roosevelt* battlegroup had been in the Adriatic; it had been sent to the Persian Gulf in March 1999 as the Kosovo crisis deepened. Clark, *supra* note 21, at 240, 421.
24. DAALDER & O'HANLON, *supra* note 23, at 103.
25. CLARK, *supra* note 21, at 212; DAALDER & O'HANLON, *supra* note 23, at 127.
26. DAALDER & O'HANLON, *supra* note 23, at 231.
27. The SFRY had been warned of the risks. *See supra* note 21.

Although NATO land-based aircraft (for the United States, US Air Force and US Marine shore-based aircraft) predominantly conducted strike operations, "Navy carrier-based aircraft, Marine . . . sea-based strike aircraft and cruise-missile equipped ships and submarines played a significant role."[28] Navy electronic warfare aircraft, operating off the carriers, protected NATO aircraft from attack by Yugoslav air defenses. These aircraft were the only US platforms able to use electronic jamming to suppress enemy air defenses. Naval aircraft also launched air defense suppression support for strike aircraft.[29] The Navy flew unmanned aerial vehicles (UAVs) to identify Yugoslav naval vessels, survey potential landing areas for Marines if amphibious landings were ordered, and to target coastal defense radar sites. Navy F-14 aircraft with the Tactical Air Reconnaissance Pod System identified targets; Navy maritime patrol aircraft made significant intelligence, surveillance and reconnaissance (ISR) collection contributions.[30] Although never used for at-sea interdiction, these assets were available to contribute to that effort, besides warships in the Adriatic.

There were differences of opinion at NATO headquarters after the 1999 NATO summit on the possibility of boarding ships in the Adriatic "to enforce the maritime blockade of Yugoslavia. . . ."[31] Oil reached Serbia through Montenegro's port of Bar; the "stop and search" regime would have aimed to halt this. However, there was concern over provoking Russia, Serbia's principal oil supplier.[32] This was reflected at national levels. In the Danish parliament, e.g.,

> [a] minor controversy arose over the possible contribution to a naval blockade and the modes of its implementation. Not only was this blockade probably a violation of international law; it also [was seen to entail] risks of a direct confrontation with the Russian Navy. As a compromise it was decided (by NATO) to enforce the blockade only with . . . countries . . . parties to the [prior] sanctions regime, on which basis Denmark decided . . . to participate.

---

28. After-Action Report, *supra* note 22, at 55, 79, 92–3.
29. *Id.* at 66–7.
30. *Id.* at 57–8.
31. Nicola Butler, *NATO: From Collective Defence to Peace Enforcement*, in KOSOVO AND THE CHALLENGE OF HUMANITARIAN INTERVENTION 279 (Albrecht Schnabel & Ramesh Thakur eds., 2000) [hereinafter KOSOVO AND THE CHALLENGE]. *See also Continued NATO Air-Strikes on Yugoslavia*, 45 Keesing's Record of World Events 42901 (1999) [hereinafter 45 Keesing].
32. *Continued NATO Air-Strikes on Yugoslavia*, *supra* note 31, at 42901.

Denmark promised a corvette from July 1999 onwards, but the conflict ended first. Later its navy contributed a mine-clearing vessel and a minelayer to clear NATO munitions dumped in the Adriatic.[33] Poland was not "asked to participate in the maritime blockade against Yugoslavia."[34]

After the Alliance pledged to impose a binding naval embargo in its April statement, European Union (EU) foreign ministers met April 26 and proposed an embargo, to begin April 30, to cut off oil shipments to the SFRY, coming primarily from Italy and Greece. The EU ministers also approved economic measures targeting Milosevic and his family and closing loopholes halting export credits and investment flows to the SFRY previously agreed in 1998. A statement offered support to Montenegro and pledged EU upgrade of EU relations with Albania and Macedonia through association agreements.[35] The naval embargo

> became a somewhat hollow promise . . . when NATO decided it would not physically enforce [it] through a blockade at Montenegro's two main ports, Bar and Kotor Bay. But all was not lost. It did go into effect and was joined by a number of non-EU and non-NATO countries. . . . [T]he voluntary "visit and search" scheme at least had the benefit of preventing profiteers using ships flagged in cooperating countries from shipping oil into Montenegro.

NATO also used its influence and NATO SFOR troops in Bosnia-Herzegovina to cut off oil coming from there to the SFRY.[36]

2. Proposed NATO Naval Interdiction during Allied Force: A Lawful Option

There were two principles concerning any projected naval interdiction during Allied Force. First, would vessel interdiction, considered with other aspects of Operation Allied Force, i.e., the aerial bombing campaign, have been a necessary and proportional part of the campaign when the overall goal of collective humanitarian intervention under state of necessity was taken into

---

33. Bjorn Moller, *The Nordic Countries: Whither the West's Conscience?*, in KOSOVO AND THE CHALLENGE, *supra* note 31, at 156.
34. Peter Talas & Laszlo Valki, *The New Entrants: Hungary, Poland, and the Czech Republic*, in KOSOVO AND THE CHALLENGE, *supra* note 31, at 207.
35. They encouraged EU members not to organize sports events with SFRY participation. DAALDER & O'HANLON, *supra* note 23, at 146; *Continued NATO Air-Strikes on Yugoslavia*, *supra* note 31, at 42901.
36. DAALDER & O'HANLON, *supra* note 23, at 146.

account? If the response is Yes (and the record suggests this), the second principle is that under the view that parties to a humanitarian intervention should follow the law of armed conflict for these operations,[37] NATO could have imposed vessel interdiction, visit and search, and capture or diversion, subject to the usual law of armed conflict rules and limitations.[38]

Blockade was an option discussed outside NATO circles, probably reflecting media and others' confusion between blockade and interdiction. If NATO wanted to establish a blockade, traditional rules—notice of start and end, grace period, area, impartiality, effectiveness, limitation to belligerents' coasts and ports and other requirements or limitations[39]—would have been required under law of armed conflict standards after an affirmative answer to the first question on blockade's place in necessity and proportionality, etc., for Allied

---

37. See supra Part A.
38. See generally Convention for Amelioration of Wounded, Sick & Shipwrecked Members of Armed Forces at Sea, Aug. 12, 1949, art. 31, 6 U.S.T. 3217, 3226, 3230, 3234, 75 U.N.T.S. at 85, 92–96 [hereinafter Second Convention]; Convention Concerning Rights & Duties of Neutral Powers in Naval War (Hague XIII), Oct. 18, 1907, 36 Stat. 2415; Convention Relative to Certain Restrictions with Regard to Exercise of the Right of Capture in Naval War (Hague XI), Oct. 18, 1907, id. 2396; Convention for Adaptation to Maritime Warfare of Principles of the Geneva Convention (Hague X), Oct. 18, 1907, art. 4, id. 2371, 2384; Hague Cultural Property Convention, supra note 8, art. 14(2), 249 U.N.T.S. at 252; Convention on Maritime Neutrality, Feb. 20, 1928, 47 Stat. 1989, 135 L.N.T.S. 187; Commission of Jurists, Hague Rules of Air Warfare, Dec. 1922 - Feb. 1923, arts. 49–50, reprinted in THE LAWS OF ARMED CONFLICTS, supra note 15, at 207, 215 [hereinafter Hague Air Rules]; International Law Association Committee on Maritime Neutrality, Final Report: Helsinki Principles on Maritime Neutrality, reprinted in International Law Association, Report of the Sixty-Eighth Conference Held at Taipei, Taiwan, Republic of China 497, Principles 1.4, 2.1–2.4, 5.2.1-5.2.9 (1998) [hereinafter Helsinki Principles]; Institute of International Law, The Laws of Naval Warfare Concerning the Relations Between Belligerents, Aug. 9, 1913, art. 41, reprinted in id. at 857, 864 [hereinafter Oxford Naval Manual]; ANNOTATED SUPPLEMENT, supra note 9, ¶¶ 7.6–7.6.2, 7.10–7.10.2; 2 PICTET, supra note 12, at 181–84 (1960); SAN REMO MANUAL, supra note 12, ¶¶ 112–34; WALKER, supra note 8, at 357–64.
39. See generally Hague XI, supra note 38, art. 1, 36 Stat. at 2408; Declaration Concerning Maritime Law, Apr. 16, 1856, ¶ 4, 115 Consol. T.S. 1, 3; Declaration Concerning Laws of Naval War (Declaration of London), Feb. 26, 1909, Annex, arts. 1–21, 208 Consol. T.S. 338, 341, 343–44, reprinted in THE LAWS OF ARMED CONFLICTS, supra note 15, at 843, 846–47, never in force; Hague Air Rules, supra note 38, art. 53(i), id. at 215; Helsinki Principles, supra note 38, Principles 5.2.10, 5.3; BOTHE ET AL., supra note 12, at 432–39, 694–97; ANNOTATED SUPPLEMENT, supra note 9, ¶¶ 7.7–7.7.5; Oxford Naval Manual, supra note 38, arts. 30, 53, 92, at 862, 866, 872; 4 PICTET, supra note 13, at 309–12, 318–24; PILLOUD ET AL., supra note 12, at 812–36, 1476–81; SAN REMO MANUAL, supra note 12, ¶¶ 93–104; WALKER, supra note 8, at 389–94.

Force's overall goals for intervention which laid primary stress on humanitarian intervention.[40] Any blockade imposed during Operation Allied Force would not have been a "pacific blockade," i.e., a blockade imposed on an adversary's coasts during time of peace, generally thought to be unlawful under the Charter.[41]

C. Captured Armed Forces Members' Entitlement to Prisoner of War Status

SFRY forces took three NATO ground service personnel into custody during Allied Force, perhaps kidnapping them across the Macedonia border. The three suffered beatings at the hands of their captors.[42] Two downed NATO pilots risked capture before NATO rescued them.[43] NATO forces later took SFRY army personnel into custody after moving into Kosovo. On May 16, 1999 President Clinton authorized releasing two SFRY force members the Kosovo Liberation Army (KLA) captured in April.[44] Although the record is not clear, it is likely that the SFRY captured members of the KLA and that the KLA captured other SFRY armed forces members.

---

40. See generally North Atlantic Council, Statement on Kosovo, Apr. 23, 1999, reprinted in DAALDER & O'HANLON, supra note 23, at 262 (2000); NATO Secretary-General Javier Solana, Statement by NATO Secretary General, Mar. 23, 1999, 45 Keesing, supra note 31, at 42847; After-Action Report, supra note 22, at 10; supra notes 31–36 and accompanying text.
41. 2 O'CONNELL, supra note 13, at 1157–58, citing UN Charter Article 2(4); ANTHONY D'AMATO, INTERNATIONAL LAW: PROCESS AND PROSPECT 43–46 (1987) (same, listing rules for permissible blockades); WALKER, supra note 8, at 389; but see COLOMBOS, supra note 13, §§ 484–88B; 2 LASSA OPPENHEIM, INTERNATIONAL LAW §§ 44–49, 52b–52e, 52l (Hersch Lauterpacht ed., 7th ed. 1952); U.S. Department of the Navy, Law of Naval Warfare: NWIP 10-2, ¶ 632a n.26 (1955 through Change 6, 1974). UN Charter Article 42 authorizes the Security Council to impose a blockade. See also GOODRICH ET AL., supra note 5, at 314–17; THE CHARTER OF THE UNITED NATIONS, supra note 5, at 629–36. ANNOTATED SUPPLEMENT, supra note 9, ¶ 7.7.2.1 n.131 correctly says, "It is not possible to say whether, or to what extent, a U.N. blockade would be governed by the traditional rules." See also The Charter of the United Nations, supra at 632. This is an example of how a Council decision can trump LOAC treaty rules. UN Charter arts. 25, 48, 103. See supra note 5 and accompanying text.
42. Reverend Jesse Jackson, US President Bill Clinton's friend, was involved in negotiating their release; there had been fears the detainees would be held hostage. CLARK, supra note 21, at 229, 286–87; DAALDER & O'HANLON, supra note 23, at 119, 146; Continued NATO Air-Strikes Against Yugoslavia, supra note 31, at 42957; Continued NATO Air-Strikes on Yugoslavia, supra note 31, at 42900.
43. CLARK, supra note 21, at 214–18, 274.
44. Id. at 286; DAALDER & O'HANLON, supra note 23, at 146, 233.

These personnel were entitled to those parts of the 1949 Geneva Conventions, other applicable humanitarian law treaties, and customary law or general principles of law governing them, absent a Security Council decision to the contrary.[45] (There was none.)

1. NATO-SFRY Aspects of Allied Force

First, as between NATO and the SFRY, the 1949 Geneva Conventions applied. Although Operation Allied Force was not a war in the traditional sense, Common Article 2 declares their provisions apply to "other" international armed conflicts. For example, the Third Convention, establishing prisoner of war treatment standards, provides in part in Article 2:

> In addition to the provisions which shall be implemented in peace time, the present Convention shall apply to all cases of declared war or of any other conflict which may arise between two or more of the High Contracting Parties, even if the state of war is not recognized by one of them.
>
> [It] shall also apply to all cases of partial or total occupation of the territory of a ... Party, even if the said occupation meets with no armed resistance.
>
> Although one ... Power ... in the conflict may not be a Party to the ... Convention, the Powers that are parties thereto shall remain bound by it in their mutual relations. They shall furthermore be bound by the Convention in relation to the said Power, if the latter accepts and applies the provisions thereof.[46]

The SFRY and all NATO States were parties to the 1949 Conventions before the SFRY's dissolution.[47] Although there was no official record of the SFRY's having accepted and applied the Conventions in accordance with

---

45. UN CHARTER arts. 25, 48, 103. *See supra* note 5 and accompanying text.
46. Convention Relative to Treatment of Prisoners of War, Aug. 12, 1949, art. 2, 6 U.S.T. 3316, 3318, 75 U.N.T.S. 135, 136 (hereinafter Third Convention). *See also* Convention for Amelioration of Condition of Wounded & Sick in Armed Forces in the Field, Aug. 12, 1949, art. 2, 6 U.S.T. 3114, 3116, 75 U.N.T.S. 31, 32 (hereinafter First Convention); Second Convention, *supra* note 38, art. 2, *id.* at 3220, 75 U.N.T.S. at 86; Convention Relative to Protection of Civilian Persons in Time of War, Aug. 12, 1949, art. 2, 6 U.S.T. 3516, 3518, 75 U.N.T.S. 287, 288 (hereinafter Fourth Convention)
47. TIF, *supra* note 17, at 330, 450–52.

Article 2 before or during the NATO campaign, after Allied Force ended, the SFRY accepted them retroactive to 1992 on October 16, 2001.[48] Nevertheless, treaty succession principles,[49] even if the SFRY and other States had formal acceptance of the former country's treaties under review at the time of Allied Force,[50] may have bound the SFRY during the NATO campaign. The SFRY was also bound to the extent the Conventions restated custom or general principles of law.[51] The general view is that much, but maybe not all, of the Third Convention restates customary rules or general principles of law.[52] Therefore, it bound the SFRY and NATO to that extent as custom or general principles. The Third Convention also has a Martens clause; even denunciation of the Convention "shall in no way impair the obligations which the Parties to the conflict shall remain bound to fulfil by virtue of the principles of the law of nations, as they result from the usages established among civilized peoples, from the laws of humanity and the dictates of the public conscience."[53] The clause may reflect a general principle of law or custom.[54] If so, the SFRY was bound to apply principles of humanity for detainees' treatment, even if not bound by the Conventions as treaty law.

Not all States party to NATO-SFRY aspects of Allied Force, e.g., the United States, were parties to 1977 Protocol I to the 1949 Conventions. The

---

48. International Committee of the Red Cross website, *supra* note 18. *See also* Christopher Greenwood, *The Applicability of International Humanitarian Law and the Law of Neutrality to the Kosovo Campaign* in the present volume. When this paper was researched and delivered in June 2001, the SFRY's acceptance had not been deposited. The ensuing and sometimes convoluted discussion based on treaty succession principles and the Conventions and Protocols as restating custom or general principles of law demonstrates the importance of the Conventions and Protocols as treaty law.
49. *See generally* Symposium, *State Succession in the Former Soviet Union and in Eastern Europe*, 33 VIRGINIA JOURNAL OF INTERNATIONAL LAW 253 (1993); Walker, *supra* note 5.
50. TIF, *supra* note 17, at 330, 450–52.
51. Today 189 States are party to the four 1949 Geneva Conventions. International Committee of the Red Cross website, *supra* note 18. This suggests that many if not all of their provisions represent customary norms. BROWNLIE, *supra* note 5, at 5; RESTATEMENT (THIRD), *supra* note 5, § 102 cmts. f, i; 1 OPPENHEIM *supra* note 5, § 10, at 28, 31; George Walker, *Anticipatory Collective Self-Defense in the Charter Era:What the Treaties Have Said*, 31 CORNELL INTERNATIONAL LAW JOURNAL 321, 367–68 (1998); THE LAW OF MILITARY OPERATIONS, *supra* note 13, at 391–92. *See also* ANNOTATED SUPPLEMENT, *supra* note 9, ¶¶ 8.5.1.1, 8.5.1.4–8.5.1.5, 11.2–11.3.
52. *See* ANNOTATED SUPPLEMENT, *supra* note 9, ¶¶ 11.4, 11.7–11.7.4; *supra* note 51.
53. Third Convention, *supra* note 46, art. 142, 6 U.S.T. at 3424, 75 U.N.T.S. at 242. *See also* 1 PICTET, *supra* note 12, at 411–13; 2 *id.*, *supra* note 38, at 281–83; 3 *id.*, *supra* note 12, at 647–48 (1960); 4 *id.*, *supra* note 13, at 624–26.
54. BOTHE ET AL., *supra* note 12, at 44. *See also* I.C.J. Statute, art. 38(1); RESTATEMENT (THIRD), *supra* note 5, §§ 102–03.

former Yugoslavia was,[55] but this is subject to treaty succession principles and other considerations as to whether the SFRY was bound in 1999.[56] To the extent the Protocol's terms relating to prisoners of war[57] reflected custom or general principles,[58] they bound States involved in Allied Force, including NATO countries and the SFRY. Protocol I also has a Martens clause: "In cases not covered by this Protocol or by other international agreements, civilians and combatants remain under the protection and authority of the principles of international law derived from established custom, from the principles of humanity and from the dictates of public conscience."[59] The clause may reflect a general principle of law or custom;[60] if so, like the analysis applied to its Third Convention counterpart,[61] the SFRY was required to treat its prisoners of war with humanity even if Protocol I did not apply as treaty law.

The same principles apply to the 1907 Hague IV Regulations relating to prisoners of war, insofar as they reflected custom.[62] Yugoslavia was not a formal party to them, but, e.g., the Regulations' provision forbidding killing or wounding those who have laid down arms, or who no longer have means of

---

55. *Signatures, Ratifications and Accessions Concerning the Protocols I and II Additional to the Geneva Conventions, 1977*, in THE LAWS OF ARMED CONFLICT, *supra* note 15, at 703. The SFRY accepted Protocol I, *supra* note 11, on October 16, 2001, retroactive to 1992, but was also bound by customary and general principles norms stated in Protocol I. As in the case of the 1949 Conventions, the ensuing and sometimes convoluted discussion based on treaty succession principles and the Protocol as restating custom or general principles of law demonstrates the importance of Protocol I as treaty law. *See supra* note 48 and accompanying text

56. TIF, *supra* note 17, at 330; Symposium, *State Succession*, *supra* note 48; Walker, *supra* note 5.

57. Protocol I, *supra* note 11, arts. 8–11, 1125 U.N.T.S. at 10–12, 22–24. *See also* ANNOTATED SUPPLEMENT, *supra* note 9, ¶¶ 11.4, 11.7; BOTHE ET AL., *supra* note 12, at 82–116, 216–62; PILLOUD ET AL., *supra* note 12, at 107–63, 473–559.

58. *See supra* notes 5, 11–15, 19, 53 and accompanying text.

59. Protocol I, *supra* note 11, art. 1(2), 1125 U.N.T.S. at 7. *See also supra* note 53 and accompanying text.

60. *See supra* note 54 and accompanying text.

61. *See supra* notes 53-54 and accompanying text.

62. BROWNLIE, *supra* note 5, at 5; RESTATEMENT (THIRD), *supra* note 5, § 102 cmts. f, i; 1 OPPENHEIM, *supra* note 5, § 10, at 28, 31; Walker, *supra* note 51, 31, *supra* note 13, CORNELL INTERNATIONAL LAW JOURNAL at 367–68; THE LAW OF MILITARY OPERATIONS at 391–92.

defense,[63] bound the SFRY and NATO States as a customary norm.[64] The Third 1949 Convention and Protocol I are complementary to the extent that they do not supersede the 1907 Hague IV Regulations.[65] Moreover, Hague IV's preamble, and its 1899 predecessor's preamble include Martens clauses.[66] To the extent these clauses reflect custom or a general principle of law,[67] the SFRY was bound to apply principles of humanity in its custody of prisoners of war whether the Hague treaties were binding as treaty law or not.

2. The SFRY-KLA Aspects of Allied Force

Common Article 3 to the 1949 Geneva Conventions establishes minimum criteria for armed conflicts that are not of an international nature; e.g., the Second Convention relating to prisoners of war says:

---

63. Hague Convention (IV) Respecting Laws & Customs of War on Land, Oct. 18, 1907, Regulations, art. 23(c).
64. ANNOTATED SUPPLEMENT, *supra* note 9, ¶ 11.4. *See also* Protocol I, *supra* note 11, arts. 40–41, 1125 U.N.T.S. at 22; BOTHE ET AL., *supra* note 12, at 216–24; PILLOUD ET AL., *supra* note 12, at 473–91; SAN REMO MANUAL, *supra* note 12, ¶ 47(i), cmt. 47.56; Horace B. Robertson, Jr., *The Obligation to Accept Surrender*, in READINGS FROM THE NAVAL WAR COLLEGE REVIEW ch. 40 (John Moore & Robert Turner eds., 1994)(Vol. 68, US Naval War College International Law Studies); *supra* note 62 and accompanying text. Serbia was a party, but the Ottoman Empire, predecessor State to modern Turkey, a NATO member, and some areas today within the SFRY, only signed 1899 Hague Convention II with Respect to Laws & Customs of War on Land, July 29, 1899, 32 Stat. 1803 (hereinafter 1899 Hague II), Regulations, art. 23(c), 32 Stat. at 1811, 1817, identical with Hague IV, *supra* note 62, Regulations, art. 23(c), 36 *id*. at 2301–02, which Montenegro, Serbia and the Ottoman Empire signed but did not ratify. Austria-Hungary, a predecessor State to parts of the SFRY and its successor States and Hungary, a NATO member, was party to the 1899 and 1907 Conventions. *See Convention of 1899, Convention of 1907: Signatures, Ratifications and Accessions*, in THE LAWS OF ARMED CONFLICTS, *supra* note 15, at 94–98. There is a circuitous argument that the SFRY, constituted as it was in 1999, was bound by treaty succession principles as well as custom. *See generally* Symposium, *State Succession*, *supra* note 49; Walker, *supra* note 5. The same kind of issues might plague analysis within NATO because of, e.g., Canada's status as a NATO member; Canada had a different status a century ago within the British Empire. TIF, *supra* note 17, at 455 does not list Canada, Montenegro, Serbia or Yugoslavia but does list Turkey as Hague IV parties; 1899 Hague II is not listed.
65. Third Convention, *supra* note 46, art. 135, 6 U.S.T. at 3422, 75 U.N.T.S. at 240; Protocol I, *supra* note 11, art. 96, 1125 U.N.T.S. at 46. *See also* BOTHE ET AL., *supra* note 12, at 554–57; 3 PICTET, *supra* note 53, at 636–40; PILLOUD ET AL., *supra* note 12, at 1084–92
66. Hague IV, *supra* note 63, preamble, 36 Stat. at 2277–80; 1899 Hague II, *supra* note 64, preamble, 32 *id*. at 1803–05. *See also supra* notes 53, 59 and accompanying text.
67. *See supra* notes 54, 60 and accompanying text.

In the case of armed conflict not of an international character occurring in the territory of one of the High Contracting Parties, each Party to the conflict shall be bound to apply, as a minimum, the following provisions:

(1) Persons taking no active part in the hostilities, including members of armed forces who have laid down their arms and those placed hors de combat by sickness, wounds, detention, or any other cause, shall in all circumstances be treated humanely, without any adverse distinction founded on race, color, religion or faith, sex, birth or wealth, or any other similar criteria. To this end the following acts are and shall remain prohibited at any time and in any place . . . with respect to the above-mentioned persons:

(a) violence to life and person, in particular murder of all kinds, mutilation, cruel treatment and torture;

(b) taking of hostages;

(c) outrages upon personal dignity; in particular, humiliating and degrading treatment;

(d) the passing of sentences and the carrying out of executions without previous judgment pronounced by a regularly constituted court affording all the judicial guarantees . . . recognized as indispensable by civilized peoples.

(2) The wounded and sick shall be collected and cared for.

. . . .

Parties to the conflict should further endeavor to bring into force, by means of special agreements, all or part of the other provisions of [this] . . . Convention.

The application of the preceding provisions shall not affect the legal status of the Parties to the conflict.[68]

If Allied Force was not an international armed conflict with respect to KLA-SFRY confrontations but would be within the Common Article 3

---

68. Third Convention, *supra* note 46, art. 3, 6 U.S.T. at 3319, 75 U.N.T.S. at 136. *See also* First Convention, *supra* note 46, art. 3, *id.* at 3116, 75 U.N.T.S. at 32; Second Convention, *supra* note 38, art. 3, *id.* at 3220, 75 U.N.T.S. at 86; Fourth Convention, *supra* note 46, art. 3, *id.* at 3518, 75 U.N.T.S. at 288; 1 PICTET, *supra* note 12, at 38–61; 2 *id.*, *supra* note 38, at 33–38; 3 *id.*, *supra* note 53, at 28–44; 4 *id.*, *supra* note 13, at 26–44.

definition, its standards applied to those taken into custody, e.g., KLA members the SFRY captured, or SFRY armed forces members the KLA captured.

It is doubtful whether the SFRY and the KLA negotiated Article 3 special arrangements. Article 3 recites minimum standards; other provisions of the Third Convention reciting customary law may also have applied to these persons. Protocol II, applying to non-international conflicts as a supplement to the Third Convention,[69] lists additional protections.[70] The former Yugoslavia was a Protocol II party subject to a declaration,[71] but this is also subject to treaty succession principles and other considerations as to whether the SFRY was bound in 1999.[72] To the extent Protocol II standards recited custom,[73] the SFRY and the KLA were bound. The SFRY and the KLA were also bound by the Martens clause principle ("in cases not covered by the law in force, the human person remains under the protection of the principles of humanity and the dictates of the public conscience") stated in Protocol II,[74] even if they were not bound under Protocol II or other formal treaty rules.

Conclusions

Operation Allied Force's legitimacy under international law is, as US sports commentators would say, a close call. Because of its history, intervention, like

---

69. Protocol Additional (II) to Geneva Conventions of 12 August 1949, & Relating to Protection of Victims of Non-International Armed Conflicts, June 8, 1977, art. 1, 1125 U.N.T.S. 609, 611 [hereinafter Protocol II]. *See also* BOTHE ET AL., *supra* note 12, at 604–08, 623–29; PILLOUD ET AL., *supra* note 12, at 1319–36, 1343–46.
70. Protocol II, *supra* note 69, arts. 4–11, 1125 U.N.T.S. at 612–15. *See also* BOTHE ET AL., *supra* note 12, at 640–64; PILLOUD ET AL., *supra* note 12, at 1368–1436.
71. *Signatures, supra* note 55, at 703, 718.
72. TIF, *supra* note 17, at 330; Symposium, *State Succession, supra* note 49; Walker, *supra* note 5. The SFRY accepted Protocol II, *supra* note 69, on October 16, 2001, retroactive to 1992, but was also bound by customary and general principles norms stated in Protocol II. As in the case of the 1949 Conventions, the ensuing and sometimes convoluted discussion based on treaty succession principles and the Protocol as restating custom or general principles of law demonstrates the importance of Protocol II as treaty law. See *supra* note 48 and accompanying text
73. See *supra* notes 62–64 and accompanying text.
74. Protocol II, *supra* note 69, preamble, 1125 U.N.T.S. at 611, which does not add "established custom" as in other Martens clauses, because of the relative newness of law applying to non-international armed conflicts, although time since 1977 may argue for including that norm as well. *See also* BOTHE ET AL., *supra* note 12, at 44, 620; PILLOUD ET AL., *supra* note 12, at 1341–42; *supra* notes 53–54, 59–61, 66–67 and accompanying text.

war, is a loaded word for many States or commentators and in many contexts. Today, in the UN Charter era, intervention in some contexts may be less lawful than it was before 1945, given Charter provisions on sovereignty, territorial integrity and the political independence of States. On the other hand, the growing body of the law of human rights, also recognized in the Charter, and humanitarian law, recognized by UN organizations' resolutions, within the world arena must be considered. Under the perhaps (and hopefully) unique circumstances of Kosovo, the NATO campaign was legitimate under principles of collective humanitarian intervention under state of necessity.

With regard to the application of the law of armed conflict, as an operation involving the use of force, Allied Force certainly met the threshold of Common Article 2 of the 1949 Geneva Conventions. Therefore NATO was obligated to conduct its campaign in accordance with the standards of that body of law. Additionally, state of necessity principles mandated that NATO operations, to be considered legitimate, must have been undertaken only when necessary and proportional to Operation Allied Force's overall goal of protecting the Albanian Kosovars from the depredations of Serbian forces. Under law of armed conflict standards and consistent with that objective, NATO, although choosing to implement only voluntary measures, could have conducted traditional visit and search ship interdiction operations to halt the shipment of oil to the SFRY. On the issue of the status of captured NATO and SFRY military personnel, the Third Convention was binding as either treaty or customary law on both sides; thus captured personnel were entitled to prisoner of war status. The situation with regard to KLA personnel is more complex. If the KLA-SFRY conflict is viewed as an international armed conflict, then captured KLA personnel would also be prisoners of war and entitled to the protections of the Third Convention. If, however, that conflict is considered to be non-international in nature, then detained KLA personnel would be subject to the more general protective standards of Common Article 3.

Intervention to protect indigenous nationals such as occurred in 1999 in the SFRY creates two distinct legal issues for the international community. First, is the intervention itself lawful? I believe that long-accepted state of necessity principles would apply and that interventions that meet state of necessity criteria are legitimate. This will limit humanitarian interventions to the most immediate and egregious situations when no reasonable alternative to intervention exists. Second, what law applies to the use of military force during humanitarian interventions? Except in the most extraordinary circumstances (none of which I can currently envision), it must be the law of armed conflict applicable to international armed conflicts. It is that body of law to which military forces train, and it is that body of law that provides the greatest protections to both combatants and noncombatants. Any lesser standard risks inflicting greater harm than the good sought to be accomplished.

Commentary

Judith A. Miller

In several instances during this colloquium scholars have alluded to UN Security Council Resolutions as having the impact "as law." I'm not sure that I would be willing to accord the Security Council such overarching authority. I certainly agree that the member States of the United Nations, in Article 24 of the Charter, conferred on the Security Council the primary responsibility for the maintenance of international peace and security, and *agreed* that the Security Council, in carrying out its responsibility, acts on their behalf. Furthermore, member States *agreed*, in Article 25, to accept and carry out the decisions of the Security Council in accordance with the Charter. In Chapter VI of the Charter the member States conferred on the Security Council the authority and responsibility to inquire into disputes which may endanger international peace and security, and to investigate those disputes and recommend measures with a view towards pacific settlement. Member States also conferred on the Security Council in Chapter VII the responsibility to determine the existence of a breach of the peace or act of aggression, make recommendations, and decide what measures shall be taken pursuant to Articles 41 and 42 of the Charter, which we all know involve non-forcible and forcible measures to maintain or restore international peace and security.

The international security paradigm established by the Charter, in my view, is an *international mutual security agreement*, in which sovereign States members of the UN have by mutual agreement conferred on the UN Security Council certain responsibilities for the maintenance and restoration of international peace and security, and have agreed to abide by the decisions of the Security Council in this respect. I do not read the Charter, however, as conferring law-making authority on the UN Security Council. In my view, neither the UN Security Council nor the UN General Assembly commands the authority or the responsibility to establish rules of law applicable to the international community or to any particular State. The Security Council, of course, may by its decisions reinforce applicable principles of international law, and may even advance developing principles of international law.

Each dispute or threat to international peace and security addressed by the Security Council is unique, having its own factual basis. UN Security Council decisions in respect to those factual situations must of necessity be tailored to the factual situation at hand. Because of this, and because decisions of the Security Council often do not reach out and touch all members of the international community, the resolutions of the Security Council do not and should not establish principles of international law applicable to all members of the international community. I think it is a stretch, and a dangerous one at that, to read into the UN Charter authority and responsibility which is not articulated, and which was never intended for those institutions established therein. Even the decisions of the International Court of Justice are applicable only to the parties to a case before the Court, although those decisions can be powerfully persuasive evidence of applicable international legal principles. And, although some may disagree, Article 13 of the Charter authorizes the General Assembly *only* to initiate studies and make recommendations concerning the progressive development of international law and its codification—it is not a law-making body.

I am sure everyone is aware of the difficulty we are now experiencing in the International Criminal Court Preparatory Committee in arriving at a sufficiently precise definition of the crime of aggression. One of the difficulties is the insistence of some States on adopting the definition of aggression embodied in UN General Assembly Resolution 3314 of December 14, 1974, arguing that the resolution articulates the international legal principle defining aggression. If one looks into the preparatory work on the definition, the debate in the General Assembly, and the interventions by States after its adoption by consensus, one would clearly discern that the definition does not represent by any means a definitive statement of aggression, much less the crime of aggression.

This is but one example of the difficulties posed by UN General Assembly declarations purporting to reflect the state of the law. Such pronouncements are so often political in nature, not supported by State practice or the realities of international discourse, and so tainted by underlying political agendas as to be highly suspect. Yet we are confronted with such pronouncements years later as definitive statements of the law. The same would hold true of UN

Security Council decisions, and I would hope that we would not lose our perspective on just how limited UN Security Council resolutions are intended to be, the fact that they too are political statements, and that they do not have the force and effect of law.

Turning now to the applicability of the law of armed conflict to the Kosovo air operation, I think that the appropriate point of departure must be the applicable rules of engagement. Since this was a NATO operation, the NATO rules of engagement were applicable and were employed by all NATO forces. In this respect, the NATO ROE specify that: "ROE first must be lawful. International law defines the lawful limits for the use of force during military operations. . . . The conduct of military operations is circumscribed by international law, to include the applicable provisions of the law of armed conflict. . . . NATO ROE, and the application of them, never permit the use of force which violates applicable international law." Furthermore, each NATO member is bound by its own domestic law, which may further constrain the use of force in certain circumstances and complicate the conduct of combined operations. For United States armed forces, service regulations specify that the international law of armed conflict applies to the use of force in hostilities, and that at all times, commanders shall observe, and require their commands to observe, the principles of international law, including the observation and enforcement of the law of armed conflict.

So from the outset of hostilities on March 24, 1999, indeed during the planning process in preparation for Operation Allied Force, there was no question that the law of armed conflict was fully applicable and that it was incumbent that there be scrupulous compliance with the principles of the law of armed conflict at all times. This was particularly important in the selection of targets, in weaponizing those targets, in choosing aimpoints, and in employing weapons against those targets. US Department of Defense (DoD) attorneys played a critical role in conducting legal reviews and analyses during the entire targeting process, and applied the traditional principles of the law of armed conflict throughout. Allow me to briefly provide you with a couple of examples of the target sets which were attacked during Allied Force, and walk you through the legal issues and concerns posed by those target sets.

In addition to targeting purely military objectives (i.e., tanks, barracks, bunkers, fighter aircraft, etc.) NATO targeted so-called "dual-use" infrastructure assets such as command, control and communication (C3), electric power, industrial plant, leadership lines of communication (LOCs) and petroleum, oil and lubricant (POL) facilities. This immediately raised issues of discrimination and the prohibitions against attacking civilians and civilian objects. We were also acutely aware of the rules of proportionality—that collateral damage to civilians and civilian objects was not to be excessive in light of the military advantage anticipated.

It is no secret that NATO targeted electrical power facilities. Such facilities are normally targeted during hostilities, because they do provide energy resources to military forces, and their destruction has a direct military advantage. Nevertheless, during Kosovo, we were careful to avoid undue and prolonged power outages which would have a disproportionate effect on the civilian population. In most cases, attacks on electrical power facilities employed "soft kill" capabilities, which could take the system down for a few hours or a day or two, but would not permanently shut down the power grid. We also were mindful of the possible cascading effects of the attacks on power grids, which could spill power outages over into neighboring countries not involved in the hostilities, and we were careful to ensure that these outages did not occur. There were some "hard kill" power grid attacks, and NATO did shut down the grid throughout Serbia at one point, but the outage was not permanent.

I will readily admit that, aside from directly damaging the military electrical power infrastructure, NATO wanted the civilian population to experience discomfort, so that the population would pressure Milosevic and the Serbian leadership to accede to UN Security Council Resolution 1244, but the intended effects on the civilian population were secondary to the military advantage gained by attacking the electrical power infrastructure.

Likewise, NATO mounted attacks on "dual-use" industrial facilities, those having both military and civilian purposes. But each and every target of this nature was carefully scrutinized by our lawyers, both at the Joint Staff level and in my office (DoD General Counsel). In each case a direct military link was required, or only those portions of the facility having military utility, or conducting military work, were targeted. An example of this type facility was the Kragujevac Arms/Motor Vehicle Plant—one side of which produced automobiles while the other side produced tanks. NATO targeted only that side of the plant producing tanks. I might add that initially this facility was identified as a heavy bomber target, but later disapproved as such because of the proximity of civilian housing.

You might find it interesting to review a recently published RAND study by Stephen T. Hosmer, entitled "Why Milosevic Decided to Settle When He Did." Hosmer concluded that it was the attacks and the threat of attacks on "dual-use" infrastructure targets that generated the decisive pressure for war termination. Furthermore, Milosevic and the Serbian leadership capitulated because they expected an unconstrained bombing campaign of even greater magnitude, including carpet bombing of Belgrade, if they rejected the NATO ultimatum delivered by Chermnomyrdin and Ahtisaari on June 2, 1999. This study also concluded that the air campaign against military targets did not significantly influence Milosevic's decision to come to terms. This in my view, has significant and disturbing implications for the application of the law of armed conflict in future conflicts of this type. There very well could be serious consequences for the civilian population should decision makers no longer appreciate the military utility of striking military targets, and applying military pressure solely against military objectives.

These are but two examples of the application of the law of armed conflict during the targeting process for Operation Allied Force. I wish to assure all of you that careful and thorough legal reviews of all targets were conducted at every echelon of command, from the Supreme Allied Commander up through the Joint Staff and in my office prior to the target lists being sent over to the US National Command Authorities (President and Secretary of Defense) for final approval. In many cases sound legal advice led to the deletion of targets, change of ordnance assigned, adjustment of aimpoints, or disapproval of targets because of law of armed conflict concerns. Principles of distinction, proportionality and military advantage were applied on a daily basis throughout the conflict. Although mistakes were made, and weapons did not always perform as accurately as we had hoped, in my view NATO scrupulously complied with the law of armed conflict in every instance. We should be gratified that civilian casualties were kept remarkably low considering the intensity of the air campaign. In many ways, we have the lawyers, and the incredibly talented and dedicated targeteers, to thank for such a superb effort.

One final comment. You undoubtedly are aware of, and may have read the Final Report to the Prosecutor by the Committee Established to Review the NATO Bombing Campaign Against the FRY.[1] The Report concludes that for several reasons, not the least because the law of armed conflict in the area of "dual-use" targets is not clear, no "in-depth" investigation of the NATO air campaign as a whole was warranted, nor should there be further investigations into specific incidents. While I found this aspect of the Report to the Prosecutor gratifying, the manner in which the committee reached its conclusions is deeply disturbing. To have twenty-twenty hindsight scrutiny, done at leisure,

---

1. Final Report to the Prosecutor by the Committee Established to Review the NATO Bombing Campaign Against the Federal Republic of Yugoslavia, 39 INTERNATIONAL LEGAL MATERIALS 1257 (2000), *reprinted* herein as Appendix A.

of decisions and determinations made in the fog of war, often under instantaneous time constraints and life-threatening conditions by military commanders, pilots, soldiers and airmen, based on allegations by those who do not hold Western nations in very high regard, is a chilling and frightening prospect. I fear that the reservations of the United States with respect to the International Criminal Court are well-founded, based on the aftermath of the Kosovo conflict. I also fear that a precedent has been established, and we can expect such allegations in future instances where the use of force is employed, even in instances of humanitarian assistance. The prospects for Western participation in peacekeeping or peace enforcement operations do not necessarily look good, and one wonders if this bodes well for the force and effect of international law for the future.

Commentary

Natalino Ronzitti

In order to assess the relevance of the Hague and Geneva Conventions and Protocol I to the Kosovo conflict, one has to ascertain, first of all, the nature of the conflict. Without a doubt, the hostilities between NATO countries and the Federal Republic of Yugoslavia (FRY) should be qualified as an international armed conflict.

On the contrary, the qualification of hostilities between the FRY and the Kosovo Liberation Army (KLA) is more controversial. At first glance, it would seem that it should be regarded as an internal conflict, since the conflict took place between the constituted government and an insurgent community within a State. Can the hostilities between the FRY and the KLA be qualified as an international armed conflict, since Article 1(4) of Protocol I applies?[1] Article 1(4) refers to peoples under colonial domination or alien occupation and racist regime fighting for the implementation of their right to self-determination. It does not apply to mere secessionist movements. The question, therefore, is whether the Kosovars are a people entitled to self-determination, or whether they are simply a minority.

The distinction between people and minority is a moot point and international law, while conferring different categories of rights on peoples and minorities, does not define either peoples or minorities. It is true that UN Security Council Resolution 1244[2] qualifies the inhabitants of Kosovo as "people."

---

1. Protocol Additional to the Geneva Conventions of 12 August 1949, and Relating to the Protection of Victims of International Conflicts, Dec. 12, 1977, 1125 U.N.T.S. 3, DOCUMENTS ON THE LAWS OF WAR 422 (Adam Roberts & Richard Guelff eds., 3d ed. 2000) [hereinafter Protocol I].
2. S.C. Res. 1244 (June 10, 1999), U.N. Doc. S/RES/1244 (1999).

Commentary

However, it does not clarify whether this people enjoys the right of self-determination. It only says that the people of Kosovo should enjoy "substantial autonomy." Autonomy fits more with the rights of minorities than with those of people. Be that as it may, the KLA, as a liberation movement representing Kosovo's "people," did not address any declaration to the depositary of Protocol I in order to bring into effect both the Geneva Conventions and the Protocol, as required by Article 96(3) of Protocol I.

The other possibility is to consider the KLA as being so close to NATO countries that the Kosovar militias, under the control of NATO, did not represent an autonomous party to the conflict. The Appeals Chamber of the ICTY, in the *Tadic* case relied on the control criterion to qualify the conflict, which took place in Bosnia and Herzegovina between the Bosnian Serb Army and Bosnia-Herzegovina, as international.[3] Since the Bosnian Serb Army was under the strict control of the FRY, the conflict was in reality between the FRY, on one hand, and Bosnia-Herzegovina on the other. The FRY did not regard the conflict against the KLA as international. NATO countries, on the other hand, did not take any stance on that point. Hence, the dual qualification of the Kosovo conflict (NATO countries-FRY; FRY-KLA) still holds good, unless contradicted by a future judgment of the ICTY.

I will now turn my attention to the applicability of the relevant instruments of international humanitarian law (IHL). While the Hague Conventions are mostly regarded as declaratory of customary international law, this is only true in part for the Geneva Conventions and in particular for Protocol I. All NATO countries are party to the Geneva Conventions. As for Protocol I, all were party to it at the time of Operation Allied Force except for France, Turkey and the United States.[4] All the NATO countries which conducted hostilities against the FRY are parties to Protocol II except the United States, although the United States does consider its provisions to be reflective of customary international law.

The FRY was admitted to the United Nations in 2000 as a new State. However, during the hostilities the FRY considered itself the continuation of the former Yugoslavia, which was party to the Geneva Conventions and to Protocols I and II. If one disregards the continuity claim, other principles could be applied to affirm that the FRY was obliged, during hostilities, to abide by the Geneva Conventions and the two Additional Protocols. Article 34 of the

---

3. *See* Prosecutor v. Tadic, Jurisdiction, 105 INTERNATIONAL LAW REPORTS 453, ¶ 70 (1997).
4. France acceded to Protocol I on April 11, 2001.

1978 Vienna Convention on the Succession of States,[5] imposing the rule of automatic succession in case of dissolution of States, is regarded as declaratory of customary international law, or it could be argued that the declaration by the FRY that it would honor the treaties stipulated by the former Yugoslavia should be considered equivalent to a declaration of succession to all multilateral treaties binding the predecessor State.

As far as conduct of hostilities is concerned, the Kosovo war consisted mostly of air warfare, with the exception of cruise missiles launched by warships in the Adriatic, which fall under the aegis of naval warfare. Hague Convention IX regulates naval bombardment. For air bombardment there are no conventional rules, although some commentators have argued that the 1923 Hague Rules on Aerial Warfare are declaratory of customary international law.[6] Protocol I, Article 49(3) subjects all three kinds of attacks (land, naval and air) to the same rules. Is that provision declaratory of customary international law? The point is important, since France and the United States were not parties to Protocol I. However, the very fact that all NATO countries were not parties to the same conventional instruments, did not raise any serious problem as far as the legal interoperability of forces (for instance, targeting) was concerned.

Three US soldiers were captured on March 31, 1999 at the Macedonia-Yugoslavia border. They were entitled to prisoner of war status. They were wearing uniforms and could not be considered spies. The pretense by Milosevic, subsequently abandoned, to subject them to criminal proceedings was without any legal foundation. Given the nature of the operations, the allies did not capture any FRY soldier. Personnel captured by the KLA and handed over to NATO countries were entitled to prisoner of war status. KLA personnel were covered by Common Article 3 of the Geneva Conventions and by Protocol II. As previously mentioned, the conflict between the FRY and the KLA should be regarded as an internal one.

The Kosovo conflict raised a new problem, that of the interface of the law of neutrality and peacekeeping operations. The case in point refers to the status of military personnel, belonging to a party to the conflict, in the territory of a non-participating State. During the Kosovo war, personnel belonging to NATO countries were stationed in foreign territory, close to the theater of war. They were either part of a peacekeeping operation, such as SFOR in

---

5. Vienna Convention on Succession of States in Respect of Treaties, Aug. 22, 1978, U.N. Doc. A/CONF.80/31/Corr 2 (1978), 17 INTERNATIONAL LEGAL MATERIALS 1448 (1978).
6. See authorities cited *infra* note 14.

Bosnia-Herzegovina, or dispatched as a measure of preventive deployment, such as UNPREDEP in Macedonia, whose mandate was terminated on February 28, just before the commencement of hostilities.

According to the customary law of neutrality and the rules of the Hague Convention V, belligerent military units present in neutral territory should be interned. Is the same principle applicable to units, belonging to a party to the conflict, but part of a peacekeeping force? The danger for the enemy is that the military unit might be diverted to a combat mission and take part in the hostilities.

This is a new problem, which should be resolved taking into account the principles embodied in Article 11 of the Hague Convention V of 1907, on the one hand, and the law of the UN Charter, on the other. The resolution of the issue could be along the following lines:

- If personnel are under the command and control of UN Headquarters, the danger that troops be diverted to take part in combat operations is remote;
- The same is true, however with difficulty, if the force, even though under national command and control, is mandated by the United Nations;
- A further line of reasoning could be to invoke Charter Article 103, overriding the law of neutrality, on this point;
- A policy of non-belligerency might also be invoked by the neutral State, hosting foreign troops, insofar as they do not commit any warring act.

During the conflict, NATO aircraft dropped weapons, not used during their mission in Serbia, in the Adriatic, before landing at Aviano, Italy. Landing with the weapons represented a hazard to the safety of the aircraft. The weapons were dropped in jettison areas that had been identified by NATO in previous years on the high seas.

The use of the high seas for military purposes is without any doubt lawful. Therefore one may conclude that jettison areas are not contrary to international law. However, the weapons dropped by NATO aircraft lie on the continental shelf of both Italy and Croatia. Italy was a member of the warring coalition, which took part in the identification of jettison areas, and consented to the weapon dropping. However, the case of Croatia, a State that did not take part in the armed conflict, is different. Could the continental shelf of a neutral State be used for warring activities? Our answer is yes, since the continental shelf is not under the sovereignty of the coastal State, which only enjoys sovereign rights on it. The same solution proposed for mines or other devices on the continental shelf should be followed. Military activities on the continental shelf of a foreign State are lawful, provided that the economic activities of the coastal State are not irremediably impaired. The principle of "due regard" should be taken into account.

Unlike total exclusion zones, jettison areas are a new phenomenon. Should they be regulated? The first problem is whether there is a duty of notification. Incidents may occur, as happened with Italian trawlers in the upper Adriatic, which caught a number of weapons in their nets. A duty of notification of minefields, as soon as military exigencies permit, is established under Article 3 of the Hague Convention VIII. The same rationale could be invoked as far as dropping of weapons is concerned, even though the danger is more remote than with mines. It should also be taken into account that in the *Corfu Channel* case, the International Court of Justice (ICJ) stated that Albania had the duty to notify of the danger to navigation represented by mines floating in its territorial waters.[7]

The second problem is whether there is a duty to remove weapons dumped in the high seas at the end of hostilities. Article 5 of the Hague Convention VIII establishes a generic duty to remove mines. De-mining is a duty, which has been rendered more stringent by new conventions on land mines. Environmental considerations play a role, not only during the armed conflict (Articles 35(3) and 55 of Protocol I), but also after its termination. After the termination of hostilities, Italy and other NATO countries dispatched 13 minesweepers to remove the weapons dropped during the war. However, that operation was considered a sort of exercise and not regarded by NATO as a duty imposed by international law.

The law of neutrality has not been abolished by the entry into force of the United Nations Charter. The ICJ reaffirmed the permanent validity of this body of law in 1996 in its advisory opinion on *Nuclear Weapons*, even though the Court took into consideration only the rights of neutral States and not those of belligerents vis-à-vis neutrals.[8] The right to visit and search neutral shipping in order to confiscate contraband of war is a well-established right under the law of neutrality, which has also been exercised during naval conflicts that have occurred since the entry into force of the UN Charter.

During the Kosovo war, NATO envisaged exercising belligerent rights against neutral shipping in order to stop the oil supply to FRY. This position was opposed

---

7. *See* Corfu Channel (U.K. v. Albania), 1949 I.C.J. 4, 22 (Dec. 5).
8. Advisory Opinion on the Legality of the Threat or Use of Nuclear Weapons, 1996 I.C.J. 78 (July 8).

by the Russian Federation, according to which the control of shipping bound for the port of Bar could be enforced only if authorized by a UN Security Council resolution. Also, among NATO allies, France and Italy were not enthusiastic. Resolution 1160 established an embargo on the sale and supply of war material to FRY, but did not authorize any enforcement measures, except those which could be exerted by a country on its own shipping.[9]

It is true that foreign shipping may not be visited and searched, unless a Security Council resolution authorizes appropriate measures to enforce an embargo established by the Security Council. This is a well established practice going back to the Rhodesia case[10] and implemented more recently against Iraq,[11] the former Yugoslavia[12] and the FRY.[13] However, this statement holds true in time of peace, i.e., in a situation in which there is no armed conflict. In such a case, in the absence of a Security Council resolution, States are authorized to control shipping flying their flag or belonging to foreign countries, which agree that their ships, usually under reciprocity, may be visited. A completely different situation arises when an armed conflict is going on. Warring States, as practice shows, are entitled to exercise belligerent rights, including visit and search. One can only discuss whether there is any geographical limitation or whether visiting and searching may be conducted anywhere. This depends on the scale of hostilities. The principle of necessity and proportionality might advise that those activities be conducted close to the theater of war.

A blockade of the port of Bar was also envisaged by NATO countries to impede the oil supply to the FRY. This idea was immediately qualified by the Russian Federation as contrary to international law and was also opposed by France and Denmark within the Alliance. Lacking a Security Council resolution, those countries did not regard a blockade as in keeping with international law. A blockade is still considered a lawful measure, at least when established by the United Nations, as it is one of the measures referred to in Article 42 of the Charter. But a blockade is a far more intrusive measure than visit and search and might contribute to an escalation of the conflict. Yet these are policy considerations. From a legal viewpoint, the considerations

---

9. S.C. Res. 1160 (Mar. 31, 1998), U.N. Doc. S/RES/1160 (1998) ¶ 8. This was restated in paragraph 7 of S.C. Res. 1199 (Sep. 23, 1998), U.N. Doc. S/RES/1199 (1998) without any mention of enforcement measures.
10. S.C. Res. 221 (Apr. 9, 1966), U.N. Doc. S/RES/221 (1966).
11. S.C. Res. 665 (Aug. 25, 1990), U.N. Doc. S/RES/665 (1990).
12. S.C. Res. 713 (Sep. 25, 1991), U.N. Doc. S/RES/713 (1991); S.C. Res. 757 (May 30, 1992), U.N. Doc. S/RES/757 (1992).
13. S.C. Res. 787 (Nov. 16, 1992), U.N. Doc. S/RES/787 (1992).

made before, in relation to visit and search, are also valid, *mutatis mutandis*, with regard to blockade. In time of peace, a blockade to enforce an embargo requires an authorization by the Security Council; in time of armed conflict, Security Council authorization is not necessary.

The Kosovo conflict once again brought attention to the question of the use of neutral territory as a base for hostile operations or in a manner contrary to neutrality rules. The 1923 Hague Rules on Aerial Warfare, regarded by several writers as declaratory of customary international law, establish two basic principles, as far as neutrality is concerned.[14] Belligerent military aircraft are forbidden to enter the jurisdiction of a neutral State (Article 40); a neutral State should prevent the entry into its jurisdiction of belligerent military aircraft (Article 42).

Austria and Switzerland did not permit NATO aircraft to over fly their territory. This posture is in keeping with law of neutrality, as proven by the Hague rules. On the contrary, Bulgaria, Hungary, Romania and Slovenia agreed that their airspace could be used by NATO aircraft. This practice might be justified only if one admits that a policy of non-belligerency is in keeping with international law. If a deviation from the rule of impartiality is the consequence of a Security Council resolution, non-belligerency does not raise any particular difficulty. Security Council Resolution 1160 established an arms embargo against the FRY. Consequently, States not taking part in the hostilities were forbidden to supply the FRY with war material, but were allowed to sell weapons to NATO countries (something which did not happen in practice). It is more difficult to justify derogation from neutrality rules, in the absence of a Security Council resolution, imposing sanctions on the enemy and/or qualifying it as an aggressor. Even if it is argued that non-belligerency does not constitute a violation of international law, one has to admit that the belligerent, without infringing any neutrality rule, would be allowed to react against non-belligerent States, since their territory is being used by the adversary for warlike purposes.

---

14. Remigiusz Bierzanek, *Commentary to the 1923 Hague Rules for Aerial Warfare*, in THE LAW OF NAVAL WARFARE 404–6 (Natalino Ronzitti ed., 1988). R.R. Baxter says in commenting on the Rules: "While these Rules were never put in treaty form, they nevertheless had a profound impact on the customary international law governing aerial bombardment." This passage is quoted by Yoram Dinstein, *The Law of Air, Missile and Nuclear Warfare*, 27 ISRAEL YEARBOOK ON HUMAN RIGHTS 1 n.2 (1977). See also the decision by the Tokyo District Court, December 7, 1963 in the Shimoda Case, *in* 8 THE JAPANESE ANNUAL OF INTERNATIONAL LAW 212ff (1964).

Commentary

Richard Sorenson

I am going to shift the focus just a little bit to what is appropriate for my background as a military operational law attorney. During Operation Allied Force, I served at the headquarters of the United States Air Forces in Europe, at Ramstein Air Base in Germany. Along with Lieutenant Colonel Tony Montgomery, I worked targeting issues in theater in concert with NATO. Tony Montgomery from the US European Command and myself down at the air component level can discuss what we did to comply with the law of armed conflict as we planned and executed this operation.

By way of background, both NATO and the United States were doing detailed planning in June 1998 to address the situation in Kosovo. It was simply untenable to accept another Srebrenica, where five to eight thousand individuals were taken out and slaughtered wholesale. As you know, the International Tribunal for the former Yugoslavia (ICTY) convicted General Krstic for his activities at Srebrenica on August 2, 2001. Neither NATO nor the United States, individually, could allow another Srebrenica. In the event we were unable to get consensus in NATO to go with military action, the United States was also planning for the possibility of a US-only operation. My principal role was in planning and executing the US portion of the operation.

The United States had over forty air campaigns developed as a result of detailed planned during the ten months preceding Operation Allied Force. US and NATO planning was occurring in parallel. We had very detailed intelligence information at very high levels of classification. We also had lawyers looking at each and every individual target throughout that time period. There is no question that we had more scrutiny of every single target in Operation Allied Force than has ever been done in the history of warfare.

Military planners and lawyers applied the *jus in bello* as we considered military necessity and proportionality. Every effort was made to eliminate unnecessary suffering whenever possible and to discriminate between military and non-military objectives. There is no question that Operation Allied Force was a successful campaign—it covered seventy-eight days, thirty-eight thousand aircraft sorties, over ten thousand strike sorties, and yet resulted in the unintended deaths of only about 500 civilians. While the loss of every civilian life is regrettable, the proportion of unintended deaths relative to the scale of the operation is unprecedented in warfare.

To plan for those strike sorties we conducted target analysis using a predictive model for collateral damage. The United States used this targeting process with its four-tier collateral damage model to look at each and every target. We used imagery and distance rings around the proposed target to determine whether we had non-military objects within range of the targets. We then would analyze the type of weapon we were putting against the target and adjust our aim point or the weapon employed as required to minimize collateral damage. The model would, for example, predict the damage likely from the use of a particular weapon against a particular building—whether it would cause panel collapse, glass breakage, or eardrum rupture.

Regarding the obligation to discriminate between military and non-military objects, it is difficult to discriminate regardless of what altitude you're flying when you have a high threat level in a very sophisticated air defense environment. Since emissions are created every time a bomb is dropped or a target is otherwise taken down, aircrews are exposed to increased risk with every successive mission. Regardless of risk to our own forces, however, we still have to comply with the law of armed conflict during offensive operations and we did.

Weapons reliability is always an issue during proportionality analysis. You can talk about the possibility of using missiles that are 100% reliable; however, even the United States cannot afford to buy 100% reliable weapons because the costs are about one to three million dollars per weapon. No country in the world is required by the law of armed conflict to have 100% reliable weapons.

Another problem with weapon accuracy is the delivery system. When you have pilots in the cockpit dropping ordinance or submarines launching Tomahawk land attack missiles, the systems don't always function as advertised when you hit the switch to launch the missile or you "pickle off" the bomb. But, again, the law of armed conflict does not require weapons and delivery systems with 100% reliability, rather it requires the acquisition of weapons systems that are lawful under international law and the exercise of due care when utilizing them. Once it is determined that a target is a legitimate military objective, we must then determine that any unnecessary damage to non-military objects or loss of civilian lives caused by either the choice of weapon, delivery system, or reliability is not excessive in relation to the military advantage anticipated. Of course we must avoid civilian casualties whenever possible and we did that during Operation Allied Force.

The applicability of Protocol I[1] was not an issue from my perspective, because all NATO States applied a common understanding based on customary international law. It is well known that the United States has some reservations with regard to Protocol I, but as far as the execution of Allied Force with our NATO allies, we were able to reach common ground on all the important issues. Every nation signed up to the common NATO rules of engagement developed for Operation Allied Force. These rules also allowed for national reservations when appropriate so that if a country's national laws or policies didn't allow for certain activities, then its national forces would be exempted from those functions.

In summary, I agree with Professor Greenwood's remarks that the law of armed conflict was fully applicable during Operation Allied Force. The targeting analysis was conducted the same as in any other conflict and the captured military personnel were entitled to be treated as prisoners of war.

---

1. Protocol Additional (I) to the Geneva Conventions of 12 August 1949, and Relating to the Protection of Victims of International Conflicts, Jun. 8, 1977, 1125 U.N.T.S. 3, DOCUMENTS ON THE LAWS OF WAR 422 (Adam Roberts & Richard Guelff eds., 3d ed. 2000).

Discussion

The UN Security Council and the Creation of International Law

John Murphy:

Regarding Judy Miller's comment about the United Nations Security Council and its powers of law creation, I would suggest with respect that the Security Council of the United Nations—at least if it's acting under Chapter VII—has the authority to debate, decide, and enforce international law. For more on this issue, I would recommend the two-volume book *United Nations Legal Order*[1] edited by Oscar Schachter and Chris Joyner, which goes into the authority of the UN Security Council and other bodies of the United Nations to create, to interpret, to apply and enforce international law.

George Walker:

I think I agree that Security Council's decisions under Chapter VII are law. Any other resolution of the Security Council, any General Assembly resolution except those governing United Nations governments and most other organizations unless the participants have agreed that they are law, are either supportive of law or the like. General Assembly resolutions may never declare law and they are not law in their own light, but I believe that on the political side of things they can contribute to soft law.

The Law of Neutrality Under the UN Charter

Christopher Greenwood:

Regarding the question of the application of the law of neutrality in an environment where you have Security Council action. I think it is clear that if the Security Council adopts a decision under Chapter VII, that decision or

---

1. UNITED NATIONS LEGAL ORDER (2 vols.), (Oscar Schachter and Christopher C. Joyner eds., 1995).

rather the obligation to comply with it prevails over any other rule of international law. There is, therefore, no difficulty if you have a Security Council decision which, for example, prohibits the delivery of particular goods to a particular State. That is why I have some reservation in trying to draw lessons from what happened in the second Gulf conflict and applying them to the conflict in Kosovo.

In the second Gulf conflict, you had a very clear, unambiguous Security Council Resolution 661,[2] which forbid the delivery of virtually anything to Iraq or Kuwait, and a second resolution, 665,[3] which authorized navies of governments cooperating with the government of Kuwait to enforce 661. Now neither of those conditions was satisfied in the Kosovo conflict. Resolution 1160[4] only applied to the delivery of weapons and military equipment to Yugoslavia and there was no equivalent of 665. So on the critical point about intercepting deliveries of oil to Yugoslavia, there was no Security Council authority. For legal basis, you would have had to fall back on the customary international law principles. That's where I would suggest there is a real difficulty in practice.

Peacekeepers or an Occupying Force?

Christopher Greenwood:

I would just like to say something about the situation after Resolution 1244[5] was adopted because we've only briefly touched on that so far. It seems to me that 1244 moved the goalposts completely with respect to Kosovo because it meant that when ground troops went into Kosovo, they did so under a Security Council mandate. Had that not happened, then I think the legal position would have been a very murky one indeed. Suppose that the Yugoslav government had capitulated as it did, but we had not been able to get a resolution through the Security Council because of the Chinese veto. You would then, I think, be in a position where the troops that now make up KFOR would have been there in effect as belligerent occupants or at least under a regime of belligerent occupation tempered by whatever Yugoslavia had agreed to. That would have been an extremely uncomfortable position indeed. However much we might find 1244 limiting, the law of belligerent occupation would have been a limit a great deal more difficult to live with.

---

2. S.C. Res. 661 (Aug. 6, 1990), U.N. Doc. S/RES/661 (1990).
3. S.C. Res. 665 (Aug. 25, 1990), U.N. Doc. S/RES/665 (1990).
4. S.C. Res. 1160 (Mar. 31, 1998), U.N. Doc. S/RES/1160 (1998).
5. S.C. Res. 1244 (June 10, 1999), U.N. Doc. S/RES/1244 (1999).

Discussion

The Legality of Blockade or Visit & Search

Adam Roberts:

As I recall the way the issue of visit and search arose during the Kosovo events of 1999, there should have been no problem about the application of most of the law of armed conflict because it applies when there is fighting. But I recall it being said that one of the difficulties was that numerous Western leaders in their wisdom had proclaimed that this was not a war. In the United Kingdom we had, for example, a Minister of Defence then, now Secretary-General of NATO, proclaiming repetitiously that this was not a war. Then the suggestion was made that it was particularly difficult to exercise rights of visit and search when Western leaders had been so industriously and, in my opinion, so absurdly claiming that this was not a war. I wonder if there was a connection there between this *jus ad bellum* problem and the application of that particular branch of *jus in bello*.

Christopher Greenwood:

Well I don't think it has anything to do with whether there was a state of war in the formal sense. I really think that is an issue which has become almost completely a museum piece. Having said that, I think that if you repeatedly say in public we are not fighting a war, you are not simply saying there is no technical state of war in being. You are trying to damp down expectations of the level of violence that is going to occur. If you do that, then you almost invariably as a matter of political reality—if not a matter of law—constrain your freedom of action in the future.

Wolff H. von Heinegg:

Let me address the subject of visit and search. I really don't understand this debate over the legal issues involved, because when we are just concentrating upon the legal issues and not on the policies, it is quite clear that at least that part of the law of neutrality would strictly be labeled the law of maritime neutrality. If you look at the law of maritime neutrality and if you look at the works of the International Law Association as well as the San Remo Manual,[6] there is no doubt that as soon as a belligerent decides to conduct visit and search operations it is perfectly in order and in conformity with the existing

---

6. SAN REMO MANUAL ON INTERNATIONAL LAW APPLICABLE TO ARMED CONFLICTS AT SEA ¶¶ 93–104 (Louise Doswald-Beck ed., 1995).

law. In my opinion, this is customary law and there is a customary right of belligerents to conduct visit and search operations.

Now when it comes to certain legal limitations that have been suggested this morning, well I warn you against mixing up self limitations with legal obligations. A belligerent would be entitled to conduct visit and search operations with regard to neutral shipping everywhere in the high seas outside neutral territorial waters. Of course, he probably would not do that in the Atlantic if he is engaged in the Indian Ocean, but that is just a self limitation and nothing else. So when it comes to this part of the law of neutrality that means maritime neutrality, I think there can be no real doubt about the legality of conducting visit and search operations.

Natalino Ronzitti:

We both agree that visit and search is legal as soon as there is an armed conflict. About the legal limitation, there is some practice and precedent that you are entitled to search a ship within the limits of self defense, but it's very difficult to exemplify what these limitations are.

Christopher Greenwood:

I take the point that there are any number of texts from the Naval Commander's Handbook[7] in the United States to the International Law Association to the San Remo Manual that talk about rights of visit and search. I subscribe to the views that the right could have been exercised in these circumstances if it was really necessary to do so. The problem was more a political than a legal one. But I do think we have to go into this with our eyes open. Our own governments would be exceptionally reluctant to accept the exercise of those kind of belligerent rights if we were on the receiving end of them in conflicts in which we were neutral. It is simply not the case today that one can give the kind of confident advice that "don't worry this right is clearly established in customary international law, nothing else to bother about." I think that that would not today be responsible advice for a lawyer to give. Also, I don't accept that limitations as to area are purely politically self-imposed imitations. I think that if Iran had sent frigates to the Mediterranean during the first Gulf war, which it could just about have done, and made a few token visit

---

7. ANNOTATED SUPPLEMENT TO THE COMMANDER'S HANDBOOK ON THE LAW OF NAVAL OPERATIONS (A.R. Thomas and James Duncan eds., 1999) (Vol. 73, US Naval War College International Law Studies).

and searches there, we would not have accepted the legality of that in Britain. The United States would not have accepted its legality either.

Ove Bring:

I think I rather stand on the line with Chris Greenwood being more cautious of the applicability of the law of neutrality in warfare than Wolff von Heinegg who takes a more cock-sure attitude that the traditional law of neutrality is still in place. I take this view because the law of 1907 was adopted at a time when there was no law of collective security—there was no UN Charter. In 1907 the use of force for visit and search purposes was not doubted at all. What has happened since then is that we have the law of collective security: belligerents may not automatically, or perhaps should not automatically at least, rely on the option of the use of force in relationship to States that are not involved in the armed conflict. There is a tension between the law of 1907 and the law of 1945, and that is a logical, legal and ideological tension. I'm not sure that this has resulted in state practice confirming one thing or the other, but it is a matter that should be discussed in legal circles because I think that it is a problem.

Christopher Greenwood:

First of all, without looking to get into the argument about whether the NATO operation in Yugoslavia was lawful or not, I agree entirely that there is a real problem if you have a State that maintains that there is no right of humanitarian intervention at all, or that, if there is, it doesn't apply to Yugoslavia, and then takes the position "what right have you to stop us from trading with an existing trading partner?". But that same problem arises where you have a State not involved in the conflict that says we don't accept your self-defense argument. Obviously you can't contend that there is no right of self-defense in international law.

Exactly the same problem arises if a neutral country says it doesn't accept that Iran is acting in self-defense against Iraq. "We don't accept Iraq is acting in self-defense against Iran, thus what power do you have to prevent us from trading with an existing trading partner." It is, I think, the question mark that hangs over this area of the law of neutrality in the twenty-first century. Now there is an answer to that, and the answer is that the customary international law of neutrality continues to provide certain elements of rights to belligerents irrespective of the legality of the resort to force. If you didn't have some principle of that kind, then you would in effect be scrapping the law of neutrality all together. But I come back to a point I made in my opening statement. Where you have a combination of real doubt—admittedly doubt I don't share, but real doubt nonetheless—about the legal basis for an operation in the first place, coupled with doubts about how far the law of neutrality has survived into the modern era in relation to intercepting ships and doubts about the necessity for such action, then you have a real problem about stopping neutral ships irrespective of what your lawyers tell you.

Applying the LOAC: A Question of Intent or Act?

Ruth Wedgwood:

I had a question for Judy Miller and for anybody else who wants to comment on it. When I recently spoke to Dejan Sahovic who's the new Yugoslav Permanent Representative to the United Nations, he concurred essentially with the conclusion of the Rand Study. His answer to the question "why did Milosevic ultimately step down from the campaign?" was that he thought that Milosevic doubted the ultimate loyalty of the Yugoslav Army. The disloyalty was not ideologically based, but rather that they would fear for the safety and comfort of their own families.

My question is the old catholic question of motive versus purpose, or intention versus act. If in fact we succeeded because the Serbs believed we would reduce Belgrade to a flattened version of Frankfurt or Hamburg after the Second World War, was that a licit kind of animation? The threat of force versus the actual use of force, because we may indeed have chosen our target. I know we chose our targets with great care, but if the Serbs believed we would not let up until everything they used in civilian life was destroyed, then we may have won the war by intimating, or allowing them to conclude, that we would use force in a much more unrelenting way that would raise far greater questions of proportionality.

Judith Miller:

I don't think objectively speaking that the people of Yugoslavia should have had that fear. In point of fact we were not razing parts of Belgrade. In fact, NATO and the United States were saying throughout—and we were saying it because it was true—that we were going to follow the law of armed conflict. So I can't account for the belief, if it occurred, among the army and the civilian population that we were going to practice total war. That simply wasn't in the cards from anyone's perspective, or from anyone's formal or informal statements.

I do think that if in fact somehow that perception is what really drove Milosevic to relent, then that does create some issues for people going forward because you're presumably going to hear military commanders say that we want to do X or Y. We're going to have lawyers even harder pressed to explain you can't do that because it's not allowed under the law of armed conflict. I think it does challenge one's ideas about what it is to engage in hostilities in a world where our every move is covered on CNN and reported instantaneously. It may have reverberations that are somewhat different than we've been accustomed to previously.

Enforcement of the Laws of Armed Conflict and 20/20 Hindsight

Christopher Greenwood:

If I may respond to something Judy Miller said on the question of enforcement. I take the point entirely, and I recognize the difficulty for a civilian in speaking on a subject of this kind to a predominantly military audience. I recognize entirely that it is uncomfortable to have the idea of a judge and a court with twenty-twenty hindsight second guessing the decisions you took in the heat of the moment, but I don't think we should be afraid of this. I don't think we should be worried by the sight of our own shadow.

If you take for example what was happening in Northern Ireland over the last thirty years; any British soldier firing a weapon at somebody in Northern Ireland did so knowing that the decision that he took in the heat of the moment was likely to be hauled over afterwards in great detail by people with twenty-twenty hindsight. The fact of the matter is, it didn't chill all military activity in Northern Ireland. It may have produced some circumstances and cases where we would question the result, but the fact of the matter is that it hasn't handicapped the British forces in what they set out to do. And I don't think the prospect of an International Criminal Court or the International Criminal Tribunal for the former Yugoslavia is going to have that effect on military action in general. Perhaps a more important point is that whether we like it or not, this is a fact of life. It's not something we're going to be able to escape from and there's no point in our pretending otherwise.

W. Hays Parks:

I agree that we often times are judged in law enforcement situations with twenty-twenty hindsight. Every law enforcement officer in the United States, any soldier who uses force in the United States, is subject to a line of cases that govern whether that person should have used deadly force in that circumstance. We have those processes at both the state and federal level. We are not blessed like you are with a European Court of Human Rights. That's your burden. You can have it; we don't want it. The example I can think of is the 1988 SAS killing of the three Irish Republican Army terrorists in Gibraltar. There was a very political 10 to 9 decision that found the use of force unlawful.[8] That's the kind of chilling decision that we are concerned about when talking about judging decisions that commanders make in the fog of war.

Christopher Greenwood:

First, I understand where you're coming from and the answer is you need to make sure you get the right judges. You need to make sure you have people who are not there just because they have a political axe to grind, but are genuinely seeking to apply the law impartially. Then I think you have nothing to fear provided that you get over the second hurdle. It has got to be clearly understood by everybody concerned that you are looking at an event after it happened. Therefore, there is inevitably a degree of detachment and a degree of hindsight, but you have got to apply a test that is actually capable of being applied by somebody in the heat of the moment. There's an English case on self defense from about thirty years ago which contains the passage that detached reflection is not to be expected in the face of an uplifted knife. I think it's essential to appreciate that that is the standard which has to be applied, for example, to any investigation of a pilot's decision to fire a missile on the basis of a couple of seconds in which he had a chance to appreciate the situation in front of him.

Judith Miller:

The problem I have with the International Criminal Court (ICC) is that as it's currently constituted it does not have the sort of ground rules that Christopher Greenwood has pointed to. Impartial judges, impartial prosecutors, and a body of law that is knowable in advance and fairly applied has not been guaranteed by the ICC as currently envisioned and embraced by so many people in the world. I regret personally that we are in this situation. I do not believe the United States is entitled to do what it wants to do without scrutiny. I simply want to have an institution set up that we can rely on, and everyone else in the world can rely on, to do it in a fair way.

---

8. *See* McCann and Others v. the United Kingdom, 324 Eur. Ct. H.R. (ser. A) (1995) holding by only ten votes to nine that United Kingdom had violated the European Convention on Human Rights. The European Commission on Human Rights had previously voted eleven to six that the use of lethal force was "no more than 'absolutely necessary.'" McCann and Others v. the United Kingdom, App. No. 18984/91, Eur. Comm'n. H.R. (Mar. 4, 1994), p. 251.

Discussion

My point about the Report to the Prosecutor is that you must look at that and think about it from the point of view of a lawyer in the Department of Defense trying to give good advice to the secretary and the chairman and everyone else trying to carry out a military mission. If you read that Report and try to figure out what kind of advice you're going to give, then I think it raises a lot of serious questions. So the point I'm making is that there are issues that it raises and approaches that it took that I think are not necessarily the obvious way to interpret the law of armed conflict and apply it in individual instances.

Are the Laws of War a Constraint?

Adam Roberts:

There has been an implication that the laws of armed conflict are essentially a constraining factor on the waging of war. Of course they are a constraining factor, but there are two sub-aspects of that that should be brought out. One is that some of the most important parts of the law of armed conflict don't deal with combat as such, but with the treatment of victims of war, prisoners of war, inhabitants of occupied territory and so on. Those crucially important bits of the law of armed conflict are not as it were affected by this critique, but the law of armed conflict is still constraining in a number of respects.

It's also true that the law of armed conflict is a very important means whereby the conduct of war can be kept within limits which Western publics will accept. In that sense, it is enabling and not constraining. We've seen plenty of evidence of that in the at least three major wars in which Western democracies have been involved in the last twenty years—the Falklands War, the 1991 Gulf War and Kosovo. In all three, a sense that the forces involved were fighting within certain constraints and were treating prisoners honorably and everything else was an important precondition for continued public support for the operations. So while it is true that the laws of war may be constraining, we should not think of them as exclusively a constraining and restraining factor.

PART III

TARGETING

Introduction

Robert F. Turner

This panel will focus on the legal and ethical lessons of NATO's Kosovo campaign as they concern targeting—the *jus in bello* issues of what objects may lawfully be attacked by weapons that are themselves not prohibited by the *jus in bello*.

In my view, no development in US national security law in recent decades has been more important than the development and growth of the field of operational law in the military and the cooperative relationship between the finest legal minds in the US military and the leading scholars on these issues from the United States and around the world has been truly remarkable. The Naval War College anticipated the benefits of such cooperative relationships decades ago with the establishment of the Stockton Chair of International Law and this remarkable colloquium is but a continuation of that tradition.

Legitimate Military Objectives Under The Current Jus In Bello

Yoram Dinstein

The Principle of Distinction and Military Objectives

In its Advisory Opinion of 1996 on *Legality of the Threat or Use of Nuclear Weapons*, the International Court of Justice recognized the "principle of distinction"—between combatants and noncombatants (civilians)—as a fundamental and "intransgressible" principle of customary international law.[1] The requirement of distinction between combatants and civilians lies at the root of the *jus in bello*. It is reflected in Article 48 of Protocol Additional I of 1977 to the 1949 Geneva Conventions for the Protection of War Victims, entitled "Basic rule:" "the Parties to the conflict shall at all times distinguish between the civilian population and combatants and between civilian objects and military objectives and accordingly shall direct their operations only against military objectives."[2] There is no doubt that, irrespective of objections to sundry other

---

1. Advisory Opinion on Legality of the Threat or Use of Nuclear Weapons, 1996 I.C.J. Reports 226, 257 (July 8).
2. Protocol Additional to the Geneva Conventions of 12 August 1949, and Relating to the Protection of Victims of International Armed Conflict, June 8, 1977, 1125 U.N.T.S. 3, DOCUMENTS ON THE LAWS OF WAR 447 (Adam Roberts and Richard Guelff eds., 3d. ed. 2000) [hereinafter Protocol I].

stipulations of Protocol I,[3] "the principle of the military objective has become a part of customary international law for armed conflict" whether on land, at sea or in the air.[4]

The coinage "military objectives" first came into use in the non-binding 1923 Rules of Air Warfare, drawn up at The Hague by a Commission of Jurists[5] (set up in 1922 by the Washington Conference on the Limitation of Armament). It also appears in the 1949 Geneva Conventions for the Protection of War Victims[6] (which fail to define it[7]), the 1954 Hague Convention for the Protection of Cultural Property in the Event of Armed Conflict[8] and especially the 1999 Second Protocol appended to the Cultural Property Convention,[9] as well as the 1998 Rome Statute of the International Criminal Court.[10]

A binding definition of military objectives was crafted in 1977, in Article 52(2) of Protocol I:

> Attacks shall be limited strictly to military objectives. In so far as objects are concerned, military objectives are limited to those objects which by their nature, location, purpose or use make an effective contribution to military

---

3. *See, e.g.*, Guy Roberts, *The New Rules for Waging War: The Case against Ratification of Additional Protocol I*, 26 VIRGINIA JOURNAL OF INTERNATIONAL LAW 109, 124–170 (1985–1986).

4. *See* Horace Robertson, *The Principle of the Military Objective in the Law of Armed Conflict* 197, 207, *in* THE LAW OF MILITARY OPERATIONS, LIBER AMICORUM PROFESSOR JACK GRUNAWALT (Michael Schmitt ed., 1998) (Vol. 72, US Naval War College International Law Studies).

5. Hague Rules of Air Warfare, 1923, DOCUMENTS ON THE LAWS OF WAR, *supra* note 2, art. 24(1), at 139, 144.

6. *See* Geneva Convention (I) for the Amelioration of the Condition of the Wounded and Sick in Armed Forces in the Field, Aug. 12, 1949, DOCUMENTS ON THE LAWS OF WAR, *supra* note 2, art. 19 2d para., at 195, 205; Geneva Convention (IV) Relative to the Protection of Civilian Persons in Time of War, Aug. 12, 1949, *id.*, art. 18 5th para., at 299, 308. Both texts refer to the perils to which medical establishments may be exposed by being situated close to "military objectives."

7. *See* EDWARD KWAKWA, THE INTERNATIONAL LAW OF ARMED CONFLICT: PERSONAL AND MATERIAL FIELDS OF APPLICATION 141 (1992).

8. Hague Convention for the Protection of Cultural Property in the Event of Armed Conflict, May 14, 1954, DOCUMENTS ON THE LAWS OF WAR, *supra* note 2, art. 8(1)(a), at 371, 376.

9. Second Protocol to the Hague Convention of 1954 for the Protection of Cultural Property in the Event of Armed Conflict, Mar. 26, 1999, DOCUMENTS ON THE LAWS OF WAR, *supra* note 2, art. 6(a), 8, 13(1)(b), at 699, 702, 703–4, 706.

10. Rome Statute of the International Criminal Court, Jul. 17, 1998, DOCUMENTS ON THE LAWS OF WAR, *supra* note 2, art. 8(2)(b)(ii), (v), (ix), at 667, 676–7.

action and whose total or partial destruction, capture or neutralization, in the circumstances ruling at the time, offers a definite military advantage.[11]

The term "attacks" is defined in Article 49(1) of the Protocol as "acts of violence against the adversary, whether in offence or in defence."[12] Any act of violence fits this matrix: not only massive air attacks or artillery barrages, but also small-scale attacks (like a sniper firing a single bullet). As Article 52(2) elucidates, all attacks must be strictly limited to military objectives.

The definition of military objectives appearing in Article 52(2) is repeated word-for-word in several subsequent instruments: Protocols II and III, Annexed to the 1980 Convention on Prohibitions or Restrictions on the Use of Certain Conventional Weapons Which May Be Deemed to be Excessively Injurious or to Have Indiscriminate Effects;[13] and the 1999 Second Protocol to the Hague Cultural Property Convention.[14] It is also replicated in the (non-binding) San Remo Manual of 1995 on International Law Applicable to Armed Conflicts at Sea.[15] Many scholars regard the definition as embodying customary international law.[16] With one significant textual modification—to be examined *infra*—that is also the view of the United States, which objects on other grounds to Protocol I.[17]

Notwithstanding its authoritative status, Article 52(2)'s definition leaves a lot to be desired. It is an exaggeration to claim (as does Antonio Cassese) that "[t]his definition is so sweeping that it can cover practically anything."[18] Still, it is regrettable that the wording is abstract and generic, and no list of specific military objectives is provided (if only on an illustrative, non-exhaustive basis). Under Article 57(2)(a)(i) of the Protocol, those who plan or decide upon an

---

11. Protocol I, *supra* note 2, at 450.
12. *Id.* at 447.
13. Convention on Prohibitions or Restrictions on the Use of Certain Conventional Weapons Which May Be Deemed to be Excessively Injurious or to Have Indiscriminate Effects, Oct. 10, 1980, DOCUMENTS ON THE LAWS OF WAR, *supra* note 2, at 515; Protocol II on Prohibitions or Restrictions on the Use of Mines, Booby Traps and Other Devices, *id.*, art. 2(4), at 528; Protocol III on Prohibitions or Restrictions on the Use of Incendiary Weapons, *id.*, art. 1(3), at 533.
14. Second Protocol, *supra* note 9, art. 1(f), at 701.
15. SAN REMO MANUAL ON INTERNATIONAL LAW APPLICABLE TO ARMED CONFLICTS AT SEA 114 (Louis Doswald-Beck ed., 1995).
16. *See* THEODOR MERON, HUMAN RIGHTS AND HUMANITARIAN NORMS AS CUSTOMARY LAW 64–65 (1989).
17. *See* ANNOTATED SUPPLEMENT TO THE COMMANDER'S HANDBOOK ON THE LAW OF NAVAL OPERATIONS 402 n.9 (A.R. Thomas & J.C. Duncan eds., 1999) (Vol. 73, US Naval War College International Law Studies).
18. ANTONIO CASSESE, INTERNATIONAL LAW 339 (2001).

attack must "do everything feasible to verify that the objectives to be attacked ... are military objectives within the meaning of paragraph 2 of Article 52."[19] Due to its abstract character, the definition in Article 52(2) does not produce a workable acid test for such verification. The text lends itself to "divergent interpretations" in application, and, needless to say, perhaps, "[a]mbiguous language encourages abuse."[20]

The relative advantages of a general definition versus an enumeration of military objectives—or a combination of both—have been thoroughly discussed in connection with the preparation of the San Remo Manual.[21] The present writer believes that only a composite definition—combining an abstract statement with a non-exhaustive catalogue of concrete illustrations[22]—can effectively avoid vagueness, on the one hand, and inability to anticipate future scenarios, on the other. No abstract definition standing by itself (unaccompanied by actual examples) can possibly offer a practical solution to real problems emerging—often in dismaying rapidity—on the battlefield.

The noun "objects," used in the definition, clearly encompasses material and tangible things.[23] However, the phrase "military objectives" is certainly not limited to inanimate objects,[24] and it is wrong to suggest that the Protocol's language fails to cover enemy military personnel.[25] To be on the safe side, the framers of Article 52(2) added the (otherwise superfluous) words "[i]n so far as objects are concerned," underscoring that not only inanimate objects constitute military objectives. Human beings can categorically come within

---

19. Protocol I, *supra* note 2, at 452.
20. ESBJORN ROSENBLAD, INTERNATIONAL HUMANITARIAN LAW OF ARMED CONFLICT 71 (1979).
21. SAN REMO MANUAL, *supra* note 15, at 114–116. See also William Fenrick, *Military Objectives in the Law of Naval Warfare*, in THE MILITARY OBJECTIVE AND THE PRINCIPLE OF DISTINCTION IN THE LAW OF NAVAL WARFARE: REPORT, COMMENTARIES AND PROCEEDINGS OF THE ROUND-TABLE OF EXPERTS ON INTERNATIONAL HUMANITARIAN LAW APPLICABLE TO ARMED CONFLICTS AT SEA 1, 4–5 (Wolff Heintschel v. Heinegg ed., 1991).
22. This legal technique is epitomized in Articles 2–3 of the 1974 General Assembly consensus Definition of Aggression, G.A. Resolution 3314 (XXIX), 15 UNITED NATIONS RESOLUTIONS: SERIES I, RESOLUTIONS ADOPTED BY THE GENERAL ASSEMBLY 392, 393 (Dusan Djonovich ed., 1984).
23. Claude Pilloud & Jean Pictet, *Article 52*, in COMMENTARY ON THE ADDITIONAL PROTOCOLS OF 8 JUNE 1977 TO THE GENEVA CONVENTIONS OF 12 AUGUST 1949, at 633–4 (Yves Sandoz et al. eds., 1987).
24. *See* A.P.V. ROGERS, LAW ON THE BATTLEFIELD 33 (1996).
25. Such a suggestion is made by Hamilton DeSaussure, *Comment*, 31 AMERICAN UNIVERSITY LAW REVIEW 883, 885 (1981–1982).

the ambit of military objectives.[26] Indeed, human beings are not the only living creatures that do. Certain types of animals—cavalry horses and pack mules in particular—can also be legitimate targets.

The pivotal issue is what ingredient or dimension serves to identify a military objective. On the face of it, under Article 52(2), an object must fulfill two cumulative criteria in order to qualify as a military objective: (a) by nature, location, purpose or use it must make an effective contribution to military action; and (b) its destruction, capture or neutralization, in the circumstances ruling at the time, must offer a definite military advantage.[27] However,

> In practice . . . one cannot imagine that the destruction, capture, or neutralization of an object contributing to the military action of one side would not be militarily advantageous for the enemy; it is just as difficult to imagine how the destruction, capture, or neutralization of an object could be a military advantage for one side if that same object did not somehow contribute to the military action of the enemy.[28]

Article 52(2) refers to "a definite military advantage" that must be gained from the (total or partial) destruction, capture or neutralization[29] of the targets. The expression "a definite military advantage" (like "military objectives") is derived from the Hague Rules of Air Warfare, which resorted to the formula "a distinct military advantage."[30] There is no apparent difference in the present context between the adjectives "distinct" and "definite" or, for that matter, several other alternatives pondered by the framers of Article 52(2).[31] Whatever the adjective preferred, the idea conveyed is that of "a concrete and perceptible military advantage rather than a hypothetical and

---

26. See Elmar Rauch, *Attack Restraints, Target Limitations and Prohibitions or Restrictions of Use of Certain Conventional Weapons*, 18 REVUE DE DROIT PÉNAL MILITAIRE ET DE DROIT DE LA GUERRE 51, 55 (1979).
27. See MARCO SASSÒLI & ANTOINE BOUVIER, HOW DOES LAW PROTECT IN WAR: CASES, DOCUMENTS, AND TEACHING MATERIALS ON CONTEMPORARY PRACTICE IN INTERNATIONAL HUMANITARIAN LAW 161 (1999).
28. *Id.* at 140.
29. The term "neutralization" in this setting means denial of use of an objective to the enemy without destroying it. See Waldemar Solf, *Article 52*, in NEW RULES FOR VICTIMS OF ARMED CONFLICTS: COMMENTARY ON THE TWO 1977 PROTOCOLS ADDITIONAL TO THE GENEVA CONVENTIONS OF 1949, at 318, 325 (Michael Bothe, Karl Partsch & Waldemar Solf eds., 1982).
30. Hague Rules of Air Warfare, *supra* note 5, art. 24(1), at 144.
31. See Frits Kalshoven, *Reaffirmation and Development of International Humanitarian Law Applicable in Armed Conflicts: The Diplomatic Conference, Geneva, 1974–1977, Part II*, 9 NETHERLANDS YEARBOOK OF INTERNATIONAL LAW 107, 111 (1978).

speculative one."[32] The advantage gained must be military and not, say, purely political[33] (hence, "forcing a change in the negotiating attitudes" of the adverse party[34] cannot be deemed a proper military advantage). But when coalition war is being waged, the military advantage may accrue to the benefit of an allied country—or the alliance in general—rather than the attacking party itself.[35]

The process of appraising military advantage must be made against the background of the circumstances prevailing at the time, so that the same object may be legitimately attacked in one temporal framework but not in others.[36] A church, as a place of worship, is not a military objective; nor is it a military objective when converted into a hospital; yet, if the church steeple is used by snipers, it becomes a military objective.[37] In this sense, the definition of military objectives is "relativized:"[38] there is "no fixed borderline between civilian objects and military objectives."[39]

The trouble is that the notion of "military advantage" is not singularly helpful. Surely, military advantage is not restricted to tactical gains.[40] The spectrum is necessarily wide, and it extends to the security of the attacking force.[41] The key problem is that the outlook of the attacking party is unlikely to match that of the party under attack in evaluating the long-term military benefits of any action contemplated.[42] Moreover, the dominant view is that assessment of the military advantage can be made in light of "an attack as a

---

32. Solf, *supra* note 29, at 326.
33. *See* Hamilton DeSaussure, *Remarks*, 2 AMERICAN UNIVERSITY JOURNAL OF INTERNATIONAL LAW AND POLICY 511, 513–514 (1987).
34. Forcing such a change is viewed (wrongly) as a legitimate military advantage by Burrus Carnahan, *'Linebacker II' and Protocol I: The Convergence of Law and Professionalism*, 31 AMERICAN UNIVERSITY LAW REVIEW 861, 867 (1981–1982).
35. *See* Henri Meyrowitz, *Le Bombardement Stratégique d'après le Protocole Additionnel I aux Conventions de Genève*, 41 ZEITSCHRIFT FÜR AUSLÄNDISCHES ÖFFENTLICHES RECHT UND VÖLKERRECHT (ZAÖRV) 1, 41 (1981).
36. *See* DeSaussure, *supra* note 33, at 513.
37. *See* B.A. Wortley, *Observations on the Revision of the 1949 Geneva 'Red Cross' Conventions*, 54 BRITISH YEAR BOOK OF INTERNATIONAL LAW 143, 154 (1983).
38. GEOFFREY BEST, WAR AND LAW SINCE 1945, at 272 (1994).
39. Albrecht Randelzhofer, *Civilian Objects*, in 1 ENCYCLOPEDIA OF PUBLIC INTERNATIONAL LAW 603, 604 (Rudolf Bernhardt ed., 1992).
40. *See* James Burger, *International Humanitarian Law and the Kosovo Crisis: Lessons Learned or to Be Learned*, 82 INTERNATIONAL REVIEW OF THE RED CROSS 129, 132 (2000).
41. *See* ANNOTATED SUPPLEMENT TO THE COMMANDER'S HANDBOOK ON THE LAW OF NAVAL OPERATIONS, *supra* note 17, at 402.
42. *See* Dieter Fleck, *Strategic Bombing and the Definition of Military Objectives*, 27 ISRAEL YEARBOOK ON HUMAN RIGHTS 41, 48 (1997).

whole," as distinct from "isolated or specific parts of the attack."[43] The attacking party may thus argue, e.g., that an air raid of no perceptible military advantage in itself is justified by having misled the enemy to shift its strategic gaze to the wrong sector of the front.[44] Nonetheless, "an attack as a whole" is a finite event, not to be confused with the entire war.[45]

The Definition of Military Objectives by Nature, Location, Purpose and Use

The text of Article 52(2) incorporates helpful definitional guidelines by adverting to the nature, location, purpose and use of military objectives "making an effective contribution to military action." The requirement of effective contribution relates to military action in general, and there need be no "direct connection" with specific combat operations.[46] All the same, an American attempt (reflected in the United States' Commander's Handbook on the Law of Naval Operations[47]) to substitute the words "military action" by the idiom "war-fighting or war-sustaining capability," goes too far.[48] The "war-fighting" limb can pass muster, since it may be looked upon as equivalent to military action.[49] But the "war-sustaining" portion is too broad. The American position is that "[e]conomic targets of the enemy that indirectly but effectively support and sustain the enemy's war-fighting capability may also be attacked," and the example offered is that of the destruction of raw cotton within Confederate territory by Union forces during the Civil War on the ground that the sale of cotton provided funds for almost all Confederate arms and ammunition.[50] As will be seen *infra*, multiple economic objects do constitute military objectives, inasmuch as they directly support military action. Yet, the raw cotton illustration (which may be substituted today by the instance of a country relying

---

43. See Stefan Oeter, *Methods and Means of Combat, in* THE HANDBOOK OF HUMANITARIAN LAW IN ARMED CONFLICTS 105, 162 (Dieter Fleck ed., 1995).
44. See Solf, *supra* note 29, at 325.
45. See Francoise Hampson, *Means and Methods of Warfare in the Conflict in the Gulf, in* THE GULF WAR 1990–91 IN INTERNATIONAL AND ENGLISH LAW 89, 94 (Peter Rowe ed., 1993).
46. See Solf, *supra* note 29, at 324.
47. ANNOTATED SUPPLEMENT TO THE COMMANDER'S HANDBOOK ON THE LAW OF NAVAL OPERATIONS, *supra* note 17, at 402.
48. See JAMES BUSUTTIL, NAVAL WEAPONS SYSTEMS AND THE CONTEMPORARY LAW OF WAR 148 (1998).
49. Roberts, *supra* note 4, at 209.
50. ANNOTATED SUPPLEMENT TO THE COMMANDER'S HANDBOOK ON THE LAW OF NAVAL OPERATIONS, *supra* note 17, at 403.

almost entirely on the export of coffee beans or bananas)[51] displays the danger of introducing the slippery-slope concept of "war-sustaining capability." The connection between military action and exports, required to finance the war effort, is "too remote."[52] Had raw cotton been acknowledged as a valid military objective, almost every civilian activity might be construed by the enemy as indirectly sustaining the war effort (especially when hostilities are protracted). For an object to qualify as a military objective, there must exist a proximate nexus to military action (or "war-fighting"). No wonder that the San Remo Manual rejected an attempt to incorporate the wording "war-sustaining effort."[53]

As far as "nature, location, purpose or use" are concerned, each of these terms deserves a closer look.

1. The Nature of the Objective

"Nature" denotes the intrinsic character of the military objective. To meet this yardstick, an object (or living creature) must be endowed with some inherent attribute which *eo ipso* makes an effective contribution to military action. As such, the object, person, etc., automatically constitutes a legitimate target for attack in wartime.

Although no list of military objectives by nature has been compiled in a binding manner, the following non-exhaustive enumeration is believed by the present writer to reflect current legal thinking:[54]

(a) Fixed military fortifications, bases, barracks[55] and installations, including training and war-gaming facilities;

(b) Temporary military camps, entrenchments, staging areas, deployment positions, and embarkation points;

---

51. See ROGERS, *supra* note 24, at 41.
52. See SAN REMO MANUAL, *supra* note 15, at 161.
53. *Id.* at 150.
54. Compare the various lists of legitimate military objectives offered by ANNOTATED SUPPLEMENT TO THE COMMANDER'S HANDBOOK ON THE LAW OF NAVAL OPERATIONS, *supra* note 17, at 402; A.P.V. ROGERS & PAUL MALHERBE, MODEL MANUAL ON THE LAW OF ARMED CONFLICT 72 (1999). *See also* LESLIE GREEN, THE CONTEMPORARY LAW OF ARMED CONFLICT 191 (2d ed. 2000).
55. A question has been raised about the status of deserted military barracks (*see* Konstantin Obradovic, *International Humanitarian Law and the Kosovo Crisis*, 82 INTERNATIONAL REVIEW OF THE RED CROSS 699, 720 (2000)). But the whole point about military barracks is that they constitute a military objective *per se*, irrespective of being deserted. When military units are stationed there, they qualify as military objectives by themselves (see (c)).

(c) Military units and individual members of the armed forces, whether stationed or mobile;

(d) Weapon systems, military equipment and ordnance, armor and artillery, and military vehicles of all types;

(e) Military aircraft and missiles of all types;

(f) Military airfields and missile launching sites;

(g) Warships (whether surface vessels or submarines) of all types;

(h) Military ports and docks;

(i) Military depots, munitions dumps, warehouses or stockrooms for the storage of weapons, ordnance, military equipment and supplies (including raw materials for military use, such as petroleum);

(j) Factories (even when privately owned) engaged in the manufacture of arms, munitions and military supplies;

(k) Laboratories or other facilities for the research and development of new weapons and military devices;

(l) Military repair facilities;

(m) Power plants (electric, hydroelectric, etc.) serving the military;

(n) Arteries of transportation of strategic importance, principally mainline railroads and rail marshaling yards, major motorways (like the interstate highways in the US,[56] the *Autobahnen* in Germany and the *autostradas* in Italy), navigable rivers and canals (including the tunnels and bridges of railways and trunk roads);

(o) Ministries of Defense and any national, regional or local operational or coordination center of command, control and communication relating to running the war (including computer centers, as well as telephone and telegraph exchanges, for military use);

(p) Intelligence-gathering centers (even when not run by the military establishment).

---

56. Appropriately enough, the mammoth US interstate highway network (with a total length of more than 45,000 miles)—initiated by President Eisenhower—is formally known as the National System of Interstate and Defense Highways. *See* 26 THE NEW ENCYCLOPEDIA BRITANNICA 324 (15th ed. 1997).

2. The Purpose of the Objective

More often than not, the "purpose" of a military objective is determined either by its (inherent) nature or by its (de facto) use. But if the word "purpose" in Article 52(2) is not redundant, it must be distinguished from both nature and use. The present writer is of the opinion that the purpose of an object—as a separate ground for classifying it as a military target—is determined after the crystallization of its original nature, yet prior to actual use. In other words, the military purpose is assumed not to be stamped on the objective from the outset (otherwise, the target would be military by nature). Military purpose is deduced from an established intention of a belligerent as regards future use. As pointed out by the official ICRC Commentary: "the criterion of *purpose* is concerned with the intended future use of an object, while that of *use* is concerned with its present function."[57]

At times, enemy intentions are crystal clear, and then the branding of an object (by purpose) as a military target becomes rather easy. A good illustration might be that of a civilian luxury liner, which a belligerent overtly plans (already in peacetime) to turn into a troop ship at the moment of general mobilization. Although by nature a civilian object, and not yet in use as a troop ship, it may be attacked as a military objective at the outbreak of hostilities (assuming that it is no longer serving as a passenger liner).

Unfortunately, most enemy intentions are not so easy to decipher, and then much depends on the gathering and analysis of intelligence which may be faulty. In case of doubt, caution is called for. Thus, field intelligence revealing that the enemy intends to use a particular school as a munitions depot does not justify an attack against the school as long as the munitions have not been moved in.[58] The Allied bombing in 1944 of the famous Abbey of Monte Cassino is a notorious case of a decision founded on flimsy intelligence reports, linked to a firm supposition ("the abbey made such a perfect observation point that surely no army could have refrained from using it") which turned out to have been entirely false.[59] This writer cannot accept the conclusion that the Abbey was a military objective only because it appeared to be important to deny its potential use to an enemy (who in reality refrained from using it).[60] Purpose is predicated on intentions known to guide the adversary, and not on those figured out hypothetically in contingency plans based on a "worst case scenario."

---

57. Pilloud & Pictet, *supra* note 23, at 636.
58. *See* ROGERS, *supra* note 24, at 36.
59. *Id.* at 54–55.
60. *Id.* at 55.

3. The Use of the Objective

Actual "use" of an objective does not depend necessarily on its original nature or on any (later) intended purpose. A leading example is that of the celebrated "Taxis of the Marne" commandeered in September 1914 to transport French reserves to the frontline, thereby saving Paris from the advancing German forces.[61] "So long as these privately owned taxicabs were operated for profit and served their normal purposes, they were not military equipment. Once they were requisitioned for the transportation of French troops, their function changed."[62] They became military objectives through use.

Article 52(3) of the Protocol prescribes: "In case of doubt whether an object which is normally dedicated to civilian purposes, such as a place of worship, a house or other dwelling or a school, is being used to make an effective contribution to military action, it shall be presumed not to be so used."[63] There are three elements here:

(a) Certain objects are normally (by nature) dedicated to civilian purposes and, as long as they fulfill only their essential function, they must not be treated as military targets. The examples given are places of worship, civilian dwellings and schools.

(b) The same objects may nevertheless be used in actuality in a manner making an effective contribution to military action. When (and as long as) they are subject to such use, outside their original function, they can be treated as military objectives. The dominant consideration should be "the circumstances ruling at the time" (referred to in the text of Article 52(2)).

(c) Article 52(3) adds a caveat that, in case of doubt whether an object normally dedicated to civilian purposes is actually used to make an effective contribution to military action, it must "be presumed not to be so used." The presumption has given rise to controversy at the time of the drafting of this clause, and an attempt to create an exception with respect to objects located in the contact zone failed in the ensuing vote.[64] While the results of the vote may reflect a "[r]efusal to recognize the realities of combat" in some situations,[65] it must be taken into account that the presumption (which is rebuttable) comes into play only in case of doubt. Often there is no doubt at all, especially when combatants are exposed to direct fire from a supposedly

---

61. *See* GEORGE SCHWARZENBERGER, 2 INTERNATIONAL LAW AS APPLIED BY INTERNATIONAL COURTS AND TRIBUNALS: THE LAW OF ARMED CONFLICT 112 (1968).
62. *Id.* at 113.
63. Protocol I, *supra* note 2, at 450.
64. *See* Solf, *supra* note 29, at 326–327.
65. *See* W. Hays Parks, *Air War and the Law of War*, 32 AIR FORCE LAW REVIEW 1, 137 (1990).

civilian object.[66] If, for instance, the minaret of a mosque is used as a sniper's nest, the presumption is rebutted and the enemy is entitled to treat it as a military objective.[67] The degree of doubt that has to exist prior to the emergence of the (rebuttable) presumption is by no means clear. But surely that doubt has to exist in the mind of the attacker, based upon "the circumstances ruling at the time."

It follows that, by dint of military use (or, more precisely, abuse), virtually every civilian object—albeit, innately, deemed worthy of protection by the *jus in bello*—can become a military objective.[68]

4. The Location of the Objective

"Location" of an objective must be factored in, irrespective of the nature, purpose and use thereof. Logic dictates that, if a civilian-by-nature object (like a supermarket) is located within a sprawling military base, it cannot be immune from attack. If a merchant vessel is anchored in a military port, it becomes a military objective by location.

The real issue with respect to location goes beyond these elementary observations. The notion underlying the reference to location is that a specific land area can be regarded per se as a military objective.[69] Surely, the incidence of such locations cannot be too widespread: there must be a distinctive feature turning a piece of land into a military objective (e.g., a mountain pass, a specific hill of strategic value, a bridgehead or a spit of land controlling the entrance of a harbor).[70]

5. Bridges

The quadruple subdivision of military objectives by nature, purpose, use and location is not as neat as it sounds, and certain objectives can be catalogued within more than one subset. Bridges may serve as a prime illustration. Bridges constructed for the engineering needs of major motorways and rail tracks are surely integrated in the overall network: like the roads and the tracks that they serve, they constitute military objectives by nature. But even where bridges connect non-arterial lines of transportation, as long as they are

---

66. *See* Solf, *supra* note 29, at 327.
67. Countless other examples can be postulated. Rogers refers to the case of a cathedral used as divisional headquarters. ROGERS, *supra* note 24, at 35.
68. *See* SASSÒLI & BOUVIER, *supra* note 27, at 161.
69. For the underlying reasons, see ROGERS, *supra* note 24, at 38–39.
70. See Elmar Rauch, *The Protection of the Civilian Population in International Armed Conflicts and the Use of Landmines*, 24 GERMAN YEARBOOK OF INTERNATIONAL LAW 262, 273–277 (1981).

apt to have a perceptible role in the transport of military reinforcements and supplies, their destruction is almost self-explanatory as a measure playing havoc with enemy logistics. It is wrong to assume (as does Michael Bothe in the context of bridges targeted during the Kosovo air campaign of 1999) that bridges can be attacked only "where supplies destined for the front must pass over" them.[71] The destruction of bridges can be effected to disrupt any movements of troops and military supplies, not necessarily in the direction of the front.

If not by nature, most bridges may qualify as military objectives by purpose, use or—above all—location.[72] Every significant waterway or similar geophysical obstruction to traffic (like a ravine) must be perceived as a possible military barrier, and there comes a time when the strategy of either belligerent would dictate that all bridges (even the smallest pedestrian overpass) across the obstacle have to be destroyed or neutralized. Surely, there is nothing wrong in a military policy striving to effect a fragmentation of enemy land forces through the destruction of all bridges—however minor in themselves—spanning a wide river. Thus, in the Gulf War in 1991, destruction of bridges over the Euphrates River impeded the deployment of Iraqi forces and their supplies (severing also communications cables).[73]

It has been asserted that "[b]ridges are not, as such, military objectives,"[74] and that a bridge is like a school: the question whether it "represents a military objective depends entirely on the actual situation."[75] However, the comparison between bridges and schools is meretricious. A school is recognized as a military objective only in the extraordinary circumstances of military use by the adverse party. A bridge, as a rule, would qualify as a military objective (by nature, location, purpose or use). It would fail to be a military objective only under exceptional conditions, when it is neither actually nor potentially of any military use to the enemy.

---

71. Michael Bothe, *The Protection of the Civilian Population and NATO Bombing on Yugoslavia: Comments on a Report to the Prosecutor of the ICTY*, 12 EUROPEAN JOURNAL OF INTERNATIONAL LAW 531, 534 (2001).
72. For the view that bridges are military objectives by location, see Pilloud & Pictet, *supra* note 23, at 636.
73. *See* ROGERS, *supra* note 24, at 42.
74. Francoise Hampson, *Proportionality and Necessity in the Gulf Conflict*, 86 PROCEEDINGS OF THE AMERICAN SOCIETY OF INTERNATIONAL LAW 45, 49 (1992).
75. FRITS KALSHOVEN, CONSTRAINTS ON THE WAGING OF WAR 90 (1987).

6. Military Objectives Exempt from Attack

The determination that an object constitutes a military objective is not always conclusive in legitimizing an attack. Some objects are exempted from attack, notwithstanding their distinct character as military objectives. The most extreme illustration appears in Article 56(1) of the Protocol:

> Works or installations containing dangerous forces, namely dams, dykes and nuclear electrical generating stations, shall not be made the object of attack, even where these objects are military objectives, if such attack may cause the release of dangerous forces and consequent severe losses among the civilian population. Other military objectives located at or in the vicinity of these works and installations shall not be made the object of attack if such attack may cause the release of dangerous forces from the works or installations and consequent severe losses among the civilian population.[76]

Granted, according to Article 56(2), the special protection is not unqualified: it ceases when the dam, dyke or nuclear electrical generating station regularly, significantly and directly supports military operations, and there is no other feasible way to terminate such support.[77] In any event, the entire stipulation of Article 56 is innovative and binding only on contracting Parties.

For their part, the Geneva Conventions prohibit attacks against protected military persons, i.e., those combatants who become *hors de combat*, either by choice (through surrender) or by force of circumstances (being wounded, sick or shipwrecked);[78] fixed establishments and mobile military medical units of the Medical Service;[79] hospital ships;[80] medical aircraft;[81] medical personnel engaged in the treatment of the wounded and sick;[82] and chaplains attached to the armed forces[83] (to name the most important categories). Protection

---

76. Protocol I, *supra* note 2, at 451.
77. Id.
78. Geneva Convention (I), art. 12, *supra* note 6, at 379; Geneva Convention (II) for the Amelioration of the Condition of Wounded, Sick and Shipwrecked Members of Armed Forces at Sea, Aug. 12, 1949, art. 12, DOCUMENTS ON THE LAWS OF WAR, *supra* note 2, at 221, 226–7; Geneva Convention (III) Relative to the Treatment of Prisoners of War, Aug. 12, 1949, *id.* art. 13, at 243, 250.
79. Geneva Convention (I), *supra* note 6, art. 19, at 205.
80. Geneva Convention (II), *supra* note 78, art. 22, at 230.
81. Geneva Convention (I), *supra* note 6, art. 36, at 210–1.
82. Id., art. 24, at 207.
83. Id.

from attack is also granted by customary international law to other categories, like cartel ships.[84]

Additionally, an attack against a military objective—which is not protected as such—may be illicit owing to the principle of proportionality, whereby the "collateral damage" or injury to civilians (or civilian objects) must not be excessive. This issue is dealt with separately by the present writer.

General Problems Relating to the Scope of Military Objectives

The definition of military objectives, as discussed *supra*, raises a number of question marks:

1. Retreating troops

It is sometimes contended that when an army has been routed, and its soldiers are retreating in disarray—as epitomized by the Iraqi land forces during the Gulf War—they should not be further attacked.[85] But this is a serious misconception. The only way for members of the armed forces to immunize themselves from further attack is to surrender, thereby becoming *hors de combat*.[86] Otherwise, as the Gulf War amply demonstrates, the fleeing soldiers of today are likely to regroup tomorrow as viable military units.

2. Targeting Individuals

Is it permissible to target specific individuals who are members of the armed forces? As a rule, when a person takes up arms or merely dons a uniform as a member of the armed forces, he automatically exposes himself to enemy attack (even if he does not participate in actual hostilities and does not pose an immediate threat to the enemy). The *jus in bello* prohibits treacherous assassination, yet nothing prevents singling out as a target an individual enemy combatant (provided that the attack is carried out by combatants).[87] The prohibition of assassination does not cover "attacks, by regular armed military forces, on specific individuals who are themselves legitimate military targets."[88] The United States was, consequently, well within its rights during

---

84. *See* Louise Doswald-Beck, *Vessels, Aircraft and Persons Entitled to Protection during Armed Conflicts at Sea*, 65 BRITISH YEAR BOOK OF INTERNATIONAL LAW 211, 239 (1994).
85. *See* ERIC DAVID, PRINCIPES DE DROIT DES CONFLITS ARMÉS 246 (2d ed. 1999).
86. *See* Peter Barber, *Scuds, Shelters and Retreating Soldiers: The Laws of Aerial Bombardment in the Gulf War*, 31 ALBERTA LAW REVIEW 662, 690 (1993).
87. *See* ROGERS & MALHERBE, *supra* note 54, at 62.
88. Burrus Carnahan, *Correspondent's Report*, 2 YEARBOOK OF INTERNATIONAL HUMANITARIAN LAW 423, 424 (1999).

World War II when it specifically targeted the Commander-in-Chief of the Japanese Fleet, Admiral Yamamoto, whose plane was ambushed (subsequent to the successful breaking of the Japanese communication codes) and shot down over Bougainville in 1943.[89] The ambush of the car of SS General Heydrich in 1942 is different, but only because he was killed by members of the Free Czechoslovak army (parachuted from London) who were not wearing uniforms and were therefore not lawful combatants: otherwise, Heydrich—as a military officer—was a legitimate target, just like Yamamoto.[90]

3. Police

Can police officers and other law enforcement agents be subsumed under the heading of members of armed forces (who are legitimately subject to attack)? The answer to the question depends on whether the policemen have been officially incorporated into the armed forces[91] or (despite the absence of official incorporation) have taken part in hostilities.[92] If integrated into the armed forces, policemen—like all combatants—"may be attacked at any time simply because they have that particular status."[93]

4. Industrial plants

It is exceedingly difficult to draw a dividing line between military and civilian industries. Sometimes, even the facts are hard to establish. Who is to say whether a textile factory is producing military uniforms or civilian clothing? In wartime, civilian consumption gives way as a matter of course to military priorities. Can one seriously asseverate that certain steel works ought not to be classified as military objectives only because their output has heretofore been channeled to the civilian market? The long-time civilian-oriented character of an industrial center in peacetime provides no guarantee that production would not transition in the course of hostilities into war materials. A line of production, even when introduced for plainly civilian ends (e.g., tractors for agricultural use), can often be swiftly adjusted to military use (in this

---

89. *See* Joseph Kelly, *Assassination in War Time*, 30 MILITARY LAW REVIEW 101, 102–103 (1965).
90. *See* Patricia Zengel, *Assassination and the Law of Armed Conflict*, 43 MERCER LAW REVIEW 615, 628 (1991–1992).
91. On such incorporation, *cf.* Article 43(3) of Protocol I, *supra* note 2, at 444.
92. See Peter Rowe, *Kosovo 1999: The Air Campaign*, 82 INTERNATIONAL REVIEW OF THE RED CROSS 147, 150–151 (2000).
93. *Id.* at 151.

instance, the assembly of tracked vehicles, such as tanks). The children's toys factory of today may become tomorrow's leading manufacturer of electronic precision-munitions. Besides, in the present era of high technology, the construction of any computer hardware architecture or software program can turn into a central pillar of the war effort.[94] "The problem is that the [computer] technology capable of performing ... [military] functions differs little, if at all, from that used in the civilian community."[95] If that is not enough, subcontracting in the manufacture of components of modern weapon systems causes a dispersion in the fabrication of war materials which is almost impossible to trail.[96] All in all, it is easy to object to the automatic removal of any industrial plant from the list of military objectives.

5. Oil, coal and other minerals

What is the status of oil fields and rigs, refineries, coal mines, and other mineral extraction plants, which are not ostensibly tied to military production? In the final analysis, despite their civilian bearings, all of them can be deemed to constitute the infrastructure of the military industry. It can well be argued that "oil installations of every kind are in fact legitimate military objectives open to destruction by any belligerent."[97] As for petrol filling stations, only those functioning in civilian residential areas—away from major motorways—may be exempted from attack.

6. Electric grids

Can power plants in civilian metropolitan areas be set apart from military power plants? During the Gulf War, the Coalition air campaign in 1991 treated as a military target the integrated Iraqi national grid generating and distributing electricity (used both by the armed forces and civilians).[98] Undeniably, an integrated power grid makes an effective contribution to modern military action:[99] any shortfall in military requirements can be compensated at

---

94. As regards the growing military reliance on computers, see Michael Schmitt, *Computer Network Attacks and the Use of Force in International Law: Thoughts on a Normative Framework*, 37 COLUMBIA JOURNAL OF TRANSNATIONAL LAW 885, 887 (1998–1999).
95. Michael Schmitt, *Future War and the Principle of Discrimination*, 28 ISRAEL YEARBOOK ON HUMAN RIGHTS 51, 68 (1998).
96. See Parks, *supra* note 65, at 140.
97. Leslie Green, *The Environment and the Law of Conventional Warfare*, 29 CANADIAN YEARBOOK OF INTERNATIONAL LAW 222, 233 (1991).
98. See Christopher Greenwood, *Customary International Law and the First Geneva Protocol of 1977 in the Gulf Conflict*, in THE GULF WAR 1990–91, *supra* note 45, at 63, 73.
99. *Id.* at 74.

the expense of civilian needs. Indeed, the Coalition attacks against Iraqi power generating plants and transformer stations had a great impact on the Iraqi air defense structure (supported by computers), unconventional weapons research and development facilities, and telecommunications systems.[100] The large-scale attacks also had unintended—albeit inevitable—non-military consequences, such as the disruption of water supply (due to loss of electric pumps) and the inability to segregate the electricity that powers a hospital from "other" electricity in the same lines.[101] But these unfortunate results did not detract from the standing of the Iraqi electric grid system as a military objective.[102]

7. Civilian airports and maritime ports

It would be imprudent to disregard the possibility that civilian airports and maritime ports can become hubs of military operations, side by side with continued civilian activities (which can conceivably be a fig leaf). No wonder that the 1954 Hague Cultural Property Convention refers to "an aerodrome" or "a port"—in a generic fashion—as a military objective.[103]

8. Trains, trucks and barges

If strategic arteries of transportation come within the bounds of military objectives (as stated), should the definition not incorporate all the railroad rolling stock, the truck fleets which are the backbone of motorway traffic, and the barges plying the rivers and canals? The consequences for civilian traffic are palpable. Unlike passenger liners or airliners (mentioned *infra*), passenger trains do not have any visible hallmarks setting them apart from troop-carrying trains. If an inter-urban train (as distinct from a city tram) is sighted from the air, there being no telling signs of the civilian identity of the train riders, this writer believes that the train would be a legitimate military objective. In the Kosovo air campaign of 1999, a passenger train (not targeted as such) was struck while crossing a railway bridge.[104] In analyzing the case,

---

100. *See* Daniel Kuehl, *Airpower vs. Electricity: Electric Power as a Target for Strategic Air Operations*, 18 JOURNAL OF STRATEGIC STUDIES 237, 251–252 (1995).
101. *Id.* at 254.
102. *See* Christopher Greenwood, *Current Issues in the Law of Armed Conflict: Weapons, Targets and International Criminal Liability*, 1 SINGAPORE JOURNAL OF INTERNATIONAL AND COMPARATIVE LAW 441, 461 (1997).
103. Hague Cultural Property Convention, art. 8(1)(a), *supra* note 8, at 376.
104. *See* Final Report to the Prosecutor by the Committee Established to Review the NATO Bombing Campaign Against the Federal Republic of Yugoslavia, ¶¶ 58–62, 39 INTERNATIONAL LEGAL MATERIALS 1257, 1273–1275 (2000), *reprinted* herein as Appendix A [hereinafter Report to the Prosecutor].

Natalino Ronzitti seems to take the position that—although the bridge was no doubt a legitimate military objective—a passenger train should not be attacked.[105] However, in the opinion of this writer it would all depend on whether or not the passengers were identified by the aviators as civilians.

9. Civilian television and radio stations

In wartime, control of civilian broadcasting stations can at any time be assumed by the military apparatus, which may wish to use it in communications (e.g., summoning reservists to service), in pursuit of psychological warfare, and for other purposes. In April 1999, NATO intentionally bombed the (State-owned) Serbian Television and Radio Station in Belgrade.[106] Was the bombing legally warranted? The Committee Established to Review the NATO Bombing Campaign against the Federal Republic of Yugoslavia averred that if the attack was carried out because the station played a role in the Serbian propaganda machinery, its legality might well be questioned.[107] In the Committee's opinion, the attack could be justified only if the TV and radio transmitters were integrated into the military command and control communications network.[108] However, it is noteworthy that the Hague Cultural Property Convention of 1954 refers to any "broadcasting station" as a military objective (in the same breath with an aerodrome and a port).[109] The phrase clearly covers civilian TV and radio stations.[110]

10. Government offices

It is occasionally questioned "whether government buildings are excluded under any clear rule of law from enemy attack."[111] But this sweeping statement is wrong. Government offices can be considered a legitimate target for attack only when used in pursuance or support of military functions. The premises of the Ministry of Defense have already been mentioned. Any subordinate or independent Department of the Army, Navy, Air Force, Munitions and so forth

---

105. Natalino Ronzitti, *Is the Non Liquet of the Final Report by the Committee Established to Review the NATO Bombing Campaign against the Federal Republic of Yugoslavia Acceptable?*, 82 INTERNATIONAL REVIEW OF THE RED CROSS 1017, 1025 (2000).
106. *See* Report to the Prosecutor, Appendix A, ¶ 75.
107. *Id.*, ¶ 76.
108. *Id.*, ¶ 75.
109. Hague Cultural Property Convention, art. 8(1)(a), *supra* note 8, at 376.
110. For reference to a radio broadcasting station in the Vatican City, see the UNESCO Commentary on the Hague Cultural Property Convention: THE PROTECTION OF CULTURAL PROPERTY IN THE EVENT OF ARMED CONFLICT: COMMENTARY 106 (Jiri Toman ed., 1996).
111. INGRID DETTER, THE LAW OF WAR 294 (2d ed. 2000).

is embraced. As for the edifice of the Head of State, circumstances vary from one country to another. Whereas the White House in Washington would constitute a legitimate military target (since the American President is the Commander–in-Chief of all US armed forces), Buckingham Palace in London would not (inasmuch as the Queen has no similar role).

11. Political leadership

Obviously, members of the political leadership of the enemy country can be attacked (even individually) if they serve in the armed forces.[112] Additionally, when civilian leaders are present in any military installations or government offices constituting military objectives—or when they are visiting either the front line or munitions factories in the rear areas, when they board military aircraft or are driven by military command cars, etc.—they expose themselves to danger. However, notwithstanding the personal risk run when present in a military objective, a civilian member of the political leadership does not become a military objective by himself and cannot be targeted away from such objective.

Defended and Undefended Localities in Land Warfare

The real test in land warfare is whether a given place, inhabited by civilians, is actually defended by military personnel. Should that be the case, the civil object becomes—owing to its use—a military objective. The criterion of the defense of an otherwise civilian place is highlighted in Article 25 of the Hague Regulations: "The attack or bombardment, by whatever means, of towns, villages, dwellings, or buildings which are undefended is prohibited."[113]

Similar language appears in Article 3(c) of the Statute of the International Criminal Tribunal for the former Yugoslavia (ICTY).[114] Article 8(2)(b)(v) of the Rome Statute brands as a war crime: "Attacking or bombarding, by whatever means, towns, villages, dwellings or buildings which are undefended and

---

112. See ROGERS & MALHERBE, *supra* note 54, at 62.
113. Hague Regulations Respecting the Laws and Customs of War on Land, Annexed to 1899 Hague Convention (II) and 1907 Hague Convention (IV) Respecting the Laws and Customs of War on Land, THE LAWS OF ARMED CONFLICTS: A COLLECTION OF CONVENTIONS, RESOLUTIONS AND OTHER DOCUMENTS 63, 83–84 (Dietrich Schindler & Jiri Toman eds., 3d ed. 1988). The words "by whatever means" were added to the text in 1907.
114. Statute of the International Tribunal for the Prosecution of Persons Responsible for Serious Violations of International Humanitarian Law Committed in the Territory of the Former Yugoslavia since 1991 (ICTY), Report of the Secretary-General Pursuant to Paragraph 2 of Security Council Resolution 808 (1993), 32 INTERNATIONAL LEGAL MATERIALS 1159, 1193 (1993).

which are not military objectives."[115] The last words are plainly an addition to the original Hague formula. They sharpen the issue by denoting that some undefended civilian habitations may still constitute military objectives.

Article 59(1) of Protocol I sets forth: "It is prohibited for the Parties to the conflict to attack, by any means whatsoever, non-defended localities."[116] Once more it is the Hague criterion of defending a place that counts: if a place is defended, it may be attacked. But the expression "localities," employed by the Protocol, is wider than single buildings, albeit narrower than a whole city or town. This is important to bear in mind, for land warfare cannot always be analyzed on a building-by-building basis. Not infrequently, large-scale combat is conducted in an extensive built-up area, particularly a large city. It goes without saying that "any building sheltering combatants becomes a military objective."[117] In extreme cases, when fierce fighting is conducted from house to house (*à la* Stalingrad), a whole city block—or even section—may be regarded as a single military objective: partly by (actual) use and partly by purpose (namely, potential use). The fact that, in the meantime, a given building within that block or section is not yet occupied by any military unit is immaterial. The reasonable expectation is that, as soon as the tide of battle gets nearer, it would be converted into a military stronghold. Hence, it may be bombarded even prior to that eventuality. Yet, the old Hague sweeping reference to a town *in toto* (defended or undefended) must be regarded as obsolete.[118]

A belligerent desirous of not defending a city—with a view to saving it from harm's way—can convey that message effectively to the enemy. Article 59(2) of the Protocol prescribes:

> The appropriate authorities of a Party to the conflict may declare as a non-defended locality any inhabited place near or in a zone where armed forces are in contact which is open for occupation by an adverse Party. Such a locality shall fulfill the following conditions:
>
> (a) all combatants, as well as mobile weapons and mobile military equipment, must have been evacuated;
>
> (b) no hostile use shall be made of fixed military installations or establishments;

---

115. Rome Statute, *supra* note 10, at 676.
116. Protocol I, *supra* note 2, at 454.
117. Pilloud & Pictet, *supra* note 23, at 699, 701.
118. *See* Oeter, *supra* note 43, at 171.

(c) no acts of hostility shall be committed by the authorities or by the population; and

(d) no activities in support of military operations shall be undertaken.[119]

There seem to be some complementary implicit conditions not enumerated in the text: roads and railroads crossing the locality must not be used for military purposes, and factories situated there must not manufacture products of military significance.[120] Nevertheless, the presence in the non-defended locality of police forces retained for the sole purpose of maintaining law and order is permissible under Article 59(3).[121]

Apart from the explicit and implicit cumulative conditions, it is *sine qua non* that (i) the declared non-defended locality would be in or near the contact zone,[122] and that (ii) it would be open for occupation.[123] A declared non-defended locality cannot be situated in the *hinterland*—far away from the contact zone—for the simple reason that it is not yet within "the effective grasp of the attacker's land forces."[124] *Au fond*, a non-defended locality cannot be established in anticipation of future events, but only "in the 'heat of the moment', i.e., when the fighting comes close."[125]

Article 59(4) goes on to state that the declaration mentioned in paragraph (2)—defining as precisely as possible the limits of the non-defended locality—is to be addressed to the adverse party, which must treat the locality as non-defended unless the prerequisite conditions are not in fact fulfilled.[126] The outcome is that, subject to the observation of all the conditions (specified and unspecified in the text), the unilateral declaration of a locality as non-defended binds the adverse party by virtue of the Protocol.[127]

---

119. Protocol I, *supra* note 2, at 454.
120. *See* Pilloud & Pictet, *supra* note 23, at 702.
121. Protocol I, *supra* note 2, at 454.
122. A contact zone means the area where the most forward elements of the armed forces of both sides are in contact with each other. *See* Pilloud & Pictet, *supra* note 23, at 701 n.2.
123. Indeed, prior to Protocol I, the expression commonly used was not a "non-defended locality" but an "open city." For the transition in terminology, see J. Starke, *The Concept of Open Cities in International Humanitarian Law*, 56 AUSTRALIAN LAW JOURNAL 593–597 (1982).
124. JULIUS STONE, LEGAL CONTROLS OF INTERNATIONAL CONFLICT: A TREATISE ON THE DYNAMICS OF DISPUTE—AND WAR—LAW 622 (2d ed. 1959). The comment was made prior to the drafting of Protocol I, but it is still valid.
125. Claude Pilloud & Jean Pictet, *Localities and Zones under Special Protection*, in COMMENTARY ON THE ADDITIONAL PROTOCOLS, *supra* note 23, at 697. *See also* M. Torrelli, *Les Zones de Sécurité*, 99 REVUE GÉNÉRALE DE DROIT INTERNATIONAL PUBLIC 787, 795 (1995).
126. Protocol I, *supra* note 2, at 454.
127. Solf, *Article 59*, *supra* note 29, at 379, 383–384.

Article 59(5) adds that the two parties to the conflict may agree on the establishment of non-defended localities, even when the conditions are not met.[128] But manifestly, in that case, it is the bilateral agreement (as distinct from the unilateral declaration) that is decisive. Article 15 of Geneva Convention (IV)[129] provides that the belligerents may establish in the combat zone neutralized areas intended to serve as a shelter for (combatant or noncombatant) sick and wounded, as well as for civilians who perform no work of a military character, but the creation of such areas and their demarcation is contingent on the agreement of the parties.

Special Problems Relating to Sea Warfare

1. Areas of Naval Warfare

Hostile actions by naval forces may be conducted in or over the internal waters, the territorial sea, the continental shelf, the exclusive economic zone and (where applicable) the archipelagic waters of the belligerent States; the high seas; and (subject to certain conditions) even the continental shelf and the exclusive economic zone of neutral States.[130] Military objectives at sea include not only vessels but also fixed installations (especially weapon facilities and detection or communication devices), which can be emplaced on—or beneath—the seabed, anywhere within the areas of naval warfare.[131] Cables and pipelines laid on the seabed and serving a belligerent may also constitute legitimate military objectives.[132]

2. Warships

Every warship is a military objective. The locution "warships" covers all military floating platforms, including submarines, light craft (e.g., torpedo boats), and even unarmed auxiliary naval vessels (except hospital ships). A warship can be attacked on sight and sunk (within the areas of naval warfare). "These attacks may be exercised without warning and without regard to the safety of the enemy crew."[133]

---

128. Protocol I, *supra* note 2, at 454.
129. Geneva Convention (IV), *supra* note 6, at 307.
130. *See* SAN REMO MANUAL, *supra* note 15, at 80.
131. *See* Tullio Treves, *Military Installations, Structures, and Devices on the Seabed*, 74 AMERICAN JOURNAL OF INTERNATIONAL LAW 808, 809, 819 ff (1980).
132. *See* SAN REMO MANUAL, *supra* note 15, at 111.
133. William Fenrick, *Legal Aspects of Targeting in the Law of Naval Warfare*, 29 CANADIAN YEARBOOK OF INTERNATIONAL LAW 238, 269 (1991).

3. Enemy Merchant Vessels

Enemy merchant vessels are generally deemed to be civilian objects, and are therefore exempt from attack (even though they are subject to capture as prize).[134] Still, the San Remo Manual lists no less than seven exceptions to the rule.[135] In these seven instances, merchant vessels may be attacked and sunk as military objectives:

(a) When an enemy merchant vessel is engaged directly in belligerent acts (e.g., laying mines or minesweeping).

(b) When an enemy merchant vessel acts as an auxiliary to the enemy armed forces (e.g., carrying troops or replenishing warships).

(c) When an enemy merchant vessel engages in reconnaissance or otherwise assists in intelligence gathering for the enemy armed forces.

(d) When an enemy merchant vessel refuses an order to stop or actively resists capture.

(e) When an enemy merchant vessel is armed to an extent that it can inflict damage on a warship (especially a submarine).

(f) When an enemy merchant vessel travels under a convoy escorted by warships, thereby benefiting from the (more powerful) armament of the latter.

(g) When an enemy merchant vessel makes an effective contribution to military action (e.g., by carrying military materials).[136]

Some vessels—above all, passenger liners exclusively engaged in carrying civilian passengers—are generally exempted from attack.[137] Even if the passenger liner is carrying a military cargo in breach of the requirement of

---

134. *See* Natalino Ronzitti, *Le Droit Humanitaire Applicable aux Conflits Armés en Mer*, 242 RECUEIL DES COURS 9, 69–71 (1993).
135. SAN REMO MANUAL, *supra* note 15, at 146–151.
136. The war materials under this rubric cannot be exports. Except in the context of refusing an order to stop while blockade running, a private tanker would not constitute a military objective when carrying oil exported from a belligerent oil-producing State, even though the revenue derived from the export may prove essential to sustaining the war effort. *See* Michael Bothe, *Neutrality in Naval Warfare: What Is Left of Traditional International Law?*, *in* HUMANITARIAN LAW OF ARMED CONFLICT CHALLENGES AHEAD: ESSAYS IN HONOUR OF FRITS KALSHOVEN 387, 401 (Astrid Delissen & Gerard Tanja eds., 1991). *Cf.* the comments *supra* about raw cotton in the American Civil War.
137. On passenger liners, see SAN REMO MANUAL, *supra* note 15, at 132.

exclusive civilian engagement, an attack against it may be unlawful because it would be clearly disproportionate to the military advantage expected.[138]

4. Neutral Merchant Vessels

Neutral merchant vessels are generally immune from attack, although subject to visit and search by belligerent warships (and military aircraft) and possible capture for adjudication as prize in appropriate circumstances.[139] Nevertheless, according to the San Remo Manual, neutral merchant vessels are liable to attack—as if they were enemy military objectives—in the six following cases:[140]

(a) When a neutral merchant vessel is engaged in belligerent acts on behalf of the enemy.

(b) When a neutral merchant vessel acts as an auxiliary to the enemy armed forces.

(c) When a neutral merchant vessel assists the enemy's intelligence system.

(d) When a neutral merchant vessel is suspected of breaching a blockade or of carrying contraband and clearly refuses an order to stop, or resists visit, search or capture.

(e) When a neutral merchant vessel travels under a convoy escorted by enemy warships.

(f) When a neutral merchant vessel makes an effective contribution to the enemy's military action (e.g., by carrying military materials).[141]

Thus, "[t]he mere fact that a neutral merchant vessel is armed provides no grounds for attacking it."[142] As for traveling under convoy, the entitlement to attack a neutral merchant vessel exists only when the convoy is escorted by enemy warships. Neutral merchant vessels traveling under convoy escorted by neutral warships, in transit to neutral ports, cannot be attacked (and are not subject to visit and search).[143] The neutral escort can also belong to a State other than the State of the flag.[144] During the Iran-Iraq War, the practice developed of reflagging the merchant vessels of one neutral State (like Kuwait)

---

138. See id.
139. See id. at 154, 212–213.
140. Id. at 154–161.
141. See supra note 136.
142. SAN REMO MANUAL, supra note 15, at 161.
143. See GEORGE POLITAKIS, MODERN ASPECTS OF THE LAWS OF NAVAL WARFARE AND MARITIME NEUTRALITY 560–561 (1998).
144. See id. at 571–575.

escorted by warships of another (like the United States).[145] But reflagging (in the absence of a "genuine link" between the merchant vessels and their new flag State[146]) is not strictly necessary. Suffice it for the two neutral States to conclude an agreement enabling the flag State of the escorting warships to verify and warrant that the merchant vessel (flying a different neutral flag) is not carrying contraband and is not otherwise engaged in activities inconsistent with its neutral status.[147]

Of course, neutral passenger liners would benefit from special protection.[148]

5. Destruction of Enemy Merchant Vessels after Capture

When enemy merchant vessels are protected from attack that does not mean that they cannot be destroyed. The rule is that warships (and military aircraft) have a right to capture enemy merchant vessels, with a view to taking them into port for adjudication and condemnation as prize.[149] As an exceptional measure, when circumstances preclude taking it into port, the captured merchant vessel may be destroyed.[150] The legality of the destruction of the captured ship is to be adjudicated by the prize court.[151]

There is a vital distinction between the destruction of an enemy merchant vessel subsequent to capture and an attack launched against it on the ground that it constitutes a military objective. An enemy merchant vessel liable to attack as a military objective can be sunk at sight with all those on board. Conversely, the destruction of an enemy merchant vessel in the exceptional circumstances following capture can only take place subject to the dual condition that (i) the safety of passengers and crew is assured; (ii) the documents and papers relating to the prize proceedings are safeguarded.[152] A special

---

145. See id. at 560–571.
146. See Myron Nordquist & Margaret Wachenfeld, *Legal Aspects of Reflagging Kuwaiti Tankers and Laying of Mines in the Persian Gulf*, 31 GERMAN YEARBOOK OF INTERNATIONAL LAW 138, 140–151 (1988).
147. See SAN REMO MANUAL, *supra* note 15, at 197–199.
148. See George Walker, *Information Warfare and Neutrality*, 33 VANDERBILT JOURNAL OF TRANSNATIONAL LAW 1079, 1164 (2000).
149. SAN REMO MANUAL, *supra* note 15, at 205, 208.
150. See id. at 209.
151. See Wolff Heintschel von Heinegg, *Visit, Search, Diversion, and Capture in Naval Warfare: Part I, The Traditional Law*, 29 CANADIAN YEARBOOK OF INTERNATIONAL LAW 283, 309 (1991).
152. See SAN REMO MANUAL, *supra* note 15, at 209.

Procès-Verbal of 1936 applies this general rule to submarine warfare.[153] The *Procès-Verbal* specifies that the ship's boats are not regarded as a place of safety for the passengers and crew unless that safety is assured by the existing sea and weather conditions, the proximity of land, or the presence of another vessel in a position to take them on board.[154] The San Remo Manual follows the *Procès-Verbal*, adding an important caveat: the vessel subject to destruction must not be a passenger liner.[155]

6. Exclusion Zones

The San Remo Manual rejects the notion that a belligerent may absolve itself of its duties under international humanitarian law by establishing maritime "exclusion zones," which might enable it to attack enemy merchant vessels and even neutral ships entering the zones.[156] The practice of establishing exclusion zones evolved during World Wars I and II, and was resorted to—albeit with considerable conceptual differences—in the Iran-Iraq War and in the Falkland Islands War.[157] It is clear from the 1946 Judgment of the International Military Tribunal at Nuremberg that the sinking of neutral merchant vessels without warning when entering unilaterally proclaimed exclusion zones, is unlawful.[158] This holding is not germane, however, to enemy merchant vessels in such zones.[159]

Most commentators agree that, given the on-going practice, the legality of exclusion zones should be acknowledged in some manner.[160] The San Remo Manual itself concedes that belligerents may establish exclusion zones as exceptional measures, subject to the condition that no new rights be acquired—and no existing duties be absolved—through such establishment.[161]

---

153. *Procès-Verbal* Relating to the Rules of Submarine Warfare Set Forth in Part IV of the Treaty of London of 22 April 1930, 1936, THE LAWS OF ARMED CONFLICTS, *supra* note 113, at 883, 884.
154. *Id.*
155. SAN REMO MANUAL, *supra* note 15, at 210.
156. *Id.* at 181.
157. *See* William Fenrick, *The Exclusion Zone Device in the Law of Naval Warfare*, 24 CANADIAN YEARBOOK OF INTERNATIONAL LAW 91–126 (1986).
158. International Military Tribunal (Nuremberg), Judgment and Sentence, 41 AMERICAN JOURNAL OF INTERNATIONAL LAW 172, 304 (1947).
159. *See* Edwin Nwogugu, *1936 London Procès-Verbal Relating to the Rules of Submarine Warfare Set Forth in Part IV of the Treaty of London of 22 April 1930*, in THE LAW OF NAVAL WARFARE: A COLLECTION OF AGREEMENTS AND DOCUMENTS WITH COMMENTARIES 349, 358–359 (Natalino Ronzitti ed., 1988).
160. *See* POLITAKIS, *supra* note 143, at 145.
161. SAN REMO MANUAL, *supra* note 15, at 181–182.

The condition is somewhat softened when the Manual adds that, should a belligerent create an exclusion zone, "it might be more likely to presume that ships or aircraft in the area without permission were there for hostile purposes."[162] This proviso "allows a 'grey area,'"[163] although incontestably exclusion zones must not become "free-fire zones," and specified sea lanes ensuring safe passage to hospital ships, neutral shipping, etc., must be made available.[164] Evidently, the specifics of a new law regarding exclusion zones have not yet crystallized.[165] Until the new law emerges in detail, the *lex lata* remains valid, so that "an otherwise protected platform does not lose that protection by crossing an imaginary line drawn in the ocean by a belligerent."[166]

The reverse side of the coin is that enemy warships—being military objectives subject to attack at sight—do not gain any protection by staying away from an exclusion zone. Consequently, there was no legal fault in the sinking by the British of the Argentine cruiser *ARA General Belgrano* outside a proclaimed exclusion zone (in the course of the Falkland Islands War of 1982): an enemy warship "has no right to consider itself immune" from attack beyond the range of an exclusion zone.[167]

7. Bombardment of Coastal Areas

A special problem arises with respect to the bombardment from the sea of enemy coastal areas. The matter is governed by Hague Convention (IX) of 1907, which sets forth in Article 1: "The bombardment by naval forces of undefended ports, towns, villages, dwellings, or buildings is forbidden."[168] Article 2, for its part, clarifies that military works, military or naval establishments, depots of arms or war materials, workshops or plants which can be utilized for the needs of the hostile fleet or army, and warships in the harbor, are excluded

---

162. *Id.* at 181.
163. Fausto Pocar, *Missile Warfare and Exclusion Zones in Naval Warfare*, 27 ISRAEL YEARBOOK ON HUMAN RIGHTS 215, 223 (1997).
164. *See* Wolff Heintschel von Heinegg, *The Law of Armed Conflicts at Sea*, *in* THE HANDBOOK OF HUMANITARIAN LAW IN ARMED CONFLICTS, *supra* note 43, at 405, 468.
165. *See* L.F.E. Goldie, *Maritime War Zones & Exclusion Zones*, *in* THE LAW OF NAVAL OPERATIONS 156, 193–194 (Horace B. Robertson ed., 1991) (Vol. 64, US Naval War College International Law Studies).
166. ANNOTATED SUPPLEMENT TO THE COMMANDER'S HANDBOOK ON THE LAW OF NAVAL OPERATIONS, *supra* note 17, at 395–396.
167. *See* Howard Levie, *The Falklands Crisis and the Laws of War*, *in* THE FALKLANDS WAR: LESSONS FOR STRATEGY, DIPLOMACY AND INTERNATIONAL LAW 64, 66 (Alberto Coll & Anthony Arend eds., 1985).
168. Hague Convention (IX) Concerning Bombardment by Naval Forces in Time of War, Oct. 18, 1907, DOCUMENTS ON THE LAWS OF WAR, *supra* note 2, at 111, 113.

from this prohibition.[169] Article 3—which is "a throwback to a bygone era of naval warfare"[170]—permits the bombardment of ports, towns, etc., if the local authorities (having been summoned to do so) fail to furnish supplies to the naval force before them.[171]

Article 1 of Hague Convention (IX) applies to coastal bombardment a land warfare rule, laid down in Article 25 of Hague Convention (IV). As noted, the sweeping reference in the Hague Conventions to entire towns as either defended or undefended (and accordingly subject to, or exempted from, attack) is obsolete, and the term "localities"—employed by Protocol I—is more precise. Additionally, coastal bombardments are in general different from land warfare. Whereas on land a bombardment usually serves as a prelude to assault on the target with a view to its occupation, naval bombardment is more frequently intended to inflict sheer destruction on the enemy rear (only exceptionally is the intention to land troops).[172] If there is room for some elasticity in treating whole sections of a city as a single military objective—when house-to-house combat is raging—no similar impetus affects coastal bombardment. The grafting of a land warfare rule onto coastal bombardment is therefore inappropriate.[173]

A specific issue in the context of coastal bombardment is that of lighthouses. Can they be treated as military objectives? On the one hand, they deserve protection as installations designed to ensure the safety of navigation in general.[174] On the other hand, the French Court of Cassation held in 1948 that a lighthouse is a military objective, since it can be used for the needs of a hostile fleet.[175] The present practice of States is certainly not conclusive.

---

169. Id.
170. Horace Robertson, *1907 Hague Convention IX Concerning Bombardment by Naval Forces in Time of War*, in THE LAW OF NAVAL WARFARE, *supra* note 159, at 149, 166.
171. Hague Convention (IX), *supra* note 168, at 113.
172. See ROBERT TUCKER, THE LAW OF WAR AND NEUTRALITY AT SEA 143 (1955) (Vol. 50, US Naval War College International Law Studies).
173. See Robertson, *supra* note 170, at 163–164.
174. See Matthias Hartwig, *Lighthouses and Lightships*, in 3 ENCYCLOPEDIA OF PUBLIC INTERNATIONAL LAW 220 (Rudolph Bernhardt ed., 1997).
175. *In re Gross-Brauckmann* (France, Court of Cassation [Criminal Division], 1948), 1948 ANNUAL DIGEST AND REPORTS OF PUBLIC INTERNATIONAL LAW CASES 687, 688.

Special Problems Relating to Air Warfare

1. Military Aircraft

Enemy military aircraft—and any other military aerial platforms, including gliders, drones, blimps, dirigibles, etc.—are legitimate targets for attack. In fact, air combat is intrinsically different from land or sea combat, considering that (i) it is most difficult for a military aircraft in flight to convey a wish to surrender (*i.e.*, there is no effective counterpart in the air to the land or sea method of hoisting a white flag, striking colors or—in the case of submarines—surfacing); and (ii) it is generally permissible to continue to fire upon a military aircraft even after it has become clearly disabled.[176] (Although, under Article 42 of Protocol I, persons parachuting from an aircraft in distress—in contradistinction to airborne troops—must not be made the object of attack during their descent, and upon reaching hostile ground must be given an opportunity to surrender.[177])

2. Civilian Aircraft

Enemy civilian aircraft per se do not constitute military objectives. Still, civilian aircraft are subject to rather stringent strictures under the non-binding Hague Rules of Air Warfare, whereby enemy civilian aircraft in flight are liable to be fired upon—as if they were military objectives—in the following circumstances:

(a) When flying within the jurisdiction of their own State, should enemy military aircraft approach and they do not make the nearest available landing.[178]

(b) When flying (i) within the jurisdiction of the enemy; or (ii) in the immediate vicinity thereof and outside the jurisdiction of their own State; or (iii) in the immediate vicinity of the military operations of the enemy by land or sea (the exceptional right of prompt landing is inapplicable).[179]

Even neutral civilian aircraft are exposed to the risk of being fired upon if they are flying within the jurisdiction of a belligerent, are warned of the approach of military aircraft of the opposing side, and do not land

---

176. *See* ANNOTATED SUPPLEMENT TO THE COMMANDER'S HANDBOOK ON THE LAW OF NAVAL OPERATIONS, *supra* note 17, at 407–408.
177. Protocol I, *supra* note 2, at 444.
178. Hague Rules of Air Warfare, *supra* note 5, art. 33, at 147.
179. *Id.*, art. 34.

immediately.[180] Thus, the only advantage that neutral civilian aircraft have over belligerent civilian aircraft within enemy airspace is that the neutral civilian aircraft must be warned first (belligerent civilian aircraft in that situation must establish at their own peril whether the enemy military aircraft are approaching).

These provisions have been criticized as impractical, addressing an improbable contingency (of civilian aircraft venturing into the enemy's jurisdiction), and creating new and difficult categories (what is the vicinity of the enemy's jurisdiction?).[181] Although the Hague Rules have generally had a substantial influence on the evolution of customary international law[182]—and their impact on the terminology adopted by the framers of Protocol I has been noted—it is impossible to forget that they were enunciated in 1923, at the dawn of civil aviation and prior to the exponential growth of passenger traffic by air. The normal modern procedure of declaring air exclusion zones in wartime is supposed to preclude any type of undesirable overflight in sensitive areas.[183] But even within a "no-fly" zone, it is arguable that attack against civilian aircraft in flight should follow a due warning.[184] Outside "no-fly" zones, the contemporary *jus in bello* (as corroborated by military manuals) forbids attacks against civilian aircraft in flight unless they are utilized for military purposes or refuse to respond to interception signals; and civilian airliners (engaged in passenger traffic) are singled out for special protection.[185] Still, as demonstrated by the lamentable 1988 incident of the US cruiser *USS Vincennes* shooting down an Iranian passenger aircraft (with 290 civilians on board), the speed of modern electronics often creates insurmountable problems of erroneous identification.[186]

The status of civilian aircraft is different when they are not in flight (nor in the process of taking off or landing with passengers), but parked on the

---

180. *Id.*, art. 35, at 148.
181. *See* J.M. Spaight, Air Power and War Rights 402 (3d ed. 1947).
182. *See* Richard Baxter, *The Duties of Combatants and the Conduct of Hostilities (Law of the Hague)*, in International Dimensions of Humanitarian Law 93, 115 (1988).
183. *See* F.J.S. Gómez, *The Law of Air Warfare*, 38 International Review of the Red Cross 347, 356 (1998).
184. *See* Torsten Stein, *No-Fly-Zones*, 27 Israel Yearbook on Human Rights 193, 196 (1997).
185. *See* Horace Robertson, *The Status of Civil Aircraft in Armed Conflict*, 27 Israel Yearbook on Human Rights 113, 125–126 (1997).
186. On this incident, see Jose Reilly & R.A. Moreno, *Commentary*, in The Military Objective and the Principle of Distinction in the Law of Naval Warfare, *supra* note 21, at 111, 114–115.

ground. It must be recalled that the airport in which they are parked is liable to be deemed a military objective, so the civilian aircraft may be at risk owing to its mere presence there.[187] Moreover, irrespective of where they are situated, civilian aircraft are often viewed as constituting "an important part of the infrastructure supporting an enemy's war-fighting capability," since they can be used later for the transport of troops or military supplies.[188]

3. Strategic and "Target Area" Bombing

The most crucial issue of air warfare is that of strategic bombing, to wit, bombing of targets in the interior, beyond the front line (the contact zone). Conditions of air warfare have always defied the logic of the distinction between defended and undefended sites, enshrined in the traditional law of Article 25 of the 1907 Hague Regulations, although the words "by whatever means" were inserted into the Article with the deliberate intention of covering "attack from balloons."[189] After all, there is no real meaning to lack of defenses *in situ* as long as the front line remains a great distance away. First, a rear zone is actually defended (however remotely) by the land forces facing the enemy on the front line. Secondly, the fact that a place in the interior is undefended by land forces while the front line is far-off is no indication of future events: it may still be converted into an impregnable citadel once the front line gets nearer. Thirdly, and most significantly for air warfare, the emplacement of anti-aircraft guns and fighter squadrons *en route* from the front line to the rear zone may serve as a more effective screen against intruding bombers than any defense mechanism provided locally.[190]

For these and other reasons, the Hague Rules of Air Warfare introduced the concept of military objectives, endorsed and further elaborated—with a new definition—by Protocol I. However, strategic bombing triggers the complementary question whether it is permissible to treat a cluster of military objectives in relative spatial proximity to each other as a single "target area." The issue arises occasionally in some settings of long-range artillery bombardment. But it is particularly apposite to air warfare, in which target identification may be detrimentally affected by poor visibility (especially as a result of

---

187. *Cf.* Leslie Green, *Aerial Considerations in the Law of Armed Conflict*, 5 ANNALS OF AIR AND SPACE LAW 89, 109 (1980).
188. Robertson, *supra* note 185, at 127.
189. THOMAS HOLLAND, THE LAWS OF WAR ON LAND (WRITTEN AND UNWRITTEN) 46 (1908).
190. *See* R.Y. Jennings, *Open Towns*, 22 BRITISH YEAR BOOK OF INTERNATIONAL LAW 258, 261 (1945).

inclement weather), effective air defense systems, failure of electronic devices (sometimes because of enemy jamming), sophisticated camouflage, etc. Thus, when the target is screened by determined air defense, the attacking force may be compelled to conduct a raid from the highest possible altitudes, compromising precision bombing (especially when "smart bombs" are unavailable).[191] The practice which evolved during World War II was that of "saturation bombings," aimed at large "target areas" in which there were heavy concentrations of military objectives (as well as civilian objects).[192] Such air attacks were designed to blanket or envelop the entire area where military objectives abounded, rather than search for a point target.[193] The operating assumption was that, if one military objective would be missed, others stood a good chance of being hit. This practice (entailing, as it did, immense civilian casualties by way of "collateral damage") was harshly criticized after the war.[194]

The World War II experience may create the impression that "target area" bombing is relevant mostly to sizeable tracts of land—like the Ruhr Valley in Germany—where the preponderant presence of first-class military objectives stamps an indelible mark on their surroundings, thereby creating "an indivisible whole."[195] But the dilemma whether or not to lump together as a single target several military objectives may be prompted even by run-of-the-mill objects when they are located at a relatively small distance from each other. The dilemma is addressed by Article 51(5)(a) of Protocol I, where it is prohibited to conduct "an attack by bombardment by any methods or means which treats as a single military objective a number of clearly separated and distinct military objectives located in a city, town, village or other area containing a similar concentration of civilians or civilian objects."[196]

While placing a reasonable limitation on the concept of "target area" bombing, Article 51(5)(a) does not completely ban it. "Target area" bombing is still legitimate when the military objectives are not clearly separated and

---

191. It must be appreciated that "smart bombs" are not a panacea: much can go wrong even when they are available. See A.P.V. Rogers, *Zero-Casualty Warfare*, 82 INTERNATIONAL REVIEW OF THE RED CROSS 165, 170–172 (2000).
192. See STONE, *supra* note 124, at 626–627.
193. See E. Rosenblad, *Area Bombing and International Law*, 15 REVUE DE DROIT PÉNAL MILITAIRE ET DE DROIT DE LA GUERRE 53, 63 (1976).
194. See, e.g., Hans Blix, *Area Bombardment: Rules and Reasons*, 49 BRITISH YEAR BOOK OF INTERNATIONAL LAW 31, 58–61 (1978).
195. MORRIS GREENSPAN, THE MODERN LAW OF LAND WARFARE 335–336 (1959).
196. Protocol I, *supra* note 2, at 651.

distinct. Understandably, "the interpretation of the words 'clearly separated and distinct' leaves some degree of latitude to those mounting an attack."[197] In particular, the adverb "clearly" blurs the issue: is the prerequisite clarity a matter of objective determination or subjective appreciation (depending, e.g., on the degree of visibility when weather conditions are poor)?[198] Another question is what a "similar concentration" of civilian objects within the "target area" means in practice. The ambiguities are regrettable, keeping in mind that "target area" bombing stretches to the limit the principle of distinction between military objectives and civilian objects.

Conclusion

It is difficult to overstate the importance of establishing authoritatively the compass of military objectives in conformity with the *jus in bello*. In exposing military objectives to attack, and (as a corollary) immunizing civilian objects, the principle of distinction provides the main line of defense against methods of barbarism in warfare. The validity of the principle cannot be seriously contested today, and it may be regarded as lying at the epicenter of the law regulating the conduct of hostilities. Unfortunately, the Devil is in the detail. As this paper should amply demonstrate, the detail is far from resolved by the current *lex scripta* (specifically Protocol I). There is an evident need for further expounding quite a few aspects of the accepted definition of military objectives. This need becomes more urgent with the dramatic changes in the modern techniques of combat. The *jus in bello* cannot afford to lag far behind the changing conditions of combat.

---

197. *See* Pilloud & Pictet, *supra* note 23, at 613, 624.
198. *See* Hamilton DeSaussure, *Belligerent Air Operations and the 1977 Geneva Protocol I*, 4 ANNALS OF AIR AND SPACE LAW 459, 471–472 (1979).

Targeting

Michael Bothe

The international legal rules which determine whether certain targets may or may not be lawfully attacked are based on one of the pillars of the international law applicable in armed conflicts, namely the distinction between the civilian population on the one hand and the military effort of the State on the other. The development of this distinction is a historical and cultural achievement of the age of enlightenment. This fact needs to be emphasized when there is a temptation to consider certain consequences of this distinction as too cumbersome for what is supposed to be a necessary military operation.

Distinction

In the centuries before the enlightenment, war was often, and then lawfully so, conducted in a way that made the "civilian" population suffer very drastically.[1] It was in particular the philosopher Jean Jacques Rousseau who, in the second half of the 18th century, developed the idea that war did not constitute a confrontation between peoples, but between States and their rulers ("sovereign's war").[2] This principle limited both the group of persons entitled to perform acts harmful to the enemy (combatants) and the scope of persons and objects which may be the target of such acts (combatants/military objectives).

In the 18th and early 19th century, this distinction corresponded to the reality of the conflicts of those days. It was possible and practicable to keep

---
1. Fritz Münch, *War, Laws of, History*, in 4 ENCYCLOPEDIA OF PUBLIC INTERNATIONAL LAW 1386 et seq. (Rudolf Bernhardt ed., 2000).
2. WILHELM GREWE, THE EPOCHS OF INTERNATIONAL LAW 267 (2000).

military activities well apart from the day-to-day life of the citizens, unless such unusual things as a *levée en masse* occurred. It was the technological developments of the late 19th and early 20th century which created the fundamental challenge to this distinction, namely the development of long-range weapons, in particular air warfare. The first rather comprehensive reaction to this challenge was an attempt at international rule making, the so-called Hague Rules of Air Warfare of 1923,[3] drafted by a group of experts based on a mandate given by the 1922 Washington Conference on Disarmament. These rules constituted a confirmation of the old distinction and developed its concrete application to the new situation. Rules elaborated by scientific bodies such as the International Law Association were formulated along the same lines.[4]

The great practical challenge to the traditional principle of distinction occurred during the Second World War. There were so many violations of the traditional principle that it was quite appropriate to ask the question whether that rule had survived or whether it had become obsolete.[5] The biggest challenge to the traditional rule of distinction was the development of nuclear weapons. It is, thus, necessary to critically analyze the attitude which States and other relevant actors adopted after the war in relation to that rule.

State practice immediately following the Second World War was somewhat puzzled and puzzling. The definition of war crimes in the Statute of the International Military Tribunal is based on the assumption that the rule of distinction was applicable ("wanton destruction of cities, towns or villages, or devastation not justified by military necessity"). But neither the judgment of the International Military Tribunal nor the judgments of the American military courts really address the principle of distinction as a limitation on the choice of targets for bombardments.[6] Furthermore, there was a kind of resounding silence of States in relation to that rule. The Geneva Conventions of 1949, which in many ways clarify and develop the law taking into account the experience of the Second World War, do not address the question, yet most

---

3. DOCUMENTS ON THE LAWS OF WAR 139 (Adam Roberts and Richard Guelff eds., 3d. ed. 2000).
4. Draft Convention for the Protection of the Civilian Population Against New Engines of War, adopted by the 40th Conference of the International Law Association, Amsterdam 1938. THE LAW OF ARMED CONFLICTS: A COLLECTION OF CONVENTIONS, RESOLUTIONS AND OTHER DOCUMENTS 223 (Dietrich Schindler & Jiri Toman eds., 3d ed. 1988).
5. For a brief analysis of the practice, see ERIK CASTRÉN, THE PRESENT LAW OF WAR AND NEUTRALITY 402 *et seq* (1954).
6. COMMENTARY ON THE ADDITIONAL PROTOCOLS OF 8 JUNE 1977 TO THE GENEVA CONVENTIONS OF 12 AUGUST 1949, ¶ 1828 (Yves Sandoz et al. eds., 1987).

writers were loath to accept that the bombing practices of the war had changed the law.[7]

In 1956, the International Committee of the Red Cross (ICRC) made an attempt to have the question of the validity of the principle of distinction clarified by what was meant to become the Delhi Rules for the Limitation of the Dangers Incurred by the Civilian Population in Time of War.[8] This attempt was based on the assumption that the traditional rule of distinction was still valid, but it failed. It became, so to say, the victim of the development of nuclear weapons or, more precisely, of a dispute concerning their legality. The military establishment of the day, it appears, remained completely outside the legal discourse concerning the legality of those nuclear weapons, of which the resolution of the Institut de Droit International of 1969[9] concerning the prohibition of weapons of mass destruction is a lively testimony.

That insulation of the legal discourse disappeared when the issue of the reaffirmation and development of international humanitarian law came on the political agenda as a consequence of the debate about the conduct of the Vietnam War and the issue of "human rights in occupied territory."[10] In 1968, the United Nations General Assembly reaffirmed the traditional principle in its resolution "Respect for Human Rights in Armed Conflicts," which declared: "That it is prohibited to launch attacks against the civilian population as such; That distinction must be made at all times between persons taking part in the hostilities and members of the civilian population...."[11]

The negotiations from 1974 to 1977 that led to the Additional Protocol I to the 1949 Geneva Conventions[12] and the reactions of States, including major military powers, after the adoption of the Protocol in 1977 are clearly based on the assumption that the basic content of the rule of distinction is part of customary international law. This is, in particular, reflected in the formulation of the declarations made by the United States and the United Kingdom on the occasion of the signature of the Protocol. In respect of so-called

---

7. CASTRÉN, *supra* note 5, at 200 *et seq.*
8. THE LAW OF ARMED CONFLICTS, *supra* note 4, at 251.
9. The Distinction between Military Objectives and Non-Military Objects in General and particularly the Problems Associated with Weapons of Mass Destruction, Resolution adopted by the Institut de Droit International at its session at Edinburg on September 9, 1969. *Id.* at 265.
10. Michael Bothe *in* MICHAEL BOTHE, KARL PARTSCH AND WALDEMAR SOLF, NEW RULES FOR VICTIMS OF ARMED CONFLICTS 2 (1982).
11. G.A. Res. 2444, U.N. GAOR, 23rd Sess., Supp. No. 18, at 50, U.N. Doc. A/7128 (1969).
12. Protocol Additional to the Geneva Conventions of 12 August 1949, and Relating to the Protection of Victims of International Armed Conflict, June 8, 1977, 1125 U.N.T.S. 3, DOCUMENTS ON THE LAWS OF WAR, *supra* note 3, at 422 [hereinafter Protocol I].

non-conventional weapons, they deny that the "new rules" of the Protocol apply to those weapons, the clear implication being that the "old," i.e., customary law rules do apply. It is made clear that the principle of distinction figures among these old rules.[13]

In addition, a legal discourse developed which now included military lawyers dealing with practical implications of this rule. Military lawyers explained and continued to explain that major bombing campaigns like those during the Vietnam[14] and 1991 Persian Gulf[15] wars were indeed conducted on the basis of these rules. Thus, it can safely be concluded that the rule has survived all major challenges; that it is still part and parcel of customary law. This, however, raises the question of the interpretation of the rule in the light of changing circumstances.

The Two-Pronged Test of the Military Objective

As to the selection of targets in general and in air warfare in particular, the basic rule that follows from the distinction between the civilian population and the military effort is the distinction between military objectives and civilian objects. That distinction is to be made on the basis of two interrelated elements, namely the effective contribution the military objective makes to military action and the "definite military advantage" that the total or partial destruction, capture or neutralization of the objective offers. There is no doubt that this is a rule of customary international law and its binding force is, thus, not limited to the parties to Protocol I, which formulates this very principle as follows in Article 52(2): "military objectives are limited to those objects which by their nature, location, purpose or use make an effective contribution to military action and whose total or partial destruction, capture or neutralization, in the circumstances ruling at the time, offers a definite military advantage."[16]

---

13. *See inter alios* Waldemar Solf, *in* BOTHE, PARTSCH AND SOLF, *supra* note 10, at 276, 282.
14. Burrus Carnahan, *"Linebacker II" and Protocol I: the Convergence of Law and Professionalism*, 31 AMERICAN UNIVERSITY LAW REVIEW 861 (1982).
15. *See* Theodor Meron, *The Time Has Come for the United States to Ratify Geneva Protocol I*, 88 AMERICAN JOURNAL OF INTERNATIONAL LAW 678, 681 (1994).
16. Protocol I, *supra* note 12, at 450.

The most recent practical confirmation of the customary law character of these principles is the experts report[17] published by the Chief Prosecutor of the Criminal Tribunal for the former Yugoslavia concerning the question whether the NATO bombing campaign against the Federal Republic of Yugoslavia (FRY) involved the commission of crimes which were subject to the jurisdiction of the Tribunal—a report which constitutes an important document if lessons are to be drawn from the Kosovo experience.

The difficulty of the Article 52(2) definition is its general character. There are, of course, clear cases of "pure" military objectives: military barracks, trenches in a battlefield, etcetera. Where objects are used or usable for different, military and non-military purposes (dual-use objects), their qualification as a military objective or civilian object becomes more difficult. What constitutes an "effective contribution" to military action? What is a "definite" military advantage? What is the difference, if any, between an "indefinite" or a "definite" military advantage? This brings us to the crucial problems of targeting. It must be realized that the application of rules formulated in general terms is a problem lawyers often encounter, not only in the law of war, but also in international law in general—even law in general. Legal rules expressed in general clauses need concretization for their practical application. The question, thus, is how to render the general principle of distinction more concrete in order to have secure standards for targeting.

A standard legislative method of rendering a general rule more concrete is the establishment of a list of cases of application, be it exhaustive or illustrative. This approach has been proposed by Professor Dinstein.[18] It presents a few problems of its own. An illustrative list may be useful for certain purposes, but it cannot terminate the discussion because the qualification of items that are not on the list remains open. The exhaustive list is dangerous, because it

---

17. Final Report to the Prosecutor by the Committee Established to Review the NATO Bombing Campaign against the Federal Republic of Yugoslavia, 39 INTERNATIONAL LEGAL MATERIALS 1257 (2000), *reprinted* herein as Appendix A [hereinafter Report to the Prosecutor]. For an analysis, see, *inter alia, Symposium: The International Legal Fallout from Kosovo*, 12 EUROPEAN JOURNAL OF INTERNATIONAL LAW 391 (2001), in particular the contributions by William Fenrick, *Targeting and Proportionality during the NATO Bombing Campaign against Yugoslavia*, at 489, Paolo Benvenuti, *The ICTY's Prosecutor and the Review of the NATO Bombing Campaign against the Federal Republic of Yugoslavia*, at 503, and Michael Bothe, *The Protection of the Civilian Population and NATO Bombing on Yugoslavia: Comments on a Report to the Prosecutor of the ICTY*, at 531. In addition, see Natalino Ronzitti, *Is the non liquet of the Final Report Established to Review the NATO Bombing Campaign Against the Federal Republic of Yugoslavia Acceptable?*, 82 INTERNATIONAL REVIEW OF THE RED CROSS 1017 (2000).

18. *See, e.g.* Professor Dinstein's paper in this volume.

can exclude clear cases falling under the general rule, which were just forgotten or not foreseen when the list was drafted. Thus, there is often a tendency to add a catchall clause at the end of a list.[19] At that point one is for all practical purposes back to the illustrative list.

Despite these deficiencies of the list method, the ICRC in 1956 attempted to draft such a list of military objectives.[20] In relation to the difficult or controversial questions, this list shows all the problems of this method. The list is based on the undisputed fact that there are certain typical military objectives which can indeed be listed, but this is possible only to a limited extent. There are objects that in one context may constitute a military objective, making an effective contribution to military action, while in other circumstances they do not. This is clearly shown in the items on the list that have become quite controversial in the context of the Kosovo campaign, namely lines and means of communication and in particular telecommunication facilities.

As to traffic infrastructure, the formulation of the ICRC list is as follows: "Those of the lines and means of communications (railway lines, roads, bridges, tunnels and canals) which are of fundamental military importance." Thus, a distinction has to be made between those lines and means of communications that are of fundamental military importance and those that are not. Only those lines of communication that are of fundamental military importance are military objectives. This is clearly stated in Article 7, Paragraph 3 of the ICRC Draft Rules to which the list was to be annexed: "However, even if they belong to one of those categories, they cannot be considered as a military objective where their total or partial destruction, in the circumstances ruling at the time, offers no military advantage."

As a consequence, in every instance the question of the military importance of a bridge or railway line is unavoidable. It is submitted that to ask this very question is the only correct application of the rule of distinction. There is no rule saying that railway lines and bridges are always a military objective. Their military importance has to be ascertained in each particular case. This is

---

19. *See, e.g.,* Article 61(a) (xv) of Protocol I ("complementary activities necessary to carry out any of the tasks mentioned above, including, but not limited to, planning and organization").

20. The list was drafted by the ICRC "as a model" to be annexed to the "Draft Rules for the Limitation of the Dangers Incurred by the Civilian Population in Times of Armed Conflict" (see note 8 *supra*) which the ICRC submitted in 1956 for consideration by the Red Cross Conference of 1957. *See* ICRC COMMENTARY, *supra* note 6, ¶ 2002. These rules became the victim of bitter controversies between governments during that conference (*see* J. Pokštefl and Michael Bothe, *Bericht über Entwicklungen und Tendenzen des Kriegsrechts seit den Nachkriegskodifikationen*, 35 ZEITSCHRIFT FÜR AUSLÄNDISCHES ÖFFENTLICHES RECHT UND VÖLKERRECHT 574, 575, 601 (1975).

the crucial problem of dual-use facilities. This problem applies to traffic infrastructure, telecommunication infrastructure and also to energy production and transmission facilities.

In the traditional context of land warfare, the military importance of traffic infrastructure is quite obvious. This traffic infrastructure is needed in order to bring supplies to the front or, as the case may be, to allow a swift retreat of the troops which may then reorganize afterwards. The examples given by Professor Dinstein[21] in order to prove his thesis are all taken from this context. During the so-called Christmas bombing of Hanoi, it was the use of railway lines for logistical support that was put forward as a justification for choosing certain targets (mainly railroads) in the very center of this city.[22] But what was the military importance of the many bridges crossing the Danube River that were destroyed during the Kosovo campaign? There was no front to which supplies could have been moved. It was the declared policy of the NATO States not to create such a front but to renounce to ground operations and to restrict military action to an air campaign. In such a situation, it is very hard to see any military importance of this traffic infrastructure. If there is no such military importance, these means of communication are civilian objects, not military objectives.

With respect to the telecommunication network, the situation may be somewhat different. This network is of military importance even in the context of a conflict where one side uses the strategy of air warfare only, while the other side, by necessity, would have to rely on anti-aircraft defense. This defense certainly depends on telecommunications, but it remains questionable whether each facility using telecommunications equipment that may be found in the country belongs, for that reason, to a network of military significance. Is there a kind of presumption that telecommunication facilities are always, unless the contrary is apparent, related to the military network?

This seems to be the underlying rationale of the Report to the Prosecutor.[23] It brings us to a question of precautionary duties, duties of due diligence in evaluating the military importance of certain objects and more generally the decision-making process to which we will revert below. This was the crucial problem in evaluating the lawfulness of the attack against the television facilities in Belgrade. Could the target selectors just proceed on the basis of the assumption or presumption that the technical equipment of this station was so

---

21. See Professor Dinstein's paper in the present volume.
22. Carnahan, *supra* note 14, at 864 *et seq.*
23. Report to the Prosecutor, Appendix A, ¶ 72.

closely linked to the military network that, although there was an obvious civilian use, its military importance was significant enough that its destruction provided a definite military advantage?

So far, the notion of contribution to the military effort or of military advantage has been discussed in tactical or operational terms. The question then arises whether this notion could also be understood in a broader sense. Can objects that are not related to specific military operations also "contribute to the military effort?" Air attacks have a definite impact on the morale of the entire population and, thus, also on political and military decision-makers. It may well be argued that it was not only the diplomatic efforts by Chernomyrdin and Ahtassari, but also or even mainly the impact of the bombing campaign that finally induced Milosevic to agree to a withdrawal of the Serbian military and police forces from Kosovo. Did the bombing for that reason provide a "definite military advantage"?

As is rightly pointed out by Professor Dinstein and the Report to the Prosecutor,[24] this type of "advantage" is political, not military. The morale of the population and of political decision-makers is not a contribution to "military action." Thus, the advantage of softening the adversary's will to resist is not a "military" one and, thus, cannot be used as a legitimation for any targeting decision. If it were otherwise, it would be all too easy to legitimize military action which uses bombing just as a psychological weapon—and there are other words for this.

The practical importance of this limitation is considerable and not new. It would indeed be impossible to make any meaningful distinction between civilian objects and military objectives as the psychological effect can be produced by an attack on any target, including entirely civilian living quarters. The morale of the civilian population and of political decision-makers was the main target of the nuclear bombs dropped on Hiroshima and Nagasaki—not a legitimate one. During the bombing of North Vietnamese targets, already mentioned, in addition to the military significance of the traffic infrastructure as channels for military supplies, "forcing a change in the negotiating attitudes of the North Vietnamese leadership" was also recognized as a goal of the bombing campaigns against that country.[25] The NATO bombing campaign against the FRY was also designed to induce the Belgrade leadership to accept a settlement of the status of the Kosovo along the lines of NATO terms. Although

---

24. Professor Dinstein's paper in the present volume and Report to the Prosecutor, *id.*, ¶ 55 ("civilian objects and civilian morale . . . are not legitimate military objectives").
25. Carnahan, *supra* note 14, at 867.

the psychological impact of a certain attack may be a legitimate consideration in choosing between targets that are for other reasons of a military character, that impact alone is not sufficient to establish the qualification of a certain target as a military objective.

This legal situation introduces a basic ambiguity, or a fictitious character, into targeting decisions to be made within the framework of an armed conflict conducted for humanitarian purposes. As the goal of such a "war" is not the military defeat of an adversary, but the protection of the human rights of the population, the traditional notion of military advantage loses much of its significance. In the Kosovo campaign target selection was made on the basis of the fiction that military advantages and military victory in the traditional sense were sought, although this was not the case. The only real goal was a change of attitude of the Belgrade government. Thus, the question of what really constitutes a military objective within the framework of a humanitarian intervention has to be asked. It would better correspond to the specific character of that particular type of military operation if only "pure" military objectives, in the sense mentioned already above, were considered to be legitimate targets.

The Environment—A Military Objective?

An additional comment is necessary concerning the environment as a military objective or civilian object. The rules of Protocol I relating to the protection of the environment, i.e., Articles 35(3) and 55, not only limit the permissible collateral damage to the environment caused by attacks against military objectives, but also limit permissible attacks where the environment itself constitutes a military objective, which is quite possible. Military objectives are not just persons or manmade structures: a piece of land can become a military objective if its neutralization offers a definite military advantage. Interdiction fire is an example. This type of military action is not directly targeted at combatants. The military usefulness consists of the fact that by bringing a certain area under constant fire, the enemy is deterred from entering that area. Cutting down, or defoliating, trees in order to deprive the enemy of cover is another example. The consequences of such actions for the environment may be disastrous. In such cases, for the reasons indicated, the rules of Articles 35(3) and 55 protect the environment when it is a military objective.

An attack against the environment, however, is unlawful only where the damage caused or expected is "widespread, long-term and severe." These three conditions are cumulative. All three must be met for there to be a violation. Therefore, we are back to the problem of general clauses and their concretization. It is true that many of the delegations present at the conference in Geneva that drafted Protocol I favored a very high threshold.[26] It appears that the Kosovo campaign has not really given any new impetus to concretize this threshold, as the actual environmental damage remained below that limit. The threshold is still an open question, but the very fact that the Report to the Prosecutor starts its legal assessment of the bombing campaign by analyzing the question of environmental destruction[27] shows that environmental considerations have indeed become an important restraint on military activities, although the legal reasoning of the report in this respect is highly questionable.[28]

In a first approach, the Report to the Prosecutor uses Articles 35(3) and 55 of Protocol I as the basic yardstick to determine the legality of any damage caused to the environment. It does not give a final answer to the question whether these provisions have become a rule of customary international law. The report simply finds that the damage caused by the NATO air campaign does not meet the triple cumulative threshold established by these provisions of being "widespread, long-term and severe."

If one takes the factual findings of the Balkan Task Force established by the United Nations Environment Programme, this conclusion is probably unavoidable. What is interesting, however, is that the assessment made by the committee does not stop at this point. It also analyses environmental damage in the light of the proportionality principle which is the usual test for the admissibility of collateral damage caused by attacks against military targets. This, as a matter of principle, is a valid point. This line of argument could be used as a means to lower the difficult threshold of Articles 35 and 55. Once it was established that collateral environmental damage was excessive in relation to a military advantage anticipated, it would also be unlawful even it was not widespread, long-lasting and severe.

A systematic interpretation of Protocol I would lead to the conclusion that the environment is protected by the combined effect of the general provision limiting admissible collateral damage and the particular provision on environmental damage. It would mean that in a concrete case, the stricter limitation

---

26. BOTHE, PARTSCH AND SOLF, *supra* note 10, at 346 *et seq.*
27. Report to the Prosecutor, Appendix A, ¶¶ 14–25.
28. Bothe, *supra* note 17, at 532 *et seq.*; Thilo Marauhn, *Environmental damage in times of armed conflict – not "really" a matter of criminal responsibility?*, 82 INTERNATIONAL REVIEW OF THE RED CROSS 1029 (2000).

would apply. Unfortunately, the report does not draw this conclusion. Instead, it refers to the formulation of Article 8(2)(b)(iv) of the International Criminal Court (ICC) Statute as "an authoritative indicator of evolving customary international law."[29] This provision, which is quite unfortunate from the point of view of environmental protection, creates a different type of cumulative effect of the rules on the protection of the environment and the proportionality principle. Causing environmental damage is only a war crime if it goes, first, beyond the threshold established by the triple cumulative conditions and, second, beyond what is permissible according to the proportionality principle. In the light of the reservations which the military establishment shows vis-à-vis taking into account environmental concerns as a limitation on military violence, this is probably as far as one could go in the definition of a war crime. It should be stressed, however, that this stance can be accepted only for the definition of the war crime, not as far as the interpretation of the primary rules of behavior relating to the protection of the environment in times of armed conflicts are concerned. The damage caused to the environment is unlawful if it is either excessive or widespread, long-term and severe. Causing the damage, however, is a war crime only if damage fulfils both criteria.

Decision-Making: Ascertaining Relevant Facts

As already pointed out, a targeting decision must involve a certain factual evaluation of the actual or potential use of specific objects as to whether they make or do not make a contribution to military action. Protocol I prescribes that efforts have to be made in order to ascertain the military character of an objective.[30] On the other hand, the targeting decision is certainly one which has to be taken in a context of uncertainty. It is unrealistic to require absolute certainty concerning the military importance of a specific object before it can be lawfully attacked, but not requiring absolute certainty is not the same as permitting disregard of the facts.

Whatever the actual standard of due diligence, there is an obligation of due diligence in ascertaining the character of a proposed target. This question arises, in modern decision making, on two different levels, that of target selection at the command level and that of launching the actual attack, which is not the same, as the case of the attack on a bridge which also hit a civilian

---

29. Report to the Prosecutor, Appendix A, ¶ 21.
30. Article 57(2)(a)(i).

train (not a selected target) demonstrates.[31] A violation of this duty of due diligence is a violation of the law of armed conflict. In such cases as the attack against the Chinese Embassy in Belgrade, there are reasons to believe that indeed the selection of that particular building as a target was due to a violation of this obligation of due diligence and therefore a negligent violation of the law of armed conflict.

Decision-Making: Balancing Processes and Value Judgments

The evaluation of the military advantage to be derived from an attack is not only a matter of the relevant facts, but also a matter of value judgments. What constitutes an advantage is a matter of subjective evaluation. This raises the question of "whose values matter?" In a somewhat different context, namely the value judgment involved in the assessment of proportionality, the Report to the Prosecutor states that this must be the judgment of the "reasonable military commander."[32] This statement, plausible as it may appear at a first glance, is problematic. In a democratic system, the value judgment which matters most is that of the majority of the society at large. The military cannot and may not constitute a value system of its own, separated by waterproof walls from that of civil society. Such separation would be to the disadvantage of both the military and civil society. A dialogue between the two, critical and constructive in both directions, is needed.

This is essential for a number of reasons. There is no denying the fact that public opinion in many countries views the military with a critical eye. This is particularly true for certain organizations of civil society engaged in the promotion of human rights. It is certainly in the interest of both the military and civil society organizations to avoid a situation where such critique is based on a lack of understanding and on misconceptions.[33] Furthermore, the practice observed in recent conflicts indeed recognizes that targeting decisions have political implications. This is why certain decisions are reserved to persons

---

31. Report to the Prosecutor, Appendix A, ¶¶ 58–62.
32. Id., ¶ 50.
33. A good example for the problem was the case of a German organization for the preservation of the language which chose "collateral damage" as the "bad expression of the year" for 1999. See the Unwort des Jahres website at http://www.unwortdesjahres.org. The mistake was on both sides. The organization was unaware of the technical character and meaning of the term, and the NATO spokesmen who had used it did not realize that the term transported a wrong message to the public, namely that damage to the civilian population and civilian objects were something which was unimportant and negligible for those who decided on targets in the Kosovo conflict.

that are very high in the governmental hierarchy. Targeting decisions engage the political responsibility to the electorate, i.e., civil society, of those holding high governmental offices. Therefore, these decisions have to be understandable and acceptable to civil society; hence the need for a dialogue.

The Problem of Errors

The question of values or value judgments leads to the problem of error or mistake in judgment. Such an error may relate to the facts or to the law. In the case of the Chinese Embassy, it was an error of fact. When the decision was made to attack a particular building, the decision-makers thought, or at least this is what we were told, that the building had a military use. The decision-makers did not know that it was the Chinese Embassy, which was obviously not a military objective.

In relation to attacks against railways and bridges, another question arises, namely the error of law. In this case, there was probably no erroneous evaluation of the actual use of those bridges and railway lines as a matter of fact. The essential error, if the view submitted by this paper is correct, consisted in a mistaken view of the law that considered traffic infrastructure as military objectives without asking the question of their military importance in the concrete context. As a matter of principle, an error of law does not exclude responsibility. *Ignorantia iuris* is no excuse or even circumstance excluding the wrongfulness of the behavior.

What are the consequences of these problems of due diligence and error on criminal accountability? The definition of war crimes contained in the statute of the permanent International Criminal Court[34] requires intent.[35] Violations of the laws of war committed by negligence are not subject to the jurisdiction of that court. The situation is, however, different with respect to the ad hoc International Criminal Tribunal for the former Yugoslavia (ICTY). Any violation of the laws and customs of war comes within the jurisdiction of that court according to Article 3 of its statute.[36] Thus, the ICTY would have had jurisdiction to prosecute and punish negligent violations of the laws of war which, as indicated, appear to be quite possible in this case. It is in this context that the question of error becomes most relevant. An error concerning the facts

---

34. U.N. Doc. A/CONF/183/9, July 17, 1998, DOCUMENTS ON THE LAWS OF WAR, *supra* note 3, at 667.
35. *Id.*, art. 30, at 690.
36. Statute of the International Tribunal, U.N. Doc. S/25704, May 3, 1993. The text of the Statute is *reprinted in* 32 INTERNATIONAL LEGAL MATERIALS 1192 (1993).

may entail a negligent violation of the respective rule, an error concerning the law, as a rule, does not constitute a valid defense.

The Law of War and Humanitarian Intervention—Some General Reflections

It must be stressed that all these considerations concerning lawful means and methods of combat are independent from the question whether the Kosovo air campaign was or was not a violation of the rules of the United Nations Charter prohibiting the use of force. *Jus ad bellum* and *jus in bello* have to be kept separate. This is the essential basis for a realistic approach to the law of armed conflict that has to treat both parties to a conflict on an equal footing. Questions of the legality or illegality of the use of force in a particular context have to be raised in other contexts, not in that of the application of the *jus in bello*. The equality of the parties in relation to the *jus in bello* is an essential precondition to the effective functioning of this body of law. This is why the Preamble to Protocol I reaffirms this principle in no uncertain terms: "*Reaffirming* that the provisions of the Geneva Conventions of 12 August 1949 and of this Protocol must be fully applied in all circumstances . . ., without any adverse distinction based on the nature or origin of the armed conflict or on the causes espoused by or attributed to the Parties to the conflict."

The principle of the equality of the parties to a conflict does not exclude the need to consider the entire context of a conflict, its intrinsic character, when determining the concept of military objective. Military advantage, as already pointed out, is a contextual notion. Where the declared purpose of a military action is limited from the outset, where the goal pursued is not just victory, but something else, it is difficult to ignore this limitation when it comes to the question what constitutes an advantage in that particular context. Thus, where the exclusive purpose of a military operation is to safeguard the human rights of a certain population, this very context excludes, it is submitted, a legal construction of the notion of military advantage or contribution to the military effort which disregards the life and health of this very population. In other words, in this context, the notion of military objective has to be construed in a much narrower way than in other types of conflict.

This contextual concept of military advantage is, it is submitted, *lex lata*. It must not be confused with proposals *de lege ferenda* demanding special rules for the conduct of so-called humanitarian interventions. If such rules were to be adopted, they could only mean an additional unilateral restraint imposed on those States or organizations which intervene for the sake of safeguarding the human rights of a certain population. Such rules could not and should not affect the rights and duties of the other party to the conflict.

More critical review of the notion of military advantage is needed. If the law were to be developed by a specific legal instrument relating to humanitarian intervention, why not impose on the forces maintaining the rule of law and human rights, obligations that are stricter than the usual rules of targeting valid for any belligerent?

Legal Perspective from the EUCOM Targeting Cell

Tony Montgomery

The Beginnings

During Operation Allied Force I was assigned to Headquarters, US European Command (EUCOM) as the Deputy Staff Judge Advocate and Chief, Operations Law. My responsibilities included being the legal member of the group that reviewed all fixed targets. In early July 1998, I attended one of the first meetings of the Kosovo Planning Group. This cross-functional group of officers was formed to evaluate the situation in Kosovo and make recommendations on possible courses of action (COAs). As the months passed, and a military confrontation seemed more likely, sets of targets were developed to support each of the various COAs. Target sets were refined, modified and discussed along with each COA.

The legal advisor's role/responsibility in this process is to offer well-reasoned advice, based on relevant data, in accordance with existing law and policy guidance. In the target development process, legal advisors help to ensure that a decision to attack a target or set of targets is based on known facts or reasonable assumptions. Usually, only after sifting through the facts do the assumptions come to light. There are always assumptions: about the weather, weapon effectiveness, absence or presence of people, impact on the enemy and others. Legal advisors identify and then voice concerns when the assumptions being made go beyond the reasonable person standard. This requires knowing the law, awareness of other restrictions, understanding of the military and political objectives, familiarity with the methods of achieving those objectives and, finally, the ability to synthesize and make a recommendation on a target or set of targets.

Actions at the time of the attack will be held to the standard of reasonableness; based on the evidence available at the time, factoring in the situation, time to attack and enemy actions. A commander must be reasonable in uncovering facts but clairvoyance is not a requirement. The legal advisor—if doing their job—will point out where in the rush for victory the line of reasonableness appears about to be crossed. Legal advisors provide recommendations on whether the proposed use of force abides by the law of war and do this by offering advice on both restraint and the right to use force.

Of course, the final decision on attacking a target is the subjective one of assessing the value of innocent human lives against the value of capturing/destroying a particular military objective. To assist a commander in making this subjective determination, a legal advisor—just like anyone involved—can provide an opinion and, a recommendation on a target or any other aspect of the operation. However, the final decision will always be the commander's. Legal advisors do not set the political or military objectives of a campaign, nor do they approve or disapprove targets.

Targeting—Some Basics

For those with no personal experience, it may come as a surprise to know that targeting is more than just looking at some "things" and deciding that today those will be destroyed. Objects are selected as targets based on campaign goals, intent, guidance, military objectives, and compliance with the law of war. Targeting is the process that identifies, detects, selects, and prioritizes targets in order to achieve a specific result based on the commander's objectives, guidance, and intent, then matches weapons systems to achieve that result, and finally assesses the results. Target selection is not at all haphazard—at least not at the planning level.

The current theory around which targets were developed during Operation Allied Force is known as "effects based targeting." Effects based targeting theorizes that by attacking specific links, nodes, or objects the effect or combination of effects will achieve the desired objective. If the theory is correct, following this approach will conserve resources, reduce the overall risk to friendly forces and civilians and, ultimately, shorten the conflict. However, the increasing ability to routinely hit targets with great accuracy has not been matched by a commensurate understanding of exactly which targets must be hit to achieve specific outcomes. Establishing a causal link between targeting some "thing" and achieving the desired ultimate political outcome is still the challenge.

I say "challenge" because once a decision to use force has been made, understanding the enemy well enough to accurately predict the enemy's reaction to being bombed is key to the overall efficacy of effects based targeting. Ultimately the goal of Operation Allied Force was to coerce Milosevic to comply with the demands of NATO. Without Milosevic explicitly telling us why he yielded when he did, we simply do not know for sure. We know NATO did achieve its principal military objective of a Serbian withdrawal from Kosovo; however, we were not able to halt ethnic cleansing before it was essentially complete.

The Mechanics of the Operation Allied Force Targeting Process

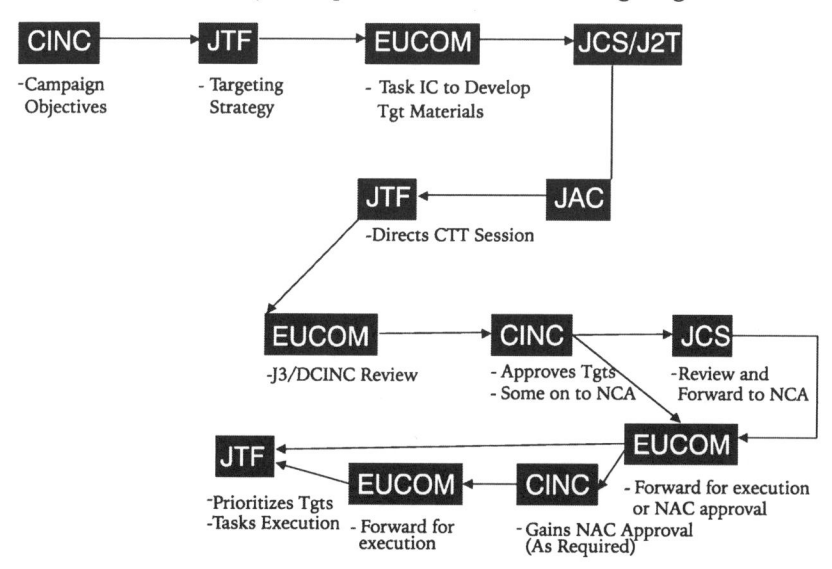

```
CINC → JTF → EUCOM → JCS/J2T
-Campaign   - Targeting   - Task IC to Develop
 Objectives  Strategy     Tgt Materials

              JTF ← JAC
              -Directs CTT Session

EUCOM → CINC → JCS
-J3/DCINC Review   - Approves Tgts   -Review and
                   - Some on to NCA   Forward to NCA

                                     EUCOM
JTF ← EUCOM ← CINC   - Forward for execution
-Prioritizes Tgts                     or NAC approval
-Tasks Execution  - Forward for   - Gains NAC Approval
                    execution       (As Required)
```

Figure 3.1

Recognizing the acronyms in Figure 3.1 is not as important as knowing that each fixed target basically followed the above route to approval. During Allied Force, those who had authorized the use of force very much wanted to limit the consequences and this process helped achieve that objective. Legal input was embedded throughout the process, with issues being addressed at the point where they were identified. However, this paper will focus on the efforts related to obtaining the approval of the commander of the United States European Command (EUCOM/CINC).

Once the air campaign began, a daily list of proposed new targets (or targets that had been previously reviewed, but additional information had been obtained on) was provided to those working within the targeting group. All target nominations were maintained on a spreadsheet that was electronically updated and available for review on a classified website. I would review the information on the new targets using this list.

Early and unfettered access to data is critical for an effective and efficient target review. During Operation Allied Force, target data was stored on and accessed through our classified computer system. Those with access to the system had the ability to have most of the data on any individual target available for review with just a few keystrokes and mouse clicks. This information consisted of imagery, descriptions of the facility and its functions, analysis on impact (military advantage anticipated) if destroyed, possible collateral damage concerns, and historical information on the target. There, literally at my fingertips, was all the data needed to make a good initial legal evaluation of the target.

The results of the legal reviews were inputted into the targeting process using two primary methods. A spreadsheet format that was provided to those working within the targeting group and updated as new targets were proposed. This spreadsheet contained the target identification information, collateral damage concerns, justification for attack, and a law of war determination or recommendation. This method ensured a permanent record for each target reviewed and provided an easy means of recalling inputs on each target.

The second method of input was through the collaborative targeting (CTT) sessions. These sessions were an outgrowth of Serbia's failure to acquiesce as quickly as some had hoped would happen. Continuing the conflict translated into a demand for more and better targets, and faster identification.

Increasing the pace of target development meant, in part, more people devoted to the task. Throwing more people into the mix initially created additional problems. Groups worked and coordinated target products in a serial fashion. One group would forward its work as e-mail attachments, message traffic, fax, and/or phone calls to others with responsibility for different portions of the process. The next group would make changes and forward (or, depending on the changes, return to the first group for reconsideration) to other groups involved in the process. This process continued until the lead group believed the proposed target was ready for decision-maker review. Decision-makers would receive an e-mail with the attached product information and would either accept the product information or send it back for further development.

The disadvantages of this early process were information overload, uncertainty, and duplication of effort. Using a serial workflow extended the process timeline and provided more opportunities for confusion, ambiguities and errors. There was no consensus among the participants on the rationale for attacking targets. While no illegal targets were attacked during this period, others and myself were concerned that as the tempo increased our ability to provide the necessary oversight would continue to degrade.

The solution to this serial process was the development of the collaborative targeting sessions. The CTT sessions ensured all targeting organizations had a common understanding of objectives and guidance, built consensus, validated targeting assessments and integrated operational and legal concerns early into the targeting process. Using NetMeeting, a Microsoft product, on the classified internet system, the sessions "virtually" united representatives from commands throughout the theatre and the United States. Similar in concept and format to an internet "chat room" conducted over our classified computer system, these sessions brought all of the players into the same "virtual" room at the same time. All participants could see the proposed target on their computer monitor, could talk via headsets in real time to each other, and could ask questions and resolve issues. This format enabled everyone's input—including legal—to get to all those involved at the same time. With all the relevant functional experts gathered together, questions could be asked and resolutions made in minutes rather than days. What might have taken a week before could be done in one night's session.

Collaborative targeting sessions were generally conducted every night. During a CTT session, the group reviewed proposed targets to determine whether they could be forwarded for approval. For each target, discussion revolved around three issues: 1) the linkage to military effects—the key to gaining legal approval, 2) the collateral damage estimate, and 3) the unintended civilian casualty estimate. The one aspect of this process that consumed most of the time was the collateral damage estimate. Whether it was the nature of the conflict, an outgrowth of the ever increasing visibility of the results of military actions, over sensitivity by political authorities, the desire to make a decision based on some objective "number" (no matter how unscientifically reached or misunderstood) rather than a subjective "value," or a combination of the above, the collateral damage estimate quickly became central to much of the targeting process. An integral part of this estimate was the Tier System.

Legal Perspective from the EUCOM Targeting Cell

The Tier System was developed prior to Operation Allied Force as an effort to standardize the methodology to be used for estimating collateral damage. Though some aspects of this methodology are classified, the unclassified information provides a general understanding. The system currently has four tiers or levels. Each tier represents an ever-increasing level of analysis. Tier 1 consists of a 1500-foot circle drawn around the outer boundary of a proposed target. If there is no collateral damage concern within that circle, then there is no need to move on to the next tier. Tier 2 involves applying fragmentation data of a specific munition to the actual target. This results in a smaller circle being drawn around the target. If a collateral damage concern still exists, then Tier 3 is used. This involves taking a specific munition, applying its record of accuracy, along with the possibility of error, and determining the probable or possible extent of collateral damage. Finally, if the level of possible collateral damage is still viewed as unacceptable; and the target in question is deemed of sufficient value, then a Tier 4 analysis, involving computer simulation and modeling can be conducted.

Here is an illustrative analogy: Tier 1 is like looking at an object with the naked eye, Tier 2 is like using a hand held magnifying glass, Tier 3 is like using a microscope, while Tier 4 is like using a high-powered electron microscope. The tier system is a useful tool that provides a methodology for evaluating the structural collateral damage and possible effects upon any human within the target area. However, it does not provide the actual number of injuries. Also, just because a target is Tier 1 or Tier 4 does not tell the reviewer anything about the actual value of striking that target within the context of the ongoing campaign. Whether or not destroying a particular target is going to achieve the stated military or political objective is not a part of the tier system analysis.

A target may have zero possibility of collateral damage, but if it also has zero impact on the campaign, then bombing that target is wasting resources, putting aircrews and civilians in danger, and possibly violating the law of war. Still, it is very tempting to point to the tier level of some target and make a value judgment solely on those criteria.

Returning to the target approval process, once a collaborative targeting session approved a target, it was sent forward to the decision authority. Obtaining approval from both the appropriate authorities within the United States and NATO was required before any target could be attacked. (Note that as I was not involved in the NATO process, my discussions are focused exclusively on the US process.) Upon this final approval, the Joint Task Force (JTF) could add the target to the master list and schedule it for attack.

However, approval to strike meant much more than just satisfying the rather low thresholds set out by the law of war. The intense concern over the issue of collateral damage meant that targets were approved for strike only at a certain tier level. To achieve that level often meant that only a certain type of munition could be used or the target could only be attacked at certain times of the day. Thus, something as simple as a change in munition could raise the level of collateral damage above what had been approved and, thus, remove a target from the "approved for strike" category.

As a result, though not listed as an official step in the targeting process, reviewing the daily list of proposed strikes for the next two days became a part of the process. This review was simply a quality check—not because people would intentionally ignore orders, but because people enter the data into the computers, people hit the wrong keys and people make mistakes. A single wrong entry or a miscommunication to the personnel who actually had to execute the mission could mean an attack occurring that had not been approved. This is not saying that a law of war violation would occur, just that a target would be struck in a manner that our civilian authorities had not authorized.

In contrast to the hi-tech world of the collaborative targeting sessions, this review was a simple line-by-line comparison of the strike list to the approved target list and the legal review. Usually, this review found no discrepancies; however, on occasion targets listed as approved for attack had not yet been approved at the appropriate level or were being attacked with a munition that raised the possible collateral damage above that approved for the target. When such discrepancies were found, the target would be expedited through the approval process if possible, or the munition would be changed to bring the collateral damage estimate back down. Sometimes this necessitated canceling a strike. After this quality review, the proposed new list of targets would arrive and the process would begin for another day.

Conclusion

After giving this presentation to various audiences, I have found that there is generally surprise at how the targeting process worked. People are surprised to hear that such effort was devoted to each individual target. Of the nearly 2000 fixed targets that were reviewed, each received an independent evaluation within the requirements of the law of war. Is the target a military objective? What military value or advantage is gained from destroying this target? Are we being proportional? Are there any issues with distinction/discrimination?

For those who disagree with the decisions to attack individual targets, I would simply suggest that the laws of war are certainly subject to different interpretations. It is easy to state that there must be an acceptable relation between the legitimate destructive effect and undesirable collateral effects. In reality, whether a specific set of results is "acceptable" is going to depend on the objectives being sought, as well as both the military and political risk those in charge are willing to take. Human rights activists and experienced combat commanders will often not agree on individual targeting decisions. The legal advisor must keep both views in mind and still be able to make a recommendation on a target without losing perspective.

Legal involvement in the targeting process was not limited to just my level. Just as each level of command has its own operators and intelligence officers, so too do they have their own legal advisor. The legal advisors were in constant contact discussing both the broad impact of changes in guidance, as well as specific issues on individual targets.

Operation Allied Force had its share of mistakes, errors, miscalculations and systems malfunctions. Those usually made the evening news and are the subject of continuing, intense discussion and condemnation. The literally thousands of decisions that were made in order to reduce casualties, to limit effects and to deflect the impact do not make the news. The result can be that those who are listening or watching come away with a very one-sided view of the events.

This, in my own view, was—and still is—our biggest miscalculation. Failing to explain before, during and after the fact the efforts that went into the bombing campaign allowed others to interpret it as they saw fit. It did not take being clairvoyant to know that no matter how "just" our cause (at least in the minds of some), our actions would be scrutinized. No one liked what was going on in Kosovo but no one wanted Serbia bombed to oblivion either. This simple truth apparently came as a surprise when the International Criminal Tribunal for the former Yugoslavia—in compliance with its charter—asked questions about the bombing.

Even when we make some feeble attempt at explaining our efforts, we do not provide the depth or detail necessary. Saying we will comply with the law of war is a conclusion that does not do justice to the efforts expended. Further, as a conclusion, there is nothing for people to evaluate and judge. What does the statement "we will comply with the law of war" actually mean? What steps are in place, what guidelines, what processes to ensure compliance?

The assumption that just because we think our cause is "just" that people are going to blindly accept everything we do is born out of arrogance. The price paid for that arrogance is a lack of trust, a disbelief, a lingering disquiet that may be kept at bay only so long as those being opposed can be viewed as the "bad" guy. If we care about our obligations under the law of war, then learning the lesson from Kosovo means that the next time we will do a better job of educating people about the process ahead of time. I am confident that this lesson has not been learned.

Commentary

Harvey Dalton

As I am standing in for Admiral Michael Lohr, I want to approach this from the standpoint of the legal counsel to the Chairman of the Joint Chiefs of Staff—the position that then Captain Lohr held during Operation Allied Force. I will explain the process he employed in providing legal advice to the Chairman and to the General Counsel of the Department of Defense with respect to targeting in Kosovo. We have heard from the former General Counsel, Ms. Judy Miller, from Judge Jamie Baker who provided the National Security Council point of view, and from Lieutenant Colonel Tony Montgomery who provided the US European Command point of view. So this is another link in the legal chain in terms of targeting and the approval of targets at the national level.

At the outset of the conflict, it was expected that Operation Allied Force was going to be quick and easy. There were about fifty to seventy-five pre-designated targets approved in advance. These were very traditional targets that were chosen for immediate military impact. They involved command and control, integrated air defense system, airfields, and aircraft—thoroughly traditional military targets. But Operation Allied Force was not quick and short lived. We realized very quickly that the Serbs were not going to leave Kosovo easily. This caused two things to happen: there was a need for more targets, and there was a need to move to different type of targets other than just the traditional military targets.

The requirement for more targets led to two routes for approval. Most targets, mainly the traditional military targets, were approved in the theater by the US European Command. These targets did not come up to the Joint Staff level, or up to the General Counsel level, or to the Secretary of Defense or president. So this idea that the president approved each and every target is simply not true. The vast majority of targets were approved in-theater. Some targets did have to come back to the Pentagon for review and approval. The military industrial targets, the electric power grids, certain infrastructure, any targets within Belgrade, and those targets that were assessed to have a high potential for collateral damage did have to be reviewed by the Pentagon.

When a target came to the Pentagon, and this is a little bit different from what happened at the European Command, two things happened. The J2, which is our intelligence division, and the Joint Staff immediately began an independent assessment of the target. Aside from what the European Command had done in-theater, the Joint Staff intelligence division started an immediate assessment of the target. This included what Lieutenant Colonel Montgomery referred to as the four-tier assessment. That is a refined assessment that tries to determine as accurately as possible the potential collateral damage that might be sustained in attacking a target. Slides were then produced for briefing the Chairman of the Joint Chiefs of Staff and, if necessary, the secretary of defense and the president. The contents of the slides showed the objective or military linkage of the target. Was it command and control, was it integrated air defense, was it industrial-military, and what was the collateral damage estimate? The assessment might include "high collateral damage," or it might include a specific number of anticipated unintended civilian casualties. The slide would also have a casualty estimate which would include sometimes both the combatants and the noncombatants.

The Joint Staff then produced a matrix, which I don't think they did at European Command. This matrix rated the military significance of the particular target, i.e., whether it was so important that it might cause the termination of hostilities or whether it was a target that merely sustained the military or sustained the Serbian operations in Kosovo. Collateral damage was given a rating of high, medium, or low.

Next came the risk assessment of outliers—the potential for a bomb or missile to miss its target and land somewhere else. This assessment was particularly important where we were using bombs or missiles and where there was a heavily built-up area with large urban structures around the target. There was a greater risk of outliers in those situations. Finally, the matrix would indicate whether the recommendation was to approve the target, disapprove the target, ask for more information, or hold it while we received additional information.

Based upon this information, and based upon the target folders that were received by the Joint Staff, the legal counsel would conduct a legal assessment.

This was a basic law of armed conflict legal assessment: operations may be directed only against military objectives, the civilian population is not to be the object of attack, there can be no intent to spread terror among the civilian population, indiscriminate attacks are prohibited, and the damage to civilian property cannot be excessive in light of the anticipated military advantage. Military objectives were those objectives which by their nature, location, purpose or use make an effective contribution to the military action and whose destruction in the circumstances ruling at the time offered a definite military advantage. That was the rule that was employed in terms of what is a military objective. Take all precautions in means and methods of attack to avoid and minimize incidental injury and death and damage to civilians. This in many cases influenced the aim points of the weapons to try to direct the weapons and the effects of the weapons away from civilians, civilian objects, civilian places.

A number of targets were sent up for further review by the secretary of defense and, occasionally, the president. The four-tier analysis was part of those target packages. The four-tier analysis tried to estimate the damage by fragmentary blast, skin piercing fragments from the blast, window breakage (because that could create a lot of damage and incidental injury), building collapse (the possibility of building collapse or which buildings would be expected to collapse), and eardrum rupture, which obviously causes civilian injuries. Those were the four types of injuries that were modeled and simulated by computer with each type of weapon that was considered as a possible weapon to be employed. This made a lot of difference. It was all visualized, displayed, and we could actually determine to a reasonable degree the extent of collateral damage.

This was the type of analysis that was done by the lawyers, the intelligence community, and the operators. This is what went to the Chairman of the Joint Chiefs of Staff. There may have been ten targets every four or five days that were carried to the president. The chairman would brief those targets to the president, and the president would make the decision to approve, disapprove, request more information, or hold the target. That was essentially the process that the chairman's legal counsel was involved in.

Of course the military objective overall was to force the Serbs to withdraw from Kosovo. NATO in no way unleashed an unlimited war; it was very tightly controlled. There was always some element of political control at all times, which was necessary because we had to hold the coalition together. We did target some of the propaganda capabilities of the Serbs primarily through information operations—non-lethal type attacks. We hit military industrial, dual-use electric power, petroleum because petroleum always supplies the military and the military runs on petroleum products, and infrastructure.

Note the comments by Professor Bothe about the type of infrastructure that can be targeted. In our targeting and in our legal review there were a number of bridges, roads, infrastructures that had no military value whatsoever. We had a couple of targets nominated that were two-lane wooden bridges across drainage ditches. They had no military value whatsoever, and those targets were not approved. So even though it was hostilities, we did not go after all military objects. We went after those that counted, or least the ones we thought counted.

One final comment—I hope you don't get the impression that we are patting ourselves on the back. We did not come here to talk about the wonderful job we did. We came to talk about the process that we went through, and the process that we will hopefully go through and approve each time we employ the use of force. I do think it is necessary that people are aware of the great care and the great effort that goes into targeting, including its legal analysis.

Commentary

Wolff H. von Heinegg

I must congratulate our presenters for their most remarkable contributions; however, congratulation does not mean agreement. This again does not mean that I'm in complete disagreement with all three of them, rather to say that my agreement varies. I will not be able to touch upon all the issues addressed. Hence, I will briefly refer to some details, and then I will close with some more general remarks on some fundamental issues that I'm afraid are too often left out of sight. I will not go into the question of the relevance of Hague Convention IX. I will start with the natural environment.

Professor Bothe is seemingly willing to apply the rules contained in Protocol I[1] on the natural environment as customary international law. First, it needs to be emphasized that Articles 35(3) and Article 55 of Protocol I are so-called "new rules" and, thus, binding only upon States parties to the Protocol. But even when Protocol I is formally applicable, in an international armed conflict, the question remains as to the possible practical impact of these provisions. Remember, they merely prohibit the employment of methods and means of warfare that do or may inflict damage to the natural environment that is "widespread, long-term and severe."[2] There is no conventional method or means of warfare the use of which will clearly be illegal under this prohibition. Even the sinking of an oil tanker cannot always be subsumed under those rules. Moreover, I still have not seen a convincing definition of natural environment. The often-used term "ecosystem" is not a definition, but merely a

---

1. Protocol Additional to the Geneva Conventions of 12 August 1949, and Relating to the Protection of Victims of International Conflicts, Dec. 12, 1977, 1125 U.N.T.S. 3, DOCUMENTS ON THE LAWS OF WAR 422 (Adam Roberts & Richard Guelff eds., 3d ed. 2000).
2. Id., arts. 35(3) and 55.

substitute and not of much help. Hence, the only fairly secure statement on the legal status of the natural environment during international armed conflict is that which is contained in the United States Navy's Commander's Handbook.[3] Please note that while the wanton destruction of the natural environment is illegal because it cannot be justified by reason of military necessity, it is of course never a war crime entailing individual criminal responsibility.

Secondly, I would like to address the list approach. The combined list approach suggested by Professor Dinstein seems to be based on quite a condensing logic. Professor Dinstein correctly referred in his paper to the San Remo process and the very intense discussion on whether it was preferable to merely have an abstract definition of military objectives or to also have a non-exhaustive and merely illustrative list of objects that would usually qualify as military objectives.[4] I believe that the decision of the Round Table to be satisfied with an abstract definition was correct. Such lists would be counterproductive because in the eyes of many, the exclusion of certain objects will mean that they may be attacked in exceptional cases only. All legal methodology will not prevent them from such a misunderstanding. I cannot imagine two or more international lawyers, not to speak of government officials, who could reach an agreement on such a list. The papers presented by Professors Bothe and Dinstein illustrate this point.

Thirdly, let us come to the definition of military objectives. First the question of effective contribution to military action. I fully agree with Professor Dinstein that the concept of war-sustaining capability is much too wide, and more importantly has no foundation in international law. This follows from the simple truth that objects such as raw cotton or, to take a more contemporary example, oil, only under exceptional preconditions and circumstances are subject to military measures, i.e., only if they are used for military purposes. In naval warfare, to give but one example, oil exports are not subject to capture if transported on neutral vessels. Only in the case of a breach of a blockade is there the opportunity to capture it. Capture, however, has to be strictly distinguished from targeting even though I must admit that the dividing line is not always so clear.

---

3. ANNOTATED SUPPLEMENT TO THE COMMANDER'S HANDBOOK ON THE LAW OF NAVAL OPERATIONS 405 (A.R. Thomas and James Duncan eds., 1999) (Vol. 73, US Naval War College International Law Studies).
4. See Professor Dinstein's paper in this volume.

Professor Bothe also maintains in his paper that there are no standing or permanent military objectives.[5] I am unable to agree with such a statement if made in such an absolute form. It is beyond any doubt that there are quite an impressive number of objects that always qualify as legitimate military objectives because by their nature, and by their very nature, they effectively contribute to military action. To give but one example, take a warship or a military airplane. A discussion like that following the sinking of the *General Belgrano* in the Falklands War should not be repeated, and that discussion should not contribute to casting doubt upon this fact of law and life.

Let me shortly refer to the definite military advantage and the circumstances ruling at the time. Here as with regard to the effective contribution to military action, Professors Bothe and Dinstein have presented quite different positions. I must confess that I'd rather follow the Dinstein approach because of fundamental considerations. To start with the details and by concentrating on the broadcasting station, I would like to add and emphasize that we must admit that under the laws of war, enemy means of communication have always been and always will be considered legitimate military objectives. It must also be emphasized that this is true regardless of the overall aim of the war or of the armed conflict. Professor Bothe maintains that tradition should not be overestimated, but, in my opinion, tradition has a lot to do with State practice, which is not only of significance when it comes to the formation of rules of customary international law.

Let me finally turn to some fundamental issues. Even though Professor Bothe correctly holds that the *jus in bello* and the *jus ad bellum* have to be distinguished and kept apart from each other, I wonder whether he doesn't pay just lip service to that distinction. In view of his further thesis, I have some doubts. In any event, the distinction may not be brushed aside. Moreover, the overall aim that led one of the parties to an armed conflict to resort to use of armed force is irrelevant when it comes to the question whether certain objects effectively contribute to military action of the adversary or whether their neutralization offers a definite military advantage. Apart from the problem that such aims will be merely political, the actual or potential tactics and strategies taken by the adversary or the attacker are decisive. We should not forget that the law of armed conflict is designed as a order of necessity that comes into operation if for whatever reasons States are unwilling or unable to refrain from the use of armed force. It is, so to speak, the ultimate legal yardstick that customary international law is willing to accept.

---

5. See Professor Bothe's paper in this volume.

The law of armed conflict does not ask for motives, political aims, or the legality of the first use of force. It takes as a fact that the *jus ad bellum* has failed to function properly. Thus, it accepts that the parties to an international armed conflict do apply certain methods and means of warfare in order to harm the respective enemy and by keeping to a minimum one's own losses. This means that the law of armed conflict sets up certain limits, but it has never been designed to prevent armed conflict.

We as international lawyers should never forget that international law is made by States – that means by those who are bound by it. But if the consensus of States can only be verified, let us say to have reached a certain level, we are not allowed as international lawyers to ignore this and to replace the missing basis by pure hermeneutics or to equate what we wish the law to be with the existing law.

Commentary

Henry Shue

Focusing on dual-purpose targets, I would like to do two things. First, I want to do a little bit of abstract worrying, which is inconclusive and really just a plea for other people to tell me whether there is a real issue here or not. Secondly, I want to go onto something that is fairly concrete. When Professor Dinstein began, he made the traditional point that today we are talking about discrimination and tomorrow we will talk about proportionality. Normally that is how we think about things. It seems to me that it is not absolutely clear that proportionality is as separate in the case of dual-purpose targets as it is in the case of other targets although maybe that is so.

I would just like to raise this question. In the really clear case where you have an object, and you ask if this thing is civilian or military and the answer is that this thing is clearly military, so it is eligible to be a legitimate target. Now we ask if we can destroy this thing without causing collateral damage to some other objects which are civilian. So there is a military object, there are other civilian objects located nearby, and so we ask how much damage will there be to the co-located civilian objects? That is the discussion about proportionality. But the thing about dual-purpose targets is that they are undoubtedly military, but they are also undoubtedly civilian. So rather than having two different objects, we have one object that has two different purposes. Now maybe there is no reason not to treat this in essentially the same way, but I am sort of bothered by that. That is, you can say just as we first ask is this object military, and then we go and look at whether the damage to civilian objects will be disproportionate—why can't we just say okay, here we have a military purpose.

Now let's talk about whether the frustration of the civilian purpose, which this same object also plays, is proportional. But because this is after all only one object, I wonder whether the proportionality shouldn't come up a bit sooner. One way of raising the question is to ask something about Professor Dinstein's list. I do not think I am actually disagreeing with him, but the question is what does it mean to say a certain object is, for example, by nature a military objective. If that just means it's over the first hurdle—that it's now eligible for consideration of whether destroying it will cause proportional damage or not—then that's fine. That is, if all we're saying is that everything that's on the list are military objects about which we now need to ask about proportionality, then that's okay.

It seems to me there's some danger—though maybe this is just an unfair reading of the list—that when one says that all the main railroad lines are by nature military objectives, then one may think that the burden of proof lies especially on proportionality. In order to establish that the civilian damage will be disproportional, one somehow has to show more than one would have had to show if this thing was not already on the list. I hope that's just a misreading of what Professor Dinstein is saying. If not, then I would be a bit worried.

I wonder about the role of proportionality with respect to dual-purpose targets in particular. Now to get a little more concrete and specific, I ask this because it does seem to me that in the case of the dual-purpose targets, everything really turns on proportionality. Academic theorists tend to think that proportionality is not much of a task—that it's so vague that it's not going to really do much work. I want to say two things. The first is that I do take some comfort from what has been said by Lieutenant Colonel Montgomery, Ms Judith Miller and Colonel Sorenson. Based on their testimony anyway, it does appear that in the case of the Kosovo bombing campaign proportionality really did do serious work. To the extent that this is true, I guess I do disagree with Professor Dinstein's comment that World War II would still be going on if the same review had been applied.

I certainly don't think we should take the targeting in World War II as any kind of example of acceptable targeting. There was a lot of targeting in World War II that was completely disproportionate. My understanding is that the war might have ended a lot sooner if we had wasted less stuff trying to break civilian morale and used it in more militarily useful ways. So whether or not this whole process, which I don't pretend I actually understood, is needed, I don't know. That there is some such process seems to me to be actually quite a good thing.

Why do we have the *jus in bello*? We have it because we're trying to avoid having total war. The point of *jus in bello* is that some semblance of normal civilian life should continue even during the war, even while the fighting is occurring on the land and the sea and in the air. Babies are to be born. Old people should be able to finish out their lives. People who need medical attention should be able to get medical attention. There has to be at least some civilian life that is protected from the war. So one of the questions about proportionality is "would the elimination of a particular target make it impossible for even elemental civilian processes to continue?" It seems to me that if it would, the answer is that damage is not proportional unless the military value is of some extraordinary significance of a kind rarely found. It seems to me that this is almost always true of the basic energy sources of the society and especially the electrical grid, the destruction of which makes it impossible to purify the water so children will get waterborne diseases and hospitals are put out of business. It is going to be a rare military advantage that is actually proportional to that.

I am not saying we did the contrary in Kosovo. Maybe not. I worry a little bit about the change in the way we bombed electrical facilities toward the end of the war, but I'm not even sure that there's any objection there. It does sound as if we pretty much made a point of not permanently causing prolonged damage.

Just one final point. I have not seen the RAND study Ms. Judith Miller was talking about this morning that apparently argues that a fear about the extent of the civilian damage was part of the reason that Milosevic conceded.[1] I am very impressed with the argument in Robert Pape's *Bombing to Win* book that I am sure many of you know. His thesis is basically that strategic bombing has never succeeded.[2] That is that the attempt to break the will has never succeeded. Pape's argument mainly being that there is a missing mechanism. The argument is that if you caused the civilians enough pain, then they will want to change the government or end the war, so they will. But the "so they will" part is what is usually not there. In the case of many governments if they could have done that, they might have done it a long time ago. It's especially unlikely they'll be able to do it under the conditions of a national security emergency.

So I doubt very much that that was true in the case of Serbia, although obviously I need to look at that report. If so, of course, that is very different from

---

1. See Ms. Miller's commentary in this volume.
2. ROBERT PAPE, BOMBING TO WIN: AIR POWER AND COERCION IN WAR (1996).

the position that says the civilian damage is unintended but proportional. If you're hoping for this effect, then you are hoping for the civilian damage. That then has become strategic bombing of the World War II sort, not an example of unintentional civilian damage that might then be proportional. That is a very different matter and, as far as I can see, an unacceptable way to proceed.

Discussion

Reasonable Military Commanders and Reasonable Civilians

Charles Dunlap:

I found Professor Bothe's comment about the reasonable military commander and that we ought to have reasonable civilians very interesting. What kind of training regime would you suggest for the civilians to have the competence of the reasonable military commander? Because we find it very difficult to teach even lawyers the art of war sufficiently so that they can render appropriate legal advice.

Michael Bothe:

The point with the "training," I think is not well taken. What is required indeed is a dialogue. This is a two-way street, of course, but "training" implies that I know better and I have to teach the others. That's not the point in a democratic system. We have to have two-way communications and to start a dialogue on that assumption. "I know better" is just the wrong way. I am quite well prepared to tell the same story to some of the human rights organizations who think they know better. This is a lesson I think that both sides should learn.

Harvey Dalton:

I'm a bit worried about that answer. A military commander knows how to employ the Tomahawk land attack missile (TLAM) better. I'm going to defer to his judgment in terms of weaponizing and employing TLAM. I may provide him my legal advice in respect to targeting, but he knows better in terms of that weapon.

Leslie Green:

I, too, am worried about this "reasonable civilian"—this idea of the ordinary civilian and the ordinary soldier. It reminds me of the attitude sanctioned by too many war crimes tribunals. What was the thought of a reasonable man? A reasonable man is the man on a downtown bus; that is not the reasonable soldier. One of the reasons that I don't like civilian judges trying military offenses is that they don't know the circumstances that were prevailing at the time that led to the soldier's actions. The question of what is reasonable in times of conflict depends on what is reasonable in the eyes of the man who is involved in that conflict. That would only be accepted by those who have similar background knowledge, not by one who has been securely moved up in some Inn of Court.

Michael Bothe:
Maybe I'm too much under the impact of the constitutional development of my country after the war. One of the lessons that the persons who drafted the German constitution after the war wanted to draw from historic experience was to integrate the military into a civilian system of values, not to have the military as a state within the State. Arguing that military matters are something which the military knows and the civilian doesn't is utterly a step in the wrong direction.

Natalino Ronzitti:
Ruth Wedgwood and Admiral Robertson have advocated the wisdom of having military people sitting on courts that apply international humanitarian law. I have mixed feelings on this point because you are referring to your American tradition. You have military people with the necessary knowledge of international humanitarian law, but I don't know if in other countries there are military people or military judges who have a good knowledge of international humanitarian law.

I guess I'm more concerned because not all wartime crimes are battlefield crimes. There are courts such as the ICC and ICTY that are competent to try not only war crimes, but also crimes against humanity and genocide. Genocide is very, very hard to establish. It is easy to define, but it is really difficult to prove that the person, the head of State, has committed genocide. So I believe that civilian judges can play a role, but you can have special chambers to deal with battlefield crimes. In those cases it would be best to rely on the opinion of the experts.

Discussion

Legal Advisors and Time-Sensitive Targets

Charles Dunlap:

Kosovo was in many ways a sort of a set-piece operation where you had the luxury of multilevel reviews of targets and so forth, but we are building technological systems to try to close the decision loop in the Air Operations Center to literally minutes where, at best, we are going to be able to have a JAG at the table to try to provide some instantaneous advice regarding targets of opportunity. I'm not sure how these processes will be able to work except by having the JAG being able to make some kind of instantaneous judgment, but this again reflects back on training and the need to know the operational art.

Harvey Dalton:

The dynamic during Kosovo was that we would get these nominations maybe two to three days in advance and we had a constant input of nominated targets. So what we reviewed and approved would be the targets two days down the road. Your point is well taken about the timeline and the fact it's going to get faster. My only suggestion would be that we're going to have to have a lawyer in the loop twenty-four hours a day, seven days a week. It will be a continuous review process and the lawyer can be there for the targets of opportunity. But for the most part this process is a revolving process that may be two days ahead of when you actually use the weapon.

Tony Montgomery:

For time-sensitive targeting in Kosovo, these issues did not even come up to the European Command, much less go to the Joint Staff. Time-sensitive targets or mobile targets were delegated down and the guys on the ground could address those using the same practices they've always used, which are basically using their best judgment. There were people in the Combined Air Operations Center that provided legal advice to General Short.

What the targeting process that everyone and I have been talking about relates to what we think of as strategic targets, not the ones that pop up and we hit opportunistically. Though I will say that the issue of dealing with the tanks and artillery in houses and how to deal with that from a political level as opposed to just if you see a tank in the house you go and whack it, that did get up to the higher levels just because of the consequences that would fall from NATO forces being seen to go in and take down some houses that supposedly had tanks inside of them.

Discussion

Coalition Approval of Targets

Charles Kogan:

It appears that there was a certain dissatisfaction on the part of the Europeans with some aspects of their input into the target approval process. This, I believe, came out in the French after-action report by their defense ministry stating that the B-1 raids from Missouri were conducted outside the NATO chain-of-command. I wonder if Lieutenant Colonel Montgomery could comment on that?

Tony Montgomery:

As far as I know, and I have to qualify it in that way, there was no target struck unilaterally by the United States. What I mean is that everything that was struck had some approval by NATO. Now that does not necessarily mean that each of the nineteen countries sat down and approved each of the individual targets. The Supreme Allied Commander for Europe (SACEUR) had been delegated certain authority. The NATO Secretary-General had been delegated certain authority. Since the US European Command (EUCOM) was not in that chain of command, I have never seen and I have no real idea just how much authority SACEUR had been delegated. I am aware of the French after-action report. I have read it. I am just not aware of any instance where there was a unilateral attack by the United States. I would be surprised if there had been one.

There was a great deal of effort made to do as much as possible to provide information, but EUCOM did not work for NATO. All of my efforts and all of the efforts of the EUCOM targeting cell were directed solely towards satisfying the US desire for information on the targets. We did not provide that targeting data directly to NATO. We were never authorized to do that and we did not take that step. Our data went to the Joint Staff. It went to our political authorities and our military authorities. We were aware that there was some dissatisfaction within certain NATO channels concerning the targeting process, but we could not fix that ourselves.

When Civilian Objects Become Military Objectives

Charles Garraway:

I would like to discuss objects because there has been considerable confusion over the definition of military objective in Article 55(2) of Protocol I. I think the problem has been slightly expanded by some of the language used today such as "traditional military objects" and "dual-use facilities." The problem with the definition is between military objectives and civilian objects. Civilian objects are defined as anything that is not a military objective. Not all military objects are military objectives. I would suggest that the USS *Constitution* in Boston Harbor is a military object, but not necessarily a military objective. Similarly, a civilian house, which may not be being used by the military in any way but may be interrupting a tank advance, can by its location be a military objective. So certainly on the European side of the pond, there is a lot of confusion about military objects and civilian objects with people saying that civilian objects cannot ever be attacked, forgetting about the distinction between civilian objects as defined in Protocol I and civilian objects as used in the ordinary common sense term. Would the panel have anything to say on that?

Yoram Dinstein:
A few words about defended and undefended localities on the frontline. It must be understood that in a frontline situation, as a rule, the pertinent issue is less whether an object constitutes a military objective and more whether it is part of a defended locality. The term "locality" (introduced in Protocol I) is narrower than the expression "village, town or city" originally employed by the Hague Regulations. Whatever language is used, the point is that if a prescribed area is defended, any building within the area (other than an assembly point for the collection of wounded, marked as such) would be exposed to attack, irrespective of its ostensible status as a civilian object.

This is particularly relevant to scenario of house-to-house fighting epitomized by Stalingrad. If house-to-house fighting goes on in a particular city block, there is no need to evaluate the legal standing of every edifice within the block. Any such edifice can be shelled, bombed or otherwise attacked notwithstanding the fact that for the moment it does not serve a military function. The reason is the underlying expectation that the tide of house-to-house fighting will ultimately engulf it although, as yet, this has not come to pass. Obviously, the result can be grave collateral damage to civilians.

The issue of collateral damage to civilians is tied in with that of proportionality. The phrase proportionality is often misunderstood. Protocol I does not mention proportionality at all. The only expression used there is "excessive." The question is whether the injury to civilians or damage to civilian objects is excessive compared to the military advantage anticipated. Many people tend to confuse excessive with extensive. However, injury/damage to non-combatants can be exceedingly extensive without being excessive, simply because the military advantage anticipated is of paramount importance.

Consider the rudimentary example of the bombing of a major munitions factory. The factory may have thousands of civilian employees who are liable to be injured in an air raid. Notwithstanding the enormous civilian casualties likely to ensue, the enemy air force is allowed to strike the factory.

A related point is that of shielding combatants with civilians. A belligerent party shielding a military objective with civilians is acting in breach of the law of armed conflict, and it bears full responsibility for the civilian blood shed by an enemy attack against that military objective. Coming back to my Stalingrad example, once the Soviets decided to turn the city into a battlefield, it was their responsibility to remove civilians from the line of fire. A residential locality on the frontline can be saved from destruction by being declared non-defended. But a belligerent party cannot eat the cake and have it. Logic and experience militate against an attempt to defend a place to the hilt and at the same time expecting the civilian population *in situ* to be protected from the ravages of war.

Relating the Permissible Mission to the Military Advantage

Christopher Greenwood:

There is surely a difference between taking into account what a belligerent is seeking to achieve and trying to determine whether a particular attack will give it a military advantage. Professor Bothe seemed to suggest that we must account for what the belligerent is entitled to seek to achieve. Now it seems to me that an attack does not offer a military advantage if you will destroy something, when its destruction is not going to make the blindest difference to your own military tactics, or to what you expect the enemy's military tactics to be. To say that a State must not destroy something that does indeed interfere with its game plan because that should not have been its game plan in the first place because, for example, it is acting out of humanitarian motives, that seems to me to be an entirely different matter. I would be grateful to see some clarification of the distinction between the two.

Michael Bothe:

This is of course the fundamental issue: how far does the context of the military operation have an impact on the notion of military advantage? I think that the overall context of a military operation has an impact on what can be considered as advantage in this particular context. What you are suggesting is that any conflict is like any other conflict. This is also the basis of the objection of Professor von Heinegg in his Commentary. You say for the purposes of

Discussion

the *jus in bello*, any armed conflict is like the other. There is no distinction. I recognize that if I try to make distinctions, then I am very close to mixing *jus in bello* and *jus ad bellum*. I repeat that is something I do not want to do because it means foregoing one of the essential bases of the application of the *jus in bello*, which is reciprocity. Anything which risks negatively affecting reciprocity, I think, should be out.

There, I agree with all the objections that have been made. But this being so, I am still not convinced that you can take the notion of military advantage out of its context. If the declared purpose of a military operation is limited, as it was in Kosovo, you cannot divorce the notion of advantage from that purpose. It is not just the subjective intent; it is the objective character of the entire mission. The Independent Commission on Kosovo comes up with something similar and even goes a little further. They say there should be a protocol three on humanitarian intervention, because it is not appropriate to have the whole spectrum of otherwise lawful means of combat for an exclusively humanitarian intervention. I am not sure whether I would go that far, but I think that without changing the law, my interpretation of military advantage is a possible restraint.

This brings me to the more fundamental question which was asked by Wolff von Heinegg. Is it wishful thinking? Or is it a real development of the law? This is a distinction that sometimes is hard to make if we are in a situation of transition. We do not yet know whether Kosovo is transition or not. Operation Allied Force was for some something novel. It is a part of a process, as the United Nations Secretary-General put it, of redefining sovereignty and drawing different conclusions from the requirements of sovereignty than we did before. I am not so sure whether this is the case, but we are entering the question of the *jus ad bellum* here, and I refrain from commenting on that. If new types of military operations are developing, having completely different purposes from traditional war, then it is not only a matter of the *jus ad bellum*. It's also a matter of the means how these conflicts are conducted.

This also goes into the question of the ethical considerations which are discussed in relation to Kosovo. The standard objection from the moral point of view is from the traditional *bellum iustum* theory (there was a just cause but not a just means). This is standard in the literature on that subject. So these things are linked. And the relationship between *jus ad bellum* and *jus in bello* is not one watertight compartment. That is wishful thinking. We are at a point where the law might change, and I think it's absolutely legitimate to think about the direction in which it changes. My conclusion is formulated farther in terms of the question than in terms of a statement of *lex lata*.

Discussion

Yoram Dinstein:

I have already tried to underscore in my paper the relativistic nature of a military advantage. Let me add here that often, whereas you do not know for sure what's good for you, you clearly perceive what you would like to deny to the other side. Thus, a military advantage to one belligerent party would simply be a mirror image of a military disadvantage to the adverse side. This brings me to my disagreement with Professor Bothe regarding the issue of bridges and railroads. At a certain juncture in the course of hostilities a bridge may just be standing there, without anyone appreciating its military value. It is only when a belligerent party calculates of what value the bridge could be to the enemy at a later stage that it dawns on military commanders that they'd better do something to eliminate the risk. The issue is not always destruction or capture: neutralization of a bridge to the enemy is another form of military advantage.

The momentous significance of some bridges should be manifest to all when it is borne in mind that World War II may have been prolonged by some six months only because of a British failure to capture a crucial bridge on the Rhine ("a bridge too far"). And it may as well be added that, had not the US Army captured intact the rail bridge at Remagen, the issue of the crossing of the Rhine might possibly have plagued the Allies a lot longer than it did.

What is true of bridges may also be true of railroads. The Panzer divisions in the Battle of Normandy fought superbly. But since the rail system had been paralyzed by Allied bombings, the Panzers had to reach the frontline—sometimes from the other side of France—on their own power. This took a long time (in some cases, up to two weeks), denying the Germans the opportunity to stop the Allied forces at the beaches. Moreover, by the time that the German armored units arrived at the frontline, they were (1) out of fuel, (2) in dire need of repair of many machines (while lacking the facilities to undertake the repair), and (3) the crews were tired and in some instances expecting defeat. In all, the dramatic Allied victory in June 1944 probably owes more to the systematic bombings of the French railroads than to the actual matching of tanks against tanks.

"Dual-Purpose" Targets

Yoram Dinstein:

A question was posed to me about "dual purpose" targets. I am not enamored of this phrase and have not used it in my paper. It appears neither in Protocol I nor in any other LOAC instrument that I am familiar with. I do not know where "dual use" comes from, and can only surmise that it has penetrated the lingo through articles published by human rights (rather than law of armed conflicts) scholars. To the best of my knowledge, references to "dual use" started with ill-founded criticisms of coalition bombings of the electric grid in Iraq in 1991. Since the electric grid in Iraq was totally integrated, attacks against it—and its installations—resulted not only in a tremendous military advantage (shutting down radar stations, military computers, etc.), but also extensive damage to civilians: hospitals stopped operating, water pumping and filtering facilities came to a standstill, etc. From a legal viewpoint, a "dual use" of Iraq's electric grid did not alter its singular and unequivocal status as a military objective. There was, as usual with military objectives, the question of proportionality where collateral damage to civilians is concerned. But the extensive damage to civilians was not excessive in relation to the military advantage anticipated. What was true of Iraq is equally true of Kosovo.

One has to constantly bear in mind that war is war; not a chess game. There is always a price-tag in human suffering. Admittedly, Kosovo is not a very appropriate backdrop for such a point to be made, inasmuch as the war was conducted on NATO's part on the assumption of zero casualties (although that meant zero casualties to NATO). In any event, no serious war can be founded on such an assumption. Some wars are more unfortunate than others in terms of actual bloodshed, but in the long run civilian suffering cannot be utterly avoided.

John Murphy mentioned that in present-day wars it may paradoxically be safer to be a combatant than a civilian. This shocking truth has become a governing factor of modern hostilities only since the outbreak of World War II. Earlier, the situation was entirely different. As late as World War I, in the Western Front at least, civilian casualties were mild while a whole generation of young combatants was destroyed in the trenches.

The current disproportion of the civilian/combatant ratio of casualties is totally unacceptable. Anyone even mildly interested in international humanitarian law must strive to bring about a better world in which civilized losses in war are minimized. Nevertheless, the realistic goal is to minimize civilian casualties, not to eliminate them altogether. There is no way to eliminate civilian deaths and injuries due to legitimate collateral damage, mistake, accident and just sheer bad luck.

Discussion

Targeting Regime Elites

John Norton Moore:
As we seek to stop aggressive war and to end the all too frequent slaughter of civilian populations as we saw in Bosnia and had begun to see in Kosovo before the NATO intervention, there has been increasing theoretical interest in the focusing of deterrents, including intra-war deterrents, on the regime elites who were ordering the aggressive war or the genocide in the first place. From that observation, I have a couple of questions for any member of the panel who would like to respond. First, did NATO in fact consider that in relation to targeting Milosevic or his assets or his principal henchmen? Second, did the laws of war constrain NATO in any way from targeting the regime elites in Serbia if NATO had wanted to do so? And third, if there were any such constraints, do you believe that it is necessary to modify the law of war to permit the kinds of targeting of assets of regime elites or at least those that are ordering the continuation of such wars? And if so, what kinds of constraints or restraints if any would you put on them?

Michael Bothe:
Well, I cannot of course comment on what NATO considerations in this respect were, as these were not privy to me. As far as the law of war is concerned, targeting the elite is perhaps not the right term in this respect. It matters whether the persons in question are combatants or military commanders. If the president happens to be the military commander, as said earlier today, he or she can be targeted. If not, no. This is of course a certain constraint. I think it is a healthy constraint if you ask me. I would not like to see the laws of war modified in this respect because that would really open the door to do away with the distinction which I think is a healthy one.

Robert F. Turner:
We are trying to distinguish *jus ad bellum* and *jus in bello*, but the modern view is (at least when you're dealing within the setting of aggression) that the prevailing responsibility of States is not to be neutral but to be in opposition to aggression. You are not obliged to send troops, but you are not supposed to be in favor of the aggressor. If you are in a setting where international law allows the use of lethal force in self-defense or collective self-defense in response to the aggression, then the question becomes not are you assassinating a leader, which is by definition murder, but rather which target do you use lethal force against. If one of your choices in your best professional judgment is that we

can stop this aggression by taking out the head aggressor, the head war criminal—even if he doesn't wear a uniform, but is the person who made the decision to commit the aggressive act—are you saying that it is in every instance preferable to say no, we would rather slaughter twenty or thirty thousand soldiers out on the field who may have had nothing to do with the policy and may have had no chance of going to Canada? Saddam Hussein, for example, was rough on his deserters. How do you deal with the doctrine of proportionality when you say it is better to kill thirty thousand innocent soldiers than to endanger the key war criminal who started the entire attack? Does that change anybody's attitude?

Wolff H. von Heinegg:

What you just asked only at first glance seems to be logical, because it does not matter. What the law of armed conflict has achieved from 1977 and beyond is something that we should not underestimate. There is the principle of distinction not only with regard to targeting, but also with regard to the question of distinction between combatants and noncombatants. So if there is a person that is not a combatant, a noncombatant I must say, then this person may not be attacked—period. It doesn't matter whether this decision will lead to twenty thousand deaths in the field, because those who are dying in the field or in the air or in the sea are combatants. They are legitimate military targets.

If we are trying to modify the existing law by such considerations, then what we have achieved until now will be destroyed very easily. As soon as you accept that *jus ad bellum* considerations play a role when it comes to the question of applicability of the *jus in bello*, the *jus in bello* is lessened. It is being deformed. Suddenly it doesn't depend only on the parties to the conflict, but on somebody else (like Her Majesty's government, for example) to determine whether certain measures taken during armed conflict by the parties to the conflict are legal or not under the laws of war. I say we must rather leave the laws of war and leave the law of armed conflict as it is with the principle of distinction between combatants and noncombatants and not modify it with any considerations taken from outside the law of armed conflict.

Robert F. Turner:

The concept of the noncombatant was one of innocence. It was that this person's life has no effect on the outcome of the war, and therefore they should not be harmed. If you trace the history of the law or the rule that says you cannot touch the other guy's king, Vattel and Grotius and others point out this is not the logical rule of law. This is an agreement that the leaders made to protect their own safety in an era where waging aggressive war was the sovereign prerogative of kings. What I am saying is now that we have moved on to make waging aggressive war a war crime, why do we still decide that the head war criminal is an innocent party who should be given the same protection as a Red Cross worker at the expense of all these young kids that get sent out there and slaughtered?

Harvey Dalton:

The study that Judith Miller cited this morning did conclude that there was an effort to impose pressure on the elites of Yugoslavia so as to have them impose pressure on Milosevic to terminate the conflict. That was done by targeting military-industrial plants and facilities owned or run by these elites and, as Ms Miller mentioned this morning, the Rand Study found that that was in fact more effective than the attacks on the military objectives. Now that is a very disturbing conclusion. I think it is very disturbing, because I do think the laws of armed conflict still apply. At least from our standpoint in targeting and approving these targets, there had to be a very clear military link between these industrial facilities and the war effort. We required that, but the pressure later on may be otherwise.

John Norton Moore:

I think this does raise some very important questions because all that we have and all that we do and all that we should do in the law of war, as in any other area of law, needs to serve a variety of important goals. We are trying to serve the humanitarian goals of preventing aggressive war, of minimizing casualties and preventing genocide. If, in fact, we discover as a significant body of newer information such as the Rand study is suggesting that a focus on regime elites, including the head of the State if necessary, is more effective than a variety of other applications, then it seems to me that is something that deserves very careful consideration.

PART IV

COLLATERAL DAMAGE

Introduction

John Norton Moore

We have a distinguished panel of experts addressing issues associated with collateral damage. That general rubric would include issues that are dealt with in Protocol I, referred to as excessive civilian damage in attacks on otherwise lawful targets, and issues regarding feasible precautions in attacking.

I have three brief points that I would like to put before us before turning to the panelists. The first is for us to consider just how far we have come in relation to the systematic inclusion of the laws of war in military operations and to reflect for a moment on the creation of the field called operational law in the United States. As I think everyone in this room knows full well, the United States and particularly the US military had a sorry experience in Vietnam. When the war was over and we looked back and sought to look at the lessons learned about Vietnam, a number of things emerged that were very important in relation to the laws of war. The first of those is that we had not trained as adequately in the laws of war as we should have. The result was a My Lai which had enormous cost for the United States in that war. We also found that one of the problems was a series of areas of advice given and constraints placed on the United States military ostensibly designed for ethical and law of war reasons, but in fact uninformed about proper targeting and correct operation of the law of war. The result was a series of inhibitions that were not required by the law of war and which dramatically stretched out the war and perhaps in the end cost the United States the war in Vietnam.

After Vietnam there was a review, led for the most part by the US military, that said in effect "We're going to have to in the future have a cadre of people that are extraordinarily well trained in the law of war so that we won't be making the mistakes on either side of this equation—either unnecessarily prohibiting targeting that is essential for warfighting, or on the other hand not controlling activities that are violations of the laws of war." The result has been an extraordinary input of good legal advice regarding US military activities. Indeed I think we can say that the first real test of this came during the Gulf War in which we saw extremely careful vetting of virtually every target with equal emphasis on both sides of the equation—permitting effective warfighting on the one hand, and on the other hand preventing problems that could be serious humanitarian violations that would undermine the war effort.

It seems to me that the same thing has happened again in Kosovo. As we put this in perspective, the real starting point is to notice that there has never been a military campaign in the history of the world that has had such a careful input and consideration of targeting, proportionality and all of the other issues than in the Gulf War and again in the Kosovo operation under NATO. It is a sea change.

My second point is that while this colloquium is quite properly focused on the issue of lessons from the NATO campaign in Kosovo, let us at least remind ourselves that there is—quite apart from NATO activities—a very serious enforcement problem in relation to massive noncompliance with the laws of war by the opponents that we were facing. We can go all the way back to Vietnam and the massive violations of the laws of war by North Vietnam, not unintended by the government as in the case of My Lai, which was carried out by an out-of-control second lieutenant who was poorly trained. We saw the same problem in Bosnia with the slaughter of people in that conflict. We saw it in Kosovo, and we saw it in Rwanda. It has not gone away. It is still with us in the modern world. So one of the jobs for us as academics and members of the government and those that are interested seriously in humanitarian law is never to forget that we have a fundamental enforcement problem in relation to the non-democratic governments that are still committing democide, genocide and other massive insults in relation to the laws of war.

The third and final context point I would like to make is simply to remind us that as with all law, the laws of war are intended to serve important goals. They must be judged in the end by their effectiveness in serving those goals. In this context of the laws of war, all of us know that there is in fact a careful balance that has to be met. For a variety of ethical, moral and other reasons we want to make sure that we protect against unnecessary and excessive damage. All of us are very aware of principles of discrimination, of proportionality, of avoidance of unnecessary suffering and other important principles of the laws of war that lead in that direction. Let me just suggest that there is another

Introduction

critical reason for democracies to support such laws. That is for democracies it is essential that they comply with humanitarian objectives in wartime. To fail to do that has extraordinary cost for the democracies and the entire political-military effort. If we learned anything from the Vietnam context, it is the great importance of democracies fighting wars in strict compliance with humanitarian objectives.

There is another consideration that makes the issue far more complex and far more difficult because we also learned in the Vietnam context that excessive constraints can be highly costly. If all we had was the one side of the equation, it would be tempting simply to say that we can always keep placing more and more constraints on the warfighting effort. Unfortunately we know in the real world that if we place too many constraints on that effort it will have costs that will undermine the very goals that we seek to support through the laws of war. We can endanger our own military when we have constraints that are too great. In addition, we may end up prolonging the war—mitigating the shock value necessary to promptly end the conflict—and as a consequence end up with many, many more combatants and civilians killed than if the war had been properly fought and ended at an early time.

I was the Counselor on International Law to the US Department of State during the Vietnam War and I witnessed with great interest what happened in a three-week period when the President of the United States, President Nixon, suddenly decided to fight the war the proper way—not by violating the laws of war or engaging in carpet bombing or anything of that sort—but instead by doing what the Joint Chiefs had suggested that he do many years before. He simply mined Haiphong Harbor, which as far as I know had zero casualties on all sides but suddenly prevented 90% to 95% of all the importation of war supplies into North Vietnam. In addition to that, he carried out the "Christmas" bombing, which was not an area bombing of Hanoi or Haiphong, but was instead a careful attack on rail lines in the Hanoi area. The result was North Vietnam came to the table for the first time in the entire history of the war seriously seeking the end of the war. Within three weeks, the Paris accords were agreed and the United States decided the war was over and came home. The point is this could have been done at any point in the preceding years of the war and casualties on all sides would have been reduced very dramatically.

There is yet another problem if the constraints are too excessive. At some point if the cost of war fighting by the democracies in resisting aggression, genocide and democide is too high, we will in fact discourage the democracies from undertaking those efforts. That of course in the end is what happened in

Vietnam when the United States finally came home. The other party then simply had a regular army invasion of the south and the result was a bloodbath, which we now know resulted in at least one hundred thousand killed in the south, a million boat people, with a half million dying at sea, and somewhere between one and three million dying in Cambodia. So what we do in relation to advice on the laws of war is important in terms of the real world and real human lives and real effectiveness in preventing aggression, stopping aggression and in fact stopping genocide as well. I simply place these points in front of you as context as we move forward to our discussion on collateral damage.

Some Legal (And A Few Ethical) Dimensions Of The Collateral Damage Resulting From NATO's Kosovo Campaign

John F. Murphy

Introduction

Any analysis of the legal dimensions of NATO's Kosovo campaign should first distinguish between the *jus ad bellum*, the law of resort to the use of armed force, and *the jus in bello*, the law regulating the way the armed force is employed, of that conflict. To be sure, there is no "Chinese wall" separating the *jus ad bellum* and *jus in bello* aspects of the Kosovo campaign. For example, assuming *arguendo*, as some have argued,[1] that international law recognizes a doctrine of humanitarian intervention, and this doctrine serves as a justification for NATO's resort to armed force in the Kosovo campaign, it is arguable that the military action undertaken must be designed to prevent the humanitarian catastrophe unfolding.[2] Nonetheless, the focus of this paper is not the effectiveness, or lack thereof, of the bombing to prevent or minimize Serbian "ethnic cleansing" or other war crimes in Kosovo. Rather, it is on the collateral damage to civilians caused by this bombing.

According to the organizers of this colloquium, this panel is to address in particular the following issues:

---

* The author would like to thank Kevin Jarboe, a graduate of Villanova University School of Law and Andrew Kenis, a third year student at the Law School, for research and assistance on this paper.
1. *See, e.g.*, Michael Glennon, *The New Interventionism: The Search for a Just International Law*, 78 FOREIGN AFFAIRS 2 (May–June 1999).
2. I have so argued in my chapter on *Kosovo Agonistes*, in TRILATERAL PERSPECTIVES ON INTERNATIONAL LEGAL ISSUES (Chi Carmody, Yuji Iwasawa, and Sylvia Rhodes eds., 2002).

(1) Does the use of precision-guided munitions (so-called "smart bombs") lead to a duty to use those types of weapons exclusively in future conflicts?

(2) If so, does it mean that two adversaries may be subjected to differing legal and ethical regimes, dependent on their relative level of technological sophistication?

(3) What degree of injury and damage to civilians can be regarded as excessive, and consequently disproportionate, as compared to the military advantage gained?

(4) What are the legal and ethical implications of NATO's apparent efforts to minimize its own combat casualties through high-altitude bombing and avoidance of a ground campaign, and did this greatly increase the risk of civilian casualties?

Each of these issues, along with issues related thereto, will be addressed seriatim in this paper.

Precision-Guided Munitions and International Law

Before turning to the issue of whether international law does or should require the use of precision-guided munitions in future conflicts, we need to define a few terms. The US Department of Defense defines precision-guided munitions as "a weapon that uses a seeker to detect electromagnetic energy reflected from a target or reference point, and through processing, provides guidance commands to a control system that guides the weapon to the target."[3] Like Stuart Belt, in his extensive treatment of the subject,[4] this paper does not discuss the use of air-to-air missiles, because they normally do not produce collateral damage. Rather, the focus of the paper is on air-to-ground munitions. Again like Belt, this paper does not distinguish between smart, accurate, or precision weapons but instead groups them together as precision-guided weapons. It does distinguish the precision-guided weapon from an

---

3. Precision Weapons, *available at* http://www.dtic.mil/doctrine/jel/doddict/data/p/04864.html, last visited Dec. 27, 1999, and *quoted in* Stuart Belt, Missiles Over Kosovo: Emergence, Lex Lata, of a Customary Norm Requiring the Use of Precision Munitions in Urban Areas, 47 NAVAL LAW REVIEW 115, 118 (2000).

4. Belt, *supra* note 3, at 118.

unguided weapon by noting that the former has some type of in-flight guidance system. This in-flight guidance system may or may not be powered. The so-called Paveway series of weapons, for example, are laser guided.[5] For a detailed discussion of various kinds of precision-guided munitions, the reader should consult Belt's article.

In his article, Belt notes that US military operations or US-led military operations have seen a dramatic increase in the use of precision-guided munitions from the "opening salvo of Operation Desert Storm" to the "closing shot of Kosovo"[6]—a five-fold increase to be precise. Between the Desert Storm and Kosovo campaigns, Belt points out, there was Operation Desert Fox, an intensive four-day US bombing campaign against Iraq, with the stated goal "to degrade Saddam's capacity to develop and deliver weapons of mass destruction, and to degrade his ability to threaten his neighbors."[7] According to Belt, Operation Desert Fox offered the US military an opportunity to "battle-test some new smart weapons and reaffirm lessons learned in Desert Storm."[8] Belt quotes David Isby, writing for Jane's Missiles and Rockets, who reportedly stated: "Operation Desert Fox was the largest air offensive to be waged largely with guided weapons rather than 'dumb' munitions that [had] predominated in all previous major offensive uses of air power, including the 1991 Gulf War."[9]

As elaborately detailed by Belt, there seems to be no question that the United States has made increasingly heavy use of precision-guided munitions in recent military operations. Whether it now has an obligation under international law to do so in future conflicts is the issue to which we now turn.

Does International Law Now Require the Use of Precision-Guided Munitions in Future Conflicts?

It is clear that there is no requirement under international law that precision-guided munitions be used exclusively in future conflicts. A strong advocate of the use of precision-guided munitions, Belt admits that they have their limitations:

---

5. *Id.* at 118–19.
6. *Id.* at 126.
7. Statement by President William Clinton, quoted by Richard Newman, in *Bombs over Baghdad*, U.S. NEWS AND WORLD REPORT, Dec. 28, 1998, at 32, *cited in id.* at 131 n.108.
8. Belt, *supra* note 3, at 131.
9. David Isby, *Cruise Missiles Flew Half the Desert Fox Strike Missions*, JANE'S MISSILES AND ROCKETS (1999), *cited in id.* at 132 n.110.

The function of the precision-guided weapon, however, has its limitations. There are limitations on its efficacy and missions that are clearly better suited for mass bombing. Large maneuvering units in the field are excellent targets for unguided, gravity bombs (carpet bombing) and much less so for precision-guided weapons. Not only does the carpet-bombing produce favorable psychological impact, but also the number of precision-guided weapons required to hit the large number of open field targets would be prohibitively expensive. This idea was confirmed by W. Hays Parks, who concluded that B-52s were the right platform to use because they were able to drop a large number of bombs into an area where no protected objects existed and where Iraqi troops were entrenched in the desert and difficult to attack. In essence, the use of precision-guided weapons and that of unguided, en masse bombs have a complementary role. Precision-guided weapons are particularly useful against strategic targets that often times have a locus near heavily populated civilian areas whereas en masse bombing is useful for targets where the goal is widespread damage and the demoralization of troops. This was the practice during Operation Desert Storm.[10]

Accordingly, the issue should be restated as whether there is an obligation under international law to use precision-guided munitions in attacks on urban areas. Belt is of the opinion that there is.

At the risk of oversimplification, one may say that treaties and norms of customary international law are the primary sources of international law, as reflected in the Statute of the International Court of Justice.[11] Both sources have played a major role in the law of armed conflict. We begin with norms of customary international law.

---

10. *Id.* at 130.
11. Article 38(1) of the Statute of the International Court of Justice, 59 Stat. 1055, T.S. 993, 3 Bevans 1179, provides:

    1. The Court, whose function is to decide in accordance with international law such disputes as are submitted to it, shall apply:

    (a) international conventions, whether general or particular, establishing rules expressly recognized by the contesting states;

    (b) international custom, as evidence of a general practice accepted as law;

    (c) the general principles of law recognized by civilized nations;

    (d) subject to provisions of article 59 [which states that "The decision of the Court has no binding force except between the parties and in respect of that particular case"], judicial decisions and the teaching of the most highly qualified publicists of the various nations, as subsidiary means for the determination of the rules of law.

A. *Customary International Law*

Parenthetically, it should be noted that the basic concept of customary international law has recently come under attack, and one commentator has gone so far as to call for its elimination as a source of international law.[12] Be that as it may, the law of armed conflict has long recognized the importance of customary international law through the so-called "Martens Clause," which appears in the preambles to both the 1899 and 1907 Hague Conventions on Laws and Customs of War on Land, as well as in Article 1(2) of the 1977 Protocol I Additional to the Geneva Conventions of 12 August 1949, and which provides in pertinent part: "In cases not included in the Regulations ... the inhabitants and belligerents remain under the protection and the rule of the principles of the law of nations, as they result from the usages established among civilized peoples, from the laws of humanity, and the dictates of the public conscience."[13] The practical significance of the Martens Clause is that "it contains a built-in mechanism to fill in the lacunae existing in the law of war at any particular time."[14] For the United States, the Martens Clause may take on added importance at the present time, since it is not a party to either of the 1977 Additional Protocols.

The classic description of the process of creating customary international law is that of Manley O. Hudson, a Judge on the International Court of Justice and an eminent authority on international law. According to Hudson, the essential elements of the customary international law process include:

1. concordant practice by a number of States with reference to a type of situation falling within the domain of international relations;

2. continuation or repetition of the practice over a considerable period of time;

3. conception that the practice is required by, or consistent with, prevailing international law; and

4. general acquiescence in the practice by other States.[15]

---

12. J. Patrick Kelly, *The Twilight of Customary International Law*, 40 VIRGINIA JOURNAL OF INTERNATIONAL LAW 449 (2000).
13. For a brief discussion of the Martens Clause, see Howard Levie, *The Laws of War and Neutrality*, in NATIONAL SECURITY LAW 307 (John Moore, Frederick Tipson, and Robert Turner eds., 1990).
14. EDWARD KWAKWA, THE INTERNATIONAL LAW OF ARMED CONFLICT: PERSONAL AND MATERIAL FIELDS OF APPLICATION 12 (1992).
15. Manley Hudson, [1950] 2 YEARBOOK OF THE INTERNATIONAL LAW COMMISSION 26, U.N. Doc. A/CN.4/Ser.A/Ser. A/1950/Add.1.

There is general agreement that the first, third and fourth of Hudson's elements are the most crucial under modern approaches to the customary international law process. At the same time, however, each of these three elements has been subject to critical scrutiny and debate.

There is, for example, no agreement on what constitutes State practice.[16] The US Department of State emphasizes the acts of governments but not UN resolutions. This approach supports the claims of States, such as the United States, with strong centralized governments. In contrast, some scholars and less powerful States would include as State practice normative statements in drafts of the International Law Commission, resolutions of the United Nations General Assembly, and recitals in international instruments.[17]

Hudson's requirements that States engage in a practice with an understanding that it is required by, or consistent with, prevailing international law and that there be general acquiescence in the practice by other States raises the complex issue of *opinio juris*, which is the general acceptance of a norm as a legal obligation by the world community. The concept of *opinio juris* introduces a subjective element in the customary international law process because it requires that States when engaging in or refraining from a particular practice do so under an understanding that they have a legal right to engage in the practice or a legal obligation to refrain from engaging in the practice.

With respect to the methodological problem of determining *opinio juris*, Professor Anthony D'Amato has suggested that, as a requirement for a finding of *opinio juris*, an objective claim of legality be articulated in advance of, or concurrently with, the State practice allegedly required or permitted by customary international law.[18] Interestingly, under D'Amato's approach, the articulation of a claim of legality could be made either by a State, a recognized writer, or a court.[19] To others, however, this "'claims approach' defines away the requirement of the normative conviction of the community."[20] Moreover, D'Amato concedes that it is not possible to determine if a majority of States are conscious of any international obligation.[21]

Other commentators would dismiss or at least minimize the importance of an articulation of a claim of legality on the ground that the "best evidence of

---

16. See Kelly, *supra* note 12, at 500–07.
17. *Id.* at 501.
18. ANTHONY D'AMATO, THE CONCEPT OF CUSTOM IN INTERNATIONAL LAW 77, 85 (1971).
19. *Id.*
20. See, e.g., Kelly, *supra* note 12, at 479.
21. D'AMATO, *supra* note 18, at 82–85.

opinio juris is actual practice consistently and generally followed."[22] According to this view, a record of consistent and widespread practice raises strong inferences of *opinio juris* without need of further evidence. Before turning to a consideration of whether customary international law requires the use of precision-guided munitions in aerial attacks on urban or other highly populated areas, it may be appropriate to keep in mind a famous statement of the Permanent Court of International Justice in the *Lotus* case:

> International law governs relations between independent States. The rules of law binding upon States therefore emanate from their own free will as expressed in conventions or by usages generally accepted as expressing principles of law and established in order to regulate the relations between these co-existing independent communities or with a view to the achievement of common aims. Restrictions on the independence of States cannot therefore be presumed.[23]

Although the *Lotus* case has been "strongly criticized for its 'extreme positivism' and especially for asserting that restrictions on the freedom of states cannot be presumed,"[24] it has never been repudiated by the International Court of Justice. Moreover, its positivist approach may be particularly well suited to issues of the law of armed conflict, which, by their very nature, implicate the vital interests of States.

Let us turn then to State practice regarding the use of precision-guided munitions. As noted previously, the United States has made increasingly heavy use of precision weapons in aerial attacks on targets in urban or other heavily populated areas, and this was especially the case in the Kosovo campaign. What is less clear is the extent to which other States have made use of precision-guided weapons in armed conflict. Belt reports that more than 34 countries are using or have access to the Paveway laser guided bomb series and gives other examples of precision-guided weapons used by various countries.[25] His study is extremely thin, however, on the extent of actual use by countries of precision weapons in armed conflict. On the contrary, Belt admits that Russia has made relatively little use of precision weapons in Chechnya, although he attempts to explain this away by noting that there has been some Russian use of such weapons in the conflict and that Russia has never asserted the right to

---

22. Oscar Schachter, *Entangled Treaty and Custom, in* INTERNATIONAL LAW AT A TIME OF PERPLEXITY: ESSAYS IN HONOR OF SHABTAI ROSENNE 717, 731 (Yoram Dinstein ed., 1989).
23. The S.S. Lotus (Fr v. Turk.), P.C.I.J. (Ser. A) No. 10, at 18 (Sep. 7).
24. LOUIS HENKIN ET AL., INTERNATIONAL LAW 70 (3d ed., 1993).
25. Belt, *supra* note 3, at 125.

use non-precision bombs indiscriminately near civilian areas.[26] The limited evidence of use of precision-guided munitions to date would seem to indicate an absence of any widespread State practice. Significantly, the International Court of Justice has stated that: "Although the passage of only a short period of time is not necessarily . . . a bar to the formulation of a new rule of customary international law . . . State practice . . . should have been both extensive and virtually uniform. . . ."[27]

Assuming *arguendo* the existence of sufficient State practice to support the existence of a norm of customary international law requiring the use of precision weapons in attacks on urban or other heavily populated areas, even Belt admits that the "harder issue" is whether *opinio juris* is present.[28] In his attempt to prove the existence of *opinio juris*, Belt cites statements by US officials or statements in US government documents that confirm the US desire to conduct the Gulf War in a manner consistent with international legal obligations or that recognize the long-standing customary law of armed conflict principle of distinction or discrimination that commanders and others planning an attack take all possible feasible steps, consistent with allowable risk to aircraft and aircrews, to minimize the risk of injury to noncombatants.[29] He fails to cite any statements by US officials regarding the Gulf War, Desert Fox, or Kosovo campaigns that in any way recognize a legal obligation to use precision-guided munitions. To be sure, with respect to the Kosovo campaign, Belt is able to quote Lord Robertson, who, when serving as NATO Secretary-General, said that "international law and public opinion" required the use of precision weapons in the Kosovo campaign.[30] With respect, this appears to be a weak reed upon which to lean.

---

26. *Id.* at 161.
27. North Sea Continental Shelf (F.R.G. v. Den./F.R.G. v. Neth.), 1969 I.C.J. 3, 43 (Feb. 20).
28. Belt, *supra* note 3, at 163.
29. *Id.* at 163–64. Belt quotes from a study of the Gulf War commissioned by the Department of Defense that concluded:

> Coalition forces took several steps to minimize the risk of injury to noncombatants. To the degree possible and consistent with allowable risk to aircraft and aircrews, aircraft and munitions were selected so that attacks on targets within populated areas would provide the greatest possible accuracy and the least risk to civilian objects and the civilian population.

30. Vago Muradian, *Robertson: Europe Must Spend More Wisely to Achieve Gains*, DEFENSE DAILY, Dec. 8, 1999, at 6, *quoted* and *cited in id.* at 165 nn.294, 295.

B. Treaties and Conventions

A major problem one faces in analyzing treaty law to determine whether the United States has an international obligation to use precision weapons is that the United States is not a party to Additional Protocol I, the most recent major treaty on the law of armed conflict. Nonetheless, in the section of his article discussing the relevance of treaty law to precision weapons, Belt focuses his primary attention on Protocol I. Obviously, for the United States, Protocol I would be apposite only if its relevant provisions represent a codification of customary international law. Belt appears to assume *sub silentio* that they do, a highly debatable proposition, as we shall see. Before turning to this issue, however, we need to examine briefly some treaties and conventions that the United States has ratified.

A primary premise of the 1907 Hague Convention IV Respecting the Laws and Customs of War on Land[31] is that "the right of belligerents to adopt means of injuring the enemy is not unlimited."[32] Although the 1907 Hague Convention is a relatively (for the time) comprehensive codification of laws governing land warfare, Articles 25 and 27 apply as well to aerial bombardment.[33] Article 25 provides that "the attack or bombardment, by whatever means, of towns, villages, dwellings, or buildings which are undefended is prohibited." Article 27 states that

> In sieges and bombardments all necessary steps must be taken to spare, as far as possible, buildings dedicated to religion, art, science, or charitable purposes, historic monuments, hospitals, and places where the sick and wounded are collected, provided they are not being used at the same time for military purposes.

For its part, Article 2 of Hague Convention IX of 1907 Concerning Bombardment by Naval Forces in Time of War[34] built upon and improved the

---

31. Hague Convention (IV) Respecting the Laws and Customs of War on Land, Oct. 18, 1907, 36 Stat. 2277, DOCUMENTS ON THE LAWS OF WAR 69 (Adam Roberts and Richard Guelff eds., 3d. ed. 2000).
32. *Id.*, art. 22.
33. Much of this discussion of the 1907 Hague Convention draws from Danielle Infeld, *Precision-Guided Munitions Demonstrated Their Pinpoint Accuracy in Desert Storm; But is a Country Obligated to use Precision Technology to Minimize Collateral Civilian Injury and Damage?*, 26 GEORGE WASHINGTON JOURNAL OF INTERNATIONAL LAW & ECONOMICS 109 (1992). Ms. Infeld in turn relies heavily on the magisterial examination of applicable law in W. Hays Parks, *Air War and the Law of War*, 32 AIR FORCE LAW REVIEW 1 (1990).
34. Hague Convention (IX) concerning Bombardment by Naval Forces in Time of War, Oct. 18, 1907, 26 Stat. 2351, DOCUMENTS ON THE LAWS OF WAR, *supra* note 31, at 122.

approach taken by Hague Convention IV in that it "identified particular military objects that could be attacked, and recognized the inevitability of collateral damage in the execution of such attacks."[35] In addition, Article 2 explicitly absolved the attacker of responsibility for "unavoidable" collateral damage resulting from the attack of such military objects.[36] Also, as Hays Parks has noted, these and other provisions in the two Hague Conventions placed primary responsibility for collateral damage on the defender because it had the superior ability to control the civilian population.[37] The civilian population itself also had, to the extent possible, to take steps to remove itself from the conflict. Only if he engaged in an indiscriminate attack would the commander be responsible for collateral damage. In Parks' view, "responsibility for avoidance of collateral civilian casualties or damage to civilian objects . . . is a shared obligation of the attacker, defender, and the civilian population."[38]

This "shared obligation" approach continued under subsequent treaty developments in the law of armed conflict. In particular, the Geneva Convention Relative to the Protection of Civilian Persons in Time of War (Geneva Convention IV)[39] defines a person protected by the Convention as anyone who, during a conflict or occupation, is "in the hands of a Party to the conflict or Occupying Power of which they are not nationals."[40] Any person suspected of, or engaged in, activities hostile to the security of the State will not be afforded protection as a civilian.[41] For their part, States are required to take steps to ensure that their private citizens do not take part in hostilities in a way that could endanger innocent civilians.[42]

According to Hays Parks, however, this tradition of shared obligation was broken with the adoption of Additional Protocol I. In a lengthy exegesis of the Protocol, especially Articles 48 through 58, the articles most directly relating to combat operations, Parks demonstrates that these provisions shift the

---

35. Parks, *supra* note 33, at 17.
36. The second paragraph of Article 2 of Hague Convention IX provides that the commander "incurs no responsibility for any unavoidable damage which may be caused by a bombardment under such circumstances."
37. Parks, *supra* note 33, at 28–29.
38. *Id.*
39. Convention Relative to the Protection of Civilian Persons in Time of War, Geneva, Aug. 12, 1949, 6 U.S.T. 3516, 75 U.N.T.S. 287, DOCUMENTS ON THE LAWS OF WAR, *supra* note 31, at 301.
40. *Id.*, art. 4.
41. *Id.*, art. 5.
42. Parks, *supra* note 33, at 118.

responsibility for the protection of the civilian population away from the defender almost exclusively to the attacker.[43] He concludes:

> Customary international law requires that an attacker exercise ordinary care in the attack of military objectives located near the civilian population, to minimize injury to individual civilians or the civilian population as such incidental to the attack. The defender's responsibility is to exercise an equal degree of care to separate individual civilians and the civilian population as such from the vicinity of military objectives. Where a defender purposely places military objectives in the vicinity of the civilian population or places civilians in proximity to military objectives, in either case for the purpose of shielding military objectives from attack, an attacker is not relieved from his obligation to exercise ordinary care. Responsibility for death or injury resulting from the illegal action of the defender lies with the defender, however. The language of Protocol I—particularly as it has been interpreted by the ICRC and many of the nations known in the course of the Diplomatic Conference as the Group of 77—casts doubt upon whether the limited credibility of the law of war relating to war-fighting *per se* will survive any serious challenge.[44]

Interestingly, in his discussion of relevant provisions of Protocol I, Belt does not acknowledge, in text or footnotes, Parks' critique or that dissatisfaction with Articles 48 to 58 was a primary reason for the US decision not to ratify the Protocol.[45] Nonetheless, he concludes that

> The language in Protocol I was not specific enough, either in form or from a review of *travaux preparatoires*, to mandate the exclusive use of precision-guided munitions (PGMs) in urban areas. Therefore, even if it were declaratory of customary international law norms at the time of its signing in 1977, it would not be dispositive as to use of PGMs.[46]

Accordingly, Belt and Parks appear to be in agreement that treaty law does not require the use of precision-guided munitions in future conflicts. They disagree as to whether customary international law requires the use of

---

43. *Id.* at 112–202.
44. *Id.* at 168.
45. Belt, *supra* note 3, at 145–51. For other commentary on why the United States decided not to ratify Protocol I, see Michael Matheson, *Session One: The United States Position on the Relation of Customary International Law to the 1977 Protocols Additional to the 1949 Geneva Conventions*, 2 AMERICAN UNIVERSITY JOURNAL OF INTERNATIONAL LAW & POLICY 419 (1987); Abraham Sofaer, *Agora: The U.S. Decision Not to Ratify Protocol I to the Geneva Conventions on the Protections of War Victims*, 82 AMERICAN JOURNAL OF INTERNATIONAL LAW 784 (1988).
46. Belt, *supra* note 3, at 167.

precision-guided weapons in attacks on urban or other highly populated areas. Belt, as we have seen, believes that it does. Parks has indicated that he agrees with Danielle Infeld that it does not.[47] Previously in this paper, I have expressed my agreement with the Parks/Infeld position as to the *lex lata* (existing law). Still to be considered, however, is whether the Belt position has merit as a *lex ferenda* (law in formation) proposition.

C. *Should International Law Require the Use of Precision-guided Munitions in Urban or Other Highly Populated Areas?*

There seems to be little disagreement that, as a policy matter, precision-guided weapons should normally be used in aerial attacks on urban or other highly populated areas. Under many, perhaps most, circumstances, there is a happy congruence between the needs of military efficiency and the avoidance of unnecessary injury to civilian persons or property.[48] That is, the use of precision-guided weapons will more thoroughly destroy the target, while avoiding or minimizing collateral damage, than will so-called "dumb" bombs. In such cases, the attack is being conducted in complete accord with Article 57(2)(a)(iii) of Additional Protocol I, which requires commanders and others planning an attack to "take all feasible precautions in the choice of means and methods of attack with a view to avoiding, and in any event to minimizing, incidental loss of civilian life, injury to civilians and damage to civilian objects." The problem is that in some circumstances this happy congruence is not present.

Belt admits that precision-guided weapons are not suitable for all circumstances, and indeed cites Hays Parks in acknowledging this fact.[49] His acknowledgment, however, appears to be limited to attacks on targets far from heavily populated areas, such as large maneuvering units in the field. In contrast, Parks has discussed in detail several circumstances when the use of precision-guided weapons might not be suitable, even in attacks on highly populated areas.[50] These circumstances include, in particular, adverse weather conditions, technological malfunction, human error, or heavy anti-aircraft fire that requires pilots to zigzag, which decreases the accuracy of an attack.[51] When such circumstances are present, an attacker might reasonably conclude that the use of precision-guided weapons would not be

---

47. See W. Hays Parks, *The Protection of Civilians from Air Warfare*, 27 ISRAEL YEARBOOK ON HUMAN RIGHTS 65, 85–86 n.57 (1998).
48. For examples, see Belt, *supra* note 3, at 117–37.
49. *Id.* at 130.
50. Parks, *supra* note 33, at 185–202.
51. For further discussion, see Infeld, *supra* note 33, at 131–33.

appropriate. A hard and fast "black letter rule" requiring the use of precision-guided weapons in any attack on an urban area would be dysfunctional under such circumstances. Better perhaps to rely on the judgment of the commander in such cases. Hays Parks emphatically states his view:

> Article 57, paragraph 2(a)(iii) [of Protocol I] requires commanders and others planning an attack to "take all feasible precautions in the choice of means and methods of attack with a view to avoiding, and in any event to minimizing, incidental loss of civilian life, injury to civilians and damage to civilian objects." An inevitable question is, "If a commander has a choice between two means for attacking a target, one less accurate than the other, is he obligated to use the most precise means?" Common sense, the definition of *feasible* by many States in the process of their respective ratification or accession—a definition subsequently adopted by the community of nations in their drafting of Protocol III on Incendiary Weapons to the 1980 United Nations Conventional Weapons Convention—and a reading of the relevant punitive provisions of Additional Protocol I clearly indicate that not to be the case. A commander's good faith judgment remains essential to effective implementation of this provision.[52]

The definitions of feasible referred to by Parks lend substantial support to his position. In a footnote, he quotes the statement of Italy accompanying its ratification of Protocol I that it "understands . . . that the word 'feasible' is to be understood as practicable or practically possible, taking into account all circumstances ruling at the time, including humanitarian and military considerations."[53] Similarly, Article 1(3) of Protocol III on Incendiary Weapons to the 1980 United Nations Conventional Weapons Convention defines "feasible precautions" as "those precautions which are practicable or practically possible taking into account all circumstances ruling at the time, including humanitarian and military considerations."[54] This recognition that combat decisions vary depending on the "humanitarian and military considerations" existing at the time argues in favor of maximizing the discretion of the commander rather than imposing a hard and fast rule. Finally, Article 85(3)(b) of Protocol I, which classifies an action as a grave breach only if it involves "launching an indiscriminate attack affecting the civilian population or civilian objects in the knowledge that such attack will cause excessive loss of life,

---

52. Parks, *supra* note 47, at 85–86.
53. *Id.* at 85 n.54.
54. *Id.* at 86 n.55.

injury to civilians or damage to civilian objects,"[55] lends a measure of support to this thesis.

To this commentator, Parks and Infeld have the better of the argument. It appears to be the case that the use of precision-guided weapons is not always suitable, even with respect to targets in heavily populated areas. Moreover, it also appears to be impossible to predict in advance of an attack what circumstances might arise that would make the use of precision-guided weapons inappropriate. If these two propositions are correct, it would make no sense to have a "black letter" rule requiring the use of precision-guided weapons, since this would introduce a degree of undesirable rigidity into the law of armed conflict. The better approach is to leave the decision whether to employ precision-guided weapons to the individual commander whose decision turns on the particular circumstances he faces at the time of armed conflict.

Since he contends that present customary international law requires the use of precision-guided weapons in attacks on urban areas, Belt recognizes that this raises the second issue the organizers of the colloquium have posed: whether two adversaries may be subjected to differing legal and ethical regimes, dependent upon their relative level of technological sophistication. Belt contends that they may.[56] He suggests that the problem may be minimized if not eliminated by technology transfer that narrows the gap between the level of technological sophistication of developed countries and that of developing countries, quoting one writer who urges that developed countries provide subsidies to developing countries to enable them to acquire precision weapons.[57] In Belt's view, however, the "most balanced approach" is:

> The one similar to the environmental stance of "common but differentiated responsibilities." This has been coined in the law of war arena as "normative relativism." As the divide between countries grows in regard to military prowess and capability, "there will be subtle stressors that encourage an interpretation of the law of armed conflict relative to the state to which it is applied." In the end the same standard applies to both states (developed vs. less developed)—that is the need to minimize collateral damage—but there will be a higher standard on the developed state. The theory of normative relativism essentially supports the conclusion that "belligerents are held to the standards to which they are capable of reasonably rising."[58]

---

55. Id. at 86 n.56.
56. Belt, *supra* note 3, at 167–73.
57. R. George Wright, *Noncombatant Immunity: A Case Study in the Relation Between International Law and Morality*, 67 NOTRE DAME LAW REVIEW 335, 336–37 (1991), *quoted in id.* at 172.
58. Belt, *supra* note 3, at 172–73.

In sharp contrast, Michael Schmitt has contended, "[i]t is simply beyond credulity to suggest that the acceptability of striking a particular type of target or causing a certain amount of collateral damage or incidental injury might one day depend on the characteristics of the attacking state."[59] For his part, Hays Parks has observed that: "Lawful combat actions are not subject to some sort of 'fairness doctrine,' and neither the law of war in general nor the concept of proportionality in particular imposes a legal or moral obligation on a nation to sacrifice manpower, firepower, or technological superiority over an opponent."[60] It might be suggested further that Belt's reliance on "common but differentiated responsibilities" in the field of international environmental law seems misplaced. It is one thing to suggest that developed States should be subjected to more onerous standards than developing countries in protecting or cleaning up the environment. It is quite another to propose that developed countries should accept standards that could disadvantage them in armed conflict. Since many, perhaps most, developing countries would be unable to comply with a rule requiring the use of precision weapons in attacks on urban areas, this is a good reason not to have such a rule in the first place.

What Degree of Injury and Damage to Civilians Can be Regarded as Excessive, and Consequently Disproportionate, as Compared to Military Advantage Gained?

The question of what degree of injury to civilians is "excessive" and therefore "disproportionate" to the military advantage gained by an armed attack cannot, of course, be answered in the abstract. It raises in sharp relief, however, the issue of the role the principle of proportionality does or should play in the law of armed conflict. Judith Gail Gardam has suggested that proportionality is a "fundamental" component of the *jus in bello* and described it as "the

---

59. Michael Schmitt, *The Principle of Discrimination in 21st Century Warfare*, 2 YALE HUMAN RIGHTS & DEVELOPMENT LAW JOURNAL 143, 176 (1999).
60. Parks, *supra* note 33, at 169–70. As an egregious example of the misuse of the concept of proportionality, Parks sets forth the following hypothetical that was presented by an inexperienced Army instructor at The Judge Advocate General's School of the U.S. Army:

> An enemy platoon of forty men is in a defensive position on a hill, armed only with small arms. You have been assigned the mission of capturing the hill. You have the capability of attacking the hill with a company of two hundred men, supported by artillery, tanks, helicopter gunships and close air support fixed-wing aircraft. The "rule"of proportionality requires you to eschew the use of anything more than an infantry platoon armed with small arms.

balance to be struck between the achievement of a military goal and the cost in terms of lives."[61] Although she acknowledges that some civilian casualties have always been accepted as the inevitable consequence of a military attack, she contends that "the concept of proportionality . . . has assumed the pivotal role in determining the extent to which civilians are entitled to be protected from the collateral effects of armed conflict."[62]

Hays Parks is much more skeptical. He reports that the American military review of Protocol I concluded that the concept of proportionality is not a rule of customary international law and argues that, judged by US domestic law standards, "the concept of proportionality as contained in Protocol I would be constitutionally void for vagueness."[63] To support his "void for vagueness" argument, Parks further contends that

> [F]ollowing more than a decade of research [as of 1990] and meetings of international military experts who are anxious to implement the language contained in Protocol I to the extent it advances the law of war and the protection of the civilian population, there remains a substantial lack of agreement as to the meaning of the provisions in Protocol I relating to proportionality. This is a rather disconcerting situation given that other lawyers are claiming that the concept of proportionality is customary international law.[64]

For her part, Gardam acknowledges the significant juridical impact the US position has had on the role the concept of proportionality plays in the law of armed conflict. She concludes:

> In the final analysis, it appears that the interpretation by the United States and its allies of their legal obligations concerning the prevention of collateral casualties and the concept of proportionality comprehends only two types of attacks: first, those that intentionally target civilians; and second, those that involve negligent behavior in ascertaining the nature of a target or the conduct of the attack itself, so as to amount to the direct targeting of civilians. The conduct of hostilities in the Gulf conflict indicates that the concept of "excessive casualties" was restricted to that context; the military advantage always outweighed the civilian casualties as long as civilians were not directly

---

61. Judith Gardam, *Proportionality and Force in International Law*, 87 AMERICAN JOURNAL OF INTERNATIONAL LAW 391 (1993).
62. *Id.* at 398.
63. Parks, *supra* note 33, at 173.
64. *Id.* at 175.

targeted and care was taken in assessing the nature of the target and the carrying out of the attack itself.

The impact of the practice of states such as the United States and its coalition partners on the formation of custom is considerable and cannot be overlooked. It seems inevitable that the concept of proportionality as a customary norm is currently limited to the situations outlined above. Moreover, it seems likely that the interpretation of the conventional requirements of Articles 51 and 57 with respect to "excessive casualties" may be similarly limited.[65]

Michael Schmitt approaches the problem of "excessive casualties" with a focus on the principle of discrimination that mandates discrimination between civilians and their property and legitimate targets.[66] He suggests that the principle of discrimination comprises two primary facets. The first facet limits or prohibits the use of weapons that are by their nature indiscriminate. One example he gives is "biological weapons that spread contagious diseases, for such weapons are incapable of afflicting only combatants and difficult to control."[67] The second facet of the principle prohibits the indiscriminate use of weapons, regardless of their innate ability to discriminate. As an example, he cites Iraq's use of SCUD missiles against Israel during the Gulf War. This second facet of discrimination, he suggests, in turn consists of three components: distinction, proportionality, and minimizing collateral damage and incidental injury.

The concept of distinction, which prohibits direct attacks on civilians or civilian objects, finds its primary expression in Article 48 of Protocol I, which provides that parties to a conflict must "distinguish between the civilian populations and combatants and between civilian objects and military objectives and accordingly direct their operations only against military objectives." Under Article 52(2), military objectives are "those objects which by their nature, location, purpose or use make an effective contribution to military action and whose total or partial destruction, capture or neutralization, in the circumstances ruling at the time, offers a definite military advantage."

---

65. Gardam, *supra* note 61, at 410. In footnote 102 Gardam recognizes that there is disagreement among scholars as to whether the practice of specially affected States is more important in the formation of custom from conventional norms than that of other States but suggests that it "may, however, be more influential in reality by virtue of being more frequent and better publicized."
66. Schmitt, *supra* note 59.
67. *Id.* at 147.

Seemingly straightforward and unobjectionable as an abstract proposition, the concept of distinction has given rise to considerable controversy. For example, the International Committee of the Red Cross (ICRC) defines the terms "effective" and "definite" narrowly. In the ICRC's Commentary on Protocol I, effective contribution includes objects "directly used by the armed forces" (e.g., weapons and equipment), locations of "special importance for military operations" (e.g., bridges), and objects intended for use or being used for military purposes."[68] The Commentary also interprets the phrase "definite military advantage" to exclude those attacks offering only "potential or indeterminate advantages."[69] Under Article 51(3) of Protocol I, civilians are legally protected from attack unless they take a "direct part in the hostilities." According to the ICRC Commentary, such participation is limited to "acts of war which by their nature or purpose are likely to cause actual harm to the personnel and equipment of the enemy armed forces."[70] Under Article 50(1) of Protocol I doubts as to the character of an individual are resolved in favor of finding civilian status, and Article 52(3) provides the same presumption for civilian objects.

The ICRC interpretation has been subject to scathing criticism.[71] In temperate tones, Schmitt has noted:

> Others take a less protective approach to the limitations. The United States, for example, would include economic facilities that "indirectly but effectively support and sustain the enemy's war-fighting capability" within the ambit of appropriate targets. Similarly, some have cited mission-essential civilians working at a base during hostilities, even though not directly engaging in acts of war, as legitimate targets. Thus, while there is general agreement that the Protocol accurately states customary international law principles, notable disagreement persists over exactly what those standards are.[72]

Schmitt goes on to suggest that proportionality differs from distinction in terms of *scienter*, i.e, the issue of proportionality arises in situations where the attacker knows that an attack on a legitimate military target will result in injury to civilians or civilian property. To Schmitt, this

---

68. COMMENTARY ON THE ADDITIONAL PROTOCOLS OF 8 JUNE 1977 TO THE GENEVA CONVENTIONS OF 12 AUGUST 1949, at 636 (Yves Sandoz et al. eds., 1987), cited and quoted in id. at 148.
69. Id., quoted and cited in Schmitt, supra note 59, at 149.
70. Id. at 619, quoted and cited in Schmitt, supra note 59, at 149.
71. See especially Parks, supra note 33, at 113–45.
72. Schmitt, supra note 59, at 150.

[R]enders the discrimination decision matrix much more complex. With the first tier of discrimination analysis, the question is: 'May I lawfully target an object or person?' With proportionality, an additional query must occur: 'Even if I conclude that targeting the person or object is unlawful, may I nevertheless knowingly cause him or it injury or damage in my attack on a legitimate objective?'[73]

The difficulty of answering the additional query arises in particular because

[T]he actor must not only struggle with issues of inclusiveness (what are the concrete and direct consequences?), but he must also conduct a difficult jurisprudential balancing test. Optimally, balancing tests compare like values. However, proportionality calculations are heterogeneous, because dissimilar value genres—military and humanitarian—are being weighed against each other.[74]

To be sure, in some cases the proportionality calculation would be relatively simple. Hays Parks cites as the "classic example" of a disproportionate action the destruction of a village of 500 persons simply to destroy a single enemy sniper or machine gun.[75] But what if the likely cost in civilian lives lost were five? Would (should) this be regarded as "excessive" and disproportionate to the military advantage gained? In such a case, a clash between the military and humanitarian "value genres" referred to by Schmitt might well arise.

Moreover, Parks has suggested three "fundamental" problems with implementation of the concept of proportionality.[76] The first is the definition of military advantage, and the level at which a determination should be made (tactical or strategic), the second is who should be responsible for the probable civilian losses resulting from the attack (the attacker, defender, or the civilians themselves), and the third concerns what Parks calls the "friction of war." To Parks, this friction is caused in large measure by uncertainty, and he quotes Clausewitz's observation that "War is the realm of uncertainty; three quarters of the factors on which action in war is based are wrapped in a fog of greater or lesser uncertainty."[77] This uncertainty is based in considerable part on a lack of information regarding the enemy and greatly complicates the decision making process. To Parks, it also counsels against any attempt "to establish an

---

73. Id.
74. Id. at 151.
75. Parks, *supra* note 33, at 168.
76. Id. at 175.
77. CLAUSEWITZ, ON WAR 119–20 (M.Howard & P. Paret trans., 1976), *quoted in id.* at 183.

unrealistic form of accountability for civilian casualties that occur incidental to legitimate military operations."[78] In his view, this is what Protocol I, especially as interpreted by the ICRC, attempts to do.

In my view, it is not necessary to decide whether "proportionality" is part of customary international law or simply a policy consideration or a "principle" that commanders should take into account during the course of armed conflict. The conscientious commander will make every effort to avoid launching an armed attack when the likely outcome is a clearly disproportionate amount of collateral damage. Under any other than the easy case scenario, however, as Parks and especially Schmitt have noted, the calculation of whether a particular attack will result in proportionate or disproportionate collateral damage becomes exceedingly difficult and problematic. It must also be remembered that a mistaken calculation of proportionality could result in individual liability for a war crime for the commander or in liability for a violation of the law of armed conflict by the commander's country. Accordingly, it would seem best to limit such liability to the circumstances summarized by Gardam as the US position: where civilians are deliberately targeted or there is negligent behavior in ascertaining the nature of a target or the conduct of the attack itself that amounts to the direct targeting of civilians. Any other standard would pose an unacceptable dilemma for the commander operating under exceedingly stressful conditions.

To return to the point made at the beginning of this section of the paper, the question of what degree of injury to civilians is excessive and therefore disproportionate to the military advantage gained by an armed attack cannot be answered in the abstract. Accordingly, in the next section we turn to the legal and ethical implications of NATO's apparent efforts to minimize its own combat casualties through high-altitude bombing and avoidance of a ground campaign.

What Are the Legal and Ethical Implications of NATO's Apparent Efforts to Minimize Its Own Combat Casualties Through High-Altitude Bombing and Avoidance of a Ground Campaign and Did This Greatly Increase the Risk of Civilian Casualties?

At the outset of our discussion in this section, it should be noted that there is a crucial factual issue to be addressed: did NATO's high-altitude bombing and avoidance of a ground campaign in fact greatly increase the risk of civilian

---

78. Parks, *supra* note 33, at 202.

casualties? Some critics of the Kosovo campaign have so alleged.[79] Charles Dunlap, however, has challenged this thesis.[80] According to Dunlap, lower altitude attacks were attempted but did not prove very effective. On the contrary, he contends, the nature of precision-guided munitions is such that they are often optimally targeted at the altitudes NATO employed. He further suggests that flying at lower altitudes would have increased the chances of success for Serbia's antiaircraft and short range missile systems and that "[a] crippled twenty or thirty-ton airplane loaded with fuel and high explosives crashing out-of-control into an urban neighborhood can create as much or more devastation among civilians as any errant bomb."[81] Similarly, in his view, a ground assault would have increased the risk of civilian casualties because the weapons of land warfare—artillery, multiple rocket launchers, and machine guns and other small arms—lack the precision quality of high-altitude bombing, and ground combat in an urban environment is a casualty-intensive affair for both combatants and civilians. Finally, Dunlap notes that reportedly, out of the more than 25,000 weapons used in Kosovo, only twenty resulted in collateral damage incidents, "a phenomenal record in the history of warfare."[82]

Let us assume *arguendo* that the critics are right and the high-altitude bombing and the avoidance of a ground campaign did increase the risk of civilian casualties. What, if any, are the legal and ethical implications of these decisions? We turn to the legal implications first.

A. Legal Implications

There seems to be little question that the decision to engage in high-altitude bombing did not by itself constitute a violation of the law of armed conflict. As Dunlap points out, although the law of armed conflict seeks to protect noncombatant civilians from the adverse effects of war, there is "nothing in that

---

79. *See, e.g.*, HUMAN RIGHTS WATCH, CIVILIAN DEATHS IN THE NATO AIR CAMPAIGN 2 (2000), *available at* http://www.hrw.org/reports/2000/nato/; AMNESTY INTERNATIONAL, NATO/Federal Republic of Yugoslavia: "Collateral Damage" or Unlawful Killings?, Violations OF THE LAWS OF WAR BY NATO DURING OPERATION ALLIED FORCE 17 (2000), available at http://www.amnesty.org/ailib/intcam/kosovo/docs/natorep_all.doc; Richard Bilder, *Kosovo and the New Interventionism: Promise or Peril?*, 9 JOURNAL OF TRANSNATIONAL LAW & POLICY 153, 171 (1999); Ved Nanda, *NATO's Armed Intervention in Kosovo and International Law*, 10 US AIR FORCE ACADEMY JOURNAL OF LEGAL STUDIES 1, 9 (1999/2000).
80. Charles Dunlap, *Kosovo, Casualty Aversion, and the American Military Ethos: A Perspective*, 10 US AIR FORCE ACADEMY JOURNAL OF LEGAL STUDIES 95 (1999/2000).
81. *Id.* at 97.
82. *Id.* at 103.

legal regime [that] expressly requires an assumption of more risk by a combatant than a noncombatant."[83] Similarly, the Final Report to the Prosecutor by the Committee Established to Review the NATO Bombing Campaign Against the Federal Republic of Yugoslavia (hereinafter ICTY Final Report) concluded "there is nothing inherently unlawful about flying above the height which can be reached by enemy defenses."[84] To be sure, the Committee recognized that the principle of distinction required NATO air commanders to "take practicable measures to distinguish military objectives from civilians or civilian objectives," and that the 15,000 feet minimum altitude adopted for part of the campaign may have meant the target could not be verified by the naked eye. But it concluded that "with the use of modern technology, the obligation to distinguish was effectively carried out in the vast majority of cases during the bombing campaign."[85] Lastly, the Report of the Independent International Commission on Kosovo, established at the initiative of the Prime Minister of Sweden, Mr. Goran Persson, concluded that the "high-altitude tactic does not seem to have legal significance. . . ."[86]

The legal issue, then, would seem to be whether the bombing campaign resulted in injury and damage to civilians that can be regarded as excessive and therefore disproportionate to the military advantage gained—more or less the same issue we considered in the abstract in the previous section of this paper. Any determination as to whether injury and damage to civilians is "excessive" in relation to the military advantage gained by the bombing necessarily includes a measure of subjectivity that may lead reasonable persons to differ over the proper conclusion to be reached. It is accordingly noteworthy that the Independent International Commission on Kosovo was

> [I]mpressed by the relatively small scale of civilian damage considering the magnitude of the war and its duration. It is further of the view that NATO succeeded better than any air war in history in selective targeting that adhered to principles of discrimination, proportionality, and necessity, with only relatively minor breaches that were themselves reasonable interpretations of 'military necessity' in the context.[87]

---

83. *Id.* at 99.
84. Final Report to the Prosecutor by the Committee Established to Review the NATO Bombing Campaign against the Federal Republic of Yugoslavia, 39 INTERNATIONAL LEGAL MATERIALS ¶ 55 (2000), *reprinted* herein as Appendix A [hereinafter Report to the Prosecutor].
85. *Id.*
86. THE INDEPENDENT INTERNATIONAL COMMISSION ON KOSOVO, THE KOSOVO REPORT 181 (2000).
87. *Id.* at 183–84.

For its part, the ICTY Final Report noted that the NATO bombing campaign involved 38,400 sorties, including 10,484 strike sorties, and the release of 23,614 air munitions, yet only approximately 500 civilians were killed during the campaign. The conclusion of the Report was that "[t]hese figures do not indicate that NATO may have conducted a campaign aimed at causing substantial civilian casualties either directly or incidentally."[88]

One of the allegations that led to the establishment of the Committee that issued the ICTY Final Report was that NATO forces "deliberately or recklessly caused excessive civilian casualties in disregard of the rule of proportionality by trying to fight a 'zero casualty war' for their own side."[89] Interestingly, in its discussion of the "principle [not rule] of proportionality," the Committee expressed some of the same concerns and reservations that have troubled Hays Parks and the US military in their review of Protocol I. They are worth quoting at length.

> 48. The main problem with the principle of proportionality is not whether or not it exists but what it means and how it is to be applied. It is relatively simple to state that there must be an acceptable relation between the legitimate destructive effect and undesirable collateral effects. For example, bombing a refugee camp is obviously prohibited if its only military significance is that people in the camp are knitting socks for soldiers. Conversely, an air strike on an ammunition dump should not be prohibited merely because a farmer is plowing a field in the area. Unfortunately, most applications of the principle of proportionality are not quite so clear-cut. It is much easier to formulate the principle of proportionality in general terms than it is to apply it to a particular set of circumstances because the comparison is often between unlike quantities and values. One cannot easily assess the value of innocent human lives as opposed to capturing a particular military objective.
>
> 49. The questions which remain unresolved once one decides to apply the principle of proportionality include the following:
>
> (a) What are the relative values to be assigned to the military advantage gained and the injury to noncombatants and/or the damage to civilian objects?
>
> (b) What do you include or exclude in totaling your sums?
>
> (c) What is the standard of measurement in time or space? and

---

88. Report to the Prosecutor, Appendix A, ¶ 54.
89. Id., ¶ 2.

(d) To what extent is a military commander obligated to expose his own forces to danger in order to limit civilian casualties or damage to civilian objects?

50. The answers to these questions are not simple. It may be necessary to resolve them on a case by case basis, and the answers may differ depending on the background and values of the decision maker. It is unlikely that a human rights lawyer and an experienced combat commander would assign the same relative values to military advantage and to injury to noncombatants. Further, it is unlikely that military commanders with different doctrinal backgrounds and differing degrees of combat experience or national military histories would always agree in close cases. It is suggested that the determination of relative values must be that of the "reasonable military commander." Although there will be room for argument in close cases, there will be many cases where reasonable military commanders will agree that the injury to noncombatants or the damage to civilian objects was clearly disproportionate to the military advantage gained.

51. Much of the material submitted to the OTP [Office of the Prosecutor] consisted of reports that civilians had been killed, often inviting the conclusion to be drawn that crimes had therefore been committed. Collateral casualties to civilians and collateral damage to civilian objects can occur for a variety of reasons. Despite an obligation to avoid locating military objectives within or near densely populated areas, to remove civilians from the vicinity of military objectives, and to protect their civilians from the dangers of military operations, very little prevention may be feasible in many cases. Today's technological society has given rise to many dual-use facilities and resources. City planners rarely pay heed to the possibility of future warfare. Military objectives are often located in densely populated areas and fighting occasionally occurs in such areas. Civilians present within or near military objectives must, however, be taken into account in the proportionality equation even if a party to the conflict has failed to exercise its obligation to remove them.

52. In the *Kupreskic* Judgement (Case No: IT-95-16-T 14 Jan 2000) the Trial Chamber addressed the issue of proportionality as follows:

> "526. As an example of the way in which the Martens clause may be utilized, regard might be had to considerations such as the cumulative effect of attacks on military objectives causing incidental damage to civilians. In other words, it may happen that single attacks on military objectives causing incidental damage to civilians, although they may raise doubts as to their lawfulness, nevertheless do not appear on their face to fall foul *per se* of the loose prescriptions of Articles 57 and 58 (or of the corresponding customary rules). However, in case of repeated

attacks, all or most of them falling within the grey area between indisputable legality and unlawfulness, it might be warranted to conclude that the cumulative effect of such acts entails that they may not be in keeping with international law. Indeed, this pattern of military conduct may turn out to jeopardize excessively the lives and assets of civilians, contrary to demands of humanity."

This formation in *Kupreskic* can be regarded as a progressive statement of the applicable law with regard to the obligation to protect civilians. Its practical import, however, is somewhat ambiguous and its application far from clear. It is the committee's view that where individual (and legitimate) attacks on military objectives are concerned, the mere *cumulation* of such instances, all of which are deemed to have been lawful, cannot *ipso facto* be said to amount to a crime. The committee understands the above formulation, instead, to refer to an *overall* assessment of the totality of civilian victims as against the goals of the military campaign.[90]

One may assume that the Committee's acknowledgment of the ambiguous and controversial nature of the principle of proportionality contributed to its conclusion that NATO had not conducted "a campaign aimed at causing substantial civilian casualties either directly or indirectly."

For its part, the Independent International Commission on Kosovo accepted "the view of the Final Report of the ICTY that there is no basis in available evidence for charging specific individuals with criminal violations of the laws of war during the NATO campaign." It did add, however, rather cryptically, that "some practices do seem vulnerable to the allegation that violations might have occurred, and depend for final assessment upon the availability of further evidence."[91]

Pending the presentation of further evidence, one may safely conclude that the injury and damage to civilians caused by the NATO bombing campaign were not excessive but rather proportionate to the military advantage gained. Hence the bombing did not violate the law of armed conflict merely because it resulted in collateral damage.

B. Ethical Implications

There remains the issue of the ethical implications of the high-altitude bombing and the avoidance of a ground campaign. According to the Independent

---

90. *Id.*, ¶¶ 48–52.
91. THE INDEPENDENT INTERNATIONAL COMMISSION ON KOSOVO, *supra* note 86, at 184.

International Commission on Kosovo, although the high-altitude bombing lacked legal significance, "it does weaken the claim of humanitarianism to the extent it appears to value the lives of the NATO combatants more than those of the civilian population in Kosovo and Serbia. . . ."[92] If, however, Charles Dunlap's claim that the high-altitude bombing was more protective of civilians than lower level bombing would have been is correct, the suggestion of the Commission is clearly invalid. Moreover, even if he is incorrect and the high-altitude bombing and the avoidance of a ground war resulted in a higher number of civilian casualties than would have been the case if low level bombing and a ground campaign had been launched, it does not necessarily follow that such a decision violated ethical or moral precepts. As Dunlap points out, "Americans do not instinctively draw a distinction that finds its soldiers' lives less precious than those of the citizens of an enemy state. This is traceable to the American concept of who composes its military: citizens with just as much right to life as enemy citizens."[93] Reasonable persons may disagree with Dunlap's reasoning and the values it reflects. But at a minimum the ethical and moral case against NATO's high-altitude bombing and avoidance of a ground campaign on the ground that they caused excessive collateral damage is debatable.

A Few Concluding Thoughts

Regardless of whether they have an international law obligation to do so, it is likely that the United States, other NATO members, and developed States in general will make greater and greater use of precision-guided munitions in future conflicts because as the technology develops—in Michael Schmitt's words, "the weapons of future wars will be more than smart—they will be 'brilliant'"[94]—the "happy congruence" between the needs of military efficiency and the avoidance of unnecessary injury to civilian persons or property will increasingly be present. At the same time, however, as also noted by Schmitt, the protections the law of armed conflict affords to civilian persons and property are likely to be less and less effective in practice. This is because the technologically weaker States, as well as terrorists or other non-governmental actors, may increasingly conclude that they must attack the civilian

---

92. *Id.* at 181.
93. Dunlap, *supra* note 80, at 100.
94. Schmitt, *supra* note 59, at 164.

population of the enemy State to offset the latter's great advantage in firepower. As Schmitt puts it,

> [I]n many cases, their only hope is not to prevail in combat, but rather to raise the costs for their opponents to an unacceptable level. The fewer targets the States with lesser technology are permitted to strike, the less opportunity they will have to impose costs on their advantaged opponents. By the same token, the more limits placed upon their opponents, the greater the advantage to these States.[95]

This "normative relativism," Schmitt suggests, bodes ill for the principle of discrimination in the future.[96]

To this observer, it is ironic that so much attention has been devoted to the issue of whether NATO complied with the *jus in bello* in its Kosovo campaign. For when one looks at practices in other armed conflicts around the world—Chechnya, Afghanistan, the Sudan, the Congo, and Sierra Leone, to name just a few—one sees not only no effort to comply with the *jus in bello* but barbaric practices that flout even the most elementary dictates of humanity. Accordingly, the most strenuous efforts should be made to induce States and other combatants to adhere to at least the ethical and moral dimensions of international humanitarian law, regardless of the presence or absence of a formal legal obligation to do so. Steps that might be taken to this end are beyond the scope of this paper.[97]

---

95. *Id.* at 171.
96. *Id.* at 172.
97. For discussion of some steps that might be taken, see my chapter on *Kosovo Agonistes*, *supra* note 2.

International Humanitarian Law After Kosovo: Is Lex Lata Sufficient?

Ove Bring

This presentation will build on the earlier discussion of relevant international humanitarian law principles as they relate to what happened in Kosovo. My approach will be a functional one: did the generally recognized combat rules of international humanitarian law function during the conflict? Were they complied with? Did they prove to be adequate for the Kosovo intervention type of armed conflict? Is there a need for a *de lege ferenda* discussion on rules protecting the civilian population in interventionist types of conflicts? These are the issues I would like to address.

The Additional Protocol I of 1977[1] has codified three somewhat overlapping principles of customary law in the field of targeting and the protection of civilians: the principle of distinction, the principle of proportionality and the principle of feasible precautions. The principle of distinction is closely linked to the definition of military objectives. In fact, the principle would be meaningless if it were not substantiated by a set of norms clearly indicating where the line should be drawn between protected civilian lives and objects on the one hand, and legitimate military objectives on the other. This issue should be addressed first since much of the criticism directed against NATO's methods of warfare in Kosovo was based on the perception that many of the attacks

---

1. Protocol Additional (I) to the Geneva Conventions of 12 August 1949, and Relating to the Protection of Victims of International Armed Conflict, June 8, 1977, 1125 U.N.T.S. 3, DOCUMENTS ON THE LAWS OF WAR 422 (A. Roberts and R. Guelff eds., 3d. ed. 2000) [hereinafter Protocol I].

were directed against people, houses and materiel that were protected under international humanitarian law.

Another focal point of criticism, both during and after the conflict, was the extent of damage caused incidentally by attacks against military objectives—the issue of collateral damage. This issue, as an element of the overarching principles of proportionality and feasible precautions, will be discussed later in this paper.

Distinction

The principle that a distinction shall always be made in military operations between protected and non-protected values is found in Article 48 of Protocol I. It includes the following language: "In order to ensure respect for and protection of the civilian population and civilian objects, the Parties to the conflict shall at all times distinguish . . . and accordingly shall direct their operations only against military objectives." During the Kosovo air campaign, NATO complied with this principle in the sense that it attempted to attack only objectives that it perceived to be of a military nature. In other words, NATO tried to distinguish.

Basically, a violation of the principle of distinction implies action *mala fide*, an intentional disregard for civilian values (e.g., attacks of terror against civilians) or a reckless disregard for such values (e.g., attacks of a nature to strike military objectives and civilians without distinction). The latter aspect—the prohibition against indiscriminate attacks—is covered by Article 51(4) of Protocol I. This prohibition flows from the principle of distinction and could include both intentional violations and reckless behavior. The Gulf War offers some examples on *mala fide* behavior in this respect. Saddam Hussein was not sensitive to the prohibition of Article 51(4), outlawing, *inter alia*, attacks "which employ a method or means of combat which cannot be directed at a specific military objective." Iraq fired SCUD missiles into Saudi Arabian and Israeli territory, well knowing that these missiles could hit military targets only through sheer luck. Clearly, NATO did not act in this way during the Kosovo conflict. Nevertheless, the media reporting that came out of Belgrade gave the impression that NATO was not in compliance with the prohibition against indiscriminate attacks. The alleged compliance or collateral damage problems that were at issue were not linked to the principle of distinction as such, but rather to the definition of military objectives.

Definition of Military Objectives

As has been stated already, the definition of military objectives is a corollary to the principle of distinction. Article 52(2) of Protocol I states that:

> Attacks shall be limited strictly to military objectives. In so far as objects are concerned, military objectives are limited to those objects which by their nature, location, purpose or use make an *effective contribution* to military action and whose total or partial destruction, capture or neutralization, in the circumstances ruling at the time, offers a *definite military advantage*.[2]

Thus, the requirements of "effective contribution" and "definite military advantage" are of crucial importance. As the ICRC Commentary to Protocol I points out: "Whenever these two elements are simultaneously present, there is a military objective in the sense of the Protocol."[3] Together the two elements seem to produce quite a strict rule. However, the current interpretation of the rule is not so strict. It includes the right to attack objectives that have a *potential* of being militarily useful at some point in the future. This does not explicitly follow from the text, although the ICRC Commentary has indicated that the phrase "objects which by their nature, location, purpose or use" should be given the following interpretation: "The criterion of *purpose* is concerned with the intended future use of an object, while that of *use* is concerned with its present function."[4] This may be true, but even so the quoted phrase is subordinate to the proviso that the objects so defined shall "make" (in the present tense) "an effective contribution to military action," and it is further required that their destruction "offers" (in the present tense) "a definite military advantage." The Protocol's definition of military objectives has often been perceived as a codification of traditional customary law applied during World War II and earlier. This perception is probably correct, but it brings with it this flexible and future-oriented interpretation of legitimate military targets that does not explicitly follow from the text of Article 52(2).

---

2. Emphasis added.
3. COMMENTARY ON THE ADDITIONAL PROTOCOLS of 8 June 1977 to the Geneva Conventions of 12 August 1949, at 635 (Y. Sandoz, C. Swinarski and B. Zimmerman eds., 1987) [hereinafter ICRC COMMENTARY].
4. *Id.* at 636, ¶ 2022. See also Anthony Rogers who accepts the ICRC view that "purpose" means future intended use of an object. He adds, however, "[i]t is hard to think of an example or a case where 'purpose' will be the deciding factor, especially given the limitation of 'in the circumstances ruling at the time'." A.P.V. ROGERS, LAW ON THE BATTLEFIELD 35–36 (1996).

The future-oriented approach was clearly manifested during the Kosovo crisis. At a NATO press conference on March 26, 1999, it was said that the armed attacks were directed against the adversary's *"ability* to coordinate his military forces in the field, his *ability* to attack innocent civilians" and "his *ability* to command and control his military forces."[5] This liberal view on what constitutes legitimate military objectives was as typical for the NATO air campaign as it was typical for World War II. In Kosovo it tended to include a large number of dual-use targets, i.e., objects which besides their ordinary civilian use had a military potential. A few of these targets were controversial as to their military potential and it was sometimes argued that they were not to be considered as legitimate military objectives.

The requirements of "effective contribution" and "definite military advantage" have to be met no less with regard to attacks against dual-use or dual-purpose objects. Typical dual-use objects are transportation systems like roads, bridges and railway lines, oil and other power installations, and communication installations like radio, television, telephone and telegraph stations. Although it is clear that broadcasting facilities could have a military function, NATO's bombing on April 23, 1999 of the Serb Radio and Television Station (RTS) in Belgrade seems difficult to justify under the circumstances ruling at the time. The Serb media was hardly—to quote from the Report to the ICTY Prosecutor—"the nerve system that keeps a war-monger in power and thus perpetuates the war effort" nor was it "used to incite crimes, as in Rwanda."[6] Any or both of these things could of course have materialized later, but at the time of the attack on April 23, when 10–17 civilians were killed, the military nature of the RTS was in some doubt. At a press conference on April 27, NATO officials justified the attack with the need to disrupt and degrade the Yugoslav command, control and communications (C3) network The argumentation was partly of a general nature: "everything is wired in through dual use. Most of the commercial system serves the military and the military system can be put to use for the commercial system."[7] It was not clear, in concrete

---

5. Emphasis added. *See* www.nato.int/kosovo/press/p990326a.htm.
6. Final Report to the Prosecutor by the Committee Established to Review the NATO Bombing Campaign against the Federal Republic of Yugoslavia, 39 INTERNATIONAL LEGAL MATERIALS, ¶ 55 (2000), *reprinted* herein as Appendix A [hereinafter Report to the Prosecutor]. *Cf.* also the comment by William Fenrick that it is "highly debatable that the media in the FRY, which was state-controlled to a degree, constituted a legitimate military objective even if it was re-labeled as a propaganda source. To be a military objective, it must be more than a symbol of the regime." William Fenrick, *Targeting and Proportionality during the NATO Bombing Campaign against Yugoslavia*, 12 EUROPEAN JOURNAL OF INTERNATIONAL LAW 497 (2001).
7. Report to the Prosecutor, Appendix A, ¶ 72.

terms, the degree to which the attack against the RTS was militarily useful. The ICRC Commentary states with regard to Article 52(2) of Protocol I that the destruction in question:

> [M]ust offer a *definite military advantage* in the circumstances ruling at the time. In other words, it is not legitimate to launch an attack that only offers potential or indeterminate advantages. Those ordering or executing the attack must have sufficient information available to take this requirement into account; in case of doubt, the safety of the civilian population, which is the aim of the Protocol, must be taken into consideration.[8]

Another dual-use discussion during and after the Kosovo bombings focused on whether or not different bridges in Serbia that were attacked by missiles really made an effective contribution to military action. NATO spokesmen have said that bridges and roads were used to send military forces into Kosovo and that those put on the target lists had been thoroughly screened and found militarily useful. Some bridges may have been selected because they were conduits for communication cables.[9] Nevertheless, in order for the attacks to be lawful the objects in question had to make—in each instance—an "effective contribution to military action." Was this really the case in Kosovo? Human Rights Watch reported in February 2000 that seven of the bridges that were attacked had no military functions at the time and could not be classified as military targets.[10]

With regard to dual-purpose objects, Article 52(3) of Protocol I adds the following to the definition of military objectives: "In case of doubt whether an object which is normally dedicated to civilian purposes . . . is being used to make an effective contribution to military action, it shall be presumed not to be so used." In other words, in case of doubt there is a presumption of civilian status. It is more than doubtful whether NATO always complied with this rule of doubt or principle of presumption. On the other hand, it is also doubtful whether this rule of doubt has the status of customary law and thus is binding for non-parties to the Protocol.

---

8. ICRC COMMENTARY, *supra* note 3, at 636.
9. HUMAN RIGHTS WATCH, CIVILIAN DEATHS IN THE NATO AIR CAMPAIGN 10–11 (2000), *available at* http://www.hrw.org/reports/2000/nato/.
10. *Id.* at 1.

Proportionality and Collateral Damage

A general impression conveyed by the media during the Kosovo crisis was that there was a lot of collateral damage. Amnesty International's report on Kosovo of June 2000 is titled "Collateral Damage or Unlawful Killings? Violations of the Laws of War by NATO during Operation Allied Force." Amnesty International believed that in the course of the operation "civilian deaths could have been significantly reduced if NATO forces had fully adhered to the laws of war."[11] Some collateral damage—even extensive damage in certain case—is permitted under the principle of proportionality, but the proportionality issue was not discussed as such in relation to the media coverage at the time. The impression of unnecessary civilian losses during the spring of 1999 has to be tested against the frequent (but occasionally politically biased) accusations that NATO was not acting in compliance with basic international humanitarian law principles.

The principle of proportionality flows from the prohibition against indiscriminate attacks. In fact, in Protocol I it is presented as a part of that prohibition. Article 51(5)(b) prohibits "an attack which may be expected to cause incidental loss of civilian life, injury to civilians, damage to civilian objects, or a combination thereof, which would be excessive in relation to the concrete and direct military advantage anticipated." Although the term "proportionality" is not used, the text clearly conveys a proportionality message. The principle expressed here is arguably a codification of traditional customary law. In this context the concept of "collateral damage" is always referred to, although that terminology is not used either in the Protocol. The language of Article 51 focuses on what may be called "incidental damage," a certain amount of which is legally accepted as it is unintended and perhaps unavoidable in the circumstances at the time.

Another way of describing the principle of proportionality is to start with a presumption that the attacker is complying with the principle of distinction. In fact, the principle of proportionality rests on that presumption. So, even when military planners make sure that an attack is directed against a military objective, the commanders must avoid an attack where the military advantage cannot outweigh the civilian damage that can be expected from the attack. In

---

11. AMNESTY INTERNATIONAL, NATO/FEDERAL REPUBLIC OF YUGOSLAVIA, "COLLATERAL DAMAGE" OR UNLAWFUL KILLINGS? VIOLATIONS OF THE LAWS OF WAR BY NATO DURING OPERATION ALLIED FORCE 29 (2000), *available at* http://www.amnesty.org/ailib/intcam/kosovo/docs/natorep_all.doc.

other words, decision-makers should ensure that civilian casualties should not be disproportionate in relation to the military advantage anticipated.

Although the principle of distinction was complied with during the NATO campaign over Kosovo, it is submitted that this was perhaps not always the case with regard to the principle of proportionality. In comparison, the proportionality requirements were not always complied with during the Gulf War, e.g., when coalition attacks deprived Iraqi hospitals of electricity and generated adverse cumulative effects on civilians in those hospitals. Proportionality assessments are difficult to accomplish. To the extent things went wrong in Kosovo, these things may be easier to grasp and discuss under a heading of "the principle of feasible precautions," rather than under the principle of proportionality.

Feasible Precautions

The principle of feasible precautions requires that military commanders plan their attacks in such a way that constant care is taken to spare the civilian population, civilians and civilian objects. A summary of Article 57(2) of Protocol I has to focus on the following requirements that were all of special relevance during the Kosovo operation:

Those who plan or decide upon an attack shall:

(1) do everything feasible to verify that the objectives to be attacked are military objectives;

(2) take all feasible precautions in the choice of means and methods of attack with a view to avoiding, and in any event minimizing, incidental loss of civilian life;

(3 refrain from deciding to launch an attack that may be expected to cause such incidental loss, which would be excessive in relation to the concrete and direct military advantage anticipated;

(4) suspend an attack if it becomes apparent that it may be expected to cause incidental loss of civilian life, damage to civilian objects, or a combination thereof, "which would be excessive in relation to the concrete and direct military advantage anticipated;" and

(5) in addition, "effective advance warning shall be given of attacks which may affect the civilian population, unless circumstances do not permit."

Since there were a number of mistakes in targeting in Kosovo, the principle of feasible precautions seems to be the one most clearly deviated from during the air campaign. The mistakes included the two air strikes hitting a train on the Grdelica bridge in southern Serbia on April 12; an attack on vehicles in a convoy of refugees near Djakovica in Kosovo on April 14; an attack south of Belgrade on April 28 hitting a residential area instead of army barracks; an attack against the Lusana Bridge north of Pristina on May 1 hitting a civilian bus; a cluster bomb attack against the Nis airfield on May 7 hitting a market place and a hospital; and the attack on the Chinese Embassy in Belgrade on May 8. In the case of the Embassy, NATO used inaccurate intelligence information and believed that it was attacking the Federal Directorate of Supply and Procurement for the Yugoslav Army. Further cases where there may have been a lack of necessary precautions are the bombing of the village of Korisa in Kosovo on May 13, the attack on the Varvarin bridge in Serbia on May 30, and the attack against military barracks in Surdulica on May 30 in which a hospital was struck. In all these attacks there were civilian casualties.[12]

When evaluating these and other mistakes in targeting, however, they must be related not only to the number of civilian casualties, but also to the total number of air strikes, and to the military efficiency of these strikes. In that regard, between March 24 and June 9, 1999, 10,484 strike sorties were flown by NATO aircraft and 23,614 munitions were released. No NATO casualties were reported arising out of these strikes. The damage caused to the Yugoslav forces in Kosovo alone was reported to include 181 tanks, 317 armored personnel carriers, 600 military vehicles and 857 artillery and mortar pieces.[13]

When in February 2000 Human Rights Watch published its report "Civilian Deaths in the NATO Air Campaign," it became clear that about 500 civilian lives were lost as a consequence of the campaign, a much higher figure than NATO had previously admitted. By comparison, the numbers of civilian deaths given by the authorities in Belgrade varied between 1,200 and 5,000. Even the lower number of 500 civilian deaths raises questions of efficiency with regard to precautionary measures. It could also be argued that, even if 500 civilian casualties is not a high figure for an international armed conflict lasting about three months, it is arguably too high a figure for a military operation with humanitarian motives; for an operation that many would classify as a "humanitarian intervention."

---

12. See the case studies in id. at 33–74.
13. NATO Press Conference held on 16 September 1999.

The Human Rights Watch report claimed that the casualties had occurred during 90 separate occasions, and that 50% of the victims died in circumstances where the identification of targets as military was questionable. Controversial cases included the attacks on the New Belgrade heating plant and the Serb TV and Radio Station (RTS) in Belgrade. With regard to the latter, it has already been indicated that no assessments seem to have been made to clarify to what extent the RTS dual-use facility actually was contributing to the Yugoslav military effort. An indirect early warning of the attack seems to have been communicated to the authorities in Belgrade, but since the attack did not occur shortly thereafter, the warning was not effective. Civilian employees working the night shift, who had emptied the building at an earlier point in time, had during the night of the attack returned to the building.[14] In this case, it seems far from clear that NATO, in accordance with Article 57(2)(c), communicated an "effective advance warning."

The RTS case signifies a mix of intentional damage (the building) and collateral damage (the 10 or more civilian casualties). Like in some of the other cases that resulted in civilian casualties, it is not clear whether there was compliance with the precautions in attack required by Article 57. There seem to be enough dubious cases to warrant a conclusion that violations of international humanitarian law precautionary standards did in fact take place.

The Moral Dimension: "Ready to Kill But Not to Die"

In London, the Foreign Secretary admitted during the Kosovo conflict that only a small number of the aircraft available to NATO had a precision-bombing capability. In Kosovo, as in the Gulf War, events have shown that even with smart bombs and missiles, air attacks do result in unplanned damage and loss of civilian life. High-tech developments increase the possibilities for successful target discrimination and better protection of the civilian population,

---

14. According to the committee which prepared the Report to the Prosecutor,

> [I]t would... appear that some Yugoslav officials may have expected that the building was about to be struck.... Although knowledge on the part of Yugoslav officials of the impending attack would not divest NATO of its obligation to forewarn civilians under Article 57(2), it may nevertheless imply that the Yugoslav authorities may be partially responsible for the civilian casualties resulting from the attack and may suggest that the advance notice given by NATO may have in fact been sufficient under the circumstances.

Report to the Prosecutor, Appendix A, ¶ 77. The latter part of this statement seems far from uncontroversial.

but individual civilians will never know whether this phenomenon will in fact protect them.

In Kosovo, the risk of unwanted damage increased due to the minimum altitude of 15,000 feet at which NATO aircraft operated most of the time. It has been argued that by setting this 15,000 feet level NATO politicians managed to avoid aircrew casualties, but in so doing, were transferring the risks to the civilian population. However, the British Ministry of Defence has stated that some aircraft "operated down to 6,000 feet when target identification or a weapons delivery profile required it."[15] Nevertheless, "the no-body-bags policy" posed and poses a moral dilemma. It implies that the lives of your own pilots are worth more than the lives of the innocent civilians on the ground, since the acceptance of some collateral damage relates to the "others", while the aim of "zero-casualty warfare" only relates to "yourself." The discrepancy is troublesome and indicates that future humanitarian interventions or peace-enforcement actions should rely also on low flying aircraft to make possible genuine target identification—and arguably also ground troops—if that is necessary in order to protect the civilian population. One expert on the law of the battlefield has written that in taking care to protect civilians, "soldiers must accept some element of risk to themselves."[16] He notes that the law is unclear as to what degree of care is required of a soldier and what degree of risk he must take—"Everything depends on the target, the urgency of the moment, the available technology and so on."[17]

In the autumn 1999 issue of the Canadian International Journal Mr. Paul Robinson of Toronto wrote an article with a sensational heading: "Ready to kill but not to die."[18] The author was of course referring to the NATO strategy in Kosovo. Robinson made the point that in high-tech, standoff warfare there is no chivalry, no military honor. In Kosovo NATO pilots did not see the people they were fighting. This type of warfare, it was argued, is problematical not only from a humanitarian but also from a security point of view. Its clinical character results in a temptation to resort to military force in international crises. It lowers the threshold for military force as such. Although this conclusion does not seem to be empirically sound, the broader argument raises the question whether existing international humanitarian law is appropriate for

---

15. LORD ROBERTSON, KOSOVO: AN ACCOUNT OF THE CRISIS (1999).
16. A.P.U. Rogers, *Zero-casualty warfare*, 82 INTERNATIONAL REVIEW OF THE RED CROSS 165, 177 (2000).
17. Id.
18. Paul Robinson, *'Ready to kill but not to die'*: NATO strategy in Kosovo, 54 INTERNATIONAL JOURNAL 671 (1999).

dealing with high-tech warfare. An increased use of standoff weapons is not to the advantage of civilians. The solution is not a prohibition of such weapons, but rather a reconsideration of the parameters for modern warfare as it affects civilians.

Did Protocol I Mean Anything in Kosovo?

International humanitarian law as it related to the Kosovo crisis was discussed in the March 2000 issue of the International Review of the Red Cross. A perspective *de lege ferenda* was put forward in an article by Peter Rowe, Professor of Law at the University of Lancaster. Rowe first put the question of whether in fact the constraints of modern IHL influenced NATO behavior during the conflict. The subtitle of his article is: "Have the provisions of Additional Protocol I withstood the test?"[19] Rowe's position is that Protocol I did not add anything to the protection of the civilian population beyond the customary law protection that was already applicable before 1977. He concludes that the Protocol had little impact or influence upon the decisions of the air campaign—that "all the detailed rules so carefully drafted in 1977 were of little consequence."[20] In his view, the objects that military commanders for military reasons wished to attack were attacked. There was nothing more to it.

If this argumentation is intended to imply that modern international law played no part in the crisis, it should be refuted. International humanitarian law clearly influenced decision-makers in Kosovo. Moreover, Additional Protocol I contributed to the role that law played in decision-making. During the conflict, as during the Gulf War, legal advice was sought and considered. In both cases it was extremely important, for political and public image reasons, to be seen as acting in conformity with international law. The opposite would imply a political cost and setback that had to be avoided at a time when political support was essential. During the Gulf War General Schwarzkopf was adamant that "we didn't want any war crimes on our hands."[21] The same feeling obviously dominated NATO thinking in the spring of 1999. Protocol I, although it has not been ratified by all NATO States (not by the United States, France and Turkey at the time; France is now a party), has contributed much to the awareness of IHL standards in military and political circles. The United

---

19. Peter Rowe, *Kosovo 1999: The air campaign*, 82 INTERNATIONAL REVIEW OF THE RED CROSS 147 (2000).
20. *Id.* at 159.
21. NORMAN SCHWARZKOPF, IT DOESN'T TAKE A HERO 465 (1992).

States position is that many of the rules of Protocol I are applicable as customary law. Moreover, the non-governmental organizations and informed public opinion are very much aware of the IHL standards. They continuously monitor relevant situations—and the politicians know it. Thus, it was in the self-interest of NATO to involve its legal advisers in the planning and targeting process.

The US military lawyer James Burger has written in the same March issue of the International Review of the Red Cross the following: "While there may be disagreement over the application of the rules by commentators who write about it after the event, there can be no doubt that full consideration was given, as required by the laws of armed conflict, to the advice of legal counsel and the application of the rules."[22] We can probably safely conclude that in Kosovo there was a greater respect for humanitarian normative restraints than would have been the case had the adoption of Protocol I never taken place.

The Weakness of Protocol I and the Need for Reform

The Protocol only offers weak protection for civilians. Here one could easily agree with Peter Rowe, when he argues that the Protocol, when it comes to the test, is very weak in determining what may and what may not be attacked. "It is when civilians are most likely to be placed in danger that Protocol I, designed to protect them, shows its faults."[23] One reason for this is that the Protocol sets the dividing line between legal and illegal attacks on the basis of military expectations before the attack is commenced. As Rowe states: "At this stage of military operations those planning the attack are at their most optimistic and civilians are at most risk."[24] This criticism mainly relates to the principle of proportionality and the acceptance of collateral damage. An even more important flaw with the Protocol, in this writer's view, is the wide interpretations of legitimate military objectives that the Protocol harbors. This interpretation flows only indirectly from the text of Article 52, but rather through a perception that the Protocol has codified a liberal customary law regime. The effect is an increased risk of extensive collateral damage.

With regard to Kosovo it has already been indicated that collateral damage was a serious problem, but that the problem was not so much related to

---

22. James Burger, *International humanitarian law and the Kosovo crisis: Lessons learned or to be learned*, 82 INTERNATIONAL REVIEW OF THE RED CROSS 129 (2000).
23. Rowe, *supra* note 19, at 160.
24. Id.

violations of IHL standards as it was to the flexible interpretation of the definition of military objectives. Should a reform of IHL be considered to address these matters, one point of departure would be that Additional Protocol I should stand as it is. A revision of the Protocol is neither realistic nor necessary. There is another way to approach the problem.

Suggestions De Lege Ferenda

Rowe suggests a new additional protocol to the 1980 Conventional Weapons Convention. Such an additional protocol would be adapted to the use of air-delivered "smart" weapons and it would introduce the same restrictions on such weapons as now exist with regard to air-delivered incendiary weapons. The relevant formulation would then read as follows:

> It is prohibited to make any military objective located within a concentration of civilians the object of attack, except when such military objective is clearly separated from the concentration of civilians, and all feasible precautions are taken with a view to limiting the effects of the attack to the military objective and to avoiding, and in any event to minimizing, incidental loss of civilian life, injury to civilians and damage to civilian objects.[25]

The suggested text almost copies the 1980 restrictions on incendiaries.[26] It would be a *lex specialis* for mainly air warfare, overriding the balancing act of the principle of proportionality, a principle that has its main application in air warfare. According to such a *lex specialis*—and rethinking air warfare in history—no buildings in Berlin, Baghdad or Belgrade could be attacked. It is difficult to believe that States would be willing to accept an erosion of the principle of proportionality and give up their military freedom of assessing military advantage against civilian damage. Protocol I has established a sort of balance between military necessity and proportionality and also between proportionality and feasible precautions. It does not seem realistic to expect that States would be willing to renounce the advantages of that approach.

Another problem with the text suggested by Rowe is that it is envisaged as a protocol additional to the 1980 Weapons Convention, although the text only

---

25. *Id.* at 162.
26. *Cf.* Article 2(3), Protocol III on Prohibitions or Restrictions on the Use of Incendiary Weapons, annexed to the Convention on Prohibition or Restriction on the Use of Certain Conventional Weapons Which May Be Deemed to be Excessively Injurious or to Have Indiscriminate Effects, Oct. 10, 1980, 1342 U.N.T.S. 137, DOCUMENTS ON THE LAWS OF WAR, *supra* note 1, at 533.

covers *methods* and not *means* of warfare. It does not (like the other Protocols attached to the Weapons Convention) refer to a specific weapon category, although it may indirectly focus on air-delivered "smart" weapons.

On the other hand, one could imagine another solution. The Independent International Commission on Kosovo has suggested the drafting of an additional protocol III to the Geneva Conventions.[27] Such a protocol would not detract from or compete with Protocol I, because the new protocol would have another scope of application. It would be limited to conflicts of an interventionist nature where the intervening side is a coalition enforcing a mandate against a militarily inferior party to the conflict. The coalition would not be fighting for its national security, vital interests or political survival, but for the purpose of limited crisis management. The new protocol would be limited to peace-enforcement operations conducted on behalf of the international community, or other interventions within the framework of regional crisis management, whether they are labeled humanitarian or not. It is important to state that such a new protocol would not address the *jus ad bellum* legality of humanitarian or other interventions (it would not introduce a "Just War" doctrine); it would stick to the traditional IHL method of describing a scope of application based on factual circumstances. In this case the scope of application would be linked to the limited nature of the international armed conflict. Should the State under attack plead self-defense and respond with counter-attacks, thus escalating the level of armed conflict, the limited scope of application of the new protocol would no longer describe the situation accurately and Protocol I would become applicable. In line with this thinking Michael Hoffman, the American Red Cross Officer for International Humanitarian Law, has suggested that we may witness emerging rules for "interventional armed conflict," for example in peace enforcement operations, whether authorized by the UN Security Council or conducted otherwise by regional organizations.[28]

The UK Secretary of State for Defence said about the Kosovo air campaign on March 25, 1999 that "This is not a war, it is an operation designed to prevent what everybody recognizes is about to be a humanitarian catastrophe: ethnic cleansing, savagery. . . . That is what we are in there to prevent, that

---

27. THE INDEPENDENT INTERNATIONAL COMMISSION ON KOSOVO, THE KOSOVO REPORT, 5, 31, 165–66 (2000).
28. Michael Hoffman, *Peace-enforcement actions and humanitarian law: Emerging rules for "interventional armed conflict,"* 82 INTERNATIONAL REVIEW OF THE RED CROSS 193, 200–203 (2000).

is not war, it is a humanitarian objective very clearly defined as such."[29] Nevertheless, NATO relied on the traditional law of war developed for inter-State armed conflict during the air campaign, including the definition of military objectives and the rules on targeting, proportionality and collateral damage linked to that definition. The liberal definition of military objectives and the generous acceptance of collateral damage are part of a legal regime that envisages a full-scale war. The Geneva Conventions and Additional Protocol I were drafted against the background of World War II and partly with a possible clash between NATO and the Warsaw Pact in mind.

International humanitarian law is built upon a balance between acceptance of military interests on the one hand and humanitarian concerns on the other. NATO's "no-body-bag policy" showed that this balance was upset in the Kosovo conflict's limited type of war. NATO could use the liberal definition of military objectives—thus benefiting from the rules favorable to the military interest—while at the same time attacking from such altitudes that humanitarian concerns could not be met. This problem could be addressed in a new protocol for interventional types of conflict, through a sharpening of the definition of military objectives. One could require that only those objectives be attacked which *are* making an effective contribution to military action, or which imminently are about to make such a contribution.[30] A requirement of imminence should be added, somewhat along the lines of the famous *Caroline* case. This would protect a number of dual-use objects and increase the protection of the civilian population.

Such a sharpening of the definition of legitimate military objectives would have its consequences with regard to the implementation of the principles of proportionality and feasible precautions. A stricter application of these two principles will follow from a more strict definition of military objectives. A stricter application of the principle of proportionality would somewhat reduce the problem of collateral damage flowing from that principle. The concepts of proportionality and feasible precautions would not themselves need to be sharpened. They would stand as they are today—in all types of international armed conflict. However, in interventionist conflicts a better balance with regard to precautionary measures would result from the suggested change; i.e.,

---

29. *Quoted in* Hoffman, *id.* at 195.
30. *Cf.* the ICRC Commentary to Article 51(5)(b) of Additional Protocol I that the military advantage "should be substantial and relatively close, and that advantages which are hardly perceptible and those which would only appear in the long term should be disregarded." ICRC COMMENTARY, *supra* note 3, ¶ 2209.

precautionary measures would, as intended by the drafters of Protocol I, genuinely protect civilians on the ground, and not only the attackers flying high.

Although the above suggestion is the main *de lege ferenda* thrust of this paper, it should be mentioned that a further additional protocol could be imagined—a protocol attached to the 1980 Weapons Convention that would explicitly prohibit the use of cluster bombs. This type of multiple sub-munitions affected the civilian population in Kosovo and Serbia on several occasions, often more so than the intended military targets. A protocol on multiple weapons was in fact debated, in the years 1977 – 1980, as a follow-up to Additional Protocols I and II for inclusion in the 1980 Conventional Weapons Convention. But time was not ripe for it then, during the Cold War, and the situation does not seem to have changed that much today. Or has it? During the Kosovo air campaign, after alarming media reports about civilian casualties caused by cluster bombs, some decision-makers reconsidered things. The NATO attack targeted on the Nis airfield on May 7 went wrong. The cluster bomb container opened right away after release from the aircraft, instead of opening over the airfield. As a consequence it projected the sub-munitions into the city of Nis. Following the media coverage of this incident there was a decision by the White House to prohibit the further use of cluster bombs during the conflict. However, this was a unilateral US decision. The British command in London did not follow suit and more cluster bombs were dropped on targets in Serbia and Kosovo in the spring of 1999.

Whether States in the future may in fact be willing to forgo weapons of the cluster bomb type in interventionist types of conflicts is not clear. Further thinking on this issue of means of warfare could perhaps usefully be channeled into the kind of discussion I have tried to promote in this paper, a discussion on the possibilities of increased protections for civilians in conflicts of a limited nature.

Commentary

Yves Sandoz

As I have been Director of International Law and Communication at the International Committee of the Red Cross (ICRC), an institution which devotes much energy to promote the Geneva Conventions of 1949 and their Additional Protocols of 1977, for 16 years and as I am co-editor of the Commentary to those Protocols, you will not be surprised that I don't share the negative views expressed by John Murphy, echoing those of Hays Parks, on both the Additional Protocols and their Commentary, even if they are certainly far from being perfect.

What can at least be said about the Additional Protocols of 1977 in a few words is that it is not possible simply to affirm that they are or that they are not part of international customary law. As stated in the title of the Diplomatic Conference of 1974–1977, which negotiated and adopted the Protocols, this Conference had the double ambition to reaffirm and to develop international humanitarian law (IHL). That means that in part the Protocols reaffirm and clarify customary rules of IHL and in part they develop that law. For the first part their rules bind all States, for the second only the States parties to the Protocols are bound. But the borderline is not always easy to determine for two reasons. The first is that the Diplomatic Conference has not clearly declared what was reaffirmation and what was development. The second is that some rules which were considered as a development in 1977 may be considered today as part of customary law. But being commentator I will now base my next points on the very good papers presented by John Murphy and Ove Bring and enter into discussion on the Protocols and their Commentary only on the occasion of remarks to those papers.

Let me start with some words on international customary law. John Murphy has quoted an author who went as far as questioning even the existence of international customary law. I will not comment on this not very serious declaration, but I would have something to add on the description given by John Murphy on how to establish that there is customary law, with a particular focus on the difficulty of establishing State practice.

A reference to the notion of "specially affected States" by the ICJ in the *North Sea Continental Shelf* case would be, for example, an important additional element to mention. I will not go further here and now on that question, but I wish to mention that lawyers from the ICRC are finalizing a broad study on the customary rules of IHL, done with the contribution of legal and governmental experts, and based on the work of working groups, from all regions of the world. This study will be published next year. Of course, the question to know how to establish the practice and the *opinio juris* of States is discussed in that study to determine the existence of customary rules and the criteria taken into account will be explained. That being said and without entering into the substance of this study, I would like to stress three points. First, the aim of the study is to determine if a rule can or cannot be considered as a customary rule, but not to give an in-depth interpretation of that rule. For that reason we cannot expect too much from this study for the clarification of the exact and practical meaning of existing rules, which is the central problem debated by this colloquium. Secondly, there will always remain a certain degree of uncertainty as to the customary nature of certain rules, and therefore customary law is not a substitute to the formal adoption by States of treaties aiming to be universally accepted, as those of IHL. Thirdly, the problem of the existence or not of a normative restriction is particularly delicate with the emergence of new weapons, due to the fact that there cannot be a largely established practice during a long period of time in those cases. I will come back to this last question later.

My next remark will be on the principle of proportionality, to affirm my strong conviction that this principle does exist in *jus ad bellum*—a State which has to use force as a last resort does not have the right to do more than what is imposed by the situation—as in jus *in bello*—there is an obligation in military operations to keep a balance between the military advantages anticipated and the expected incidental civilian damages. It is even a central principle of those laws. I was therefore surprised to read in the paper of John Murphy that Hays Parks has reported that "the American military review of Protocol I concluded that the concept of proportionality is not a rule of customary international law." All that I read and even what we heard yesterday from James Baker reinforce my conviction. James Baker reminded us that this principle was at the center of the discussions on legitimate targets during the Kosovo bombings, as well for NATO members party to Additional Protocol I as for those, like the United States, that were not. Therefore I can conclude in quoting Bill Fenrick, the well-known Senior Legal Adviser of the Office of the Prosecutor of the International Criminal Court on Yugoslavia: "That the principle of proportionality exists is not seriously disputed." The problem we have to address is the *interpretation* of the principle, not its existence.

Without entering in-depth into this issue, I would signal that another problem is the confusion in some military operations between the political objective and the military objectives *stricto sensu*. Such confusion took place in the NATO operations in Kosovo, where the political objective—to oblige Milosevic to accept conditions previously fixed—was not well distinguished from military objectives. In fact, the question was not to win the war, but to put enough pressure on Milosevic to cause him to end the conflict. Therefore traditional notions of military objective and military advantage were used in an ambiguous way. This question would need serious consideration for operations of this nature. But I do not pretend to start a serious discussion here and now. It would require in-depth analysis of this and other concrete cases.

My next remark is that I cannot agree with the affirmation that the balance between the obligations of the defenders and those of the attackers has been broken down in Additional Protocol I of 1977 to the detriment of the attackers. In reality, the obligations of the defenders are very clearly stated in Protocol I, as we can read particularly in Article 51(7):

> The presence or movements of the civilian population or individuals civilians shall not be used to render certain points or areas immune from military operations, in particular in attempts to shield military objectives from attacks or to shield, favor or impede military operations. The Parties to the conflict shall not direct movement of the civilian population or individual civilians in order to attempt to shield military objectives from attacks or to shield military operations.

Article 58 then goes on to provide:

> The Parties to the conflict shall, to the maximum extent feasible; (a) without prejudice to Article 49 of the Fourth Convention, endeavour to remove the civilian population, individual civilians and civilian objects under their control from the vicinity of military objectives; (b) avoid locating military objectives within or near densely populated areas; (c) take the other necessary precautions

to protect the civilian population, individual civilians and civilian objects under their control against the dangers resulting from military operations.

Thus, as we can see, the Protocol is very clear in imposing on a Party to the conflict a requirement not to use civilians to protect its military objectives. Nevertheless, it is also true that it requires as well that the attackers take into consideration the situation as it is in reality. They can't just ignore the fact that civilians are used as "human shields." But this is common sense. Imagine your own citizens being used; you cannot pretend you just don't care. And it is also true if innocent civilians of one party, particularly children, are used for this purpose. This element has to be taken into account in the balance and the crime of your enemy does not give you the right to ignore the situation created by that crime. But the Protocol doesn't prohibit action; it requires that all of these elements be taken into account in the appreciation of the situation. I think, as was clearly explained yesterday, that this position was adopted without hesitation by those deciding on the NATO bombings in Kosovo.

Where I am in total agreement with John Murphy is that a real and crucial problem of clarification remains for the definition of a military advantage, and ascertaining the level where a decision must be taken or the determination of responsibilities. These are undoubtedly delicate questions which can only be clarified through practical examples in order to establish a kind of jurisprudence. We could certainly add some other questions to the list, as the one just mentioned by Ove Bring on the dual-use objects, which precisely has, in my opinion, a close link with the principle of proportionality—in fact the attack of a dual-use object can be considered as the attack of a military objective with collateral damages.

Mentioning again the principle of proportionality I want to stress another element of this principle, the fact that it has to be observed at different levels. Some would confine this principle to the strategic level and I cannot agree with that opinion. There is no doubt, for example, that a soldier cannot blow up a school full of children under the pretext that an enemy solider has entered the school. Such a restriction is an application of the principle—the military advantage being overthrown in such a hypothesis by the expected collateral damages—even if the enemy soldier has himself committed a violation of the law in taking children as a shield.

That being said, I don't deny that the appreciation of those rules is complex, but we cannot totally avoid such complexity. War is complex; life is complex; and the complexity of a problem is not a good reason to refuse facing it. We have to solve those questions because they are at the heart of the necessary limitations in war.

On the other hand, I am the first to admit that the military must have precise orders and that the trend to take more seriously the obligation to punish war crimes renders still more indispensable this clarity, even if I cannot share the criticisms of the ICRC lawyer's commentary, in particular on the meaning of military objectives. In reality, the recent German military manual goes exactly in the same direction, as well as the excellent commentary written by Michael Bothe, who is present with us, and by the late Karl Josef Partsch and Waldemar Solf, the latter playing, as you know, a very important role in the American delegation to the 1974–1977 Diplomatic Conference. That being said, I do agree that this Commentary does not give a precise reply to all those delicate questions.

Therefore we have to go further and to find the best way to do it. And for that, I think it is worth reading what Bill Fenrick has written in a recent article:

> If the application of the law applicable to targeting and proportionality is to become more transparent and, one hopes, more humane, outsiders, including military experts and legal advisers not directly involved in particular conflicts, should learn from the military planning process. A vigorous informed discussion of targeting and proportionality issues based on case studies, both historical and hypothetical, can contribute substantially to clarification of how the law can and should be applied.

Then Fenrick draws the conclusion that "[t]he law applicable to targeting and proportionality must be brought down to earth." I totally agree with this statement and I think that the Naval War College is precisely the type of place where the discussion suggested by Fenrick could take place.

I will not really enter into the problem of high-altitude air bombings, as I have not the basic factual elements to do it seriously. But I think nevertheless that it is important to reaffirm at this occasion at least one basic principle on which a certain confusion emerged in the discussion on those bombings: one cannot affirm that the security of its own soldiers have an absolute priority over the protection of the civilian population. Both elements have to be put into the balance and taken into account. If the price to absolute security of one's own soldiers is heavy casualties among civilians, this price is too high.

Allow me then a further comment on the issue of precision-guided ammunition. I agree with John Murphy that there is no obligation to use it exclusively. In fact there are many interdictions and restrictions on the use of weapons in IHL, but no obligation to use a specific weapon. I don't think those weapons are an exception. But that does not mean the possession of these weapons is without legal consequence in certain circumstances. It may help, for example, to keep the military action in conformity with IHL, particularly in densely populated areas, in changing favorably the balance between the anticipated military advantages and the expected civilian collateral damages.

Another question is the following: if you have the choice between weapons causing more or less collateral damages to obtain the *same* military advantage, have you an obligation to use the second? My reply is yes, and that even if the principle of proportionality would still be in a favorable balance with the use of weapons of the first type—i.e., that the anticipated military advantage would overcome the expected incidental civilian damages. This affirmation is based on another principle which has been reaffirmed in Protocol I and which is often confused with the principle of proportionality, the principle of the least feasible damage, which is clearly stated at Article 57(2)(ii). This provision requires those who plan or decide upon an attack to "take all feasible precautions in the choice of means and methods of attack with a view to avoiding, and in any event to minimizing, incidental loss of civilian life, injury to civilians and damage to civilian objects."

Let me now say a few words on the ethical dimension of the question. My opinion is that the problem has not been correctly posed. To have or not to have a weapon doesn't change the ethical basis of your action, even if it can change your behavior, because this one depends on one hand on your ethical values, which remain constant, but on the other hand on the means you have at your disposal, which vary. As an example I would take a medical doctor. If he practices here or in a region of Africa far from any well-equipped medical center, he will keep the same ethic. But his decision and responsibility will be different if he has the capacity to test blood before an emergency transfusion or if he hasn't, with the same objective to best serve the interest of his patient. It is exactly the same if you have or don't have certain weapons.

Finally I would like to make some comments on the future. I heard with sympathy the suggestions made by Ove Bring. I agree with him that some specific rules could be elaborated, or at least that an agreed interpretation of existing rules should be discussed, about enforcement measures, where there remain some unsolved questions. That being said, I am not sure that the best way to do it would be to start the drafting of an additional protocol III to the Geneva Conventions.

Just recently the Secretary-General of the UN promulgated in a bulletin the rules of IHL which must be applied by UN forces engaged in enforcement operations. This was the result of fruitful informal discussions organized by the ICRC between senior UN officials, military experts, the ICRC and other legal experts. This informal and smooth way to deal with such problems could inspire us for other necessary clarifications or developments. I am afraid that if we open formally the procedure to adopt a third additional protocol (or even a fourth as we know that there are ongoing discussions on the elaboration of a third additional protocol on the protective emblems) so many obstacles and oppositions will emerge that it would require very long and tremendous work for an end result which has a good chance to be very disappointing. My hesitation, therefore, is on the procedure, not on the necessity to clarify the points mentioned by Ove Bring.

My second remark for the future is to insist again on the importance to discuss further the practical meaning of some IHL provisions on the conduct of hostilities and to find the right place to do it. I insist again on the fact that a place like this prestigious Naval War College would be ideal for such discussions.

Finally my last remark is the following. There are no doubts for me that the United States has to play a leading role in further discussions on IHL provisions, particularly those concerning the conduct of hostilities. It is the greatest military power, with many recent war experiences. But those discussions and this leading role would be much easier and more credible if everyone accepted the same basic rules. The crucial problem nowadays is the *application* of the rules as we have seen in the discussion on the NATO operations in Kosovo. But as long as the United States is not party to Additional Protocol I, there will be some hesitations on what rules can be taken as a basis for this discussion.

I know that there are still many obstacles to United States' ratification of the 1977 Additional Protocols, but I cannot refrain from affirming again my conviction that the US could ratify them without endangering its own security in using, where deemed necessary, the possibility of express reservations, as many other States did. Over this internal problem, I would stress also my conviction that the ratification of the United States would have a decisive effect on the uniformity of IHL in the whole world, in the universal acceptance of this law, and on the possibility for United States to play a leading role in the necessary clarification of some of its provisions. We need the United States in that role.

I hope you will accept my apology for using this opportunity to reaffirm my strong conviction on this issue and I thank you very much for your patience.

Commentary

W. Hays Parks

It is the role of a commentator to comment on the program offered, the topic before the panel, or the papers offered before that panel. While my emphasis will be on the latter, necessarily it will range over all three.

The premise for this conference—lessons learned from Operation Allied Force, the NATO air campaign against Serbian forces in Kosovo—raises many questions. Allied Force may be a classic example of the adage, "Bad cases make bad law," with few valid lessons. As NATO's first military operation, a prime objective was keeping the nineteen-member alliance intact. Another was continuation of the Clinton Administration's objective in each of its peace operations after Somalia of using military force, but with the admonition to commanders to "do no harm," a flawed philosophy akin to wanting to make an omelet without breaking any eggs. In Allied Force, uncommon steps were taken by NATO forces to reduce to an absolute minimum collateral civilian casualties and collateral damage to civilian objects, and in some instances avoiding Serbian military casualties as well.[1] These steps could be

---

1. This generated considerable criticism in the official Air Force evaluation. *See* HEADQUARTERS UNITED STATES AIR FORCE, INITIAL REPORT: THE AIR WAR OVER SERBIA, AEROSPACE POWER IN OPERATION ALLIED FORCE pp. x, 54 (2000). Of particular note is the following (p. x):

> Traditionally, air planners have assumed that political conditions will allow the most efficient employment of aerospace power, giving planners the latitude to optimize survivability, target effects, and and collateral damage considerations. During the air war over Serbia, such latitude did not exist. Not all members of the 19-nation Alliance would have accepted the intensity and violence required to fight this war if military planning had followed optimum Air Force doctrine. As long as Serbia was unable to inflict significant Allied casualties, NATO accepted some operational inefficiencies associated with those political restraints.

taken because the United States and one or two of its allies had the capability to do so, not because they necessarily felt legally obligated to do so. Professor Murphy's articulation of the essential elements of the customary international law process would indicate that these voluntary actions offer little, if any, precedent as to future law of war interpretation.[2]

The questions my two colleagues were asked are somewhat troubling, as they limit the scope of the inquiry. Specifically, they focus entirely on the obligations of the force engaged in offensive operations, to the neglect of the defending ground force.[3] This flows in part from the incorrect, perhaps intentional, use of the word "attacks" in the 1977 Additional Protocol I[4] to refer to actions taken either by an attacker or defender.[5] Use of "attacks" to refer to acts of defense is etymologically inconsistent with its definition and customary use in any of the six official languages of Additional Protocol I, a point conceded in the *Official Commentary* of the International Committee of the Red Cross.[6] Limiting the definition of attacks to "acts of violence against the adversary" is inconsistent with the customary law principle of *distinction*, partially codified in Article 48,[7] and other provisions of Additional Protocol I that prohibit the use of the civilian population or individual civilians as human

---

2. See Professor Murphy's paper in this volume.
3. This unfortunate and incorrect effect is demonstrated in articles critiquing Operation Allied Force. See, for example, Peter Rowe, *Kosovo 1999: The air campaign*, 82 INTERNATIONAL REVIEW OF THE RED CROSS 147 (2000) and A. Rogers, *Zero-casualty warfare*, 82 INTERNATIONAl REVIEW OF THE RED CROSS 165, 176 (2000). The former examines only the efforts of the attacker to reduce collateral civilian casualties, while the latter offers only three sentences on the obligation of the defender.
4. Protocol Additional (I) to the Geneva Conventions of 12 August 1949, and Relating to the Protection of Victims of International Armed Conflict, June 8, 1977, 1125 U.N.T.S. 3, DOCUMENTS ON THE LAWS OF WAR 422 (A. Roberts and R. Guelff eds., 3d. ed. 2000) [hereinafter Protocol I].
5. Article 49, paragraph 1 of Additional Protocol I states, "'Attacks' means acts of violence against the adversary, whether in offense or defense."
6. COMMENTARY ON THE ADDITIONAL PROTOCOLS OF 8 JUNE 1977 TO THE GENEVA CONVENTIONS OF 12 AUGUST 1949, at 603 (Yves Sandoz et al. eds., 1987).
7. Article 48 states: "In order to ensure respect for and protection of the civilian population and civilian objects, the Parties to the conflict shall at all times distinguish between the civilian population and combatants and between civilian objects and military objectives and accordingly shall direct their operations only against military objectives." Using the term "Parties to the conflict" rather than "States Parties" (to the Protocol) ignores the customary law obligation of a government to take reasonable measures to separate military objectives from civilian objects, and vice versa, in peacetime and war.

shields.[8] That this definition was the beginning of a slippery slope to erode the customary law principle of *distinction* is evident not only in the questions framed for this session, but also in the answers of the two primary presentations. Professor Murphy notes this inconsistency. Others, including some of the sources he cites, have failed to do so.

This second point is offered to emphasize a concluding comment of Professor Murphy. As he notes,[9] it is ironic that a nation committed to the rule of law, that has spent billions of dollars—in all likelihood more money than all other nations combined—to develop the most sophisticated target intelligence systems, weapons systems capable of the most accurate weapons delivery, precision-guide munitions, that provides the best training for the men and women who operate them, and employs a multi-level, redundant, disciplined target approval process, has its operations placed under a post-conflict microscope, while the illegal actions of its opponent in using human shields, and gross violations of the law of war in other conflicts occurring simultaneously around the world, are ignored. It is doubtful that others who purport to follow the rule of law could have conducted the same campaign with fewer collateral civilian casualties. This "Do as I say, not as I can't do" approach

---

8. Article 51, paragraph 7 states:

The presence or movements of the civilian population or individual civilians shall not be used to render certain points or areas immune from military operations, in particular in attempts to shield military objectives from attacks or to shield, favor or impede military operations. The Parties to the conflict shall not direct the movement of the civilian population or individual civilians in order to attempt to shield military objectives from attacks or to shield military operations.

Article 58 provides:

The Parties to the conflict shall, to the maximum extent feasible:

(a) . . . endeavor to remove the civilian population, individual civilians and civilian objects under their control from the vicinity of military objectives;

(b) avoid locating military objectives within or near densely populated areas;

(c) take the other necessary precautions to protect the civilian population, individual civilians and civilian objects under their control against the dangers resulting from military operations.

9. Professor Murphy's paper in this volume.

also suggests a double standard—a very high standard for the United States and a limited number of other Western democracies, and a lower standard for the rest of the world.[10] Hence the adage "Be careful what you ask for" is appropriate in considering the law related to collateral casualties with respect to the precedent of Allied Force.

Emphasis on the predominantly airpower focus of Allied Force neglects the historic lesson that ground force operations cause greater civilian casualties than air operations.[11] For this reason, historically a distinction was made between the risks to the civilian population in the "operational zone," that is, within enemy artillery range, and civilians more distant from the line between opposing forces.[12] The former were assumed to remain at their own risk. Several efforts have been made to define the degree of protection afforded civilians not within the zone of operations, the most recent being Additional Protocol I.[13] This historic struggle has not been answered satisfactorily to date, but seems to have been lost in the post-Kosovo debate and in the questions posed at this conference.

---

10. This is true within NATO itself. Targeting and collateral damage limitations insisted upon by some NATO governments during Allied Force, as noted in footnote 1, contrast markedly with their inability to meet the same standards. As the Air Force report states:

> Interoperability achieved many successes in terms of Alliance cooperation, but also fell short in areas such as precision munitions.... As the United States military continues to move toward a 21st century force propelled by the revolution in military affairs, the resulting gaps in capabilities with its Allied must be addressed. In future conflicts, the U.S. Air Force must also discover methods to integrate its assets with those of less-technologically advanced allies . . . without resorting to a "lowest common denominator" solution. In the face of a more sophisticated threat, this could be an increasingly significant limitation for those states expecting to participate in a coalition with the United States.

INITIAL REPORT, *supra* note 1, at 47.
Post-conflict reviews of law of war compliance is particularly hypocritical when the criticism comes from citizens of or private organizations in a neutral nation, whose government and people have "opted out" of assuming their share of responsibility for a safer world.
11. See this author's *Air War and the Law of War*, 32 AIR FORCE LAW REVIEW 1 n.1 (1990) providing World War II German casualty figures and Charles J. Dunlap, *Kosovo, Casualty Aversion, and the American Military Ethos: A Perspective*, 10 UNITED STATES AIR FORCE ACADEMY JOURNAL OF LEGAL STUDIES 95, 103 (1999/2000).
12. See, for example, M. W. Royse, *Consultation, in* LA PROTECTION DES POPULATIONS CIVILES CONTRE LES BOMBARDMENTS 72, 88 (1930). This program of contributions by international law experts was hosted by the International Committee of the Red Cross.
13. This history is summarized and analyzed in Parks, *supra* note 11.

To close this portion of my remarks, the picture posed by the questions, the responses thereto, and sources cited therein, offer a clearer picture than the one seen by the battlefield commander. Appreciating the fog of war in which a commander must operate, the threshold for violation of the law of war is high, whether in the grave breach provisions of the 1949 Geneva Conventions or the 1977 Additional Protocol I, each of which requires *mens rea*.[14] In establishing *mens rea*, a commander's decisions must be based upon information reasonably available to him at the time, and not what may be learned—or alleged—long after the conflict has ended.[15]

---

14. Article 147, GC, defines a grave breach as "... those involving any of the following acts, if committed against persons or property protected by the present Convention: willful killing, torture or inhuman treatment ... *willfully* causing great suffering or serious bodily injury to body or health ... [or] extensive destruction and appropriation of property, not justified by military necessity and carried out *unlawfully and wantonly*" [emphasis supplied].

Article 85, paragraph 3, Additional Protocol I, defines a grave breach (for the circumstances of this panel) as "(a) making the civilian population or individual civilians the object of attack; [or]

(b) launching an indiscriminate attack affecting the civilian population or civilian objects *in the knowledge* that such attack will cause excessive loss of life, injury to civilians or damage to civilian objects, as defined in Article 57, paragraph 2(a)(iii)....."[emphasis added].

15. See, for example, the reservation taken by Switzerland upon ratification of Additional Protocol I (February 17, 1982), which states, "The provisions of Article 57, paragraph 2, create obligations only for commanding officers at the battalion or group level and above. The information available to commanding officers at the time of their decision is determinative." Similarly, at the time of its ratification (January 28, 1998), the United Kingdom declared that "Military commanders and others responsible for planning, deciding upon, or executing attacks necessarily have to reach decisions on the basis of their assessment of the information from all sources which is reasonably available to them at the relevant time." This approach was taken in the Final Report to the Prosecutor by the Committee Established to Review the NATO Bombing Campaign Against the Federal Republic of Yugoslavia, 39 INTERNATIONAL LEGAL MATERIALS 1257 (2000), *reprinted* herein as Appendix A [hereinafter Report to the Prosecutor], with respect to NATO's mistaken attack of the Chinese Embassy in Belgrade on July 5, 1999. See *id.*, ¶¶ 80–85, which found no criminal responsibility.

Commentary

In considering ways in which to reduce collateral civilian casualties, *distinction* must be placed in its historic context. It is a mutual obligation, as seen in the following:

Distinction[16]

Attacker's obligations	Defender's obligations
Design/employment of weapon systems	Separation of civilian population military objectives
Training	
Target intelligence	
Target acquisition	Air raid precautions
Warning to civilian population[17]	shelters
	evacuation
	civil defense

The United States has done more than its fair share to fulfill its obligations with respect to improving bombing accuracy:[18]

U.S. Bombing Accuracy

War	Number of Bombs[19]	Circular Error Probable[20]
World War II	9,070	3,3000 feet
Korean War	1,100	1,000 feet
Viet Nam War	176	400 feet
Desert Storm	30	200 feet

Modern weapons systems, such as the McDonnell-Douglas F15E Strike Eagle, using the Global Positioning System (GPS), account for ever-increasing accuracy with gravity (so-called "dumb") bombs. Today, the circular error probable (CEP) for US strike aircraft dropping "dumb" bombs is less than forty feet. I say this to note an error made in a source of Professor Murphy's that incorrectly assumed that increased bombing accuracy has occurred only through use of precision-guided munitions.[21]

---

16. W. Hays Parks, *The Protection of Civilians from Air Warfare*, 27 ISRAEL YEARBOOK ON HUMAN RIGHTS 65, 88 (1998).

17. Hague Convention (IV) Respecting the Laws of Customs of War on Land, Oct. 18, 1907, Annex, art. 26, DOCUMENTS ON THE LAWS OF WAR, *supra* note 5, at 69, 78; Protocol I, *supra* note 5, art. 57(2)(c).

18. R. P. HALLION, STORM OVER IRAQ: AIR POWER AND THE GULF WAR 283 (1992).

19. Table computed for 90% probability of a single bomb striking a 60x100 foot target, dropping 500-lb. unguided bombs. For discussion of the relative accuracy of World War II strategic bombing, see W. Hays Parks, *'Precision' and 'Area' Bombing: Who did Which, and When?*, 18 JOURNAL OF STRATEGIC STUDIES 147–174 (1995).

20. *Circular error probable* is "the radius of a circle within which one-half of an aircraft's or missile's projectiles are expected to fall." U.S. Department of Defense, Joint Publication 1-02, Department of Defense Dictionary of Military and Associated Terms (1994).

21. Professor Murphy's paper in this volume quoting Stuart Belt, *Missiles Over Kosovo: Emergence, Lex Lata, of a Customary Norm Requiring the Use of Precision Munitions in Urban Areas*, 47 NAVAL LAW REVIEW 115, 118 (2000).

Precision-guided munitions were used with great effect during the 1972 Linebacker campaigns over North Viet Nam. They received greater public attention during the 1991 Coalition war to liberate Kuwait, and have been improved since that time. Today the CEP "norm" for a laser-guided precision munitions (PGM) is three meters, with at least eighty per cent (rather than the CEP standard of fifty per cent) within that circle. But PGMs are not a panacea weapon. When a precision-guided munition goes awry, it is considerably less accurate than gravity bombs. For example, in the April 15, 1986 air strike against terrorist-related targets in Libya, the Mk-84 2,000-pound precision-guided bombs of one F-111F assigned to attack Aziziyah Barracks struck 7,400 feet long and 3,700 feet left of the intended target.[22] PGM accuracy may be affected by weather and/or defeated by simple countermeasures. Obscurants, such as smoke, may defeat laser-guided bombs, while electro-optical munitions have similar vulnerabilities.[23] As is true of many aspects of warfare, the simple answer often masks myriad complexities. Who bears the responsibility for collateral civilian casualties resulting from successful obscurant use to defeat precision-guided munitions?

Part of the problem in suggesting an obligation to use precision-guided munitions is neglect of the factors that can result in collateral civilian casualties, almost all of which were evident to one degree or another in Allied Force:

Factors Affecting Collateral Damage and Collateral Civilian Casualties[24]

Target intelligence	Distance to target	Target winds, weather
Planning time	Force training, experience	Effects of previous strikes
Force integrity	Weapon availability	Enemy defenses
Target identification	Target acquisition	Rules of engagement
Enemy intermingling[25]	Human factor	Equipment failure
Fog of war		

Not all are within the attacking force's control. As Professor Adam Roberts noted in a presentation at the US Institute of Peace on March 1, 2001, there is a "rush to judgment that anything that affects the civilian population is illegal.

---

22. BRIAN L. DAVIS, QADDAFI, TERRORISM, AND THE ORIGINS OF THE U.S. ATTACK ON LIBYA (1990).
23. Gary S. Ziegler, *Weather Problems Affecting Use of Precision Guided Munitions*, 32 NAVAL WAR COLLEGE REVIEW (May–June 1979), at 95; John P. Bulger, *Obscurants: Countermeasures to Modern Weapons*, 62 MILITARY REVIEW (May 1982), at 45.
24. Parks, *supra* note 11, at 184–202.
25. That is, enemy intermingling of military objectives with civilian objects and the civilian population, including the use of human shields. Photographic examples are contained in Parks, *supra* note 16, at 112–113.

It is an error to assume that the law of war provides absolute protection for everything that may be civilian." It also is an error to view every civilian casualty as a war crime, and/or to place the entire responsibility for civilian casualties on the party to the conflict that has the least control over them.

Offsetting the law of war principle of distinction is the continuing emergence of a 'counter' targeting practice by some governments. In order to reduce or defeat an opponent's military superiority, particularly with respect to airpower, many governments have taken no or limited air raid precautions or steps to evacuate the civilian population. Some have purposely located objects of strategic importance in urban areas, in order to use the civilian population as human shields. This practice became evident in the Korean War. It was experienced in the Vietnam War, both in the air campaigns over North Vietnam and in air and ground operations in South Vietnam; in the 1991 Persian Gulf conflict; and in Allied Force.[26] It is not unique to air operations, as members of Task Force Ranger discovered in their battle in Mogadishu on October 3, 1993 (relearning a lesson experienced a generation earlier in Vietnam). In April 1986, just prior to the US air strike against terrorist-related targets in Libya, Libyan dictator Moammar Gadhafi threatened to round up all foreign nationals and place them in and around his most important facilities. In the last decade, members of United Nations peacekeeping forces in the Balkans were taken hostage and placed adjacent to military objectives as human shields. In one nation, one of the first to ratify Additional Protocol I, an entire downtown city block was razed. A major military command and control center was built underground. The structures that existed on that block previously were meticulously rebuilt, including a school and a mosque. The intent was clear: to use civilian objects and the civilian population to shield this important military objective, and to exploit damage to them and civilian casualties should the military objective be attacked.[27]

Article 51, paragraph 8 of Additional Protocol I states that even where a party to a conflict fails to fulfill its obligations to separate military objectives from the civilian population or, worse, uses the civilian population as human shields, the opposing party is not released from its legal obligations with respect to the civilian population and civilians. Although the United States is not a State Party to Additional Protocol I, this statement is consistent with its

---

26. See, for example, W. Hays Parks, *Rolling Thunder and the Law of War*, 33 AIR UNIVERSITY REVIEW (Jan.–Feb. 1982), at 2 (Vietnam War); and U.S. DEPARTMENT OF DEFENSE, FINAL REPORT TO CONGRESS: CONDUCT OF THE PERSIAN GULF WAR 608, 614, 615 (1992).
27. See, for example, W. Hays Parks, *Crossing the Line*, U.S. NAVAL INSTITUTE PROCEEDINGS (Nov. 1986), at 40, 50, and DAVIS, *supra* note 22, at 15, 18, 19.

post-World War II practice. A point this conference might have addressed is: In light of the increasing, illegal reliance upon human shields by some, to what extent can it be expected that the other side can assume the responsibility for minimizing collateral civilian casualties beyond its legal obligation?

Professor Bring suggests a new additional protocol to limit (if not prohibit) attacks on military objectives in urban areas.[28] Recent State practice suggests this would merely exacerbate the problem, encouraging many to make increased use of civilian objects and the civilian population to shield military objectives from attack.

Professor Bring also suggests more effective warnings. I differ from his reading of the Final Report to the ICTY Prosecutor regarding Allied Force regarding NATO's attack on the Serbian Television and Radio Station in Belgrade, which I see as corroborating General Wesley Clark's statement that as a result of NATO warnings that the Serb Television and Radio Station building was about to be attacked, the Serbs ordered international journalists to report to the building, using them as human shields.[29]

---

28. Professor Bring's paper in this volume.
29. WESLEY CLARK, WAGING MODERN WAR 264 (2001) and Alex Todorovic, *Serb TV Chief Accused Over Air Raid*, THE DAILY TELEGRAPH (London), Feb. 14, 2001, at 19. The ICTY Prosecutor's report does not support Professor Bring's argument. The report states in part:

> [S]ome doubts have been expressed as to the specificity of the warning given to civilians by NATO of its intended strike, and whether the notice would have constituted "effective warning . . . of attacks which may affect the civilian population, unless circumstances do not permit" as required by Article 57(2) of Additional Protocol I.
>
> Evidence on this point is somewhat contradictory. On the one hand, NATO officials in Brussels are alleged to have told Amnesty International that they did not give a specific warning as it would have endangered the pilots. . . On this view, it is possible that casualties among civilians working at the [radio and television station] may have been heightened because of NATO's apparent failure to provide clear advance warning of the attack, as required by Article 57(2).
>
> On the other hand, foreign media representatives were apparently forewarned of the attack. . . . As Western journalists were reportedly warned by their employers to stay away from the television station before the attack, it would also appear that some Yugoslav officials may have expected that the building was about to be struck. Consequently, UK Prime Minister Tony Blair blamed Yugoslav officials for not evacuating the building, claiming that "[t]hey could have moved those people out of the building. They knew it was a target and they didn't. . . . [I]t was probably for . . . very clear propaganda reasons." . . . Although knowledge on the part of Yugoslav officials of the impending attack would not divest NATO of its obligation to forewarn civilians . . ., it may nevertheless imply that the Yugoslav authorities may be partially responsible for the civilian casualties resulting from the attack and may suggest that the advance warning given by NATO may have been sufficient under the circumstances.

Report to the Prosecutor, Appendix A, ¶ 77.

This issue is not new, nor changed by Additional Protocol I. Hugh Trenchard, Marshal of the Royal Air Force, identified the problem in 1928:

> As regards the question of legality, no authority would contend it is unlawful to bomb military objectives, wherever situated. Such objectives may be situated in centers of population in which the destruction from the air will result in casualties also in the neighboring civilian population. The fact that air attack may have this result is no reason for regarding the bombing as illegitimate provided all reasonable care is taken to confine the scope of the bombing to the military objective. Otherwise a belligerent would be able to secure complete immunity for his war manufactures and depots merely by locating them in a large city . . . a position which the opposing belligerent would never accept.[30]

A parallel issue relating to interpretation of Additional Protocol I with respect to precision-guided munition use was raised between World Wars I and II. Professor M. W. Royse, a World War I Marine Corps aviator, went on to a long and respected academic career at Harvard. In 1928 he authored what remains the best work on the law of war as it relates to aerial bombardment.[31] Speaking at a 1930 conference of international legal experts hosted by the International Committee of the Red Cross, Royse noted "It is possible to gauge the immunity of civil populations by noting restrictions on 'permissible violence.' Rules of war restrict the means and methods of warfare only . . . when the rule does not have the effect of placing one or more States at a disadvantage."[32] The increasing conduct of some States in using human shields, and some interpretations of Additional Protocol I offered in this meeting that place the entire responsibility for civilian casualty avoidance on nations employing more advanced weaponry, are likely to erode rather than enhance respect for the law of war and civilian protection.

Comments also are necessary regarding two arguments made by Professor Bring in his paper. The first concerns counting civilian deaths within a military objective as "collateral civilian casualties."[33] It is clear that the Pentagon would be a military objective in war. It should be equally obvious that a

---

30. Charles Webster and Noble Frankland, THE STRATEGIC AIR OFFENSIVE AGAINST GERMANY 1939–1945, Vol. IV, Annexes and Appendices, 73 (1961).
31. M. W. ROYSE, AERIAL BOMBARDMENT AND THE INTERNATIONAL REGULATION OF WARFARE (1928). This comment is made with full and great appreciation and respect for the many works by James Maloney Spaight, including his three-edition AIR POWER AND WAR RIGHTS, published in 1924, 1933 and 1947.
32. Royse, *supra* note 12, at 77.
33. See Professor Bring's paper in this volume.

civilian working there assumes a certain risk. His or her presence would not change the nature of the Pentagon as a legitimate target. Civilians killed within an obvious military objective are not "collateral civilian casualties." Counting civilians employed within a military objective as "collateral civilian casualties" would only encourage increased civilian presence in a military objective in order to make its attack prohibitive in terms of collateral civilian casualties.

Finally, Professor Bring declares without any documentation or authoritative reference that the proportionality language contained in Article 51, paragraph 5(b) of Additional Protocol I is "arguably a codification of traditional customary law."[34] The principle of proportionality has gained importance over the past thirty-five years, but within the limited audience of Western democracies. The principle of proportionality is important today to the US and its NATO allies. I do not disagree with its intent. I do disagree with some of the radical interpretations being offered of it. To suggest that it is customary law is bad history, as I have shown elsewhere.[35]

One question asked by conference planners is: "Does the use of precision-guided munitions lead to a duty to use those types of weapons exclusively in future conflicts?" The answer should not be viewed solely through the US defense budget, which (misguidedly) some see as unlimited. Were I a lawyer for another government, my advice to that government would be: Don't buy them. There is no legal obligation to acquire them. But if you do buy them, you may be required to use them or face criminal prosecution for failure to use them when some believe you should have. Also, it may encourage an opponent to use human shields to offset your technological advantage.

Another answer is a question: How far does one take this argument? Two of the most precise attacks in recent years were the 1983 truck bomb attack on United States peacekeepers in Beirut, and last year's suicide barge attack on the *USS Cole*. Had a State party to an armed conflict carried those out, would it be legally obligated to continue precision suicide attacks? Similarly, on April 16, 1988, an Israeli special operations team entered the home of Khalil el-Wazir, also known as Abu Jihad, the military commander and chief of

---

34. See Professor Bring's paper in this volume. Following the colloquium, Professor Bring advised me that this statement was based upon the argument offered by Hans Blix in his *Area Bombardment: Rules and Reasons*, 49 BRITISH YEAR BOOK OF INTERNATIONAL LAW 1978, at 31–69 (1980). While I hold both Hans Blix and Professor Bring in the highest respect, the practice of nations offers no evidence to substantiate this claim.

35. Parks, *supra* note 16, at 90–97.

operations for the Palestine Liberation Organization, in Sidi Boussaid, Tunisia. Abu Jihad was killed as he reached for his weapon. His wife and two children, present in the room, were left unharmed. That is the epitome of *distinction*. Is it not a logical and inevitable extension of the question posed to this panel to suggest that a nation that has such a special operations capability would be legally obligated to use it against military objectives in urban areas even before resorting to precision-guided munitions? Such a suggestion is absurd, of course, but no less than the argument some have made with respect to precision guided munitions.

I will close with one final comment, and that is to suggest that air power advocates to some degree may be victims of their own hype. Promising degrees of accuracy that cannot always be met raises public expectations, and allows critics to argue that collateral civilian casualties resulting from the friction of war may have been intentional. Touting technological precision may lead to expectations that are unrealistic.[36] It is a case of let the advocate or proponent beware.

---

36. The official US Air Force analysis of Allied Force, received after this author's comments were given, agrees: "The benchmark for high bombing accuracy and low collateral damage, however, may create unrealistic expectations for political leaders and the public at large in future air operations fought under very different circumstances...." INITIAL REPORT, *supra* note 1, at 54.

Commentary

Barry Strauss

I would first like to thank Professors Murphy and Bring for such excellent papers, and the organizers for having invited me. This is an act of faith on their part because I am neither a warrior nor a lawyer. I know that most of you in this room fit one or the other if not both of these categories, so I'll direct my remarks towards you. In particular, I will try to avail myself with the Socratic method or as some would put it the 'Jeopardy approach.' That is, I'll pose my comment in the form of questions.

Let me point out first that I am a historian. And as a historian, it's my duty to tell you that I represent a guild that has a fundamental skepticism about our enterprise here because historians are famously cautious about the possibility of learning from history. Historians would ask can we learn any lessons from the Kosovo conflict? Some of you will know the anecdote about the historian who was asked, 'What do you think of the French Revolution?' And he replied, 'It's too soon to tell.' Well, it may or may not be too soon to tell about Kosovo, but we need to ask about the Kosovo conflict—what can we learn from it?

We begin by asking what can we learn about the role of lawyers? Professor Moore has told us that lawyers played a unique role in the Kosovo conflict in the history of modern warfare or indeed the history of warfare, in the role they played in advising on the tactics of this conflict. We need to ask is Kosovo the wave of the future? Will lawyers play a similar role in future wars? Or was Kosovo unique? Was it an abrogation? To what extent do the unique characteristics of the Kosovo warfare shape what happened there? In particular let me pose a question—what would have happened during the Kosovo war if groups of Serb terrorists had bombed hospitals in NATO countries? Would this have affected NATO's tactics in this war? Would lawyers have been able to convince commanders and indeed to convince politicians to be similarly restrained in their response in Serbia? More generally—and this is my second question—when we think about the Kosovo war, should we think of it as fundamentally a humanitarian intervention, or should we think of it as a political conflict whose aim was to stabilize NATO's volatile southeastern flank? I think we have to ask this question when we look more broadly at the strategy of the Kosovo conflict.

Some of the questions and comments that arose yesterday I think would cause us to ask whether NATO's strategy in Kosovo was strictly military or was it rather following a political and psychological strategy? Did NATO plan to win the war by destroying Serbia's military potential for action in Kosovo, or was NATO rather aiming at delivering a message to Mr Milosevic and other members of the Serb elite that if the war were to continue, that eventually NATO would flatten the economic infrastructure of Serbia? I think we need to ask that as a factual question. We also need to ask it as an ethical question. What about the ethics of NATO's strategy in this war? In particular we need to ask it about the question of dual-use targets. NATO did target a number of dual-use facilities that had military use and so was legally proper to target, but they also were very important for the Serb economy. The question is to what extent were they targeted because of their military use? To what extent were they targeted because of their economic and therefore their political use? If this targeting was legal, was it also ethical?

To turn the question around, to ask it in a somewhat different way, we've heard that the strategy in this war was not to strike a quick devastating knock-out blow, but rather it was a strategy of slow escalation. The war lasted seventy-eight days when it could possibly have ended much sooner. We need to ask the ethics of this strategy and in particular how many additional Kosovars suffered or died as a result of the prolongation of the war? How would we balance that number against the number of civilians who were perhaps spared in Serbia because of the particular strategy that NATO followed?

Now let's turn from strategy to tactics and look more specifically at collateral damage. On the subject of collateral damage, let me be forgiven for just stating the obvious. The term collateral damage is a euphemism—if not indeed Orwellian. We're asking of course how many civilian casualties, how many deaths, how many injuries, how much civilian suffering is permitted in the conduct of war? The figure of five hundred civilian deaths in Serbia is before us. We need to ask the question, was this an excessive number of deaths in this conflict? Or does it reflect restraint? Does it reflect admirable restraint?

From this we need to ask about NATO commanders. In their behavior in this war were there significant deviations from the rules of proportionality and feasible precautions.? Was there to a significant degree too liberal an interpretation of what a military objective was in Serbia and Kosovo?

From this we need to go to a factual question. It's one that's been raised before, but I think we need to raise it again and ask for clarification from the experts. It's a factual question regarding high-altitude bombing. That is, by bombing at 15,000 feet rather than going lower as a general rule, did NATO increase the possibility of civilian casualties? Did it increase the number of civilian casualties? Depending on what our answer to that question is, I think we come up with a serious ethical question. That is, how do we weigh in the balance concern for the safety of soldiers' lives as opposed to concern for civilian lives? To ask the question in a different way, just what risks can we ethically ask soldiers to undertake? Can we for example ask soldiers to expose themselves to hostile fire from other soldiers in order to minimize the number of civilian casualties? Is that a fair and ethical thing for us to demand? To go a step further, is it a democratic thing for us to demand?

Now I raise the question of whether it's a democratic thing to demand because the question of chivalry has come up—the question of chivalry and military honor. To my ears, these strike me as rather unusual terms to hear in talking about modern warfare. When I hear about chivalry and military honor, I have to ask myself whether these are appropriate terms or whether they are not instead aristocratic hangovers from an age of gentlemen warriors. We can certainly ask soldiers never to deliberately target civilians. We certainly must ask soldiers never to deliberately target civilians. We must ask commanders to follow the laws of armed conflict in choosing their targets. But again, can we ask soldiers to knowingly risk their own lives in order to minimize civilian casualties?

Moving on from this, I wanted to ask some questions about Professor Bring's proposal for defining military objectives more tightly in future multinational humanitarian interventions. In particular I wanted to ask the following questions. What would the effect of his proposal be on the safety of soldiers following this much more restricted definition of military objectives? What would its effect have been in the Kosovo campaign? What would its effect have been on Kosovars in prolonging the campaign? And what would its effect have been on enemy power?

Turning to Professor Murphy's discussion of the role of precision-guided munitions in urban and highly populated areas, it may indeed be the case that we ought not to employ any black letter rule in demanding that precision-guided munitions be used. But would it not make sense to say that depending upon feasibility—the feasibility of using them and upon the discretion of the commanders—that indeed precision-guided munitions should be used in urban and highly populated areas whenever possible. So not a black letter rule, but something that should be striven for in the interest of minimizing civilian casualties. A follow-up question on that for the experts would be to what extent would finances make this possible or impossible?

The question of finances brings me to my final question. That is one about the differences of the different kinds of States that fight war, the differences in ethics might be expected between technologically poor States and technologically rich and sophisticated States. In particular, should we expect democratic countries to fight their wars by democratic principles? Should we expect democratic countries particularly when they are engaging in humanitarian interventions to fight wars by humanitarian principles? Or rather, should we say that it's simply impossible to expect that of democratic countries and unfair to expect that of democratic countries? Should we say that war is not a humanitarian business and that the proper role of democratic principles in the conduct of war is making democratic political decisions about the nature of war, the aims of war, the purpose of war and having made those decisions to fight war cleanly and fairly and according to the laws of armed conflict, but fighting the war using all force at a country's disposal in order to win the war as quickly as possible, to achieve a political goal that is in and of itself humanitarian and humane? I'll leave that as my final question. I'm sure the discussion will take it further.

Discussion

Modern Technology: Is There An Obligation to Use It?

Brian O'Donnell:[1]
We had some discussion on the precision-guided munitions issue and I'd like to turn that to the targeting analysis issue for collateral damage purposes. Colonel Montgomery's presentation yesterday discussed the highly technical nature of some of the new technology that we've used to determine the blast patterns of buildings whether it's going to be walls falling in, walls falling out and so forth. Are we establishing in the panel's opinion—probably Hays Parks would be the best person to answer this—a new standard that if we don't take advantage of that new technology in future operations, then we have failed to utilize all reasonable means to minimize collateral damage?

W. Hays Parks:
I don't know enough about the formulas for determining how many civilians are likely to be inside an objective or how many collateral civilian casualties there may be. I will note that years ago I looked at the Top Secret original target package for North Vietnam. It was written in August of 1964 and gave an estimate that there were 2.7 persons living in each structure. I feel sorry for that .7 person whoever that may be. I'll let Tony Montgomery really respond more to that, but I feel that we know what munitions can do. The JDAM that we have is very well developed, quite sophisticated. So I feel fairly good about that side of it provided you have accurate delivery. I have not seen the formulations for how we determine that there's going to be X number of civilians in a particular structure or how likely it is we'll have X amount of collateral civilian casualties. I do think that we may be again creating expectations there

---

1. Lieutenant Commander, United States Navy; International Law Advisor, Naval Warfare Development Command.

that when these formula do not work, people will look at them in the most negative fashion.

Mike Newton:[2]

In fulfilling the obligation of the law to take all feasible measures, it's easy to jump to precision-guided munitions which I think is what the media and much of the public has done. But in point of fact, I think the targeteers and our Air Force colleagues would agree that what really is done is an assessment of how to weaponeer a target, how to attack it, when to attack it in the way most likely to minimize collateral damage. I would give you just one example—the MUP [Yugoslav Ministry of Internal Affairs police forces] police station in Jackavitza. If you attacked it on an east-west axis, there were four-story civilian apartment buildings on either side. They didn't do that. They attacked it with five hundred pound dumb bombs on a north-south access. There's a big bomb crater in the road in front of the building. The building is devastated. There's a big bomb crater in the parking lot behind the building. Beautiful weaponeering, and the civilians on either side weren't affected—the windows weren't even broken. I think that's an example of the kinds of things that US militaries do precisely to minimize collateral damage which lead into a question really for the panel as a whole.

Human Shields: Can Abuse of the Law of War Be a Force Multiplier?

Mike Newton:

There was press reporting on the attack on the RTS station where, when you look at what happened, the US military took steps to minimize collateral damage. It was press reporting that in fact Slobodan Milosevic had advance notice of the attack on the RTS station and the casualties that were caused were caused by the fact that he took people, rounded them up and locked them in the station—literally locked them into the station—as a propaganda vehicle to then exploit to the world media, which he did successfully. I mean the very fact that people perceive of that as an unlawful attack; the very fact that we're still discussing it is, I think, an indicator of Milosevic's success.

If you do go down the road of pursuing future legal developments, how do you envision using the law? I mean it's pretty clear to me that people are using the laws as a force multiplier to actually assist an unethical defendant. How

---

2. Lieutenant Colonel, United States Army; Office of War Crimes Issues, Department of State.

would you guard against that because very clearly that's what we're seeing in the practicality on the ground—an unethical defender is using the law as a way to limit and constrain the attacker even when the attacker is making a huge effort to comply with the law? So how would you address that as a matter of law if you do try to come up with an additional protocol or further targeting restrictions?

W. Hays Parks:

I think the one thing that I would look at if we were rewriting additional Protocol I, I would make it a grave breach to use human shields. I think that's not in there. You could perhaps interpret that from using the grave breach provision of the Civilians' Convention if you're on occupied territory. But if you're not, I think the dilemma you have is that some nations felt then and feel now that if I can draft my men and women into my military and have them die in my defense, I can use my civilians the same way. If those are civilians of another country—as happened both I think in Yugoslavia and also happened in Iraq in 1990 when hostages were taken and used as human shields—then you have a grave breach of Article 147. I think, however, we still have the unresolved dilemma that existed at the time of negotiation of Additional Protocol I as to what extent can the leadership of an enemy nation use its own population as human shields.

John Murphy:

The only comment I'll make on the situation that's been posed here is that it illustrates the difficulty of getting the facts straight in an armed conflict. Part of the problem in the situation you pose is that Mr Milosevic was successful in getting a certain element of the press to believe the story and that if all the facts had come out, then there really would have been no valid charge that the United States forces had violated the law of armed conflict. In fact, quite the contrary would have been charged. But of course getting the facts straight during any crisis, certainly during armed conflict, continues to be a major—perhaps irresolvable—problem.

Yves Sandoz:

The problem is not so much a need to change the law but to implement it. There are too many violations; but it's not drafting new laws that will change this. We have to find better ways to react to violations of the law. That is the key issue.

Discussion

Michael Bothe:

I must admit, I have not quite seen where this problem of human shields comes in. This is in violation of the laws of war certainly. In Yugoslavia, this is a subject for the jurisdiction of the ICTY. As it is a violation of the laws of war, it comes under the definition of the crimes which are subject to the jurisdiction of that Court under Article 3 of the Statute of the ICTY. Having said that, I entirely agree that much more attention should be paid to this current practice.

Do We Need An Additional Protocol For Humanitarian Intervention?

Christopher Greenwood:

This question is for Ove Bring regarding his proposal for drafting an additional protocol for humanitarian interventions. Which body of law would apply to States toward which the intervention is directed? In a Kosovo type of case if the coalition which is carrying out the intervention is governed by a new protocol as envisioned on interventions because they are acting in a humanitarian capacity and not self-defense, which body of law would apply to the country in which the intervention is being carried out? Will it be subject to the same body of rules about intervention because it is the intervenee, or will it be able to say that in it's own view that it is acting in self-defense indeed for it's own national survival and thus subject only to the more lenient standards that are the general rule in Protocol I?

Ove Bring:

First, I would like to say that if we could imagine an additional protocol III in this context, it needs to be a balanced protocol relating to what we've just talked about—the need to get rid of human shields as a way of defense during international conflicts. That issue has to be addressed in the same kind of protocol. But I'm not married to the idea that it must be a negotiated text. It could also be some common statement on how operations should be conducted. That kind of document would not compete with international humanitarian law proper. It would only be something in addition to it with very specific messages being signaled to the parties to that conflict.

I agree that you have a very good point there with regard to who is governed by what body of law. How would Yugoslavia in this case consider the situation in legal terms? They would probably look upon this as a right of self-defense. Although this protocol I'm talking about is not relating to aggression or self-defense for humanitarian intervention or the opposite, they would certainly find themselves having the right to conduct warfare under the normal standards of self-defense. I agree with you that that is a problem that has to be looked into further.

If you have a kind of new protocol trying to limit the situation to a certain kind of intervention, that will presume that the armed conflict will stay within the confines of the scope of application that has been drafted in that protocol. If the Yugoslav authorities start to upgrade and escalate the fighting under the principle of self-defense, then that scope of application will fall. You will not find yourself within those parameters any more. You will go back to the ordinary law of armed conflict.

John Murphy:

The briefest of comments regarding this interesting proposal. I have problems with it just as others have expressed problems. One thing I think hasn't been noticed is it seems to be that in the case of where the motivation for the intervention is primarily humanitarian, to change the rules to make it more difficult for there to be military efficiency would obstruct bringing the humanitarian violations to an end quickly. That it seems to me would be dysfunctional and unfortunate. It does seem to me that Professor Bring's proposal brings with it a little bit of the just war concept with all of the difficulties that raises.

Ove Bring:

There have been a lot of points of view put forward with regard to the proposed additional protocol III. Perhaps that suggestion should be looked upon in perspective. Probably the main focus on my paper was the definition of military objectives. At the end of the paper, I wanted to address the ethical lessons of the Kosovo conflicts since that is part of our agenda here. During such an assessment of the ethical dimension of the Kosovo conflict, I think it's appropriate to bring up the idea that is already floating around in the international community about such an additional protocol III. I have taken the many reservations and critical points with regard to it—it might be totally unrealistic and it might be counterproductive in certain respects. Still, I think it addresses the matter of improper balance with regard to the rights of attackers against the hazards that the civilians on the ground are experiencing. But in order to address that problem, if you admit it is a problem in these situations, we don't have to be stuck to a certain legal solution. Additional protocol III that we've been discussing would be a treaty. Another way would be, as I said, perhaps to have a code of conduct which perhaps could get rid of some of the more technical devaluating effects that a treaty text would have on international humanitarian law as a whole. Or one could imagine having the Secretary-General of the United Nations issue another bulletin on observance by UN forces on international humanitarian law principles in armed conflict. That kind of bulletin could refer exactly to these enforcement operations and it could be a sort of a guideline for other kinds of similar interventions. That was in the general perspective.

Reciprocity in War and the Law of War

Leslie Green:

In any future conflict, particularly one with a coalition character, we've got to carry the public with us. From this point of view I want to raise a question. I'm thinking of the issue of these "clever," or, to use Mike Schmitt's term, "brilliant" bombs. We've got them. By way of contrast, if we are involved in a conflict against an enemy that doesn't have them, are we under an obligation to use only deliberative resources that are available to him? This is reciprocity par excellence! It's merely a modern application of the old Asian idea that elephants should only be used against elephants and men against men. Where do we stand from our propaganda point of view in persuading the public when we have the means to wipe them out, but they only have the means to kick us?

W. Hays Parks:

Leslie, I don't recall where that was. I've seen various versions of that. One of them of course was the proposal during the negotiation of Additional Protocol I that was made by Togo, which argued that if two nations were in a war and one of them had an air force and the other did not, the one that had the air force could not use it—nice try!

There's a rather famous quote by Churchill about a disarmament conference where the lion wanted another animal to give up its teeth. And the bear said we all just ought to hug each other—this kind of thing. So, there's a great deal of that. I think the dilemma we have is that unfortunately our opponents do not always follow our doctrine. They don't play to our strong suit. Mr Milosevic would have loved to have neutralized our airpower capabilities to force us into a ground campaign. That's the dilemma you have. However we feel about the obligation to use precision-guided munitions in every case; I think all of us would agree that we are not going to say we'll not use them because we do want to hold down the collateral casualties as much as we can.

Discussion

Yves Sandoz:

I have two points. First, the question of determining how a poor country, without important military means, could defend itself without violating IHL was at the heart of negotiations which took place during the 1974-1977 Diplomatic Conference. The result of those negotiations was the introduction in Additional Protocol I of 1977 of rules accepting guerilla warfare as a legitimate means of warfare. The principles remain the same, as I mentioned before, but they have to be implemented in relation to the means available. Quite clearly, if the fighting is unbalanced, there is a great risk, as I think John Murphy mentioned too, that respect for the law will decrease and that we will enter into an era of terrorist attacks.

The second point is the following: the NATO action in Kosovo will probably remain a special case. I do not think we will have many cases in which this emergency humanitarian intervention doctrine will be applied. Basically, it is an intervention to ensure the application of the law in stopping a violation of it. This type of intervention is unbalanced by nature. There is no comparison between NATO and Yugoslavian forces. But the fundamental questions for the credibility of such interventions in world public opinion are clarity and impartiality. Clarity in setting forth the threshold over which a State may not step without encountering such enforcement actions and establishing who has the right to decide those actions. And impartiality in taking measures corresponding only to the gravity of the situation and not to the economic or political interest of those deciding and undertaking the action.

John Norton Moore:

When we look at imbalance, we need, for example, to talk about the imbalance of the Iraq Army invading Kuwait. If we talk about the imbalance, talk about the imbalance of the massive human rights violations in Bosnia with 200,000 killed in disregard of the law of war. If we talk about the imbalance, we might talk about the imbalance of a regular army police force directed toward killing civilians in Kosovo in a massive way that we're trying to stop. It seems to me that the real key is to look at what the goals of the democracies are in trying to stop democide and genocide, trying to stop aggressive war. The reality is we want to win those as rapidly as we possibly can at the lowest cost to all involved.

Michael Bothe:

The question of differentiated or equal obligations has been with us all the time because although legally speaking, parties to a conflict are equal, militarily speaking they never are. We've had that in different prospects and different respects. For instance the question whether poor countries can afford to provide adequate standards of treatment for prisoners of war if they cannot nourish their own armies. That is one version of that. There is a tension between reciprocity and the fundamental principle of no reciprocity which is also inherent in the laws of war. You do not mete out bad treatment to the other guy as a reaction to bad treatment if you can do better. I think this is all very well covered by Article 57 of Protocol I which says in relation to the attacks that all feasible precautions have to be taken in order to minimize civilian casualties. Now what is feasible for one party is not necessarily feasible for the other party, but this does not lower the standard for the party for which this is feasible.

Target Priority and Collateral Damage

Michael Glennon:

Assume that a list of lawfully vetted targets is assembled. Assume further that some of the targets on the list are known to carry a substantially greater risk of collateral damage and civilian deaths. Can those targets be assigned a higher priority? Can they be moved up on the list and hit sooner rather than later because the belief is the war will therefore be ended sooner saving ultimately a greater number of military and civilian lives.

Yves Sandoz:

If I understood the question, you have a reply in Article 57(3) of Protocol I, which states that "when a choice is possible between several military objectives for obtaining a similar military advantage, the objective to be selected shall be that the attack on which may be expected to cause the least danger to civilian lives and to civilian objects." I think that answers your question.

"No Body Bags" War and the Value of Human Lives

Adam Roberts:

I want to raise the question of whether this really was a "no body bags" war as Ove Bring stated it in his paper. Of course it was in the sense that we know that allied forces did not suffer any combat casualties, but whether it was a clear policy from the beginning that it was a "no body bags" war is a much more debatable proposition. Those embarking on the decision to engage in war knew that they were taking a risk with their own servicemen's lives. I think I'm right in recalling that that was stated in some of the speeches at the beginning of the war including I think in President Clinton's. So one has to be very careful before one adopts the *ex post facto* wisdom which assumes that this was clearly understood to be a "no body bag" war at the time. I do not think that it was. On the other hand, the desire to protect the servicemen and women of allied countries was in my view entirely understandable. Again, I don't think it's self-evident, and I'd like the opinions of the panel on this, but just because there was a desire to protect their lives doesn't mean they were being viewed superior in value to the lives of others. And it's far from self-evident that keeping airmen in a position of relative safety increases the risk to the population below. It is possible that in a position of relative safety aircrews could make decisions that were calm and informed as distinct from being made in haste. I come from a country with a tradition of low-level bombing and the risks associated with that low-level bombing are well known. They include risks to those on the ground as well as those performing it.

Ove Bring:

Professor Barry Strauss asked me if you have this kind of solution, what will be the safety of the soldiers, the safety of the Kosovars? Will there be a prolongation of the conflict, etcetera? Well, these are all issues that need to be discussed from this ethical perspective. With regard to the safety of soldiers, I quoted Tony Rogers who said that under international humanitarian law, we have to realize that certain risks will have to be taken. I'm arguing here for a solution that would increase the risk to soldiers and pilots. That is clear. It's a political problem of course for those States as to whether they will or not embark in the beginning on a "no body bags" policy or something close to that. They will have terrific problems in democratic States to accept these increased risks for pilots and soldiers. Still, I think what we need in this international community of today is more political leadership—more political willingness to take risks in order to secure common values of the international community. So that is something which I would like to see more of and I think that many individuals would be prepared to take risks personally in order to achieve things like saving people from genocide or whatever. The safety of the Kosovars in this kind of situation could have been much better with my suggestion, but of course the Kosovo conflict as Yves Sandoz said was unique. It probably will not repeat itself again. I mean there was almost a gigantic humanitarian catastrophe with regard to the refugees in the beginning due to the fact that there were no ground troops. My argument goes in the direction that political leadership has to consider ground troops in situations like this. That could actually shorten the conflict and it could give much better protection. It would signal something to the Milosevic regime in this case that would deter them from going further on the track of ethic cleansing. All these are possibilities.

Chuck Kogan:

Listening to the discussions this morning and particularly the remarks of Mr. Strauss and Mr. Parks, I'd like to make the following observation. The Kosovo war was fought on the basis that coalition lives are more valuable than lives on the other side. This is what war is all about.

W. Hays Parks:

I have to disagree with that. The Kosovo campaign was conducted to save lives. Although it may have cost 500, it probably saved many thousands more than that. I think that's something that's been neglected in these discussions.

Does Kosovo Provide Lessons For The Future?

Barry Strauss:

I'd like to return to my point that the lessons of this war must be very limited because Serbia's inability to respond massively to NATO attacks leaves us with one dimension unknown. We don't know how NATO would respond if it was provoked in ways that Serbia couldn't provoke it. So from the point of view of what we've learned for the future, the answer is we don't know about that yet.

Cluster Bombs and Long-Term Collateral Damage

Adam Roberts:

I just wanted to raise an issue about this discussion and the focus here on collateral damage and the way in which the discussion has gone. One dimension of damage got largely but not entirely excluded: that is the long-term damage that may flow from use of certain types of weapons and may have an impact long after the conflict. Ove Bring mentioned in his paper the effect of cluster bombs. The principal problem with regard to cluster bombs is not the immediate collateral damage, but rather the long-term effect. That is one issue that I think does arise very clearly from the Kosovo war. So there are other aspects to unintended damage besides the immediate collateral damage that certainly require attention.

Discussion

W. Hays Parks:

The answer to the question of cluster munitions is threefold: it's historical, it's technical, and it's ongoing diplomatic initiatives. Unexploded ordnance—what we are calling now, explosive remnants of war—are of course part of everyone's history. I think the French have been clearing something like a half million rounds of unexploded ordnance from their own territory for the last fifty some odd years. We recognized it more after Kosovo for the very simple reason that many of the people who lived in Kosovo were allowed to go back to their homes before the areas were cleared thus placing themselves at risk.

I just finished reading Anthony Beevor's book on the battle of Stalingrad.[3] Even in the dead of winter when that battle was over, the Soviet Army did not let the civilians return to their homes until the unexploded ordnance was cleared. That of course is a responsibility of a sovereign nation to do that. We have the gap in Kosovo because there was no sovereign there to prevent people from returning. The United Nations and others, however, have noted the activities of the United States and a number of other nations in going in to clear not only antipersonnel landmines but to assist in clearance of all unexploded ordnance, and they've been praised for that effort.

Lastly, the diplomatic part. Last September the International Committee of the Red Cross hosted a meeting in Leone that was chaired by Yves Sandoz. While its original focus was on cluster munitions, the issue eventually evolved to explosive remnants of war. We are in the middle of the second review conference to the UN Conventional Weapons Convention now where this issue is under consideration. One of the things that we're looking at—and it will be a long-term solution—is requiring some sort of a self-destruct or self-neutralization device on all ordnance. That could be very expensive, but in the long run it will save lives and save money. It costs roughly $500 to clear one piece of unexploded ordnance whereas something like this would be less than $50 a round. We're looking at it very seriously. We have not only a humanitarian and technological interest in doing it, but also a military interest. No commanding officer likes to have his own troops advance through their own unexploded ordnance. So this may be one of those places where all of this will come together. It may take some time because obviously some people will say we can't afford that. It may take twenty years to do it. It's an issue being focused on. It is certainly not related just to cluster munitions.

---

3. ANTONY BEEVOR, STALINGRAD: THE FATEFUL SIEGE, 1942–1943, at 407 (1998).

Discussion

The Principle of Proportionality

John Murphy:

I want to clarify a point with respect to Yves Sandoz' comments. I'm an agnostic as to the debate that you have with Hays Parks on whether there is or is not a rule of customary international law called the rule of proportionality. I'll leave it up to you folks to continue to do battle on that. I am similarly an agnostic because I think it's really beyond my technical competence to get into the question of whether Protocol I strikes an improper balance between the obligations of the attackers and the obligations of the defenders. I did note that in my paper. I will say this in respect to the rule of proportionality. It does seem to me that it is applied, whatever its status, in terms of a question of whether the collateral damage is excessive compared to the military advantage. I think it is a very difficult rule to interpret and apply and I think that's been brought out in the course of our discussions not only this morning but at other times and no doubt it will arise again.

Henry Shue:

I would like to say a bit more about the role that the considerations of proportionality play in target selection. A lot of us were fairly skeptical about how important proportionality can be because it is so vague. But you all say that proportionality absolutely did come into consideration. There's kind of two ways it can work. One, effective proportionality can be that you decide that rather than hitting a particular target the way you would like to, you hit it some other way—at night instead of in the day, or with a precision weapon instead of a non-precise one—but you still go ahead and hit it. Were there very many cases in which you said of a dual-purpose target, "Yes, it has military value, but its civilian value is so great that we shouldn't hit it at all with consideration to proportionality?" Were any targets ever totally ruled out rather than just hit some other way? It sounds as if for example the electrical grid was treated that way until the end of the bombing campaign.

Judith Miller:

Proportionality was key in respect to any targeting decision that I am aware of in Kosovo or in any other context in which military force was used by the United States in conjunction with its allies while I was at DoD. And while it may sound vague, I think we all have very much in mind that it is a principle that needs to be applied. You can't say, "Well, there are X human lives at stake or civilians versus an enormous military value." There's no way to boil that down to a formula. But our intelligence people, the people who put together target folders and background information, and the modeling that we've done have allowed us to actually think in specifics not just generalities. We knew that there were housing developments close to something that we cared about attacking and there were a number of occasions where targets were rejected.

I'm confident there were a number of targets rejected before they ever got to my level because we had so many other good lawyers and target people working in the field, which is the first line of the appraisal. But there were some targets that came through from the field that we asked questions about, looked at, and ultimately concluded that they were not appropriate targets to take on. So while it's not a science, I think certainly everyone I worked with on the operational side and the Joint Staff, in the policy world of DoD, and the legal community felt that that was the guiding principle of really paramount importance.

Richard Sorenson:

We closely scrutinized each and every target. That of course started out fundamentally with military necessity, but then would go down to the number of military casualties that would happen and the number of civilians that potentially would die. We were really looking at "effects based targeting." We're not looking at simply blowing up a particular building or whatever. If we can achieve the desired effect with some other means that minimizes the unnecessary suffering, then that was also considered. So if we could go with alternative means to achieve the same effect that's required by military necessity. And that was considered throughout the campaign. The bottom line is we had a lot of data.

Flying At 15,000 Feet

Susan Fink:[4]

As a military pilot who's been in academia for about a year now, I've been struck by the number of times I've heard that one of the things that we need to really think about in humanitarian intervention is how we can put our pilots at 15,000 feet and knowingly kill hundreds of people when the reason for this is humanitarian intervention, not just a regular international war, but

---

4. Lieutenant Commander, United States Navy; Fletcher School of Law and Diplomacy.

humanitarian in purpose. When I dig a little deeper, I find that the argument is two-fold. First, it's a moral and ethical one that must be taken into account when decision makers at the highest level entertain a thought of humanitarian intervention. And then deeper it is that the altitude at which pilots fly actually increases the number of civilians killed. Pressing this a little further, there is some ambiguity about whether there were precision-guided munitions available or whether we'd run out of those at this point and were reverting to other weapons, etcetera. But my question is this—it's probably more appropriate to ask this of a moral and ethical panel—but I would like to ask the legal experts whether you entertain this from a legal standpoint. Secondly, what advice would you give to those who live in the land of the doable—those who live in the land of the political who have to make these decisions—what advice you would give them to either rebut, entertain or take this into account when making a decision to go in to humanitarian intervention?

Richard Sorenson:

Let me start out by saying that I don't think there are facts to support that in reality in particular with Kosovo. The problems with hitting the convoys from fifteen thousand feet occurred when Milosevic intentionally intermingled combatants with noncombatants—it was difficult to discriminate. I think there were relatively few civilians killed as a result of those strikes from fifteen thousand. And in fact, the pilots did go down to six thousand. They had binoculars. They were in fact complying with their obligations under the law of armed conflict to discriminate between combatants and noncombatants. So I don't think the facts are out there. It makes great newspaper copy, sells newspapers, airtime and interviews, but the facts just simply aren't there to suggest that by keeping our pilots at 15,000 feet to protect them we were engaging in basically carpet bombing. I understand what carpet bombing is and that did not happen. The A-10 pilots did not pickle off their general-purpose bombs anywhere. They had specific targets that they had spotted and were releasing their ordnance against those military targets that they had identified. Sometimes there was misidentification and that goes with the fog of war. The military commanders that are in command of military forces, and the pilots that are flying planes and releasing ordnance, use their best military judgment at the time, assessing all the facts, knowing that they cannot intentionally target civilians due to the training they have received on the law of armed conflict. Plus targeting reviews happened at all levels, including during the operations going after field forces in Kosovo proper, to ensure we were distinguishing between military and civilian targets.

PART V

COALITION OPERATIONS

Introduction

Nicholas Rostow

Our topic is coalition warfare. We will examine such issues as what rules to follow when different members of the coalition have different international legal obligations. A particular focus will be Protocol I since some NATO members are parties, while others are not. We will also examine the extent to which Protocol I is customary international law.

This whole issue of coalition warfare of course is an old one. There have been coalitions since I suppose the beginning of recorded military history. They always raise very interesting political-military issues. Commanders always complain bitterly about political interference. One need only read Winston Churchill's book on the life of Marlborough to learn what real political interference was. I would just offer Churchill's comment that the only thing worse than fighting with allies is fighting without them—that is on your side.

Coalition Warfare and Differing Legal Obligations of Coalition Members Under International Humanitarian Law

Torsten Stein

Wars were fought by alliances or "coalitions," both before and at Waterloo. Indeed, coalition warfare has been a dominant theme of armed conflict in the 19th and 20th centuries and is represented at the end of the last millennium in Operation Allied Force. It is, however, a more recent development that coalition partners do not necessarily operate separately and in clearly distinct segments of the theater or battlefield. Today's coalitions "inter-operate" so closely that it may be difficult, if not impossible, for adversaries and outsiders, such as the International Committee of the Red Cross (ICRC) that seek to monitor the observance of obligations under international humanitarian law, to identify who did what and to whom.

Admittedly, the coalition partners have (almost) a clear understanding of such matters. Moreover a participating State would, due to the pressure from a public at home which demands answers, either admit to its own wrongdoing, deny responsibility and point out the responsible party, or make a plausible denial of responsibility without putting the blame on any specific State or actor. If the coalition consists of democracies, that process should make it easier to place the blame within a relatively short period of time. Theoretically, however, one cannot leave out the possibility that the coalition may manage to build a wall of denial or silence.

Increasing the problems further, the various members of a coalition waging war might have differing legal obligations under the law of armed conflict;

obligations which are treaty-based. Some coalitions might be more homogeneous in this respect, others less so. The coalition conducting Operation Allied Force was certainly more homogenous, even if not all participating members were contracting parties to the 1977 Additional Protocol I the 1949 Geneva Conventions, than the coalition which is currently providing troops for the Kosovo International Security Force (KFOR).

At the end of the day Protocol I may not be the biggest problem. What about the 1980 UN Conventional Weapons Convention and its Protocols? Or the 1997 Ottawa Convention on anti-personnel mines? The diversity of respective obligations arising from these conventions might be much greater in a coalition of over 30 States than with regard to Protocol I.

Can there be differing legal standards for various members of a given coalition? Could the commander-in-chief (CINC) of such a coalition ask (or even order) those force-providing States not parties to the restricting treaties to undertake actions which violate those treaties, while all the others live up to their treaty obligations? Does it make a difference if the coalition is a "UN force" or at least authorized by the Security Council to use force? Are there other reasons why the strictest legal standard should govern a coalition war because the coalition derives the legality of its use of force from being a regional arrangement, or from its humanitarian purpose? Or because reprisals of the other side would be indiscriminate? And to whom would possible internationally wrongful acts be attributed? To the coalition if it is an international organization, to all members of the coalition or only to the flag State?

This paper will discuss all these questions using NATO's Kosovo campaign as an example, which includes the air campaign of Operation Allied Force, as well as KFOR, the ground force authorized by the UN Security Council to use force, if necessary. There can be no doubt that the whole of the law of armed conflicts applies to the air campaign, although NATO spokesmen avoided calling it a "war" and insisted that it was a "humanitarian action." I will attempt to treat the questions under a somewhat broader perspective, because there will be other (and different) coalitions in the future, and the same rules will probably apply to all of them; as would, by the way, customary international law rules emerging out of Operation Allied Force.

The Factual Setting

Examples of the diversity of obligations during the Kosovo campaign include: France, the United States and Turkey were not parties to Protocol I; Turkey is not a party to the UN Conventional Weapons Convention or any of its Protocols; Russia (as was the former Soviet Union) is not a party to Protocols II and IV, nor is Poland; Yugoslavia and all its former Republics are not parties to Protocols II and V with the exception of Bosnia, which is a party to Protocol II; and the United States is not a party to Protocol IV. One could go on naming other force-providing States among the over 30 contributing to KFOR and the various choices they have made with respect to ratifying the Conventional Weapons Convention and its protocols.

It is also a fact that for probably different reasons foreign offices and defense ministries carefully compared armed forces manuals. However, as the second KFOR Commander confirmed,[1] while rules of engagement contained numerous restrictions premised on grounds of domestic law, none expressly refer to obligations under international humanitarian law. General Clark, who served as Supreme Allied Commander Europe, reports that while there was resistance among NATO States when he tried to get additional targets approved, the rationale did not include "we can't do it because some of us are bound by Protocol I."[2] Nonetheless, the legal restraints of Protocol I were observed, even if they found no expression at the CINC-level.

Has Protocol I Become Customary International Law?

Differing treaty obligations of members of a coalition would not pose a problem if a treaty such as Protocol I has become customary international law. No one, however, has thus far maintained that the UN Conventional Weapons Convention and its Protocols, or the 1997 Ottawa Convention, have become binding upon non-parties.[3] It is widely accepted in international law that, as Article 38 of the Vienna Convention on the Law of Treaties confirms, treaty obligations and customary law obligations may coincide, because the treaty codifies already existing customary law, or because new customary international law is generated in the aftermath of a treaty.

It is appropriate to dwell for a moment on the process of creating customary international law. As stated in Article 38 (1)(b) of the Statute for the International Court of Justice (ICJ), such law requires both custom and the subjective element of following this custom because one is so obliged by law—*opinio iuris*. In this respect, it is interesting to note the practice of the same court in the

---

1. Personal interview; cf. also GENERAL KLAUS REINHARDT, KFOR - STREITKRÄFTE FUR DEN FRIEDEN (2001).
2. WESLEY CLARK, WAGING MODERN WAR 201 (2001).
3. The dubious process of instant customary international law will thus not be investigated here.

"de-emphasising of material practice as a constitutive element combined with the tendency to "count" the articulation of a rule twice, so to speak, not only as an expression *opinio juris* but also as State practice itself."[4]

In the *Nicaragua* case, the International Court of Justice (ICJ) disregarded the view of some lawyers[5] as to the non-relevance of General Assembly resolutions in the process of evolving customary international law, when it referred to non-binding resolutions as evidence of this kind of law.[6] The question of who's practice is relevant in the formation of customary law is central in this process. The ICJ stated in its *North Sea Continental Shelf* case[7] that the practice of non-parties is essential in the development of this law. With treaties of universal acceptance like the 1949 Geneva Conventions,[8] and to a lesser extent the Additional Protocols of 1977,[9] there are only a few States left to create this kind of custom and *opinio iuris*. This Baxter paradox[10] has, however, not been seen as blocking the evolution of customary law, as exemplified by the above-mentioned decisions of the Court. The focus has instead shifted to the activities of both the parties and the non-parties, considering a wide range of sources as evidence for both custom and *opinio iuris*. With a distinct unwillingness to focus solely on what the belligerents actually do, which is probably bound up with a policy of enhancing the protection of noncombatants and combatants alike, the ICJ, and lately as well the International Criminal Tribunal for the former Yugoslavia (ICTY),[11] have decided to direct their focus at other sources of "evidence" for the necessary custom and *opinio iuris*. Amongst these, the number of ratifications to international treaties and the dictates of military manuals have been referred to in order to

---

4. Bruno Simma & Philip Alston, *The Sources of Human Rights Law: Custom, Jus Cogens and General Principles*, 12 AUSTRALIAN YEAR BOOK OF INTERNATIONAL LAW 82, 96 (1992).
5. E.g, Gaetano Arangio-Ruiz, *The Normative Role of the General Assembly of the United Nations and the Development of Principles of Friendly Relations*, 137 RECUEIL DES COURS 431 (1972).
6. Military and Paramilitary Activities (Nicar. v. U.S.) 1986 I.C.J. 99–100 (June 27) [hereinafter Nicaragua case]. Though, as stated by Wolfke,"[t]he evaluation of the sufficiency of such evidence must, however, always be carried out 'with all due caution,' especially as far as the evidentiary value of non-binding resolutions is concerned." Karol Wolfke, CUSTOM IN PRESENT INTERNATIONAL LAW 152 (2d ed. 1993).
7. North Sea Continental Shelf (F.R.G. v. Den., F.R.G. v. Neth.) 1969 I.C.J. 43 (Feb. 20).
8. According to a search of the official ICRC website (http://www.icrc.org) on October 18 2001, there are 189 Parties to the 1949 Geneva Conventions.
9. There are 159 Parties to Additional Protocol I and 151 Parties to Additional Protocol II. *Id.*
10. Richard Baxter, *Treaties and Custom*, 129 RECUEIL DES COURS 27, 73 (1970).
11. Prosecutor v. Tadic, Appeal on Jurisdiction, Case No. IT-94-1-AR72 (Oct. 2, 1995), *reprinted in* 35 INTERNATIONAL LEGAL MATERIALS 32, 55 (1996).

ascertain what States consider to be binding on themselves.[12]

Customary international law may also emerge from treaties because a great number of identical bilateral treaties establish a widespread *opinio iuris*, or because a multilateral treaty has been ratified by the overwhelming majority of States. Thus, quite a number of authors conclude from the fact that the Geneva Conventions of 1949 have been ratified by more States than virtually any other convention (the Convention on the Right of the Child being one of the rare exceptions[13]) that a great number of their rules have become recognized as customary rules, even as *ius cogens*. In some instances this might be the result of occasional confusion provoked by renaming the "law of war" or "law of armed conflict" as "international humanitarian law," thus blurring the distinction between "humanitarian" and "human rights" law.[14] Common Article 3 to the four Geneva Conventions, which does constitute a kind of human rights provision, might have contributed to that confusion, since, as the ICJ held in the *Nicaragua* case, it reflects "elementary considerations of humanity"[15] and constitutes "the minimum yardstick"[16] for armed conflict. And again in the *Nuclear Weapons* advisory opinion, the ICJ pronounced that:

> [A] great many rules of humanitarian law in armed conflict are so fundamental to the respect of the human person... that... these fundamental rules are to be observed by all States whether or not they have ratified the conventions that contain them, because they constitute intransgressible principles of international customary law.[17]

---

12. *Id.*, and Report on the follow-up to the International Conference for the Protection of War Victims, 26th International Conference of the Red Cross and Red Crescent, Commission I, Item 2, Doc 95/c.I/2/2, at 7–8 (1995).
13. Mention should as well be made of the Constitution of the Universal Postal Union and the Constitution of the International Telecommunication Union, both of which have 189 parties, as stated on their homepages http://www.itu.int and http://www.upu.int, respectively.
14. Dietrich Schindler, *Significance of the Geneva Conventions for the Contemporary World*, 81 INTERNATIONAL REVIEW OF THE RED CROSS 717 (1999). The process is well described by Meron, who states that "the recognition of norms based in international human rights as customary may affect the intepretation and even the status of the parallel norms in instruments of international humanitarian law through a sort of osmosis or application by analogy." THEODOR MERON, HUMAN RIGHTS AND HUMANITARIAN NORMS AS CUSTOMARY INTERNATIONAL LAW 68, (1989).
15. Nicaragua case, *supra* note 6, at 104.
16. *Id.*
17. Legality of the Use by a State of Nuclear Weapons in Armed Conflict, 1996 I.C.J. 257, ¶ 99 (July 8).

The International Tribunal for the former Yugoslavia joined the ICJ in this view in the *Tadic* case.[18] The question remains, however, whether this is of much help in determining whether all the provisions of Protocol I, and in particular those that might not have been properly observed in Operation Allied Force, are intransgressible principles of customary international law.

The gap between those coalition partners who have ratified Protocol I, and those who have not, might not be as wide as it seems, since, for example, the US Air Force's Intelligence Targeting Guide has incorporated almost verbatim many relevant articles from the Protocol.[19] It is of interest here to note that its Attachment 4.2.2 on military objects is—almost to the letter—a restatement of Protocol I, Article 52(2). Attachment 4.3.1.2 on precautions and proportionality does not mention the trinity of "excessive," "concrete," and "direct," though these are mentioned in US Army Judge Advocate General's School's Operational Law Handbook 2002,[20] as well as in the US Army's Field Manual 27-10.[21] The Handbook states that "[t]he U.S. considers these provisions customary international law." Admittedly, this statement indicates only that the US recognizes its *own* interpretation of these principles/rules as part of customary international law.[22]

As mentioned above, the pronouncement of a rule in a national manual of a non-party to a treaty has special relevance in the process of establishing customary international law, notwithstanding the assertion in *United States v. List et al.*[23] The fact that the entries are motivated by more than just legal considerations does not seem to limit their legal significance.[24]

---

18. Tadic case, *supra* note 11, ¶¶ 96–137.
19. TARGETING DIVISION, HEADQUARTERS 497 INTELLIGENCE GROUP, AIR INTELLIGENCE AGENCY, USAF INTELLIGENCE TARGETING GUIDE (Air Force Pamphlet 14-210), Feb 1, 1998, *available at* http://www.fas.org/irp/doddir/usaf/afpam14-210/.
20. INTERNATIONAL AND OPERATIONAL LAW DEPARTMENT, THE JUDGE ADVOCATE GENERAL'S SCHOOL, OPERATIONAL LAW HANDBOOK 9 (2002), *available at* http://www.jagcnet.army.mil/CLAMO-Public.
21. HEADQUARTERS, DEPARTMENT OF THE ARMY, THE LAW OF LAND WARFARE (Department of the Army Field Manual 27-10) para. 41 (1956), *available at* http://www.adtdl.army.mil/cgi-bin/atdl.dll/fm/27-10/Ch1.htm.
22. OPERATIONAL LAW HANDBOOK, *supra* note 20, at 9.
23. U.S. v List et al. [The Hostage case] (1948), Trials of War Criminals before the Nuernberg Military Tribunals under Control Council Law No. 10, vol. 11 (1950), 1230 at 1237. See as well Theodor Meron, *The Geneva Conventions as Customary Law*, 81 AMERICAN JOURNAL OF INTERNATIONAL LAW 361 (1987).
24. Compare this with the ICJ's accceptance of statements made by State representatives in international fora as constitutive of *opinio iuris*, although these statements are motived by a wide range of different reasons, I.C.J. Report 1986 at 98–108, ¶¶ 187–205.

But even if national military manuals may increasingly be looked at as important evidence of customary international law, this will only be of limited help such as, for example, regarding the status of collateral damage.

The problem here is whether those provisions of Protocol I that came into focus during Operation Allied Force are eligible for consideration as customary law, given that terms like "military significance," "definite military advantage," and "effective contribution to military action" are not defined, not even by non-exhaustive examples as for "indiscriminate attacks?" If one takes only the declaration made by Germany and the United Kingdom, according to which "the military advantage anticipated from an attack is intended to refer to the advantage anticipated from the attack as a whole and not only from isolated or particular parts of the attack,"[25] what then is the meaning or interpretation that could become customary law for non-parties? Could it be that non-parties have to observe stricter obligations than those who have ratified Protocol I, but with admissible and accepted reservations or declarations? As stated by Baxter, "[i]t would be paradoxical in the extreme if a non-party were to be regarded as bound unqualifiedly by the obligations of the conventions, while a party might limit its duties by the entry of reservations."[26]

It could be argued that there would not be any significant problems binding non-parties to the same extent as far as the States having made reservations are bound. The understanding that collateral casualties are both legal and unavoidable, as long as they are below a certain threshold, would thus stand. Admittedly, only a few of the parties to Protocol I have made the above-mentioned reservations. A case could thus be made for binding the non-parties to a stricter code, i.e., what the parties without a reservation are bound by, as long as customary international law can be established.

Both alternatives, however, incorporate a degree of uncertainty as regards the precise limits of the obligations, as the proportionality principle "creates serious difficulties in practice, since it necessarily remains loosely defined and is subject to subjective assessment and balancing. In the framework of the required evaluation, the actors enjoy a considerable margin of appreciation."[27] It may be correct to say that the fundamental principles repeatedly mentioned

---

25. See DOCUMENTS ON THE LAWS OF WAR 505 and 511, respectively (Adam Roberts & Richard Guelff eds., 3d ed. 2000). Similar statements were made by Australia, Belgium, Canada, Italy, the Netherlands, New Zealand and Spain. *Id.* at 500–509.
26. Richard Baxter, *Multilateral Treaties as Evidence of Customary International Law*, 41 BRITISH YEARBOOK OF INTERNATIONAL LAW 285 (1965–66).
27. Stefan Oeter, *Methods and Means of Combat*, in THE HANDBOOK OF HUMANITARIAN LAW IN ARMED CONFLICTS 178–9 (Dieter Fleck ed., 1995). See *id.* for further references.

by the ICJ, the basic distinction between civilians and combatants, the prohibition against directly attacking civilians, and the rule of proportionality, are customary international law. But it is very doubtful whether the same can be said about all the other provisions of Protocol I—in particular those dealing with collateral damage.[28]

If Protocol I is not, at least not as a whole, customary international law, differing legal standards for various members of a given coalition remain—even leaving aside other restrictions on weapons and means of warfare. But there might be other reasons why the same standard of legal obligations should apply to such a coalition.

Does "same standard" always mean "maximum standard" in the sense of a "most favored nation clause?" The answer probably depends upon if and to what extent the reciprocity principle is (still) applicable to the international humanitarian law as it certainly was to the traditional law of war. Article 96 of Protocol I provides that parties to a conflict which are bound by the Protocol remain so bound vis-à-vis adverse parties also bound thereby, even if one or more allied or adverse parties are not party to the Protocol. Consequently, States bound by the Protocol participating in a coalition which includes States not party thereto, are not relieved of their Protocol I obligations. But it has been said that, because Iraq has not accepted Protocol I, those States in the opposition coalition during the Gulf War which were bound by that Protocol, were not directly obliged to apply it, whatever "directly" means in that context.[29] I will come back to the reciprocity problem later with respect to reprisals.

A Single (Maximum) Standard for "UN Forces"?

For quite some time it has been debated whether UN forces were not only morally, but legally bound to respect the existing humanitarian law, even if some or all of the force-providing States were not. But before addressing that issue, a few words should be devoted to the differentiation of forces operating under a United Nations mandate. Since no standing UN force has been established under UN Charter Articles 43 and 45, the UN has had to rely on

---

28. For a comprehensive analysis of the customary status of the Additional Protocols, see Christopher Greenwood, *Customary Law Status of the 1977 Additional Protocols*, in HUMANITARIAN LAW OF ARMED CONFLICT, CHALLENGES AHEAD 93 (Astrid J.M. Delissen & Gerard J. Tanja eds., 1991).
29. Christopher Greenwood, *Historical Developments and Legal Basis*, in HANDBOOK OF HUMANITARIAN LAW, *supra* note 27, at 26.

coalitions of the willing whenever it decided armed force was needed.[30] In only one instance did such a coalition of the willing operate under anything resembling UN command and control.[31] These Chapter VII actions have in general been carried out under UN authority—through the mandate itself—but under no tangible UN control. Such was the case with Operation Desert Storm in 1991. State practice seemed to be founded on the idea that armed forces acting under Chapter VII are not bound by the Geneva Conventions or other treaty-based international humanitarian law, as they act for the UN rather than as State actors bound by those rules.[32]

The doctrine has, on the other hand, often claimed binding effect of international humanitarian law in these situations.[33] This claim is often based on the obligation of parties to the 1949 Geneva Conventions to ensure observance of these rules in all situations.[34] It can also be said to be presumed by the adoption of the 1994 Convention on the Safety of United Nations and Associated Personnel, which in its Article 2(2) excludes its application to missions authorized by the Security Council as an enforcement action under Chapter VII of the Charter of the United Nations in which any of the personnel are engaged as combatants against organized armed forces and to which *the laws of international armed conflicts applies.*"[35]

---

30. The regime regulating UN authorized peace-keeping forces will not be examined here.
31. The US-led coalition forces in Korea during 1950–53.
32. Michael Hoffman, *Peace-enforcement actions and humanitarian law: Emerging rules for "interventional armed conflict"*, 82 INTERNATIONAL REVIEW OF THE RED CROSS 193 (2000).
33. E.g., LESLIE GREEN, THE CONTEMPORARY LAW OF ARMED CONFLICT 319 (1993). Seyersted stated that "[n]one of the States participationg in the United Nations action in Korea maintained during that action that it was not governed by the general laws of war, on the contrary, they acted on the assumption that it was." FINN SEYERSTED, UNITED NATIONS FORCES IN THE LAW OF PEACE AND WAR 204 (1966). The binding effect of international customary law seems furthermore to follow from UN Charter Article 103, which seems to allow the UN obligations to supersede other obligations only when these other obligations result from treaties. *But see* Paul Szasz, *UN Forces and International Humanitarian Law*, in INTERNATIONAL LAW ACROSS THE SPECTRUM OF CONFLICT: ESSAYS IN HONOUR OF PROFESSOR L.C. GREEN ON THE OCCASION OF HIS EIGHTIETH BIRTHDAY 513 (Michael Schmitt ed., 2000) (Vol. 75, U.S. Naval War College International Law Studies). This in itself leaves open the question of how the UN can be bound by the treaty obligations of international humanitarian law that do not (yet) have a customary status.
34. Common Article 1 to all four Conventions. *See e.g.*, Greenwood, *supra* note 29, at 46.
35. Emphasis provided by the present author. The main problem with respect to the determination of which law is to apply to UN missions is considered by Greenwood to relate to those situations where the mission is neither an enforcement mission which undertakes military actions resembling an armed conflict, nor a peacekeeping mission which strives to act neutrally. Christopher Greenwood, *International Law and the Conduct of Military Operation: Stocktaking at the Start of a New Millennium*, in INTERNATIONAL LAW ACROSS THE SPECTRUM OF CONFLICT, *supra* note 33, at 192.

The UN Secretary-General's Bulletin on the "Observance by United Nations forces of international humanitarian law" of August 6, 1999,[36] provides only partial answers. First of all, the Bulletin is restricted to forces conducting operations under UN command and control,[37] which is, as stated above, the exception rather than the rule. What about forces under national or NATO command, authorized, as KFOR, "to monitor and ensure compliance with this [the Military Technical] Agreement and to respond promptly to any violations and restore compliance, using military force if required"?[38] Secondly, the Bulletin is said not to replace the national laws by which military personnel remain bound throughout the operation.[39] What if the army, air force, navy or marine corps manuals of States which are not a party to some or most of the treaties on humanitarian law allow for actions and operations prohibited under those treaties? Are the manuals to prevail? Because this Section seems to be included in order to ensure that obligations resting on parties that are more far reaching than those flowing from the Bulletin's provisions will not be abrogated from, the object thus being the application of as much international humanitarian law as possible to the relevant force, it is therefore submitted that such manuals cannot validly derogate from the obligations under the Bulletin.

The substantive Sections 5 to 9 of the Bulletin combine fundamental principles that might be classified as customary law with rules prohibiting or restricting the use of certain weapons, rules which are hardly customary law.[40] This raises the question as to whether the Secretary-General can issue rules and regulations for the conduct of State-deployed forces on UN missions if some of the provisions rely on treaties that have not been ratified by all States participating in Chapter VII or peacekeeping operations?[41] Some authors

---

36. 38 INTERNATIONAL LEGAL MATERIALS 1659 (1999) [hereinafter Bulletin].
37. *Id.*, Section 1.
38. The Military Technical Agreement Between the International Security Force ("KFOR") and the Governments of the Federal Republic of Yugoslavia and the Republic of Serbia, Appendix B(4), *available at* http://www.nato.int/kfor/resources/documents/mta.htm.
39. Bulletin, *supra* note 36, Section 2.
40. See especially Bulletin, *id.*, Section 6.
41. Hoffman, *supra* note 32, at 201.

seem to claim so when focusing on the Secretary-General's function as "commander-in-chief" of operations carried out under UN authority and command—which currently includes only peacekeeping operations.[42] It should be pointed out here that in those situations where a coalition has been authorized by the UN, but has not been obliged to operate under its control/command, a right for the Secretary-General to instruct the force does not exist, which is presumed by the exclusion of missions outside "United Nations command and control" from the Bulletin's applicability.[43]

A solution could be seen in the status-of-forces agreements mentioned in Section 3, which are treaties by themselves and which are designed to ensure that the force will conduct its operations with full respect for the principles and rules of the general conventions applicable to the conduct of military personnel. But then, also under Section 3, the obligation to respect such principles and rules is applicable even in the absence of a status-of-forces agreement. And, finally, the Guidance has serious lacunae, not least because it is silent on military occupation and KFOR is an occupation force *par excellence*.

One obvious way to bind the forces operating under a UN mandate to the highest level of international humanitarian law would be to mandate such compliance in the Security Council resolutions which authorize the use of force in the first place. This way, contributing States which are non-parties to the relevant treaties would be obliged to act in accordance with these treaties for the purpose of the specific mission. On the other hand, such a policy could effectively undermine the interest of these States in participating in UN missions, thus leading to a shortage of voluntary forces.[44]

It remains more or less a gut feeling that UN or UN-authorized forces should abide by all existing principles and rules of international humanitarian law. The legal foundation of such an obligation—as well as the legal status of the Secretary-General's Bulletin—is still open to debate.

---

42. Szasz, *supra* note 33, at 519. As UN Force Protection (UNPROFOR) I and II in the former Yugoslavia have shown, enforcement actions can become necessary even in the course of peacekeeping operations.
43. Bulletin, *supra* note 36, Preamble.
44. The Security Council could as well decide to relieve the participating members of their humanitarian treaty obligations through UN Charter Article 103, though it is submitted here that this is only a theoretical possibility.

A Single (Maximum) Standard for "Coalitions"?

There are, as we have witnessed in Operation Allied Force, coalitions that have no UN authorization whatsoever. The legality of such operations will not be the subject of this paper. Rather, the focus here is whether the fact alone that States form a coalition for the joint use of force oblige them to apply a single maximum standard in humanitarian law? In general, a State does not lose or gain rights and obligations when it operates together with other States as opposed to undertaking operations alone. Some arguments in favor of such an obligation are, however, conceivable. NATO drew some legitimacy (if not legality) for Allied Force from the fact that the UN Security Council was veto-blocked, unable to do what common sense and the humanitarian agenda of present day politics and law expected,[45] and that the regional arrangement (NATO) had to step in; that this was not the use of force by a single State for selfish purposes, but the use of force by a coalition of like-minded, democratic, law-abiding States for a good purpose, a "small UN." This might, or might not, overcome the missing UN mandate and might end up setting a problematic precedent, but since it is at least not entirely clear whether even UN forces have to apply a maximum standard of humanitarian law, being a coalition alone does not seem to be a convincing argument in that respect.

More compelling could be the argument that the coalition used force for humanitarian purposes, that its very purpose was to end gross violations of human rights.[46] The fact that NATO was intervening in the name of human rights implied a perhaps heavier moral burden to respect the rules of humanitarian law, but did it also imply a legal obligation to do so? Would the same reasoning apply if a coalition is not intervening in the name of human rights, but participating in collective self-defense?

In the specific case of NATO's Operation Allied Force, one motive for respecting a high standard of humanitarian law was certainly to avoid the loss of the support of even a single ally, and NATO's unanimity rule in targeting decisions also guaranteed that the concerns of each member were taken seriously. It also has been reported from the Gulf War that the Royal Air Force

---

45. Bruno Simma, *NATO, the UN and the Use of Force: Legal Aspects*, 10 EUROPEAN JOURNAL OF INTERNATIONAL LAW 1 (1999).
46. V. Kröning, *Kosovo and International Humanitarian Law*, in Forum: HUMANITÄRES VÖLKERRECHT - INFORMATIONSSCHRIFTEN HEFT1/2000, at 45 (2000).

refused at least twice to bomb targets given it by American commanders because the risk of collateral damage was too high.[47]

A policy argument that would still have some importance is the need to streamline the planning structure of a coalition of forces. Thus, it is preferable to have only one set of rules upon which to formulate plans, and since the parties with the most comprehensive legal bindings cannot derogate from their obligations, unless these bindings are dependent upon reciprocity and the other party is not bound, the maximum level should be chosen.

But the strongest incentive for a coalition to apply the maximum standard, if it is also the one applied by the other side, is, I believe, still "positive reciprocity" and the risk of reprisals. Quite a few argue that since the law of war has been transformed into a human rights oriented law, belligerent reprisals are prohibited and reciprocity has therefore lost its relevance.[48] This may be correct to a certain extent for the Geneva Conventions and Protocols, which expressly prohibit reprisals against civilians, wounded, prisoners of war, indispensable objects, the natural environment and installations containing dangerous objects, etc.[49] Hostile forces, however, still may become the object of reprisals. But beyond "Geneva Law," there is the UN Conventional Weapons Convention and its Protocols. An adversary might not want, or might not be able, to distinguish between coalition partners if it decides to respond to the use of a prohibited weapon in the same manner.

Responsibility

Another reason, finally, for applying a single (maximum) standard of international humanitarian law in a given coalition might be responsibility for possible internationally wrongful acts. To whom will non-compliance with humanitarian law rules, which bind some but not all in a coalition, be attributed?

---

47. H.L.Debs, Vol. 600, col. 907, May 6, 1999, as mentioned in Peter Rowe, *Kosovo 1999: The Air Campaign—Have the Provisions of Additional Protocol I Withstood the Test?*, 82 INTERNATIONAL REVIEW OF THE RED CROSS 158 n.41 (2000). It should here be mentioned that one of the reasons for the US to limit the amount of States participating in the attacks on the Taliban regime in Afganistan in the fall of 2001 seems to be "the lesson US military planners took from Nato's bombing campaign in Kosovo in 1999 [which] was that a large alliance complicates and delays the choice of objectives" as stated in the FINANCIAL TIMES (London), Sep. 22/23, 2001, at 1.
48. Schindler, *supra* note 14, at 725.
49. Articles 46, 47, 13 and 33 of the 1949 Geneva Conventions I, II, III and IV, respectively, and Articles 20 and 41–56 of Protocol I.

To the "coalition" if it is, as in the case of NATO, an international organization? To all members of the coalition or only to the respective flag State?

A. Responsibility of international organizations in general

It seems to be widely accepted today that the rules of State responsibility can be applied *mutatis mutandis* to intergovernmental organizations having a legal capacity of their own in international law. One relevant principle that applies here is that nobody should be able to evade liability or responsibility by transferring activities to a separate legal entity which he has co-founded and which operates in pursuit of his own goals and under his influence in the organs of that entity. This, again in principle, entails that an international organization is responsible for its internationally wrongful acts in the same way as would be its member States had they acted individually instead as of members of the organization.[50]

The attribution of responsibility to international organizations has been justified on several grounds. With the major role of international organizations in contemporary international relations, the international community could not tolerate a situation in which such active actors in the global system could violate binding international norms without bearing the consequences; otherwise the basic aims of international responsibility (i.e., deterrence and provision of remedies) would be undermined.[51] Others base their reasoning for attributing responsibility to international organizations on their international legal personality, which entails rights and obligations, one of the obligations being international responsibility in certain cases.[52] Again others hold that the same "general principles of law" that are the basis of State responsibility apply also to international organizations which, being subjects of international law, are governed by identical principles.[53] Since treaties or agreements which explicitly establish the responsibility of international organizations are scarce,[54]

---

50. See Werner Meng, *Internationale Organisationen im völkerrechtlichen Deliktsrecht* 45, 324–57 ZIETSCHRIFT FÜR AUSLÄNDISCHES ÖFFENTLICHES RECHT UND VÖLKERRECHT 324 et seq (1985) and MOSHE HIRSCH, THE RESPONSIBILITY OF INTERNATIONAL ORGANIZATIONS TOWARD THIRD PARTIES: SOME BASIC PRINCIPLES *passim* (1995).
51. See HIRSCH, *supra* note 50, at 8.
52. See Konrad Ginther, *International Organizations, Responsibility*, in ENCYCLOPEDIA OF PUBLIC INTERNATIONAL LAW 1336 et seq (Rudolph Bernhardt ed., 1995).
53. See Mahnoush Arsanjani, *Claims Against International Organizations*, 7 YALE JOURNAL OF WORLD PUBLIC ORDER 131 (1981).
54. See Convention on International Liability for Damages Caused by Space Objects, Jan. 29, 1972, 18 U.S.T. 2410, 610 U.N.T.S. 205, and the United Nations Convention on the Law of the Sea, *opened for signature* Dec. 10, 1982, U.N. Doc. A/conf.62/122, *reprinted in* 21 INTERNATIONAL LEGAL MATERIALS 1261–1354 (1982).

the principle that international organizations may be held internationally responsible for their acts is mostly classified as being part of international customary law. But practice in this field is also rare and, furthermore, not consistent, since "responsibility" and "liability" are not always clearly distinguished.[55]

A number of preconditions seem to be unanimously required for the responsibility of international organizations, the first one being that the organization has legal personality, i.e., a legal capacity of its own. There is little doubt that the member States of an international organization in most cases have accepted that legal status by either founding the organization or by joining it later on. But what about third States? The majority opinion still appears to be that international organizations have legal capacity with respect to third States only if those third States have recognized the organization, either explicitly or implicitly through establishing diplomatic relations or entering into treaties with the organization.[56] One might add that an implicit recognition could also be found if a third State raises claims against an international organization.

Another precondition is that the act that caused damage is attributable[57] to the international organization. Likewise, in this respect, it does not seem to be decisive whether the act was within the power, function or mandate of the organization, or rather constituted an *ultra vires* act;[58] rather, it is necessary that the international organization had "effective control" over the act. One of the notable shortcomings of international organizations, in comparison with States, lies in their limited resources.[59] Most international organizations lack personnel, means, and in particular troops to administer large-scale operations. The practical solution that has been found is that the organization "borrows" the necessary resources from its member States.[60] The question that then arises is who shall bear international responsibility, i.e., who has command and control, the organization or the "sending State?"

---

55. The International Law Commission makes a distinction, using "responsibility" for cases involving a breach of obligations and "liability" in connection with activities which have caused damage, but are otherwise lawful. See HIRSCH, *supra* note 50, at 7 n.34.
56. But see IGNAZ SEIDL-HOHENVELDERN & GERHARD LOIBL, RECHT DER INTERNATIONALEN ORGANISATIONEN 90 *et seq.* (2000).
57. KNUT IPSEN, VÖLKERRECHT 573 (1999).
58. See HIRSCH, *supra* note 50, at 88 *et seq.*
59. See Torsten Stein, *Decentralized International Law Enforcement: The Changing Role of the State as Law Enforcement Agent*, in ALLOCATION OF LAW ENFORCEMENT AUTHORITY IN THE INTERNATIONAL SYSTEM 107 *et seq.* (Jost Delbrück ed., 1995).
60. See HIRSCH, *supra* note 50, at 66 *et seq.*

A slightly different question is who will bear responsibility if the organization directs or "orders" its members to implement a decision of the organization. The crucial factor for the determination of responsibility for the implementing act is the measure of discretion left to the members.[61]

B. Is NATO responsible?

If a precondition for the responsibility of international organizations is that they have legal personality with regard to the claimant third party, the fulfillment of that condition vis-à-vis Yugoslavia can by no means be taken for granted. There is no evidence that Yugoslavia, as a non-aligned State, ever formally recognized NATO as a subject of international law. And Yugoslavia remained excluded from the vast and rapidly developing net of NATO's cooperation agreements with Central and Eastern European countries (North Atlantic Cooperation Council and Partnership for Peace).[62] Yugoslavia has not, in any event not yet, raised claims arising out of Operation Allied Force against NATO, but instead—before the ICJ—against NATO's member States.[63] This is certainly also due to the fact that NATO is neither a possible respondent before the ICJ, nor a possible defendant before the International Criminal Tribunal for the former Yugoslavia (ICTY). Only States can be parties to a legal dispute before the ICJ, and the Yugoslavia Tribunal's jurisdiction is limited to the individual criminal responsibility of those who have committed grave breaches against international humanitarian law.[64] Proceedings have also been introduced before the European Court of Human Rights.[65]

---

61. *See id.* at 82.
62. For details, see NORTH ATLANTIC TREATY ORGANIZATION, NATO HANDBOOK 43 *et seq.* (1995).
63. For details, see Peter Bekker, International Decisions, *Legality of Use of Force - International Court of Justice, June 2, 1999*, 93 AMERICAN JOURNAL OF INTERNATIONAL LAW 928 (1999).
64. Nevertheless, in May 1999, the chief prosecutor for the ICTY established a committee to examine and assess charges that NATO's conduct of the air campaign violated the laws of war. On June 2, 2000, the ICTY prosecutor reported to the UN Security Council that, based on the committee's report, she found that there was no basis to open a criminal investigation into any aspect of the NATO campaign. Although NATO had made some mistakes, the prosecutor determined that NATO had not deliberately targeted civilians. For details, see Sean Murphy, Contemporary Practice of the United States Relating to International Law, *NATO Air Campaign Against Serbia and the Laws of War*, 94 AMERICAN JOURNAL OF INTERNATIONAL LAW 690 (2000).
65. Application No. 5220/99 (Bankovic and others—Belgium, Czech Republic, Denmark, France, Gemany, Greece, Hungary, Iceland, Italy, Luxembourg, Netherlands, Norway, Poland, Portugal, Spain, Turkey and United Kingdom). The applicants alleged violations of Articles 1, 2, 10 and 13 of the Convention. The application has been communicated to the respondent States and transferred to the Grand Chamber of the Court (see Information Note No. 24 on the case-law of the Court, November 2000). The Court held hearings on the admissibility on October 25, 2001.

Another question would be whether NATO acted within the framework of its functions and powers, both defined and fixed in the North Atlantic Treaty,[66] since some writers maintain that an international organization's responsibility presupposes that the organization has acted according to its statute. Here, again, the answer is not that easy. The main purpose of the North Atlantic Treaty is "to safeguard the freedom, common heritage and civilization of their (the parties) peoples. . . ."[67] There is nothing in the NATO Treaty to suggest that another of NATO's purposes is to protect human rights through the use of force "out of area," as was the case with Operation Allied Force. To be able to say that this too is one of NATO's purposes, one will have to add the "New Strategic Concept"[68] adopted during the Washington summit in April 1999, to the existing Treaty, although it is not a formal amendment of the Treaty, duly ratified in each member State. In its "New Strategic Concept" NATO pledges to fulfill "non-Article 5 missions" in case of a crisis outside the NATO Treaty area. Although the new concept is a political, not a legal commitment, one could not say that Operation Allied Force has been an *ultra vires* act of one of NATO's organs. All NATO member States agreed, otherwise the operation would not have taken place. But NATO looked more like an instrument than the author of or the driving force behind the operation.

Be that as it may, the next question is whether the alleged violations of international law would be attributable to NATO, because the relevant rules of international law are binding also on NATO, and because NATO had "effective control" over the act that could subsequently be qualified as internationally wrongful. Is NATO bound by the 1977 Additional Protocols even though not all of its members are? The relevant question here is "targeting." NATO has been accused of having selected targets for air strikes that were not, or at least not strictly, military targets (bridges, power stations, radio and TV

---

66. North Atlantic Treaty, Apr. 24, 1949, 63 Stat. 2241, 34 U.N.T.S. 243.
67. See paragraph 2 of the preambula. *Id.*
68. Bulletin des Presse- und Informationsamtes der Bundesregierung Nr. 24 vom 3.5.1999, 222 *et seq. See also* Eckart Klein & Stefanie Schmahl, *Die neue NATO-Strategie und ihre völkerrechtlichen und verfassungsrechtlichen Implikationen,* 35 RECHT UND POLITIK 198 (1999).

stations). Most of these targets certainly served both military and civilian uses, and attacking dual-use objects is not necessarily unlawful, provided that they meet the definition of military objectives in Article 52, paragraph 2 of Protocol I, that the principle of proportionality is observed, and that collateral damage is minimized.[69] But did the television studios make an effective contribution to Serbian military action and did the attacks offer a definite military advantage? If they were targeted merely because they were spreading propaganda to the civilian population, it appears at least doubtful whether their destruction offered a definite military advantage.[70]

If these attacks were in breach of Protocol I, did NATO have "effective control?" The targeting procedure was as follows: NATO's military planners identified and requested specific targets. These targets were or were not approved by the permanent representatives of the member States, sometimes after consulting with their respective governments. If only one Representative cast a negative vote, the target was not attacked. If the target was approved, the task force received an order to attack. Every air force contingent had its own "national commander in theater" and the pilots received their mission orders from him. The national commander could, in theory, decide not to attack a specific target because he was of the opinion that it was not a military objective. Does this discretion of member States' authorities to implement or not a decision of the organization remove the organization's responsibility? In reality the commander gave the order, because he knew that his government had approved the target and because the target could be classified as a dual-use object. So the decision was in fact taken at the NATO level, and NATO, provided that all other preconditions were fulfilled, could be responsible for "illegal" targeting.

The last category of possible internationally wrongful acts are what one might call "pilot errors." A number of such errors were reported and some had to do with the fact that for reasons of "force protection" NATO had decided to execute the missions from a very high altitude. One pilot attacked what he thought was a Serbian military convoy; it turned out to be a convoy of refugees. Another pilot attacked a bridge (certainly a dual-use object) at the very moment at which a civilian train entered the bridge. Both bridge and train were destroyed. It is not clear whether the pilot had the possibility to break off

---

69. *See* Theodor Meron, *The Humanization of Humanitarian Law*, 94 AMERICAN JOURNAL OF INTERNATIONAL LAW 239, 276 (2000).
70. *See* George Aldrich, *Yugoslavia's Television Studios as Military Objectives*, 1 INTERNATIONAL LAW FORUM 149–50 (1999).

the attack. If these and other attacks constituted violations of the humanitarian law applicable in armed conflicts, did NATO—given the chain of command—have "effective control?" Even if this should be so, NATO does not possess one mode of reparation that might be required in such a case:[71] disciplinary and penal jurisdiction remain with the force-providing State.

C. The responsibility of NATO's member States

Responsibility of member States for "their" international organizations actions can be direct, if it turns out that the organization itself is for one or another reason not responsible in a situation in which the members acted through the organization. Responsibility can also be concurrent, with the consequence that a third party which is the victim of an internationally wrongful act can choose whether to seek redress from the organization or its members. Responsibility of the member States can be secondary in cases in which the organization is primarily responsible, but, for example, lacks the necessary funds to pay compensation.

This is not the place to discuss in detail the distribution of responsibility between international organizations and its member States.[72] It is, however, beyond doubt that member States would be responsible if, for general reasons, NATO should not be responsible at all. A so-called "negative conflict" would not be acceptable, i.e., that both sides, the organization and its members, point fingers at one another. It seems equally beyond doubt that, should it be their turn, all NATO member States are responsible for the decision to use force against Yugoslavia; it was a unanimous decision of all member States. The same is true for "targeting" decisions, which also, as has been shown above, required unanimity. But not all member States took part in Operation Allied Force. Iceland, for example, does not maintain armed forces at all.[73] And not all of the NATO member States who do maintain an air force participated.

The situation becomes even more complicated by the fact that not all member States have accepted the same treaty obligations. The United States, whose air force flew most of the missions, has not ratified Protocol I under

---

71. See Protocol I, art. 87(3).
72. See in this respect MATTHIAS HARTWIG, DIE HAFTUNG DER MITGLIEDSTAATEN FüR INTERNATIONALE ORGANISATIONEN *passim* (1993), and HIRSCH, *supra* note 50, at 96 *et seq*. See also C.F. Amerasinghe, *Liability to Third Parties of Member States of International Organizations: Practice, Principle and Judicial Precedent*, 85 AMERICAN JOURNAL OF INTERNATIONAL LAW 259–280 (1991).
73. Iceland is a respondent in the application pending before the European Court of Human Rights (see *supra* note 65).

which targeting decisions, as well as decisions taken by pilots during their mission, appear to be at least problematic. The same was true for France and Turkey. Are those member States who approved the targets and are bound by Protocol I, responsible, but not the nation that eventually attacked these targets because it is not a party to the Protocol? Does NATO have to disclose who attacked which target?[74] Can, at the end of the day, only those States carry responsibility that have accepted the jurisdiction of the ICJ and could, therefore, be sued there?[75]

The only reasonable solution seems to be that all NATO member States are responsible for any internationally wrongful acts committed during Operation Allied Force. NATO as such is not recognized by the possible claimant (Yugoslavia). NATO is not an organization that has been created "to do business" with third States and which third States have accepted as such. NATO is not the "international tin council."[76] Therefore, the concept that has been developed in international law for the sole responsibility of international organizations, and which has borrowed much from national commercial law,[77] does not really fit NATO. NATO's budget could certainly not accommodate all claims for pecuniary compensation.[78] If it comes to individual wrongful decisions made by pilots, other NATO States could, of course, invoke the flag-State principle, but they should consider that NATO will also in the future have to rely on a few actors for common operations. If those who agree "to do the job" will afterwards be left alone to face responsibility on account of possible internationally wrongful acts, their readiness will disappear. Although, for these reasons, joint responsibility advocates strongly for a common standard, the concept of responsibility under international law as such does

---

74. Amnesty International concluded that NATO's command structure appears to contribute to confusion over legal responsibility and recommended that NATO clarify its chain of command so that there are clear lines of responsibility, known within and outside the organization, for each State and each individual involved in military operations conducted under its aegis (*cf.* Murphy, *supra* note 64, at 692).
75. The ICJ has dismissed, *inter alia*, Yugoslavia's claims against the United States for lack of jurisdiction (*see* Bekker, *supra* note 63). *See also* Nicholas Alexander, *Airstrikes and Environmental Damage: Can the United States Be Held Liable for Operation Allied Force?*, 11 COLORADO JOURNAL OF INTERNATIONAL ENVIRONMENTAL LAW AND POLICY 471 (2000).
76. *See* HARTWIG, *supra* note 72, at 307 *et seq.* and Amerasinghe, *supra* note 72.
77. *See* MENG, *supra* note 50.
78. Financing 85% of the costs for making the Danube again navigable has been estimated by the European Union as requiring 22 Million Euro (Agence Europe No. 7724 of 25 May 2000, at 11).

not legally mandate a single (maximum) legal standard for all members of a coalition in case of differing individual legal obligations.[79]

Conclusion

It is, for practical as well as legal purposes, preferable that the same (maximum) legal standard of obligations under international humanitarian law apply to all members of a given coalition, provided that the other side is bound to obey the same rules. To the extent that treaty-based rules of humanitarian law are at the same time regarded as declaratory of custom, the uniformity of the legal standard is guaranteed, but it is doubtful whether this would reach much beyond the most fundamental principles. In those instances when humanitarian law obligations arise only from treaties, other possible reasons for why a coalition should apply the same (maximum) standard do not individually seem to be compelling, although perhaps taken together, they may be.

A solution for future coalitions could be found in the idea which underlies Article 96(2) and also 96(3) of Protocol I: status-of-forces agreements as well as rules of engagement should provide that the maximum standard of obligations of one or more members of a coalition applies to all its members during a given conflict. Members of a coalition who so wish may make it clear that they do not intend, by accepting the maximum standard, to contribute to the emergence of additional customary law, but that they accept and apply the relevant rules only for coalition purposes. Such an ad hoc solution might be more helpful than a possible "third protocol" to the Geneva conventions on rules applicable to coalition warfare. Such a protocol would be only another treaty, with few ratifications at the beginning and probably not in force for a long time, and would give rise later to the old question whether and when it might become part of customary law.

---

79. For more on this topic by the present author, see Torsten Stein, *Kosovo and the International Community. The Attribution of Possible Internationally Wrongful Acts: Responsibility of NATO or of its Member States*, in KOSOVO AND THE INTERNATIONAL COMMUNITY 181 et seq (C. Tomuschat ed., 2002).

* I am very much indebted to Magne Frostad, a doctoral student who served in the Norwegian Judge Advocate's Corps, for his great support in finalizing this paper.

To What Extent Is Protocol I Customary International Law?

The Honorable Fausto Pocar

To what extent does Protocol I[1] reflect customary international law, such that it may be regarded as binding on non-party States? The question has been discussed since the early days following the entry into force of Protocol I, when the number of ratifying States was still rather thin.[2] Indeed the frequent involvement of non-ratifying States in international armed conflicts made an answer to that question urgent, in order to establish the scope of application of the principles that the Protocol enshrines in a given situation. Notwithstanding the increase in the number of States parties,[3] the problem continues to be topical, in particular because the countries that have not yet ratified the instrument, including some major actors in international relations, maintain serious reservations as to the binding force of one or more principles expressed and regulated therein.[4] In this context, it has to be pointed out that attention has mainly focused on Part III (Articles 35 to 47) of Protocol I, dealing with methods and means of warfare and with the status of combatants and prisoners of war, as well as on Part IV (Articles 48 to 79), concerned with the

---

1. Protocol Additional (I) to the Geneva Conventions of 12 August 1949, and Relating to the Protection of Victims of International Conflicts, June 8, 1977, 1125 U.N.T.S. 3, DOCUMENTS ON THE LAWS OF WAR 422 (A. Roberts & R. Guelff eds., 3d ed. 2000) [hereinafter Protocol I].
2. Protocol I entered into force on December 7, 1978. By 1980 only 16 States had become parties to Protocol I; they were Bahamas, Bangladesh, Botswana, Cyprus, Ecuador, El Salvador, Finland, Gabon, Ghana, Jordan, Laos, Libya, Niger, Sweden, Tunisia and Yugoslavia.
3. 59 States were parties to Protocol I as of August 21, 2001.
4. India, Indonesia, Iran, Iraq, Israel, Japan, Pakistan, Turkey and the United States are some of the States which have not ratified Protocol I so far.

protection to be afforded to civilian populations; these two parts of the Protocol being in many respects linked to each other.

It is undisputed that Protocol I is aimed both at codifying existing international law relating to the protection of victims of international armed conflicts and at developing such law in order to increase their protection. As the Preamble clearly states, the instrument is based on the necessity "to *reaffirm* and *develop* the provisions protecting the victims of armed conflicts."[5] Thus, Protocol I itself explains that not all of its provisions simply codify existing law, though it declares at the same time that a number of them do so.

One is therefore confronted with a problem common to the interpretation of all so-called codification conventions, i.e., the problem of identifying the treaty provisions that reflect customary international law, as opposed to those that make innovations or contain additional elements, thus developing the law's scope and content.[6] The former will have general value in that they reproduce customary rules, while the binding force of the latter will be limited to the States having ratified or acceded to the convention. This is in accordance with the general rule that treaties do not create either obligations or rights for a third State without its consent and that their effects are limited to State parties (*pacta tertiis nec nocent nec prosunt*).[7]

In making this assertion, however, some points must be borne in mind. First, the abovementioned status of a treaty provision as reproducing or developing customary international law may change according to the time at which its status is assessed. A provision that did not reflect customary law when it was drafted may subsequently become a customary rule through its general application by States. Similarly, although less frequently, a provision which codified principles forming part of customary law when it was drafted may not reflect them at a later stage due to changes in general State practice. In dealing with this issue, reference should therefore be made to the point in time at which the question of the binding force of a specific treaty provision for non-contracting States arises.

---

5. Emphasis added.
6. *See* Richard Baxter, *Treaties and Custom*, 129 RECUEIL DES COURS 36 ff. (1970); Karl Zemanek, Die Bedeutung der Kodifizierung des Völkerrechts für seine Anwendung, *in* FESTSCHRIFT VERDROSS 565 (1971); Roberto Ago, *Nouvelles réflexions sur la codification du droit international*, 92 REVUE GÉNÉRALE DE DROIT INTERNATIONAL PUBLIC 539 (1988).
7. According to Article 34 of the Vienna Convention on the Law of Treaties (May 23, 1969, 1155 U.N.T.S. 331), "A treaty does not create either obligations or rights for a third State without its consent."

Secondly, even when a treaty provision can be considered as codifying a norm of customary law, it is the latter that finds application as regards non-party States and not the treaty provision as such. As the International Court of Justice clarified in the *Nicaragua* case,[8] the two norms derive from distinct sources of law and each continues to belong to a separate body of rules. Indeed, the Court stated:

> Even if the customary norm and the treaty norm were to have exactly the same content, this would not be a reason for the Court to hold that the incorporation of the customary norm into treaty-law must deprive the customary norm of its applicability as distinct from that of the treaty norm. . . . [T]here are no grounds for holding that when customary international law is comprised of rules identical to those of treaty law, the latter 'supervenes' the former, so that the customary international law has no further existence of its own.[9]

Thus, their interpretation and application may be subject to different principles, although the treaty provision will have an impact in this context in that it constitutes an assessment of the relevant rule or principle made by the States which have entered into the treaty.

Thirdly, as the codification process necessarily requires an assessment of the customary rule or principle concerned as well as a written definition thereof, the resulting written text may be regarded as affecting its scope and content. Consequently, any precision or new element that may have been added—as is normally the case—by the treaty provision to the principle of customary law which it codifies must be checked carefully in order to establish whether it has come to be accepted as generally applicable. However, the addition of new elements by a treaty provision to a customary principle should be distinguished from specifications deriving by necessary implication from the accepted general customary principle. As it has been pointed out,[10] such specifications could not be regarded as requiring acceptance of the treaty in order to become applicable to a State. A different conclusion would result in allowing a limitation of the already accepted general principle that derives from

---

8. Military and Paramilitary Activities (Nicar. v. U.S.), 1986 I.C.J. 14, 94–5 (June 27) [hereinafter Nicaragua case].
9. Id. at 95.
10. See Georges Abi-Saab, *The 1977 Additional Protocols and General International Law: Some Preliminary Reflections*, in HUMANITARIAN LAW OF ARMED CONFLICTS: CHALLENGES AHEAD, ESSAYS IN HONOUR OF FRITS KALSHOVEN 120 (Astrid J.M. Delissen & Gerard J. Tanja eds., 1991), who mentions in this regard the rules concerning the protection of civilians against aerial bombardments in Protocol I.

customary law. The inclusion of such necessary implications in a treaty provision cannot reduce in any way for non-party States the obligations they would have under the general principles from which those implications derive.

The elements and factors to be taken into consideration in assessing State practice for the purposes of establishing the existence of customary rules and principles have been widely discussed in international legal doctrine and case law. This paper does not aim at revisiting all the features and implications of the problems arising in this area, including the issue of defining State practice. The main principles governing the matter have been already laid down by the International Court of Justice in the *North Sea Continental Shelf* case[11] and in the *Nicaragua* case,[12] whereby the Court has stressed the respective role of the practice of States and *opinio juris* as factors for identifying a customary rule of international law, as well as the place of treaty provisions codifying customary law in this regard. Following these judgments, there is no doubt that for a rule to exist as a norm of customary international law both its recognition as a legal obligation by States and the latter's conduct which is consistent with the rule are required.[13]

Some issues deserve special consideration as far as the relationship between codified and customary rules is concerned. In this context, it has been discussed whether the practice of all States, including those which are parties to the treaty (in our case Protocol I), should be taken into account for the purposes of establishing the existence of a customary norm. A negative answer would diminish the number of States whose practice is relevant to this end and would make it more difficult to determine the status of customary law, as

---

11. *See* North Sea Continental Shelf (F.R.G. v. Den., F.R.G. v. Neth.), 1969 I.C.J. 3, 44 (Feb. 20).
12. *See* Nicaragua case, *supra* note 8, at 97–8.
13. In particular, the Court in the *Nicaragua* case stated:

> The mere fact that States declare their recognition of certain rules is not sufficient for the court to consider these as being part of customary international law, and as applicable as such to those States. Bound as it is by Article 38 of its Statute to apply, *inter alia*, international custom 'as evidence of a general practice accepted as law', the Court may not disregard the essential role played by general practice.... The Court must satisfy itself that the existence of the rule in the *opinio juris* of States is confirmed by practice.... In order to deduce the existence of customary rules, the Court deems it sufficient that the conduct of States should, in general, be consistent with such rules, and that instances of State conduct inconsistent with a given rule should generally have been treated as breaches of that rule, not as indications of the recognition of a new rule.

Nicaragua case, *supra* note 8, at 97–8.

the acceptance of the treaty increases. However, such a conclusion (the so-called Baxter paradox[14]) would disregard both the fact that the treaty itself is an important piece of State practice for the determination of customary law, although its role in this regard must be carefully assessed,[15] and the impact that any subsequent practice of the contracting States in the application of the treaty which establishes their agreement or disagreement regarding its interpretation[16] may bear on the development of a customary norm. Therefore, it is submitted that customary international humanitarian law should not be determined on the sole basis of the practice of the States that have not ratified Protocol I.

In addition to the practice of State parties in their application of Protocol I and the behavior of other States vis-à-vis the Protocol itself, any other element being evidence of State practice may come into play. Special importance should however be attached to the case law, although limited, of international courts, such as the International Criminal Tribunal for the former Yugoslavia

---

14. According to the Baxter paradox, "[A]s the number of parties to a treaty increases, it becomes more difficult to demonstrate what is the state of customary international law dehors the treaty." In addition, "[a]s the express acceptance of the treaty increases, the number of states not parties whose practice is relevant diminishes. There will be less scope for the development of international law dehors the treaty...." See Baxter, *supra* note 6, at 64, 73.

15. See Theodor Meron, *The Geneva Conventions as Customary Law*, 81 AMERICAN JOURNAL OF INTERNATIONAL LAW 367 (1987), which points out that although acts concordant with a treaty obviously are indistinguishable from acts in the application of the treaty, the demonstration that an act by State parties is regarded by them as required not only by their conventional obligations but also by general international law would show the existence of an *opinio juris*, which should be given probative weight for the formation of customary law.

16. *Cf.* Article 31(3)(b) of the Vienna Convention on the Law of Treaties (*supra* note 7), concerning general rules of interpretation, which states: "There shall be taken into account, together with the context . . . [a]ny subsequent practice in the application of the treaty which establishes the agreement of the parties regarding its interpretation." See on this provision Francesco Capotorti, *Sul valore della prassi applicativa dei trattati secondo la convenzione di Vienna*, in INTERNATIONAL LAW AT THE TIME OF ITS CODIFICATION. ESSAYS IN HONOUR OF ROBERTO AGO 197 ff. (A. Giuffré ed., 1987); Fausto Pocar, *Codification of Human Rights Law by the United Nations*, in PERSPECTIVES ON INTERNATIONAL LAW 153 (Nandasiri Jasentuliyana ed., 1995).

(ICTY) and the International Criminal Tribunal for Rwanda (ICTR).[17] As has been pointed out, the assessment of the customary nature of treaty provisions made by international courts has frequently proved to be regarded as determinative in subsequent debates.[18] However, even in respect of case law, it has to be stressed that previous decisions of international courts cannot be relied on as having the authority of precedents in order to establish a principle of law. The current structure of the international community, which clearly lacks a hierarchical judicial system, does not allow consideration of judicial precedent as a distinct source of law. Therefore, prior case law may only constitute evidence of a customary rule in that it may reflect the existence of *opinio juris* and international practice, but cannot be regarded per se as having precedential authority in international criminal adjudication. As has been pointed out, international criminal courts must always carefully appraise decisions of other

---

17. The limited number of ICTY decisions dealing with the issue considered in this paper, i.e., whether Protocol I reflects customary law, depend on the consideration that the Protocol was referred to by the ICTY as conventional law rather than as evidence of customary international law. *See e.g.* Prosecutor v. Blaskic, Judgement, I.C.T.Y. No. IT-95-14-T, Mar. 3, 2000, ¶ 172 [hereinafter Blaškic case], where it is stated that Croatia and Bosnia-Herzegovina ratified Protocol I and Protocol II (which is applicable to non-international armed conflicts) in 1992 and that "consequently, as of January 1993, the two parties were bound by the provisions of the two Protocols, whatever their status within customary international law." See also Prosecutor v. Kordic and Cerkez, Decision on the Joint Defence Motion to Dismiss for Lack of Jurisdiction Portions of the Amended Indictment Alleging "Failure to Punish" Liability, I.C.T.Y. No. IT-95-14/2-PT, Mar. 2, 1999, ¶ 13, where it is stated that "both the Republic of Croatia and Bosnia and Herzegovina are bound by Additional Protocol I as successor States of the Socialist Republic of Yugoslavia, which had ratified the Protocol on 11 June 1979." In this context see also Prosecutor v. Delalic et al., Appeal Judgement, I.C.T.Y. No. IT-96-21-A, Feb. 20, 2001, ¶¶ 111–113, where it is stated that Bosnia and Herzegovina would have in any event succeeded to the Geneva Conventions of 1949 (to which Yugoslavia was a party) irrespective of any findings as to formal succession. The Appeals Chamber considered that "in international law there is automatic State succession to multilateral humanitarian treaties in the broad sense, i.e., treaties of universal character which express fundamental human rights" and that "in light of the object and purpose of the Geneva Conventions, which is to guarantee the protection of certain fundamental values common to mankind in times of armed conflict, . . . the Appeals Chamber is in no doubt that State succession has no impact on obligations arising out from these fundamental humanitarian conventions."

18. *See* THEODOR MERON, HUMAN RIGHTS AND HUMANITARIAN NORMS AS CUSTOMARY INTERNATIONAL LAW 43 (1989). See also Christopher Greenwood, *Customary Law Status of the 1977 Geneva Protocols, in* HUMANITARIAN LAW OF ARMED CONFLICTS, *supra* note 10, at 99, where it is noted that no decisions of the ICJ or of other authoritative international tribunals existed regarding Protocol I and points out that international decisions are rare in respect to any of the humanitarian law treaties, except for the decisions on war crimes cases issued after World War II. Later on, as mentioned in the text, the international criminal tribunals established by the Security Council have sometimes dealt with the Protocols.

courts before relying on their persuasive authority as to existing law.[19] Consequently, although judicial decisions of international courts may have a special weight, they must be regarded as one of the elements that have to be taken into account in the assessment of the existence of a customary rule.

Looking at the provisions of Protocol I from the perspective of existing customary international humanitarian law, it is certainly possible to identify different groups of norms. The first and largest group encompasses the rules whose customary nature is undisputed. It is widely recognized that much of the Protocol is a codification of general international law. Even States that hesitate to accept the instrument or have decided not to ratify it, such as the United States,[20] have expressed the view that many of its provisions are either settled customary international law or eligible for their ultimate recognition as customary international law.[21]

A customary status should clearly be accorded, in the first place, to the provisions that echo or restate the Hague Regulations annexed to the Fourth Hague Convention of 1907, which are generally regarded as reflecting

---

19. *See* Prosecutor v. Kupreskic et al., Judgement, I.C.T.Y. No. IT-95-16-T, Jan. 14, 2000, ¶ 542 [hereinafter Kupreskic case].
20. *See* Letter of Transmittal of Protocol II by President Reagan to the Senate, dated January 29, 1987, *reprinted in* 81 AMERICAN JOURNAL OF INTERNATIONAL LAW 910 (1987), and Hans-Peter Gasser, *An Appeal for Ratification by the United States*, 81 AMERICAN JOURNAL OF INTERNATIONAL LAW 912 (1987). See also George Aldrich, *Prospects for United States Ratification of Additional Protocol I to the 1949 Geneva Conventions*, 85 AMERICAN JOURNAL OF INTERNATIONAL LAW 1 (1991), where the difficulties encountered by the United States are discussed with a view to overcoming them by means of reservations.
21. Indeed, it has been noted that statements of United States officials following the announcement that the United States would not ratify Protocol I are evidence that "the United States regards Articles 37 (perfidy), 40 (refusal of quarter), 42 (on persons parachuting from a disabled aircraft), 59 (non-defended localities), 60 (demilitarised zones), 73 (refugees), 75 (fundamental guarantees) and 79 (journalists) as declaratory of custom." *See* Greenwood, *supra* note 18, at 103. *See also* EDWARD KWAKWA, THE INTERNATIONAL LAW OF ARMED CONFLICT: PERSONAL AND MATERIAL FIELDS OF APPLICATION 26 (1992); THEODOR MERON, WAR CRIMES LAW COMES OF AGE 179–80 (1998).

customary law.[22] This applies, for example, to the basic rules that concern methods and means of warfare, such as those contained in Article 35(1), which declares that the right of the parties to a conflict to choose methods or means of warfare is not unlimited, and to Article 35(2), which prohibits the employment of weapons, projectiles and material and methods of warfare that are of a nature to cause superfluous injury or unnecessary suffering. These provisions basically follow Articles 22 and 23(e) of the Hague Regulations, which excluded the unlimited use of means of warfare and contained the prohibition on employing arms, projectiles or material calculated to cause unnecessary suffering. It is true that Protocol I uses, additionally, the term "methods of warfare" in order to define the scope of the prohibition and that the addition could be regarded as introducing a new element, which would only have the status of a treaty rule.[23] It is submitted, however, that the addition is a mere clarification of the already existing customary rule reflected in the Hague Regulations rather than a new rule aiming at its development. Indeed, the prohibition against employing certain means of warfare appears to include both the choice of weapons and the way in which weapons are employed.[24]

---

22. It has to be noted that a Trial Chamber of the ICTY has considered that:

> [I]t is the Hague Convention (IV) of 1907 respecting the Laws and Customs of War on Land (hereinafter "the Regulations of The Hague"), as interpreted and applied by the Nuremberg Tribunal, which is the basis for Article 3 of the Statute. Hence, although Article 3 of the Statute subsumes Common Article 3, it nevertheless remains a broader provision inasmuch as it is also based on the Regulations of The Hague which, in the opinion of the Trial Chamber, also undoubtedly form part of customary international law.

See Blaskic case, *supra* note 17, ¶ 168.

23. See Henri Meyrowitz, *The Principle of Superfluous Injury or Unnecessary Suffering: From the Declaration of St. Petersburg of 1868 to Additional Protocol I of 1977*, 299 INTERNATIONAL REVIEW OF THE RED CROSS 98 (1994), where it is stated that "while this rule derives from the principle expressed in HR, Article 23(e), international legislation was required to make it positive law."

24. See Greenwood, *supra* note 18, at 104. It has to be noted in this context that Article 35 was adopted by consensus at the Geneva Diplomatic Conference and that some participating States made declarations that confirm the customary nature of paragraphs (1) and (2) of Article 35. In particular, the Federal Republic of Germany joined the consensus with the "understanding that paragraphs 1 and 2 reaffirm customary international law" and that paragraph 3 constitutes a new conventional rule. It should also be noted that the addition of the term "superfluous injury" to the term "unnecessary suffering" is to be regarded as simply aiming at rendering in English the expression *"maux superflus"* contained in the French text of Article 23(e). See Meyrowitz, *supra* note 23, at 104–5.

Similar considerations apply in this context to the provisions prohibiting acts that go beyond ruses of war and amount to perfidy (Article 37) or declarations that no quarter will be given (Article 40), and others that clearly follow the corresponding provisions of the Hague Regulations. Equally, most of the provisions concerning combatant and prisoner-of-war status (Articles 43 to 47) restate rules already expressed in the Hague Regulations or in the Geneva Conventions of 1949, which are largely considered as reflecting customary international law[25] even though the customary nature of some additions have been questioned in legal doctrine. This is the case, in particular, of the provision of Article 44(3) concerning the requirement that combatants distinguish themselves from the civilian population. While this requirement clearly reflects an existing principle, the provision differs from customary international law especially as regards the situation in which combatants are unable to distinguish themselves; therefore, the criteria set forth in Protocol I have to be regarded as new conventional rules.[26]

As regards the protection of civilians and the civilian population against the effects of hostilities, there is no doubt that the principle of distinction as set forth in Article 48 of Protocol I, both as regards the distinction between combatants and noncombatants and between civilian objects and non-civilian objects, reaffirms a general rule of international law that has never been questioned despite being frequently disregarded in State practice. The same applies in this context, at least in general terms, to the definition of civilians and the civilian population (Article 50) and to the general protection they shall enjoy against dangers arising from military operations (Article 51), in particular through the prohibition of indiscriminate attacks, as well as to the general rule on protection of civilian objects (Article 52). The specificity of these provisions appear mainly to be detailed clarifications of existing recognized rules rather than additions aimed at their development.[27]

---

25. See e.g., Jean-Marie Henckaerts, *Study on Customary Rules of International Humanitarian Law: Purpose, Coverage and Methodology*, 81 INTERNATIONAL REVIEW OF THE RED CROSS 660 (1999).
26. See in particular L. Penna, *Customary International Law and Protocol I: An Analysis of Some Provisions*, in STUDIES AND ESSAYS ON INTERNATIONAL HUMANITARIAN LAW AND RED CROSS PRINCIPLES, IN HONOUR OF JEAN PICTET 214–5 (Christophe Swinarski ed., 1984); and Greenwood, *supra* note 18, at 107, where it is also noted that Article 44(3) was one of the most controversial provisions inserted in Protocol I, and has been identified by the United States as a major reason for its decision not to ratify the Protocol.
27. As to the role of Protocol I in clarifying pre-existing customary law, see Hans-Peter Gasser, *Negotiating the 1977 Additional Protocols: Was it a Waste of Time?*, in HUMANITARIAN LAW OF ARMED CONFLICTS, *supra* note 10, at 85–6.

It has to be noted in this regard that a Trial Chamber of the ICTY has, with respect to Articles 51(2) and 52(1) of the Protocol, expressed the view that these provisions "are based on Hague law relating to the conduct of warfare, which is considered as part of customary law." The Chamber concluded that:

> [T]o the extent that these provisions ... echo the Hague Regulations, they can be considered as reflecting customary law. It is indisputable that the general prohibition of attacks against the civilian population and the prohibition of indiscriminate attacks or attacks on civilian objects are generally accepted obligations. As a consequence, there is no possible doubt as to the customary status of these specific provisions as they reflect core principles of humanitarian law that can be considered as applying to all armed conflicts, whether intended to be international or non-international conflicts.[28]

A similar consideration can be made as concerns the principle of proportionality as set forth in Article 51(5)(b), according to which an attack on a military objective is prohibited when it would cause excessive injury to civilians or damage to civilian objects in relation to the concrete and direct military advantage anticipated.[29] Admittedly, the extent to which these provisions correspond to customary law has been questioned, because the formulation adopted appears to contain a number of specifications that can not be found in previous declarations of the same principles. However, it has also been pointed out that such specifications are aimed at clarifying the scope of the principles rather than at adding new elements that would lead to the modification of their content or effects.[30] While it is possible that the interpretation of certain expressions used in Protocol I may lead to improvements that could result in a departure from existing customary law principles, it is certain that such improvements would be considered as forming part of the natural development of customary law rather than as constituting mere treaty provisions.

In the same line of reasoning, it may be assumed that the provisions of Articles 57 and 58, prescribing that precautionary measures should be taken in conducting an attack, as well as against the effects of attacks, are mere qualifications of the general principles of distinction and proportionality, although

---

28. Prosecutor v. Kordic and Cerkez, Decision on the Joint Defence Motion to Dismiss the Amended Indictment for Lack of Jurisdiction Based on the Limited Jurisdictional Reach of Articles 2 and 3, I.C.T.Y. No. IT-95-14/2-PT, Mar. 2, 1999, ¶ 31.
29. See Greenwood, *supra* note 18, at 109; Penna, *supra* note 26, at 220.
30. As to the specifications contained in Article 51(5)(b), see, e.g., MERON, *supra* note 18, at 65.

they may be seen as going beyond customary law.[31] It is interesting to note that the customary nature of these provisions has been recently affirmed by a Trial Chamber of the ICTY, not only because they specify pre-existing norms, but also because they appear to be uncontested by States, even non-ratifying States. The Chamber went on to state that when a rule of international humanitarian law is somewhat imprecise, it must be defined with reference to the laws of humanity and dictates of public conscience espoused in the celebrated "Martens clause,"[32] which constitutes customary law. As a result, the Chamber concluded that the prescriptions of Articles 57 and 58, and of the corresponding customary rules, must be interpreted "so as to construe as narrowly as possible the discretionary power to attack belligerents and, by the same token, so as to expand the protection accorded to civilians."[33]

While most of Protocol I can undoubtedly be regarded as essentially reflecting customary international law, there are areas where this conclusion is subject to debate for two reasons. First, Protocol I clearly sets forth some new rules. Secondly, the specificity of Protocol I's provisions add new elements to principles that, while well established in customary law, leave margins of discretion to belligerent States. Belligerent States are then free to argue that such specifications will limit or may limit discretion if they are given certain interpretations. The scope and impact of these additions is therefore controversial and may be the basis for the hesitations of some States to ratify Protocol I. Indeed, Protocol I's ratification would require that the interpretation of its principles should be conducted according to the relevant criteria of the law of treaties, which are not applicable to the corresponding rules as recognized in customary international law.

Some areas appear to be especially significant in this respect, in particular those relating to the protection of the civilian population and civilian objects. For instance, the presumption expressed in Article 50(1) that in case of doubt as to whether a person is a civilian, that person should be considered as having

---

31. See Greenwood, *supra* note 18, at 111.

32. The Martens clause first appeared in the preamble to the Hague Convention (II) of 1899. It states:

> Until a more complete code of the laws of war is issued, the High Contracting Parties think it right to declare that in cases not included in the Regulations adopted by them, populations and belligerents remain under the protection and empire of the principles of international law, as they result from the usages established between civilised nations, from the law of humanity, and the requirements of the public conscience.

33. Kupreskic case, *supra* note 19, ¶¶ 521–25. The issue was not considered on appeal. See Prosecutor v. Kupreskic et al., Appeal Judgement, I.C.T.Y. No. IT-95-16-A, Oct. 23, 2001.

such status, and the provision of Article 52(3) that an object normally dedicated to civilian purposes shall, in case of doubt as to its being used to contribute to military action, be presumed not to be so used. These provisions do not seem to derive automatically—although it would certainly be desirable[34]—from the principle of distinction as settled in customary international law, which appears to leave it to the attacker to decide how to determine the status of the military objective.

There seems to be no doubt that the definition of military objectives contained in Article 52(2) corresponds to existing principles as reflected in customary international law and simply clarifies them. However, if the clarifications of the definition are considered as being open to different interpretations of the scope of the obligations imposed on the attacker, then that would be incompatible with a consideration of the provision as fully reflecting customary law. Expressions such as "effective contribution to military action" or "definite military advantage" may not be sufficiently precise for the purpose of establishing a safe basis for a rule of customary international law.[35] On the other hand, it has also been submitted that the definition enshrined in the second sentence of Article 52(2) is such that it should be deemed to include not only civilians, but combatants as well. If, indeed, the implicit *ratio legis* for such provision is the same that underlies the principle that superfluous injury or unnecessary suffering should be avoided, there is no reason why the provision should not apply to attacks against members of armed forces as well.[36]

Similarly, the obligation to protect the natural environment against widespread, long-term and severe damage, which includes the prohibition of the use of methods or means of warfare which are intended or may be expected to

---

34. See in particular Frits Kalshoven, *Reaffirmation and Development of Humanitarian Laws Applicable in Armed Conflicts*, 9 NETHERLANDS YEARBOOK OF INTERNATIONAL LAW 112 (1978).
35. The possibility of a wide interpretation of legitimate objectives under Protocol I is underlined, among others, by Peter Rowe, *Kosovo 1999: The Air Campaign: Have the provisions of Additional Protocol I withstood the test?*, 82 INTERNATIONAL REVIEW OF THE RED CROSS 147 (2000). See also Penna, *supra* note 26, at 219, who points out that Article 52(2) may be regarded as customary law, but recognizes that the definition of military objectives contained therein is far from being precise and that "customary international law at present allows belligerents to regard legitimate civilian objects serving directly or indirectly the enemy war effort as 'military objectives'."
36. For this approach see Meyrowitz, *supra* note 23, at 115, who states that "strictly speaking, the extension of the rule stated in Article 52(2) to combatants would not have the purpose of protecting them, but of excluding them, under certain circumstances, from the definition of military objectives that may lawfully be attacked."

cause such damage (Article 35(3)), in particular when the health or survival of the population may be prejudiced (Article 55), finds no clear precedent in existing customary law, as was acknowledged by some States who participated in the drafting of Protocol I.[37] Although subsequent development of a customary principle of respect for the environment in warfare may be in progress,[38] its scope is certainly far from being assessed and recognized. It may be also noted, in this connection, that the said provisions appear to affirm a principle of protection in absolute terms, applicable irrespective of a reference both to the principles of proportionality and of distinction. It must be noted, in this respect, that Article 55 refers to population without the qualification "civilian."

A final area that may deserve special attention, since it is subject to debate, concerns the prohibition of reprisals against civilians and protected objects, which are referred to in Articles 51 to 56 of Protocol I. It is well known that the controversy on this matter has been and still is important, and different views have been expressed both at the Geneva Diplomatic Conference where Protocol I was negotiated and subsequently. The dominant view is probably that the provisions of Protocol I neither reflect pre-existing customary law nor have subsequently reached that nature, but contain significant developments in this regard.[39]

Interestingly, the issue was considered by a Trial Chamber of the ICTY,[40] which discussed whether the Protocol's provisions on reprisals against

---

37. *See* Greenwood, *supra* note 18, at 101, where it is stated:

> Article 35(3) . . . is more contentious and, unlike the rest of Article 35, was not based upon the provisions of earlier treaties. Nor could it be said that State practice prior to 1977 provided much support for the existence of such a rule. Although the Article was adopted by consensus, the Federal Republic of Germany stated that it participated in that consensus on the understanding that Article 35(3) introduced a new rule. Subsequent United States statements regarding Article 35(3) take the same position. . . . Article 55 is closely linked to Article 35(3) and should be regarded as having the same status.

38. *See* NATALINO RONZITTI, DIRITTO INTERNAZIONALE DEI CONFLITTI ARMATI 161 (2d ed. 2001).

39. For the state of international customary law before Protocol I, see FRITS KALSHOVEN, BELLIGERENT REPRISALS 375 (1971), who concludes, after a thorough consideration of State practice, that belligerent reprisals have not so far come under a total prohibition, and further notes that "the power of belligerents to resort to belligerent reprisals can only be effectively abolished to the extent that other adequate means take over their function of law enforcement." For a recent consideration of the issue, see RONZITTI, *supra* note 38, at 180.

40. Kupreskic case, *supra* note 19, ¶¶ 527–36. The issue has not been raised on appeal. *See* the Appeal Judgment, *supra* note 33.

civilians in combat zones (Article 51(6)) and reprisals against civilian objects (Article 52(1)) have been subsequently transformed into general rules of international law. Assuming that the mentioned provisions were not declaratory of customary law, the Chamber expressed the view that the universal revulsion towards reprisals, as well as their trampling on the most fundamental principles of human rights, have contributed to the emergence of customary law on the matter. The Chamber also recalled the requirements of humanity and dictates of public conscience espoused in the Martens clause, stating that the pressure stemming therefrom has resulted in the formation of customary law on reprisals. It further maintained that *opinio juris* existed to support the view that these rules have become a part of customary law. It pointed to circumscriptions on reprisals in modern warfare contained in the military manuals of States, including the United States; the adoption by the United Nations General Assembly of a resolution in 1970 stating that civilian populations should not be the object of reprisals; and the ratification of Protocol I by a large number of States. It further pointed out that another Trial Chamber also held the view that reprisals against civilians must always be prohibited.[41] In addition, it stated that in the armed conflicts of the last fifty years, States have normally not asserted the right to undertake reprisals against enemy civilians in the combat area. Whatever consideration be given to this judgment,[42] it is undeniable that it may play an important role in assessing the legitimacy of reprisals against civilians and protected objects, and in developing customary international law that reflects the provisions of Protocol I in this area.

Other examples could be cited in examining the extent to which Protocol I reflects pre-existing customary international law and its contributions to clarifying the content and scope of customary law. However, at this stage it seems that some conclusions can be drawn in light of the present practice. A slow but continuous trend towards recognizing the general value of the provisions contained in Protocol I, especially as far as they are intended to set forth well established customary principles or improve their definitions, is largely

---

41. *See* Prosecutor v. Milan Martic, Review of Indictment Pursuant to Rule 61, I.C.T.Y. No. IT-95-11-R61, Mar. 8, 1996, ¶¶ 10–18.
42. For the position that the invocation of the Martens clause can hardly justify the conclusion that the combined effect of the clause and *opinio juris* can transform the prohibition on reprisals against civilian objects into customary law binding on States that have not ratified Protocol I or have dissented from the prohibition of reprisals, see Theodor Meron, *The Humanization of Humanitarian Law*, 94 AMERICAN JOURNAL OF INTERNATIONAL LAW 250 (2000).

discernible in international practice and legal doctrine.[43] The increasing number of State ratifications is corroborative of this growing trend, together with the emerging case law of international judicial bodies, which tends to more frequently underline human values in assessing the content of customary international law.

Except perhaps in some cases where it is clear that no customary rule exists, the areas in which Protocol I has encountered the most difficulty in developing into customary law appear to be the areas where the Protocol itself, because its provisions and the definitions contained therein are not sufficiently clear and well shaped, is subject to different interpretations. In other words, the diverging approach to such provisions lies in their interpretation. In this regard, it has to be noted that the resistance to ratify Protocol I may also lie in the different rules of interpretation that would apply in establishing the scope of the principles enshrined in the Protocol, should the latter be regarded as treaty provisions instead of principles of customary international law.

In light of these conclusions drawn twenty-five years after Protocol I was adopted, one can doubt whether it was drafted in a way intended to help the development of customary law. Unclear treaty rules can hardly develop into customary law and may frequently be opposed by States which may fear being bound by interpretations they would not be in the position to accept. By way of example, a list of military objectives would have helped the formation of customary law, at least as far as the list is concerned, even though it would have been necessary to recognize that the list was not exhaustive. The lack of such a list, due to only partially different views of States as to its scope, does not provide any help in this regard. [44] Although it cannot be denied that Protocol I has had an impact on pre-existing customary law,[45] it may be submitted that Protocol I could have made a far greater contribution to its development.

---

43. In this connection, the potential impact of Protocol I on the state of customary law has been stressed by Gasser, *supra* note 27, at 87.
44. For a different view, see FRITS KALSHOVEN AND LIESBETH ZEGVELD, CONSTRAINTS ON THE WAGING OF WAR 101 (2001).
45. For a discussion of this issue, see Yoram Dinstein, *The New Geneva Protocols: A Step Forward or Backwards?*, 33 YEAR BOOK OF WORLD AFFAIRS 269 (1979); and, with regard to reprisals against civilians, *Commentaires au sujet du Protocole I*, 79 REVUE INTERNATIONALE DE LA CROIX ROUGE 553 (1997).

Commentary

Rudolf Dolzer

As I agree with most points made by Professor Stein and Judge Pocar, I shall limit my comments to two points. The first one concerns the methodology and sources of international humanitarian law in general. The second one relates more specifically to the evolving diversity of goals and functions of humanitarian law and the necessity to understand and apply the existing rules in the current policy context.

The first point on the sources of humanitarian law starts out from the basic premise that no special rules exist, or should be recognized, in this area which would in principle depart in any way from those recognized for public international law in general. In other words, the canon of principles laid down in Article 38 of the Statute of the International Court of Justice will apply to humanitarian law as well. The jurisprudence of the ICJ has been consistent with this postulate. As to the relationship between treaty law and customary law in particular, the rulings in the *North Sea Continental Shelf* case,[1] the *Nicaragua* case[2] and the *Nuclear Weapons* advisory opinion[3] do not point to any divergence in the Court's approach between humanitarian law and other areas of public international law. The nuances of these three decisions may not be always identical. It has been noticed rightly that the *North Sea Continental Shelf* decision, for instance, seems to require a more comprehensive and detailed examination of State practice than the *Nicaragua* decision. All three

---

1. North Sea Continental Shelf (F.R.G. v. Den., F.R.G. v. Neth.), 1969 I.C.J. 3 (Feb. 20).
2. Military and Paramilitary Activities (Nicar. v. U.S.), 1986 I.C.J. 14 (June 27) [hereinafter Nicaragua case].
3. Legality of the Use by a State of Nuclear Weapons in Armed Conflict, 1996 I.C.J. 78 (July 8).

decisions converge inasmuch as they are based on the same view that "it should not lightly be assumed that treaty law evolves into customary law."[4] Widespread practice and corresponding *opinio iuris* will be required for the formation of customary law, with or without parallel treaty law. This maxim has to be adapted to the circumstances of the context in regard to the number and characteristics of relevant States, and the practice of the major States will have to be given considerable weight.

At the same time, it is appropriate to assume that the rules on the persistent objector will also be operative in the context of humanitarian law. While we all agree that the strengthening and expansion of the rules protecting the victims and the innocents deserve our support, it is also clear that behind these rules lie carefully balanced compromises which take into account the nature of warfare. Against this background, it should not be generally presumed that States are inclined to interpret those rules in *favoram humanitatem* at the cost of their freedom in the means and methods of warfare.

Special issues may arise in those areas of customary law and treaty law which are frequently disregarded in State practice. In such a setting it will be necessary to examine carefully to the extent possible whether States assume that the relevant rule is valid in principle, and point to special justifications for their departure from the rule, or clarify whether it must be concluded that States do not consider themselves to be bound in general. Of course, the first alternative describes the setting of considerable State practice regarding the prohibition of the use of force. Many governments act contrary to a rule, but nonetheless accept it in principle by way of pointing to one of the justifications that allow them, or would allow them if the relevant facts existed, to act contrary to the rule. The issue will become more complex if no attempt to justify the conduct is made. In case a considerable number of States fall into this category, it will have to be assumed that the rule has been eroded. Such a process of derogation may take different forms, depending on the precise circumstances.

In the extreme setting, it is possible that the rule as such can no longer be considered to be valid and that States are no longer bound by any norm in the relevant context. Another version of a process of this kind will exist where States do not flatly disregard the rule but apply it frequently in a generally restricting manner; under such circumstances, the understanding of the rule will have to be adapted to the practice. This will also be the case if State practice disregards the rule in a specific area of application. Evidence of such

---

4. North Sea Continental Shelf, *supra* note 1, at 41, No. 71.

different types of derogation can be found in various areas of humanitarian law. The common denominator of all such developments lies in the requirement to take into account State practice in identifying and interpreting the rules of humanitarian law. In the context of treaty law, Article 31 of the Vienna Convention on the Law of Treaties[5] points in the same direction.

The second part of my remarks concerns the diversity of goals, functions and faces of humanitarian law. The essential point which I wish to make is that the various branches of humanitarian law resulting from this diversity need to be viewed in an integrated context so that the development of the law as a whole will be kept and tied together.

The diversity and the branches to which I refer essentially consists of the following three parts:

(1) The protection of potential victims, being the primary goal of humanitarian law as it has evolved historically, remains the key concern.

(2) The necessity to leave room to fight a war for a good cause in an efficient manner must be preserved. This concerns Professor Dinstein's point that we do not want a war to last forever, and John Norton Moore's emphasis on the need to fight effective wars in our contemporary world.

(3) Following the developments in the past decade, we need to view humanitarian law increasingly through the lenses of international criminal law, as the two areas are increasingly linked together.

Why is it necessary to point to the distinctness of these diverse goals and branches? The concern here is a fragmentation in the outlook on humanitarian law that may occur when the three segments noted above are seen in isolation without regard to the necessity to fashion and design the rules so as to reflect the existence and the special needs of all three branches. In practice, the three perspectives have their own "constituencies" which may or may not be prepared in practice to accept that their own concerns need to be merged with the policies and considerations underlying the two other concerns. As to the protective dimension of humanitarian law, it is widely known that its causes are championed especially in scholarly circles, but also by a number of

---

5. Vienna Convention on the Law of Treaties, May 23, 1969, 1155 U.N.T.S. 331.

governments. Perhaps it is fair to say that the favorite clause of this part of the international humanitarian law community is the Martens Clause drafted in 1899 for the first time and phrased in Article 1(2) of Protocol I[6] as follows: "In cases not covered by this Protocol, civilians and combatants enjoy the protection of the principles of international law derived from the established custom, from the principles of humanity and from the dictates of public conscience."[7] This emphasis on humanity and the public conscience as the overarching goal of humanitarian law echoes the fundamental purpose of humanitarian law, and from an abstract point of view no one will disagree with the noble cause expressed by the Martens Clause.

Nevertheless, it will not be denied that another part of the community concerned with humanitarian law may have priorities in practice which highlight factors additional to those reflected in the Martens Clause. I refer to the military sector and to the actors on the ground. Any realistic consideration will have to conclude that it is not surprising that this community is often less concerned with the principles of the Martens Clause than with the interpretation of the law in a manner which allows flexibility, military advantage and ultimately the operation and conclusion of a successful military operation ended within an appropriate timeframe.

The third branch of the contemporary humanitarian law relates, of course, to the enforcement community, charged with the application of the modern rules of international criminal law. It appears that the application and interpretation of this dimension of international humanitarian law may present the most difficult challenge for the entire body of rules in the coming years. The universe of criminal law as generally accepted in most parts of the world is characterized by distinct principles such as the prohibition of *ex post facto* laws, the presumption of innocence, the prohibition of vagueness of criminal rules and an emphasis on the subjective perception of the individual concerned. Should the rules of international criminal law based on the laws of war be

---

6. Protocol Additional (I) to the Geneva Conventions of 12 August 1949, and Relating to the Protection of Victims of International Conflicts, June 8, 1977, 1125 U.N.T.S. 3, DOCUMENTS ON THE LAWS OF WAR 422 (A. Roberts & R. Guelff eds., 3d ed. 2000) [hereinafter Protocol I].
7. The Martens clause first appeared in the preamble to the Hague Convention (II) of 1899. It states:

> Until a more complete code of the laws of war is issued, the High Contracting Parties think it right to declare that in cases not included in the Regulations adopted by them, populations and belligerents remain under the protection and empire of the principles of international law, as they result from the usages established between civilised nations, from the law of humanity, and the requirements of the public conscience.

fashioned so as to be as transparent and predictable as possible? Should these rules be construed so as to allow a wide margin of appreciation and an emphasis *ex ante* for the actor on the ground?[8] Should the main emphasis in the interpretation concern the broad protection of the victim, even though this would be at the expense of the special guarantees characteristic of criminal law and also at the expense of chilling the enthusiasm of those States willing to wage a just war?

These three modes of interpreting international criminal law are emphasized here only for the sake of separating and isolating the potential perspectives. In reality, these approaches will be blended in one way or another in the application of the law. What is remarkable, however, is that the International Criminal Tribunal for the former Yugoslavia (ICTY) has come fairly close to emphasising the third, the "humanitarian approach" in the context of applying Articles 57 and 58 of Protocol I dealing with the necessity of feasible precautions for the civilian population. Generally speaking, the Tribunal was faced in this context with an unusually generally worded, imprecise rule, uncharacteristic for language typical of criminal law. The court would have had the opportunity to narrow down the meaning of the two articles by way of a narrow construction. It would have been possible to interpret the rules taking into account the necessity of military efficiency, and an approach respecting the rule of the margin of appreciation would also have been conceivable.

In the *Kupreskic* case referred to by Judge Pocar, the ICTY chose to interpret Articles 57 and 58 in the specific light of the Martens Clause laid down in Article 2 of Protocol I.[9] In effect, this reading of the rules led to a very broad understanding and to an emphasis on the protective dimension of Protocol I, with no special regard for the first and second branch of international humanitarian law in the sense mentioned above. The ICTY found that these rules must be interpreted "so as to construe as narrowly as possible the discretionary power to attack belligerents and, by the same token, so as to expand the protection accorded to civilians."[10] Clearly, for purposes of enforcement, the ICTY thus has underlined a distinctly humanitarian approach to the interpretation of the Protocol I. The ruling shows no apparent regard for the classical

---

8. The concept of the margin of appreciation has been widely used by the European Court of Human Rights in the context of the application of human rights norms which, in the view of the court, must be interpreted to take into account the special situation of the member States as they apply the law.
9. See Prosecutor v. Kupreskic et al., Judgement, I.C.T.Y. No. IT-95-16-T, Jan. 14, 2000, ¶ 525.
10. Id.

requirements of criminal law, nor was any attention paid, it appears, to any approach favoring a margin of appreciation for those who have to render decisions during times of war. As to the wording of the Martens Clause in the modern sense, as reflected in Protocol I, the literal reading leaves no doubt that the clause will only be applied in cases "not covered by this Protocol."[11] Thus it has to be assumed that the Martens Clause must be applied only in areas not addressed by the written rules. This is quite different from assuming, as the ICTY did, that the Martens Clause must serve as a rule of interpretation for the written rules which are written in a manner so as to be in need of interpretation. The implication of the ICTY's approach is indeed then to broaden the protective dimension of the humanitarian rules in a general manner, without attention to the other branches of this body of rules. It is more than doubtful whether such an approach is consistent with the original intention of the Martens Clause and with the contemporary need to integrate all concerns embodied in humanitarian law.

When we speak about the lessons of the Kosovo, the humanitarian approach adopted by this decision of the ICTY reflects our general hope that this decision has taught former President Milosevic and his disciples a lesson which future warmongers and warlords and dictators will eventually remember. The urgent question, however, remains whether this approach satisfies all goals and functions present in humanitarian law. What about the chilling effect for those who are willing to fight a war with a just cause? What are the consequences of such a chilling effect? Does such an approach in an unintended way protect a dictator from those who may be called upon to fight him? And, more generally, what is the effect of such an approach to humanitarian law doctrine on the acceptance by governments of an international criminal system?

There are no clear-cut answers to these questions, but they need to be addressed because they concern serious questions. We are living through a period of fundamental changes in the laws of armed conflict, and it is important that the implication of all these changes are thought through in a broad debate where the requirements of criminal law guarantees are discussed, where the realities of military conduct are taken into account and where not only the noble humanitarian aspirations in an isolated sense are highlighted. Possibly, the international community will decide to adopt the humanitarian approach favored by the ICTY, but we must do so in a manner which is responsive to all elements and dimensions of the laws of war as they will operate in practice. I

---

11. Protocol I, *supra* note 6, art. 1(2).

submit that our reflections on the choices to be made in the future are still at an early stage. Whoever wishes to take the moral high ground for the development of humanitarian law is also under moral pressure to consider the implications in all their various facets on international relations. This requires, in particular, both a focus on the impact of any change of law on those national leaders who are most likely to start an illegal war and to cause unnecessary suffering, and also on the conduct of those leaders and nations who are most likely to defend potential victims against an illegal war and thus to end unnecessary suffering.

Commentary

Leslie C. Green

As had been forewarned, the immediate effect of Operation Allied Force, which was in fact directed against targets in Serbia as well as Kosovo province, was an increase in the terror directed against the Muslim Albanian population. While NATO claimed that only military targets were being attacked, it soon became clear that civilians and civilian objects were suffering damage—sometimes because of "clever" bombs going astray but also, it seems, from NATO's desire to avoid casualties among its own personnel, which led to aircraft flying beyond anti-aircraft range resulting in mistakes in targeting. Cluster bombs, the range of which is difficult or impossible to control, were among the ordinance dropped rendering civilian casualties virtually inevitable. While it was claimed that bridges over the Danube, television studios and electricity-generating establishments were legitimate military objectives, questions regarding the rule of proportionality in relation to collateral damage, both under customary law and Protocols I and II, have to be examined.

The Economist Intelligence Unit reported, perhaps in the light of more recent developments with some exaggeration, that the NATO bombing "inflicted enormous damage on Yugoslavia's economy and infrastructure.... Yugoslavia will sink below Albania and become the poorest country in Europe."[1] The Secretary General of the United Nations stated in a press release of April 28, 1999:

> The civilian death toll is rising, as is the number of displaced. There is increasing devastation to the country's infrastructure, and huge damage to [its] economy. For example, Mr. Sommarugua [President of the International Committee of

---

1. *Globe and Mail* (Toronto), 23 August 1999.

the Red Cross after visiting Yugoslavia] told me that the destruction of the three bridges in Novi Sad also cut off the fresh water supply to half of that city's population of 90,000 people.[2]

No fewer than 350 cluster bomb attacks were launched against Serb forces (it was later discovered that NATO claims of destruction of Serb tanks and other military installations were unrealistic) and:

> [O]fficially it is acknowledged that between five and ten per cent of the bombs would have failed to detonate, although unofficial estimates put it higher. . . . Although the civilian casualty toll from incidents involving unexploded munitions has dropped from five a day in the first month after the air campaign ended to the present one or two a day Lt. Col. Flanagan [Australian program manager of the United Nations mine action coordinate center in Pristina] said he needed NATO's help to meet the challenge of making Kosovo safe for the population, especially in rural areas, 'Any help we could get from NATO would be appreciated, but at the moment KFOR [Kosovo Protection Force] is not addressing the problem unless there is an emergency humanitarian or operational reason'. He said 'children were being maimed because the cluster bombs looked like toys and were extremely sensitive. If you pick up a cluster bomb it will explode, it is even more dangerous than a mine. Anything can detonate a cluster bomb'. Colonel Flanagan said NATO had supplied the coordinates for the cluster bomb attacks which had helped his teams to trace some of the unexploded bomblets. However, not all the coordinates had proved accurate.[3]

Given the nature of this statement, one is inclined to enquire whether it did not embarrass those participants in the NATO campaign which were parties to Protocol II as amended[4] of the 1990 Conventional Weapons Convention.[5]

---

2. Statement by Secretary-General Kofi Annan on Kosovo Crisis, Press Release SG/SM/6972, Apr. 28, 1999, available at http://www.globalpolicy.org/security/issues/Kosovo334.htm. For a breakdown of the damage done to Yugoslavia's economy, see Ved Nanda, *Legal Implications of NATO's Armed Intervention in Kosovo*, in INTERNATIONAL LAW ACROSS THE SPECTRUM OF CONFLICT: ESSAYS IN HONOUR OF PROFESSOR L.C. GREEN ON THE OCCASION OF HIS EIGHTIETH BIRTHDAY 313, 319 (M. Schmitt ed., 2000)(Vol. 75, US Naval War College International Law Studies).
3. Michael Evans, *NATO Bombs Still Killing Kosovars*, THE TIMES (London), Aug. 16, 1999.
4. Protocol on Prohibitions or Restrictions on the Use of Mines, Booby-Traps and Other Devices, *adopted* May 3, 1996, 35 INTERNATIONAL LEGAL MATERIALS 1206, 1209 (1996).
5. Convention on Prohibitions or Restrictions on the Use of Certain Conventional Weapons Which May be Deemed to be Excessively Injurious or to Have Indiscriminate Effects, *adopted* Oct. 10, 1980, 1342 U.N.T.S. 137, *reprinted in* THE LAWS OF ARMED CONFLICT 179 (D. Schindler and J. Toman eds., 3d ed. 1988). The unamended Protocol II is at 185.

While NATO certainly did not use booby-traps, Colonel Flanagan's description of cluster bombs as "toy-like and attractive to children" brings them very close to the definition of such weapons: "any device or material which is designed, constructed, or adapted to kill or injure, and which functions unexpectedly when a person disturbs or approaches an apparently harmless object or performs an apparently safe act."[6]

Colonel Flanagan also expressed some criticism of NATO's unwillingness to assist in clearing these weapons which again draws attention to the Protocol and its obligation to give notice of a minefield and arrange for its clearance:

1. Without delay after the cessation of active hostilities, all minefields, mined areas, mines, booby-traps and other devices shall be cleared, removed, destroyed. . . .

2. High Contracting Parties and parties to a conflict bear such responsibility with respect to minefields, mined areas, mines, booby-traps and other devices in areas under their control.

3. With respect to minefields, mined areas, mines, booby-traps and other devices laid by a party in areas over which it no longer exercises control, such party shall provide to the party in control of the area . . . to the extent permitted by such party, technical and material assistance necessary to fulfill such responsibility.[7]

For the main part, KFOR and those members of NATO contributing thereto remained in control of most of Kosovo and would appear, at least at the time of Colonel Flanagan's remarks, as not being as cooperative as some of them are obligated to be. Finally, it may be asked whether by using weapons coated in depleted uranium there has not been a breach of the basic principle of customary law that weapons likely to cause unnecessary suffering may not be used, while for parties to Protocol I[8] there would appear to have been also a breach of Article 35, which forbids "methods or means of warfare which are intended *or may be expected*, to cause widespread, long-term and severe damage to the environment" (emphasis added) as such usage must have envisaged.

As has been pointed out, the bombing campaign was not as successful as NATO might have hoped. It extended over seventy-eight days and at no time

---

6. *Id.*, art. 2(4).
7. *Id.*, art. 10.
8. Protocol Additional (I) to the Geneva Conventions of 12 August 1949, and Relating to the Protection of Victims of International Conflicts, Dec. 12, 1977, 1125 U.N.T.S. 3, 16 INTERNATIONAL LEGAL MATERIALS 1391 (1977) [hereinafter Protocol I].

was there any contact between ground troops and no fatalities were suffered by NATO air personnel. Since the aerial campaign was affected by weather conditions as well as the accuracy of the crews, observation of targets was sometimes difficult.[9] While the United States was not a party to Protocol I, both Canada and the United Kingdom were. It is therefore necessary as regards these participants to refer to the relevant Articles of that instrument. It should also be noted that in so far as the United States was concerned it was under the customary law obligation to confine its offensive activities to military and not civilian targets. In accordance with Protocol I:

Article 48 - Basic rule

[T]he Parties to the conflict shall at all times distinguish between the civilian population and combatants and between civilian objects and military objectives and accordingly shall direct their operations only against military objectives.

Article 51 - Protection of the civilian population

1. The civilian population and individual civilians shall enjoy general protection against dangers arising from military operations.

. . . .

3. The civilian population as such, as well as individual civilians, shall not be the object of attack. Acts or threat of violence the primary purpose of which is to spread terror among the civilian population is prohibited.

There has never been any suggestion that NATO operations were in any way directed at causing terror, but NATO never concealed that there was inherent in its policy an intention to create a situation in which the Yugoslav population would be so discomforted as to rise up and overthrow the government seated in Belgrade. This eventually occurred but not as a direct consequence of the bombing campaign.

Article 51 continues:

4. Indiscriminate attacks are prohibited. Indiscriminate attacks are:

   (a) those which are not directed at a specific military objective;

   (b) those which employ a method or means of combat which cannot be directed at a specific military objective; or

---

9. *See, e.g.,* Nanda, *supra* note 2, at 319.

(c) those which are employ a method or means of combat the effects of which cannot be limited as required by this Protocol;

and consequently, in each case, are of a nature to strike military objectives and civilian objectives and civilians or civilian objects without distinction.

5. Among others, the following types of attacks are to be considered as indiscriminate:

(a) an attack by bombardment by any methods or means which treats as a single military objective a number of clearly separated and distinct military objectives located in a city, town, village or other area containing a similar concentration of civilians or civilian objects; and

(b) an attack which may be expected to cause incidental loss of civilian life, injury to civilians, damage to civilian objects, or a combination thereof, which would be excessive[10] in relation to the concrete and direct military advantage anticipated.

Article 52 - General protection of civilian objects

. . . .

2. Attacks shall be limited strictly to military objectives. In so far as objects are concerned, military objectives are limited to those objects which by their nature, location, purpose or use make an effective contribution to military action and whose total or partial destruction, capture or neutralization, in the circumstances ruling at the time, offers a definite military advantage.

3. In case of doubt whether an object which is normally dedicated to civilian purposes . . . is being used to make an effective contribution to military action, it shall be presumed not to be so used.

In the case of the bombing campaign undertaken by NATO, it would often appear, *prima facie*, that the question may also be asked whether the distinction demanded by Protocol I of those States which were parties to it was always respected.

Perhaps one of the clearest instances of acceptance of ethical principles in modern international law is that which governs the punishment of those guilty of war crimes, genocide and crimes against humanity. To the extent that Serbian or Kosovar Albanians committed any of these offenses, they must answer at a trial before the International Criminal Tribunal for the former

---

10. *See, e.g.,* William Fenrick, *The Rule of Proportionality and Protocol I in Conventional Warfare,* 98 MILITARY LAW REVIEW 91 (1982).

Yugoslavia (ICTY) established by the United Nations. The ICTY has no *dies ad quem* and so enjoys jurisdiction until it is declared *functus officio* or there is a clear statement that conflict in the territories of the former Yugoslavia has come to an end. *Prima facie*, members of the NATO forces who may have committed offenses against the law of armed conflict are as amenable to the jurisdiction of the Tribunal as are any other offenders. In fact, the ICTY established a committee to investigate this issue, which, concluded that no further investigation was necessary and no attempt has been made to indict any NATO personnel.[11]

Since the operation was essentially aerial, the ambit subject to the law of armed conflict was somewhat limited. The provision of Protocol I defining grave breaches is almost certainly an expression of the customary law with regard to protection of civilians and so is not confined solely to parties to the Protocol. However, that instrument's language is specific:

3. [T]he following acts shall be regarded as grave breaches of this Protocol, when committed willfully . . . and causing death or serious injury to body or health:

   (a) making the civilian population or individual civilians the object of attack;

   (b) launching an indiscriminate attack affecting the civilian population or civilian objects in the knowledge that such attack will cause excessive loss of life, injury to civilians or danger to civilian objects. . . . [12]

One English newspaper report lends support to the argument that such breaches did occur: "So wild was the bombing that ministers found themselves having to call journalists, make-up girls, hospital staff and even whole villages 'legitimate targets of war', blithely rewriting the Geneva Convention to suit themselves."[13]

There can be no doubt that if the rule of law or ethical standards are to prevail in the future, it is essential that the law concerning war crimes, genocide and crimes against humanity be attached to all individuals, military, political or civilian, and not merely to those against whom "we" are taking action. As has been mentioned a committee established by the ICTY Office of

---

11. Final Report to the Prosecutor by the Committee Established to Review the NATO Bombing Campaign Against the Federal Republic of Yugoslavia, *reprinted* in 39 INTERNATIONAL LEGAL MATERIALS 1257 (2000), and *reprinted* herein as Appendix A [hereinafter Report to the Prosecutor].
12. Protocol I, *supra* note 8, art. 85 (3)(a) and (b).
13. Simon Jenkins, *A Victory for Cowards*, THE TIMES (London), June 11, 1999.

the Prosecutor (OTP) in accordance with Article 18 of its Statute[14] did investigate allegations lodged against NATO. Some of its comments bear reproduction. As regards the legality of the NATO recourse to force without United Nations sanction, the Report states

> [T]he *jus ad bellum* regulates when states may use force and is, for the most part, enshrined in the UN Charter. In general, states may use force in self defence (individual or collective) and for very few other purposes. In particular, the legitimacy of the presumed basis for the NATO bombing campaign, humanitarian intervention, without prior Security Council authorization, is hotly debated. That being said ... the crime related to an unlawful decision to use force is the crime against peace or aggression. While a person convicted of a crime against peace may, potentially, be held criminally responsible for all of the activities causing death, injury or destruction during a conflict, the ICTY does not have jurisdiction over crimes against peace.[15]

Consequently, the Report was confined to examining only allegations that NATO might have committed acts contrary to the *jus in bello*.

In so far as it was alleged that the use of depleted uranium (DU) constituted a breach of the law of armed conflict, the Report stated:

> There is no specific treaty ban on the use of DU projectiles. There is a developing scientific debate and concern expressed regarding the impact of the use of such projectiles and it is possible that, in future, there will be a consensus view in international legal circles that use of such projectiles violate general principles of the law applicable to use of weapons in armed conflict. No such consensus exists at present.... It is acknowledged that the underlying principles of the law of armed conflict such as proportionality are applicable in this context; however it is the committee's view ... based on information available at present, that the OTP should not commence an investigation into use of depleted uranium projectiles by NATO.[16]

A similar hesitancy to condemn the use of cluster bombs is to be found in the Report.

---

14. "The Prosecutor shall initiate investigations *ex officio* or on the basis of information obtained from any source, particularly from Governments, United Nations organs, intergovernmental and non-governmental organizations. The Prosecutor shall assess the information received or obtained and decide whether there is sufficient basis to proceed." S.C. Res. 827 (May 25, 1993), U.N. Doc. S/25704, at 36-40 (1993), *reprinted in* 32 INTERNATIONAL LEGAL MATERIALS 1165, 1192 (1993).
15. Report to the Prosecutor, Appendix A, ¶ 30.
16. *Id.*, ¶ 26.

> There is no specific treaty provision which prohibits or restricts the use of cluster bombs, although, of course, cluster bombs must be in compliance with the general principles applicable to the use of all weapons. Human Rights Watch [which had submitted documentary evidence concerning alleged NATO offences] has condemned the use of cluster bombs alleging that the high 'dud' or failure rate of the submunitions (bomblets) contained inside cluster bombs converts these submunitions into antipersonnel landmines which it asserts, are now prohibited under customary international law. Whether antipersonnel landmines are prohibited under current customary international law is debatable, although there is a strong trend in that direction. There is, however, no general legal consensus that cluster bombs are, in legal terms, equivalent to antipersonnel landmines . . . . It is the opinion of the committee, based on information presently available, that the OTP should not commence an investigation into use of cluster bombs as such by NATO.[17]

While it was hesitant to condemn the use of particular weaponry, the committee did make some general comments concerning legal issues relating to target selection. Here we may detect some hints of a commander's responsibility to have concern for ethical principles.

> [I]n combat, military commanders are required a) to direct their operations against military objectives, and b) when directing their operations against military objectives, to ensure that the losses to the civilian population and the damage to civilian property are not disproportionate to the concrete and direct military advantage anticipated. Attacks which are not directed against military objectives (particularly attacks directed against the civilian population) and attacks which cause disproportionate civilian casualties or civilian property damage may constitute the *actus reus* for the offence under Article 3 of the ICTY Statute.[18] The *mens rea* for the offence is intention or recklessness, not simple negligence. In determining whether or not the *mens rea* requirement has been met, it should be borne in mind that commanders deciding on an attack have duties:
>
> > (a) to do everything practicable to verify that the objectives to be attacked are military objectives,
> >
> > (b) to take all practicable precautions in the choice of methods and means of warfare with a view to avoiding or, in any event to minimizing incidental civilian casualties or civilian property damage, and

---

17. *Id.*, ¶ 27.
18. Concerning violations of the laws or customs of war.

(c) to refrain from launching attacks which may be expected to cause disproportionate civilian casualties or civilian property damage.

One of the principles underlying international humanitarian law, constituting an expression of high ethical standards, is the principle of distinction, which obligates military commanders to distinguish between military objectives and civilian persons or objects. The practical application of this principle is effectively encapsulated in Article 57 of Protocol I which, in part, obligates those who plan or decide upon an attack to 'do everything feasible to verify that the objectives to be attacked are neither civilians nor civilian objects.' The obligation to do everything feasible is high but not absolute. A military commander must set up an effective intelligence gathering system to collect and evaluate information concerning potential targets. The commander must also direct his forces to use available technical means to properly identify targets during operations. Both the commander and the aircrew actually engaged in operations must have some range of discretion to determine which available resources shall be used and how they shall be used. Further, a determination that inadequate efforts have been made to distinguish between military objectives and civilians or civilian objects should not necessarily focus exclusively on a specific incident. If precautionary measures have worked adequately in a very high percentage of cases then the fact they have not worked well in a small number of cases does not necessarily mean they are generally inadequate.[19]

Once again, it would seem that the committee was unwilling to find that NATO might in fact have breached the law, even though it might be argued that the decision not to suffer casualties and to fly beyond the range of anti-aircraft artillery militated towards ineffective targeting, especially in cloudy weather. Moreover, the number of incidents listed in the Report to the prosecutor[20] involving civilian casualties, some of which were quite heavy, might suggest that the accuracy of targeting was inadequate in quite a large number of cases.[21]

---

19. Report to the Prosecutor, Appendix A, ¶¶ 28–9.
20. See id., ¶¶ 9 and 53.
21. See for example, id., ¶¶ 58–70, dealing with attacks on a civilian train and a convoy of Albanian refugees.

The Report to the Prosecutor went into some detail as to what might be defined as a military objective,[22] but once again fails to be dogmatic as to the policy adopted by NATO. Perhaps more important in so far as the future is concerned is its comments on proportionality, a concept that owes its origins to ethical standards:

> 48. The main problem with the principle of proportionality is not whether or not it exists but what it means and how it is to be applied. It is relatively simple to state that there must be an acceptable relation between the legitimate destructive effect and undesirable collateral effect. For example, bombing a refugee camp is obviously prohibited if its only military significance is that people in the camp are knitting socks for soldiers. [Is the same true if they are collecting aluminum pots to be converted into aircraft or munitions?] Conversely, an air strike on an ammunition dump should not be prohibited merely because a farmer is ploughing a field in the area. Unfortunately, most of the applications of the principle of proportionality are not quite so clear cut. It is much easier to formulate the principle of proportionality in general terms than it is to apply it to a particular set of circumstances because the comparison is often between unlike quantities and values. One cannot easily assess the value of innocent human lives as opposed to capturing a particular military objective.
>
> 49. The questions which remains unsolved once one decides to apply the principle of proportionality include the following:
>
> (a) What are the relative values to be assigned to the military advantage gained and the injury to non-combatants and or the damage to civilian objects?
>
> (b) What do you include or exclude in totaling your sums?
>
> (c) What is the standard of measurement in time or space? and
>
> (d) To what extent is a military commander obligated to expose his own forces to danger in order to limit civilian casualties or damage to civilian objects? [Once again, an ethical question for said commander]
>
> 50. The answers to these questions are not simple. It may be necessary to resolve them on a case by case basis, and the answers may differ depending on the background and values of the decision maker. It is unlikely that a human rights lawyer and an experienced combat commander would assign the same relative values to military advantage and to injury to noncombatants. Further, it is unlikely that military commanders with different doctrinal backgrounds and

---

22. See id., ¶¶ 35–47.

differing degrees of combat experience or national military histories would always agree in close cases. It is suggested that the determination of relative values must be that of the *'reasonable military commander'*.[23] Although there will be room for argument in close cases, there will be many cases where reasonable military commanders will agree that the injury to noncombatants or the damage to civilian objects was clearly disproportionate to the military advantage gained.[24]

Despite the somewhat confident expression to be found in this last sentence, the entire approach adopted in the Report to the Prosecutor emphasizes how difficult it will always be to reach an acceptable common understanding of what constitutes ethical standards of behavior.

City planners rarely pay heed to the possibility of future warfare. Military objectives are often located in intensely populated areas and fighting occasionally occurs in such areas, Civilians present within or near military objectives must, however, be taken into account in the proportionality equation even if a party to the conflict has failed to exercise its obligation to remove them.[25]

In the *Kupreskic* case the ICTY addressed the issue of proportionality as follows:

> 526. As an example of the way in which the Martens clause[26] may be utilised, regard might be had to considerations such as the cumulative effect of attacks on military objectives causing incidental damage to civilians. In other words, it may happen that single attacks on military objectives causing incidental damage to civilians, although they may raise doubts as to their lawfulness, nevertheless do not appear on their face to fall foul *per se* of the loose prescriptions of Articles 57 and 58[27] (or of the corresponding customary rules). However, in case of repeated attacks, all or most of them falling within the grey area between indisputable legality and unlawfulness, it might be warranted to conclude that they may not be in keeping with international law. Indeed, this pattern of military conduct may turn out to jeopardise

---

23. Emphasis added.
24. Report to the Prosecutor, Appendix A.
25. *Id.*, ¶ 51
26. "[I]n cases not included in the Regulation ... the inhabitants and the belligerents remain under the protection and the rule of the principles of the law of nations, *as they result from the usages established among civilized peoples, from the laws of humanity and the dictates of the public conscience."* Convention (IV) Respecting the Laws and Customs of War on Land, Oct. 18, 1907, *in* THE LAWS OF ARMED CONFLICT, *supra* note 5, at 70 (emphasis added).
27. Protocol I, *supra* note 8, regarding "Precautionary Measures."

excessively the lives and assets of civilians, contrary to the demands of humanity.'[28]

This formulation ... can be regarded as a progressive statement of the applicable law with regard to the obligation to protect civilians. Its practical import, is somewhat ambiguous and its application far from clear. It is the committee's view where individual (and legitimate) attacks on military objectives are concerned, the mere *cumulation* of such instances, all of which are deemed to have been lawful, cannot *ipso facto* be said to amount to a crime. The committee understands the above formulation, instead, to refer to an *overall* assessment of the totality of civilian victims as against the goals of the military campaign....

54. During the bombing campaign, NATO aircraft flew 38,400 sorties, including 10,484 strike sorties. During these sorties 23,614 munitions were released.... [and] it appears that approximately 500 civilians were killed during the campaign. These figures do not indicate that NATO may have conducted a campaign aimed at causing substantial civilian casualties either directly or incidentally.

55. The choice of targets by NATO includes some loosely defined categories such as military-industrial infrastructure and government ministries and some potential problem categories such as media and refineries. All targets must meet the criteria for military objectives. If they do not do so, they are unlawful. A general label is insufficient. The targeted components of the military-industrial infrastructure and of government ministries must make an effective contribution to military action and their total or partial destruction must offer a definite military advantage in the circumstances ruling at the time. Refineries are certainly traditional military objectives but tradition is not enough and due regard must be paid to environmental damage if they are attacked. The media as such is not a traditional target category.... As a bottom line, civilians, civilian objects and civilian morale as such are not legitimate military objectives. The media does have an effect on civilian morale. If that effect is merely to foster support for the war effort, the media is not a legitimate military objective. If the media is sued to incite crimes ... it can become a legitimate military objective. If the media is the nerve system that keeps a war-monger in power and thus perpetuates the war effort, it may fall within the definition of a legitimate military objective. As a general statement, in the particular incidents reviewed by the committee, it is the view of the committee that NATO was attempting to attack objects it perceived to be legitimate military objectives.

---

28. Prosecutor v. Kupreskic et al., Judgement, I.C.T.Y. No. IT-95-16-T, Jan. 14, 2000, ¶ 542.

56. The committee agrees there is nothing inherently unlawful about flying above the height which can be reached by enemy air defences. However, NATO air commanders have a duty to take practicable measures to distinguish military objectives from civilians or civilian objectives. The 15,000 feet minimum altitude adopted for part of the campaign may have meant the target could not be verified with the naked eye. However, it appears that with the use of modern technology, the obligation to distinguish was effectively carried out in the vast majority of cases during the bombing campaign.

57. In the course of its review, the committee did not come across any incident which, in its opinion, required investigation by the OTP. . . .

The committee examined five specific incidents of attacks the legality of which might have been doubtful, but in each case came to the conclusion that there was no reason to refer the matter to the Prosecutor. One is left with a somewhat uncomfortable feeling with the committee's statement in its penultimate paragraph:

[T]he committee has not assessed any particular incidents as justifying the commencement of an investigation by the OTP. NATO has admitted that mistakes did occur during the bombing campaign; errors of judgment may also have occurred. Selection of certain objectives for attack may be subject to legal debate. On the basis of the information received, however, the committee is of the opinion that neither an in-depth investigation related to the bombing campaign as a whole nor investigations related to specific incidents are justified. In all cases, either the law is not sufficiently clear or investigations are unlikely to result in the acquisition of sufficient evidence to substantiate charges against high level accused or against lower accused for particularly heinous offences.[29]

It may well be that, noting all the efforts to define proportionality and to assess the role of ethical considerations, one comes to the conclusion that the findings of the committee might be correct. However, it is submitted that one cannot but feel that the report might have contributed more to vindicating the rule of law and recognizing the significance of ethical standards as equally operative for all parties, had it recommended to the Prosecutor the possibility of referring to the ICTY some of the issues it examined. The Tribunal might not in all cases have agreed with individual recommendations, particularly in view of the fact in some instances the Report to the Prosecutor itself refers to a "trend

---

29. Report to the Prosecutor, Appendix A, ¶ 90.

developing," or to particular cases being controversial or—clearly an issue for judicial determination—that in some instances "the law is not sufficiently clear."

The Serbs, particularly as a result of pressure from Russia, its traditional ally, and in face of the threat by NATO that a land offensive would be launched, finally accepted terms almost identical with those rejected at Rambouillet prior to the commencement of the bombing campaign. Among the terms accepted was an arrangement for Kosovo to be temporarily administered by an international body supported by some military and police personnel brought in from Yugoslavia, thus preserving that State's concern with its national sovereignty. Kosovo was divided into areas of administration with civil affairs to some extent controlled by the United Nations Mission in Kosovo (UNMIK). Since it was recognized that returning Kosovar Albanians, supported by the KLA, might pursue a policy of revenge against the remaining Serb population, it was agreed that the KLA would be disarmed and that KFOR would ensure the safety of the Serbs. It was not long before it became clear that the KLA was not going to be overly cooperative regarding the surrender of arms and KFOR not excessively effective in preventing attacks on the Serbs.

Further, KLA leaders made it clear that they intended to regard themselves as an interim government determined on secession, whatever the view of NATO or KFOR. The French defense minister commented on this state of affairs:

> [T]here's an unseemly scramble for power, influence and wealth within the KLA.... The Kosovars don't understand that we're here not to support them but to support human rights for all and ensure political power is held to account. On the other hand, to expect the KLA to willingly disband when they see a continued threat from paramilitaries under effective protection by French and Russian troops [in their respective administrative areas], and to refuse to recognize provisional mayors when UNMIK hasn't assigned a single municipal administrator, is just farcical.[30]

This seems to overlook that, officially at least, it was never part of NATO's policy to assist the Kosovars in doing anything to question or endanger Yugoslavia's sovereignty over the area. As the occupation by KFOR continued, it became clear that, on paper at least, the KLA and its *soi disant* political leadership were proving a little more cooperative, although KFOR's protective activities became more and more essential for the Serb population.

---

30. THE TIMES (London), Aug. 14, 1999.

The growing willingness to allow the KLA—originally denounced as a gang of terrorists—to push its political aims and failure to prevent attacks upon the local Serbs raise questions as to the extent to which NATO was sustaining its contention that its intervention was ethical based on the needs to protect humanitarian principles. In fact, the ethical and humanitarian character of NATO's policy became even more questionable when it reneged somewhat on its promises to assist in the rehabilitation and rebuilding of Yugoslavia, unless the then government was replaced by one that was more "democratic." It is true that this has now ensued, but this fact does not lend support to the idealistic grounds on which NATO claims to have acted originally.

In assessing the validity of the NATO bombing campaign from both legal and ethical standpoints, it becomes necessary to ask whether the campaign achieved its purpose. That is to say, whatever its legality might have been, was the action justified because of what was ultimately achieved? It is clear from the above comments, and in the light of the continuing trouble in Kosovo and the threats of conflict spreading in the area, that the writer is not happy with either the legal or ethical grounds on which NATO claimed to be acting. Since similar situations denying human rights in the most obscene manner might recur, it is clearly necessary to consider what, if any, process can be introduced to prevent similar unilateral and questionable punitive or enforcement action in the future. Perhaps this might be achieved by adopting a policy somewhat like the following:

> When a government is unwilling or unable to protect, or persistently infringes the human rights of large segments of its population, or the government structure has so disintegrated that law and order have virtually ceased to exist, it may then well be time for the United Nations to take over the administration until such time as normal conditions have been restored. . . . To some extent this is already happening in Bosnia and Kosovo. . . . However it would perhaps be more desirable that this be done not on an *ad hoc* basis—nor by a group of states assuming such authority unto itself—but on the basis of a permanent United Nations body made up of trained personnel from a variety of countries. . . . The members of such administrative or governing commissions should not be drawn from nationals of the great powers among whom, despite the end of the cold war, political rivalries and maneuvering is still likely to take place.[31]

---

31. *See* Leslie Green, 23rd Annual Conference of the Canadian Council on International Law, 1994 CANADIAN COUNCIL ON INTERNATIONAL LAW PROCEEDINGS 6, 26; 26th Annual Conference of the Canadian Council on International Law, 1997 CANADIAN COUNCIL ON INTERNATIONAL LAW PROCEEDINGS 31, 37.

If such a policy were adopted, there might be less doubt as to the legal or ethical basis for the intervention and a more substantial foundation for contending that it is in accordance with the rule of law and the maintenance of ethical principles.

Commentary

David Graham

Professor Stein and Judge Pocar have done well in addressing the issue of coalition warfare and the effect that Protocol I has had on the ability of coalition partners to engage in effective operations. Central to this discussion, of course, has been the fact that the United States—a principal participant in essentially every major coalition enterprise undertaken since the coming into force of Protocol I—is not a party to the Protocol. I would hasten to add that there is no indication that the United States intends to become a party to this instrument at any time in the foreseeable future. Given this fact, I would like to offer my own thoughts concerning three specific questions and in so doing also comment on a number of the observations that have been made.

Let us turn to the first question. Since certain members of NATO are contracting parties to Protocol I, whereas the United States and some others are not, what does this signify in terms of the interoperability of coalition forces like NATO's? Upon the coming into force of Protocol I and the concomitant decision of the United States not to become a party, I can well remember the substantial hand-wringing that occurred. This action on the part of the United States sounded the death knell of the NATO Alliance, it was said. Others believed this US decision, for all intents and purposes, served to negate its Article V collective defense commitment under the North Atlantic Treaty. Why? Because, how would it be possible for the United States to engage in combat operations with its NATO allies absent an obligation to comply fully with the provisions of Protocol I? It would be impossible to mount effective NATO coalition operations when the participating States were bound by different law of armed conflict standards. The means and methods by which warfare could be conducted would vary too substantially. It would be impossible to achieve consensus even upon a set of command rules of engagement (ROE). In brief, the coalition sky was falling and it was all the result of the US decision to reject Protocol I.

What has become of these dire predictions? Time and experience have shown these concerns to have fallen into the category of "much ado about nothing." The fact that the United States is not a party to Protocol I has had no adverse effect on the ability of the United States and its coalition partners to engage in numerous effective military operations. There are three principal reasons for this. First, shortly after the United States announced its decision not to become a party to Protocol I—and prior to the time that a number of other NATO States did so—law of armed conflict experts from the United States and several NATO countries conducted a series of meetings to discuss various provisions of the Protocol. As a result of these meetings, a common understanding was reached regarding the manner in which certain of the more vague, subjective, and ill-defined articles would be interpreted and applied. (A number of these agreed interpretations were later reflected in several of the statements of understanding and reservations made by NATO members when they eventually became parties to Protocol I.) These common understandings have assisted the United States and its NATO partners in achieving a broad consensus regarding the law of armed conflict requirements applicable to coalition operations.

Coupled with these earlier meetings between US and NATO law of armed conflict experts is the fact that there has been extensive cooperation between the United States, key NATO allies, and several other countries in the updating of their respective law of war manuals. These countries have included, at various times, Australia, Canada, the United Kingdom, New Zealand, Denmark, and Israel. Again, numerous provisions of Protocol I have been discussed, in detail, and common approaches toward the manner in which these provisions would be applied during military operations have been developed. This process has served to foster a growing consensus among the States concerned that no substantive differences regarding the law of armed conflict applicable to coalition operations currently exist.

The third and perhaps most basic reason why the US decision not to become a party to Protocol I has not adversely affected its ability to engage in effective coalition operations revolves around the process through which coalition ROE are drafted, disseminated, and trained. Of primary importance is the fact that coalition military activities are conducted in accordance with mutually agreed ROE, which are largely unaffected by academic/diplomatic disagreements over nuanced interpretations of various provisions of Protocol I.

This is not to say that the drafting of coalition ROE is not often a time consuming, frustrating process. This was certainly true in the cases of SFOR (the Stabilization Force in Bosnia-Herzegovina) and KFOR (the Kosovo International Secutity Force), and was true as well during Operation Allied Force. Of note, however, is the fact that the major ROE issues that arose in the context of these operations—such as those related to targeting—did not result from differing interpretations regarding the law of armed conflict. Invariably, any delay in achieving ROE consensus resulted largely from a highly politicized decision making process driven by a desire on the part of the participating governments to minimize casualties—both military and civilian. This was not a desire mandated by law of armed conflict considerations, but by the perceived need to retain the very thin veneer of public and political support for the operation itself. In a similar vein, Professor Stein has noted that, though KFOR ROE were unquestionably restrictive in nature, these restrictions were the result of domestic law, rather than law of armed conflict concerns. In brief, coalition ROE are the product of a negotiated consensus that reflects a common understanding of coalition law of armed conflict requirements, and then disseminated to and trained on by coalition forces.

It is for these reasons that the US decision not to become a party to Protocol I has had no adverse effect on the interoperability capabilities of coalition forces. Again, experience has shown that when concerns that might affect interoperability do surface, these are driven by political or domestic law considerations, rather than disagreements over the meaning or requirements of specific international law requirements. In such cases, the coalition ROE are drafted and the forces of the participating countries deployed in such a way that such concerns are resolved and the operational capabilities of the coalition are not diminished.

Can there be differing legal standards for various members of a given coalition? This is a question that Professor Stein and Judge Pocar appeared to struggle with, for good reason, in order to arrive at a workable answer. A textbook treaty law response would most likely render effective coalition warfare exceptionally difficult to wage. Allow me to explain what I mean by this statement. The question posed immediately begs another. To what does the term "legal standards" refer in this context? That is, does there exist an international consensus as to the nature of the "legal standards" applicable to a coalition as a whole, or to individual member States of a coalition, when those States are engaged in military operations?

Commentary

This question might be answered in one of two ways. First, the textbook approach: within a coalition, the actions of each member State must be dictated by the various international conventions to which it is a party, as well as by the statements of understanding and reservations made by this State to each of these conventions. Under this approach it would seem to follow that a coalition as a whole, when developing its operations plan, must take into account each convention to which any of its members are parties, as well as the statements of understanding and reservations made by these individual members. There is little doubt that such an approach would prove to be exceptionally difficult to apply in a real-world environment. Rather than establishing clear-cut "legal standards" for a coalition as a whole, it would subject the coalition to a potentially vast array of varying interpretations of what these standards should be. Individual coalition members would be forced to function under diverse standards, a fact that would be certain to adversely affect the operational capabilities of the coalition.

In view of these inherent difficulties, might this issue be approached in a more practical way? I would submit that if there are to be uniform legal standards to which a coalition as a whole is to be held, these must be customary law of armed conflict standards. This is a workable approach—a 90% solution, if you will. Adherence to the customary law of armed conflict, of which the four 1949 Geneva Conventions are an integral part, would ensure a disciplined, effective, and lawful coalition operation. Coalition ROE could be drafted accordingly. If within a coalition there arise those situations in which individual members feel as if they are restrained from employing certain means or methods of warfare, these could be dealt with on a case-by-case basis. However, experience has shown that these situations would be few in number, and "work-arounds" could be effected. This is a common sense, legally sustainable approach toward ensuring that all coalition members, as well as the international community, fully understand the law of armed conflict applicable to coalition operations.

There are also other elements of this issue that merit comment. Professor Stein has suggested in seeking to formulate a workable response to this question that perhaps the law of armed conflict standards applicable to coalition operations may be found, in part, in the UN Secretary-General's 6 August 1999 guidance on the "Observance by United Nations forces of international humanitarian law."[1] He notes a number of problems associated with this approach, but fails to speak to the principal shortcomings of this document. It is poorly drafted and incomplete, and in a number of instances misleading and inaccurate. It does nothing to advance the development and effective implementation of the law of armed conflict. If one is searching for coalition standards, they will not be found in this guidance.

On another matter raised by Professor Stein in connection with his discussion of coalition standards, I find myself in complete agreement. He points out the potential for confusion that has resulted from what he refers to as "the re-naming" of the law of war, which has generally been referred to in the post-Charter era as the law of armed conflict. By referring to the law of armed conflict as international humanitarian law, he notes that the distinction between "humanitarian" and "human rights" law has been blurred. I would go further. The apparent attempt to make the law of armed conflict a kinder, more gentle form of jurisprudence has generated a significant degree of confusion in the minds of many.

What does the term "international humanitarian law" actually mean? Even a cursory review of this issue clearly reflects the fact that the term means different things to different people. In discussions with articulate, well-informed individuals who insist upon using this term, I have listened to sometimes passionate explanations of the term and the necessity for its use. Disturbingly, however, these explanations often differ and there appears to be no consensus as to the norms and principles embraced under this terminological umbrella. To some, it is just another "updated" name for the law of armed conflict, indicative of the "humanitarian" emphasis now placed on the regulation of armed conflict. To others it reflects the fact that the body of law applicable to armed conflict now contains many, but not all, of the elements of human rights law. There are also those who view international humanitarian law as the single embodiment of all of the law of armed conflict and human rights law.

How did we reach this point? When was the vote taken as to whether such a name change should occur? I cannot think of a single individual charged with the responsibility of giving real-world advice to military commanders on law of armed conflict issues that would have cast an affirmative vote for embracing a term that would result in blurring the legal obligations for which a commander and his staff would be held accountable in an operational environment. The use of a term that confuses and carries with it such imprecision in an area of the law that imposes so many responsibilities and often calls for life and death decisions, does a disservice to those who constantly strive to comply with this law. I'll continue to provide advice on the law of armed conflict. I know what it is and, even more importantly, what it is not.

To what extent is Protocol I customary international law, such that it may be binding on non-parties? Perhaps this question might be more accurately articulated: "can't we simply declare Protocol I, in its entirety, to be reflective of customary international law and thus declare its provisions to be binding on the United States, despite the fact that the United States has chosen not to become a party to the Protocol?" To this question, Professor Stein has provided an answer. He has expressed substantial doubt as to whether all of the provisions of Protocol I have become "intransgressible" principles of customary international law. He notes specifically that it is "very doubtful" whether many of the undefined provisions of Protocol I can be declared to be of such a nature, specifically those that were of principal concern during the conduct of Operation Allied Force.

In illustrating this point, Professor Stein refers to terms such as "military significance," "definite military advantage," "effective contribution to military action," and "indiscriminate attacks" and notes that they are not defined even by way of non-exhaustive examples. Moreover, he observes, even among those States that have become parties to Protocol I, a number have issued varying statements of understanding regarding their individual interpretations of the meaning of these terms. Given these facts, he concludes that it may be correct to state that the fundamental principles of the law of armed conflict contained within Protocol I and repeatedly referenced by the International Court of Justice—that is, the basic distinction between civilians and combatants, the prohibition against directly attacking civilians, and the rule of proportionality—are customary law of armed conflict concepts. However, he notes, "[i]t is very doubtful whether the same can be said about all of the other provisions of Protocol I. . . . " I am in complete agreement with Professor Stein on that point.

Judge Pocar, on the other hand, would appear to be much more supportive of the view that Protocol I, as a whole, is making steady progress toward becoming customary international law. He observes that in looking at the factors to be considered in making customary law determinations, "customary international humanitarian law should not be determined on the sole basis of the practice of the States that have *not* ratified the Protocol."[2] In making this statement, Judge Pocar acknowledges, in essence, the primary role played by State practice in the formulation of customary international law. Of this, there can be no doubt. Every criterion set forth for the purpose of making customary law determinations has, at its core, the concept of State practice. The primacy of this concept has been reaffirmed repeatedly by various international tribunals. To this Judge Pocar would seem to say that he agrees that

---

2. See Judge Pocar's paper in this volume (emphasis added).

State practice is the key component of any customary law determination, but that in applying this principle one must not look exclusively at the practice of those States that have chosen to challenge the customary law nature of numerous provisions of Protocol I. Fair enough. Let us take a look at those States that are parties to Protocol I.

I have never been impressed by the number of States that have, over the years, become parties to Protocol I. It is my view that the long list of signatories of this document has very little to do with State practice in the area of the law of armed conflict. The vast majority of the signatories of Protocol I are at best interested observers—bystanders, if you will—when it comes to the actual application of the law of armed conflict in combat situations. These States have not applied the provisions of Protocol I on the battlefield or, for the most part, during any form of military operation. In sum, they have not "practiced" the various provisions of Protocol I. (The same is true of the International Committee of the Red Cross (ICRC) and a host of other non-governmental organizations (NGOs).) As a result, the fact that these States are parties to Protocol I means very little when one examines the practice of such States in the context of determining whether the Protocol constitutes customary international law.

In terms of tangible State practice that substantively affects the evolution of Protocol I as customary law, I have but one thing to say: "show me the players." Not the signatories; not the observers; not the ICRC or the NGOs; but rather "show me the players." Which States in the international community actually practice or apply law of armed conflict principles on an ongoing basis in a real-world environment? The answer is very few—of which the United States is one. And the United States as a consistent law of armed conflict practitioner has just as consistently expressed the view that Protocol I, as a whole, does not reflect customary international law.

One might ask "what about those States, though relatively few in number, that have signed Protocol I and have practiced or applied the law of armed conflict in a series of military operations since the times of their signatures? Surely their status as parties to Protocol I evidences a growing acceptance of its provisions as customary law?" Again, another fair observation. However, such a premise fails to hold up under scrutiny. Examine, if you will, the States in issue. Essentially each of these States has qualified its ratification of Protocol I with a series of both reservations and statements of understanding dealing with various articles of the Protocol. Search as you may, you will find no concordant and continuous State practice regarding the application of numerous provisions of Protocol I—even among that limited number of States that are both parties and players.

Judge Pocar also notes that special importance should be attached to the case law of international tribunals, in terms of evaluating the assessment of such courts as to whether certain treaty provisions have become customary international law. Leaving aside the fact, however, that customary law is not the primary source of international law upon which international tribunals base their decisions, what have such courts looked for when they turn to an examination of whether a particular concept has become a binding principle of customary international law? Once again, these courts have sought to find the existence of concordant and continuous State practice associated with the concept in issue, and the acceptance of or acquiescence in the concept by the State(s) to which the court is being asked to apply this principle. As I have indicated previously, there exists no concordant and continuous State practice with respect to the applicability of Protocol I—and the United States has neither accepted or acquiesced in the view that the Protocol, as a whole, reflects customary international law. I do not believe that any international tribunal would find the more controversial and ill-defined articles of Protocol I to be binding customary law.

Let me speak, very briefly, as well, to Judge Pocar's summary of an opinion of a Trial Chamber of the ICTY that was dealing with law of armed conflict obligations under Articles 57 and 58 of Protocol I. The Court found that "when a rule of international humanitarian law is somewhat imprecise, it must be defined with reference to the laws of humanity and dictates of public conscience espoused in the celebrated 'Martens Clause', which is, itself, customary law." Here, I would simply call your attention to the fact that the "laws of humanity" and "the dictates of public conscience" are but the second and third components of the Martens Clause. The first, omitted component refers to the "usages established among civilized peoples", that is, customary law as established by State practice. The omission of any reference to this aspect of the Martens Clause, even if inadvertent, is certainly a significant one when the Martens Clause has been invoked to "define" the "imprecision" of certain Protocol I provisions.

I'll conclude my comments by leaving you with a quote from Judge Pocar's excellent paper, a quote that very cogently summarizes the issue of whether Protocol I, as a whole, might rightly be viewed as customary international law. Judge Pocar states:

While most of Protocol I can undoubtedly be regarded as essentially reflecting customary international law, there are areas where this conclusion is subject to debate for two reasons. First, Protocol I clearly sets forth new rules. Second, the specificity of Protocol I's provisions add new elements to principles that, while they are well established in customary law, leave margins of discretion to belligerent States. Belligerent States are then free to argue that such provisions will limit or may limit discretion if they are given certain interpretations. The scope and impact of these additions is therefore controversial and may be the basis of the hesitations of some States to ratify Protocol I.[3]

To this, I can add only, "Well said."

---

3. See Judge Pocar's paper, *supra*, at 347.

Discussion

Can a Coalition Member Be Held Responsible for the Actions of Other Members?

Ruth Wedgwood:
I have a question for Professor Stein on your approach to the problem of the potential responsibility of one coalition member for the actions of other coalition members. This is probably a statement against interest because I'm not sure this is a good line of argument for the United States. Given the manner in which the idea of command responsibility has now been liberalized to include not only direct commanders in a wiring diagram but also responsibility for actors who may be under the effective control of a commander (I have in mind here the *Blaskic* case[1] where the fact that actions may have been taken by a paramilitary was not enough to exculpate Blaskic and indeed the extension of command responsibility to a broad range of civilian officials), don't you think there is some potential liability (I suppose we shall see in the International Court of Justice) by individual coalition members for the actions of others which they might indeed have been able to stop politically?

Torsten Stein:
Well, there might be. I take a three-stage approach. Where you have an international organization, States cannot hide behind the organization and say "we will not be responsible because it's the organization that's acting, not us." The organization has no penny to pay. You cannot say "well, this was something where the organization as such acted *ultra vires*, so we are not responsible." But if you have a situation like Operation Allied Force where you say NATO is not the "international tin council," then you can't use all those rules and say NATO is responsible. You have a group of individual nations. They agree to do something together, and now they are responsible. It would make

---
1. Prosecutor v. Blaskic, Judgement, I.C.T.Y. No. IT-95-14-T, Mar. 3, 2000.

sense. Also, for political reasons, let not the one who did it stand alone in the rain because the others were not in a position to do it. I don't see a clear rule in international law that says because you are all acting together, we can just choose one out of the coalition. There are little examples for that I think. That would not be a bad rule.

Ruth Wedgwood:

I would simply issue a note of caution. There are even arguments being made that UN peacekeepers should be responsible for not having prevented the Serbs from acting out. So the command responsibility may be going horizontal as well as vertical and therefore one should be careful.

Wolff H. von Heinegg:

When it comes to NATO operations there are a variety of different instruments in force for the member States of the coalition, but it's never NATO to whom it can be attributed. It's always the national States to whom a possible violation can be attributed. Politically there may be a problem. So what the NATO countries should do, rather than having a variety of rules of engagement (even though they are standardized), they should at least try to find a common denominator as regards their different legal obligations.

Torsten Stein:

We agree that in any given coalition there can be different legal standards, and if there was no pre-existing legal obligation then one will not be held liable even for the actions of coalition partners. But it would be an awkward case indeed if one asked a State to be in the coalition primarily because that State had not ratified certain conventions, such as the one on blinding laser weapons.

The United States and Protocol I

Yves Sandoz:

Has the United States de facto recognized Protocol I? If not, are there concerns remaining that prevent the United States from ratifying Protocol I?

David Graham:

I'll answer your second question first. Yes, I think there are still concerns that we have with specific provisions to Protocol I, and I won't go through those specific concerns. I think those have appeared in the public domain on a number of different occasions. Those concerns are essentially of an operational nature.

I think there are inartfully drafted and very subjective provisions of Protocol I. Provisions that lend themselves to subjective judgments and would place commanders in a very tenuous position on the battlefield and subject to second-guessing. Just as various parties of Protocol I have expressed various interpretations of what those provisions mean in the form of statements of understanding and reservations, we have reservations with respect to whether they could ever be applied in an objective manner. I think that includes much of Protocol I given the fact that it was based on compromise and was very inartfully drafted. Those are the types of provisions that we still have reservations about because we think that it places commanders in situations that subject those commanders to subjective judgments. We can't give them clear guidance with respect to what those provisions mean.

As I said, we have met with coalition partners. We have agreed as to how we would interpret those provisions (in terms of developing consensus rules of engagement), how we would apply the use of force, and how we would not apply the use of force. But that doesn't mean that we still do not have serious reservations about some of the provisions of Protocol I.

Now with respect to your first question, I do not think that we are going to be the position of violating Protocol I because the rules of engagement that we come up with in a coalition environment will essentially reflect the interpretations that our coalition partners have with respect to the law of armed conflict. I don't see any commander that would knowingly force a coalition partner into a violation of Protocol I; knowing what governmental limitations might have been placed on that coalition partner by their capitals. I don't see that situation as occurring.

The Status of Protocol I As Customary International Law

Fausto Pocar:

I would like to clarify my remarks regarding the status of Protocol I as customary international law. I didn't say that as a whole the Protocol is becoming or is customary law. I said that there is a trend towards recognition of the general value of Protocol I as evidenced by the increasing number of ratifications and some case law in international tribunals. However, I also said that the State practice is still showing areas in which this is not true, and I referred to major actors in international relations. I maintain one should take into account also the State practice of the States that have ratified the Protocol and not only the non-ratifying States. Neither did I say that the practice of the ICTY is determinative. I only referred to arguments made by many scholars—including scholars in this room like Professor Greenwood—that referred to international case law as having been seen later on as determinative in debates, but this is not necessarily always the case. When I referred to the increase in number of State parties, I had in mind major actors as well because one of the States that has ratified Protocol I as recently as 1998 is the United Kingdom.

Leslie Green:

I only want to touch on the point of the number of ratifications. True, from the point of view of classical doctrine, there would have been a general attitude that perhaps 159 ratifications amounts to at least general international law. But when I look at those 159 ratifications, I'm not very concerned as to what Nepal thinks about the law of armed conflict nor what Iceland thinks. (I'm fascinated by the thought that Iceland recently signed a treaty of non-aggression and peace with Nepal. Somehow or another it doesn't sound very practical.) I'm much more concerned with the fact, not that the United Kingdom has ratified, but that the United States, China, and Israel have not ratified. What we have to count are those who are the contributors. If I'm looking at the law this evening, I don't care whether Switzerland has ratified a law of the sea convention. The same thing applies here. Who are the actors? If a number of senior actors don't play, then we can't call it general or universal international law.

Reprisals

Adam Roberts:

This is a question particularly directed at Judge Pocar and Colonel Graham. It touches on whether there may be a difference of emphasis between them regarding the issue of reprisals. In his paper, Judge Pocar referred to the problem of reprisals very briefly. Colonel Graham was quite right to suggest that the reservations that a number of States—and not only NATO member States but at least one other State—have made to Protocol I suggest that there is unease on this issue of reprisal and a desire to leave some room open for reprisals as a means of enforcing observance of the laws of armed conflict. This is an issue which can certainly arise in coalition warfare as evidenced in the 1991 Gulf operations where the senior partner in the operation was the United States. The United States felt an obligation to make clear that it would do something if the other side violated fundamental norms, as Secretary of State James Baker communicated to Tariq Aziz on 9 January in Geneva with respect to the use of weapons of mass destruction. My question is very simply, what scope do you think is left within the law of armed conflict for reprisals and is that a problem in coalition operations?

David Graham:

The concept of reprisals—even if you restricted it to belligerent reprisals—is an extremely difficult concept. I think I can tell you without divulging confidential information that we have debated the issue of belligerent reprisals within the Department of Defense and between Defense and the Department of State extensively. I wish I could give you an easy answer with respect to what the position is on belligerent reprisals. I will tell you that I do not think the United States has renounced the right to engage in belligerent reprisals (apart from those categories of persons and property protected in the 1949 Geneva Conventions) given certain circumstances, but that's as far as I'm prepared to go. It's a difficult issue.

Fausto Pocar:

Unfortunately I am not able to fully answer this question. I touched upon it in my paper only to show that this is an area in which the debate is open. When I referred to the decision of the Trial Chamber in *Kupreskic*,[2] I was quite prudent to say that whatever consideration is given to this judgment it may play a role in developing the law. I won't say more because this question is now before the Appeals Chamber of which I am a member.

The Martens Clause and the Margin of Appreciation

Rudolf Dolzer:

Allow me to make a brief point regarding the *Kupreskic* case. The ICTY had to interpret Protocol I, Article 57's "feasible precautions" provision. (I think this is a very broad statute with a very broad wording). What the ICTY did was interpret "feasible precautions" in the light of the Martens Clause. In other words, you interpret a very broadly worded statute in the light of a very, very broad general clause.

---

2. Prosecutor v. Kupreskic et al., Judgement, I.C.T.Y. No. IT-95-16-T, Jan. 14, 2000.

Discussion

The Martens Clause is reworded in the Protocol I. It says "[i]n cases not covered."[3] Now I'm not quite sure what it means, "in cases not covered," but I would be very careful to apply the Martens Clause in areas that are more or less specifically addressed in the Protocol. Otherwise I would probably not apply the Martens Clause. But even if I would in principle think it might be applicable in terms of applying Article 57 in the context of criminal justice, if you add the Martens Clause, you would come into a sphere of vagueness that in most domestic constitutional systems would probably be quite near to the borders that probably constitutional lawyers would find acceptable.

My remark as to margin of appreciation was meant as follows: those who have to apply Protocol I or customary law have to apply it under specific circumstances—sometimes very short-term, sometimes without very specific knowledge. I think the ICTY should do more. I would be happier if the ICTY had not supplemented Article 57 with the Martens Clause, but with a sense and spirit of the margin of appreciation approach. In other words giving some benefit of doubt to those who act under the circumstances in which they have to act. Now why do I say so again? I say so mainly not because I am sympathetic to those who are before the ICTY at the moment as very few of us are, but I think we have to keep in mind that those rules will have to be accepted. I take the ICTY very seriously. I think there is a very good chance that the jurisprudence of the Tribunal in the long-term will have a considerable influence depending upon its persuasiveness. What I'm concerned about is if the Tribunal for very good or excellent reasons comes down with an interpretation of the law that will make it difficult next time for those who are on the different side and in similar circumstances, then I think indeed those very hard cases would make very bad law.

The Relationship Between Human Rights Law and the Law of Armed Conflict

Natalino Ronzitti:

The International Court of Justice in its *Nuclear Weapons* advisory opinion has said that humanitarian law is *lex specialis* vis-à-vis human rights law, so in some cases you have to apply human rights law. This is a problem for European countries; it's not a problem for the United States. For European countries it's a real problem because we have a European Convention on Human Rights. There is a case before the European Court of Human Rights for

---

3. Protocol I, Article 1(2).

Discussion

violation of the Convention on Human Rights during Operation Allied Force. This is important also for an occupying army or also for peacekeeping operations. We cannot say that we will not apply the European Convention because in this case individuals are under the jurisdiction of the State that is occupying its territory or having its troops on their territory. So for the European States it's a very important issue. How is it possible to address this issue in a coalition?

David Graham:

I appreciate that comment Professor. I understand that you're subject to the European Convention on Human Rights and I understand that the European Court is now making a determination as to whether or not it will assume jurisdiction of the case against NATO countries for Operation Allied Force. If the European Court assumes jurisdiction, my question becomes does it apply human rights law? Does it apply the law of armed conflict? Does it apply a combination of the two? Is, in fact, the European Court on Human Rights going to make rulings with respect to the law of armed conflict and interpret the law of armed conflict? To me that's a fairly scary proposition.

My concern also is that when you combine elements of human rights law and the law of armed conflict, it makes my job of advising military commanders a very difficult job. I know what the law of armed conflict is. When I ask very, very bright people to tell me what international humanitarian law is, I get some very good answers. The problem is that they're all different. Everybody has his or her own idea with respect to what international humanitarian law is. Professor Stein has said that we have seen the transformation of the law of armed conflict into simply an element of humanitarian law. Well, that's an uncomfortable proposition for me as well because it makes my job in advising commanders a very difficult job in terms of understanding what their obligations are. That's something that continues to trouble me. I think it's something that we need to take a long hard careful look at.

Torsten Stein:

I just want to comment on one point of Colonel Graham's statement. It's absolutely clear that the Strasbourg Court will apply the European Convention and nothing else if they take up the case.[4]

---

4. See Professor Greenwood's paper in this volume.

Discussion

Fausto Pocar:

The European Court has managed to apply the European Convention on Human Rights and nothing more than that. But of course the problem—the relationship with the law of war —arises in any case because the Convention says that the state of war does not exclude the application of the Convention. So the problem of combining the Geneva conventions and the European Convention on Human Rights does exist for States that are parties to both.

Leslie Green:

I find myself very much in agreement with Colonel Graham, because from my point of view international humanitarian law is the Geneva conventions. This is treaty armed conflict law. We also have customary armed conflict law. Armed conflict law is *lex specialis*. It has been created to deal specifically with armed conflicts. If I look at the European Convention on Human Rights, it relates to a peace situation. It relates to a situation of a country dealing with its own subjects or perhaps those who are present within its territory. That was the basic view that the Convention originally took. The fact that the Court has perhaps extended it, in the same way that the Canadian Supreme Court has extended our own Charter of Rights, does not change the law. It is not the role of the European Court of Human Rights to deal with issues that are outside the field of human rights. The issue of the law of armed conflict is *lex specialis*, which applies even if the Convention on Human Rights is *lex generalis*, which I don't think it is.

Michael Bothe:

It comes as a surprise to me that we are back to this old issue of humanitarian law and human rights. Professor Green, you know what you said was wrong. We made every effort from 1974 to 1977 to have a good mix of human rights and humanitarian law. Article 75 of Protocol I and the human rights provisions of Protocol II are human rights provisions. They are drafted according to the international covenants. Their purpose is to a certain extent to exclude the suspension of the guarantee which is possible according to the European Convention on Human Rights; to reintroduce those guarantees and to make them in a certain sense immune against this type of suspension. This double guarantee or double protection of victims by humanitarian law and by human rights law was always with us. This is not new.

There is nothing like a *lex specialis*. These are two overlapping areas of international law. Now when you have overlapping areas of international law, you will get into difficult situations at some point. I think the case which is pending before the European Court of Human Rights is one of those difficult situations where you have also as a matter of fact a very old question. The relationship between the right to life and the right to kill in warfare. It's a very fundamental issue. It pops up from time to time at places where you might not have expected, but there is nothing shocking and nothing new about it. Perhaps it's an opportunity to rethink the issue. This is the fundamental side of it.

The Court has to decide the issue on a technical level because the Court will have to apply the European Convention. There the problem is whether actual fighting is something that is meant to be "subject to the jurisdiction" of a party to the Convention, or whether the scope of protection of the Convention as it is formulated really covers actual fighting. It covers action in the context of an occupation, but actual fighting is different. This would be my problem if I were a judge there. Is this really something which is within the scope of protection of the European Convention?

Leslie Green:

Professor Bothe, I know you were *Rapporteur* of that Committee. I sat in on that Committee. But I would remind you that what we did in that Committee was to take certain human rights and make them part of armed conflict law. They were taken out of the generality of human rights law from the point of view of military operations and made part of Geneva law because they appear not in a human rights document but in a Protocol attached to the Geneva conventions. They are now part of armed conflict law. They are to be considered from the point of view of the operation of the law of armed conflict, not in the light of human rights law. They may be in Pictet's definition of international humanitarian law, which he said was the Geneva conventions, but from that point of view I think you go too far in retaining it as a separate concept when it has become part of the *lex specialis* of the law of armed conflict.

Rudolf Dolzer:

To me the issue of the law of armed conflict or humanitarian law is to some extent a semantic issue in terms of interpreting the law. It is a matter of strict interpretation of the relevant treaties. The European Court will interpret the case before it in terms of its law, not more and not less.

Professor Bothe indicated that there is a serious question whether the European Convention was meant in the first place to address war or war-like situations. I would think that is not the case. The universal human rights conventions will have to interpret human rights laws in their own light. I think that we will come to the general issue of which is the more specific law.

The law of armed conflict is probably more specific, but there may be instances where the two bodies of law have to be interpreted in the light of each other. That would be a very specific issue to be determined in the light of the very specific case, but in principle one would have to assume that the law of armed conflict is much more specific than human rights law.

Fausto Pocar:

I would like to make a simple point on the relationship between human rights law and humanitarian law. We are discussing the question of the European States, but the question is not only European. We should not forget that many countries in the world—about 150 now—are parties to the UN Covenant on Civil and Political Rights. The Covenant's provisions on these matters are more or less going in the same direction as the European Convention. So the problem of combining the treaty obligation that was mentioned by Professor Bothe still exists and exists also for the United States because the United States is a party to the Covenant. So it's a point that should be stressed.

PART VI

THE ROAD AHEAD

Introduction

Joel Rosenthal

Our topic is entitled "The Road Ahead." Now I suppose if Yogi Berra were in my place he would just say, when you get to the fork in the road, take it. Say what you will about Yogi, but he's right to imagine that the road ahead is one with many forks. Legal and ethical dilemmas necessarily imply that choices must be made. I hope that this colloquium and this particular panel can help us to see these choices clearly and help us articulate the principles upon which we make our decisions.

The organizers of this colloquium sensed that the Kosovo campaign brought to the surface several inconclusive legal and ethical issues stemming primarily from rapid geopolitical and technological changes. This point has been made throughout proceedings. For example Professor Dinstein points out in his paper that the *jus in bello* cannot afford to lag behind the changing conditions of combat. Colonel Graham asked us when did we change our perspective from the law of armed conflict to international human rights law? We have seen some new language and new concepts, and we've seen some old concepts put under new strain. We are all here because we know that these changes affect our thinking about the road ahead.

The organizers also understand that in order to investigate the world between law and ethics, we would need to call upon an eclectic group. So that is why in this colloquium are included judges, philosophers, military officers, historians and even lawyers. We hope we've created a stimulating and fruitful discussion that has been interdisciplinary, inter-professional and international. Yesterday historian Barry Strauss cautioned whether we can or should even try to learn lessons from history. The organizers take that admonition seriously, but we're also confident that we can profitably reflect on the Kosovo experience in ways that might not amount strictly to lessons learned but might nevertheless shed some light on the road ahead.

The Laws of War After Kosovo

Adam Roberts

The 1999 Kosovo War between NATO members and the Federal Republic of Yugoslavia confirmed the importance of issues relating to the laws of war in contemporary conflicts, especially in coalition operations. It also exposed some problems in that body of law. A central issue in the war was the minimizing of civilian casualties. The NATO leadership recognized from the start that this was of major importance, for two main reasons: because the war was being fought with a stated purpose of protecting the inhabitants of Kosovo and also because international opinion would not have tolerated a war on civilians.[1] An underlying question raised by the war is thus the extent to which international legal considerations and institutions can assist in protecting the civilian.

The title of this paper calls for explanation. The terms "the laws of war" (*jus in bello*) and "international humanitarian law" are for most purposes interchangeable. They refer to the same body of law. Both terms are used in this paper. For most purposes I prefer the first of these terms, "laws of war" being older and simpler, and recognizing as it does that war is the central area of concern. However, the second term, "international humanitarian law," sometimes with the suffix "applicable in armed conflicts," is increasingly used in international diplomacy. In some usages, this term can also encompass relevant parts of the international law of human rights. The term may be particularly appropriate in reference to a situation (such as applied in Kosovo before March 24, 1999) in which there is no international armed conflict and only a

---

1. The importance of minimizing civilian casualties is stressed in the memoirs of the Supreme Allied Commander Europe during the period of the Kosovo War. *See* WESLEY CLARK, WAGING MODERN WAR 438–40 (2001).

small-scale civil war, but there is systematic government repression of part of its own population. Whichever term one uses, the fact remains that the scope of this body of law has significantly expanded in the past sixty years to encompass the law on crimes against humanity and on genocide as well as the laws and customs of international armed conflict; and that in the past decade this body of law has been increasingly viewed as at least partially applicable in conflicts which are partly or completely non-international in character.

Eight questions

This survey concentrates on the following eight questions which (a) arose in connection with the Kosovo War, and (b) also touch on matters which are likely to affect the way in which the law is viewed, influences events, and develops further in the future:

1. How did developments in the written laws of war which occurred in the 1990s, and the increasing international concern with implementation of the law, affect the framework within which international responses to civil wars, including in Kosovo, took place?

2. Is there now a stronger link than before between *jus in bello* and *jus ad bellum*? In particular, what are the implications of the fact that sometimes, as in Kosovo, violations of international humanitarian norms by a belligerent in an internal conflict provide part of the rationale for external military intervention?

3. If military action is embarked upon for proclaimed humanitarian purposes by a large alliance or coalition, is there a logic whereby it is carried out by low-risk, remote control methods? In particular, is the oxymoron, humanitarian war, particularly likely to take the form of bombing; and what *jus in bello* problems arise from reliance on air power?

4. Is there tension between (a) the NATO/US strategic doctrine which aims at putting pressure on the adversary's government, and not just its armed forces, and (b) the implicit assumption of the laws of war that the adversary's armed forces are the main legitimate object of attack? If so, how can this tension be addressed?

5. What lessons are to be learned from the fact that the NATO operations were subject to the jurisdiction of the International Criminal Tribunal for the former Yugoslavia (ICTY)? In particular, does the consideration of the NATO bombing campaign that was conducted under the auspices of the ICTY Prosecutor suggest that the NATO campaign was conducted largely in accord with member States' obligations under the laws of war?

6. Did the war confirm that there can be many forms of non-belligerence which differ significantly from neutrality as traditionally conceived in the laws of war?

7. Did the war expose deficiencies or omissions in the existing codifications of the laws of war? In particular, is there a need for further codification? And what are the main subject-areas that might require such codification?

8. What, if anything, might need to be done about the paradox that the United States is simultaneously a principal upholder of the obligation of States to observe the laws of war and a non-party to several important agreements on the subject?

These questions are certainly not the only important *jus in bello* ones to arise. A number of specific issues and controversies, such as the naval operations in the Adriatic and the bombing of the TV station in Belgrade, cannot be covered here in the detail they deserve.

These eight questions have to be seen against a larger background of changes in the conduct of international politics in the 1990s, and increasing international preoccupation with the problem of civil wars and with the implementation of the laws of war. These changes had a significant effect on the fact, and the form, of NATO involvement in Kosovo.

Changes in the conduct of international politics

In the 1990s four factors, none of them entirely new, reinforced the tendency of international bodies and foreign powers to get involved in wars, including particularly civil wars, and also to apply pressure for implementation of the laws of war by belligerents.

Firstly, most conflict since the end of the Cold War has had the character of civil wars, though often with international involvements on one or more sides. Since such wars cause appalling and often highly visible suffering, as well as threatening international stability in the regions in which they occur, there has been an evident need to ensure the application of certain rules of restraint in such wars.

Secondly, many contemporary wars have a particular tendency to engage the interests of outside powers because they threaten to create huge refugee flows with which our not-very-liberal societies are unwilling to cope. Whether it is northern Iraq, Bosnia, Kosovo or East Timor, an unholy alliance of humanitarianism and illiberalism makes intervention within the State undergoing conflict a possible, even imperiously necessary, option.

Thirdly, there has been a growing awareness that crimes committed by States have been among the most serious of the twentieth century. The international preoccupation with restitution for a wide range of State misdeeds is evidence of this.

Fourthly, it is widely accepted that the post-Cold War international order has to be based on values other than, or additional to, mutual respect among sovereign States. Human rights and humanitarian norms are core parts of any such system of values. It is thus very difficult for States to ignore massive violations of fundamental norms.

The challenge of implementation

The main challenge facing the laws of war today is not devising new rules—though some are needed. It is implementation of the rules that exist, and of the underlying idea of moderation in the conduct of armed conflict. Unquestionably, the preoccupation with implementation is widely shared among those who have worked in the field of the laws of war; it has had a profound effect on policy and on treaty-making in this field; and it has been reflected in a number of UN reports and in certain actions of the UN Security Council.

"Implementation" is taken to encompass (1) the normal measures taken by States, and by international bodies including the International Committee of the Red Cross (ICRC) and the United Nations, to ensure that populations and armed forces are aware of the laws of war and carry out their terms; (2) the actions taken by outside bodies, including States and international organizations, in response to systematic violations of the laws of war. My focus is mainly on this second and more difficult category, which encompasses the *enforcement* of the laws of war, but is not limited to coercive measures.

The concern with implementation should not be taken to imply support for the commonly expressed view that existing implementation is lamentable or even non-existent. In the 1999 Kosovo War there was much effective implementation. This was not only on the NATO side, but also in some instances on the Federal Republic of Yugoslavia (FRY) side. For example, in the talks at the conclusion of the war the FRY military provided extensive and accurate information about the location of minefields.[2] The central challenge is both to improve patterns of implementation, and to further develop means of coping with gross violations.

Changes in the Laws of War in the 1990s

In the decade before the war on Kosovo, there had been two striking developments in the laws of war: a tendency to make more explicit and detailed the application of the laws of war to conflicts with a partly or wholly non-international character; and a range of specific measures to improve mechanisms of implementation. Both of these developments affected the United States and NATO response to the events in Kosovo. Up to March 24, 1999 the Kosovo problem had largely the character of State repression by the Yugoslav authorities and civil war. It might thus have been perceived as a largely internal problem, about which the rest of the world should not worry. The fact that Kosovo did not escape the attention of outside powers and bodies owes something to the development of the law.

Changes in the written law

In the laws of war, as they developed from the mid-nineteenth century to the Second World War, implementation was traditionally not treated as a major topic in its own right. The general assumption, reflected in certain early agreements on the laws of war (e.g., the 1899 and 1907 Hague Conventions) was that civilized States could be relied on to ensure that their own armed forces would act in a disciplined, restrained and professional manner. That idea was called into question by the events of the twentieth century. When the State that was supposed to take action was the very one whose armed forces had committed the alleged offenses, the idea of purely national jurisdiction seemed optimistic; and when the State itself was committed to a criminal

---

2. Information from General Rupert Smith, Deputy Supreme Allied Commander Europe, June 25–27, 1999. *See also* the UN Mine Action Programme website, www.mineaction.org. Its report on Kosovo of September 2001 (*available at* the Mine Action website) showed that the Yugoslav Army handed over 620 records of minefields in Kosovo, principally but not exclusively on the Albanian and Macedonian borders. According to the final annual report on the UN Interim Administration in Kosovo Mine Action Programme, covering the period to December 15, 2001, the 620 records did not include mines laid by Ministry of Interior Police Units, or paramilitary groups. UNMIK *Mine Action Programme Annual Report – 2001* (December 2001) ¶ 10 (*available at* the Mine Action website).

policy, it was absurd. That is why since 1945 there has been a definite movement towards a system of international criminal law affecting the activities of States and armed forces.

As far as treaties are concerned, the old pattern of treating implementation casually began to change significantly after the Second World War. The 1948 Genocide Convention authorized and indeed exhorted parties to take action against offenders, including rulers and public officials; and it authorized action through the UN. The four 1949 Geneva Conventions called for: (1) universal jurisdiction as regards grave breaches, and (2) "Protecting Powers" to ensure implementation of certain parts of the agreements in wartime. However, the implementation systems specified in these treaties concluded in 1948 and 1949 have not been used much in the intervening years.

The 1977 Geneva Protocol I[3] included some provisions attempting to break the impasse. In particular, in accordance with the terms of its Article 90, the "International Humanitarian Fact-Finding Commission" was set up in 1991. Yet this too has not worked. Not a single one of the numerous problems in the decade of its existence has been referred to it. In this, as in many other ways, the actual forms of implementation that have been developed have been different from what was envisaged in treaties.

In short, the law developed before the 1990s had relatively few provisions regarding implementation, and those that existed were not effective. This does not mean that there was no implementation—many States did a capable job of developing a culture of law observance within their own armed forces. However, the war crimes and crimes against humanity of the 1990s exposed the weakness of the implementation "system."

Similarly, laws of war agreements concluded before the 1990s said relatively little about civil war. The treaty provisions explicitly applicable in civil wars were notoriously modest (being essentially Common Article 3 of the 1949 Geneva Conventions and 1977 Geneva Protocol II), and were especially weak on matters of implementation.

In the 1990s, States and international bodies made further attempts to address questions of implementation and enforcement. Eight new legally binding international documents in the area of the laws of war broadly defined were adopted by the UN Security Council or by States at international conferences. Only one of these new agreements (the 1995 Protocol on Blinding Laser

---

3. Protocol Additional (I) to the Geneva Conventions of 1949, and Relating to the Protection of Victims of International Armed Conflict, June 8, 1977, 1125 U.N.T.S. 3, DOCUMENTS ON THE LAW OF WAR 422 (Adam Roberts and Richard Guelff eds., 3d ed. 2000) [hereinafter Protocol I].

Weapons) does not deal extensively with implementation and enforcement, or with the problem of civil war.[4] The other seven new international instruments, all of which do address these issues, are:

1. The *1993 Statute of the International Criminal Tribunal for the former Yugoslavia*. Adopted by the UN Security Council in 1993.

2. The *1994 Statute of the International Criminal Tribunal for Rwanda*. Adopted by the UN Security Council in 1994.

3. The *1994 Convention on the Safety of UN and Associated Personnel*. This is not part of the laws of war as such, but closely related. It contains extensive provision for prosecution or extradition of offenders.

4. The *1996 Amended Protocol II on Landmines to the 1980 UN Convention on Certain Conventional Weapons*. This requires each party to take legislative and other measures against violations "by persons or on territory under its jurisdiction or control."

5. The *1997 Ottawa Landmines Convention*. This contains extensive provisions on transparency, compliance and dispute settlement.

6. The *1998 Rome Statute of the International Criminal Court* (entered into force July 1, 2002).

7. The *1999 Second Hague Protocol for the Protection of Cultural Property in Armed Conflict* (not yet in force). This was concluded and opened for signature during the Kosovo War, but had been negotiated and agreed well before. It contains numerous provisions regarding implementation and enforcement not just of the Second Protocol itself, but also of the Convention and the first Protocol (both of which had been concluded in 1954).

---

4. I exclude from this total documents of an essentially advisory character, such as the 1994 ICRC/UNGA Guidelines for Military Manuals and Instructions on the Protection of the Environment in Times of Armed Conflict, included in the UN Secretary-General's report of 19 August 1994 to the UN General Assembly. See U.N. Doc. A/49/323 (1994).

All seven documents have two critically important features in common. *First*, they contain some provisions that go beyond the old idea of essentially national implementation by the authorities of individual States. *Second*, they have formal application in wholly or partly non-international armed conflicts.

An unresolved problem: internationalized civil war

Most wars are much more confused in character than the simple dichotomous definition of war, as being either international or non-international, would suggest. Frequently, as in past eras, the civil wars of our time have had international dimensions: troops and command structures from outside powers have often played major roles on one or more sides. In many cases a more accurate short description of the conflict would be "internationalized civil war", although this is not a recognized category in the laws of war.

As far as the laws of war are concerned, one unhappy result of having largely separate bodies of law applying to different aspects of the conflict is that courts, especially ICTY, have had to devote enormous efforts to determining the character of the conflict in Bosnia as it arose in particular times, places and events. The wars in Bosnia and Croatia were among many which have had partly international and partly internal aspects. There must in principle be a case for applying the whole of the body of the laws of war even to armed conflicts that are substantially non-international in character, and some recent developments in the law do point in that direction. However, as far as Kosovo is concerned, the question of the character of the conflict is not especially difficult. Before March 24, 1999 it was mainly or entirely a non-international armed conflict, occurring within the territory of the Federal Republic of Yugoslavia. After that date there was, superimposed on that conflict, an international armed conflict between the NATO powers and the FRY.

The UN Security Council's involvement

In the 1990s the UN Security Council assumed a major role in attempting to ensure implementation of the laws of war, including investigation and punishment of certain violations. This role was not entirely new. For example, already during the Iran-Iraq War (1980–88) the Security Council had authorized the main official investigation into the use of chemical weapons.

In the conflicts of the 1990s the UN Security Council addressed issues relating to the implementation of international humanitarian law in at least five cases: Bosnia and Herzegovina (1992–5); Somalia (1992); Rwanda (1994); Sierra Leone (1997–2000); and Kosovo (1998–9). In addition to attacks on civilians and other similar violations, a major issue at stake in some of these cases was the refusal of parties to permit delivery of humanitarian aid—which is certainly a problem relating to the laws of war, but could also be considered a violation of other norms and agreements.

In all these cases in the 1990s the Security Council went beyond appeals to observe norms, and called for action. There were always several different stated purposes for UN-authorized action or the threat thereof, but observance of humanitarian law was one of them. The actions taken by the Council included not only the establishment of the international criminal tribunals for Yugoslavia and Rwanda, but also action of a more direct kind. Some of the cases of UN-authorized military action, and some cases of UN-imposed economic sanctions, were partly based on claims that the target State had violated fundamental norms of humanitarian law.

These forms of action under UN Security Council auspices posed problems. As regards military action, in most of these five crises a principal problem for the UN was the difficulty of finding outside forces willing to act in situations perceived to be dangerous. The failures of the UN, and of States, to act in time in respect of the crises in Rwanda in 1994 and Srebrenica in 1995 are clear examples. The enthusiasm for implementing humanitarian norms ran into the rock of national interests. In respect of Kosovo the problem was different: the main difficulty was in getting agreement in principle in the Security Council that force should be used at all in response to the unfolding crisis. This was because, more than in any of the other five cases, any military action to stop ongoing atrocities in Kosovo involved violating the sovereignty of a functioning sovereign State, Yugoslavia.

Links Between Jus in Bello and Jus ad Bellum

One consequence of the developments of the 1990s has been the strengthening of the idea that a systematic pattern of violations of the basic humanitarian norms of international humanitarian law may justify acts of military intervention. Although there were many pre-echoes of this in the nineteenth and twentieth centuries, the apparent strengthening of this link between *jus ad bellum* and *jus in bello* represents a momentous and controversial change in the terms of international debate.

The long-standing and important principle that the law relating to resort to war (*jus ad bellum*) is a separate and distinct subject from the law relating to conduct in war (*jus in bello*) remains valid and important. However, there have always been causal links between these distinct bodies of law. One such link is that aspect of the idea of proportionality that deals with the proportionality of a military response to the original grievance. The developing practice of military action as a response to violations of the law of war is another important link. Quite simply, massive violations of *jus in bello* by a belligerent can help to legitimize certain threats and uses of force by outside powers intervening to stop the violations.

In an effort to get an offending State to observe rules of restraint, the first response of outside powers may be the threat, rather than the actuality, of force. The use of pressure against States, for example in order to make them accept an intervention force, as was attempted in Kosovo and done in East Timor in 1999, raises a problem. Traditionally, international law and international lawyers have been suspicious of agreements negotiated under duress. If the host government has only given consent under extreme pressure, is its consent valid? The experience of the post-1990 period shows how necessary pressure can be to achieve international objectives, and how hard it is to eliminate certain aspects of power politics.

The change in the landscape, whereby humanitarian outrages serve in practice as a basis for threatening or using force, has not been universally recognized. This is not surprising, particularly as the whole issue poses difficult dilemmas for humanitarian workers and organizations. In some cases in the 1990s, the violations of *jus in bello* that contributed to decisions to intervene included assaults on aid workers and convoys. Any suggestion that humanitarian workers and organizations may play some part in triggering military actions challenges their deep (and in some cases legally based) commitment to impartiality and neutrality. Almost all humanitarian workers and organizations are in a state of denial about the extent to which they, and the principles and laws for which they stand, have played a part in initiating military action.

Where, following a pattern of violations, military action has been with the authorization of the UN Security Council, and/or has had the consent (however reluctant) of the host State, there has not generally been a strong objection to it in principle. These conditions were present, for example, in Bosnia in 1995 and in East Timor in September 1999. However, where these conditions were not present, as in Kosovo in March-June 1999, military intervention has been strongly contested by major and minor powers.

In respect of Kosovo, before the NATO military action there had been several UN resolutions which, in addition to many other elements, noted the violations of international humanitarian law there. For example, a long resolution on Kosovo passed by the General Assembly in December 1998 criticized the Yugoslav authorities for a variety of unacceptable practices, including violations of Common Article 3 of the 1949 Geneva Conventions, and the

1977 Protocol II; deplored the killing of humanitarian aid workers; and required the Yugoslav authorities to allow investigators from the International Criminal Tribunal access to examine alleged atrocities against civilians.[5] The Security Council resolutions on Kosovo also addressed these issues. A resolution in March 1998 condemned "the use of excessive force by Serbian police forces against civilians and peaceful demonstrators."[6] In September 1998 the Council expressed concern at "the excessive and indiscriminate use of force by Serbian security forces and the Yugoslav Army," and at "reports of increasing violations of human rights and of international humanitarian law," going on to call for a cessation of such acts.[7] This resolution, notably tough in tone, followed a first-hand presentation made to the UN Security Council by a senior representative of the United Nations High Commissioner for Refugees (UNHCR) on September 11, 1998. The next resolution, passed in October 1998, also referred repeatedly to humanitarian issues.[8] The failure of the Yugoslav authorities to comply with these resolutions was a key consideration in the decisions of NATO countries to resort to the use of military force, as they did on March 24, 1999. When President Clinton addressed the nation on that day, in a key link in his argument he asked Americans: "Imagine what would happen if we and our allies instead decided just to look the other way, as these people were massacred on NATO's doorstep."[9]

To draw attention to the connection between issues related to violations of the laws of war, and the decisions of outside countries to intervene, is not to say that there is a simple and clear doctrinal or legal link. There is not now, nor is there likely to be, a generally recognized "right" of humanitarian intervention. Such interventions may occasionally be necessary, but to suggest that they are a general "right" implies that it is possible to adjudicate in a general way between the undoubted and still important non-intervention rule on the one hand, and the demands of humanitarian considerations on the other. Any decision on forcible intervention must involve a balancing of considerations in the face of unique and urgent circumstances, not the assertion of a general right.

To suggest that there is no general right of humanitarian intervention is not to say that certain uses of force for humanitarian ends are necessarily illegal

---

5. G.A. Res. 53/164 (Dec. 8, 1998), U.N. Doc. A/RES/53/164 (1998).
6. S.C. Res. 1160 (Mar. 31, 1998), U.N. Doc. S/RES/1160 (1998).
7. S.C. Res. 1199 (Sep. 23, 1998), U.N. Doc. S/RES/1199 (1998).
8. S.C. Res. 1203 (Oct. 24, 1998), U.N. Doc. S/RES/1203 (1998).
9. THE KOSOVO CONFLICT AND INTERNATIONAL LAW: AN ANALYTICAL DOCUMENTATION 1974–1999, at 416 (Heike Krieger ed., 2001).

under international law; nor is it to assert that certain uses of force are simply beyond the scope of international law. Rather, it is to suggest that in respect of each intervention there are important, relevant but alas competing legal principles which have to be balanced against each other; and a great deal depends on the particular facts and legal considerations that relate to that particular case.

Since the Kosovo War there have been attempts to develop a "right" of humanitarian intervention by such figures as UK Prime Minister Tony Blair in his speech in Chicago on April 22, 1999; UN Secretary-General Kofi Annan in his UN report of September 8, 1999; a number of speakers in the UN General Assembly in 1999; the then Canadian Foreign Minister Lloyd Axworthy in a lecture in New York on February 10, 2000; and the then UK Foreign Secretary Robin Cook in a speech in London on July 19, 2000. Yet there is absolutely no sign of international agreement on their propositions. Moreover, the US government has never wanted a doctrine in this area that might tie its hands.

The attempt to develop a general doctrine could actually do harm to the cause of humanitarian intervention: such an attempt can imply that the legitimacy of each case of intervention is dependent on the existence of a general right. Since that right does not exist, the legitimacy of individual actions may, if anything, be reduced. Because pursuit of a defined legal right is doomed to fail, and the conditions giving rise to humanitarian intervention will not disappear, the situation is likely to remain untidy. It probably ought to do so.

The recognition of a link between *jus in bello* and *jus ad bellum* falls far short of any general recognition of a right of humanitarian intervention.[10] What has emerged from the experiences of the 1990s is a pattern of acquiescence by significant numbers of States in respect of some interventions with stated humanitarian purposes. However, there has also been strong opposition by States to particular interventions, and even stronger opposition to the granting of a general right. The distinctly uneven pattern of acquiescence is not the same thing as the recognition of a right.

The fact that an intervention may be motivated by humanitarian considerations, including a concern to stop violations of human rights and humanitarian norms, does not in any way affect the equal application of the laws of war in any resulting hostilities. During the Kosovo war there was no suggestion from any party that the United States and its allies were entitled to ignore any

---

10. *See* Adam Roberts, *The So-Called "Right" Of Humanitarian Intervention*, 3 YEARBOOK OF INTERNATIONAL HUMANITARIAN LAW 3–51 (2002).

aspects of *jus in bello* because they were engaged in what they saw as a high moral cause.[11] If anything, the logic was rather that the humanitarian elements in the stated reasons for resort to war particularly obliged the NATO members to observe the rules of war.

The Kosovo War confirmed another connection between *jus in bello* and *jus ad bellum*. In the Kosovo War, as in a number of other recent conflicts, the public's perception of the legitimacy of the operation as a whole appeared to depend in significant measure on a public understanding that the war was being fought in a disciplined and restrained manner, and in accordance with international norms. Some of the worst moments for NATO in the entire campaign were when NATO appeared to be falling short of this standard. Support for the war could easily have evaporated if there had been more incidents such as the bombing of refugee convoys.

Bombing as a Default Form of Humanitarian War

Bombing from the air formed a key part of the Western response to at least three humanitarian crises of the 1990s: *(1)* in northern and southern Iraq since 1991, as a means of maintaining "no-fly-zones," enabling refugees to return home, and limiting the activities of the Iraqi armed forces; *(2)* in Bosnia in 1995, especially in the form of NATO's Operation Deliberate Force, following the Bosnian Serbs' brutal massacre at Srebrenica and their renewed assault on Sarajevo; and *(3)* in 1999, in the war over Kosovo.

One underlying reason for reliance on air power in such cases is the reluctance of the populations and governments of Western democracies to take substantial risks, for example by using ground forces in a combat role, in what were perceived to be distant humanitarian causes. This reluctance is understandable but may at times jeopardize the effectiveness of operations. In the 1999 war it was disadvantageous to NATO, and to the inhabitants of Kosovo, that Milosevic was not confronted with a more convincing threat of land operations in the province.

Bombing as such has never been, and is not now, violative of the laws of war, but in practice it has frequently risked violating norms requiring force to

---

11. This was confirmed in the discussion of the committee established by the Prosecutor of the International Criminal Tribunal for the former Yugoslavia to review NATO actions in Yugoslavia. *See* Final Report to the Prosecutor by the Committee Established to Review the NATO Bombing Campaign Against the Federal Republic of Yugoslavia, ¶¶ 30–4, 39 INTERNATIONAL LEGAL MATERIALS 1257, 1265–6 (2000), *reprinted* herein as Appendix A [hereinafter Report to the Prosecutor].

be directed at military targets and to be used discriminately. The increased accuracy of certain air-delivered weapons in several recent conflicts, including the 1991 Gulf War, has indicated that certain uses of air power may be, or have the capacity to become, compatible with the existing rules about targeting and discrimination. This was one conclusion of the detailed UK House of Commons Foreign Affairs Committee report on Kosovo. It noted that this was the first armed conflict in which the United Kingdom had engaged since it ratified Protocol I in 1998; and after considering the main areas of controversy surrounding the bombing it concluded: "On the evidence available to us, we believe that NATO showed considerable care to comply with the 1977 Protocol and avoid civilian casualties."[12]

However, the use of air power in this war posed certain problems. Some of these were more political than legal: the controlled use of air power is an option available to very few States, and it naturally causes both fear and resentment. Some of the problems were technical, but have a major impact on evaluations of the lawfulness of particular uses of air power. As the Kosovo war demonstrated, even in the electronic age air power suffers from certain striking limitations, and it has a natural tendency to lead to unintended damage.

The 1999 Kosovo War began in an atmosphere of arrogant and ignorant illusions among Western decision-makers about the capacity of bombing to protect the inhabitants of Kosovo and/or to bring about a change in Serbian policy in a matter of days. In the end, the bombing could only succeed as a campaign of long-drawn-out coercive pressure, in which other elements were also involved.

The Kosovo War exposed certain limitations in the capacity of bombing to achieve results. Most notably, bombing was not at all effective in providing protection or relief from Serb attacks, for the hard-pressed Kosovars. The initiation of the bombing campaign was followed by an intensification of those attacks, leading to huge numbers of people fleeing from their homes. In his address on March 24 President Clinton did warn that Yugoslavia "could decide to intensify its assault on Kosovo."[13] However, the apparent belief of many Western policy-makers that NATO military action would deter Milosevic from further atrocities against the Kosovars was one of the most shocking

---

12. House of Commons Foreign Affairs Committee, Fourth Report, *Kosovo*, vol. I, *Report and Proceedings of the Committee*, HC 28-I, May 2000, ¶¶ 145, 157.
13. President Clinton, Address to the Nation, March 24, 1999. Text *in* THE KOSOVO CONFLICT AND INTERNATIONAL LAW 415–6 (Heike Krieger, ed.) (Cambridge International Documents Series, Volume 11).

lapses of the crisis.[14] One reason why the bombing failed to stop the ethnic cleansing is that it had very limited effects on movable military targets. A suppressed USAF investigation is reported to have showed that NATO forces verifiably destroyed just fourteen Serb tanks in Kosovo, eighteen armored personnel carriers, and twenty artillery pieces. As Tim Garton Ash has commented: "Even if the real figures are higher than that, it is an indisputable fact that ethnic cleansing increased under the bombing."[15] It is probably true that bombing did inhibit the mobility of Serb armor, but that is a modest achievement especially in a context in which heavy armor was not necessary for the effective pursuit of ethnic cleansing.

Partly because of its stated humanitarian purpose, the Kosovo air campaign involved many elements of restraint, including in target selection, in efforts to ensure the accuracy of bombing, and in the evident willingness to abandon sorties because of concerns about potential civilian casualties. Yet the case confirms that such bombing can cause direct damage to civilians and to non-military installations and activities in several distinct ways.

- *Unintended damage caused by bombing from high altitude.* It has been frequently asserted that the problems of damage to civilians and civilian property were made worse by NATO aircraft generally flying at a safe altitude. The potentially disastrous consequences of flying at altitude are obvious: in attacks on railway bridges, the time an air-to-ground guided weapon takes to get to the target may also be the time a passenger train takes to get onto the bridge; and in attacks on road convoys, it may be impossible at 15,000 feet to be sure that the convoy does not contain, or even consist largely of, the very civilians who are supposedly being protected. Both of these things happened in the Kosovo War, and many died as a result. Yet there may also be certain advantages in attack aircraft operating from relative safety: not just that the aircrew are safer, but also that they have more time in which to acquire targets and make decisions, can afford to make a second pass over a target if they are in doubt, and may feel less urgency about getting rid of whatever explosives they are carrying so that they can rush back to safety.

---

14. At a press conference on March 25, 1999, despite her recognition that there could be "a flood of new refugees," Secretary of State Madeleine Albright was notably optimistic on the capacity of air strikes to deter or prevent Milosevic from inflicting further horrors on the Kosovar people. *See* THE KOSOVO CONFLICT AND INTERNATIONAL LAW, *id.*, at 416 and 418.

15. Timothy Garton Ash, *Kosovo: Was it Worth It?*, NEW YORK REVIEW OF BOOKS, Sept. 21, 2000, at 58–9. The US Air Force report he cites was publicized *in* NEWSWEEK, May 15, 2000.

- *Pressure to attack fixed targets.* A major problem in Kosovo was that, because it proved relatively easy to conceal military units and movable equipment from attacks from the air, and to fabricate dummies, there was especially strong pressure on the NATO alliance to attack large fixed targets. In many cases (bridges, power stations, buildings of various types, the broadcasting station in Belgrade) these were dual-use targets which had major civilian as well as military functions.
- *Changing functions of buildings.* Even if targets are believed to be purely military and are hit accurately, as with the Amariya bunker in Baghdad in 1991 or the Chinese Embassy in Belgrade in 1999, their function proved in the event to be different from what the targeteers had believed.
- *Long-term effects of certain weapons on the civilian population.* Trying to inhibit the adversary's military movements by the use of cluster bombs and similar weapons can have a long-term adverse effect on the civilian population and on international military personnel who may be present in the territory following the end of hostilities. (The question of cluster bombs is considered further below.)

In some cases the damage to civilians or civilian objects may be completely unintended. However, in other cases (especially against certain dual-use targets) the damage may be seen by military planners as contributing to the overall goal of wearing down the adversary's will to carry on with the struggle.

Behind these problems lay a deeper and more intractable one. If the prime function of a bombing campaign is to bring about a capitulation by the government of the country, what happens when the bombing starts to run out of military targets, and seems unable to force a change of policy on the part of the target government? In such circumstances, there is bound to be heavy pressure to continue with the bombing and to direct it at targets which are doubtful or plainly illegal under the laws of war.

A particular challenge posed by the development of precision-guided munitions is that it is harder than in earlier eras to deny that there was a specific intention to hit whatever object was hit. As a result, armed forces and individuals may be more likely than before to be held responsible for specific acts of destruction. This development could have a considerable effect on how destruction is viewed by the public in allied, neutral or adversary States. It could also, at least potentially, create additional grounds for conducting inquiries, investigations and prosecutions, whether by the internal disciplinary mechanisms of States and armed forces, or by international criminal tribunals.

The exact combination of factors that led Milosevic to back down on June 3, 1999 is not yet known with any certainty. There are three obvious factors:

the bombing; the prospect of invasion of Kosovo by NATO land forces; and the isolation of Yugoslavia, especially with the abandonment of Milosevic by his last significant potential ally, Russia. General Clark considers that it was the combination of these three factors that led to the Milosevic surrender.[16] The indictment of Milosevic by ICTY announced on May 27, 1999, discussed further below, may also have contributed to the ending of the war. How these and other factors are evaluated will heavily influence any overall verdict on the lessons to be drawn from the Kosovo War, and on the importance, or the limitations, of the laws of war. As to the effect of bombing, my own provisional evaluation is that even though certain initial assumptions about how quickly a bombing campaign might achieve results were mistaken, that does not prove that the actual bombing, and the threat of more, were not important. They were. The most difficult question this raises so far as the laws of war are concerned is the following: did attacks on dual-use targets, and/or a perceived threat of further attacks directed at civilians and civilian objects, play a major part in the Yugoslav decision of June 3?[17]

In conclusion, a lesson of the bombing in the Kosovo War is that, while air power undoubtedly achieved significant results, its use involved serious problems. It did not perform particularly well against what might have been considered a relatively straightforward target, namely an army which was reliant on heavy armor and operated on at least partly conventional lines.[18] It was slow to achieve results even against a State debilitated by years of war and poor economic performance. It would be hazardous to assume that a similar air campaign would necessarily be the appropriate course in the context of another urgent humanitarian or other crisis. It appears that a systematic campaign of bombing was not a serious option when the East Timor crisis was at its gravest in September 1999.

NATO Strategic Doctrine

NATO's conduct in the 1999 Kosovo War confirms that there is continuing tension between certain contemporary strategic doctrines and the implicit vision of war contained in the laws of war. Over recent decades the United

---

16. CLARK, *supra* note 1, at 410–11.
17. For a challenging argument that the NATO bombing was a key factor in leading to the decision to back down, and that one element was a belief that the bombing would become less discriminate if Milosevic did not settle, see Stephen Hosmer, *The Conflict Over Kosovo: Why Milosevic Decided to Settle When He Did*, RAND Report MR-1351-AF, at 91–107 (2001).
18. See Clark's lugubrious comment on this in CLARK, *supra* note 1, at 412.

States and NATO have developed a conception of how force can be applied which involves putting military pressure not just on the armed forces of the adversary State, but on its government. Such an approach was evident in some official thinking about nuclear deterrence and strategic doctrine generally vis-à-vis the Soviet Union. It has also been evident in the conduct of certain operations in which NATO members have been involved, including aspects of the bombing campaign against Iraq in early 1991 as well as the Kosovo War eight years later.

The NATO approach is in tension with one underlying principle of the laws of war, as famously expressed in the 1868 St. Petersburg Declaration, "that the only legitimate object which States should endeavor to accomplish during war is to weaken the military forces of the enemy." Actually the laws of war as they have developed in the intervening years are not so restrictive as the words of the St. Petersburg Declaration might imply. In particular, they by no means exclude the application of military force against aspects of the adversary's war-making capacity and system of government. In the Kosovo campaign, the targets of operations clearly had to encompass all those taking an active part in ethnic cleansing, even if they were only police.

There is much to be said in favor of attacks against government targets. Such attacks may reach the individuals most directly responsible for the situation which has led to war. They may save lives among the adversary's armed forces, many of who will be essentially innocent individuals conscripted into the front line. They may shorten the duration of hostilities. However, there are also problems with attacks aimed at government targets. The very government whose actions caused a war may also be the only body that can end it, in which case its continued existence is vital. Attacks against government targets may have severe effects on the civilian population, and may indeed involve attacks on people or objects that are non-military in character. There is much scope for debate as to whether, for example, the homes and families of government ministers are legitimate military targets.

The key question of what is a military objective, addressed most extensively in certain provisions of Protocol I, may merit re-examination. Numerous States, including many NATO members, had already long before the Kosovo War made declarations or reservations regarding some of these provisions. NATO members, including non-parties to Protocol I such as the United States, may now need to address the question of how their conceptions of war relate to the limits on targeting that are specified in the laws of war. It may be doubted whether such an exercise would lead to specific revisions to the written laws of war, or to the reservations to Protocol I made by NATO States, but it might suggest some criteria for handling the tensions between NATO doctrine and the laws of war.

International Tribunals: ICTY

The conduct of hostilities by NATO in the Kosovo War became the subject of consideration by no less than three international courts and tribunals: the International Criminal Tribunal for the former Yugoslavia, the International Court of Justice (ICJ), and the European Court of Human Rights (ECHR). Although the ICJ case, brought by Yugoslavia, revolved mainly around matters of *jus ad bellum*, it did also involve claims concerning breaches of international humanitarian law. This ICJ case is ongoing, and demonstrates, sadly, that legal processes sometimes proceed at a pace far slower than war. The ECHR case was brought against all seventeen European NATO states by six Yugoslav citizens complaining about the bombing of the TV station in Belgrade by NATO forces on April 23, 1999, in which sixteen people were killed and another sixteen seriously injured. In its decision of December 12, 2001 the ECHR ruled that there was no jurisdictional link between the persons who were victims of the bombing and the seventeen NATO states, and therefore the application was inadmissible.

In contrast to the limited part played by ICJ and ECHR, ICTY had a number of important roles in connection with the Kosovo War. It played a significant part during the build-up of the crisis, principally through its entirely proper and widely supported insistence on recording details of atrocities in Kosovo. In March 1998 the Prosecutor, Louise Arbour, affirmed that ICTY's jurisdiction "is ongoing and covers the recent violence in Kosovo."[19] A defining moment occurred on January 18, 1999, when the Prosecutor applied for entry to Kosovo in order to "investigate the reported atrocities at Racak," but was refused. This hardened views in NATO member States that no political settlement would work unless it allowed for the deployment of a substantial NATO-led force. Even during the hostilities, ICTY investigators were active outside Kosovo in collecting evidence of crimes by the Yugoslav forces in the province.[20]

---

19. Text of ICTY Prosecutor's statement of March 10, 1998 is *in* THE KOSOVO CONFLICT AND INTERNATIONAL LAW, *supra* note 13, at 515.
20. For a useful account, see particularly David Gowan (formerly UK War Crimes Coordinator at the Foreign and Commonwealth Office, London), *Kosovo: The British Government and ICTY*, 13 LEIDEN JOURNAL OF INTERNATIONAL LAW 913–29 (2000).

The announcement on May 24, 1999 of the indictment of Slobodan Milosevic, President of the Federal Republic of Yugoslavia, and four colleagues further illustrated the way in which ICTY's role was unavoidably caught up in political and military events.[21] Milosevic was indicted in respect of the conduct of Yugoslav forces in Kosovo during the war there in 1998-9. In this particular case, despite speculation to the contrary, the indictment may have contributed to the willingness of Milosevic to make the concessions necessary for a settlement, as he did early in June 1999. The ICTY indictment, as General Clark has argued, may have hardened European resolve to continue with the struggle.[22] It is also possible that it compelled Milosevic to focus on reaching a settlement while he still had a functioning State around him which could protect him from arrest and trial; and it may also have shocked him into an erroneous belief that he could escape from the threat of trial by cutting a deal with NATO.[23] If he did entertain any such hope, he was to be disappointed. On June 28, 2001 Milosevic, by this time the former President, was extradited to The Hague to face trial, which began on February 12, 2002. This first-ever extradition of a former head of State to face trial before an international criminal tribunal is an important precedent.

The ICTY's most unusual role, its consideration of NATO actions, was particularly controversial in the United States. In 1999 the United States, having been campaigning diplomatically against the projected International Criminal Court for the previous six months on the grounds that the actions of US forces should not be subject to a foreign prosecutor and tribunal, chose to wage war in the one part of the world where ongoing war was subject to such a tribunal. The ICTY, the establishment of which the United States had actively promoted in 1993, has much stronger powers of independent investigation and prosecution than are provided for the projected International Criminal Court under the terms of the 1998 Rome Statute.[24]

---

21. For texts of the key documents relating to the indictment of Milosevic, see THE KOSOVO CONFLICT AND INTERNATIONAL LAW, *supra* note 13, at 516–29.
22. CLARK, *supra* note 1, at 327–8, where it is confirmed that the Pentagon and White House were not happy with the ICTY Prosecutor's decision to issue the indictment.
23. This is argued by James Gow of King's College, London in THE SERBIAN PROJECT AND ITS ADVERSARIES: A STRATEGY OF WAR CRIMES (2002).
24. Compare the uncomplicated provisions on jurisdiction, investigation and prosecution in Articles 1 and 18 of the 1993 ICTY Statute, U.N. Doc. S/25704, May 3, 1993, *available at* http://www.un.org/icty/basic/statut/stat2000_con.htm, with the much more heavily qualified provisions on the same subjects in the 1998 Rome Statute, U.N. Doc. A/CONF/183/9, July 17, 1998 *available at* http://www.un.org/law/icc/statute/romefra.htm.

On May 14, 1999, while hostilities in the Kosovo War were ongoing, the ICTY Prosecutor established a committee to assess the numerous allegations made against the NATO bombing campaign and the material accompanying them. It prepared an interim report which was presented to the Prosecutor on December 6, 1999. On February 1, 2000 the Prosecutor stated that there was no evidence that NATO's bombing campaign had violated international treaties on the conduct of war. The committee investigating the NATO campaign then prepared a detailed final report, published in June 2000, discussing the numerous facts and issues involved. It provided evidence for the conclusion that as a result of the NATO bombing approximately 495 civilians were killed and 820 wounded in documented instances. It recommended that "neither an in-depth investigation related to the bombing campaign as a whole nor investigations related to specific incidents are justified. In all cases, either the law is not sufficiently clear or investigations are unlikely to result in the acquisition of sufficient evidence to substantiate charges against high level accused or against lower accused for particularly heinous offences." The Report's final recommendation was that "no investigation be commenced by the OTP [Office of the Prosecutor] in relation to the NATO bombing campaign or incidents occurring during the campaign."[25] On June 2, 2000 the ICTY Prosecutor, Carla del Ponte, stated in her address to the UN Security Council that she would not open a criminal investigation into any aspect of NATO's bombing campaign, and this was confirmed eleven days later in a statement issued by the Office of the Prosecutor.[26]

The Report to the Prosecutor had many limitations, and the reactions to it showed how difficult it is to get justice done, and seen to be done, when controversial issues of war, peace and national pride are at stake. ICTY's consideration of the bombing campaign ran into two depressingly predictable lines of political criticism. First, some initial US reactions suggested a sense of outrage that any prosecutor anywhere would even contemplate the possibility of investigating a US-led military action. Because of this outrage, there was little sign that ICTY's decision not to launch any criminal investigation caused any easing of US concerns about the proposed International Criminal Court. Secondly, some reactions by countries and individuals critical of the NATO campaign suggested that the ICTY was hardly impartial, not least because NATO member States had played a significant part in creating it, financing it, and

---

25. Report to the Prosecutor, Appendix A, ¶¶ 53, 90, 91.
26. ICTY Press Release PR/PIS/510e of June 13, 2000.

arresting indicted individuals. In this view, ICTY could not realistically have embarked on prosecutions of NATO personnel.

In addition to such political criticisms, the Report to the Prosecutor was vulnerable on other grounds. It was criticized by some international lawyers as being insufficiently rigorous in its consideration of NATO actions and decision-making, especially as regards the balancing of military advantage and civilian damage.[27] Even to those, like myself, who do not quarrel with its overall recommendation, some parts of its analysis call for comment. On the question of damage to the environment it makes the common mistake of assuming that the only relevant provisions in treaty law are those provisions of Protocol I, namely Articles 35(3) and 55, which specifically mention the word "environment."[28] On the question of what is a military objective, it states (probably correctly) that Protocol I, Article 52, is "generally accepted as part of customary law," but nowhere mentions the declarations made in respect of that article by many States, including NATO members.[29] On the question of the scale and gravity of offence that brings an action within ICTY's remit, the Report says remarkably little. Indeed, the Report implies, in the concluding passage quoted above, that the reasons for not pursuing any investigation were a lack of clarity of the law, or a lack of sufficient evidence. The fundamental reason why ICTY could not act in this matter, not fully expressed in the conclusions, was that the alleged NATO offenses, because of considerations of scale, gravity and absence of criminal intent, did not pass the threshold that would have brought them into the court's remit. Despite such flaws, the committee performed a service by openly addressing a number of difficult issues raised by the NATO bombing campaign, and demonstrating that, although NATO decisions and actions were within ICTY's jurisdiction, there were serious grounds for doubt as to whether any of them was such as to merit further investigation and possible prosecution.

Ultimately ICTY's most important role in relation to Kosovo, as well as to other parts of the former Yugoslavia, may be by holding particular individuals

---

27. See particularly Michael Bothe, *The Protection of the Civilian Population and NATO Bombing on Yugoslavia: Comments on a Report to the Prosecutor of the ICTY*, 12 EUROPEAN JOURNAL OF INTERNATIONAL LAW 531–5 (2001) and Natalino Ronzitti, *Is the Non Liquet of the Final Report by the Committee Established to Review the NATO Bombing Campaign against the Federal Republic of Yugoslavia Acceptable?*, 82 INTERNATIONAL REVIEW OF THE RED CROSS 1017–28 (2000).

28. Report to the Prosecutor, Appendix A, ¶¶ 14–25. For discussion of the other parts of the laws of war that bear on damage to the environment, see my chapters in the two works on the environment mentioned in note 34 *infra*.

29. Report to the Prosecutor, Appendix A, ¶¶ 35–47. On the declarations re Protocol I, Article 42, see DOCUMENTS ON THE LAWS OF WAR, supra note 3, at 500–11.

guilty of some of the terrible crimes associated with ethnic cleansing. Only by establishing individual guilt in this way can the idea of collective guilt be effectively challenged.[30]

Variety of Forms of Non-belligerence and Neutrality

The campaign confirmed the lesson of numerous wars of the twentieth century that non-participation in war can assume many forms much more subtle and complex than the impartial neutrality spelled out in certain laws of war agreements. Two developments of the Kosovo crisis and war stand out—one typical, the other exceptional. First, in this war various non-belligerent States took part in the ongoing UN economic sanctions against the Federal Republic of Yugoslavia, and some offered some other elements of support for the NATO operations. These events thus confirmed the lesson of many other conflicts in the twentieth century, that the traditional law of neutrality, with its emphasis on impartiality, is far from covering all circumstances and cases. Secondly, one part of the Federal Republic of Yugoslavia, namely Montenegro, pursued a policy close to neutrality during the NATO bombing campaign. From the outset of hostilities NATO policy-makers recognized this remarkable, perhaps even unprecedented, state of affairs, and acted accordingly.[31] This is further evidence that the law's neat classification of States into belligerents and neutrals can be confounded by messy realities; and that the reasons for moderation in war extend far beyond *jus in bello*.

These developments show that life (in the form of conduct during war) is richer than art (in the form of legal agreements). However, they do not show that there is an urgent need to modify art to reflect the complexities of life. Neither of these developments threw up serious practical problems—certainly not those of the kind that could attract a general legal answer. In particular, it would be a brave person who dared to assert, as a matter of general right, that the component parts of a federal State should be free to declare their neutrality, especially in a war in which the parent State is under direct assault from outside. What these developments do show is that law can only provide a

---

30. A point made forcefully by Chris Patten, European Commissioner for External Affairs, in a speech to the International Crisis Group, Brussels, July 10, 2001. He credited the idea to President Stipe Mesic of Croatia.
31. See the passages praising Montenegro's independent stance and warning Serbia not to change it, which were made in US Secretary of State Madeleine Albright's press conference on Kosovo, Washington DC, March 25, 1999 *in* THE KOSOVO CONFLICT AND INTERNATIONAL LAW, *supra* note 13, at 417, 419.

partial framework for the conduct of States and individuals during war: unique situations which defy tidy legal categorization frequently occur.

New Codifications

Certain issues raised in recent wars, including the Kosovo War, have been perceived by some as pointing to lacunae in the existing law. Three major controversies arising from the Kosovo War, and which might point to the need for new codification, concerned the environmental effects of war generally, and two related issues, depleted uranium and cluster bombs.[32]

Environmental effects of war

This is a complex area, on which existing treaty law offers general principles as well as a number of relevant rules. The best available short summary of the legal framework on this subject is the 1994 ICRC/UN General Assembly document "Guidelines for Military Manuals and Instructions on the Protection of the Environment in Times of Armed Conflict."[33] In studies of the subject there has been a broad consensus against the idea of trying to negotiate a new treaty on the protection of the environment in war.[34]

Many NATO actions in the Kosovo War led to expressions of concern on environmental grounds. The actions that were most questioned included the destruction of bridges causing blockage of major rivers; attacks on power stations having serious knock-on effects on water supplies, etc.; other attacks on the infrastructure of Serbia; and the use of depleted uranium and cluster bombs, discussed separately below.

There were prompt and careful investigations of certain key issues. A study conducted under the auspices of the United Nations Environment Programme in 1999 concluded a key part of its study: "There is no evidence of an ecological catastrophe for the Danube as a result of the air strikes during the Kosovo conflict." It went on to say, however, that there were "some

---

32. All three issues were discussed in the Report to the Prosecutor, Appendix A, ¶¶ 14–27.
33. U.N. Doc. A/49/323 of 19 August 1994, at 49–53. Text in DOCUMENTS ON THE LAWS OF WAR, *supra* note 3, at 609–14.
34. See especially the two main general works on the subject: PROTECTION OF THE ENVIRONMENT DURING ARMED CONFLICT (Richard Grunawalt, John King and Ronald McClain eds., 1996) (Vol. 69, US Naval War College, International Law Studies) and THE ENVIRONMENTAL CONSEQUENCES OF WAR: LEGAL, ECONOMIC AND SCIENTIFIC PERSPECTIVES (Jay Austin and Carl Bruch eds., 2000). In the latter, see especially Carl Bruch and Jay Austin, *Epilogue: The Kosovo Conflict: A Case Study of Unresolved Issues*, at 647–64. This lays out certain general issues usefully.

serious hot spots where contamination by hazardous substances released during the air strikes poses risks for human health and the aquatic environment." It also stressed that there was long-term chronic pollution of the Danube due to factors other than the war.[35] The report was overwhelmingly concerned with describing the situation and proposing remedial action: it did not discuss existing or possible future international legal regimes governing environmental destruction in war. The Chairman of the Task Force that prepared the report stated that the exercise "marked the first time that an environmental impact assessment had been made of any war, though the UN did look at the effects of oil well fires after the Gulf War with Iraq."[36]

For the future, while no grand general treaty on the environmental effects of war is remotely probable, it seems likely that the practice of evaluating actual cases, coupled with demands for remedial action, will continue.

Depleted uranium

The military value of depleted uranium (DU) shells in piercing heavy armor is proven. At the same time the very mention of the word "uranium" arouses considerable public anxiety. The use of DU in the Kosovo War, and the various issues that it raised, was not well handled by NATO spokespersons either during or after the war.[37]

The greatest controversy in NATO member States concerned fears that exposure to DU might have been a cause of subsequent cases of cancer among their own troops. In this connection there were criticisms of official policy towards NATO/KFOR troops involved in operations in Kosovo after the end of the bombing campaign. This is not strictly speaking a laws of war issue, as it involves relations between governments and their own troops. Some member States, including the UK, were inconsistent in the briefings given to their own

---

35. UNEP/UNCHS BALKANS TASK FORCE, THE KOSOVO CONFLICT: CONSEQUENCES FOR THE ENVIRONMENT AND HUMAN SETTLEMENTS 60–1 (1999), *available at* http://www.grid.unep.ch/btf/final/index.html.
36. Pekka Haavisto, former Finnish Environment and Development Cooperation Minister and Chair of the UNEP/UNCHS Balkans Task Force, presenting the report at a press conference in Stockholm on October 14, 1999. Frances Williams, Christopher Brown-Humes and Neil Buckley, *NATO "hindered" Kosovo inquiry*, FINANCIAL TIMES (London), Oct. 15, 1999, at 30.
37. After the war, NATO spokesmen were reluctant to say anything about DU, and even cast doubt on whether it had been used at all. The UNEP/UNCHS Balkans Task Force, in its 1999 report, commented on the lack of information from NATO. *See* THE KOSOVO CONFLICT, *supra* note 35, at 61–2. The task force chairman, in his presentation on October 14, 1999, elaborated on these complaints. *See* NATO "hindered" Kosovo inquiry, *supra* note 36, at 30.

troops serving in Kosovo about possible hazards, and also about subsequent health screening.[38]

As far as *jus in bello* is concerned, the main issues raised are the possible effects of DU on adversary troops and third parties, both during and after an armed conflict. In particular, the use of DU involves a matter with which the laws of war have long dealt: the adverse effect that remnants of war may have, including on innocent civilians, long after hostilities are over. The scientific evidence about possible health effects of DU is still inconclusive, and the ICRC has been notably cautious in its statements on the matter. In view of DU's exceptionally slow rate of radioactive decay it is far from certain whether any worry should focus on its radioactivity. Grounds for concern which seem more likely to have a strong scientific basis are (a) evidence of impurities including much more highly radioactive isotopes of uranium; and (b) the possible toxicity of DU, though this is far from established. Such concerns will be increased by reports of pollution of groundwater in Kosovo. Careful scientific investigation of the effects of DU must be the first priority. Since there is at present no international consensus on its effects or on the desirability of putting legal controls on it, DU will not be a promising subject for negotiation until there has been a fuller scientific investigation.

Cluster bombs

The explosive remnants of war, a problem of long standing which has traditionally been a subject of concern in the laws of war, proved to be a serious problem in the aftermath of the Kosovo War. Cluster bombs formed one part of that problem. These weapons, which are meant to explode on impact and/or to deactivate themselves after a specific period, can cause particularly severe problems when they fail to do so. In the year after the NATO bombing campaign ended in June 1999, at least 50 people in Kosovo were killed and 101 injured by unexploded bomblets. Over 15,000 unexploded bomblets were left in Kosovo, and NATO was criticized for failing to provide sufficient information on where cluster bombs were dropped. Cluster bombs killed or maimed five times more Kosovar children than landmines. Peter Herby, head of the Red Cross anti-mines unit, said: "Anti-personnel landmines were doing what they were meant to do, but were not being used properly. Cluster bombs are causing this problem because they're not doing what they were designed to

---

38. Michael Smith and Nigel Bunyan, *Soldiers will be screened for uranium exposure*, THE DAILY TELEGRAPH (London), Jan. 9, 2001; Nicholas Watt and Richard Norton-Taylor, *Troops not told of shells' toxic risk*, THE GUARDIAN (London), Feb. 8, 2001, at 8.

do, so it's a bit more difficult to argue on humanitarian grounds."[39] Despite this difficulty, the use of cluster bombs could usefully be addressed within a laws of war framework: the harm they can do to innocents is hardly in dispute, and although complete prohibition is unlikely, means to reduce the threat they pose to civilians and others should be investigated.

The United States and Certain Laws of War Agreements

US non-participation in key treaties

Despite its conspicuous role in certain acts of enforcement of the laws of war, the United States is not a party to several important treaties on the laws of war. Its notorious difficulties in accepting international treaties produced the strange result that it took the United States forty years to ratify the 1948 Genocide Convention. The United States is still not formally a party to the following agreements.

- *The 1954 Hague Cultural Property Convention.* Parties: 103. (The United States signed in 1954, but it has not been ratified.)
- *The 1977 Geneva Protocols I & II on International and Non-international Armed Conflicts.* Parties: 159 and 152 respectively. (The United States signed both on December 12, 1977, but has not ratified either one.)
- *The 1980 Protocol III on Incendiary Weapons.* Parties: 81.
- *The 1995 Protocol IV on Blinding Laser Weapons.* Parties: 63.
- *The 1997 Ottawa Convention on Anti-personnel Land-mines.* Parties: 124.
- *The 1998 Statute of the International Criminal Court.* Parties: 75. (The United States signed on December 31, 2000, but has not ratified it. In May 2002 the United States informed the Depositary that it did not

---

39. Peter Capella, *Nato bombs "still killing" in Kosovo*, THE GUARDIAN (London), Sept. 6, 2000, at 14, commenting on a Red Cross report first issued in September 2000. A revised version of this report is INTERNATIONAL COMMITTEE OF THE RED CROSS, CLUSTER BOMBS AND LANDMINES IN KOSOVO: EXPLOSIVE REMNANTS OF WAR (2001). I have also relied here on the annual reports of the UN Mine Action Coordination Centre (MACC) in Pristina, *available at* www.mineaction.org. The final annual report on the UN Interim Administration in Kosovo Mine Action Programme, covering the period to December 15, 2001, stated that it "has successfully completed its objectives, and the problems associated with land mines, cluster munitions and other items of unexploded ordnance in Kosovo have virtually been eliminated." (¶ 4.) Over 47,000 devices were cleared. (¶ 9.) Nonetheless, there continued to be concerns about a remaining threat from unexploded cluster bomblets in Kosovo, with further finds being reported, e.g., by Richard Lloyd, Director of Landmine Action, London.

intend to become a party to the treaty and accordingly has no legal obligations arising from its signature.)[40]

It would be wrong to view the US's or any other State's non-participation in a treaty as in itself a failure. There are some questionable provisions in some treaties in this area. Although a non-party, the United States takes at least some of these accords more seriously than some States that are parties. The reasons for US non-participation go far beyond the obduracy of one single elderly Senator, and call for careful analysis rather than uncomprehending condemnation. In some cases they are based on serious arguments.

Indeed, there may be a price for like-minded States taking the lead in negotiation of particular treaties, as happened in the case of the Ottawa land-mines convention. The price is that States which are partially or wholly outside the consensus, and have particular problems which need to be addressed, feel sidelined. This also happened at the Rome conference in 1998. Add a prohibition on reservations—as was done with the Ottawa and Rome treaties—and there is a recipe for non-participation even by States, such as the United States, which have a serious record of supporting the general thrust of these projects.

Of the above agreements, the one most directly relevant to the NATO operations in the Kosovo War was the Protocol I. At the time of the Kosovo War, all NATO States were parties except the United States, Turkey and France.[41] Although the Protocol was in force between many NATO members and the FRY (which, too, was a party to Protocol I), in formal legal terms the United States was not so bound. This unevenness in the formal participation in a key treaty could in principle have posed many problems in the conduct of the Kosovo operations. In practice the fact that three NATO members were not at that time parties to Protocol I does not appear to have been a problem. This was mainly because the United States had long accepted that it would observe a high proportion of the Protocol's provisions, either because they

---

40. Information as of July 1, 2002 from ICRC, UN and UNESCO websites, *available at* www.icrc.org, www.un.org, and www.unesco.org, respectively.
41. France acceded to Protocol I on April 11, 2001.

represented customary law, or because it had been decided to apply them as a matter of policy, especially in view of the reality of coalition warfare.[42]

Of the treaties to which the United States is not a party, probably the most politically neuralgic is not the Protocol I (sensitive as that issue continues to be) but the 1998 Rome Statute of the International Criminal Court. The opposition of the United States to this treaty, marking a reversal of its earlier support for the general idea of such a court, reflects the fundamental American concern that US forces deployed in a wide range of situations globally might face unfounded or politically motivated prosecutions, over which the United States would have no control. The detailed terms of the Rome Statute contain certain safeguards against such an eventuality.[43] Because of these provisions, I am tempted to say that the United States is suffering from a case of "prosecution mania." However, in Washington DC the fear of such prosecutions was and is real. One of many US areas of concern is that in its conduct of military operations the United States might decide to attack "dual-use" targets in a country, as it did in the Kosovo War, and then face an enthusiastic prosecutor who might view this as an illegal attack on civilian objects.

Certain political and military hazards may flow from US non-participation in the Rome Statute. The US voice on certain key issues may well be muffled. In the future, US complaints about violations of the laws of war by its adversaries, and demands for the arrest of certain war criminals, may be weakened by the US refusal to accept even the potential application of international judicial procedures under the ICC to any US forces. However, the most serious consequence of US non-participation will be for the power of the court itself. Without US participation, there are bound to be questions about whether the ICC will have sufficient power to operate effectively.

---

42. A succinct exposition of US policy on the application of Protocols I and II is in the US Army's Judge Advocate General's School's OPERATIONAL LAW HANDBOOK 2002, at ch. 2, pp. 4–5, and ch. 11, pp. 13–15 (Jeanne Meyer and Brian Bill eds., 2002), *available at* the Judge Advocate General's School's website at http://www.jagcnet.army.mil/JAGCNETInternet/Homepages/AC/CLAMO-Public.nsf.

43. Among the provisions of the Rome Statute offering safeguards: Article 8 on war crimes, which requires that they be "committed as part of a plan or policy or as part of a large-scale commission of such crimes." Certain safeguards in the case of "second track jurisdiction" (i.e., where the matter has not come to the ICC from the UN Security Council): Article 16, enabling the Security Council to require the ICC to defer an investigation or prosecution; Article 17, providing that a case is inadmissible where a State is genuinely carrying out investigation or prosecution itself; and Article 18, enabling a State party to request the ICC to defer an investigation if such State is pursuing the same matter, although such deferral is left to the ICC's decision.

This pattern of US non-participation in existing treaties is, at least for this observer, worrying. Other States which have a record of foreign military activity, including the United Kingdom, manage to be parties to many more of these agreements, and have been less nervous about the possibility, remote as it may be, of seeing the actions of their forces being actually or potentially submitted to the not always tender mercies of foreign prosecutors and courts.[44] When a State such as the United States that on occasion acts as a principal guarantor of implementation of humanitarian norms itself avoids being subject to many of those norms through the regular mechanism of treaty ratification, it invites criticism.

Impact of legal norms in US-led combat operations

Whatever the US fears, the actual impact of international legal norms on US conduct of operations has often been positive. Commitment to the laws of war has contributed to the post-Vietnam rehabilitation of the US armed forces. In both the 1991 Gulf War and the 1999 war over Kosovo, the United States, though not a party to Protocol I, observed many of its provisions—whether because of their customary law status, because it was policy to support them anyway, or because of a need to harmonize targeting and other matters with allies. The experience of these wars suggested that most of these provisions represented a useful set of guidelines for professional conduct.

Conclusions

After a war, there is a need to evaluate how well belligerents observe the rules of war; and there is also a need to evaluate how appropriate or otherwise the law is to the ever-changing circumstances and forms of armed conflict.

The NATO role in the 1999 Kosovo War was in some respects remarkably successful, and did enable the overwhelming majority of people who had fled from their homes to return. However, before too many lessons are drawn from this success, it must be emphasized that it had many exceptional features, as well as some that are more typical of the new types of conflict. There is probably a danger, as Mark Twain would have put it, of seeing more wisdom in it than is there. A war in which one side had no casualties is exceptional, and hardly likely to be repeated. Equally, it is hardly typical of modern conflict for

---

44. The United Kingdom completed a key part of the Rome Statute ratification process on May 10, 2001, when the House of Commons passed the ICC Bill. Its ratification was registered with the depositary on October 4, 2001.

Western armed forces to find themselves in combat against a disciplined armed force under an organized State. With these caveats, the following conclusions are offered.

1. To a large extent NATO did succeed in the aim of avoiding damage to civilians, and the events of the war largely confirm the value and viability of the soldier/civilian distinction that is so central in the laws of war.

2. However, the war caused the death of about 495 civilians, had a huge impact on civilians in both Kosovo and Serbia, and involved extensive destruction of "dual-use" targets. It is possible that the threat of further societal destruction in Serbia played some part in the Serbian decision to capitulate: if this is correct, then it follows that the requirement of victory, and the need to observe the laws of war, could have been in considerable tension with each other. NATO strategic doctrine, in so far as it concentrates on attacking the adversary's governmental structure, can involve problems in relation to the laws of war. The question of what is a legitimate objective, addressed principally in Article 52 of 1977 Geneva Protocol I, remains a difficult one, and a subject of contestation.

3. Reliance on air power as a means of implementing an action for fundamentally humanitarian purposes raised difficult moral questions. It also proved to be something of a gamble, both because it could not protect the victims in the short term, and because many other factors were required to bring about the Milosevic capitulation. The sense that the campaign had been a close-run thing, and the product of a unique set of circumstances, contributed to a feeling in many countries that it was unlikely to be repeated.

4. Implementation of the laws of war, and humanitarian norms more generally, had a particularly high profile not only in the course of this war, but also in its beginnings and its ending. The importance of ensuring observance of international humanitarian norms contributed to the factors leading up to the initiation of the NATO military campaign. The indictment of Milosevic on May 27, 1999 may have played some part in the Yugoslav leader's decision to accept the eventual settlement.

5. Whether this war will prove to have some deterrent function in respect of potential future violations of fundamental humanitarian norms remains to be seen. It did not stop Indonesian forces from engaging in mass killings in East Timor in September 1999; though it may have given credibility to the efforts subsequently made under UN auspices to stop the killings.

6. Among the many difficult laws of war issues raised by the war, perhaps the most urgent is the explosive remnants of war, and in particular cluster

bombs. On depleted uranium, more knowledge of its impact on health is needed before that issue can be usefully addressed in the laws of war.

7. It remains an odd although not completely inexplicable paradox that the United States, which has played the key part in developing a use of air warfare that is reasonably consistent with key principles and provisions of the laws of war, is outside so many parts of the treaty regime of the laws of war. This situation calls for careful analysis, not shrill condemnation. After the experience of Kosovo, the US government could usefully re-examine the treaties to which it is not party, to see if it can bring itself more into line with a treaty regime which it has, in large measure, not merely observed but also found useful, not least in the 1999 Kosovo War. Unfortunately there has been a tendency in the United States to react negatively and defensively to the reasonably judicious ICTY review of the NATO bombing campaign; and this tendency has reinforced the US government's resistance to becoming a party to certain laws of war treaties, including the ICC Statute.

8. The Kosovo War, and the role of the laws of war in it, evoked different perceptions in different parts of the world. Some perceived the war favorably as a case of NATO coming to the aid of an oppressed population which happened to be predominantly Muslim, and maintaining certain limits in its conduct of military operations. However others viewed these events much more critically, as one further proof that the armed forces of northern countries, especially of course the United States, have established such a monopoly on the battlefield that the only effective response to their presumed dominance becomes an asymmetric one, including terrorist attacks. In this view, to the extent that the laws of war are considered at all, they are deemed to suit the north more than the south. Such a perception may be rooted in a naive and probably incorrect view of the results that are presumed to flow from terrorist attacks and other unlawful acts, but it appears to be held by many. Partly because of such perceptions, the effective US/NATO conduct of operations in the Kosovo War, in a manner deeply influenced by laws of war considerations, may paradoxically fail to discourage certain groups from conduct in which such considerations are alien.

Propositions on the Law of War after the Kosovo Campaign

Ruth Wedgwood

Jus Ad Bellum and the Personal Factor in History

After Kosovo, any purely proceduralist account of the international community's use of force must be found wanting. Belgrade's sovereign claim to Kosovo, even including the right to police the activities of the Kosovo Liberation Army (KLA), did not plausibly include the right to deport the majority of its own ethnic Albanian citizens. After the failed negotiations at Rambouillet and the beginning of the bombing campaign, Belgrade's troops and police deliberately forced 740,000 Albanian Kosovars to flee their villages and cross the borders into Albania and Macedonia—providing a *casus belli* for a continued allied campaign even if any was disputed before. Belgrade committed its clumsy acts of violence and coercion in the full sight of international officials and CNN television cameras. The tactics bore witness to Milosevic's political madness and ethical hedonism. Yet many public international lawyers have felt great difficulty in admitting any legal justification for the NATO intervention in the absence of formal endorsement by the UN Security Council.

This pure proceduralism is odd in the extreme, for even the Security Council's endorsement could not have stilled questions about the outer limits of the post-Cold War Charter of the United Nations. Council decisions may not resolve all issues of international law and ultra vires action, if one is to believe the International Court of Justice in the *Lockerbie* jurisdictional decision. Thus, even with Council endorsement, one would have to resort to the teleology of the Charter, including its strengthened embrace of human rights, to indulge the new limits of Chapter VII.

Rather than resting upon a mechanistic decision rule, legitimacy for the use of force may also be strengthened by a resort to history—in the appropriate inferences about intention, shown by an adversary's past behavior. The allied response in Kosovo has to be taken in the context of a decade's disorder. Milosevic was the excessive personality who lit the tinder for the wars in Croatia and Bosnia, and beguiled the West with a false promise of cooperation at Dayton. Though he rose to power on the back of Serbian nationalism, he sharpened its talons and started three wars. Just as Napoleon was ultimately found to be a threat to the peace of Europe, and Hitler was irrepressibly aggressive, so in this smaller neighborhood, Milosevic showed himself to be the indefatigable author of conflict. To understand the interpretive context of a legal principle, such as an emerging right of humanitarian intervention, requires some attention to history and its actors. Milosevic violated the "one-bite" rule, showing no inhibition against repeating his bouleversement of delicate ethnic balances, savaging local populations, and ignoring NATO's ultimate commitment to the area evidenced in the Bosnian air campaign in 1995. One may not wish to endorse a principle of humanitarian intervention or regional stabilization for the ordinary case, and yet may admit its validity where the antagonist has shown a hearty and unsated appetite for trouble. After the frustration of the "dual key" use of force in Bosnia, it is hardly surprising that the Security Council was not given the controlling key in yet another war.

The Consanguinity of Jus ad Bellum and Jus in Bello

It is commonly believed that the tactics of war must be judged independently of the purpose of a war. The divorce of purpose and tactics is designed to allow agreement on humanitarian limits even where there is no consensus on the merits of the underlying dispute. But this asserted independence of the two regimes may be no more than a fiction. Defeating Nazism, for example, required measures that are now seen as harsh and even punitive. Even where their legality is conceded under the earlier standards of air war, it is commonly taught in American military curricula that their repetition would now be illegal. It may be that our real judgment of their contemporaneous legality is affected by the radical evil represented by Nazism—an ideology posing an ultimate threat to human welfare. Kosovo, in its smaller venue, may be another illustration of that same quiet linkage. This was not a war to settle a commercial dispute, or remap the location of a boundary valued because of mineral deposits, but rather a war to prevent ethnic expulsions. As such, its speedy conclusion was necessary. A gradual war of attrition that might defeat

Belgrade in slow motion was unacceptable in light of the human survival at stake in the conflict itself. Whether one's framework is utilitarian or pure principle, it is possible to admit that the merits of a war make a difference in our tolerance for methods of warfighting. This teleological view can be incorporated, albeit awkwardly, in the metric for "military advantage" in judging proportionality, for surely we do not value military objectives for their own sake. But it may be better to be forthright, even at the cost of questioning homilies. The latitude allowed to a victor in a conflict is commonly dismissed as self-indulgence—supposing that the law of war is mere victor's justice, might making right. An alternative explanation is possible. Democratic leaders and publics may believe there is an important link between the legitimate purpose of a war and its allowable tactics—at least within the limits of basic humanity and the protection of civilian lives.

The Contentious Role of Civilian Tribunals

The enforcement of the law of war has traditionally been left to military judges. This was so in the proposed trial of the Kaiser after World War One. The Nuremberg and Far East trials after World War Two were conducted before military tribunals, designated as such. (Indeed, Nuremberg's limitation of jurisdiction over crimes against humanity to the period of the world war reflected the extent to which the proceeding was conceived as a military trial.) The latter-day invention of the field of "international humanitarian law" has obscured the extent to which implementation of many aspects of the law of war depend on battlefield judgments and knowledge of campaign strategy, and therefore may be suitable to military tribunals. For example, the destruction of the bridges over the Danube in the Kosovo campaign may be understood as a stratagem to force Milosevic to gamble between theatres for the placement of his armor. (He could head north to meet a possible NATO invasion from Hungary, or south to meet a NATO invasion from Albania while continuing his ethnic cleansing operations. With the severance of bridges across the Danube, he had one vulnerable flank). The dependence of the prosecutor at the International Criminal Tribunal for the former Yugoslavia on a committee of experts in evaluating allegations against NATO and in attempting to judge the legitimacy of Kosovo targeting choices shows the extent to which the law of war depends on judgments that may lie outside the experience of lay judges or prosecutors. We have overlooked that the law of war contains both bright-line rules and open-textured principles, and that only the former are so easily applied. This is a serious potential defect in the new International Criminal

Court as well, where judges are to be chosen on the basis of experience in criminal law or international humanitarian law, but not for familiarity with military operations. The dangers of professional back-scratching in evaluating battlefield events should weigh in, of course, but is limited by the commitments of the military in a democratic society.

One-Trick Ponies and Specialized Armies

To a surprising extent, military equipment is designed for specialized war fighting tasks and this, too, was shown in Kosovo. We learned the same lesson in the 1980 Iranian hostage rescue mission. NATO's weaponry was planned for a very different conflict, in which allied forces would face off against massed enemy troops on the plains of Central Europe.

Much of the academic critique of NATO's operational plans and decision-making in Kosovo ignores the unique and unexpected nature of the Kosovo tasking. This was pick-up ball, redeploying weapons systems in a context far different from their original planned use. If the West is serious about humanitarian intervention as a vocation, it will need to rethink decisions about force structure and equipment. For example, to optimize target discrimination, especially for delicate distinctions between army vehicles and civilian convoys, one would like to have more JSTARS (Joint Surveillance Target Attack Radar Systems). So, too, the ability to react against mobile targets in a mountainous and frequently cloudy terrain would be enhanced by fully integrated data systems among services and allies. The real intention of the international community to implement a new ethic of humanitarian intervention may be judged (as wanting) by the extent to which most traditional powers are cutting back on military spending and force structure. The recent decisions of European countries such as France, Italy, and Germany to reduce military budgets, cut manpower, and shorten conscription periods, do not give much credence to any claimed doctrine of humanitarian police. A lightly-armed European rapid reaction corps will not, by itself, win humanitarian wars.

Surrogate Ground Forces and Conflict Containment

In an unhappy reminiscence of Afghanistan during the Russian occupation, the Kosovo experience shows the difficulties of controlling surrogate ground forces. In the aftermath of the Kosovo war, for example, the KLA extended its "defense" of Albanian communities to northern Macedonia as well as the Presevo valley in Serbia, threatening to regionalize the war. Evaluation of the efficacy of NATO's Kosovo air strategy in any "lessons learned" must be tempered by the realization that building-up local insurgents will be costly when their long-term political agenda is vastly differ from our own.

Picking Winners

The dilemma of a post-conflict breakdown in law and order (politely termed a mid-level security gap) is familiar to veterans of most peacekeeping missions. Ambassador Bob Oakley has written a troubling survey of the problem for the National Defense University,[1] and Timor-veteran Graham Day has named "policekeeping" as the major problem in post-conflict transitions. Wherever a long-standing government has been displaced, whether in Panama, Haiti, East Timor, or Kosovo, there is a raw edge in the aftermath because basic *gendarme* functions are lacking. In the absence of an effective international police presence, with language skills and the capacity to build a network of local cooperation, it is unlikely that one can control the violent "to-and-fro" between ethnic communities except by measures such as Dayton's *de facto* segregation.

Acknowledging this incapacity to fine-tune factional disputes with an international peacekeeping force, one must be realistic about the available set of outcomes to the conflict. The only real choice, regrettably, may be to "pick a winner"—while realizing that the side favored by the international community will share many of the illiberal qualities of its antagonist. In Kosovo, NATO succeeded in stopping Belgrade's ethnic cleansing of Muslims, but the U.N. follow-on force has predictably been unable to control violent attacks against Kosovar Serbs by the KLA.

The ideal of a multi-ethnic democracy, which was so attractively packaged for media export by the Sarajevo government in the Bosnian war, is hardly characteristic of the aftermath of the Kosovo intervention. One can see something of the same problem in East Timor, where violence against the returning West Timorese and ethnic Chinese continues to be a problem, and, of course, in Rwanda. A decision to intervene must depend not on the pretense of a future multi-ethnic democracy, for that end state will often not be available. It must be on some rougher calculus of which outcome minimizes overall abuse.

---

1. POLICING THE NEW WORLD DISORDER: PEACE OPERATIONS AND PUBLIC SECURITY (R.B. Oakley, E.M. Goldberg, M. J. Dziedzic, eds. 2002).

Precision-Guided Munitions and the Transparency of Intention

In the past, technological limits have often obscured the more difficult issues of target discrimination. In the air campaigns of World War Two and the Korean conflict, the radius of uncertainty for ordnance delivery against industrial targets and transportation nodes often mooted the question whether other objects would qualify as military or civilian assets. Gravity bombs and a limited ability to see through weather left a five-mile radius for probable point of impact, and finer gradations would have seemed an intellectual construct.

But the extraordinary precision of guided munitions used in the Yugoslav campaign brings front and center the most contentious questions of targeting. Aim points are made utterly clear to potential critics, and the legal categorization of cigarette factories, television stations, urban bridges, and train depots will be mooted by skeptical observers. With a targeteer's intention made plain for the world to see, the indeterminate language of humanitarian law becomes a potential hazard for warfighters. If munitions are precise, the law is vague. The hazard is increased by the active campaign to juridicalize the law of war in international fora—including the International Criminal Court and the International Court of Justice, not to mention national courts exercising universal jurisdiction. The loose-jointed language of treaty texts provides little comfort against roving legal patrols. Additional Geneva Protocol I of 1977 describes permissible military targets as those making "an effective contribution to military action," but it is hard to know what a civilian judgment of the matter will bring.

The difficulty with attempting clarification of treaty language, or venturing a clearer restatement of customary law, is two-fold. First, the right to restate humanitarian law has lately been claimed by non-governmental organizations and a subset of States proposing a "human security" agenda that may pay little heed to active military security problems. One saw the evidence of this at Ottawa and Rome, in the debates over land mines and the international criminal court. Second, the United States' unique capabilities in air warfare and other advanced methods of war-fighting may lessen the number of supporting allies in law formation. For example, we may have few interlocuters who understand the practical problems of using air power in limited wars. In the Kosovo and Iraq campaigns, the United States flew the majority of air sorties due to the requirements of targeting and the capabilities of advanced avionics. In a world skeptical of *hyperpuissance*, few other countries may admit a shared interest in effective American warfighting, including how to secure a safe air space. Only Washington and a few other capitals will be called upon to think through the problems of linkage between an adversary's anti-aircraft capability and dual-use electrical grids. To retain a necessary operational flexibility, the United States may be cast in the role of the legal Luddite, seeking to avoid the usurpation of military law by non-military actors and by States unfamiliar with strategic security challenges.

A second concern is the general collapse of State consent as a basis for norm-setting. In recent negotiations, we have seen a "vanguard" theory of law creation—a low number of ratifications needed for treaties to come into force, a prohibition on reservations so that a package must be taken on an all-or-nothing basis, the bald assertion of third party jurisdiction, and the view that soft law can become hard law on a quick timetable. The doctrine of the persistent objector is itself under challenge if the subject matter concerns human rights, and the once narrow category of *jus cogens* (the peremptory norms binding regardless of State consent) may become a cornucopia. At the Ottawa landmines negotiation and the Rome international criminal court conference, the chairmen abandoned the view that treatymaking should proceed by consensus, or even that treaty texts should have the support of major effective actors. An attempt to restate customary law is likely to leave the United States as a prime target of rhetorical bombardment.

Timing is another problem. It is dangerous to codify the law before one knows what the practical problems will be. International armed force has lately been asked to achieve some difficult ends in limited wars—including coercing local governments to end the mistreatment of ethnic minorities and persuading host States to withdraw support from terrorist groups. In these conflicts, the likely end-state will not be unconditional surrender and long-term occupation. It's not clear that we know how to gain this new type of partial compliance, through a "tariff" theory of warfare. In traditional warfare as well, an adversary's threatened misuse of weapons of mass destruction (WMD) will present new problems in strategy. In some states, civilian facilities have been lamentably misused to shield WMD manufacture. Pesticide plants convert quickly to chemical weapons manufacture, and biological laboratories can turn from diagnostics and vaccines to preparing biological pathogens for weaponization. This dual-use imperils the traditional attempt to separate civilian and military objects. We also have little knowledge of conflict termination strategies. The radius of clear-cutting destruction in prior world wars gives us little basis for judging whether narrow targeting against a limited set of assets will dissuade an adversary from acting badly. One devoutly wishes to protect civilian populations on both sides from the hardships of war.

Yet leadership morale and regime stability are also linked to the general condition of a country's infrastructure.

Indeed, if law is to be based on accepted State practice, we should be honest about the possible mismatch between the humanitarian purposes of well-intended States in using armed force and the facts of the battlefield. Strategists of air power argue that the pinprick bombing of purely military materiel may not suffice to cause regime collapse. Targeting tanks on the battlefield may be effective in a desert war or on the plains of Europe, but it can be wholly ineffective as a strategy where the adversary's illicit behavior is carried out by unconventional means or even where the adversary happens to enjoy mountainous terrain and cloudy weather. The prudential view of choosing a fight in the most advantageous circumstances—whether against an ideological antagonist or an aggressor bent on regional or global domination—is not available if one is undertaking intervention for humanitarian ends within a civil conflict. Lacking a choice of the field of engagement, humanitarian intervention may be forced to resort to bluntly coercive methods.

Proportionality and Repair

In humanitarian intervention, the "incidental" damage to civilians will include both wartime casualties and damage to the infrastructure. (Indeed, it was anticipation of the latter that persuaded Milosevic to surrender, if we credit Belgrade's new ambassador to the United Nations and former Finnish president Martti Ahtisaari.) The hardship to civilians from infrastructure damage is likely to deepen over time, as supplies run short, weather gets colder, and civilians become exhausted in jerry-rigging alternatives. Unspent munitions also can pose a continuing danger, as we see in the case of cluster bombs.

We may wish to think of proportionality as *possessing the element of time*—and as a *dynamic* requirement. If the victorious country and its allies assist in rapid repair of the infrastructure and economy, the effective penalty of "incidental damage" will be far less harsh. The post-war clearance of unexploded munitions, though not a legal requirement as such, can also limit direct civilian damage (though continued local fighting may make it hard to do this safely or expeditiously). Proportionality in warfighting should be seen as a joint responsibility of the civilian and military sectors together, extending into the post-conflict period.

Conclusion

In a post-Kosovo world, the international community must be prepared to look at humanitarian intervention with clear eyes, in determining when it is legitimate to intervene and in thinking through the applicable standards. We must also recognize the complexity of the tasks we give our military forces in hazardous and remote environments. Any post-conflict evaluations must appreciate the difficulties inherent in the application of the rules of conventional warfare in the intricate tasks of limited war, coercive diplomacy, and humanitarian protection.

Commentary

Rein Müllerson

I find the presentations of Professor Roberts and Professor Wedgwood very stimulating indeed. There are observations with which I am in complete agreement and it only remains to me to emphasize their significance. At the same time, there are also some points in both papers that, in my opinion, call for clarification or dispute.

First, about the relationship, discussed here by various speakers, between *jus ad bellum* and *jus in bello*. These branches of international law are separate in the sense that notwithstanding the status of parties of an armed conflict in the light of *jus ad bellum* (i.e., notwithstanding whether one is an aggressor or a victim of aggression), they are equal in the light of *jus in bello*. In that respect, the International Court of Justice (ICJ) in the advisory opinion on *Nuclear Weapons* created a novelty distinguishing between "an extreme circumstance of self-defense, in which the very survival of a State would be at stake"[1] and other circumstances. Only in the former circumstances, as the Court said, it "cannot conclude definitively whether the threat or use of nuclear weapons would be lawful or unlawful."[2] Paragraph 105 (2) E of the advisory opinion seems to indicate, on the one hand, that in all other circumstances the use of (or threat to use) nuclear weapons is unlawful, i.e., contrary to international humanitarian law. On the other hand, such a formula seems to make what would otherwise be unlawful under *jus in bello* lawful (or at least not necessarily unlawful) because of different status of parties in the light of *jus ad bellum*.

---

1. Advisory Opinion on the Legality of the Threat or Use of Nuclear Weapons, 1996 I.C.J. 78, ¶ 105(2)E (July 8) [hereinafter Advisory Opinion on Nuclear Weapons].
2. Id.

In *jus ad bellum* the concept of survival of a State may be expressed through the right to self-defense. Obviously, only a victim of an armed attack, and not its perpetrator, has such a right. A State that has committed an armed attack does not have the right to self-defense even if its survival is at stake as a result of measures taken in self-defense.[3] In *jus in bello* the victim's right to survival may be expressed through the concept of military necessity. As Judge Higgins, dealing with possible use of nuclear weapons, wrote in her Dissenting Opinion:

> It must be that, in order to meet the legal requirement that a military target may not be attacked if collateral civilian casualties would be excessive in relation to military advantage, the 'military advantage' must indeed be one related to the very survival of a State or the avoidance of infliction (whether by nuclear or other weapons of mass destruction) of vast and severe suffering on its own population: and that no other method of eliminating this military target be available.[4]

This carefully formulated passage does not, however, explain why only a State acting in self-defense may use nuclear weapons as a last resort when its survival is at stake. Assuming that even a victim of an armed attack has to observe requirements of *jus in bello*, the only explanation seems to be that by committing an armed attack the aggressor has forfeited its right to survival expressed through the concept of self-defense. In that way, a wrong done in the light of *jus ad bellum* has an impact on *jus in bello* since the concept of survival crosses both branches of international law. The victim's right to survival raises the bar against which military advantage resulting, for example, from the use of nuclear weapons has to be measured. In such circumstances even significant civilian casualties may not be excessive in relation to the military advantage achieved.

---

3. The requirements of necessity and proportionality may nevertheless protect the survival even of an aggressor State. A small-scale armed attack does not give the victim the right to respond by destroying the attacker. Although Professor Dinstein writes that "once the war is raging, the exercise of self-defence may bring about 'the destruction of the enemy's army,' regardless of the condition of proportionality," he correctly points out that "it would be utterly incongruous to permit an all-out war whenever a State absorbs an isolated armed attack, however marginal.... Proportionality has to be a major consideration in pondering the legitimacy of a defensive war." (YORAM DINSTEIN, WAR, AGGRESSION AND SELF-DEFENCE 208–209 (3d ed. 2001)).

4. Advisory Opinion on Nuclear Weapons, *supra* note 1, Dissenting Opinion of Judge Higgins, ¶ 21.

Be that as it may with extreme circumstances of self-defense, it remains certain that all parties have to equally abide by the requirements of *jus in bello*.[5] In that sense these branches of international law are separate. However, this does not mean that there are no points of contact between *jus ad bellum* and *jus in bello*. For example, I find the link between *jus ad bellum* and *jus in bello* discussed in Professor Roberts's paper quite new and interesting. Indeed, extreme cases of violation of *jus in bello*, like massive violations of human rights, as he writes, "can help to legitimize certain uses of force."

Adam Roberts's conclusion is rather cautious; I would say a lawyerly one even though he is the Montegue Burton Professor of International Relations at Oxford University. He says that massive violations of *jus in bello can help* (emphasis added) to legitimize certain uses of force. This seems to suppose that other conditions (say, threats to international peace and security) have to be, if not overwhelming, then at least playing a significant role in triggering such uses of force. However, even more importantly, Roberts uses the word "legitimize" instead of, for example, "making it lawful." This seems to indicate that his views on this issue are, if not identical, then and least close to those of Thomas Franck and Nigel Rodley who wrote in the aftermath of the Indian intervention in Eastern Pakistan:

> [U]ndeniably, there are circumstances in which the unilateral use of force to overthrow injustice begins to seem less wrong than to turn aside. Like civil disobedience, however, this sense of superior 'necessity' belongs in the realm of not law but of moral choice, which nations, like individuals, must sometimes make weighing the costs and benefits of to their cause, to social fabric, and to themselves.[6]

Professor Franck made a similar comment more than a quarter of a century later observing that "NATO's action in Kosovo is not the first time illegal steps have been taken to prevent something palpably worse."[7] Bruno Simma, analyzing the Kosovo conflict, believes in the same vein that sometimes "imperative

---

5. Here I have to express my reservations to Professor Wedgwood's comment that "most leaders and publics may in fact believe there is an important link between the legitimate purpose of a war and its allowable tactics." It may be true that many people believe indeed in the existence of such a link. Osama bin Laden and his ilk seem to be convinced of the existence of such a link. However, the acceptance of such an approach would lead to the erosion of the very foundations of *jus in bello*.
6. Thomas Franck & Nigel Rodley, *After Bangladesh: the Law of Humanitarian Intervention by Military Force*, 67 AMERICAN JOURNAL OF INTERNATIONAL LAW 304 (1973).
7. Thomas Franck, *Break It, Do Not Fake It*, 78 FOREIGN AFFAIRS 118 (1999).

political and moral considerations may appear to leave no choice but to act outside law" since "legal issues presented by the Kosovo crisis are particularly impressive proof that hard cases make bad law."[8]

My comment on the last point is short. I am sure, only hard cases can make law for hard cases. If hard cases (and uses of military force are all hard cases) were to make only bad law or no law at all then there would be no *jus ad bellum* or *jus in bello*, for that matter, at all. Maritime delimitation cases or precedents on diplomatic privileges and immunities do not make law for *jus ad bellum* or *jus in bello*. Only practice involving use of force may make or change law governing use of force.

I would like to argue with Adam Roberts when he writes that "it is doubtful whether there is, or is likely to be a 'right' of humanitarian intervention" and that "the recognition of a link between *jus in bello* and *jus ad bellum* falls far short of any general recognition of a right of humanitarian intervention." Taking into account what Professors Franck, Rodley and Simma have said on the issue and Roberts's point that "massive violations of *jus in bello* can help to *legitimize* (emphasis added) certain uses of force," one may conclude either that (1) certain uses of force are not suitable (amenable) for legal regulation, i.e., they have to be considered as being beyond the realm of international law or (2) though such uses of force are contrary to international law (i.e., they are unlawful), they are nevertheless legitimate since they are morally justifiable or in some instances even necessary from the moral point of view. Such an approach also presumes that some international practice is so unique, so exceptional, that it does not, cannot, or should not contribute to changes in law.

I cannot agree with that kind of reasoning both for practical and doctrinal reasons. First, speaking from the doctrinal point of view, I do not think that there can be or there should be such a gap between legitimacy and legality—between international law and morality. In most sensitive areas (use of force, human rights, etc.) international law is heavily value-loaded. If it is generally true that in international relations practice has a tendency to become law (*ex facto jus oritur*), morally justifiable practice, even if rare and unique, should be accepted sooner rather that later. In practical terms, if there were such a gap between law and morality it would be damaging for both of them.

It seems difficult indeed to conclude that Operation Provide Comfort in Northern Iraq, ECOWAS (Economic Community of West African States) interventions in Liberia and Sierra Leone, and Operation Allied Force in the

---

8. Bruno Simma, *Nato, the UN and the Use of Force: Legal Aspects*, 10 EUROPEAN JOURNAL OF INTERNATIONAL LAW 3 (1999).

Federal Republic of Yugoslavia, together with some earlier cases of use of force where humanitarian considerations played at least some role, have led to the crystallization of a right of humanitarian intervention in international law. At the same time, these cases (and some even more ambiguous earlier examples) show that there is considerable tolerance towards interventions when humanitarian catastrophes are genuine and interventions can and do realistically alleviate the sufferings of thousands if not millions of people. Such tolerance is called in the language of international law "acquiescence" and it may contribute to changes in customary international law (or even treaty law).

If this practice and the reaction to it by the majority of States do not testify conclusively that there is a right to intervene militarily for humanitarian purposes, it means not only that at least some humanitarian interventions are legitimate (or as Roberts says, "massive violations of *jus in bello* can help to legitimize certain uses of force") but also that such interventions are not unquestionably contrary to international law. A customary norm prohibiting any humanitarian intervention could not have crystallized in such circumstances. Therefore, I find that the purpose of Operation Allied Force, if not all the modalities of its execution, was not only morally justifiable, it was also not unlawful in the light of international law. Using the wording of Nguen Quoc Dinh, Patrick Dailler and Alan Pellet, *"l'intervention d'humanité ne bénéficie pas d'une habilitation expresse, mais sa condamnation ne fait pas non plus l'objet d'un consensus suffisant pour que ce soit dégagée une opinio juris qui permaitrait d'affirmer l'illicéité de cette forme d'intervention."*[9]

Today even this cautious formula seems too restrictive. I believe that State practice, especially in the 1990s, has shown that in the case of a clash between two fundamental principles of international law—non-use of force and respect for basic human rights—it is not always the non-use of force principle that has necessarily to prevail. Massive violations of human rights or humanitarian law may justify proportionate and adequate measures involving use of military force. Here one has to balance two conflicting principles by considering all concrete circumstances that necessarily are unique and urgent.

My next comment, and related to the previous one, concerns Professor Roberts's point that "any decision of forcible intervention must involve a balancing of considerations in the face of unique and urgent circumstances, not

---

9. "Though there is no express permission of humanitarian intervention neither is there consensus concerning the condemnation of such interventions that would amount to the *opinio juris* on the illegality of this form of intervention." NGUEN QUOC DINH, PATRICK DAILLER AND ALAN PELLET, DROIT INTERNATIONAL PUBLIQUE 892 (5th ed. 1994).

the assertion of a general right." I believe that there is not necessarily a contradiction between the existence of a right and the need to balance various considerations "in the face of unique and urgent circumstances." In sensitive domains of international law and politics (and practically all issues involving use of force belong to this category) the need to balance not only various policy considerations but also different principles of international law, often indicating in opposite directions, is rather a rule than an exception. If there were no right to intervene for humanitarian purposes, then however much one balanced various considerations in the face of unique and urgent circumstances, any intervention would be unlawful.

The NATO intervention in the Federal Republic of Yugoslavia over Kosovo was the first collective intervention where humanitarian considerations were overwhelming. As it was not authorized by the Security Council, concerns for peace and stability in Europe (though they certainly played an important role) alone would not have justified this use of force. Therefore, the justifiable cause of the intervention was humanitarian. However, as humanitarian intervention has been and still is a highly contested concept, doctrinal works have so far been concentrated only on the issue of the legitimacy or legality (illegality) of the use of force for humanitarian purposes (*jus ad bellum* aspect). No attention has been paid to the legitimacy or legality of modalities of use of force for these purposes (which includes both *jus ad bellum* and *jus in bello* aspect). As Roberts has remarked, "in the long history of legal debates about humanitarian intervention, there has been a consistent failure to address directly the question of methods used in such interventions."[10]

It goes without saying that the laws of armed conflict must apply in the case of humanitarian intervention. What interests us here is whether (and if yes, then to what extent) the objective of such intervention—protection of human rights—has any impact on the modalities of the use of force?

If we compare the modalities of the use of force as a collective security measure authorized by the Security Council under Chapter VII of the UN Charter with the modalities of the use of force in self-defense, we see that there may be substantial differences depending on the purpose of the use of force. Let us take as an example the response of the Coalition to the Iraqi aggression against Kuwait. In this response, there were elements of both collective

---

10. Adam Roberts, *Nato's "Humanitarian War" over Kosovo*, 41 SURVIVAL, Autumn 1999, at 110.

self-defense and collective security.[11] The right to self-defense gave the Coalition the right (even without the Security Council authorization) to use force to liberate Kuwait, to put an end to the armed aggression and to restore the *status quo ante*. But only Security Council resolutions, as a measure of collective security under Chapter VII, created an adequate legal basis for the actions (including military) aimed at forcing the regime of Saddam Hussein to destroy its programs of production of weapons of mass destruction and missiles. These measures went beyond what a State (or States) can do in self-defense, but Security Council resolutions provided the basis for measures necessary for the restoration and maintenance of peace and security in the region.

In the area of self-defense, it is the *Caroline* formula that reflects customary international law. Secretary of State Daniel Webster wrote to Mr Fox, the British Minister to Washington, that it had to be demonstrated that there was the necessity to use force in self-defense that was "instant, overwhelming, and leaving no choice of means, and no moment for deliberation" and that the act "justified by the necessity of self-defense must be limited by that necessity, and kept clearly within it."[12] There is no reason to believe that these requirements apply only in the case of self-defense or that this formula has in mind only so-called anticipatory self-defense. It seems to be possible to generalize all these criteria by the term of adequacy which, depending on the circumstances, includes necessity, proportionality and even immediacy. Every use of force, in order to be lawful, has to be adequate to the situation that calls for the use of force. Or to put it slightly differently: the modalities of the use of force have to correspond to the purposes of its use. This requirement belongs both to *jus ad bellum* and *jus in bello*.

Analyzing self-defense, Yoram Dinstein distinguishes between "on the spot reaction," "defensive armed reprisals," responses to an "accumulation of events" and "war of self-defence" as different modalities of the use of force that can be resorted to depending on the character of the armed attack that has triggered the right to use force in self-defense.[13] The legality of these modalities of self-defense is dependent on the character of the armed attack. Judith Gardam writes that "in the Gulf conflict the massive aerial bombardment

---

11. See Rein Müllerson & David Scheffer, *The Legal Regulation of the Use of Force*, in BEYOND CONFRONTATION: INTERNATIONAL LAW FOR THE POST-COLD WAR WORLD (Lori Damrosch, Gennady Danilenko & Rein Müllerson eds., 1995).
12. JOHN BASSET MOORE, *The Caroline*, in 2 DIGEST OF INTERNATIONAL LAW 412 (1906). See also, R.Y. Jennings, *The Caroline and McLeod Cases*, 32 AMERICAN JOURNAL OF INTERNATIONAL LAW 82 (1938).
13. See DINSTEIN, supra note 3, at 192–221.

of the infrastructure of Iraq had to be balanced against its contribution to the removal of Iraq from Kuwait."[14]

A good example of the adequacy of measures undertaken may be operations to rescue one's nationals abroad, which is often considered to be a special case of self-defense. Whether one regards it as a separate ground for the lawful use of force or as being within the parameters of the right to self-defense, practically all authors agree that the purpose of the use of force (rescuing nationals) conditions the modalities that may be used. As C.H.M. Waldock wrote, measures of protection must be "strictly confined to the object of protecting them [nationals] against injury."[15]

In the light of these distinctions between modalities of self-defense depending on the character of an armed attack, it seems natural that the modalities of the use of force for humanitarian purposes must also correspond to the objectives of the use of force. They have to be adequate to these objectives. Fernando Tesón writing of humanitarian intervention observes that "the general rule is that the coercion in the operation and the consequent harm done by it have to be proportionate to the importance of the interest that is being served, both in terms of the intrinsic moral weight of the goal and in terms of the extent to which that goal is served."[16]

The objectives of Operation Allied Force, as declared by NATO and the G-8 and confirmed by the Security Council, where: (1) immediate and verifiable end of violence and repression in Kosovo; (2) withdrawal from Kosovo of military and paramilitary forces; (3) deployment in Kosovo of effective international civil and security presences, endorsed and adopted by the United Nations, capable of guaranteeing the achievement of common objectives; (4) establishment of an interim administration for Kosovo to be decided by the Security Council of the United Nations to ensure conditions for a peaceful and normal life for all inhabitants in Kosovo; (5) the safe and free return of all refugees and displaced persons and unimpeded access to Kosovo by humanitarian organizations; (6) a political process towards the establishment of an interim political framework agreement providing for a substantial self-government for Kosovo, taking full account of the Rambouillet accords and the principles of sovereignty and territorial integrity of the Federal Republic of Yugoslavia and

---

14. Judith Gardam, *Necessity and Proportionality in Jus ad Bellum and Jus in Bello*, in INTERNATIONAL LAW, THE INTERNATIONAL COURT OF JUSTICE AND NUCLEAR WEAPONS 281 (Lawrence Boisson de Chazournes & Philipe Sands eds., 1999).
15. C.H.M. Waldock, *The Regulation of the Use of Force by Individual States in International Law*, 81 RECUEIL DES COURS 455, 467 (1952).
16. FERNANDO TESÓN, A PHILOSOPHY OF INTERNATIONAL LAW 64 (1998).

the other countries of the region, and the demilitarization of the KLA; and (7) a comprehensive approach to the economic development and stabilization of the crisis region.[17]

The question is: do these objectives that are different from objectives of other types of use of force (e.g., in self-defense or as a measure of collective security) determine also what kind of force can be used? Although neither the Hague or Geneva Conventions or Additional Protocols to the latter nor customary international law contain any references to wars of self-defense, collective security operations or humanitarian interventions, distinguishing only between international armed conflicts and armed conflicts of non-international character, that does not mean that requirements of necessity, proportionality or even immediacy may not lead to distinctions between applicable law depending on the purpose of the use of force.

It seems that the NATO response was not, using the *Naulilaa* formula, "excessively disproportionate"[18] to the achievement of the objectives of this humanitarian intervention. There was not simply a potential and imminent threat to human lives in Kosovo leaving little time for deliberation; human lives were actually being lost and crimes against humanity were actually being committed before NATO intervened. The world community, represented *inter alia* by the UN Security Council, had already given peaceful diplomacy a chance but the ethnic cleansing continued unabated.

The primary or general objective of any humanitarian intervention is to stop massive human rights violations. In the case of Kosovo it was to stop ethnic cleansing and, foremost, the murder and torture through which the ethnic cleansing was being carried out. All other objectives are to be subordinated to this primary objective. They are aimed at reversing, if possible, the results of human rights violations, at ensuring that violations will not recur in the future and at punishing those who have committed acts of genocide, war crimes or crimes against humanity. But the primary objective is to stop violations (i.e., to protect victims) that have engendered the intervention.

The NATO intervention, in the end, stopped such human rights violations. But the fact that it achieved this objective only in the end seems to be the major shortcoming of Operation Allied Force. I completely agree with Professor Roberts when he believes that "in the 1999 war it was

---

17. *See* general principles on the political solution to the Kosovo crisis in Annex 1 of Security Council Resolution 1244 of 10 June 1999, U.N. Doc. S/RES/1244 (1999).
18. The Naulilaa Case (Port. V. Germ. 1928), 2 REPORTS OF INTERNATIONAL ARBITRAL AWARDS 1028 (1928).

disadvantageous to NATO, and to the inhabitants of Kosovo, that Milosevic was not confronted with a more convincing threat of land operations in the province." The openly declared refusal to use ground troops and the exclusive use of air power allowed the ethnic cleansing not only to continue unabated, but also even to intensify for a while. Earlier Roberts had emphasized that "the initial exclusion of the option of a land invasion was the most extraordinary aspect of NATO's resort to force."[19]

One has to bear in mind that the Hutu extremists in their genocidal attack against the Tutsis in 1994 killed an estimated 250,000 to 500,000 people within approximately one month.[20] Ethnic cleansing, even without massive killing of the Rwandan scale, can also be carried out with extreme speed. The Croats, for example, drove out more than 200,000 Serbs from Krajina within just three days.[21] Thus, Milosevic could have expelled or killed most of the Albanian population of Kosovo while NATO was bombing targets in Serbia proper to protect the Kosovars. In humanitarian interventions, the exclusive use of aerial bombardment without even a plausible threat to use ground troops may be a terrible gamble. Therefore, an intervention seems to be inadequate to the objectives of the use of force when it is carried out by means of bombing military and dual-purpose objectives outside the area where human rights violations are being committed in order to persuade the authorities to stop violations, without at least being ready to use force to protect immediately and directly the victims of massive human rights violations. Here the remark of Professor Wedgwood that "a gradual war of attrition that might defeat Belgrade in slow motion was unacceptable in light of human values at stake in the conflict" is rather pertinent.

What may be adequate in a war of self-defense or in a war against terrorism (also a specific form of self-defense) may be inadequate in the case of humanitarian intervention. We see that just as modalities of use of force as a countermeasure depend on the characteristics of the initial wrong, so too does *jus in bello* (the law of armed conflict) depend on *jus ad bellum* (the law on lawful causes of use of force). Here the bridge between the two branches of international law is the requirement of adequacy (including, as it was said earlier, necessity, proportionality and even immediacy)—the requirement that is central to both of them. Daniel Webster, speaking of self-defense in the *Caroline* case wrote that "the act justified by that necessity of self-defense, must be limited

---

19. Roberts, *supra* note 10, at 112.
20. Report of the Secretary-General, U.N. Doc. S/1994/640 (May 31, 1994).
21. Tim Judah, *Kosovo's Road to War*, 41 SURVIVAL, Summer 1999, at 12.

by that necessity and kept clearly within it."[22] We may paraphrase it by saying that an act justified by the necessity of humanitarian intervention must be limited by that necessity and kept clearly within it.

It seems that the bridge of adequacy between purposes of the use of force and its modalities is especially important today when threats to peace and security stem not so much from the clash of interests of superpowers or cross-border attacks by one State against another, but from internal conflicts, massive human rights violations and terrorism. Here Roberts's remark about the restrictive character of the oft-quoted expression in the 1868 St. Petersburg Declaration that "the only legitimate object which States should endeavor to accomplish during war is to weaken the military forces of the enemy" is rather pertinent. As he writes, the laws of war "by no means exclude the application of military force against the adversary's war-making capacity and system of government." I support Roberts's call to NATO members "to address the question of how their conception of war relates to the laws of war, and whether any modifications of either are indicated by this experience. The question of what is a military objective, addressed most extensively in Protocol I, is central."[23]

The Kosovo experience shows that what is and what is not a military objective is, to an extent at least, dependent on the purpose of war. In that respect Roberts rightly draws our attention to the East Timor crisis writing that "it appears that a systematic campaign of bombing was not a serious option" in that crisis. Depending on the purposes of the use of force (e.g., to rescue one's nationals abroad) the adversary's armed forces (even the concept of adversary or enemy becomes uncertain in the case of many new threats) may not be the main target at all.

Adam Roberts wrote earlier that:

[T]he main problem in Kosovo was that, because it proved relatively easy to conceal military units and movable equipment from attacks from the air, there was especially strong pressure on the Nato alliance to attack fixed targets, which in many cases (bridges, power stations, buildings of various types, the broadcasting station in Belgrade) had civilian as well as military functions.[24]

---

22. MOORE, supra note 12, at 919.
23. See Professor Roberts's paper in this volume, *supra*, at 418.
24. Id.

In the light of what I have said above, I believe that targets such as bridges, power stations and other similar dual-purpose objects, which may be legitimate targets in the case of more conventional military operations (e.g., when force is used in self-defense), should not be military objectives (save maybe exceptional circumstances) in humanitarian operations.

All interventions that have so far been analyzed as humanitarian (notwithstanding whether accepted or rejected as such) have been carried out by ground troops and not by air strikes only.[25] The point is that though massive human rights violations may be stopped at the end of the day by hitting oppressive regimes' military and dual-purpose objects in order to persuade them to stop violations, the effects of such violations (which well may continue or even exacerbate while such military force is used) can be reversed only to an extent. Those who are killed remain dead. Those who are raped remain raped. Even those who are "only" expelled remain traumatized for the rest of their life and many of them, as historical experience shows, never return.

Ruth Wedgwood raises a delicate issue of "the difficulties controlling surrogate ground forces" or local insurgents who "share many of the illiberal qualities" of their opponents. In Kosovo such a force was the so-called Kosovo Liberation Army (KLA) whom President Clinton had earlier branded (and not without serious ground) terrorists. It is a dilemma of whether or not to support bad guys against the worst guys. Cooperation with such groups may be dictated by considerations of military necessity, but one should not forget that very often those who fight against oppressors fight only for their own freedom to oppress others.

One can only hope that after the Kosovo experience and other developments pointing in the same direction[26] at least some would-be human rights violators will not rely on State sovereignty and will think twice before embarking on their murderous paths. At the same time, this experience teaches us that it is difficult to protect other peoples' lives without being ready to sacrifice lives of one's own soldiers. In our so imperfect world those who care about human rights and want to make the world safer *vis-à-vis* terrorist attacks cannot afford to become soft. Unfortunately, dictators and terrorists (often these notions overlap since dictators use terror to stay in power, while terrorists are

---

25. *See, e.g.,* ANTHONY AREND & ROBERT BECK, INTERNATIONAL LAW AND THE USE OF FORCE 112–137 (1993).
26. For example, the functioning of the two *ad hoc* International Criminal Tribunals in The Hague, the arrest of General Pinochet in London, the adoption of the Statute of the permanent International Criminal Court.

aspiring dictators who want to impose their beliefs and aims on others) understand and respect only force. Mutual hatred and respect between Stalin and Hitler was not accidental.

Commentary

Horace B. Robertson, Jr.

I shall confine my comments to the papers presented by Professors Roberts and Wedgwood. First, as to Adam Roberts's paper. Professor Roberts has laid out eight issues that arose during the Kosovo air campaign, which he asserts are likely to affect the way in which the law is viewed, influences events, and develops further in the future. I will single out three of these for my comments.

First, is there now a stronger link between *jus in bello* and *jus ad bellum*? Roberts asserts that the 1990s saw a strengthening of the idea that a systematic pattern of basic humanitarian norms may justify acts of military intervention. "Quite simply," he states, "massive violations of *jus in bello* can help to legitimize certain uses of force."[1] While I do not quarrel with Roberts's conclusion, it seems to me that while justification for intervention by another State or international entity may rest in part on a systematic pattern of violations of *jus in bello* in a civil war, that is solely an issue of *jus ad bellum*. The conduct of the intervening party once involved in the conflict is completely independent of whether or not the intervention meets the test of *jus ad bellum*. The intervening party is obligated, both by treaty and customary international law, to abide by the principles and rules of *jus in bello*. With respect to the obligations of the almost universally binding 1949 Geneva Conventions, Common Article 2 provides unequivocally: "the present Convention shall apply to all cases of declared war or of any other armed conflict which may arise between two or more of the High Contracting Parties, even if the state of war

---

1. See Professor Roberts's paper in this volume, *supra*, at 410.

is not recognized by one of them."[2]

This principle is reiterated in Articles 1(1) and 3(a) of Protocol I, which state that the Protocol shall apply "from the beginning" of any armed conflict referred to in Article 2 of the 1949 Conventions.[3] Although not all parties to the Kosovo intervention were parties to Protocol I, the principle it states seems to have been generally accepted as a part of the customary law of war. The United States CJCS Standing Rules of Engagement provide, for example: "US forces will comply with the Law of War during military operations involving armed conflict, no matter how the conflict may be characterized under international law, and will comply with its principles and spirit during all other operations."[4] The US Navy's *Commander's Handbook on the Law of Naval Operations*, likewise provides as follows: "Regardless of whether the use of armed force in a particular circumstance is prohibited by the United Nations Charter (and therefore unlawful), *the manner in which the resulting armed conflict is conducted continues to be regulated by the law of armed conflict.*"[5] This principle is valid today and should be applied in any future conflict.

Now to the second question that Professor Roberts asks that I would like to address. Is there tension between the NATO/US strategic doctrine which aims at putting pressure on the adversary's government and the implicit assumption of the laws of war that the adversary's armed forces are the main legitimate object of attack? If so, how can this tension be addressed?

My answer is that I do not believe there is a tension between the *strategic* objective of putting pressure on the enemy's leadership and the *tactical* conduct of the military campaign. After all, the ultimate object of any military campaign is some political objective; the campaign itself can be fully

---

2. Convention (I) for the Amelioration of the Condition of the Wounded and Sick in Armed Forces in the Field, signed at Geneva, 12 August 1949, authentic text in *Final Record of the Diplomatic Conference of Geneva of 1949*, vol. 1, Federal Political Department, Berne, 205–224, *reprinted in* THE LAWS OF ARMED CONFLICT: A COLLECTION OF CONVENTIONS, RESOLUTIONS AND OTHER DOCUMENTS (Dietrich Schindler and Jiri Toman eds., 1988). The provisions of Convention II (Wounded, sick and shipwrecked), Convention III (Prisoners of War) and Convention IV (Civilians) are identical.
3. Protocol Additional (I) to the Geneva Conventions of 12 August 1949, and Relating to the Protection of Victims of International Conflicts, June 8, 1977, 1125 U.N.T.S. 3, DOCUMENTS ON THE LAWS OF WAR 422 (Adam Roberts & Richard Guelff eds., 3d ed. 2000).
4. Chairman of the Joint Chiefs of Staff Instruction (CJCSI) 3121.01A, Standing Rules of Engagement for US Forces, Enclosure A, ¶ 1g (Jan. 15, 2000).
5. THE COMMANDER'S HANDBOOK ON THE LAW OF NAVAL OPERATIONS, NWP 1-14M/MCWP 5-2.1/COMDTPUB P5800.1, at ¶ 5.1 (1997) (emphasis added).

compliant with law of war in reaching this *strategic* objective. As Clausewitz wrote in his much-quoted statement, "War is not merely a political act, but also a political instrument, a continuation of political relations, a carrying out the same by other means."[6] This statement is neutral with respect to the legitimacy of the military means and methods of carrying out the campaigns. The legitimacy of the resort to armed force does not excuse the violation of the laws of war (*jus in bello*) nor does it render unlawful the compliant actions of a soldier, airman or sailor engaged in a conflict, the entry into which by his nation may be regarded as unlawful under the principles of *jus ad bellum*.

It should be noted in this connection that the Committee established by the Prosecutor of International Criminal Tribunal for the former Yugoslavia (ICTY) was asked to address the linkage between the *jus in bello* and the *jus ad bellum*.[7] The Committee was specifically asked to address the allegations that since the resort to force by NATO had not been authorized by the Security Council, the resort to force was illegal and consequently "all forceful measures taken by NATO were unlawful."[8] The Committee declined to address this issue as a matter of practice, "which we consider to be in accord with the most widely accepted and reputable legal opinion."[9]

The third question raised by Professor Roberts that I would like to address is what, if anything, might need to be done about the paradox that the United States is simultaneously a principal upholder of the obligation of States to observe the laws of war, and a non-party to several important agreements.

Professor Roberts lists a number of agreements to which the United States is not a party, the most significant being Protocol I. While the other agreements listed are important, Protocol I is the most significant because it gives concrete definition to a number of principles that traditionally formed a part of the customary laws of war governing the methods and means of warfare but which have not been codified in a single document. As Professor Roberts acknowledges, although it is not a party, "the United States takes at least some of these accords more seriously than some States that are parties."[10] As Colonel Graham has stated, the fact that the United States was not a party to

---

6. KARL VON CLAUSEWITZ, ON WAR (1832).
7. *See* Final Report to the Prosecutor by the Committee Established to Review the NATO Bombing Campaign Against the Federal Republic of Yugoslavia, ¶¶ 30-4, 39 INTERNATIONAL LEGAL MATERIALS 1257, 1265-6 (2000), *reprinted* herein as Appendix A [hereinafter Report to the Prosecutor].
8. *Id.*, ¶ 30.
9. *Id.*, ¶ 34.
10. See Professor Roberts's paper in this volume, *supra*, at 428.

Protocol I had no effect on the conduct of the war in Kosovo.[11] What the United States loses by not being a party, in my view, is the legal (and moral) authority, in taking to task non-complying States which are parties, of reliance on the implementation and enforcement provisions of these agreements. As Roberts points out, a principal feature of these latter-day agreements is their provision for implementation and enforcement measures. Adherence would enable the United States to rely on and cite specific binding agreements instead of relying on the sometimes vague and ambiguous principles of the customary international law of war.

A greater paradox in this field, and perhaps a more fruitful field for future action, is pointed out by Professor Murphy in the final paragraph of his paper submitted to this colloquium. He states:

> To this observer, it is ironic that so much attention has been devoted to the issue of whether NATO complied with the *jus in bello* in its Kosovo campaign. For when one looks at practices in other conflicts around the world—Chechnya, Afghanistan, the Sudan, the Congo, and Sierra Leone, to name just a few—one sees not only no effort to comply with the *jus in bello* but barbaric practices that flout even the most elementary dictates of humanity. Accordingly, the most strenuous efforts should be made to induce States and other combatants to adhere to at least the ethical and moral dimensions of international humanitarian law, regardless of the presence or absence of a formal legal obligation to do so.[12]

Now let me turn briefly to Professor Wedgwood's paper. I can be brief here because what I have said earlier applies to some extent to the issues she raises. She states that the "asserted independence of the two regimes [*jus ad bellum* and *jus in bello*] may be no more than a fiction."[13] She argues that the Kosovo campaign was not a war to settle a commercial or boundary dispute but one to protect basic human rights and therefore that, "[w]hether one's framework is utilitarian or pure principle, it is possible to admit that the merits of a war make a difference in our tolerance for methods of warfighting."[14]

I submit such a principle places one on a very slippery slope. Any linkage between the two principles has been universally rejected by the relevant international agreements and (in the words of the Report to the Prosecutor) "the

---

11. See Colonel Graham's comments in this volume, *supra*, at 378.
12. See Professor Murphy's paper in this volume, *supra*, at 255.
13. See Professor Wedgwood's paper in this volume, *supra*, at 434–5.
14. Id.

most widely accepted and reputable legal opinion."[15] In my comments on Professor Roberts's paper I made the point that both international agreements and customary international law have firmly settled that the rules of war apply to the conduct of hostilities regardless of whether we are assessing the conduct of those on the "good" side of the conflict or those on the "bad" (or aggressor) side. I repeat it here because I firmly believe it is well established in all of the international agreements that deal with the subject and in customary international law. I also believe it is morally justified and the only workable way of judging compliance with the law of war by subordinate participants in the conflict. Judging which is the "good" or the "bad" side of any conflict is essentially subjective. I have never heard of a national leader who did not assert that his cause was "just." Are we to judge the conduct of subordinate military officers on the ground that they find themselves fighting on the wrong side of a war? I submit that the question answers itself.

I agree, however, with Professor Wedgwood in her expressions of concern about the contentious role of civilian tribunals in the post-war trial of those accused of violations of the law of war. This problem is aggravated by the development of precision-guided munitions and the increasing transparency of targeting decisions made by military authorities resulting from almost instantaneous on-scene television reporting and analysis as well as cockpit-monitoring of strike weapons from launch to detonation. What may appear to be a reasonable and lawful targeting decision to a commander enveloped in the fog of war may take on an entirely different appearance with the advantage of hindsight. Judging whether that decision is lawful or not is certainly difficult for any tribunal but particularly so for one which may not have a full appreciation that, as Professor Wedgwood states, "implementation of many aspects of the law of war depends on battlefield judgments and knowledge of campaign strategy."[16] While it would be desirable in my view (and apparently also in Professor Wedgwood's) that such judgments should be made by a military tribunal with membership familiar with these factors, I am afraid that we have gone too far down the road toward civilian tribunals to make possible a reversal of that policy. The tribunals for Yugoslavia and Rwanda, the Statute of the International Criminal Court and the provisions of the Geneva Conventions for universal jurisdiction of "grave breaches" have set us off on a course that may be irreversible. We can, I think, however, take some temporary comfort at least from the Report to the Prosecutor, which appeared to take a

---

15. Report to the Prosecutor, Appendix A, ¶ 34.
16. See Professor Wedgwood's paper in this volume, *supra*, at 435.

knowledgeable and sophisticated approach to its analysis of allegations of war crimes by NATO forces in the air campaign.

Commentary

Harvey Dalton

I think there are three verities that we need to be aware of throughout our discussions in this area. Professor Robertson has already mentioned one—that the use of force is a continuation of political relations by other means. I think another verity is embodied in Article 2(7) of the UN Charter, which provides that domestic matters are the sole responsibility of sovereign States. I think another verity is also embodied in the UN Charter, that is the inviolability of the territorial integrity and political independence of sovereign States.

We've heard from time to time that Operation Allied Force was a humanitarian intervention and that there might be a right of humanitarian intervention. I agree with Professors Roberts and Walker that, at least in my view, there is no right of humanitarian intervention and that the situation in Kosovo was an extraordinary situation dominated by necessity. It was necessary for the NATO alliance to use force. There were no alternative means. All alternative means had been exhausted.

But assuming that Kosovo was a humanitarian intervention, there have been some comments that maybe the rules should be different when we talk about the use of force as a part of humanitarian intervention. My question is why? What makes this so different from an ordinary armed conflict that the rules should be different? If we're going to apply the *jus in bello*, it should apply on all instances of armed hostilities. In this case, the weapons were no less deadly, the systems were just as effective and just as destructive, the clash of the armed forces was just as deadly, and the effects on civilians were no different.

There seems to be some implicit criticism of NATO's decision to keep its planes above fifteen thousand feet as if NATO was not being quite correct in playing by these rules. I would like to simply point out that the Federal Republic of Yugoslavia (FRY) had one of the most sophisticated integrated air defense systems in Europe. FRY forces did put our pilots and aircraft in harm's way. They shot down two of our aircraft. There's no evidence that I'm aware of that NATO's decision to stay above fifteen thousand feet affected the accuracy of our weapons. We did have outliers (missiles or bombs that drop outside the area they were targeted at). We did have mistakes. But there's no evidence that the fifteen thousand foot restriction or ceiling affected the accuracy. The fifteen thousand foot altitude protected our aircraft against the FRY anti-aircraft artillery, but it did not protect those aircraft against surface-to-air missiles. You might contemplate that fact on your way home from this colloquium when you're flying at thirty-seven thousand feet, because an SA-2 can reach out and touch you at thirty-seven thousand feet.

As Colonel Sorenson mentioned yesterday, fifteen thousand feet is not very high. Mistakes have been made at far less than fifteen thousand feet. I would refer you to the US/UK blue-on-blue clash that occurred during Operation Desert Storm. That incident occurred at much less than fifteen thousand feet.

Finally, I would like to turn very briefly to the reference by Professor Wedgwood to the international institutions and international tribunals. I would agree with Professor Roberts that there has not been a critical review of the Committee's Report to the Prosecutor on the Kosovo operation. I'd like to give you two examples from this report. The Committee uncritically accepted the definition of environmental crime contained in the International Criminal Court statute:

> Operational reality is recognized in the Statute of the International Criminal Court, an authoritative indicator of evolving customary international law on this point, where Article 8(b)(iv) makes the infliction of incidental environmental damage an offence only if the attack is launched intentionally in the knowledge that it will cause widespread, long-term and severe damage to the natural environment which would be clearly excessive in relation to the concrete and direct overall military advantage anticipated.[1]

Now that was an uncritical acceptance of a crime that was defined in the ICC Statute, and there are a few people here that can tell you—Charles Garaway in particular—that this was a definition that was cobbled together as a

---

1. *See* Final Report to the Prosecutor by the Committee Established to Review the NATO Bombing Campaign Against the Federal Republic of Yugoslavia, ¶ 21, 39 INTERNATIONAL LEGAL MATERIALS 1257, 1263 (2000), *reprinted* herein as Appendix A.

compromise by various lawyers from likeminded States in a restaurant at the top of the Ministry of Foreign Affairs in Bonn in October 1995 or 1996. It's a compromise. Yet here's an uncritical acceptance of this definition in a statute that is not in force. We need a critical review of this Committee's Report.

Another example is the Committee's rather tight control on the attacks on propaganda and a rather critical statement concerning the attack on the RTS (Serbian TV and radio station) transmission facility. It must be known that the RTS system was critical to sustaining the war effort and the ethnic cleansing effort by the FRY. It also directed virulent propaganda against NATO with the view to breaking up the alliance or shattering our unanimity. It was part of a determined effort to conceal what was actually happening in Kosovo. I think it's very important to recognize that in an authoritative regime such as in Yugoslavia, propaganda is essential. Control of the populous is essential and propaganda is the means by doing it. Let me give you a quote from Julius Stone:

> Quite apart from the dependence of totalitarian governments on unquestioning and undeviating acceptance of their respective ideologies, preparation for modern war and the waging of it demand a high degree of solidarity of outlook and effort throughout the community. In these circumstances, the undermining of the internal social and political order of the enemy and his psychological assurance become a Military target as important as his physical industrial plant and second in importance only to his armed forces.[2]

So propaganda is a legitimate military objective—at least in this commentator's view.

One final point with respect to the International Criminal Court. Professor Dinstein in his book notes that there are certain principles that are *jus cogens*. These are fundamental principles that trump other aspects of international law. His example of a *jus cogens* principle is the territorial inviolability and the political independence of sovereign States. A final comment. I would suggest to you that there may be another principle of *jus cogens* and that is a principle that no obligation can be conferred on a sovereign State without their express written consent. That is also contained in the Vienna Convention on Treaties. It is also a fundamental principle of international law. If you take that as a principle of *jus cogens*, then those aspects of the ICC statute that purport to extend the ICC's jurisdiction over a non-party State and nationals of a non-party State are a legal nullity.

---

2. JULIUS STONE, LEGAL CONTROLS OF INTERNATIONAL CONFLICT 322 (1954).

Discussion

Does the US Have a Unilateralist Approach to International Law?

John Norton Moore:
This question is addressed to Adam Roberts who I intend to gently take to task. I do so, however, after saying that I'm an admirer of your paper in general. I say gently because actually I suspect that in terms of the purpose of your statement, you and I would have exactly the same underlying purpose to be served. We would both agree on the great importance of the United States and our European allies working together. I particularly enjoyed the entire intellectual sweep of what you were dealing with. I thought it was quite extraordinary.

My comment relates to the specifics of your statement that somehow we need to be concerned that the United States currently is set out on a course to ensure that laws apply to others, but they do not apply to the United States. I believe it's quite dangerous to be making these generalizations. I'm just back from the country of some of my good European colleagues and I know that one is hearing quite a few generalizations about American isolationism and nonparticipation in various treaties. I think that we have to actually proceed treaty-by-treaty in looking at these. There are very different reasons for US nonparticipation in a number of these treaties and the kinds of generalizations that we're hearing are not helping us move forward.

With respect to the Law of the Sea Convention, US leadership actually resulted in an effective renegotiation of Part XI. Our President then submitted the treaty to the Senate. There is no opposition of any significant kind in the United States to it. There is a peculiarity in the US Constitution over requirements in relation to how it goes through the US Senate, and I fully expect that the United States will be a party to that treaty at some point.

The landmines convention is eminently reasonable in seeking to bring under control the reckless scattering of landmines by aggressive leaders. (Saddam Hussein, for example, threw landmines around Kuwait with no records kept.) That is an entirely understandable and reasonable thing to do. On the other hand, the United States believes strongly that we need to differentiate between the uses of a variety of weapons systems. For example, our forces in South Korea maintain a well-marked mined area between North and South Korea. The laws of war and arms control ought to differentiate appropriately between those two examples. The United States did not reject the landmine convention because we want to have different laws for everyone, but because we don't think the right thing is being done.

Adam Roberts:

For the sake of brevity, I made my remarks in a way that was perhaps tactless. I agree with you that there are different reasons for nonparticipation in many of these treaty regimes and sometimes there is sound, sensible, prudential reasoning on the part of the United States in thinking seriously about the consequences of becoming party to a particular agreement. I wouldn't deny any of that for one second. And of course, the United States is not alone on the landmines treaty. Finland has similar concerns to those of the United States about the possible defensive value of landmines. So there's no suggestion that it is not a serious position.

My concern is not that the United States in fact views itself as above the law, but that there may be a perception of that because of the range and number of treaties that we're talking about and because the United States has such a peculiar—as you yourself have indicated—and slow system of ratification of treaties, which has been a nightmare for successive presidents of the United States. In respect of some of the treaties in this area, a good deal can be achieved by reservation. Not of course with the landmines treaty and not of course with the ICC statute, because, in my opinion unwisely, reservations have been excluded from those treaties. There really is a structural problem there. It is not clever of the majority of the like-minded States to exclude the possibility of reservations, because reservations, although they have had a bad name among some progressive international lawyers, are actually a very important means of bringing treaties into a relationship with the needs, interests, plans and intentions of States. So I agree with you in a large part of what you say. But I think, for example in relation to Protocol I or a number of the other treaties I listed, a good deal could be achieved by participating with reservations rather than staying formally outside the regime. I hasten to add I'm well aware that the United States, even while formally outside certain regimes, in fact has contributed very powerfully to them.

Discussion

Is There a Right of Humanitarian Intervention?

Adam Roberts:

While it is impossible to establish a general right of humanitarian intervention, in individual cases one can argue that there are powerful factors supporting intervention. I'm not sure whether they are all containable within the category of necessity. I don't think they are. But there are very powerful factors, including legal factors, which may point to a justification for the use of force in a particular case. It is the concentration on the specificities of a particular and urgent situation that seems to me to be the right legal as well as political approach.

The German Bundestag, for example, when it debated the issue of Kosovo in October, 1998, essentially said that whereas it was not asserting any general right of humanitarian intervention, in the extraordinary circumstances of Kosovo, it would support an operation and would permit the use of German forces to take part in that operation. I personally think that is a more powerful and a clearer position than the very fragile one of asserting a general right of states to engage in humanitarian intervention.

One can of course buttress such an approach by making certain general propositions about particular cases, be it Bangladesh in 1971 or northern Iraq in 1991, when a use of force without the consent of the receiving sovereign State was tolerated by the international community even though it didn't have explicit UN Security Council blessing. There is also the relevant legal consideration that an intervention may be in support of UN Security Council objectives even if it is not with the specific consent of the Security Council. There's also the relevant legal consideration that some of these actions have not been condemned. All of that falls short of a general right. But it's a considerable advance over the position that you have attributed to me, which is not the position I hold—that one simply has to throw up one's hands in despair and say these questions cannot be answered. On the contrary, in specific cases, they can be answered, and they need to be answered.

Humanitarian Intervention: Ethically Right, Although Legally Wrong?

Christopher Greenwood:

There is one lesson offered to us that seems to be a pit of vipers that we need to avoid like the plague. That is the suggestion that it may be better to proceed on the basis that something is ethically right and not worry too much if it's legally wrong. Now I can see that there are times when you have a situation where something is ethically justified, and the law has not yet caught up with that. But when that's the case, surely as lawyers we ought to be trying to ensure the law is changed in order to accommodate what we recognize as the ethical need. The suggestion that we can simply fall back on an ethical justification and think that is the end of the matter is frankly wet. It's no good at all if you've got to defend what we have done in Kosovo in front of an international court. It doesn't give the kind of steer that we ought to be giving to the people who go out and do the fighting and it's frankly an abdication of our responsibility as lawyers. It comes pretty much to saying this: "It's too difficult to formulate a rule that isn't capable of abuse, therefore it would be better if we don't formulate a rule at all." That's something which I as a lawyer simply cannot accept. We're paid to deal with difficult situations and we should face up to our responsibility in that regard.

Adam Roberts:

It's not my position that one can summarize the state of affairs and justification for the Kosovo operation as ethically right but legally dubious or legally wrong. That's a position that was advanced in a number of articles by lawyers, including the articles by Bruno Simma and Antonio Cassese in the European Journal of International Law,[1] and I think it's a very extraordinary position to take. It's perhaps a comment on the puzzling state of the law to say that something may be legally dubious, even legally wrong, but ethically right.

The position I would take is different. It is impossible to establish a general right of humanitarian intervention. There is virtually no chance of getting any significant group of states to assert a general right of humanitarian intervention and no serious effort has been made since the Kosovo war to do that. Admittedly, the NATO Parliamentary Assembly passed a resolution urging there should be such a right, but they got absolutely nowhere.[2] The reason they're getting nowhere is: first, States that fear they might be the subject of intervention, have recent memories of colonialism, or are governed by seedy dictators are never going to agree; secondly, the States that might do the intervening turn out—and especially the United States—to be not very interested in

---

1. Bruno Simma, NATO, the UN and the Use of Force: Legal Aspects, 10 EUROPEAN JOURNAL OF INTERNATIONAL LAW 1 (1999); Antonio Cassese, Ex iniuria ius oritur: Are We Moving towards International Legitimation of Forcible Humanitarian Countermeasures in the World Community?, 10 EUROPEAN JOURNAL OF INTERNATIONAL LAW 23 (1999).

2. The NATO Parliamentary Assembly is completely independent of NATO but constitutes a link between national parliaments and the Alliance. It encourages governments to take Alliance concerns into account when framing national legislation. For more information, see the NATO Handbook at http://www.nato.int/docu/handbook/2001/hb1601.htm.

propounding a general doctrine that might obligate them to act in situations where for one reason or another they may be unable or unwilling to. So there is simply no chance of getting an international agreement of the kind that lawyers might recognize as law asserting a general right.

However, one can say—and here I think we agree—that there may be a tolerated occasional practice of intervention. Here the fact that there has been no General Assembly resolution condemning the Kosovo action and the fact that the Security Council draft resolution of March 26, 1999 put forward by Russia and others condemning the Kosovo action failed, is evidence that while there is no established general right, certain cases of humanitarian intervention may be tolerated. Another example is the Indian intervention over East Bengal in 1971, which was defended partly on grounds similar to those on which the NATO action over Kosovo was defended. I think that is as far as one can go. It is not saying that there is a distinction between ethics and law, but rather that there is an odd legal situation where a practice is occasionally tolerated that cannot be asserted as a general right. One actually weakens the argument for humanitarian intervention if one makes the legitimacy of a particular intervention seem to be dependent upon the existence of the general right. I think it is a very occasional practice.

Rein Müllerson:

During my comments I supported the view now expressed by Chris Greenwood. I also think that there cannot be and there shouldn't be such difference between what is ethically or morally right and legally wrong. Adam spoke about toleration of certain interventions. The toleration of them leads to change in the law or at least it undermines, it destabilizes the existing prohibition on the use of force. I think that perhaps the least we can say today about the use of force for humanitarian purposes is that it is not unquestionably unlawful in a certain set of circumstances. Every right is general—you can't say non-general or otherwise. In international law, and I am not going into theory, there are treaties that create legal obligations. These are not general rights or obligations, but customary international law certainly is general. Therefore, every right under customary international law has to be general. There was considerable toleration of Operation Allied Force on the part of many States for very different reasons. I think that this, if it hasn't led towards the emergence of a new rule, has undermined the existence of the rule (if there was such a rule) prohibiting the use of force for humanitarian purposes.

Discussion

Leslie Green:

There probably is not at present a general or a non-general right of intervention, but when I look back, I often feel that in the humanitarian field, our classical writers were far more advanced than we are. I'm thinking now of the writings of Grotius, Vattel, Hall, Westlake, and the greatest of them all on the subject of intervention, Stowell. They would argue that if the situation is so unique and so outrageous, then while there may not be a right, perhaps we are moving into a stage where there is a duty to intervene. If we develop the law with regard to humanitarian principles we may find that in the light of Bangladesh, in the light of Kosovo, perhaps in the light of Rwanda where we should have taken stronger action, we are now in a position where the situation has become so outrageous that we go back to Hall and Westlake and say that there is a duty upon those who believe in the personality of the human being and those who believe in the rule of law; there is a duty upon us even if there are written documents that suggest we may be going outside the ambit of the law.

Michael Bothe:

If law and ethics seem to clash, then something must be wrong either with the law or with ethics. The problem we are facing here is that most of us are lawyers. We know how to make nice arguments of what the law is. My impression is that many people who speak about ethics just feel in their hearts what it is. I sometimes question whether this is the correct source for ethical principles.

Ruth Wedgwood:

Actually it's a great pity that international law doesn't really have a vocabulary with which to recapture the brilliant British distinction between law and equity that is also found in American nineteenth century jurisprudence. It is the skeptical doubt that any rule could ever capture all of the necessary instances of exception—the role of equity *contra legem* and *intra legem*. Instead we seem to lapse into almost a sociological or psychological vocabulary of acquiescence or tolerance or diplomatic signal. My own suspicion is that the flat rule against humanitarian intervention is in some ways a historical period piece. It's part of anti-colonialism.

One of the curious books in my library is a 1940 monograph by the "German Library of Information" on so-called "Polish Acts of Atrocity Against the German Minority in Poland," published in New York in 1940. The fact that humanitarian intervention was proffered by Germany as an excuse for the invasion of Czechoslovakia and Poland in World War II gave it a very bad name for a very long time. So even in Europe the feeling of Turkey or other States was that mistreatment of coreligionists would be used as an excuse for intervention. The reflex against humanitarian intervention may become less automatic as the majority of members of the United Nations system become more democratic and mature. I wouldn't go so far as to coin a duty to intervene because it's going to be breached so often.

Adam Roberts:

I was pleased that Leslie Green put this in its proper context along centuries of historical debate about the issue. Maybe in a sense we can all blame Grotius for the way in which the debate has been phrased because he was the one who actually used the term "right" in respect of intervention for what we now regard as humanitarian causes. He raised the issue in terms of whether States had a right to do it. For reasons I've indicated that may be a problematic way of looking at a very difficult issue. I do think that there is bound to be skepticism in the post-colonial era about any general assertion of such a right and for pretty good reasons. One of the most notorious episodes of European colonialism—the Belgian role in the Congo—began as a humanitarian enterprise with a congress held in Brussels on Central Africa during which the word humanitarian was uttered countless times. It can very easily happen that a cause embarked upon for humanitarian or mercy purposes can end up very nasty as we have seen in Somalia. So the nervousness about a general right seems to me to be justifiable and not just to be a fad of the present post-colonial era.

Where I think there may be scope for developing a new principle is in the direction of thinking about a duty, not to intervene, but a duty to take appropriate action (whatever that may be) in case of extreme violations of humanitarian norms. In many cases, the appropriate action will not be intervention. There may be numerous other forms of action that are better for whatever reasons—prudential reasons, tactical reasons and so on. I think it would be very unwise to promote the idea of a duty to intervene as such, but a duty to take action may make more sense.

Michael Glennon:[3]

I am a bit surprised by both Adam Roberts's and Chris Greenwood's discomfort with the notion that ethical or moral considerations may, or could

---
3. Professor of Law, University of California at Davis

under certain circumstances, provide a justification for law violation. That tradition of civil disobedience is of course one with a long-standing and rather time-honored pedigree and not simply in Anglo-Saxon jurisprudence. Why should international law not be subject to the same considerations? Is it not possible that the law has come over in the fullness of time and the course of recent events to reflect evolving social mores or whatever it is that the law seeks to correspond to? Isn't that perhaps precisely what occurred with respect to Article 2(4) when it confronted the moral justifications or the felt ethical needs of NATO leaders? I myself initially conceptualized this as kind of a problem of civil disobedience in international law. I must say on further reflection, I've come to think that the real issue is not whether there is an exception for humanitarian intervention, but whether there is a rule for which an exception could or should exist. My current conclusion I suppose would be that international law simply provides no satisfactory answer to the question of lawfulness of the NATO intervention in Yugoslavia.

Wolff H. von Heinegg:

If you read Wilhelm Grewe's book *Epochs of International Law*, which has now been translated into English by Michael Byers, you will find a chapter on humanitarian intervention. The discussion that was held in the nineteenth century and much of what has been discussed since Kosovo is identical. Even though I'm a professor of international law, I have to admit that it's not us lawyers that make international law. I have always understood international law to be made by States who are the main subjects of public international law. Necessity—I just want to remind you that the Latin phrase *opinio juris* is shortened because it is *opinio juris sive necessitates*—has to be articulated by the subject of international law, which means by States. So when it comes to humanitarian intervention in Kosovo, there were a couple of States who obviously felt the necessity to do something. Whether this will develop into a rule of international law, customary or whatever, depends on the States and not on us.

Is There a Link Between Jus ad Bellum and Jus in Bello?

Wolff H. von Heinegg:

We are not only stepping on a slippery slope (as Admiral Robertson put it) when it comes to the question of whether those who are fighting for the just cause are less bound by *jus in bello* than the one who is fighting for the unjust cause. Let me remind you once again that *jus in bello* according to the consensus of States is the utmost the international community is willing to tolerate, so everything which goes beyond these limits is clearly illegal. The lesson I have learned from this colloquium, maybe not from the Kosovo conflict, is that we should leave *jus in bello* as it is. I have problems putting stronger limits on belligerents by referring to *jus ad bellum*. I certainly do have severe problems with lightening the limits or by brushing them away and thus jeopardizing the achievements of the law of armed conflict.

Henry Shue:

I admire Professor Wedgwood's courage in saying the unconventional during her presentation. I think it's very helpful, but I'm sure she'll agree that if we're going to speak the unspeakable, we should do it very precisely. I just want to emphasize how narrow a point I think there is here. That is, I didn't take her suggestion to be that the more just one's cause, the more discretion one has about the in bello rules. I took it to be that there are exceptional cases in which one's moral responsibility is to win because one's adversary is so evil that one is justified in doing what one would otherwise not be justified in doing. I'm willing to concede that there is such a category in the abstract, which I think puts me a couple of inches away from Professor Greenwood. I would also suggest that so far there's only been one case—the Nazi's. The danger here of course is that since all nations tend to demonize their enemies anyway (it's sort of notorious that George Bush first referred to Saddam Hussein as another Hitler; while Saddam Hussein is a nasty piece of work, he's not a Hitler) we really have to be very careful. It seems to me that honorable defeat without atrocity is still preferable to victory with atrocity except in these very rare cases. So although I think you're right in principle, I'm not sure that the point shouldn't stay unspoken.

Ruth Wedgwood:

I take and agree with the point. Indeed one of the problems with codification always is that (a) it is looking for simplicity and (b) both lawyers and courts take litigating positions. They choose to enunciate bright line rules that they think will lead to the best result in the majority of cases. But most States also take the relationship between *jus in bello* and *jus ad bellum* to be broader than we ordinarily admit—because very few States (at least in the age of total war) would choose to be conquered honorably and many States would use any justifiable means if, in the last analysis, they thought there was a magic bullet that would preserve them from brutal occupation. This is grounded on strategic anticipation of an adversary's expected breach of the laws of honorable occupation.

One of the purposes of the law of war (e.g., Geneva IV's provisions protecting occupied territories) is to say to States that the alternative of being conquered isn't all that bad because civil life will go on. There will be a regime change, but your private life and private property will be preserved and your families can conduct themselves as always. This is simply a quarrel among princes. But in the age of total war, if one is skeptical about the efficacy of enforcement of Geneva IV or its first-cousin principles, then I think you would see lots of deviation from *jus in bello* for the sake of avoiding a devastating occupation and social destruction. In a way, *jus in bello* is a very, very stringent rule of exhaustion, but in the last analysis, for total war (not limited war), most countries would ultimately deviate from it, at least in detail, and within the bounds of humane standards.

Yves Sandoz:

It is a fact that the law of war is fundamentally separated between the *ad bellum* and *in bello*. I share your view that humanitarian law cannot force a country to lose a war. That's why it's so important to examine the rules for the conduct of hostilities. That's also why I cannot share your suggestion that in some cases you could violate humanitarian law because if you accept that, it's the end of humanitarian law. Every State that goes to war believes it is defending a good cause.

Ruth Wedgwood:

We've been talking about lots of different senses in which *jus in bello* and *jus ad bellum* could be linked. One was Professor Roberts' point that if there are so many systematic *in bello* violations, that itself is the *casus belli* for humanitarian intervention. There's the other argument offered at Nuremberg by the prosecution, but rejected by the judges, that in an illegal war all acts of force are illegal. Harvard Professor Sheldon Glueck makes this point in his little volume on war crimes, introduced by Justice Robert Jackson.[4] My third type of linkage was to argue that there may be cases in which the urgency of concluding the war should influence the interpretation of military necessity or the unclear borderline between civilian objects and military objects. If indeed Milosevic had continued killing people at a rapid pace and we knew or could infer that, then a rapid conclusion of the war would have been all the more urgent.

---

4. *See* SHELDON GLUECK, THE NUREMBERG TRIAL AND AGGRESSIVE WAR (1946).

Discussion

That in turn would have arguably justified designations of military targets that were realistic in light of the problems of persuading Milosevic to cease and desist. It's a sliding scale. It's at the edges, but it doesn't mean to reject what is crucial. I agree with Yves Sandoz and the others that from the point of view of educating ground-level military operators and ordinary politicians, one wants to preserve the formal distinction of *in bello* and *ad bellum*.

Critiquing the Report to the Prosecutor

Natalino Ronzitti:

Adam Roberts said that the Report of the Committee established by the ICTY Prosecutor has not been properly critiqued. I am one of those who have heavily criticized the Report to the Prosecutor in an article published in the European Journal of International Law. My main critique is that it said the facts were not well established, that is, that it is the Committee's assertion that it is very difficult to establish the facts. This is very strange because the prosecutor has the full power of the ICTY to summon people. The second critique is that the Report has said that the law is not very clear. You cannot say within a court that the law is not very clear. That, together with the anonymity of the Committee because we don't know officially who they are, is not, I'm afraid, in keeping with the prestige of this Tribunal.

Adam Roberts:

What I intended to say about the ICTY Report is that there hasn't been a full-blooded criticism of its conclusion that there were no violations justifying reference to the ICTY by those who asserted that NATO did commit war crimes. On the whole, the Report has remained inviolate against that kind of criticism and it remains a valuable comment on Operation Allied Force. I am in fact aware of the article that you have contributed on the subject, which does not set out to be the kind of full-blooded critique that I had in mind. I will certainly be referring to it.

Applying the Law of Armed Conflict in the Future

Ruth Wedgwood:

A few responses to what I thought were some very thoughtful comments. The distinction that academics face between the interior view of law and the exterior view is always there. There's a language you speak as a citizen, advocate or judge that has a crisp vocabulary, rejects alternative readings, and stabilizes the legal text for the sake of clear communication and workable guidelines for behavior. But when you step back and ask how satisfactory that framework is or what meta-principles will influence interpretation, then you can dare to be a little more dangerous. Most of my scruples about not losing wars and avoiding utterly catastrophic humanitarian harm can be accommodated by interpretation within the existing rules of *jus in bello*. The worry I suppose is the *milieu* of the decision maker. If you have someone as a war crimes judge who is deeply skeptical about the right to use force in any circumstance, who fundamentally at heart is a type of a pacifist, then you're going to get a very different reading of these rules than you will from somebody who survived World War II or the Korean War or any number of other conflicts. So my concern is how you explain the appropriate balancing to somebody who's approaching these rules as an ingénue, which I hasten to say the war crimes tribunal judges are not. Europe has lived through its wars. Don't mistake my exceptional chancellor's foot for an antinomianism wanting to overthrow the rules as such.

It would be helpful to make some clear distinctions for participants who apply the law of armed conflict. Number one, some textual statements are rules and others are principles. Some norms are bright-line rules, sharp-edged and self-executing, and others are circumstance and fact specific and will garner lots of variation in lawyers' interpretation of what they mean in a particular circumstance. Professor Dolzer's invocation of margin of appreciation indeed might be one very good way of putting it into accepted vernacular. But we have too easily given the impression that all laws of war are created equal, that they all are equally easily applied, and that all are amenable to application without experience. In general, I have to agree, we're very far down the road indeed. ICTY, ICTR, ICC, European Court—the cow is out of the barn and the only cure for the movement to "juridicalize" war may be the attempt by the military community and by extraordinary judges like Judge Pocar of really coming to learn each other's trade craft.

My advice to friends in Washington has been that of forced familiarity—to smother the ICC with seminars. Have lots of NATO gatherings in which you begin to educate the judges and persuade them that they do need military law clerks. They do need a roster of expert witnesses. They do need to go to whatever the European equivalent is of CINC conferences to come to understand some of the practical operations of the law of war. I see this as an incredibly difficult field because it requires people who are versed in history, versed in criminal law, versed in international law, versed in humanitarian law, versed in military operations and versed in military law. It requires a kind of omni-competent synthesis. Perhaps the die has been cast. But the purpose of my observation was to try to invoke a sense of modesty in civilian judges and NGO's (as well as in myself) in approaching the application of rules to battlefield operations.

If I may give a parallel New Haven anecdote: Yale used to pride itself on being the vanguard for law and psychiatry. Judge David Bazelon, and some of the other judges on the US Court of Appeals for the District of Columbia Circuit, thought that if only they could get the right kind of psychiatrists testifying about the nature of legal insanity and moral choice, they could reform the law of criminal responsibility. Ultimately the judges decided, after much gnashing of teeth, that to do so would be an abdication from their own responsibility under the law to decide about the nature of moral choice. You couldn't call a randomly-selected expert witness. This wasn't an objective question of fact. In the context of battlefield law, my worry is that if there is a great distance between the two communities of judges and military operators—if all you have is an amateur criminal lawyer, acting as prosecutor, calling random experts to say what they think should happen on the Kosovo battlefield—then that's going to inhibit necessary military planning.

APPENDIX A

International Criminal Tribunal for the former Yugoslavia (ICTY)

*Final Report to the Prosecutor by the
Committee Established to Review the NATO Bombing Campaign Against
the Federal Republic of Yugoslavia*

INTERNATIONAL CRIMINAL TRIBUNAL FOR THE FORMER
YUGOSLAVIA (ICTY)

Final Report to the Prosecutor by the
Committee Established to Review the NATO Bombing Campaign
Against the Federal Republic of Yugoslavia[1]

Table of Contents

I. Background and Mandate 485
II. Review Criteria 486
III. Work Program 487
IV. Assessment 491
   A. General Issues 491
      i. Damage to the Environment 491
      ii. Use of Depleted Uranium Projectiles 496
      iii. Use of Cluster Bombs 497
      iv. Legal Issues Related to Target Selection 497
         a. Overview of Applicable Law 497
         b. Linkage Between Law Concerning Recourse to Force
           and Law Concerning How Force May Be Used 499
         c. The Military Objective 500
         d. The Principle of Proportionality 507
      v. Casualty Figures 510
      vi. General Assesment of the Bombing Campaign 510
   B. Specific Incidents 511
      i. The Attack on a Civilian Passenger Train at the Grdelica
        Gorge on 12/4/99 512
      ii. The Attack on the Djakovica Convoy on 14/4/99. 515
      iii. The Bombing of the RTS (Serbian TV and Radio Station)
        in Belgrade on 23/4/99 518
      iv. The Attack on the Chinese Embassy on 7/5/99 524
      v. The Attack on Korisa Village on 13/5/99 527
V. Recommendations 529

---

1. This document was reproduced and reformatted from the text appearing at the ICTY website (visited January 10, 2002) http://www.un.org/icty/pressreal/nato061300.htm.

Appendix A

I Background and Mandate

1. The North Atlantic Treaty Organization (NATO) conducted a bombing campaign against the Federal Republic of Yugoslavia (FRY) from 24 March 1999 to 9 June 1999. During and since that period, the Prosecutor has received numerous requests that she investigate allegations that senior political and military figures from NATO countries committed serious violations of international humanitarian law during the campaign, and that she prepares indictments pursuant to Article 18(1) & (4) of the Statute.

2. Criticism of the NATO bombing campaign has included allegations of varying weight: a) that, as the resort to force was illegal, all NATO actions were illegal, and b) that the NATO forces deliberately attacked civilian infrastructure targets (and that such attacks were unlawful), deliberately or recklessly attacked the civilian population, and deliberately or recklessly caused excessive civilian casualties in disregard of the rule of proportionality by trying to fight a "zero casualty" war for their own side. Allegations concerning the "zero casualty" war involve suggestions that, for example, NATO aircraft operated at heights which enabled them to avoid attack by Yugoslav defences and, consequently, made it impossible for them to properly distinguish between military or civilian objects on the ground. Certain allegations went so far as to accuse NATO of crimes against humanity and genocide.

3. Article 18 of the Tribunal's Statute provides:

> "The Prosecutor shall initiate investigations *ex officio* or on the basis of information obtained from any source, particularly from Governments, United Nations organs, intergovernmental and non-governmental organizations. The Prosecutor shall assess the information received or obtained and decide whether there is sufficient basis to proceed".

On 14 May 99 the then Prosecutor established a committee to assess the allegations and material accompanying them, and advise the Prosecutor and Deputy Prosecutor whether or not there is a sufficient basis to proceed with an investigation into some or all the allegations or into other incidents related to the NATO bombing.

4. In the course of its work, the committee has not addressed in detail the issue of the fundamental legality of the use of force by NATO members against

the FRY as, if such activity was unlawful, it could constitute a crime against peace and the ICTY has no jurisdiction over this offence. (See, however, paras 30 – 34 below). It is noted that the legitimacy of the recourse to force by NATO is a subject before the International Court of Justice in a case brought by the FRY against various NATO countries.

II Review Criteria

5. In the course of its review, the committee has applied the same criteria to NATO activities that the Office of the Prosecutor (OTP) has applied to the activities of other actors in the territory of the former Yugoslavia. The committee paid particular heed to the following questions:

   a. Are the prohibitions alleged sufficiently well-established as violations of international humanitarian law to form the basis of a prosecution, and does the application of the law to the particular facts reasonably suggest that a violation of these prohibitions may have occurred?
   and
   b. upon the reasoned evaluation of the information by the committee, is the information credible and does it tend to show that crimes within the jurisdiction of the Tribunal may have been committed by individuals during the NATO bombing campaign?

This latter question reflects the earlier approach in relation to Article 18(1) of the Statute taken by the Prosecutor when asserting her right to investigate allegations of crimes committed by Serb forces in Kosovo *(Request by the Prosecutor, Pursuant to Rule 7 bis) (B) that the President Notify the Security Council That the Federal Republic of Yugoslavia Has Failed to Comply With Its Obligations Under Article 29, dated 1 February 1999)*. The threshold test expressed therein by the Prosecutor was that of "credible evidence tending to show that crimes within the jurisdiction of the Tribunal may have been committed in Kosovo". That test was advanced to explain in what situation the Prosecutor would consider, for jurisdiction purposes, that she had a legal entitlement to investigate. (As a corollary, any investigation failing to meet that test could be said to be arbitrary and capricious, and to fall outside the Prosecutor's mandate). Thus formulated, the test represents a negative cut-off point for investigations. The Prosecutor may, in her discretion require that a higher threshold be met before making a positive decision that there is sufficient basis to proceed under Article 18(1). (In fact, in relation to the situation on the ground in Kosovo, the Prosecutor was in possession of a considerable body of evidence pointing to the commission of widespread atrocities by Serb forces.) In practice, before deciding to open an investigation in any case, the Prosecutor will also take into account a number of other factors concerning the prospects for obtaining evidence sufficient to prove that the crime has been committed by an individual who merits prosecution in the international forum.

III Work Program

6. The committee has reviewed:

    a. documents sent to the OTP by persons or groups wishing the OTP to commence investigations of leading persons from NATO countries,

    b. public documents made available by NATO, the US Department of Defense and the British Ministry of Defence,

    c. documents filed by the FRY before the ICJ, a large number of other FRY documents, and also the two volume compilation of the FRY Ministry of Foreign Affairs entitled *NATO Crimes in Yugoslavia (White Book)*,

    d. various documents submitted by Human Rights Watch including a letter sent to the Secretary General of NATO during the bombing campaign, a paper on *NATO's Use of Cluster Munitions*, and a report on *Civilian Deaths in the NATO Air Campaign*,

    e. a UNEP study: *The Kosovo Conflict: Consequence for the Environment and Human Settlements*,

    f. documents submitted by a Russian Parliamentary Commission,

    g. two studies by a German national, Mr. Ekkehard Wenz, one concerning the bombing of a train at the Grdelica Gorge and the other concerning the bombing of the Djakovica Refugee Convoy,

    h. various newspaper reports and legal articles as they have come to the attention of committee members,

i. the response to a letter containing a number of questions sent to NATO by the OTP, and

j. an Amnesty International Report entitled *"Collateral Damage" or Unlawful Killings? Violations of the Laws of War by NATO during Operation Allied Force.*

7. It should be noted that the committee did not travel to the FRY and it did not solicit information from the FRY through official channels as no such channels existed during the period when the review was conducted. Most of the material reviewed by the committee was in the public domain. The committee has relied exclusively on documents. The FRY submitted to the Prosecutor a substantial amount of material concerning particular incidents. In attempting to assess what happened on the ground, the committee relied upon the Human Rights Watch Report entitled *Civilian Deaths in the NATO Air Campaign* and upon the documented accounts in the FRY Ministry of Foreign Affairs volumes entitled NATO Crimes in Yugoslavia. The committee also relied heavily on NATO press statements and on the studies done by Mr. Ekkehard Wenz. The information available was adequate for making a preliminary assessment of incidents in which civilians were killed or injured. Information related to attacks on objects where civilians were not killed or injured was difficult to obtain and very little usable information was obtained.

8. To assist in the preparation of an Interim Report, a member of the Military Analysis Team reviewed the documents available in the OTP at the time, that is, all those referred to in paragraph 6 above except the FRY volumes entitled *NATO Crimes in Yugoslavia*, the HRW report on Civilian Deaths in the NATO Air Campaign, the studies by Mr. Wenz, NATO's response to the letter sent by the OTP to NATO, and the Amnesty International Report. The analyst prepared: a) a list of key incidents, b) a list of civilian residential targets, c) a list of civilian facility targets, d) a list of cultural property targets, e) a list of power facility targets, f) a list of targets the destruction of which might significantly affect the environment, and g) a list of communications targets. Very little information was available concerning the targets in lists (b) through (g).

9. The committee reviewed the above lists and requested the preparation of a file containing all available information on certain particular incidents, and on certain target categories. (It should be noted that the use of the terms "target" or "attack" in this report does not mean that in every case the site in

Appendix A

question was deliberately struck by NATO. The terms are convenient shorthand for incidents in which it is alleged that particular locations were damaged in the course of the bombing campaign).

The key incidents and target categories were:

    a. the attack on a civilian passenger train at the Grdelica Gorge – 12/4/99 – 10 or more civilians killed, 15 or more injured,

    b. the attack on the Djakovica Convoy – 14/4/99 – 70-75 civilians killed, 100 or more injured,

    c. the attack on Surdulica, - 27/4/99 – 11 civilians killed, 100 or more injured,

    d. the attack on Cuprija – 8/4/99 – 1 civilian killed, 5 injured,

    e. the attack on the Cigota Medical Institute – 8/4/99 – 3 civilians killed,

    f. the attack on Hotels Baciste and Putnik – 13/4/99 – 1 civilian killed,

    g. the attacks on the Pancevo Petrochemical Complex and Fertilizer Company – 15/4/99 and 18/4/99 – no reported civilian casualties,

    h. the attack on the Nis Tobbaco Factory – 18/4/99 – no reported civilian casualties,

    i. the attack on the Djakovica Refugee Camp – 21/4/99 – 5 civilians killed, 16-19 injured,

    j. ·the attack on a bus at Lu`ane – 1/5/99 39 civilians killed,

    k. the attack on a bus at Pec – 3/5/99 – 17 civilians killed, 44 injured,

    l. the attack at Korisa village – 13/5/99 – 48-87 civilians killed,

    m. the attack on the Belgrade TV and Radio Station – 23/4/99 – 16 civilians killed,

n. the attack on the Chinese Embassy in Belgrade – 7/5/99 – 3 civilians killed, 15 injured,

o. attack on Nis City Centre and Hospital – 7/5/99 – 13 civilians killed, 60 injured,

p. attack on Istok Prison – 21/5/99 – at least 19 civilians killed,

q. attack on Belgrade Hospital – 20/5/99 – 3 civilians killed, several injured,

r. attack on Surdulica Sanatorium – 30/5/99 – 23 killed, many injured,

s. attack on journalists convoy Prizren-Brezovica Road – 31/5/99 – 1 civilian killed – 3 injured

t. attack on Belgrade Heating Plant – 4/4/99, - 1 killed,

u. attacks on Trade and Industry Targets.

10. On 23 July 1999, each committee member was provided with a binder including all available material. The committee members reviewed material in the binders.

11. In addition to reviewing factual information, the committee has also gathered legal materials and reviewed relevant legal issues, including the legality of the use of depleted uranium projectiles, the legality of the use of cluster munitions, whether or not the bombing campaign had an unlawfully adverse impact on the environment, and legal issues related to target selection.

12. The committee prepared an interim report on the basis of its analysis of the legal and factual material available and this was presented to the Prosecutor on 6 December 1999. At the direction of the Prosecutor, the committee then further updated the incident list and prepared a list of general questions and questions related to specific incidents. A letter enclosing the questionnaire and incident list was sent to NATO on 8 February 2000. A general reply was received on 10 May 2000.

13. It has not been possible for the committee to look at the NATO bombing campaign on a bomb by bomb basis and that was not its task. The committee has, however, reviewed public information concerning several incidents, including all the more well known incidents, with considerable care. It has also endeavored to examine, and has posed questions to NATO, concerning all other incidents in which it appears three or more civilians were killed.

In conducting its review, the committee has focused primarily on incidents in which civilian deaths were alleged and/or confirmed. The committee reviewed certain key incidents in depth for its interim report. These key incidents included 10 incidents in which 10 or more civilians were killed. The review by Human Rights Watch revealed 12 incidents in which 10 or more civilians were killed, all of the incidents identified by the committee plus two additional incidents: a) the attack on the Aleksinak "Deligrad" military barracks on 5/5/99 in which 10 civilians were killed and 30 wounded (a bomb aimed at the barracks fell short), and b) the attack on a military barracks in Novi Pazar on 31/5/99 in which 11 civilians were killed and 23 wounded (5 out of 6 munitions hit the target but one went astray). The committee's review of incidents in which it is alleged fewer than three civilians were killed has been hampered by a lack of reliable information.

IV Assessment

A. General Issues

i. Damage to the Environment

14. The NATO bombing campaign did cause some damage to the environment. For instance, attacks on industrial facilities such as chemical plants and oil installations were reported to have caused the release of pollutants, although the exact extent of this is presently unknown. The basic legal provisions applicable to protection of the environment in armed conflict are Article 35(3) of Additional Protocol I, which states that '[i]t is prohibited to employ methods or means of warfare which are intended, or may be expected, to cause widespread, long-term and severe damage to the natural environment' and Article 55 which states:

   1. Care shall be taken in warfare to protect the natural environment against widespread, long-term and severe damage. This protection

includes a prohibition of the use of methods or means of warfare which are intended or may be expected to cause such damage to the natural environment and thereby to prejudice the health or survival of the population.

2. Attacks against the natural environment by way of reprisals are prohibited

15. Neither the USA nor France has ratified Additional Protocol I. Article 55 may, nevertheless, reflect current customary law (see however the 1996 Advisory Opinion on the *Legality of Nuclear Weapons*, where the International Court of Justice appeared to suggest that it does not (*ICJ Rep.* (1996), 242, para. 31)). In any case, Articles 35(3) and 55 have a very high threshold of application. Their conditions for application are extremely stringent and their scope and contents imprecise. For instance, it is generally assumed that Articles 35(3) and 55 only cover very significant damage. The adjectives 'widespread, long-term, and severe' used in Additional Protocol I are joined by the word 'and', meaning that it is a triple, cumulative standard that needs to be fulfilled.

Consequently, it would appear extremely difficult to develop a *prima facie* case upon the basis of these provisions, even assuming they were applicable. For instance, it is thought that the notion of 'long-term' damage in Additional Protocol I would need to be measured in years rather than months, and that as such, ordinary battlefield damage of the kind caused to France in World War I would not be covered.

The great difficulty of assessing whether environmental damage exceeded the threshold of Additional Protocol I has also led to criticism by ecologists. This may partly explain the disagreement as to whether any of the damage caused by the oil spills and fires in the 1990/91 Gulf War technically crossed the threshold of Additional Protocol I.

It is the committee's view that similar difficulties would exist in applying Additional Protocol I to the present facts, even if reliable environmental assessments were to give rise to legitimate concern concerning the impact of the NATO bombing campaign. Accordingly, these effects are best considered from the underlying principles of the law of armed conflict such as necessity and proportionality.

Appendix A

16. The conclusions of the Balkan Task Force (BTF) established by UNEP to look into the Kosovo situation are:

> "Our findings indicate that the Kosovo conflict has not caused an environmental catastrophe affecting the Balkans region as a whole.
>
> Nevertheless, pollution detected at some sites is serious and poses a threat to human health.
>
> BTF was able to identify environmental 'hot spots', namely in Pancevo, Kragujevac, Novi Sad and Bor, where immediate action and also further monitoring and analyses will be necessary. At all of these sites, environmental contamination due to the consequences of the Kosovo conflict was identified.
>
> Part of the contamination identified at some sites clearly pre-dates the Kosovo conflict, and there is evidence of long-term deficiencies in the treatment and storage of hazardous waste.
>
> The problems identified require immediate attention, irrespective of their cause, if further damage to human health and the environment is to be avoided."

17. The OTP has been hampered in its assessment of the extent of environmental damage in Kosovo by a lack of alternative and corroborated sources regarding the extent of environmental contamination caused by the NATO bombing campaign. Moreover, it is quite possible that, as this campaign occurred only a year ago, the UNEP study may not be a reliable indicator of the long term environmental consequences of the NATO bombing, as accurate assessments regarding the long-term effects of this contamination may not yet be practicable.

It is the opinion of the committee, on the basis of information currently in its possession, that the environmental damage caused during the NATO bombing campaign does not reach the Additional Protocol I threshold. In addition, the UNEP Report also suggests that much of the environmental contamination which is discernible cannot unambiguously be attributed to the NATO bombing.

18. The alleged environmental effects of the NATO bombing campaign flow in many cases from NATO's striking of legitimate military targets compatible

with Article 52 of Additional Protocol I such as stores of fuel, industries of fundamental importance for the conduct of war and for the manufacture of supplies and material of a military character, factories or plant and manufacturing centres of fundamental importance for the conduct of war. Even when targeting admittedly legitimate military objectives, there is a need to avoid excessive long-term damage to the economic infrastructure and natural environment with a consequential adverse effect on the civilian population. Indeed, military objectives should not be targeted if the attack is likely to cause collateral environmental damage which would be excessive in relation to the direct military advantage which the attack is expected to produce (A.P.V. Rogers, "Zero Casualty Warfare," *IRRC*, March 2000, Vol. 82, pp. 177-8).

19. It is difficult to assess the relative values to be assigned to the military advantage gained and harm to the natural environment, and the application of the principle of proportionality is more easily stated than applied in practice. In applying this principle, it is necessary to assess the importance of the target in relation to the incidental damage expected: if the target is sufficiently important, a greater degree of risk to the environment may be justified.

20. The adverse effect of the coalition air campaign in the Gulf war upon the civilian infrastructure prompted concern on the part of some experts regarding the notion of "military objective." This has prompted some experts to argue that where the presumptive effect of hostilities upon the civilian infrastructure (and consequently the civilian population) is grave, the military advantage conferred by the destruction of the military objective would need to be decisive (see below, paras. 40–41). Similar considerations would, in the committee's view, be warranted where the grave threat to the civilian infrastructure emanated instead from excessive environmental harm resulting from the hostilities. The critical question is what kind of environmental damage can be considered to be excessive. Unfortunately, the customary rule of proportionality does not include any concrete guidelines to this effect.

21. The military worth of the target would need to be considered in relation to the circumstances prevailing at the time. If there is a choice of weapons or methods of attack available, a commander should select those which are most likely to avoid, or at least minimize, incidental damage. In doing so, however, he is entitled to take account of factors such as stocks of different weapons and likely future demands, the timeliness of attack and risks to his own forces (A.P.V. Rogers, *ibid*, at p. 178). Operational reality is recognized in the

Statute of the International Criminal Court, an authoritative indicator of evolving customary international law on this point, where Article 8(b)(iv) makes the infliction of incidental environmental damage an offence only if the attack is launched intentionally in the knowledge that it will cause widespread, long-term and severe damage to the natural environment which would be clearly excessive in relation to the concrete and direct overall military advantage anticipated. The use of the word "clearly' ensures that criminal responsibility would be entailed only in cases where the excessiveness of the incidental damage was obvious.

22. Taken together, this suggests that in order to satisfy the requirement of proportionality, attacks against military targets which are known or can reasonably be assumed to cause grave environmental harm may need to confer a very substantial military advantage in order to be considered legitimate. At a minimum, actions resulting in massive environmental destruction, especially where they do not serve a clear and important military purpose, would be questionable. The targeting by NATO of Serbian petro-chemical industries may well have served a clear and important military purpose.

23. The above considerations also suggest that the requisite *mens rea* on the part of a commander would be actual or constructive knowledge as to the grave environmental effects of a military attack; a standard which would be difficult to establish for the purposes of prosecution and which may provide an insufficient basis to prosecute military commanders inflicting environmental harm in the (mistaken) belief that such conduct was warranted by military necessity. (In the *Hostages* case before the Nuremberg Military Tribunals, for instance, the German General Rendulic was acquitted of the charge of wanton devastation on the grounds that although Rendulic may have erred in believing that there was military necessity for the widespread environmental destruction entailed by his use of a 'scorched earth' policy in the Norwegian province of Finnmark, he was not guilty of a criminal act (11 *Trials of War Criminals*, (1950), 1296)). In addition, the notion of 'excessive' environmental destruction is imprecise and the actual environmental impact, both present and long term, of the NATO bombing campaign is at present unknown and difficult to measure.

24. In order to fully evaluate such matters, it would be necessary to know the extent of the knowledge possessed by NATO as to the nature of Serbian military-industrial targets (and thus, the likelihood of environmental damage

flowing from their destruction), the extent to which NATO could reasonably have anticipated such environmental damage (for instance, could NATO have reasonably expected that toxic chemicals of the sort allegedly released into the environment by the bombing campaign would be stored alongside that military target?) and whether NATO could reasonably have resorted to other (and less environmentally damaging) methods for achieving its military objective of disabling the Serbian military-industrial infrastructure.

25. It is therefore the opinion of the committee, based on information currently available to it, that the OTP should not commence an investigation into the collateral environmental damage caused by the NATO bombing campaign.

ii. *Use of Depleted Uranium Projectiles*

26. There is evidence of use of depleted uranium (DU) projectiles by NATO aircraft during the bombing campaign. There is no specific treaty ban on the use of DU projectiles. There is a developing scientific debate and concern expressed regarding the impact of the use of such projectiles and it is possible that, in future, there will be a consensus view in international legal circles that use of such projectiles violate general principles of the law applicable to use of weapons in armed conflict. No such consensus exists at present. Indeed, even in the case of nuclear warheads and other weapons of mass-destruction – those which are universally acknowledged to have the most deleterious environmental consequences – it is difficult to argue that the prohibition of their use is in all cases absolute. (*Legality of Nuclear Weapons*, ICJ Rep. (1996), 242). In view of the uncertain state of development of the legal standards governing this area, it should be emphasised that the use of depleted uranium or other potentially hazardous substance by any adversary to conflicts within the former Yugoslavia since 1991 has not formed the basis of any charge laid by the Prosecutor. It is acknowledged that the underlying principles of the law of armed conflict such as proportionality are applicable also in this context; however, it is the committee's view that analysis undertaken above (paras. 14-25) with regard to environmental damage would apply, *mutatis mutandis*, to the use of depleted uranium projectiles by NATO. It is therefore the opinion of the committee, based on information available at present, that the OTP should not commence an investigation into use of depleted uranium projectiles by NATO.

Appendix A

iii. Use of Cluster Bombs

27. Cluster bombs were used by NATO forces during the bombing campaign. There is no specific treaty provision which prohibits or restricts the use of cluster bombs although, of course, cluster bombs must be used in compliance with the general principles applicable to the use of all weapons. Human Rights Watch has condemned the use of cluster bombs alleging that the high "dud" or failure rate of the submunitions (bomblets) contained inside cluster bombs converts these submunitions into antipersonnel landmines which, it asserts, are now prohibited under customary international law. Whether antipersonnel landmines are prohibited under current customary law is debatable, although there is a strong trend in that direction. There is, however, no general legal consensus that cluster bombs are, in legal terms, equivalent to antipersonnel landmines. It should be noted that the use of cluster bombs was an issue of sorts in the *Martic* Rule 61 Hearing Decision of Trial Chamber I on 8 March 1996. In that decision the Chamber stated there was no formal provision forbidding the use of cluster bombs as such (para. 18 of judgment) but it regarded the use of the Orkan rocket with a cluster bomb warhead in that particular case as evidence of the intent of the accused to deliberately attack the civilian population because the rocket was inaccurate, it landed in an area with no military objectives nearby, it was used as an antipersonnel weapon launched against the city of Zagreb and the accused indicated he intended to attack the city as such (paras. 23-31 of judgment). The Chamber concluded that "the use of the Orkan rocket in this case was not designed to hit military targets but to terrorise the civilians of Zagreb" (para. 31 of judgment). There is no indication cluster bombs were used in such a fashion by NATO. It is the opinion of the committee, based on information presently available, that the OTP should not commence an investigation into use of cluster bombs as such by NATO.

iv. Legal Issues Related to Target Selection

a. Overview of Applicable Law

28. In brief, in combat military commanders are required: a) to direct their operations against military objectives, and b) when directing their operations against military objectives, to ensure that the losses to the civilian population and the damage to civilian property are not disproportionate to the concrete and direct military advantage anticipated. Attacks which are not directed

against military objectives (particularly attacks directed against the civilian population) and attacks which cause disproportionate civilian casualties or civilian property damage may constitute the *actus reus* for the offence of unlawful attack under Article 3 of the ICTY Statute. The *mens rea* for the offence is intention or recklessness, not simple negligence. In determining whether or not the *mens rea* requirement has been met, it should be borne in mind that commanders deciding on an attack have duties:

a) to do everything practicable to verify that the objectives to be attacked are military objectives,

b) to take all practicable precautions in the choice of methods and means of warfare with a view to avoiding or, in any event to minimizing incidental civilian casualties or civilian property damage, and

c) to refrain from launching attacks which may be expected to cause disproportionate civilian casualties or civilian property damage.

29. One of the principles underlying international humanitarian law is the principle of distinction, which obligates military commanders to distinguish between military objectives and civilian persons or objects. The practical application of this principle is effectively encapsulated in Article 57 of Additional Protocol which, in part, obligates those who plan or decide upon an attack to "do everything feasible to verify that the objectives to be attacked are neither civilians nor civilian objects". The obligation to do everything feasible is high but not absolute. A military commander must set up an effective intelligence gathering system to collect and evaluate information concerning potential targets. The commander must also direct his forces to use available technical means to properly identify targets during operations. Both the commander and the aircrew actually engaged in operations must have some range of discretion to determine which available resources shall be used and how they shall be used. Further, a determination that inadequate efforts have been made to distinguish between military objectives and civilians or civilian objects should not necessarily focus exclusively on a specific incident. If precautionary measures have worked adequately in a very high percentage of cases then the fact they have not worked well in a small number of cases does not necessarily mean they are generally inadequate.

b. Linkage Between Law Concerning Recourse to Force and Law Concerning How Force May Be Used

30. Allegations have been made that, as NATO's resort to force was not authorized by the Security Council or in self-defence, that the resort to force was illegal and, consequently, all forceful measures taken by NATO were unlawful. These allegations justify a brief discussion of the *jus ad bellum*. In brief, the *jus ad bellum* regulates when states may use force and is, for the most part, enshrined in the UN Charter. In general, states may use force in self defence (individual or collective) and for very few other purposes. In particular, the legitimacy of the presumed basis for the NATO bombing campaign, humanitarian intervention without prior Security Council authorization, is hotly debated. That being said, as noted in paragraph 4 above, the crime related to an unlawful decision to use force is the crime against peace or aggression. While a person convicted of a crime against peace may, potentially, be held criminally responsible for all of the activities causing death, injury or destruction during a conflict, the ICTY does not have jurisdiction over crimes against peace.

31. The *jus in bello* regulates how states may use force. The ICTY has jurisdiction over serious violations of international humanitarian law as specified in Articles 2-5 of the Statute. These are *jus in bello* offences.

32. The precise linkage between *jus ad bellum* and *jus in bello* is not completely resolved. There were suggestions by the prosecution before the International Military Tribunal at Nuremberg and in some other post World War II war crimes cases that all of the killing and destruction caused by German forces were war crimes because the Germans were conducting an aggressive war. The courts were unreceptive to these arguments. Similarly, in the 1950's there was a debate concerning whether UN authorized forces were required to comply with the *jus in bello* as they represented the good side in a battle between good an evil. This debate died out as the participants realized that a certain crude reciprocity was essential if the law was to have any positive impact. An argument that the "bad" side had to comply with the law while the "good" side could violate it at will would be most unlikely to reduce human suffering in conflict.

33. More recently, a refined approach to the linkage issue has been advocated by certain law of war scholars. Using their approach, assuming that the only lawful basis for recourse to force is self defence, each use of force during a conflict must be measured by whether or not it complies with the *jus in bello* and

by whether or not it complies with the necessity and proportionality requirements of self defence. The difficulty with this approach is that it does not adequately address what should be done when it is unclear who is acting in self defence and it does not clarify the obligations of the "bad" side.

34. As a matter of practice, which we consider to be in accord with the most widely accepted and reputable legal opinion, we in the OTP have deliberately refrained from assessing *jus ad bellum* issues in our work and focused exclusively on whether or not individuals have committed serious violations of international humanitarian law as assessed within the confines of the *jus in bello*.

c. The military objective

35. The most widely accepted definition of "military objective" is that in Article 52 of Additional Protocol I which states in part:

> In so far as objects are concerned, military objectives are limited to those objects which by their nature, location, purpose or use make an effective contribution to military action and whose total or partial destruction, capture or neutralization, in the circumstances ruling at the time, offers a definite military advantage.

36. Where objects are concerned, the definition has two elements: (a) their nature, location, purpose or use must make an effective contribution to military action, and (b) their total or partial destruction, capture or neutralization must offer a definite military advantage in the circumstances ruling at the time. Although this definition does not refer to persons, in general, members of the armed forces are considered combatants, who have the right to participate directly in hostilities, and as a corollary, may also be attacked.

37. The definition is supposed to provide a means whereby informed objective observers (and decision makers in a conflict) can determine whether or not a particular object constitutes a military objective. It accomplishes this purpose in simple cases. Everyone will agree that a munitions factory is a military objective and an unoccupied church is a civilian object. When the definition is applied to dual-use objects which have some civilian uses and some actual or potential military use (communications systems, transportation systems, petrochemical complexes, manufacturing plants of some types), opinions may differ. The application of the definition to particular objects may also differ

Appendix A

depending on the scope and objectives of the conflict. Further, the scope and objectives of the conflict may change during the conflict.

38. Using the Protocol I definition and his own review of state practice, Major General A.P.V. Rogers, a former Director of British Army Legal Services has advanced a tentative list of military objectives:

> military personnel and persons who take part in the fighting without being members of the armed forces, military facilities, military equipment, including military vehicles, weapons, munitions and stores of fuel, military works, including defensive works and fortifications, military depots and establishments, including War and Supply Ministries, works producing or developing military supplies and other supplies of military value, including metallurgical, engineering and chemical industries supporting the war effort; areas of land of military significance such as hills, defiles and bridgeheads; railways, ports, airfields, bridges, main roads as well as tunnels and canals; oil and other power installations; communications installations, including broadcasting and television stations and telephone and telegraph stations used for military communications. (Rogers, *Law on the Battlefield* (1996) 37)

The list was not intended to be exhaustive. It remains a requirement that both elements of the definition must be met before a target can be properly considered an appropriate military objective.

39. In 1956, the International Committee of the Red Cross (ICRC) drew up the following proposed list of categories of military objectives:

I. The objectives belonging to the following categories are those considered to be of generally recognized military importance:

   (1) Armed forces, including auxiliary or complementary organisations, and persons who, though not belonging to the above-mentioned formations, nevertheless take part in the fighting.

   (2) Positions, installations or constructions occupied by the forces indicated in sub-paragraph 1 above, as well as combat

objectives (that is to say, those objectives which are directly contested in battle between land or sea forces including airborne forces).

(3) Installations, constructions and other works of a military nature, such as barracks, fortifications, War Ministries (e.g. Ministries of Army, Navy, Air Force, National Defence, Supply) and other organs for the direction and administration of military operations.

(4) Stores of army or military supplies, such as munition dumps, stores of equipment or fuel, vehicles parks.

(5) Airfields, rocket launching ramps and naval base installations.

(6) Those of the lines and means of communications (railway lines, roads, bridges, tunnels and canals) which are of fundamental military importance.

(7) The installations of broadcasting and television stations; telephone and telegraph exchanges of fundamental military importance.

(8) Industries of fundamental importance for the conduct of the war:

   (a) industries for the manufacture of armaments such as weapons, munitions, rockets, armoured vehicles, military aircraft, fighting ships, including the manufacture of accessories and all other war material;

   (b) industries for the manufacture of supplies and material of a military character, such as transport and communications material, equipment of the armed forces;

   (c) factories or plant constituting other production and manufacturing centres of fundamental importance for the conduct of war, such as the metallurgical, engineering and chemical industries, whose nature or purpose is essentially military;

(d) storage and transport installations whose basic function it is to serve the industries referred to in (a)-(c);

(e) installations providing energy mainly for national defence, e.g. coal, other fuels, or atomic energy, and plants producing gas or electricity mainly for military consumption.

(9) Installations constituting experimental, research centres for experiments on and the development of weapons and war material.

II. The following however, are excepted from the foregoing list:

(1) Persons, constructions, installations or transports which are protected under the Geneva Conventions I, II, III, of August 12, 1949;

(2) Non-combatants in the armed forces who obviously take no active or direct part in hostilities.

III. The above list will be reviewed at intervals of not more than ten years by a group of Experts composed of persons with a sound grasp of military strategy and of others concerned with the protection of the civilian population.

(Y. Sandoz, C. Swiniarski, B. Zimmerman, eds., *Commentary on the Additional Protocols of 8 June 1977 to the Geneva Conventions of 12 August 1949* (1987) at 632-633.

40. The Protocol I definition of military objective has been criticized by W. Hays Parks, the Special Assistant for Law of War Matters to the U.S. Army Judge Advocate General as being focused too narrowly on definite military advantage and paying too little heed to war sustaining capability, including economic targets such as export industries. (W. Hays Parks, "Air War and the Law of War," 32 A.F.L. Rev. 1, 135-45 (1990)). On the other hand, some critics of Coalition conduct in the Gulf War have suggested that the Coalition air

campaign, directed admittedly against legitimate military objectives within the scope of the Protocol I definition, caused excessive long-term damage to the Iraqi economic infrastructure with a consequential adverse effect on the civilian population. (Middle East Watch, *Needless Deaths in the Gulf War: Civilian Casualties during the Air Campaign and Violations of the Laws of War* (1991); Judith G. Gardam, "Proportionality and Force in International Law," 87 *Am. J. Int'l L.* 391, 404-10 (1993)).

41. This criticism has not gone unexplored. Françoise Hampson, a British scholar, has suggested a possible refinement of the definition:

> In order to determine whether there is a real subject of concern here, it would be necessary to establish exactly what the effect has been of the damage to the civilian infrastructure brought about by the hostilities. If that points to a need further to refine the law, it is submitted that what is needed is a qualification to the definition of military objectives. Either it should require the likely cumulative effect on the civilian population of attacks against such targets to be taken into account, or the same result might be achieved by requiring that the destruction of the object offer a definite military advantage in the context of the war aim. Françoise Hampson, "Means and Methods of Warfare in the Conflict in the Gulf," in P. Rowe, ed., *The Gulf War 1990-91 in International and English Law* 89 (1983) 100.

42. Although the Protocol I definition of military objective is not beyond criticism, it provides the contemporary standard which must be used when attempting to determine the lawfulness of particular attacks. That being said, it must be noted once again neither the USA nor France is a party to Additional Protocol I. The definition is, however, generally accepted as part of customary law.

43. To put the NATO campaign in context, it is instructive to look briefly at the approach to the military objective concept in history of air warfare. The Protocol I standard was not applicable during World War II. The bomber offensives conducted during that war were conducted with technological means which rendered attacks on targets occupying small areas almost impossible. In general, depending upon the period in the conflict, bomber attacks could be relied upon, at best, to strike within 5 miles, 2 miles or 1 mile of the designated target. The mission for the US/UK Combined Bomber Offensive from the UK was:

"To conduct a joint United States-British air offensive to accomplish the progressive destruction and dislocation of the German military, industrial and economic system, and the undermining of the morale of the German people to a point where their capacity for armed resistance is fatally weakened. This is construed as meaning so weakened as to permit initiation of final combined operations on the Continent."

(A. Verrier, *The Bomber Offensive* (1968) 330).

The principal specific objectives of the offensive were designated as:

"Submarine construction yards and bases.
German aircraft industry.
Ball bearings.
Oil.
Synthetic rubber and tires.
Military transport vehicles."

(A. Verrier, *ibid*, at 330).

Notwithstanding the designation of specific targets and the attempt, at least by US Army Air Force commanders on occasion, to conduct a precision bombing campaign, for the most part World War II bombing campaigns were aimed at area targets and intended, directly or indirectly, to affect the morale of the enemy civilian population. It is difficult to describe the fire bombing of Hamburg, Dresden and Tokyo as anything other than attacks intended to kill, terrorize or demoralize civilians. Whether or not these attacks could be justified legally in the total war context of the time, they would be unlawful if they were required to comply with Protocol I.

44. Technology, law, and the public consensus of what was acceptable, at least in demonstrably limited conflicts, had evolved by the time of the 1990-91 Gulf Conflict. Technological developments, such as precision guided munitions, and the rapid acquisition of control of the aerospace by coalition air forces significantly enhanced the precision with which targets could be attacked.

Target sets used during the Gulf Conflict were:

"Leadership; Command, Control, and Communications; Strategic Air Defenses; Airfields; Nuclear, Biological, and Chemical Research and

Production; Naval Forces and Port Facilities; Military Storage and Production; Railroads and Bridges, Electrical Power; and Oil Refining and Distribution Facilities. Schwarzkopf added the Republican Guard as a category and Scuds soon emerged as a separate target set. After the beginning of Desert Storm, two more categories appeared: fixed surface-to-air missile sites in the KTO and breaching sites for the ground offensive."

(W. Murray, *Air War in the Persian Gulf* (1995) 32)

45. In the words of the Cohen, Shelton Joint Statement on Kosovo given to the US Senate:

"At the outset of the air campaign, NATO set specific strategic objectives for its use of force in Kosovo that later served as the basis for its stated conditions to Milosevic for stopping the bombing. These objectives were to:

— Demonstrate the seriousness of NATO's opposition to Belgrade's aggression in the Balkans;
— Deter Milosevic from continuing and escalating his attacks on helpless civilians and create conditions to reverse his ethnic cleansing; and
— Damage Serbia's capacity to wage war against Kosovo in the future or spread the war to neighbors by diminishing or degrading its ability to wage military operations..."

Phases of the Campaign. Operation Allied Force was originally planned to be prosecuted in five phases under NATO's operational plan, the development of which began in the summer of 1998. Phase 0 was the deployment of air assets into the European theater. Phase 1 would establish air superiority over Kosovo and degrade command and control over the whole of the FRY. Phase 2 would attack military targets in Kosovo and those FRY forces south of 44 degrees north latitude, which were providing reinforcement to Serbian forces into Kosovo. This was to allow targeting of forces not only in Kosovo, but also in the FRY south of Belgrade. Phase 3 would expand air operations against a wide range of high-value military and security force targets throughout the FRY. Phase 4 would redeploy forces as required. A limited air response relying predominantly on cruise missiles to strike selected targets throughout the Phase 1. Within a few days of the start of NATO's campaign, alliance aircraft were striking both strategic and tactical targets throughout Serbia, as well as working to suppress and disrupt the FRY's integrated air defence system.

At the NATO Summit in Washington on April 23, 1999, alliance leaders decided to further intensify the air campaign by expanding the target set to include military-industrial infrastructure, media, and other strategic targets ...."

46. The NATO Internet Report *Kosovo One Year On* (http://www.nato.int/kosovo/repo 2000, 21 Mar 00) described the targets as:

"The air campaign set out to weaken Serb military capabilities, both strategically and tactically. Strikes on tactical targets, such as artillery and field headquarters, had a more immediate effect in disrupting the ethnic cleansing of Kosovo. Strikes against strategic targets, such as government ministries and refineries, had long term and broader impact on the Serb military machine.

The bulk of NATO's effort against tactical targets was aimed at military facilities, fielded forces, heavy weapons, and military vehicles and formations in Kosovo and southern Serbia...

Strategic targets included Serb air defences, command and control facilities, Yugoslav military (VJ) and police (MUP) forces headquarters, and supply routes".

47. Most of the targets referred to in the quotations above are clearly military objectives. The precise scope of "military-industrial infrastructure, media and other strategic targets" as referred to in the US statement and "government ministries and refineries" as referred to in the NATO statement is unclear. Whether the media constitutes a legitimate target group is a debatable issue. If the media is used to incite crimes, as in Rwanda, then it is a legitimate target. If it is merely disseminating propaganda to generate support for the war effort, it is not a legitimate target.

d. <u>The Principle of Proportionality</u>

48. The main problem with the principle of proportionality is not whether or not it exists but what it means and how it is to be applied. It is relatively simple to state that there must be an acceptable relation between the legitimate destructive effect and undesirable collateral effects. For example, bombing a

refugee camp is obviously prohibited if its only military significance is that people in the camp are knitting socks for soldiers. Conversely, an air strike on an ammunition dump should not be prohibited merely because a farmer is plowing a field in the area. Unfortunately, most applications of the principle of proportionality are not quite so clear cut. It is much easier to formulate the principle of proportionality in general terms than it is to apply it to a particular set of circumstances because the comparison is often between unlike quantities and values. One cannot easily assess the value of innocent human lives as opposed to capturing a particular military objective.

49. The questions which remain unresolved once one decides to apply the principle of proportionality include the following:

   a) What are the relative values to be assigned to the military advantage gained and the injury to non-combatants and or the damage to civilian objects?

   b) What do you include or exclude in totaling your sums?

   c) What is the standard of measurement in time or space? and

   d) To what extent is a military commander obligated to expose his own forces to danger in order to limit civilian casualties or damage to civilian objects?

50. The answers to these questions are not simple. It may be necessary to resolve them on a case by case basis, and the answers may differ depending on the background and values of the decision maker. It is unlikely that a human rights lawyer and an experienced combat commander would assign the same relative values to military advantage and to injury to noncombatants. Further, it is unlikely that military commanders with different doctrinal backgrounds and differing degrees of combat experience or national military histories would always agree in close cases. It is suggested that the determination of relative values must be that of the "reasonable military commander". Although there will be room for argument in close cases, there will be many cases where reasonable military commanders will agree that the injury to noncombatants or the damage to civilian objects was clearly disproportionate to the military advantage gained.

51. Much of the material submitted to the OTP consisted of reports that civilians had been killed, often inviting the conclusion to be drawn that crimes had therefore been committed. Collateral casualties to civilians and collateral damage to civilian objects can occur for a variety of reasons. Despite an obligation to avoid locating military objectives within or near densely populated areas, to remove civilians from the vicinity of military objectives, and to protect their civilians from the dangers of military operations, very little prevention may be feasible in many cases. Today's technological society has given rise to many dual use facilities and resources. City planners rarely pay heed to the possibility of future warfare. Military objectives are often located in densely populated areas and fighting occasionally occurs in such areas. Civilians present within or near military objectives must, however, be taken into account in the proportionality equation even if a party to the conflict has failed to exercise its obligation to remove them.

52. In the *Kupreskic* Judgment (Case No: IT-95-16-T 14 Jan 2000) the Trial Chamber addressed the issue of proportionality as follows:

> "526. As an example of the way in which the Martens clause may be utilised, regard might be had to considerations such as the cumulative effect of attacks on military objectives causing incidental damage to civilians. In other words, it may happen that single attacks on military objectives causing incidental damage to civilians, although they may raise doubts as to their lawfulness, nevertheless do not appear on their face to fall foul *per se* of the loose prescriptions of Articles 57 and 58 (or of the corresponding customary rules). However, in case of repeated attacks, all or most of them falling within the grey area between indisputable legality and unlawfulness, it might be warranted to conclude that the cumulative effect of such acts entails that they may not be in keeping with international law. Indeed, this pattern of military conduct may turn out to jeopardise excessively the lives and assets of civilians, contrary to the demands of humanity."

This formulation in *Kupreskic* can be regarded as a progressive statement of the applicable law with regard to the obligation to protect civilians. Its practical import, however, is somewhat ambiguous and its application far from clear. It is the committee's view that where individual (and legitimate) attacks on military objectives are concerned, the mere *cumulation* of such instances, all of which are deemed to have been lawful, cannot *ipso facto* be said to amount to a crime. The committee understands the above formulation, instead, to refer to an *overall* assessment of the totality of civilian victims as against the goals of the military campaign.

v. Casualty Figures

53. In its report, *Civilian Deaths in the NATO Air Campaign*, Human Rights Watch documented some 500 civilian deaths in 90 separate incidents. It concluded: "on the basis available on these ninety incidents that as few as 488 and as many as 527 Yugoslav civilians were killed as a result of NATO bombing. Between 62 and 66 percent of the total registered civilian deaths occurred in just twelve incidents. These twelve incidents accounted for 303 to 352 civilian deaths. These were the only incidents among the ninety documented in which ten or more civilian deaths were confirmed." Ten of these twelve incidents were included among the incidents which were reviewed with considerable care by the committee (see para. 9 above) and our estimate was that between 273 and 317 civilians were killed in these ten incidents. Human Rights Watch also found the FRY Ministry of Foreign Affairs publication NATO Crimes in Yugoslavia to be largely credible on the basis of its own filed research and correlation with other sources. A review of this publication indicates it provides an estimated total of approximately 495 civilians killed and 820 civilians wounded in specific documented instances. For the purposes of this report, the committee operates on the basis of the number of persons allegedly killed as found in both publications. It appears that a figure similar to both publications would be in the range of 500 civilians killed.

vi. General Assesment of the Bombing Campaign

54. During the bombing campaign, NATO aircraft flew 38,400 sorties, including 10,484 strike sorties. During these sorties, 23,614 air munitions were released (figures from NATO). As indicated in the preceding paragraph, it appears that approximately 500 civilians were killed during the campaign. These figures do not indicate that NATO may have conducted a campaign aimed at causing substantial civilian casualties either directly or incidentally.

55. The choice of targets by NATO (see paras. 38 and 39 above) includes some loosely defined categories such as military-industrial infrastructure and government ministries and some potential problem categories such as media and refineries. All targets must meet the criteria for military objectives (see

para. 28-30 above). If they do not do so, they are unlawful. A general label is insufficient. The targeted components of the military-industrial infrastructure and of government ministries must make an effective contribution to military action and their total or partial destruction must offer a definite military advantage in the circumstances ruling at the time. Refineries are certainly traditional military objectives but tradition is not enough and due regard must be paid to environmental damage if they are attacked (see paras. 14-25 above). The media as such is not a traditional target category. To the extent particular media components are part of the C3 (command, control and communications) network they are military objectives. If media components are not part of the C3 network then they may become military objectives depending upon their use. As a bottom line, civilians, civilian objects and civilian morale as such are not legitimate military objectives. The media does have an effect on civilian morale. If that effect is merely to foster support for the war effort, the media is not a legitimate military objective. If the media is used to incite crimes, as in Rwanda, it can become a legitimate military objective. If the media is the nerve system that keeps a war-monger in power and thus perpetuates the war effort, it may fall within the definition of a legitimate military objective. As a general statement, in the particular incidents reviewed by the committee, it is the view of the committee that NATO was attempting to attack objects it perceived to be legitimate military objectives.

56. The committee agrees there is nothing inherently unlawful about flying above the height which can be reached by enemy air defences. However, NATO air commanders have a duty to take practicable measures to distinguish military objectives from civilians or civilian objectives. The 15,000 feet minimum altitude adopted for part of the campaign may have meant the target could not be verified with the naked eye. However, it appears that with the use of modern technology, the obligation to distinguish was effectively carried out in the vast majority of cases during the bombing campaign.

B. Specific Incidents

57. In the course of its review, the committee did not come across any incident which, in its opinion, required investigation by the OTP. The five specific incidents discussed below are those which, in the opinion of the committee, were the most problematic. The facts cited in the discussion of each specific incident are those indicated in the information within the possession of the OTP at the time of its review.

i. The Attack on a Civilian Passenger Train at the Grdelica Gorge on 12/4/99

58. On 12 April 1999, a NATO aircraft launched two laser guided bombs at the Leskovac railway bridge over the Grdelica gorge and Juzna Morava river, in eastern Serbia. A 5-carriage passenger train, travelling from Belgrade to Ristovac on the Macedonian border, was crossing the bridge at the time, and was struck by both missiles. The various reports made of this incident concur that the incident occurred at about 11.40 a.m. At least ten people were killed in this incident and at least 15 individuals were injured. The designated target was the railway bridge, which was claimed to be part of a re-supply route being used for Serb forces in Kosovo. After launching the first bomb, the person controlling the weapon, at the last instant before impact, sighted movement on the bridge. The controller was unable to dump the bomb at that stage and it hit the train, the impact of the bomb cutting the second of the passenger coaches in half. Realising the bridge was still intact, the controller picked a second aim point on the bridge at the opposite end from where the train had come and launched the second bomb. In the meantime the train had slid forward as a result of the original impact and parts of the train were also hit by the second bomb.

59. It does not appear that the train was targeted deliberately. US Deputy Defense Secretary John Hamre stated that "one of our electro-optically guided bombs homed in on a railroad bridge just when a passenger train raced to the aim point. We never wanted to destroy that train or kill its occupants. We did want to destroy the bridge and we regret this accident." The substantive part of the explanation, both for the failure to detect the approach of the passenger train and for firing a second missile once it had been hit by the first, was given by General Wesley Clark, NATO's Supreme Allied Commander for Europe and is here reprinted in full:

> "[T]his was a case where a pilot was assigned to strike a railroad bridge that is part of the integrated communications supply network in Serbia. He launched his missile from his aircraft that was many miles away, he was not able to put his eyes on the bridge, it was a remotely directed attack. And as he stared intently at the desired target point on the bridge, and I talked to the team at Aviano who was directly engaged in this operation, as the pilot stared intently at the desired aim point on the bridge and worked it, and worked it and worked it, and all of a sudden at the very last instant with less than a second to go he caught

a flash of movement that came into the screen and it was the train coming in.

Unfortunately he couldn't dump the bomb at that point, it was locked, it was going into the target and it was an unfortunate incident which he, and the crew, and all of us very much regret. We certainly don't want to do collateral damage.

The mission was to take out the bridge. He realised when it had happened that he had not hit the bridge, but what he had hit was the train. He had another aim point on the bridge, it was a relatively long bridge and he believed he still had to accomplish his mission, the pilot circled back around. He put his aim point on the other end of the bridge from where the train had come, by the time the bomb got close to the bridge it was covered with smoke and clouds and at the last minute again in an uncanny accident, the train had slid forward from the original impact and parts of the train had moved across the bridge, and so that by striking the other end of the bridge he actually caused additional damage to the train." (Press Conference, NATO HQ, Brussels, 13 April).

General Clark then showed the cockpit video of the plane which fired on the bridge:

"The pilot in the aircraft is looking at about a 5-inch screen, he is seeing about this much and in here you can see this is the railroad bridge which is a much better view than he actually had, you can see the tracks running this way.

Look very intently at the aim point, concentrate right there and you can see how, if you were focused right on your job as a pilot, suddenly that train appeared. It was really unfortunate.

Here, he came back around to try to strike a different point on the bridge because he was trying to do a job to take the bridge down. Look at this aim point – you can see smoke and other obscuration there – he couldn't tell what this was exactly.

Focus intently right at the centre of the cross. He is bringing these two crosses together and suddenly he recognises at the very last instant that the train that was struck here has moved on across the bridge and so the engine apparently was struck by the second bomb." (Press Conference, NATO HQ, Brussels, 13 April).

60. Some doubt has since been cast on this version of events by a comprehensive technical report submitted by a German national, Mr Ekkehard Wenz, which queries the actual speed at which the events took place in relation to that suggested by the video footage of the incident released by NATO. The effect of this report is to suggest that the reaction time available to the person controlling the bombs was in fact considerably greater than that alleged by NATO. Mr. Wenz also suggests the aircraft involved was an F15E Strike Eagle with a crew of two and with the weapons being controlled by a Weapons Systems Officer (WSO) not the pilot.

61. The committee has reviewed both the material provided by NATO and the report of Mr. Wenz with considerable care. It is the opinion of the committee that it is irrelevant whether the person controlling the bomb was the pilot or the WSO. Either person would have been travelling in a high speed aircraft and likely performing several tasks simultaneously, including endeavouring to keep the aircraft in the air and safe from surrounding threats in a combat environment. If the committee accepts Mr. Wenz's estimate of the reaction time available, the person controlling the bombs still had a very short period of time, less than 7 or 8 seconds in all probability, to react. Although Mr Wenz is of the view that the WSO intentionally targeted the train, the committee's review of the frames used in the report indicates another interpretation is equally available. The cross hairs remain fixed on the bridge throughout, and it is clear from this footage that the train can be seen moving toward the bridge only as the bomb is in flight: it is only in the course of the bomb's trajectory that the image of the train becomes visible. At a point where the bomb is within a few seconds of impact, a very slight change to the bomb aiming point can be observed, in that it drops a couple of feet. This sequence regarding the bomb sights indicates that it is unlikely that the WSO was targeting the train, but instead suggests that the target was a point on the span of the bridge before the train appeared.

62. It is the opinion of the committee that the bridge was a legitimate military objective. The passenger train was not deliberately targeted. The person controlling the bombs, pilot or WSO, targeted the bridge and, over a very short period of time, failed to recognize the arrival of the train while the first bomb was in flight. The train was on the bridge when the bridge was targeted a

Appendix A

second time and the bridge length has been estimated at 50 meters (Wenz study para 6 g above at p. 25). It is the opinion of the committee that the information in relation to the attack with the first bomb does not provide a sufficient basis to initiate an investigation. The committee has divided views concerning the attack with the second bomb in relation to whether there was an element of recklessness in the conduct of the pilot or WSO. Despite this, the committee is in agreement that, based on the criteria for initiating an investigation (see para. 5 above), this incident should not be investigated. In relation to whether there is information warranting consideration of command responsibility, the committee is of the view that there is no information from which to conclude that an investigation is necessary into the criminal responsibility of persons higher in the chain of command. Based on the information available to it, it is the opinion of the committee that the attack on the train at Grdelica Gorge should not be investigated by the OTP.

ii. *The Attack on the Djakovica Convoy on 14/4/99*

63. The precise facts concerning this incident are difficult to determine. In particular, there is some confusion about the number of aircraft involved, the number of bombs dropped, and whether one or two convoys were attacked. The FRY Ministry of Foreign Affairs Report (*White Book*) describes the incident as follows:

> "On April 14, 1999 [...] on the Djakovica-Prizren road, near the villages of Madanaj and Meja, a convoy of Albanian refugees was targeted three times. Mostly women, children and old people were in the convoy, returning to their homes in cars, on tractors and carts. The first assault on the column of over 1000 people took place while they were moving through Meja village. Twelve persons were killed on that occasion. The people from the convoy scattered around and tried to find shelter in the nearby houses. But NATO warplanes launched missiles on those houses as well, killing another 7 persons in the process. The attack continued along the road boween [the] villages [of] Meja and Bistrazin. One tractor with trailer was completely destroyed. Twenty people out of several of them on the tractor were killed. In the repeated attack on the refugee vehicles, one more person was killed." (Vol 1, p.1)

Total casualty figures seem to converge around 70-75 killed with approximately 100 injured. The FRY publication NATO War Crimes in Yugoslavia states 73 were killed and 36 were wounded.

64. NATO initially denied, but later acknowledged, responsibility for this attack. Assuming the facts most appropriate to a successful prosecution, NATO aircraft flying at 15000 feet or higher to avoid Yugoslav air defences attacked two vehicle convoys, both of which contained civilian vehicles. On 15 April, NATO confirmed that the aircraft had been flying at an altitude of 15,000 feet (approximately 5 km) and that, in this attack, the pilots had viewed the target with the naked eye rather than remotely. The aim of the attack was to destroy Serb military forces, in the area of Djakovica, who had been seen by NATO aircraft setting fire to civilian houses. At a Press Conference of 15 April 1999, NATO claimed that this was an area where the Yugoslav Special Police Forces, the MUP, were conducting ethnic cleansing operations over the preceding days. The road between Prizren and Djakovica served as an important resupply and reinforcement route for the Yugoslav Army and the Special Police.

65. A reconstruction of what is known about the attack reveals that in the hours immediately prior to the attack, at around 1030, NATO forces claimed to have seen a progression of burning villages, and that a series of fires could be seen progressing to the south east. They formed the view that MUP and VJ forces were thus methodically working from the north to the south through villages, setting them ablaze and forcing all the Kosovar Albanians out of those villages. At around 1030, the pilot spotted a three-vehicle convoy near to the freshest burning house, and saw uniformly shaped dark green vehicles which appeared to be troop carrying vehicles. He thus formed the view that the convoy comprised VJ and MUP forces working their way down towards Djakovica and that they were preparing to set the next house on fire. In response, an F-16 bombed the convoy's lead vehicle at approximately 1110; the pilot relayed a threat update and the coordinates of the attack and departed the area to refuel. A second F-16 aircraft appears to have arrived on the scene around 1135, and visually assessed the target area as containing large vehicles which were located near a complex of buildings. A single GBU-12 bomb was dropped at 1148. Contemporaneously, a third aircraft identified a large convoy on a major road south east out of Djakovica and sought to identify the target. The target was verified as a VJ convoy at 1216 and an unspecified number of bombs were dropped at 1219. In the next 15 or so minutes (exact time

Appendix A

unspecified), the same aircraft appears to have destroyed one further vehicle in the convoy. Simultaneously, two Jaguar aircraft each dropped 1 GBU-12 bomb each, but both missed their targets. Between 1235 and 1245, the first F-16 aircraft appears to have dropped three further bombs, at least one of which appears to have missed its target.

66. It is claimed by one source (report on file with the OTP) that the Yugoslav TV broadcast of the attack on the Djakovica convoy on 15 April 1999 recorded a conversation between one F-16 pilot involved in the attack and the AWACs. This conversation is alleged to establish both that the attack on the convoy was deliberate and that a UK Harrier pilot had advised the F-16 pilot that the convoy was comprised solely of tractors and civilians. The F-16 pilot was then allegedly told that the convoy was nevertheless a legitimate military target and was instructed to fire on it. This same report also suggests that the convoy was attacked with cluster bombs, indicated by bomb remnants and craters left at the site. However, these claims – both with regard to the foreknowledge of the pilot as to the civilian nature of the convoy and of the weapons used – are not confirmed by any other source.

67. NATO itself claimed that although the cockpit video showed the vehicles to look like tractors, when viewed with the naked eye from the attack altitude they appeared to be military vehicles. They alleged that several characteristics indicated it to be a military convoy including movement, size, shape, colour, spacing and high speed prior to the attack. There had also been reports of Serb forces using civilian vehicles. An analysis of the Serb TV footage of the attack on Djakovica by the OTP indicates that at approximately 1240, some point during the attack, doubt was conveyed that Serb convoys do not usually travel in convoys of that size. However, the on-scene analysis of the convoy appeared to convey the impression that the convoy comprised a mix of military and civilian vehicles. At around 1300, an order appears to have been issued, suspending attacks until the target could be verified.

68. NATO has consistently claimed that it believed the Djakovica convoy to be escorted by Serb military vehicles at the time of the attack. Human Rights Watch has commented on the incident as follows:

> "General Clark stated in September that NATO consistently observed Yugoslav military vehicles moving on roads 'intermixed with civilian convoys.' After the Djakovica-Decane incident, General Clark says, 'we

got to be very, very cautious about striking objects moving on the roads.' Another NATO officer, Col. Ed Boyle, says: 'Because we were so concerned with collateral damage, the CFAC [Combined Forces Air Component Commander] at the time, General [Michael] Short, put out the guidance that if military vehicles were intermingled with civilian vehicles, they were not to be attacked, due to the collateral damage.' When this directive was actually issued remains an important question. Nevertheless, the change in NATO rules of engagement indicates that the alliance recognized that it had taken insufficient precautions in mounting this attack, in not identifying civilians present, and in assuming that the intended targets were legitimate military objectives rather than in positively identifying them."

69. It is the opinion of the committee that civilians were not deliberately attacked in this incident. While there is nothing unlawful about operating at a height above Yugoslav air defences, it is difficult for any aircrew operating an aircraft flying at several hundred miles an hour and at a substantial height to distinguish between military and civilian vehicles in a convoy. In this case, most of the attacking aircraft were F16s with a crew of one person to fly the aircraft and identify the target. As soon as the crews of the attacking aircraft became aware of the presence of civilians, the attack ceased.

70. While this incident is one where it appears the aircrews could have benefitted from lower altitude scrutiny of the target at an early stage, the committee is of the opinion that neither the aircrew nor their commanders displayed the degree of recklessness in failing to take precautionary measures which would sustain criminal charges. The committee also notes that the attack was suspended as soon as the presence of civilians in the convoy was suspected. Based on the information assessed, the committee recommends that the OTP not commence an investigation related to the Djakovica Convoy bombing.

iii. *The Bombing of the RTS (Serbian TV and Radio Station) in Belgrade on 23/4/99*

71. On 23 April 1999, at 0220, NATO intentionally bombed the central studio of the RTS (state-owned) broadcasting corporation at 1 Aberdareva Street in the centre of Belgrade. The missiles hit the entrance area, which caved in at the place where the Aberdareva Street building was connected to

the Takovska Street building. While there is some doubt over exact casualty figures, between 10 and 17 people are estimated to have been killed.

72. The bombing of the TV studio was part of a planned attack aimed at disrupting and degrading the C3 (Command, Control and Communications) network. In co-ordinated attacks, on the same night, radio relay buildings and towers were hit along with electrical power transformer stations. At a press conference on 27 April 1999, NATO officials justified this attack in terms of the dual military and civilian use to which the FRY communication system was routinely put, describing this as a

> "very hardened and redundant command and control communications system [which ...] uses commercial telephone, [...] military cable, [...] fibre optic cable, [...] high frequency radio communication, [...] microwave communication and everything can be interconnected. There are literally dozens, more than 100 radio relay sites around the country, and [...] everything is wired in through dual use. Most of the commercial system serves the military and the military system can be put to use for the commercial system [...]."

Accordingly, NATO stressed the dual-use to which such communications systems were put, describing civilian television as "heavily dependent on the military command and control system and military traffic is also routed through the civilian system" (press conference of 27 April, *ibid*).

73. At an earlier press conference on 23 April 1999, NATO officials reported that the TV building also housed a large multi-purpose communications satellite antenna dish, and that "radio relay control buildings and towers were targeted in the ongoing campaign to degrade the FRY's command, control and communications network". In a communication of 17 April 1999 to Amnesty International, NATO claimed that the RTS facilities were being used "as radio relay stations and transmitters to support the activities of the FRY military and special police forces, and therefore they represent legitimate military targets" (Amnesty International Report, *NATO/Federal Republic of Yugoslavia: Violations of the Laws of War by NATO during Operation Allied Force*, June 2000, p. 42).

74. Of the electrical power transformer stations targeted, one transformer station supplied power to the air defence co-ordination network while the other

supplied power to the northern-sector operations centre. Both these facilities were key control elements in the FRY integrated air-defence system. In this regard, NATO indicated that

> "we are not targeting the Serb people as we repeatedly have stated nor do we target President Milosevic personally, we are attacking the control system that is used to manipulate the military and security forces."

More controversially, however, the bombing was also justified on the basis of the propaganda purpose to which it was employed:

> "[We need to] directly strike at the very central nerve system of Milosovic's regime. This of course are those assets which are used to plan and direct and to create the political environment of tolerance in Yugoslavia in which these brutalities can not only be accepted but even condoned. [....] Strikes against TV transmitters and broadcast facilities are part of our campaign to dismantle the FRY propaganda machinery which is a vital part of President Milosevic's control mechanism."

In a similar statement, British Prime Minister Tony Blair was reported as saying in *The Times* that the media "is the apparatus that keeps him [Milosevic] in power and we are entirely justified as NATO allies in damaging and taking on those targets" (24 April, 1999). In a statement of 8 April 1999, NATO also indicated that the TV studios would be targeted unless they broadcast 6 hours per day of Western media reports: "If President Milosevic would provide equal time for Western news broadcasts in its programmes without censorship 3 hours a day between noon and 1800 and 3 hours a day between 1800 and midnight, then his TV could be an acceptable instrument of public information."

75. NATO intentionally bombed the Radio and TV station and the persons killed or injured were civilians. The questions are: was the station a legitimate military objective and; if it was, were the civilian casualties disproportionate to the military advantage gained by the attack? For the station to be a military objective within the definition in Article 52 of Protocol I: a) its nature, purpose or use must make an effective contribution to military action and b) its total or partial destruction must offer a definite military advantage in the circumstances ruling at the time. The 1956 ICRC list of military objectives, drafted before the Additional Protocols, included the installations of

broadcasting and television stations of fundamental military importance as military objectives (para. 39 above). The list prepared by Major General Rogers included broadcasting and television stations if they meet the military objective criteria (para. 38 above). As indicated in paras. 72 and 73 above, the attack appears to have been justified by NATO as part of a more general attack aimed at disrupting the FRY Command, Control and Communications network, the nerve centre and apparatus that keeps Miloseviæ in power, and also as an attempt to dismantle the FRY propaganda machinery. Insofar as the attack actually was aimed at disrupting the communications network, it was legally acceptable.

76. If, however, the attack was made because equal time was not provided for Western news broadcasts, that is, because the station was part of the propaganda machinery, the legal basis was more debatable. Disrupting government propaganda may help to undermine the morale of the population and the armed forces, but justifying an attack on a civilian facility on such grounds alone may not meet the "effective contribution to military action" and "definite military advantage" criteria required by the Additional Protocols (see paras. 35-36, above). The ICRC Commentary on the Additional Protocols interprets the expression "definite military advantage anticipated" to exclude "an attack which only offers potential or indeterminate advantages" and interprets the expression "concrete and direct" as intended to show that the advantage concerned should be substantial and relatively close rather than hardly perceptible and likely to appear only in the long term (ICRC Commentary on the Additional Protocols of 8 June 1977, para. 2209). While stopping such propaganda may serve to demoralize the Yugoslav population and undermine the government's political support, it is unlikely that either of these purposes would offer the "concrete and direct" military advantage necessary to make them a legitimate military objective. NATO believed that Yugoslav broadcast facilities were "used entirely to incite hatred and propaganda" and alleged that the Yugoslav government had put all private TV and radio stations in Serbia under military control (NATO press conferences of 28 and 30 April 1999). However, it was not claimed that they were being used to incite violence akin to *Radio Milles Collines* during the Rwandan genocide, which might have justified their destruction (see para. 47 above). At worst, the Yugoslav government was using the broadcasting networks to issue propaganda supportive of its war effort: a circumstance which does not, in and of itself, amount to a war crime (see in this regard the judgment of the International Military Tribunal in Nuremberg in 1946 in the case of Hans Fritzsche, who

served as a senior official in the Propaganda ministry alleged to have incited and encouraged the commission of crimes. The IMT held that although Fritzsche clearly made strong statements of a propagandistic nature, it was nevertheless not prepared to find that they were intended to incite the commission of atrocities, but rather, were aimed at arousing popular sentiment in support of Hitler and the German war effort (*American Journal of International Law*, vol. 41 (1947) 328)). The committee finds that if the attack on the RTS was justified by reference to its propaganda purpose alone, its legality might well be questioned by some experts in the field of international humanitarian law. It appears, however, that NATO's targeting of the RTS building for propaganda purposes was an incidental (albeit complementary) aim of its primary goal of disabling the Serbian military command and control system and to destroy the nerve system and apparatus that keeps Milosevic in power. In a press conference of 9 April 1999, NATO declared that TV transmitters were not targeted directly but that "in Yugoslavia military radio relay stations are often combined with TV transmitters [so] we attack the military target. If there is damage to the TV transmitters, it is a secondary effect but it is not [our] primary intention to do that." A NATO spokesperson, Jamie Shea, also wrote to the Brussels-based International Federation of Journalists on 12 April claiming that Operation Allied Force "target[ed] military targets only and television and radio towers are only struck if they [were] integrated into military facilities ... There is no policy to strike television and radio transmitters as such" (cited in Amnesty International Report, *ibid*, June 2000).

77. Assuming the station was a legitimate objective, the civilian casualties were unfortunately high but do not appear to be clearly disproportionate.

Although NATO alleged that it made "every possible effort to avoid civilian casualties and collateral damage" (Amnesty International Report, *ibid*, June 2000, p. 42), some doubts have been expressed as to the specificity of the warning given to civilians by NATO of its intended strike, and whether the notice would have constituted "effective warning ... of attacks which may affect the civililan population, unless circumstances do not permit" as required by Article 57(2) of Additional Protocol I.

Evidence on this point is somewhat contradictory. On the one hand, NATO officials in Brussels are alleged to have told Amnesty International that they did not give a specific warning as it would have endangered the pilots (Amnesty International Report, *ibid*, June 2000, at p. 47; see also para. 49 above re:

proportionality and the extent to which a military commander is obligated to expose his own forces to danger in order to limit civilian casualties or damage). On this view, it is possible that casualties among civilians working at the RTS may have been heightened because of NATO's apparent failure to provide clear advance warning of the attack, as required by Article 57(2).

On the other hand, foreign media representatives were apparently forewarned of the attack (Amnesty International Report, *ibid*). As Western journalists were reportedly warned by their employers to stay away from the television station before the attack, it would also appear that some Yugoslav officials may have expected that the building was about to be struck. Consequently, UK Prime Minister Tony Blair blamed Yugoslav officials for not evacuating the building, claiming that "[t]hey could have moved those people out of the building. They knew it was a target and they didn't ... [I]t was probably for ... very clear propaganda reasons." (*ibid*, citing *Moral combat – NATO at war*, broadcast on BBC2 on 12 March 2000). Although knowledge on the part of Yugoslav officials of the impending attack would not divest NATO of its obligation to forewarn civilians under Article 57(2), it may nevertheless imply that the Yugoslav authorities may be partially responsible for the civilian casualties resulting from the attack and may suggest that the advance notice given by NATO may have in fact been sufficient under the circumstances.

78. Assuming the RTS building to be a legitimate military target, it appeared that NATO realised that attacking the RTS building would only interrupt broadcasting for a brief period. Indeed, broadcasting allegedly recommenced within hours of the strike, thus raising the issue of the importance of the military advantage gained by the attack *vis-à-vis* the civilian casualties incurred. The FRY command and control network was alleged by NATO to comprise a complex web and that could thus not be disabled in one strike. As noted by General Wesley Clark, NATO "knew when we struck that there would be alternate means of getting the Serb Television. There's no single switch to turn off everything but we thought it was a good move to strike it and the political leadership agreed with us" (*ibid*, citing "Moral combat, NATO at War," broadcast on BBC2 on 12 March 2000). At a press conference on 27 April 1999, another NATO spokesperson similarly described the dual-use Yugoslav command and control network as "incapable of being dealt with in "a single knock-out blow (*ibid*)." The proportionality or otherwise of an attack should not necessarily focus exclusively on a specific incident. (See in this regard para. 52, above, referring to the need for an overall assessment of the totality

of civilian victims as against the goals of the military campaign). With regard to these goals, the strategic target of these attacks was the Yugoslav command and control network. The attack on the RTS building must therefore be seen as forming part of an integrated attack against numerous objects, including transmission towers and control buildings of the Yugoslav radio relay network which were "essential to Milosevic's ability to direct and control the repressive activities of his army and special police forces in Kosovo" (NATO press release, 1 May 1999) and which comprised "a key element in the Yugoslav air-defence network" (*ibid*, 1 May 1999). Attacks were also aimed at electricity grids that fed the command and control structures of the Yugoslav Army (*ibid*, 3 May 1999). Other strategic targets included additional command and control assets such as the radio and TV relay sites at Novi Pazar, Kosovaka and Krusevac (*ibid*) and command posts (*ibid*, 30 April). Of the electrical power transformer stations targeted, one transformer station supplied power to the air-defence coordination network while the other supplied power to the northern sector operations centre. Both these facilities were key control elements in the FRY integrated air-defence system (*ibid*, 23 April 1999). The radio relay and TV transmitting station near Novi Sad was also an important link in the air defence command and control communications network. Not only were these targets central to the Federal Republic of Yugoslavia's governing apparatus, but formed, from a military point of view, an integral part of the strategic communications network which enabled both the military and national command authorities to direct the repression and atrocities taking place in Kosovo (*ibid*, 21 April 1999).

79. On the basis of the above analysis and on the information currently available to it, the committee recommends that the OTP not commence an investigation related to the bombing of the Serbian TV and Radio Station.

iv. *The Attack on the Chinese Embassy on 7/5/99*

80. On 7/5/99, at 2350, NATO aircraft fired several missiles which hit the Chinese Embassy in Belgrade, killing 3 Chinese citizens, injuring an estimated 15 others, and causing extensive damage to the embassy building and other buildings in the immediate surrounds. At the moment of the attack, fifty people were reported to have been in the embassy buildings. By the admission of US Government sources, the Chinese Embassy compound was mistakenly hit. The bombing occurred because at no stage in the process was it realised that the bombs were aimed at the Chinese Embassy. The Embassy had been

Appendix A

wrongly identified as the Yugoslav Federal Directorate for Supply and Procurement (Yugoimport FDSP) at 2 Umetnosti Boulevard in New Belgrade. The FDSP was deemed by the CIA to be a legitimate target due to its role in military procurement: it was selected for its role in support of the Yugoslav military effort.

81. Under Secretary of State Thomas Pickering offered the following explanation for what occurred:

> "The bombing resulted from three basic failures. First, the technique used to locate the intended target – the headquarters of the Yugoslav Federal Directorate for Supply and Procurement (FDSP) – was severely flawed. Second, none of the military or intelligence databases used to verify target information contained the correct location of the Chinese Embassy. Third, nowhere in the target review process was either of the first two mistakes detected. No one who might have known that the targeted building was not the FDSP headquarters – but was in fact the Chinese Embassy – was ever consulted."

According to US Government sources, the street address of the intended target, the FDSP headquarters was known as Bulevar Umetnosti 2 in New Belgrade. During a mid-April "work-up" of the target to prepare a mission folder for the B-2 bomber crew, three maps were used in an attempt to physically locate this address within the neighborhood: two local commercial maps from 1989 and 1996, and one US government (National Imagery and Mapping Agency or NIMA) map produced in 1997. None of these maps had any reference to the FDSP building and none accurately identified the current location of the Chinese Embassy.

82. The root of the failures in target location appears to stem from the land navigation techniques employed by an intelligence officer in an effort to pinpoint the location of the FDSP building at Bulevar Umetnosti 2. The officer used techniques known as "intersection" and "resection" which, while appropriate to locate distant or inaccessible points or objects, are inappropriate for use in aerial targeting as they provide only an approximate location. Using this process, the individual mistakenly determined that the building which we now know to be the Chinese Embassy was the FDSP headquarters. This method of identification was not questioned or reviewed and hence this flaw in the address location process went undetected by all the others who

evaluated the FDSP headquarters as a military target. It also appears that very late in the process, an intelligence officer serendipitously came to suspect that the target had been wrongly identified and sought to raise the concern that the building had been mislocated. However, throughout a series of missed opportunities, the problem of identification was not brought to the attention of the senior managers who may have been able to intervene in time to prevent the strike.

83. Finally, reviewing elements in, *inter alia*, the Joint Staff did not uncover either the inaccurate location of the FDSP headquarters or the correct location of the Chinese Embassy. The data base reviews were limited to validating the target data sheet geographic coordinates and the information put into the data base by the NIMA analyst. Such a circular process did not serve to uncover the original error and highlighted the system's susceptibility to a single point of data base failure. The critical linchpin for both the error in identification of the building and the failure of the review mechanisms was thus the inadequacy of the supporting data bases and the mistaken assumption the information they contained would necessarily be accurate.

84. The building hit was clearly a civilian object and not a legitimate military objective. NATO, and subsequently various organs of the US Government, including the CIA, issued a formal apology, accepted full responsibility for the incident and asserted that the intended target, the Federal Directorate for Supply and Procurement, would have been a legitimate military objective. The USA has formally apologized to the Chinese Government and agreed to pay $28 million in compensation to the Chinese Government and $4.5 million to the families of those killed or injured. The CIA has also dismissed one intelligence officer and reprimanded six senior managers. The US Government also claims to have taken corrective actions in order to assign individual responsibility and to prevent mistakes such as this from occurring in the future.

85. It is the opinion of the committee that the aircrew involved in the attack should not be assigned any responsibility for the fact they were given the wrong target and that it is inappropriate to attempt to assign criminal responsibility for the incident to senior leaders because they were provided with wrong information by officials of another agency. Based on the information available to it, the committee is of the opinion that the OTP should not undertake an investigation concerning the bombing of the Chinese Embassy.

Appendix A

v. <u>The Attack on Korisa Village on 13/5/99</u>

86. On 14 May 1999, NATO aircraft dropped 10 bombs on the village of Korisa, on the highway between Prizren and Pristina. Much confusion seems to exist about this incident, and factual accounts do not seem to easily tally with each other. As many as 87 civilians, mainly refugees, were killed in this attack and approximately 60 appear to have been wounded. The primary target in this attack was asserted by NATO to be a Serbian military camp and Command Post which were located near the village of Korisa. It appears that the refugees were near the attacked object. However, unlike previous cases where NATO subsequently claimed that an error had occurred in its targeting or its military intelligence sources, NATO spokespersons continued to affirm the legitimacy of this particular attack. They maintained that this was a legitimate military target and that NATO intelligence had identified a military camp and Command Post near to the village of Korisa.

87. According to NATO officials, immediately prior to the attack, the target was identified as having military revetments. The pilot was able to see silhouettes of vehicles on the ground as the attack took place at 2330, when two laser guided bombs were dropped. Ten minutes later, another two laser guided bombs and six gravity bombs were dropped. In a press conference on 15 May, NATO stated that the attack went ahead because the target was confirmed by prior intelligence as being valid and the pilot identified vehicles present. There were never any doubts, from NATO spokespersons, as to the validity of this target.

88. Information about NATO's position on the bombardment of Korisa was released at the press conference on the following day, 15 May. At this conference, General Jertz twice affirmed that the target was, in NATO's opinion, legitimate since military facilities were present at the site:

> "As already has been mentioned, it was a legitimate military target. NATO reconnaissance and intelligence orders identified just outside Korisa a military camp and command post, including an armoured personnel carrier and 10 pieces of artillery. Follow-up intelligence confirmed this information as being a valid military target. Immediately prior to the attack at 23.30-11.30 pm – local time Thursday night an airborne forward air controller identified the target, so the identification and attack system of his aircraft, having positively identified the target

Final Report to the Prosecutor

as what looked like dug-in military reveted positions, he dropped two laser guided bombs. Approximately 10 minutes later, the third aircraft engaged the target with gravity bombs, with six gravity bombs. A total of 10 bombs were dropped on the target."

When questioned about the presence of civilians on the ground, General Jertz indicated:

"What I can say so far is when the pilot attacked the target he had to visually identify it through the attack systems which are in the aircraft, and you know it was by night, so he did see silhouettes of vehicles on the ground and as it was by prior intelligence a valid target, he did do the attack [...] it was a legitimate target. Since late April we knew there were command posts, military pieces in that area and they have been continuously used. *So for the pilot flying the attack, it was a legitimate target.* But when he is in the target area for attacking, it is his responsibility to make sure that all the cues he sees are the ones which he needs to really attack. And at night he saw the silhouettes of vehicles and that is why he was allowed to attack. Of course, and we have to be very fair, we are talking at night. If there is anybody sleeping somewhere in a house, you would not be able to see it from the perspective of a pilot. But once again, don't misinterpret it. It was a military target which had been used since the beginning of conflict over there and we have all sources used to identify this target in order to make sure that this target was still a valid target when it was attacked." (Emphasis added).

The NATO position thus appears to be that it bombed a legitimate military target, that it knew nothing of the presence of civilians and that none were observed immediately prior to the attack. Indeed, NATO stated that they believed this area to have been completely cleared of civilians. There is some information indicating that displaced Kosovar civilians were forcibly concentrated within a military camp in the village of Korisa as human shields and that Yugoslav military forces may thus be at least partially responsible for the deaths there.

89. The available information concerning this incident is in conflict. The attack occurred in the middle of the night at about 2330. The stated object of the attack was a legitimate military objective. According to NATO, all practicable precautions were taken and it was determined civilians were not

present. It appears that a relatively large number of civilians were killed. It also appears these civilians were either returning refugees or persons gathered as human shields by FRY authorities or both. The committee is of the view that the credible information available is not sufficient to tend to show that a crime within the jurisdiction of the Tribunal has been committed by the aircrew or by superiors in the NATO chain of command. Based on the information available to it, the committee is of the opinion that OTP should not undertake an investigation concerning the bombing at Korisa.

V   Recommendations

90. The committee has conducted its review relying essentially upon public documents, including statements made by NATO and NATO countries at press conferences and public documents produced by the FRY. It has tended to assume that the NATO and NATO countries' press statements are generally reliable and that explanations have been honestly given. The committee must note, however, that when the OTP requested NATO to answer specific questions about specific incidents, the NATO reply was couched in general terms and failed to address the specific incidents. The committee has not spoken to those involved in directing or carrying out the bombing campaign. The committee has also assigned substantial weight to the factual assertions made by Human Rights Watch as its investigators did spend a limited amount of time on the ground in the FRY. Further, the committee has noted that Human Rights Watch found the two volume compilation of the FRY Ministry of Foreign Affairs entitled *NATO Crimes in Yugoslavia* generally reliable and the committee has tended to rely on the casualty figures for specific incidents in this compilation. If one accepts the figures in this compilation of approximately 495 civilians killed and 820 civilians wounded in documented instances, there is simply no evidence of the necessary crime base for charges of genocide or crimes against humanity. Further, in the particular incidents reviewed by the committee with particular care (see paras. 9, and 48-76) the committee has not assessed any particular incidents as justifying the commencement of an investigation by the OTP. NATO has admitted that mistakes did occur during the bombing campaign; errors of judgment may also have occurred. Selection of certain objectives for attack may be subject to legal debate. On the basis of the information reviewed, however, the committee is of the opinion that neither an in-depth investigation related to the bombing campaign as a whole nor investigations related to specific incidents are justified. In all cases, either the law is not sufficiently clear or investigations are

unlikely to result in the acquisition of sufficient evidence to substantiate charges against high level accused or against lower accused for particularly heinous offences.

91. On the basis of information available, the committee recommends that no investigation be commenced by the OTP in relation to the NATO bombing campaign or incidents occurring during the campaign.

APPENDIX B

Contributors

Contributors

Judge James E. Baker is a judge on the United States Court of Appeals for the Armed Forces. Immediately prior to his appointment to the bench in 2000, he served for three years as Special Assistant to the President and Legal Adviser to the National Security Council (NSC), where he advised the President, the National Security Advisor and the NSC staff on United States and international law involving national security, including the use of force, the law of armed conflict, intelligence activities, foreign assistance, terrorism, arms control, human rights, and international law enforcement. His earlier public service included service as the Deputy Legal Adviser to the National Security Council, Counsel to the President's Foreign Intelligence Advisory Board and Intelligence Oversight Board, and as an Attorney Adviser in the Office of the Legal Advisor, Department of State. Judge Baker also served as an officer in the U.S. Marine Corps.

Professor Michael Bothe is Professor of Public Law at the Johann Wolfgang Goethe University in Frankfurt, Germany. Professor Bothe has served as a Visiting Professor at the University of Montreal, the University of Florida, and the Rijksuniversiteit Groningen, and was a Visiting Scholar at the University of Michigan. He is currently serving as Chairman of the Advisory Commission on Humanitarian Law of the German Red Cross; on the Scientific Advisory Board, Max Planck Institute for Comparative Public Law and International Law, Heidelberg, Germany; and as the President of the German Society of International Law. He was a member of the German delegation to the Diplomatic Conference on International Humanitarian Law (1974–77). Professor Bothe is the author and/or editor of numerous books and articles on international humanitarian law as well as international law questions relating to the maintenance of international peace and security.

Professor Ove Bring is Professor of International Law at Stockholm University and at the Swedish National Defense College. He is Chairman of the Swedish Branch of the International Law Association and has served as Special Legal Adviser at the Ministry for Foreign Affairs. He participated in the

Thomson/Blackwell humanitarian mission to the former Yugoslavia, reporting to the Committee of Senior Officials of the Conference on Security and Cooperation in Europe (CSCE) (1992–1993). In 1994 he headed a Swedish human rights mission to China and Tibet, reporting to the Swedish Ministry for Foreign Affairs. In February 1995 he was appointed Swedish Conciliator under the European Convention on Conciliation and Arbitration within the CSCE, now The Organization for Security and Cooperation in Europe (OSCE). Professor Bring was on the Central Board of Directors for the Swedish Red Cross from 1996 to 1999, and is currently a member of the Governing Council of the San Remo Institute of International Humanitarian Law and a Swedish Member of the Permanent Court of Arbitration in The Hague.

Vice Admiral Arthur K. Cebrowski, US Navy (Ret.), commanded Fighter Squadron 41 and Carrier Air Wing 8, both embarked in USS NIMITZ (CVN 68). He later commanded the assault ship USS GUAM (LPH 9) and, during Operations DESERT SHIELD and DESERT STORM, the aircraft carrier USS MIDWAY (CV 41). Following promotion to flag rank, he became Commander, Carrier Group 6 and Commander, USS America Battle Group. In addition to combat deployments to Vietnam and the Persian Gulf, he deployed in support of United Nations operations in Iraq, Somalia, and Bosnia. He served with the US Air Force; the staff of Commander in Chief, Atlantic Fleet; the staff of the Chief of Naval Operations, on four occasions; with the Joint Staff (as J6); and as Director, Navy Space, Information Warfare, and Command and Control (N6). Vice Admiral Cebrowski became the forty-seventh President of the Naval War College in July 1998. Following retirement, in November 2001 Vice Admiral Cebrowski was appointed as Director of the Office of Force Transformation within the Office of the Secretary of Defense.

Captain William H. Dalton, JAGC, US Navy (Ret.), is currently assigned to the Department of Defense Office of General Counsel, as Associate Deputy General Counsel (Intelligence). From 1965 to 1995 he served as a judge advocate in the United States Navy. His assignments included service as the Executive Officer, Naval Legal Service Office, Pearl Harbor, Hawaii; the Deputy Assistant Judge Advocate General (International Law) within the Office of the Judge Advocate General, Department of the Navy; the Staff Judge Advocate, United States Pacific Command in Hawaii; and as the Inspector General, Naval Sea Systems Command, Washington, D.C. Captain Dalton also served on the faculty of the U.S. Naval War College as the first Deputy Director, Oceans Law and Policy Department.

Professor Yoram Dinstein is currently the Charles H. Stockton Professor of International Law at the US Naval War College, an appointment he also

Appendix B

filled from 1999–2000. Previously, he served as a Humbolt Fellow at the Max Planck Institute of Foreign, Comparative and International Law in Heidelberg, Germany (2000–01) and as Professor of International Law, Yanowicz Professor of Human Rights, President (1991–98), Rector (1980–85), and Dean of the Faculty of Law (1978–80) at Tel Aviv University. Professor Dinstein started his career in Israel's Foreign Service and served as Consul of Israel in New York and a member of Israel's Permanent Mission to the United Nations (1966–70). He is a member of the Institute of International Law and the Council of the International Institute of Humanitarian Law in San Remo. He was among the group of international lawyers and naval experts that produced the San Remo Manual on International Law Applicable to Armed Conflicts at Sea. Formerly, he served as Chairman of the Israel national branch of Amnesty International and was also a member of the Executive Council of the American Society of International Law. Professor Dinstein is the editor of the Israel Yearbook of Human Rights and has written extensively on subjects relating to international law, human rights, and the law of armed conflict.

Professor Rudolf Dolzer is a Professor and the Director, Institute for International Law at the University of Bonn, Germany. He attended Gonzaga University on a Fulbright Scholarship and has been a Visiting Professor at the University of Michigan School of Law, Cornell Law School and the Massachusetts Institute of Technology. Professor Dolzer has been a Research Fellow, Max-Planck-Institute of Comparative Public Law and International Law. From 1992 to 1996 he served as Director General in the Office of the German Federal Chancellor. He is currently a member of the Directorate, German Society for Foreign Policy; the Advisory Board, Dräger-Foundation, Lübeck; the International Board, Instituto de Empresa, Madrid; the Board of Directors, International Development Law Institute, Rome; and the German Parliament's Commission of Enquiry on Globalization.

Colonel David E. Graham, US Army, is the Chief, International and Operational Law Division within the Office of The Judge Advocate General, Department of the Army and the Director, Center for Law and Military Operations, The Judge Advocate General's School of the Army, Charlottesville, Virginia. During his career in the US Army, which began in 1971, Colonel Graham's other assignments have included Chief, Strategic Planning, Office of The Judge Advocate General; Staff Judge Advocate, United States Southern Command; Legal Advisor, Multinational Force and Observers: Peacekeeping Force, Sinai; and Attorney-Advisor, International Law, Office of the Staff Judge Advocate, Headquarters, United States Army Europe and Seventh Army.

Professor Leslie C. Green is a former Charles H. Stockton Professor of International Law at the Naval War College (1996–98). After serving in the British Army during World War II, he held university appointments at the University of London; University of Singapore; University of Alberta, where he is University Professor Emeritus; Kyung Hee University, Seoul, Korea; University of Colorado; and University of Denver. Professor Green's many government appointments include Member and Legal Advisor to the Canadian delegation to the Geneva Conference on Humanitarian Law in Armed Conflict (1975–77) and special consultant to the Judge Advocate General, National Defence Headquarters. In the latter capacity, he wrote the Canadian Manual on Armed Conflict Law. Professor Green is the author of numerous books, including The Contemporary Law Of Armed Conflict, and over 320 papers and articles.

Professor Christopher Greenwood is Professor of International Law at the London School of Economics and Political Science. He is a Barrister, practicing from Essex Court Chambers in London, and has represented the United Kingdom before the International Court of Justice in the *Nuclear Weapons* and *Lockerbie* cases, as well as appearing regularly in the English courts, where his cases have included Pinochet and the Guantanamo Bay detainees case. Professor Greenwood was formerly a Fellow and Lecturer at Magdalene College, Cambridge, has been a Visiting Professor at the Universities of Marburg, West Virginia, and Mississippi, and Director of Studies and Lecturer at the Academy of International Law in The Hague. He is a regular lecturer at military colleges, has published a number of articles on international law, and is the author of a forthcoming book, The Modern Law of Armed Conflict.

Professor Wolff Heintschel von Heinegg is Professor of Public International Law at the University of Frankfurt-Oder and former Professor of Law at the University of Augsburg, Germany. He was the Rapporteur of the International Law Association Committee on Maritime Neutrality and is currently the Vice-President of the German Society of Military Law and the Law of War. Professor Heintschel von Heinegg was among a group of international lawyers and naval experts who produced the San Remo Manual on International Law Applicable to Armed Conflicts at Sea. He is a widely published author of articles and books on the law of the sea and naval warfare.

Ms. Judith A. Miller is a partner at the Williams & Connolly law firm in Washington, D.C., advising on a wide range of business and governmental issues. She returned to the firm in January 2000, after serving as the General

Counsel for the Department of Defense. As the General Counsel from 1994 to 1999, she was responsible for advising the Secretary and Deputy Secretary and their senior leadership team on the host of legal and policy issues that came before the Department of Defense, including international affairs and intelligence matters, and operations law. Ms. Miller is the Co-Chair of the Federal Practice Task Force of the American Bar Association, and a member of the Defense Science Board, the Standing Committee on Law and National Security, and the American Law Institute. She was appointed to the Civil Justice Reform Act Advisory Group for the United States District Court for the District of Columbia, and its follow-on implementation committee, and is on the Executive Committee of the American Society of International Law.

Lieutenant Colonel Tony E. Montgomery, US Air Force, is the Deputy Staff Judge Advocate, United States Special Operations Command, MacDill Air Force Base, Florida. During his career, which began in 1983, his assignments have included service as the Area Defense Counsel for Florennes Air Base, Belgium; Chief of Military Justice at Hill Air Force Base, Utah; Staff Judge Advocate for Goodfellow Air Force Base, Texas; Chief, Operations and International Law for Headquarters Air Combat Command, Langley Air Force Base, Virginia; and from 1998 to 2001, he served as the Deputy Judge Advocate and Chief, Operations Law, for the United States European Command. During the summer of 1996, Lieutenant Colonel Montgomery served as the Staff Judge Advocate to the Commander, Joint Task Force Southwest Asia.

Professor John Norton Moore is the Walter L. Brown Professor of Law at the University of Virginia School of Law, and Director of the University's Center for National Security Law and the Center for Oceans Law & Policy. Professor Moore chaired the American Bar Association's Standing Committee on Law and National Security for four terms and has been a member of the Director of Central Intelligence (DCI)'s Historical Review Board from 1998 to the present. He is the author or editor of 20 books and over 140 scholarly articles and served for two decades on the editorial board of the American Journal of International Law. He is a member of the Council on Foreign Relations, the American Law Institute, and the American Society of International Law. Professor Moore's public service includes two terms as the Chairman of the Board of Directors of the United States Institute of Peace, as the Counselor on International Law to the Department of State, as Ambassador and Deputy Special Representative of the President to the Law of the Sea Conference, and Chairman of the National Security Council Interagency Task Force on the Law of the Sea. He has served as a Consultant to both the President's

Intelligence Oversight Board and the Arms Control and Disarmament Agency.

Professor Rein Müllerson is Professor and Chair of International Law at King's College of London University where he is also the Director of the Master of Arts Program on International Peace & Security. From 1992–94 he was Visiting Centennial Professor of the London School of Economics and Political Science. He served as the First Deputy Foreign Minister of Estonia during 1991–92 and from 1988–92 Professor Müllerson was a Member of the United Nations Human Rights Committee. He is a member of the Institut de Droit International. Professor Müllerson is the author of six books on international law and politics and more than 150 articles and reviews. His latest books are Human Rights Diplomacy (1997) and Ordering Anarchy: International Law in International Society (2000).

Professor John F. Murphy is Professor of Law at Villanova University. In addition to teaching, his career has included a year in India on a Ford Foundation Fellowship, private practice in New York and Washington, D.C., and service in the Office of the Assistant Legal Adviser for United Nations Affairs, US Department of State. He was previously on the law faculty at the University of Kansas, and has been a visiting professor at Cornell University and Georgetown University. From 1980–1981 he was the Charles H. Stockton Professor of International Law at the US Naval War College. Professor Murphy is the author or editor of several books and monographs, and is also the author of numerous articles, comments, and reviews on international law and relations. Professor Murphy has served as consultant to the US Departments of State and Justice, the ABA Standing Committee on Law and National Security, and the United Nations Crime Bureau, and has testified before Congress on several occasions. He is currently the American Bar Association's Alternate Observer at the US Mission to the United Nations.

Mr. W. Hays Parks, Colonel, United States Marine Corps Reserve (Retired), is Special Assistant to The Judge Advocate General of the United States Army for Law of War Matters. He has also occupied the Naval War College's Charles H. Stockton Chair of International Law and is Adjunct Professor at both George Washington University School of Law and American University School of Law. A legal adviser for the 1986 air strike against terrorist-related targets in Libya, Mr. Parks also had primary responsibility for the investigation of Iraqi war crimes during its 1990–1991 occupation of Kuwait. He has served as a United States representative for law of war negotiations in New York, Geneva, The Hague, and Vienna. A frequent lecturer on the law of military operations at the National, Army, Air Force and Naval War

Colleges, the service staff colleges, and other service schools such as the Navy Fighter Weapons School ("Top Gun"), Mr. Parks is widely published in military and legal journals. In 2001 he became the fifth person in the history of the United States Special Operations Command to receive that command's top civilian award, the U.S. Special Operations Command Outstanding Civilian Service Medal.

Judge Fausto Pocar is currently serving as a Judge at the Appeals Chamber of the International Criminal Tribunals for the former Yugoslavia (ICTY) and for Rwanda (ICTR). He is on leave from the University of Milan where he is Professor of International Law and where he also served as the Dean of the Faculty of Political Sciences and as the Vice-President. Judge Pocar has been constantly involved in United Nations activities. Elected in 1984 as a member of the Human Rights Committee of the United Nations, its Chairman in 1991 and 1992. He also conducted various missions for the High Commissioner for Human Rights (among others in Chechnya in 1995 and in Russia in 1996). He served several times as a member of the Italian delegation to the General Assembly in New York and to the Commission on Human Rights in Geneva. Judge Pocar was also a member of the United Nations Committee on the peaceful uses of outer space. Judge Pocar taught at The Hague Academy of International Law and participated, during the past twenty years, in The Hague Conference on Private International Law. Author of numerous legal publications, Judge Pocar is a member of various associations, such as the Institut de droit international and the International Law Association.

Professor Adam Roberts is the Montague Burton Professor of International Relations at Oxford University and a Fellow of Balliol College. He has been a lecturer in International Relations at the London School of Economics and Political Science and was the Alastair Buchan Reader in International Relations and Fellow of St. Antony's College, Oxford from 1981–86. He has a three-year Leverhulme Major research Fellowship for 2000–03. He is the author of numerous articles and books including Nations in Arms: The Theory and Practice of Territorial Defence and he co-edited Documents on the Law of War.

Rear Admiral Horace B. Robertson, Jr., JAGC, US Navy (Ret.), served 31 years on active duty with the US Navy, first as a general line officer (surface warfare) and later as a law specialist and judge advocate. Included among his assignments were tours as Commanding Officer of an amphibious landing ship, Special Counsel to the Secretary of the Navy, Special Counsel to the Chief of Naval Operations, and Judge Advocate General of the Navy. Following retirement, Rear Admiral Robertson was appointed Professor of Law at

Duke University School of Law, where he assumed Emeritus status in 1990. He is the editor of The Law of Naval Operations, volume 64 of the Naval War College's International Law Studies (the "Blue Book") series. He was among a group of academics and naval experts that worked together to produce the San Remo Manual on International Law Applicable to Armed Conflicts at Sea. During 1991–92, he served as the Charles H. Stockton Professor of International Law at the US Naval War College.

Professor Natalino Ronzitti is Professor of International Law at the Luiss University, Rome, Italy. He has been a Visiting Scholar, Wolfson College, Cambridge; a Fulbright Scholar and Scholar in residence, University of Virginia School of Law, and twice been a NATO Fellow. Professor Ronzitti has been a member of numerous Italian delegations at international conferences, including the 1975 Session of the Diplomatic Conference on the Reaffirmation and Development of International Humanitarian Law Applicable in Armed Conflict; International Conference for the Suppression of Unlawful Acts against the Safety of Maritime Navigation (1988); CSCE Meetings on the Human Dimension: (Paris, 1989; Copenhagen, 1990; Moscow, 1991); Legal Adviser to the Permanent Representative of Italy to the Conference of Disarmament (Geneva), 1991–95; the XLVIIth Session of the First Committee of the United Nations General Assembly; Non-Proliferation Treaty Review and Extension Conference (New York, 1995); and the Review Conference of the Convention on Prohibition or Restriction on the Use of Certain Conventional Weapons Which May Be Deemed to Be Excessively Injurious or to Have Indiscriminate Effects (Vienna, 1995). He was also a member for the Italian Government of the Preparatory Commission for the Convention on the Prohibition of the Development, Production, Stockpiling and Use of Chemical Weapons and their Destruction (The Hague) (1993–97) and has been a consultant for various departments of the Italian Government on European Union affairs and international humanitarian law. Professor Ronzitti is a member of the Editorial board of the Italian Yearbook of International Law, of the International Spectator (Rome) and of the Journal of Conflict & Security Law.

Professor Joel H. Rosenthal is President of the Carnegie Council on Ethics and International Affairs. Founded in 1914 by Andrew Carnegie, the Carnegie Council is an independent, nonpartisan, nonprofit organization dedicated to research and education in the field of ethics and international affairs. The Carnegie Council's purpose is to promote understanding of the values and conditions that ensure peaceful relations among nations. Professor Rosenthal is editor of the journal Ethics & International Affairs and author of the book, *Righteous Realists* (1991). He is also editor of *Ethics and International Affairs: A Reader* (2nd edition, 1999). Among his current professional activities, Professor Rosenthal serves as co-director of the Carnegie Council/National War College working group on "Ethics and the Future of International Conflict," and coordinates the Council's programs on "Ethics and U.S. Foreign Policy." He also serves as Adjunct Professor in the Department of Politics at New York University.

Professor Nicholas Rostow is the General Counsel, United States Mission to the United Nations. Prior to that appointment he was the Charles H. Stockton Professor of International Law at the U.S. Naval War College. Professor Rostow has served in senior positions in both the legislative and executive branches of the United States Government. These include Staff Director of the Senate Select Committee on Intelligence; Deputy Staff Director and Counsel of the House Select Committee on U.S. National Security and Military/Commercial Concerns with the People's Republic of China (more familiarly known as the Cox Committee); Special Assistant to the State Department's Legal Adviser; as a Special Assistant to Presidents Reagan and Bush; and Legal Adviser to the National Security Council. In addition to government service, Professor Rostow has taught law and history at the University of Tulsa and the Fletcher School of Law and Diplomacy. His publications are in the fields of international law and diplomatic history.

Professor Yves Sandoz is the former Director for International Law and Communication of the International Law of the International Committee of the Red Cross (ICRC). Professor Sandoz is the author or editor of numerous publications in the field of international humanitarian law and international criminal law, including the Commentary on the Additional Protocols to of 8 June 1977 to the Geneva Conventions of 12 August 1949, which he authored in part and for which he served as co-editor. He has taught at the International Institute of Human Rights in Strasbourg, France and The Hague Academy of International Law. He actively participated in the creation of the University Center for International Humanitarian Law, in Geneva, where he is currently teaching. As of November 2002, he is a member of the ICRC.

Professor Ivan Shearer is the Challis Professor of International Law at the University of Sydney. He was formerly Professor of Law and Dean of the Faculty of Law at the University of New South Wales, where he was awarded Emeritus status in 1993. He has been a Visiting Fellow at All Souls College, Oxford, and held visiting appointments at universities in Germany and Greece. Professor Shearer is the Vice President of the International Law Association (Australian branch), and on the editorial board of three professional journals. He is a member of the International Institute of Humanitarian Law, San Remo, and was among a group of international lawyers and naval experts that produced the San Remo Manual on International Law Applicable to Armed Conflicts at Sea. He holds the rank of Captain in the Royal Australian Naval Reserve, and in that capacity gives advice within the Department of Defence and frequent lectures on the law of the sea and international law to various service bodies. During 2000–01, he served as the Charles H. Stockton Professor of International Law at the US Naval War College.

Lieutenant General Michael C. Short, US Air Force (Ret.) served as Commander Allied Forces Southern Europe, Stabilization Forces Air Component, Naples Italy and Commander, 16th Air Force and 16th Air and Space Expeditionary Task Force, US Air Forces in Europe from 1998 until his retirement on July 1, 2000. As such he was responsible for the planning and employment of NATO's air forces in the Mediterranean area of operations from Gibraltar to Eastern Turkey, including the command of operations during NATO's Kosovo air campaign. Earlier assignments as a flag officer included service as the Assistant Director of Operations, Headquarters Air Combat Command; Director of Joint Training and Exercises, US Atlantic Command; Chief of Staff, Allied Air Forces Southern Europe; and Director Of Operations, Headquarters U.S. Air Forces in Europe. Lieutenant General Short was a command pilot with more than 4,600 flying hours in fighter aircraft, including 276 combat missions in Southeast Asia.

Professor Henry Shue is Senior Research Fellow in the Department of Politics and International Relations, as well as Senior Research Fellow at Merton College, University of Oxford. He has written on dual-purpose facilities as military objectives, the morality of war and of nuclear deterrence, and the strength of obligations across national boundaries. After teaching at the University of North Carolina and Wellesley College, he was a founding member of the Institute for Philosophy and Public Policy, University of Maryland, and then the first Director of the Program on Ethics and Public Life, Cornell University. His publications include Basic Rights: Subsistence, Affluence, and U.S. Foreign Policy (1980; 2nd edition, 1996), Nuclear Deterrence and Moral Restraint (editor, 1989), and "Bombing to Rescue? NATO's 1999 Bombing of Serbia" in Ethics and Foreign Intervention (2003).

Professor Scott L. Silliman is a professor of the practice of law at the Duke University School of Law, as well as Executive Director of the Law School's Center on Law, Ethics and National Security. He also holds appointments as an Adjunct Professor of Law at the University of North Carolina at Chapel Hill and at North Carolina Central University, and as an Adjunct Lecturer in

Appendix B

Law at Wake Forest University School of Law. Professor Silliman served as a United States Air Force judge advocate from 1968 until his retirement in the grade of colonel in 1993. During his career as a military attorney, he held a variety of leadership positions, including staff judge advocate at two large installations and three major Air Force commands. In his last assignment, as the senior attorney for Air Combat Command, he was general counsel to the commander of the largest principal organization within the Air Force. Professor Silliman is a frequent commentator on national radio and television news programs on issues involving military law and national security. He is a member of the Advisory Committee to the ABA's Standing Committee on Law and National Security and of the Board of Directors of the Triangle World Affairs Council.

Colonel Richard B. Sorenson, US Air Force, is the Staff Judge Advocate, 19th Air Force, Air Education and Training Command, Randolph Air Force Base, Texas. Colonel Sorenson entered active duty with the United States Air Force in May 1976. He served as an Air Force aviator for five years before attending the University of Minnesota School of Law from which he graduated in 1984. His assignments as an Air Force judge advocate have included service as Chief, Aviation Tort Claims and Litigation, Headquarters Air Force and as Chief, Operations Law Division, Headquarters, United States Air Forces in Europe at Ramstein Air Base, Germany. Colonel Sorenson served as the lead Air Force attorney for litigation arising from the terrorist bombing of Pan Am Flight 103 over Lockerbie, Scotland.

Professor Torsten Stein holds the Chair for European Law and European Comparative Law and is the Director of the Europe Institute at the University of Saarland, Saarbrücken, Germany. He has been a Senior Research Fellow at the Max-Planck Institute for Comparative Public Law and Public International Law in Heidelberg and has often served as rapporteur for committees of the International Law Association (ILA). He is currently the Honorary Secretary and Executive Director of the ILA's German branch and a member of the ILA's Executive Council, and a member of the Advisory Boards of the Academy of European Law Trier and the European Academy Otzenhausen. Professor Stein is also a Colonel in the German Air Force Reserve.

Professor Barry S. Strauss is Professor of History and Classics at Cornell University where he was also Director of the Peace Studies Program, 1995–2002. Professor Strauss has held fellowships from the National Endowment for the Humanities and the University Center for Human Values at Princeton University, as well as research grants from the Littauer Memorial Foundation, the Korea Foundation, and the U.S. Department of Education.

He has published several books including The Anatomy of Error: The Lessons of Ancient Military Disasters for Modern Strategists (1990) and War and Democracy: A Comparative Study of the Korean War and the Peloponnesian War (2001), which he co-edited. Professor Strauss is currently writing a book on the battle of Salamis (480 B.C.) and the ancient clash of civilizations.

Professor Robert F. Turner holds both professional and academic doctorates from the University of Virginia School of Law, where in 1981 he co-founded the Center for National Security Law. He continues to serve as the Center's Associate Director. A former three-term chairman of the ABA Standing Committee on Law and National Security, and Editor of the ABA *National Security Law Report* for many years, he previously served as a Principal Deputy Assistant Secretary of State and as the first President of the congressionally-established U.S. Institute of Peace in Washington, D.C. The author or editor of more than a dozen books and numerous articles, Professor Turner has testified before more than a dozen congressional committees. During 1994–1995, he held the Charles H. Stockton Chair of International Law at the Naval War College.

Professor George K. Walker is Professor of Law, Wake Forest University School of Law. He was the Charles H. Stockton Professor of International Law at the US Naval War College from 1992–93. Professor Walker retired as a Captain in the US Naval Reserve after serving aboard destroyers, qualifying as a Surface Warfare Officer, and duty as Commanding Officer of six Naval Reserve units. He was a Woodrow Wilson fellow at Duke University and received a Sterling Fellowship while holding a research position at Yale Law School. Professor Walker has edited or written ten books and over forty book chapters, law journals, and continuing education publications, as well as several state statutes. He is the author of The Tanker War, 1980–88: Law and Policy, volume 76 of the Naval War College's International Law Studies (the "Blue Book") series. Professor Walker was among the group of international lawyers and naval experts that produced the San Remo Manual on International Law Applicable to Armed Conflicts at Sea. He has served as a vice president of the North Carolina Bar Association and on the Executive Council of the American Society of International Law. Professor Walker is also a member of the American Law Institute.

Lieutenant Andru E. Wall, JAGC, US Navy, is on the faculty of the US Naval War College as a member of the International Law Department. Lieutenant Wall was commissioned in 1997 and after graduating from the Naval Justice School he reported to the Naval Legal Service Office Mid-Atlantic. In 1999 he was assigned as Staff Judge Advocate for Commander, Amphibious

Squadron Six where he served during a Mediterranean and Red Sea deployment. Lieutenant Wall has taught international law at the US Naval War College in Newport, Rhode Island since June 2000. In addition, he serves as adjunct faculty at the International Institute of Humanitarian Law in San Remo, Italy and the Roger Williams University School of Law in Bristol, Rhode Island.

Professor Ruth G. Wedgwood is a Professor of Law at Yale Law School, and is also Senior Fellow and Director of the Project on International Organizations and Law at the Council in Foreign Relations in New York City. Currently on a leave of absence from Yale Law School, she is serving as the Edward B. Burling Professor of International Law at the Johns Hopkins University Nitze School of Advanced International Studies in Washington, D.C. Professor Wedgwood is a member of the Secretary of State's Advisory Committee on International Law, and is Vice President of the International Law Association (American branch). During 1998–99, she served as the Charles H. Stockton Professor of International Law at the US Naval War College. She has written and lectured widely on Security Council politics, United Nations peacekeeping, war crimes, and UN reform. She is a former law clerk to Judge Henry Friendly of the US Court of Appeals for the Second Circuit and Justice Harry Blackmun of the U.S. Supreme Court, and Executive Editor of the Yale Law Journal. Professor Wedgwood served as *amicus curiae* in the case of Prosecutor v. Blaskic at the International Criminal Tribunal for the former Yugoslavia.

Index

A

Adriatic Sea: 92, 93, 94–95, 115, 116–17
Aggression, definition of the crime of: 108
Aircraft: 27–28, 29
Albania: 93, 95, 117
Amnesty International: 262
Annan, Kofi: 412
Arbour, Louise: 419
Ash, Tim Garton: 415
Assassinations: 153–54
Attorney general of the United States, advice to on LOAC: 8–9, 11–12, 15
Australia: 378
Austria: 119
Aviano, Italy: 30, 115
Axworthy, Lloyd: 412

B

Badinter, Robert: 42
Badinter Commission: 42
Baker, James E.: 7–18, 199, 274–75, 390–91
Bankovic v Belgium: 66–68
Bar, FRY: 56, 57, 94, 118
Baxter, Richard: 321, 341
Belgium: 64, 65
Belgrade
    attacks on: 67–68, 157, 179–80, 184, 200, 258, 260–61, 264–65, 289
    attack on the Chinese embassy in: 21, 184, 185, 264
    fears of civilians regarding attacks on: 110–11, 130–31
Belt, Stuart: 230–32, 235, 236, 239–40, 242–43
Blair, Tony: 412
Blaskic case: 387
Blockades: 118–19, 127–30
Bombing to Win, by Robert Pape: 209
Bosnia: 115–16, 408, 410, 413, 434, 437
Bosnia case: 42–43
Bothe, Michael: 50–51, 52, 151, 173–87, 202, 203, 204, 205, 211, 212, 216–17, 281, 220, 277, 300, 303–04, 394–95, 472
Bridges, bombing of: 5–6, 22–23, 261, 264
Bring, Ove: 129, 257–72, 273, 276, 278, 279, 289, 290–91, 295, 300–302, 304–06
Burger, James: 54, 268
Bush, George H. W.: 28, 475

547

Index

C

Canada: 29, 64–65, 364–65, 378, 394
Caroline case: 449, 452–53
Carpet bombing: 27–28
Cassese, Antonio: 141, 470
Casualties, civilian
    and achievement of military goals: 23–24, 219
    assessment of potential for: 122–23, 193–94, 200, 201
    avoidance of and rules of engagement: 82–83
    caused by cluster bombs: 272, 306–07, 361, 362–63, 416, 426–27, 440
    factors affecting: 287–88, 299
    and humanitarian interventions: 229, 264–65, 266, 295–96, 301–02, 414–16, 440–41
    obligation to use feasible precautions to avoid: 263–65, 269–70, 271–72, 278, 290, 297–99, 304, 357–58, 368–69, 391–92
    and Operation Allied Force: 5–6, 250, 251–53, 264–65, 294–95, 361, 362–63, 368–69, 371–73, 401, 414–16, 421, 431
    public expectations regarding: 17, 292, 297–98, 302–03, 401
    responsibility for: 238, 293, 286, 287–89, 290
    and security of one's own soldiers: 277, 295, 304–06, 370
    and terrorists: 254–55
    and use of civilians as human shields: 216, 275–76, 282–83, 288–90, 298–302
    and use of high-altitude bombing: 248–54, 266–67, 283–84, 369, 415
Casualties, military in Operation Allied Force: 266–67
Cebrowski, Vice-Admiral Arthur: 3–6
Chairman, Joint Chiefs of Staff, legal advice to: 11, 12, 199–202
Chechnya: 235–36
Chinese embassy bombing: 21, 184, 185, 264
Churchill, Winston: 302, 313
Civil wars, international responses to: 402, 403, 405, 406–07, 408
"Civilian Deaths in the NATO Air Campaign" (Human Rights Watch report): 264–65
Civilian morale as a target of bombing: 29–30, 48, 110–11, 130–31, 180–81, 191, 209–10, 222, 275, 294, 364, 414, 416–17, 418, 440
Civilian system of values, place in military decision making: 211–12
Civilian tribunals and enforcement of the law of war: 435–36, 461–62, 464, 477–79. *See also* specific international courts.
Clark, General Wesley: 10, 21, 289, 317, 417, 420
Clausewitz, Karl von: 459
Clinton, William: 97, 304–05, 411, 414, 454
Cluster bombs: 272, 306–07, 361, 362–63, 367–68, 416, 426–27, 431–32, 440
Coalition warfare
    and applicability of customary international law: 326–27, 380
    and different treaty obligations of members: 315–17, 321–22, 377–85
    failures of: 24–26
    and the Gulf War: 24, 390–91
    and international humanitarian law: 315–35
    and KFOR: 316
    and NATO: 24–26, 326, 377–85

and Operation Allied Force: 316, 326
proposed protocol regarding: 270
and reciprocity: 327
and reprisals: 390–91
and responsibility for violations of international humanitarian law: 327–35, 387–88, 389
rules of engagement: 380, 389
UN enforcement actions: 322–25
Coastal areas, bombardment of: 166–67
Collateral damage
 assessment of potential: 192, 193–94, 195, 200, 201, 297
 commander's responsibility to use all feasible precautions to avoid or minimize: 238–39, 241, 248, 286, 297
 defender's responsibility for: 238, 239, 286, 287, 288–89
 excessive civilian damage: 219, 262–63, 268–69, 308–09
 and Operation Allied Force: 262–65, 294
 and precision guided munitions: 240–41, 249, 265–67, 277–78, 297, 299
 and principle of proportionality: 215–16, 262–63. See also Proportionality, principle of.
 and Protocol I: 262–63, 268–69
 and target approval process: 199–200
 and World War II: 174, 208, 218
Commanders
 accountability of: 15, 17–18, 89–92, 211–12, 263–64, 285, 368–69, 387–88, 438–40
 and reasonable decisions: 89–92, 238–39, 241, 248, 252, 263–64, 285, 368–69, 370–71
 responsibility to use all feasible precautions to avoid or minimize collateral damage: 238–39, 241, 248, 252, 294–95, 368–69
 role in targeting: 241–42
 and use of precision-guided munitions: 438–40
Consensus decision making
 and accountability: 92
 and creation of laws of war: 438–40
Continental shelf used as a military weapons jettison area: 116–17
Convention on Privileges and Immunities of 1946: 55
Convention on the Safety of United Nations and Associated Personnel of 1994: 55, 79–80, 81, 323, 407
Cook, Robin: 412
Corfu Channel case: 117
Crimes against humanity
 and international courts: 212
 and international law: 402
 prosecution of Milosevic for: 61
 weakness of implementation of laws against: 406
Criminal sanctions for individual servicemen: 52
Croatia: 116–17, 408, 452
Customary international law
 applicability to non-international conflicts: 45
 and case law of international courts: 341–43, 350–51, 353–55, 382, 384, 389–90

creation of through State practice: 233–36, 274, 317–18, 320–21, 338–40, 350–51, 353–55, 382–85, 389–90, 446–47, 474
and definition of military objectives: 141
derogation of: 354–55
and the environment: 182, 183, 203–04
and the law of neutrality: 116, 119, 126, 127–28, 129–30
and military manuals: 318–19, 320–21
and new weapons: 274
and objectives exempt from attack: 152–53
and *opinio juris*: 234–35, 236
and the principle of distinction: 139–40, 175–77, 238, 282–83
and the principle of proportionality: 244–45, 246, 248
process of creating: 233–34, 317–18, 337–51, 382–85, 438–40, 446
and Protocol I: 73, 175–77, 257, 259, 261, 262, 268, 273, 274–75, 282–83, 291, 317–22, 337–51, 366, 381–85, 389–90, 422, 458, 459–60
and reprisals: 349–50
and self-defense: 449
and the succession of States: 114–15
and the use of precision-guided munitions: 233–36, 238–39
and visit and search operations: 127–28, 129–30
Cyprus: 66, 68

D

D'Alema, Massimo: 21, 30
Dalton, Harvey: 199–202, 211, 213, 222, 463–65
D'Amato, Anthony: 234
Danube: 424–25
Day, Graham: 437
Dayton Accords for Bosnia-Herzegovina: 86
Delhi Rules for Limitation of the Dangers Incurred by the Civilian Population in Time of War: 175
Denmark: 94–95, 118, 378
Department of Defense
general counsel: 12, 110, 199–200
role of attorneys in target selection: 109
Department of State and the creation of customary international law: 234
Dinstein, Yoram: 139–72, 177, 179, 180, 204, 205, 207, 208, 215–16, 218–19, 355, 399, 449–50, 465
Distinction, principle of
and civilian leaders: 220–22
customary law regarding: 46–47, 257–58, 282–83, 347–48
and dual-use targets: 207–08, 214–15, 415–16
and duty of due diligence: 183–84, 185–86
and failure to distinguish between military objectives and political objectives: 275
and goal of putting pressure on the adversary's government: 110–11, 130–31, 180–81, 191, 209–10, 222, 275, 294, 364, 402, 414, 416–19, 431, 458–59

550

Index

and high-altitude bombing: 250, 284, 295, 310, 413–14
history of: 173–75, 286
and humanitarian interventions: 47–48, 50–51, 186–87
and the ICRC: 175, 178, 261
and notion of military advantage: 180–81, 184–85
and Operation Allied Force: 122–23, 179–80, 185–86, 200–201, 249–50, 259–61, 283–84, 310, 364–65, 413–14, 431
and precision-guided munitions: 438–40
and Protocol I: 46–47, 171–72, 175–78, 181–83, 214–16, 245, 257, 258, 261, 345, 347–48, 364–65
and State practice: 345
violations of: 174–75, 258
and World War II: 174–75

Dolzer, Rudolf: 353–59, 391–92, 395–96, 478

Dual-use targets
attacks on used to influence civilians to pressure Milosevic: 110–11, 130–31, 180–81, 191, 209–10, 222, 275, 294, 364, 414, 416–17, 418, 439–40
efficacy of attacks on: 110–11
electric power facilities: 110, 155–56, 200, 209, 219
factories: 16, 30, 110, 154–55, 200, 216, 439–40
and LOAC: 16, 109–12
merchant vessels: 162–63
and Operation Allied Force: 260, 264–65, 416
passenger trains: 156–57
in Persian Gulf War: 155–56
and rules of proportionality: 109–10, 207–10
standards for targeting of: 177–81, 260–61, 439–40
and target selection process: 199–200
transportation infrastructure: 150–51, 156–57, 178–79, 200

Dunlap, Charles: 211, 213, 249–50, 254

E

East Timor: 410, 417, 431, 453
Economist Intelligence Unit: 361
Ellis, Admiral Jim: 21
Environment, protection of during war: 181–83, 203–04, 348–49, 363, 422, 424–25, 464–65
Ethical considerations
in humanitarian interventions: 217, 278, 296, 300–302, 305–06, 309–10, 431, 445–46, 475, 476–77
in NATO's intervention in Kosovo: 294–96, 366–67, 366–74
Ethnic cleansing: 303, 305–06, 402, 410–11, 433, 434–35, 451–52
European Command (EUCOM) staff judge advocate: 11
European Convention on Human Rights: 392–96
European Court of Human Rights: 66–68, 130–31, 330, 392–96, 419
European Union and prosed oil embargo against the FRY: 95

Index

F

Falkland Islands War of 1982: 165, 166, 205
Fenrick, Bill: 275, 277
Final Report to the Prosecutor by the Committee Established to Review the NATO Bombing Campaign Against the Federal Republic of Yugoslavia: 33–34, 111–12, 157, 177, 179–80, 182, 183, 184, 250, 251–53, 260, 289, 366–74, 421–23, 459, 460–62, 464–65, 477
Fink, Lieutenant Commander Susan: 309–10
Finland: 468
Flanagan, Lieutenant Colonel: 362–63
France
    and proposed oil embargo: 118
    and Protocol I: 115, 267, 316, 334
    and target selection process: 26, 214
Franck, Thomas: 445, 446
French Court of Cassation: 167

G

Gadhafi, Moammar: 288
Gardam, Judith Gail: 243–45, 248, 449–50
Garraway, Charles: 214–15, 464–65
General Belgrano, ARA: 166, 205
Geneva Convention II of 1949: 101–02
Geneva Convention III of 1949: 53, 54–55, 98–99, 103, 104
Geneva Convention IV of 1949: 161, 238
Geneva Conventions of 1949
    accepted as customary international law: 345
    applicability to UN enforcement actions: 322–25
    Common Article 1: 67–68
    Common Article 2: 75–76, 98, 104, 457–58
    Common Article 3: 45, 76, 77, 101–03, 104, 115, 319, 406, 410–11
    failure to address the principle of distinction: 174–75
    implementation provisions: 406
    Martens Clause: 71–72
    military persons and equipment exempted from attack: 152–53
    proposed additional protocols to: 270
    status of FRY as a party to: 41, 43–44
    threshold of application of: 75–76, 77, 104
Geneva Protocol I Concerning International Armed Conflicts (1977). *See* Protocol I.
Genocide
    and international courts: 212
    and international law: 402
    interventions to stop: 303, 305–06, 451–55
Genocide Convention of 1948: 42–43, 63–64, 406, 427
Germany: 30, 321, 469, 472–73
Glennon, Michael: 304, 473–74

Glueck, Sheldon: 476
Graham, David: 377–85, 388–89, 391, 393, 399, 459–60
Greece: 95
Green, Leslie C.: 28, 211–12, 302, 361–76, 390, 394, 395, 472
Greenwood, Christopher: 30, 35–69, 78–79, 123, 125–26, 127, 128–30, 131, 132, 216, 300, 469–70
Grewe, Wilhelm: 474
Grotius: 472, 473
Guerrilla warfare: 303
"Guidelines for Military Manuals and Instructions on the Protection of the Environment in Times of Armed Conflict": 424

H

Hague Convention
   for the Protection of Cultural Property of 1954: 91, 140, 156, 157, 427
   Second Protocol to: 91, 140, 141, 407
Hague Convention of 1899: 60, 71, 158–59, 237–38, 405
Hague Conventions of 1907: 72, 75, 100–101, 116, 158, 166–67, 343–45, 405
   IV: 158, 167, 170, 343–44
   V: 116
   VIII: 117
   IX: 166–67, 237–38
Hague Rules on Aerial Warfare (1923): 115, 119, 140, 143, 168, 169, 170, 174
Hammarskjold, Dag: 79
Herby, Peter: 426–27
Heydrich, SS General: 154
Higgins, Rosalynn: 444
Hiroshima, Japan: 180
Hoffman, Michael: 270
Hors de combat: 153
Hosmer, Stephen T.: 110–11
Hudson, Manley O.: 233–34
Human rights
   duty to intervene to stop violations of: 472–74
   need to stop violations of as justification for Operation Allied Force: 37–38, 433, 446–47, 448, 451–52, 463, 470, 471–72
   violations of by States: 404, 410–11, 433, 445, 446–47, 451–52, 453, 454–55, 472–74
Human rights law
   and the law of armed conflict: 67–68, 381, 392–96, 401–02
Human Rights Watch: 261, 264–65, 368
Humanitarian aid, force used to permit the delivery of: 408–09, 410–11
Humanitarian interventions
   and applicability of LOAC: 88–89, 104–05, 270–71, 326, 412–13, 439–40, 441, 457–60
   and civilian casualties: 229, 264–65, 266, 295–96, 301–02, 414–16, 440–41
   and consensus decision making: 92

ethical considerations: 217, 278, 296, 300–302, 305–06, 309–10,1 431, 445–47, 448, 461, 469–74, 475, 476–77
international support for the idea of: 409–10, 411–13, 441, 446–47, 457–58, 469–74
legal right of: 434, 441, 445–48, 463, 469–74
need for an additional protocol for: 268–72, 300–302
proposed guidelines for: 375–76
public support for: 303, 413
and relationship between purpose and degree of force: 52, 448–55, 460–61, 463
and reliance on air power: 402, 413–17, 431, 452
rules of conduct during: 71–83
and standards of necessity: 88–89, 104
suggested need for stricter adherence to LOAC and international humanitarian law during: 49–51
and target selection: 181, 186–87, 294–96
Hussein, Saddam: 221, 258, 449, 467–68, 475

I

Iceland: 333
Ignatieff, Michael: 82
Independent International Commission on Kosovo: 49–50, 51, 250, 253–54, 270
Infeld, Danielle: 240, 242
Institut de Droit International, resolution of 1969: 175
International armed conflict, definition of: 39
International Committee of the Red Cross: 43
  1956 attempt to clarify the principle of distinction: 175, 178
  Commentary to Protocol I: 148, 239, 246, 248, 259, 261, 273, 282
  and depleted uranium: 426
  and explosive remnants of war: 307
  and prisoners of war: 54, 55
  and protection of the environment in time of war: 424
  study on the customary rules of international humanitarian law: 274
International Court of Justice
  and alleged violations of the Genocide Convention by FRY: 42–43
  applicability of decisions: 108
  Bosnia case: 42–43
  and charges brought against NATO States by the FRY: 62–66
  and charges related to the Genocide Convention: 63–64
  Corfu Channel case: 117
  and creation of customary international law: 236, 318–19
  Lockerbie case: 433
  Lotus case: 235
  and the NATO air campaign: 62–66, 330, 334, 419
  Nicaragua case: 318, 319, 339, 340, 353–54
  North Sea Continental Shelf case: 274, 318, 340, 353–54
  Nuclear Weapons advisory opinion: 117, 139, 319, 353–54, 392–93, 443–44
  Reparations for Injuries Suffered in the Service of the United Nations: 76

and rights of neutral States: 117
Statute: 63, 64–65, 317–18, 353
International criminal systems, factors affecting the acceptance of: 358–59
International Criminal Court: 140
   and legal scrutiny of military actions: 15
   potential effect on military actions: 130–33
   potential problems with: 112, 130–33, 435–36
   reservations fo the United States regarding: 112, 420, 421
   Statute. *See* Rome Statute of the International Criminal Court.
International Criminal Court for Rwanda: 407, 409
International Criminal Court Preparatory Committee: 108
International Criminal Tribunal for the former Yugoslavia (ICTY): 60–62, 365–66
   Appeals Chamber: 39, 45, 114
   and atrocities in Kosovo: 419
   Blaskic case: 387
   and customary international law: 318–19, 346–47
   and indictment of Milosevic: 61, 417, 420, 422–23
   jurisdiction of: 408, 419, 422
   Kupreskic case: 357–58, 371–72, 391–92
   and NATO air campaign: 61–62, 196, 330, 366–67, 402, 419–23, 432, 435, 459, 460–62, 477
   Prosecuter: 6, 44, 61–62, 177, 421
   reluctance to find that NATO might have violated the law of war: 366–74, 421–23
   and reprisals against civilians: 349–50, 391
   review of US actions: 15, 366–74, 384, 420, 432
   and Srebrenica: 121
   Statute: 158–59, 185, 300, 407
   Tadic case: 45, 114, 320
International Humanitarian Fact-Finding Commission: 406
International humanitarian law. *See also* Law of armed conflict.
   and ability to fight effective wars: 355, 356
   applicability to armed forces of member States implementing NATO decisions: 40
   applicability to hostilities between FRY and the KLA: 44–46
   applicability to Operation Desert Storm: 323
   application to operations carried out under UN authority but not UN control: 322–25
   applicability to operations under United Nations command and control: 80–81, 322–23, 324
   application of to Operation Allied Force: 38, 39–46, 266–68
   and coalition warfare: 315–35
   confusion caused by using this term for law of armed conflict: 381, 393, 401–02
   and creators' understanding of military security problems: 438–39
   effects on willingness of States to engage in humanitarian operations: 358–59
   goals and functions of: 353, 355–59
   and humanitarian interventions: 40–41, 69
   and international criminal law: 355, 356–57
   ICRC study of the customary rules of: 274
   potential violations of: 265
   and principle that civilians are not legitimate targets: 48
   and protection of potential victims of war: 353, 355–56

Index

relationship to international human rights law: 67–68
responsibility for non-compliance by a coalition: 327–35
sources of: 353–55
threshold for the application of: 39–40, 75–77, 81–83
and treaty making by consensus: 438–40
International Law Association: 127–28, 174
International Military Tribunal at Nuremberg: 165, 174
International organizations, responsibility for wrongful acts: 328–35
International Review of the Red Cross: 267, 268
Iran-Iraq War: 408
Iraq: 80, 126, 151, 153, 155–56, 219, 231, 232, 245, 258, 322, 413, 418, 446–47, 449–50, 467–68, 469
Isby, David: 231
Israel: 291–92, 378, 390
Italy: 30, 93, 95, 116, 117, 118, 241

J

Jackson, General Mike: 19
Jane's Missiles and Rockets: 231
Jettison areas: 116–17
Johnson, Admiral Jay: 4
Johnson, Lyndon B.: 8, 82
Jus ad bellum
 and applicability of international humanitarian law: 50–52, 78, 81–82
 application of to Operation Allied Force: 38–39, 127, 367
 and considerations of necessity for the use of force: 52
 and considerations of proportionality in the use of force: 52, 274
 linkage to *jus in bello*: 33–34, 38, 50, 51–52, 69, 73, 127, 216–17, 221, 402, 409–13, 434–35, 443–46, 452–53, 457–59, 460–61, 474–77
 and naval blockades: 56–57
Jus in bello
 and applicability of international humanitarian law: 40–41, 73, 78, 81–83
 and attacks against civilian aircraft: 169
 and humanitarian interventions: 52, 73, 186–87, 216–17, 434–35
 and the law of neutrality as applicable to Kosovo campaign: 38–39
 and legitimate military objectives: 139–72
 linkage to *jus ad bellum*: 33–34, 38, 50, 51–52, 69, 73, 127, 216–17, 221, 402, 409–13, 434–35, 443–46, 452–53, 457–59, 460–61, 474–77
 and principle of distinction: 139–40
 and proposed oil embargo: 56, 127
 purpose of: 209

K

Kitty Hawk, USS, battle group: 93
Kogan, Charles: 214, 306

Index

Korea, Republic of: 468
Korean War: 286, 288
Kosovo
    and cluster bombs: 272, 306–07, 362–63, 426–27
    failure of Operation Allied Force to protect Kosovars from Serb attacks: 414–15
    UNMIK responsiblities in: 59–60, 374
Kosovo International Security Force (KFOR)
    applicability of international humanitarian law to: 324–25
    creation of: 58, 126, 374–75
    and removal of cluster bombs: 362, 363
    responsibilities of: 58, 69
    rules of engagement: 317, 379
Kosovo Liberation Army
    applicability of international humanitarian law to conflict with FRY: 44–46, 113–14
    and attacks on Serbs: 374–75, 437–38
    and capture of FRY soldiers: 53, 55, 97, 102–03
    claim to be a national liberation movement: 45, 113–14
    demilitarization of: 54, 374, 436–37
Kragujevac Arms/Motor Vehicle Plant: 110
Krstic, General Radislav: 121
Kupreskic case: 252–53, 357–58, 371–72, 391
Kuwait: 80, 126, 448–50, 467–68

K

Lakenheath, Royal Air Force Base, United Kingdom: 26
Law of armed conflict. *See also* International humanitarian law.
    applicability to humanitarian interventions: 88–89
    applicability to military operations pursuant to UN Security Council decisions: 86–88
    applicability to Operation Allied Force: 33–133
    and civil wars: 406
    creation of by those unfamiliar with military concerns: 438–40
    double standards in the application of: 283–84, 293–96, 300–302
    and dual-use targets. *See* Dual-use targets.
    enforcement of: 435–36, 461
    and human rights law: 381, 392–96
    and imbalance in fighting abilities: 302–04, 306
    need for further codification of: 403, 424–27
    need to induce all States and combatants to comply with: 226, 255, 404–05, 460–61
    and obligation of due diligence in target selection: 183–84
    and principle of distinction. *See* Distinction, principle of.
    and principle of proportionality. *See* Proportionality, Principle of.
    responses to violations of: 299–300, 404–05, 408, 460–61
    and terrorists: 254–55
    and theory of normative relativism: 242–43
    training in by the US military: 225–26
    as US criminal law: 18

and use of precision-guided munitions: 231–43, 249–50
Law of belligerent occupation: 59–60, 69, 478–79
Law of neutrality
    and customary international law: 116, 119, 127–28, 129–30
    and humanitarian interventions: 88, 115–16
    and *jus in bello* in Kosovo: 38–39, 403
    and peacekeeping operations: 115–16
    and proposed NATO embargo on shipments to the FRY: 38–39, 117–18
    validity of: 117–18, 423–24
Lawyers
    role in target selection process: 8–9, 14–15, 18, 25, 26
Leskovac railway bridge, bombing of: 5–6
Liberia: 446–47
Libya: 287, 288
Lockerbie case: 433
Lohr, Admiral Michael: 12, 199
Loizidou v. Turkey: 66, 68
Lotus case: 235

M

Macedonia: 95, 97, 115–16
Macedonia, Former Yugoslav Republic of (FYROM): 53, 54
Martens, Feodor de: 71, 72
Martens Clause: 71–72, 77, 99, 100, 101, 103, 233, 347, 350, 356, 371–72, 384, 391–92
Mason, Air Vice-Marshal Tony: 17
McNamara, Robert: 28
Merchant vessels: 162–63, 164–65
Military advantage. *See also* Military objectives.
    and coalition warfare: 144
    defined: 143–45, 321
    and humanitarian interventions: 216–18
Military manuals
    common approaches to law of war issues in: 378
    and reprisals: 350
    as a resource for determining what States consider binding on themselves: 318–19, 320–21
Military objectives
    in air warfare: 168–72
    bridges: 5–6, 150–51, 156–57, 178–79, 185, 218, 261, 264
    civilian aircraft: 168–70
    civilian broadcasting stations: 157, 178, 179–80, 205, 260–61, 372
    civilian leaders: 220
    civilian morale: 29–30, 48–49, 110–11, 130–31, 180–81, 208, 209–10
    definition of: 48–49, 50–51, 140–45, 176–78, 204–05, 259–61, 268–69, 271, 277, 294, 296, 301–02, 347–48, 351, 365, 418–19, 422, 438–39, 453, 458–59, 464–65
    as different from political objectives: 275, 294
    doubts regarding: 149–50

Index

economic targets that support the enemy's war-fighting capability: 145–46
enemy merchant vessels: 162–63, 164–65
the environment as: 181–83, 203–04, 348–49, 464–65
exempt from attack: 152–53
government offices: 157–58
human beings as: 142–43
and humanitarian interventions: 181, 186–87, 216–17, 271, 294–96, 301–02, 453–55
identified by location: 150, 151, 215
identified by purpose: 148, 151, 159
identified by use: 149–50, 151, 159
individual members of the enemy's armed forces: 153–54
industrial plants: 154–55, 200, 222
ICRC attempt to draft a list of: 175, 178, 204
in land warfare: 158–61, 215
lighthouses: 167
military aircraft: 168
and military potential of targets: 259–61
need for good intelligence regarding: 148, 183–84
neutral merchant vessels: 163–64, 165–66
oil, coal, and other minerals: 155
in Operation Allied Force: 259–61, 294–95
passenger trains: 156–57
police officers: 154
political leaders: 158, 220
responsibility to remove civilians from the vicinity of: 275876
retreating troops: 153
in sea warfare: 161–67
telecommunications facilities: 157, 178, 179–80, 205
transportation infrastructure: 150–51, 156–57, 170, 178–79, 185, 200, 218
types of objectives whose nature makes them legitimate targets: 146–47
and use of civilians as human shields: 275–76
warships: 161, 166
Military Operations Other than War: 73–74
Miller, Judith A.: 107–12, 125, 130–31, 132–33, 199, 208, 209, 222, 308–09
Milosevic, Slobodan: 19, 20, 22, 41, 85, 95, 115, 130, 433–34
    indicted for war crimes: 61, 417, 420, 431
    power of as target of Operation Allied Force: 20, 22, 29, 191, 220
    and use of civilians as human shields: 22–24, 298–99
    use of targeting to stimulate the population to pressure: 48, 110–11, 130–31, 180–81, 191, 209–10, 222, 275, 294, 364, 414, 416–17, 418, 440
Mogadishu, Somalia: 288
Montenegro: 56, 94, 95, 423
Montgomery, Lieutenant Colonel Tony: 121, 189–97, 199, 200, 208, 213, 214, 297
Moore, John Norton: 220, 222, 225–28, 293, 303, 355, 467
Morale, civilian: 29–30, 110–11, 130–31, 180–81, 208, 209–10
Müllerson, Rein: 443–55, 471

Index

Murphy, John: 125, 219, 229–55, 273, 274, 276, 277–78, 282, 283, 286, 295–96, 299, 301, 303, 308, 460

N

Nagasaki, Japan: 180
National security advisor: 8–9
National Security Council, and target selection process: 8, 14, 15
Naval embargo: 55–57, 117–18
Naval interdiction, laws applicable to use of during Operation Allied Force: 95–97
Naval War College
    role in studying application of the law of war: 277, 279
    Stockton Chair of International Law: 137
Netherlands: 64, 65
Neutral States, and proposed naval embargo: 55–57, 117–18
New Zealand: 378
Newton, Lieutenant Colonel Mike: 298–99
Nicaragua case: 318, 319, 339, 340, 353–54
Nis airfield: 22, 272
Nixon, Richard M.: 227
Non-belligerence, new forms of: 119, 403, 423–24
North Atlantic Treaty Organization
    applicability of international humanitarian law to the armed forces of any member State implementing NATO decisions: 40
    bound by provisions of the Third Geneva Convention: 98–99
    and clearing of cluster bombs after hostilities ended: 362–63, 426–27
    compliance with the LOAC in targeting: 109–12, 326–27, 378
    compliance with Protocol I: 377–79, 414
    effect of use of high-altitude bombing on risk to civilians: 248–54, 305, 414–15
    failure to stop ethnic cleansing in Kosovo: 414–15
    interpretation of what is a military objective: 259–61
    and KFOR: 58
    and the KLA: 45–46, 436–37
    legal justifications advanced for resort to force in Kosovo: 36–39
    and nature of coalition warfare: 24–6, 29, 326–27, 333
    need to hold the alliance together while carrying out Operation Allied Force: 10, 13–14, 24–26, 201–02, 281, 326–27, 379
    New Strategic Concept: 331
    objectives in Operation Allied Force: 16, 19, 20, 47–48, 294, 375
    Operation Allied Force. *See* Operation Allied Force.
    Operation Deliberate Force: 413
    planning for Operation Allied Force: 121, 267–68
    policies in the post-hostilities period: 374–75
    and prisoners of war: 98–101
    and proposed oil embargo: 38–39, 55–57, 69, 92, 94–95
    Protocol I and the interoperability of coalition forces: 377–79, 428–29
    removal of weapons dumped in the high seas: 117

responsibility of member States for the wrongful actions of: 330–35, 387–88
role of national policies in target selection: 10, 11, 12–13, 15–16, 20, 22–24, 25, 332
and review of operatiosn by the International Criminal Tribunal for the former Yugoslavia: 33–34, 111–12, 157, 177, 179–80, 182, 183, 184, 250, 251–53, 260, 289, 366–74, 402
and right of humanitarian intervention: 470
rules of engagement: 109, 123, 377–79
Secretary-General: 40, 214
strategic doctrine: 402, 417–19, 431, 436, 451–52, 453, 458–59, 463–64
and use of cluster bombs: 361, 362–63, 426–27
and use of depleted uranium: 425
warnings of attacks by: 289
North Atlantic Council: 5–6, 40
North Atlantic Treaty: 331
North Sea Continental Shelf case: 274, 318, 340, 353–54
Nuclear weapons and the principle of distinction: 174, 175
Nuclear Weapons advisory opinion: 117, 139, 319, 353–54, 392–93, 443–44

O

Oakley, Bob: 437
"Observance by the United Nations forces of international humanitarian law" (UN Secretary-General's Bulletin): 80–81
O'Donnell, Brian: 27, 297
Oil embargo, proposed: 55–57, 69, 92, 94–95, 117–18
Operation Allied Force
    accountability of commanders: 92
    applicability of LOAC to: 3, 39–41, 88, 109, 121–23, 283–84, 326
    and application of the principle of distinction: 179, 257–58, 265, 270–71, 294–95, 372–73, 414–15, 416
    civilian casualties: 179, 250, 251–54, 264–65, 281–82, 283–84, 294–95, 361, 362–63, 368–69, 371–73
    and consensus decision making: 92, 281
    effect on Yugoslavia's economy: 361–62
    effects of the use of high-altitude bombing on civilian casualties: 248–54, 265–67, 332–33, 361, 463–64
    efforts to avoid military casualties: 277, 295, 304–05, 361, 463–64
    and environmental damage: 182, 424–25
    failures of: 414–15, 451–52
    failures to take feasible precautions to avoid civilian casualties and damage: 263–65, 268–69, 271
    legitimacy under international law: 103–04, 446–47, 448, 470, 473–74, 477
    naval support for: 93–95
    NATO responsibility for claims arising from: 330–33
    planning for: 121–22, 189–90, 199, 267–68
    political objectives: 110–11, 130–31, 180–81, 191, 209–10, 222, 275
    and Protocol I: 267–68, 275, 317, 331–33
    purpose of: 47–48, 191, 201–02, 364, 450–51

Index

rules of engagement: 379
strategy of: 47, 266–67, 294, 401, 413
target selection process: 190–95, 196, 199–202, 415
and use of cluster bombs: 272
and violations of human rights laws: 392–93
warnings of attacks by: 289
Operation Desert Fox: 231, 236
Operation Desert Storm: 231, 232, 236
Operation Provide Comfort: 446–47
Operational law, role in the military: 137, 225–26
Opinio juris: 234–35, 236, 317–18, 318–19, 340, 342, 350, 354, 447, 474
Ottawa Convention on Anti-personnel Land-mines of 1997: 317, 407, 427, 428, 438–39, 467–68

P

Pape, Robert: 209
Parks, W. Hays: 131–32, 232, 238–43, 244, 247–48, 251, 273, 274, 281–92, 297–98, 299, 302, 306, 307, 308
Peace Conference for the Former Yugoslavia, Arbitration Commission: 42
Peace-enforcement operations: 80, 270
Peacekeeping operations
  and applicability of Geneva Conventions and Protocol I: 74, 77–78, 81, 322–25
  and law of neutrality: 115–16
  and minimization of overall abuse: 437
Persian Gulf War: 24, 151
  and *jus ad bellum*: 38
  bombing accuracy in: 286, 287
  and military objectives: 153, 155–56, 219
  and principle distinction: 176
  and principle of proportionality: 244–45
  and Protocol I: 82, 267, 322
  rules of engagement: 82
  and retreating troops: 153
  target selection process: 28, 226
  and UN Secretary-General's Bulletin of 1999: 80
Pilots, mistakes made by: 21, 332–33
Pocar, Fausto: 337–51, 357, 379, 382–83, 384–85, 389–90, 391, 394, 396, 478
Poland: 95, 317
Ponte, Carla del: 421
Portugal: 64, 65
Precision-guided munitions
  defined: 230–31
  and minimization of collateral damage: 240–41, 249, 265–67, 277–78, 287
  need for commander to determine the appropriate use of: 241–42
  proposed protocols regarding the use of: 269–70
  and Protocol I: 237, 238–40, 241

Index

responsibility of individuals for the use of: 416
should they be required by international law: 231–43, 277–78, 287–88, 291–92, 295–96, 297–99
State practice regarding the use of: 235
and target selection: 27–28
transparency of the intentions of the users of: 438–40, 461
used in Operation Allied Force: 235, 249, 265–66
used in the Persian Gulf War: 231, 232, 236, 287

President of the United States
and relations with NATO allies: 8, 13–14
and review of targets: 8–9, 10–14, 18, 20, 21–22, 199–200, 201

Presson, Goran: 49, 250

Principals and deputies committees: 8–9, 10, 11

Prisoners of war
and the Geneva Conventions: 98–103, 104
members of FRY forces captured by the KLA and turned over to US forces: 53, 55, 97–98, 102–03, 115
status as: 53–55, 69, 97–103, 104, 115
United Nations personnel: 54–55
US soldiers captured by FRY forces: 53–54, 97–98, 115

Procès-Verbal of 1936: 164–65

Proportionality, principle of
and customary international law: 244–45, 246, 248, 274–75, 291, 346
and determination of excessiveness: 243–48, 251–53, 254, 308–09, 443–46
and dual-use targets: 207–10, 219, 270–72, 276, 371–73
and environmental damage: 181–83
and humanitarian interventions: 47–48, 50–51, 440–41
and *jus ad bellum*: 52, 274
and merchant vessels: 162–63
and Operation Allied Force: 122, 200–201, 209–10, 250, 262–63, 275, 308–09
and the Persian Gulf war: 263
and political considerations: 15–16, 17, 292, 297–98, 302–03, 401
problems in the application of: 244, 246–48, 275–79, 308–09, 321–22, 370–74
and Protocol I: 47, 215–16, 244, 245, 262, 278
and security of one's own soldiers: 277, 295, 304–06, 370

Protocol I, 1977 Protocol Additional to the Geneva Conventions of 1949
applicability to NATO actions: 331–32, 357–58
Article 1(4): 113
Article 35: 181, 182, 203, 344, 348–49, 363, 422
Article 37: 345
Article 40: 345
Article 42: 163
Article 44: 345
Article 48: 46, 139–40, 245, 258, 282–83, 345, 364
Article 49(1): 141
Article 49(3): 115
Article 50: 246, 345, 347–48

Article 51: 89–90, 285, 288–89, 345, 364–65
Article 51(2): 46, 346
Article 51(3): 246
Article 51(4): 258
Article 51(5)(a): 171–72
Article 51(5)(b): 47, 51, 52, 262, 291, 346
Article 51(6): 349–50
Article 51(7): 275
Article 52: 89–90, 268, 345–46, 349–50, 365, 422
Article 52(2): 47, 48, 51, 140–45, 148, 149, 176–77, 245, 259, 261, 320, 348
Article 52(3): 149, 246, 261, 347–48
Article 55: 181, 182, 203, 214–15, 348–49, 422
Article 56(1): 152
Article 56(2): 152
Article 57: 89–90, 141–42, 240, 241, 245, 263, 265, 278, 304, 346–47, 357, 369, 384, 391–92
Article 58: 275–76, 346–47, 357, 384
Article 59: 159–61
Article 75: 394
Article 85: 241–42
Article 90: 406
Article 96: 76, 114, 322, 335
and guerrilla warfare: 303
Martens Clause: 72, 100, 233, 356, 357–58
negotiations regarding: 51
and obligation to use precision-guided munitions: 237
and Operation Allied Force: 267–68, 275, 317, 331–33
parts of regarded as customary law: 73, 115, 175–77, 237, 257, 259, 261, 262, 268, 273, 291, 317–22, 337–51, 366, 381–85, 389–90, 422, 458, 459–60
and the Persian Gulf war: 82, 267, 322
principle of distinction in targeting: 46–47, 48–49, 51, 52, 175–76, 245, 259, 261, 282–83, 438
and principle of proportionality in targeting: 47, 48–49, 51, 52, 215–16, 244, 245, 248
and protection of the environment: 181–83, 348–49
and reciprocity provision: 322
and reprisals: 349–50, 390–91
and responsibility for collateral damage: 238–39, 241–42, 275–76
statements of understanding and reservations: 378, 383–84, 389, 418–19, 422, 468
status of FRY as a party to: 41, 43–44, 99–100
threshold of application: 75–76, 77
United States not party to: 99–100, 237, 239, 267, 279, 316, 377–85, 388–89, 427, 459–60
weakness of protection for civilians: 268–69
Protocol II, 1977 Protocol Additional to the Geneva Conventions of 1949
and civil wars: 406, 410–11
and human rights: 394
and prisoners of war: 103, 115
and threshold of application of: 76–77, 114
Protocol on Blinding Laser Weapons: 406–07, 427

Public opinion
    and coalition warfare: 315, 379
    and humanitarian interventions: 184–85, 267–68, 292, 297–98, 302–03, 305–06
    role in strategy: 302–03, 305–06l, 379
    role in target selection: 184–85, 267–68

R

Radio Televizije Srbije (RTS): 66–68, 157, 260–61, 265, 289, 298, 465
RAND study: 110–11, 130, 209, 222
Refugees
    civil wars as creators of: 403, 433
Report of the Independent International Commission on Kosovo: 250
Reprisals, prohibitions against: 349–50, 390–91
"Respect for Human Rights in Armed Conflicts," UN General Assembly resolution (1968): 175
Roberts, Adam: 127, 133, 287–88, 304–05, 306, 390–91, 401–32, 445, 446–48, 451–52, 453–54, 457, 458–61, 463, 464, 468, 469, 470–71, 473, 476, 477
Robertson, Horace B., Jr.: 212, 236, 457–62, 463
Robinson, Paul: 266
Rodley, Nigel: 445, 446
Rogers, Tony: 305
Rome Statute of the International Criminal Court (1998): 140, 158–59, 183, 185, 407, 420, 427–28, 429, 438–40, 464–65, 468
Ronzitti, Natalino: 113–19, 128, 156–57, 212, 392–93, 477
Rosenthal, Joel: 399
Rostow, Nicholas: 313
Rousseau, Jean Jacques: 173
Rowe, Peter: 267, 268, 269–70
Royse, M. W.: 290
Rules of engagement
    and avoidance of casualties: 82–83, 379
    and the law of armed conflict: 82–83, 109, 123, 458
    NATO: 109, 123, 377–79
    US military: 458
Russia: 317
    naval forces in the Mediterranean Sea: 93
    and the proposed naval embargo: 56, 94, 117–18
    and use of precision-guided munitions: 235–36
Rwanda: 408–09, 437, 452, 472

S

Sahovic, Dejan: 130
St. Petersburg Declaration of 1868: 418, 453
San Remo Manual: 92, 127–28, 141, 142, 146, 162, 163, 165–66, 204
Sandoz, Yves: 273–79, 299, 303, 304, 307, 308, 388, 476
Schmitt, Michael: 243, 245, 246–47, 248, 254–55, 302

Index

Schwarzkopf, General Norman: 267
Sea warfare
    military objectives in: 161–67
    exclusion zones: 165–66
Secretary of Defense: 199–200, 201
Secretary of State, and target approval process: 10
Self-defense: 448–50, 451, 452–53
Serbia: 5–6, 27–28, 56, 94, 194, 452. *See also* Belgrade.
Serbian Television and Radio Station (Belgrade): 66–68, 157, 260–61, 265, 289, 298, 465
Shearer, Ivan: 71–83
Short, Lt. Gen. Michael, USAF (Ret): 19–26, 27–28, 29–30, 213
Shue, Henry: 207–10, 308, 475
Sierra Leone: 408–09, 446–47
Silliman, Scott: 33–34
Simma, Bruno: 445–46, 470
Somalia: 408–09, 473
Sorenson, Colonel Richard: 29, 30, 121–23, 208, 308, 309, 464
Spain: 64, 65, 66
Srebrenica: 121, 409, 413
Stabilization Force in Bosnia-Herzegovina (SFOR): 379
Stalingrad, Russia: 215, 216
State practice
    and the creation of customary international law: 233–36, 274, 317–18, 320–21, 338–40, 350–51, 353–55, 382–85, 389–90, 446–47
    and use of precision-guided munitions: 235, 243
Status-of-forces agreements: 325, 335
Stein, Torsten: 315–35, 379, 380, 381, 382, 387–88, 393–94
Stone, Julius: 465
Strategic bombing: 170–72
Strauss, Barry: 293–96, 305, 306, 399
Supreme Allied Commander Europe (SACEUR): 40, 214
Sweden
    Prime Minister of: 49, 250
Switzerland: 119

T

Tadic case: 45, 114
Target selection process
    and assessment of collateral damage: 192, 193–94, 195
    and balance between military efficacy and civilian control: 13, 21–22, 28–29, 199–202
    described: 190–95, 199–200
    for Operation Allied Force: 190–95, 196, 213, 214
    role of lawyers in: 8–9, 14–15, 18, 25, 26, 121–23, 189–91, 191–95, 196–97, 199–202, 213, 268
    role of military commanders in: 20, 21–22, 25
    role of NATO member's national policies in: 10, 11, 12–13, 20, 25

Index

    role of Department of Defense attorneys in: 109
    role of the US president in: 8–15, 18, 20
    within the US government: 7, 8–18, 109–10, 122
    use of collateral damage model: 122
Targeting
    and civilian morale: 29–30, 110–11
    and compliance with the law of war: 10, 12, 16, 109, 111, 122–23, 199–202, 267–68
    and criminal liability of commanders: 5, 15, 17–18, 331–33
    of dual-use objects. *See* Dual-use targets.
    effects-based: 16, 20, 190–91
    errors in: 185–86
    and humanitarian interventions: 181, 186–87, 216–17
    inappropriateness of targets selected in terms of achieving the aims of Operation Allied Force: 20
    need to limit collateral damage. *See* Proportionality, principle of.
    need to minimize risk of collateral casualties: 12–13, 17–18, 22–24, 122–23
    NATO responsibility for compliance with international humanitarian law in: 331–33
    political constraints on: 9–10, 11, 15–16, 17, 22–24, 184–85, 196–97, 213, 267–68
    obligation of due diligence: 183–84, 185–86
    and politically significant objectives: 48
    and principle of distinction: 46–47, 48, 50–51, 122–23, 171–72, 173–87, 200–201, 207, 209–10, 214–16, 220–22
    and the principle of proportionality: 46, 47, 50–51, 122, 162–63, 182–83, 200, 207–10, 215–16, 219, 308–09
    and provisions of Protocol I: 46–47, 48, 123, 171–72, 331–32
    role of psychological impact in: 180–81
    role of US policy concerns in: 12–13, 17
    time-sensitive targets of opportunity: 213
    and weapons reliability: 122–23
Telecommunication facilities: 66–68, 157, 178, 179–80, 260–61, 265
Terrorists: 254–55, 303
Tesón, Fernando: 450
Theodore Roosevelt, USS battle group: 93
Togo: 302
Treaties, applicability to non-party States: 337–51
Trenchard, Marshal Hugh, Royal Air Force: 290
Turkey: 66, 68, 267, 316–17, 334
Turner, Robert F.: 137, 220–22

U

United Kingdom: 64, 65
    House of Commons Foreign Affairs Committee report on Kosovo: 414
    and conformance with international humanitarian law: 40
    law of war manual: 378
    Minister of Defence: 127
    Ministry of Defence: 266

Index

Permanent Representative to the United Nations: 37–38
and Protocol I: 175–76, 321, 364–65, 390
Royal Air Force: 326–27
Royal Navy units: 93
Secretary of State for Defence: 270–71
statements to the UN Security Council regarding Operation Allied Force: 37–38
and target selection process: 26, 30
United Nations
General Assembly: 42, 108–09, 125, 175, 234, 350, 424
not a contracting party to the Geneva Conventions and Protocol I: 76, 77–79
peacekeeping operations: 77–78, 79–80, 81
Secretary-General: 58–59, 361–62
Secretary-General's Bulletin of 1999: 80–81, 278–79, 324–25, 380–81
United Nations Charter
and armed conflict: 75
Article 2(7): 463
Article 13: 108
Article 24: 107
Article 25: 86, 107
Article 41: 107
Article 42: 107, 118
Article 48: 86
Article 103: 86–87, 116
Chapter VI: 107
Chapter VII: 59–60, 78, 107, 125–26, 323, 324–25, 433, 449
United Nations Convention on Civil and Political Rights: 396
United Nations Conventional Weapons Convention (1980): 91–92, 307, 316–17, 327, 427
proposed protocol to: 269–70, 272
Protocol II on landmines, booby-traps and other devices: 362–63, 407
Protocol III on Incendiary Weapons: 241
United Nations Environment
Programme: 424–25
Balkan Task Force: 182
United Nations High Commissioner for Refugees: 411
United Nations Mission in Kosovo (UNMIK): 58–59, 69, 374
United Nations Preventative Deployment Force (UNPREDEP): 53, 54–55, 115–16
United Nations Security Council
applicability of LOAC to military operations pursuant to decisions of the: 86–88, 322–25, 449
and blockades: 118–19
economic sanctions imposed by: 409, 423
enforcement actions undertaken by authority of: 78, 80, 322–25, 410
and FRY as the continuation of SFRY: 42
and the ICTY: 44
and Kosovo: 37–38, 408–09, 410–11, 471
and proposed oil embargo against FRY: 117–18, 126
Resolution 661: 126

Index

    Resolution 665: 126
    Resolution 687: 38
    Resolution 827: 61
    Resolution 1160: 37, 61, 118, 119, 126
    Resolution 1199: 37, 61
    Resolution 1203: 37
    Resolution 1244: 37, 57–60, 69, 113–14, 126
    resolutions of law: 107–09, 125
    role of : 107–08, 408–09
United States
    and application of the principle of distinction: 364–65
    and bombing accuracy: 286–87
    failure to become a party to treaties regarding the law of war: 403, 427–30, 432, 438–40, 459–60, 467–68
    and ICTY investigation of Operation Allied Force: 420, 421–22, 432
    and international humanitarian law: 279, 286, 288–89
    law of war manuals: 378, 458
    not party to Protocol I: 115, 175–76, 316, 333–34, 343, 377–85, 388–89, 459
    opposition to the International Criminal Court: 420, 429, 432
    and principle of distinction: 246–47
    and principle of proportionality: 244–45, 246–47, 248, 251
    prisoners of war in the custody of: 53, 55
    and reprisals: 390–91
    strategic doctrine: 417–19
    use of precision-guided munitions: 231, 232, 235, 236
United States Air Forces in Europe: 121
United States' Commander's Handbook of the Law of Naval Operations: 145, 204, 458
US Air Force, Intelligence Targeting Guide: 320
US Army, Field Manual 27-10: 320
US Army Judge Advocate General's School, Operational Law Handbook 2002: 320
US European Command
    and planning for Operation Allied Force: 121, 189, 191–95
    target selection process: 189–97, 199–200, 214
US National Command Authorities, and target approval process: 5–6, 18
US Navy support operations for Operation Allied Force: 93–95
United States v. List et al.: 320
Uranium, use of depleted: 363, 367, 425–26, 432

V

Vienna Convention on the Law of Treaties: 317, 355, 464
Vienna Convention on the Succession of States (1978): 114–15
Vietnam War
    and application of the law of war: 175, 225, 227
    and bombing accuracy: 286, 287
    and principle of distinction: 175, 176, 179, 180
    and use of civilians as shields: 288

Index

Vincennes, USS: 169
Visit and search of ships: 56–57, 69, 94–95, 117–19, 127–30, 163
von Heinegg, Wolff H.: 127–28, 129, 203–06, 216, 217, 221, 388, 474–75

W

Waging Modern War, by General Wesley Clark: 10
Waldock, C. H. M.: 450
Walker, George: 85–105, 125, 463
War crimes
    and bombing of the Leskovac bridge: 6
    conclusions of the Committee Established to Review the NATO Bombing Campaign Against the Federal Republic of Yugoslavia regarding: 34
    defined: 158–59, 174, 185–86, 277
    environmental damage as: 183, 204
    and international humanitarian law: 353, 355, 356–57
    indictment of Milosevic for: 61, 417, 420, 431
    and standard of reasonableness: 211–12
    as violations of US criminal law: 10
    weakness of enforcement of laws against: 406
War criminals as military targets: 220–22
Washington Conference on Disarmament (1922): 174
Webster, Daniel: 449, 452–53
Wedgwood, Ruth: 29, 130, 212, 387, 388, 433–41, 452, 454, 457, 460–61, 464, 472–73, 475–79
World War II
    and the principle of distinction: 174, 259, 260
    and the principle of proportionality: 208
    targeting practices in: 174, 208, 218

Y

Yamamoto, Admiral (Japanese): 153–54
Yugoslavia, Federal Republic of (FRY)
    absence of attacks on NATO forces outside the FRY: 47, 50
    admitted to the United Nations: 42–43
    applicability of international humanitarian law to conflict with KLA: 44–45, 113–19
    arms embargo imposed on: 37
    bound by the Third Geneva Convention: 98–99
    and capture of US soldiers: 53–54, 97, 115
    and claims against NATO member States: 62–66, 330, 334
    compliance with the laws of war: 404–05
    as continuation of the Socialist Federal Republic of Yugoslavia: 41–43, 64–65, 114–15
    effect of Operation Allied Force on the economy of: 361–62
    and the Genocide Convention: 42–43
    humanitarian situation in as justification for Operation Allied Force: 37–38, 433, 446–47, 448, 451–52, 463, 470, 471–72
    nature of conflict with KLA: 113–14

Index

Operation Allied Force strategy to change the policy of: 47–48, 110–11, 130–31, 180–81, 191, 209–10, 222, 275, 294, 364, 414, 416–17, 418, 440
post-Milosevic government acceptance of FRY as a new State: 42–43
and prisoners of war: 53–54, 97–101, 115
proposed embargo on shipments to: 38–39, 44–95, 117–18
proposed naval operations against: 55–57, 92, 94–95
relationship with NATO: 330
status as a party to Protocol I of 1977: 41–44, 114–15
status as a party to the Geneva Conventions: 41–44, 114–15
and UN Security Council mandates: 36–37
Yugoslavia, Socialist Federal Republic of (SFRY), FRY as successor to: 41–44